Criminal Justice Act 2003

(2003 c.44)

A Current Law Statute Guide

THOMSON
™
SWEET & MAXWELL

Published in 2004 by Sweet & Maxwell Ltd
of 100 Avenue Road, London NW3 3PF
Typeset by MFK Information Services Ltd, Gunnels Wood Road, Stevenage, Hertfordshire SG1 2BH.
Printed in Great Britain by Hobbs, Totton, Hampshire.

No natural forests were destroyed to make this product; only farmed timber was used and replanted

ISBN 0421878509

This Annotated Act is correct as at Royal Assent (November 20, 2003)

The Criminal Justice Act 2003 (c.44) was annotated by:

D.A. Thomas Q.C., LL.B
Rudi F. Firtson LL.B (Hons.), Barrister

Please note that since the Act received Royal Assent some further amendments have been made by correction slip. These changes have not been incorporated into the text and they are as follows:

Schedule 30
Page 362, paragraph 3(3)(b), "section 198 or 200" should read "section 226 or 228".

Schedule 32
Page 399, paragraph 135, "Schedule 11" should read "Schedule 12".

ISBN 0-421-87850-9

9 780421 878501

©
Sweet & Maxwell Ltd.
2004

CRIMINAL JUSTICE ACT 2003*

(2003 c.44)

CONTENTS

PART 1

AMENDMENTS OF POLICE AND CRIMINAL EVIDENCE ACT 1984

PART 2

BAIL

PART 3

CONDITIONAL CAUTIONS

PART 4

CHARGING ETC

PART 5

DISCLOSURE

---

* Annotations by Rudi Fortson, LL.B, Barrister, 25 Bedford Row (Parts 1–11, 13 and 14) and D A Thomas, Q.C., LL.B (Part 12).

PART 10

RETRIAL FOR SERIOUS OFFENCES

Cases that may be retried

Application for retrial

Retrial

Investigations

Arrest, custody and bail

Part 10: supplementary

PART 11

EVIDENCE

CHAPTER 1

EVIDENCE OF BAD CHARACTER

Introductory

Persons other than defendants

Defendants

CHAPTER 2

HEARSAY EVIDENCE

Hearsay: main provisions

Principal categories of admissibility

Supplementary

Miscellaneous

General

CHAPTER 3

MISCELLANEOUS AND SUPPLEMENTAL

PART 12

SENTENCING

CHAPTER 1

GENERAL PROVISIONS ABOUT SENTENCING

Matters to be taken into account in sentencing

General restrictions on community sentences

General restrictions on discretionary custodial sentences

General limit on magistrates' court's power to impose imprisonment

Procedural requirements for imposing community sentences and discretionary custodial sentences

Disclosure of pre-sentence reports etc.

Pre-sentence drug testing

Fines

Savings for power to mitigate etc.

Sentencing and allocation guidelines

CHAPTER 2

COMMUNITY ORDERS: OFFENDERS AGED 16 OR OVER

CHAPTER 3

PRISON SENTENCES OF LESS THAN 12 MONTHS

CHAPTER 4

FURTHER PROVISIONS ABOUT ORDERS UNDER CHAPTERS 2 AND 3

CHAPTER 7

EFFECT OF LIFE SENTENCE

CHAPTER 8

OTHER PROVISIONS ABOUT SENTENCING

Deferment of sentence

An Act to make provision about criminal justice (including the powers and duties of the police) and about dealing with offenders; to amend Chapter 1 of Part 1 of the Crime and Disorder Act 1998 and Part 5 of the Police Act 1997; to make provision about civil proceedings brought by offenders; and for connected purposes. [20th November 2003]

PARLIAMENTARY DEBATES

Hansard, HC, Vol. 394 col.800 (1R); Vol. 395 col.912 (2R) (PM) (MR); Vol. 400 col.930 (PM); Vol. 402 cols.925 (PM), 929 (Rep.); Vol. 405 cols.668 (Remaining Stages), 865 (3R).

HL, Vol. 648 col.835 (1R); Vol. 649 col.558 (2R); Vol. 650 cols.139 (MfA), 601, 607 (Comm.); Vol. 651 cols.12, 36, 98, 645, 715, 768, 837 (Comm.); Vol. 651 cols.1009, 1039 (Comm.); Vol. 652 cols. 687, 737, 1081 (Comm.); Vol. 653 cols.22, 296, 377, 768, 858, 890, 945, 1037 (Comm.); Vol. 653 col.1725.

INTRODUCTION AND GENERAL NOTE

The Criminal Justice Act 2003 is a landmark Act which introduces wide-ranging reforms to court procedure and sentencing. As to the former, Parliament's aim is to improve the management of cases and to "ensure that criminal trials are run more efficiently and to reduce the scope for abuse of the system" (Explanatory Notes, para.5). The Act is not just about improving the management of criminal trials, but is an attempt to encourage professionals operating inside the criminal justice system, to focus on outcomes and to revise rules relating to process that are judged not only to be unnecessary but impede the search for truth (consider the remarks of the Home Secretary on Radio 4, the Today programme, November 22, 2003 at 8:30am; see *Hansard*, HC, Vol. 413, col.1025 (November 20, 2003) and see the Government's White Paper "*Justice for All*" Cm.5563 (2002)). Unsurprisingly, there is much in the 2003 Act that is controversial, resulting in many heated debates (even acrimony), when the provisions of the Act were debated in Parliament (*Hansard*, HC, Vol. 413, col.1026 (November 20, 2003)).

In its White Paper, the Government state that "[the] process will be geared towards getting to the truth, convicting the offender as early as we possibly can, and minimizing opportunities for anyone to impede efforts to achieve that. We will put the victims, who suffer most from crime, at the heart of the system and do everything we can to support and inform them, and we will respect and protect the witnesses without whom the CJS would not function" (para.0.2). As to how this is to be achieved the Government wrote (Executive Summary):

"To convict more of the guilty we will:
- improve defence and prosecution disclosure by increasing incentives and sanctions to ensure compliance;
- allow the use of reported evidence ('hearsay') where there is a good reason, such as where a witness cannot appear personally;
- allow for trial by judge alone in serious and complex fraud trials, some other complex and lengthy trials or where the jury is at risk of intimidation; and
- extend the availability of preparatory hearings to ensure that serious cases such as drug trafficking as well as complex ones can be properly prepared.

At the trial we will:

- allow the court to be informed of a defendant's previous convictions where appropriate;
- remove the double jeopardy rule for serious cases if compelling new evidence comes to light;
- give witnesses greater access to their original statements at trial;
- give the prosecution the right of appeal against rulings which terminate the prosecution case before the jury decides; and
- increase the proportion of the population eligible for jury service."

All of the above are the subject of provisions in the 2003 Act. Changes to rules of evidence are premised on confidence that fact-finders (lay and professional) can be trusted to correctly evaluate evidence, whether hearsay or not, and notwithstanding that the evidence relates to the bad character of a defendant or a witness. Changes to trial procedure and practice, are premised on the philosophy that a criminal trial is not a game, but "a search for truth in accordance with the twin principles that the prosecution must prove its case and that defendants are not obliged to incriminate themselves. The object must be to convict the guilty and acquit the innocent" (*Justice For All*, p.32; and see the Review of the Criminal Courts of England and Wales, Lord Justice Auld, Ch.10, para.154; and see Ch.11, paras 78, 101, 103). Interpreting what this statement actually means, in practical terms, is considered elsewhere in the annotations. Nothing in the 2003 Act is intended to change the adversarial nature of a criminal trial.

Although changes to the rules of hearsay evidence largely follow the recommendations of the Law Commission in its Final Report (No.245; Ch.2 to Pt 11 of the 2003 Act), the Government has, for the most part, steered its own course in relation to many other reforms introduced by the Act. Changes to rules of evidence relating to bad character of defendants and non-defendant witnesses, represent the Government's approach to this difficult topic: it will therefore be seen that rules relating to evidence of bad character set out in Ch.1 to Pt 11 of the 2003 Act often depart from the proposals of the Law Commission in its Consultation Paper (No.141), and in its Final Report and draft Bill (Report No.273). Provisions of the 2003 Act that enact rules relating to (i) court procedure, (ii) the allocation of court business, (iii) rules on disclosure by the prosecution and by the defence, (iv) the right of appeal for the prosecution against judicial decisions relating to criminal trials, (v) the power to retry a person acquitted of certain very serious offences if there is new and compelling evidence of an accused's guilt, are enacted mindful of (but frequently do not mirror) recommendations and proposals in many consultation documents, reports, and studies: Review of the Criminal Courts of England and Wales (Sir Robin Auld, 2001); the *Report of the Royal Commission on Criminal Procedure*, Cmnd.8092 (1981); the *Report of the Royal Commission on Criminal Justice* Cm.2263 (1983); the *Fraud Trials Committee Report* (HMSO, 1986); the *Report of the Joint Home Office/Cabinet Office Review of PACE* (2002); *Prosecution Appeals Against Judges' Rulings* (Law Commission, Consultation Paper No.158); *Double Jeopardy and Prosecution Appeals* (Law Commission, Report No.267); *Double Jeopardy* (Law Commission Consultation Paper No.156); *Evidence of Bad Character in Criminal Proceedings* (Law Commission Report No.273); *Evidence in Criminal Proceedings: Hearsay and Related Topics* (Law Commission Report No.245). If practitioners hope that the new rules of evidence enacted in Part 11 of the 2003 Act will be less complex, and easier to apply in practice than hitherto, they are going to be disappointed.

Part 12 of the Act includes numerous provisions dealing with a sentencing, many of them based on the Review of the Sentencing Framework for England and Wales (2001), commonly known as the Halliday report. Chapter 1 sets out the purposes of sentencing, and the matters which should be considered by a court in determining of the seriousness of an offence. Other provisions of Ch.1 substantially reproduce existing provisions of the Powers of Criminal Courts (Sentencing) Act 2000 (c.6). The powers of magistrates courts in relation to the terms of imprisonment which may be imposed on summary conviction are extended. Sections 167–173 provide for the creation of a Sentencing Guidelines Council, which will have the task of publishing guidelines which must be taken into account by sentencing courts. Section 174 imposes on courts duties to give various explanations when imposing sentence.

Chapter 2 of Pt 12 makes provision for a new scheme of community orders. Existing forms of community orders will be grouped together a single form of community order, and courts will be empowered to impose a wide for range of requirements in conjunction with a community order.

Chapter 3 makes provisions for short sentences of imprisonment, providing for what will be known as "custody plus orders", intermittent custody and suspended sentences.

Chapter 4 makes detailed provision for the various requirements which may be imposed in conjunction with community orders or custody plus or similar orders.

Chapter 5 makes new provision for dangerous offenders, introducing a new sentence of "imprisonment for public protection" for offenders convicted of certain offences from whom the public need protection from serious harm.

Chapter 6 substantially changes the law relating to release on licence. Under the new parole scheme, the distinction between short term and long-term prisoners will disappear, and all prisoners serving determinate sentences will be released after having served half of their sentences, and remain on licence until the end of the whole term of the sentence. In some circumstances prisoners will be eligible for discretionary release before they have served half of the sentence.

Chapter 7 deals with mandatory life sentences, introducing a new scheme for determining the minimum term to be served by a person sentenced to a mandatory life sentence on conviction of murder. The term will be set by the sentencing court in accordance with Sch.21 to the Act, which lays down a detailed framework of considerations. A minimum term fixed by a court will be subject to appeal and the possibility of a reference by the Attorney General. The role of the Secretary of State in the release of persons sentenced to life imprisonment for murder disappears. Once a prisoner has served the minimum term determined by the court, the Parole Board may direct his release if it is satisfied that it is not necessarily for the protection of the public for him to remain in custody.

Chapter 8 makes numerous miscellaneous changes in sentencing law, increasing the penalties for certain offences, including causing death by dangerous driving, and introducing a minimum sentence of five years imprisonment, (or three years detention in the case of an offender aged over 16 and under 18) on conviction for an offence of possessing a prohibited weapon. Numerous minor changes are made to other statutory provisions relating to you sentencing.

COMMENCEMENT

The Criminal Justice Act 2003 received Royal Assent on November 20, 2003. A number of provisions came into force on the passing of the Act, these were ss.168(1), 168(2), 183(8), 307(1)–(3), 307(5), 307(6), 330, 331(1)–(5), 334–339, and the repeal in Pt 9 of Sch.37 of s.91(2) and (3) of the Countryside and Rights of Way Act 2000 (c.37) (and s.332 so far as relating to that repeal), and paras 1 and 6 of Sch.38 (and s.333(6) so far as relating to those paragraphs).

A number of provisions also came into force at the end of a period of four weeks beginning with the day on which this Act was passed (*i.e.* December 18, 2003). Theses were as follows: Ch.7 of Pt 12 (and Schs 21 and 22); s.303(b)(i) and (ii); paras 42, 43(3), 66, 83(1)–(3), 84, 109(2), 109(3)(b), 109(4) and 104(5) of Sch.32 (and s.304 so far as relating to those provisions); Pt.8 of Sch.37 (and s.332 so far as relating to that Part of that Schedule).

The remaining provisions in the Act will be brought into force by order. A commencement order may make different provision for different purposes or different areas.

ABBREVIATIONS

"ACPO"	:	Association of Chief Police Officers
"PACE"	:	Police And Criminal Evidence Act 1984 (c.60)
"the 2003 Act"	:	Criminal Justice Act 2003 (c.44)
"the 1976 Act"	:	Bail Act 1976 (c.63)
"the 1996 Act"	:	Criminal Procedure and Investigations Act 1996 (c.25)
"the Review of PACE"	:	Home Office/Cabinet Office, *PACE Review: Report of the Joint Home Office/Cabinet Office Review of the Police and Criminal Evidence Act 1984*, (2002)

PART 1

AMENDMENTS OF POLICE AND CRIMINAL EVIDENCE ACT 1984

1   Extension of powers to stop and search

(1) In this Part, "the 1984 Act" means the Police and Criminal Evidence Act 1984 (c. 60).

(2) In section 1(8) of the 1984 Act (offences for purpose of definition of prohibited article), at the end of paragraph (d) there is inserted "; and

(e) offences under section 1 of the Criminal Damage Act 1971 (destroying or damaging property)."

DEFINITIONS
  "prohibited article": s.1(7) PACE
  "the 1984 Act": s.1(1)

GENERAL NOTE

This section has its origins in the Review of Police And Criminal Evidence Act 1984 (c.60) ("PACE") conducted in the early part of 2002 (see the Home Office/Cabinet Office, *PACE Review: Report of the Joint Home Office/Cabinet Office Review of the Police and Criminal Evidence Act 1984*, (2002) ("the Review of PACE"). The purpose of that Review "without compromising the rights of those that the Act protects" was to simplify police procedures, to reduce procedural and administrative burdens on the police, to save police resources, and to speed up the process of justice (Executive Summary, para.2). PACE has been criticised for being too rigid and that the Act would benefit from greater fluidity of application. This would include giving the police and the courts greater discretion over the interpretation and application of the statutory provisions in PACE, and the PACE codes.

A highly controversial aspect of PACE has been the general power to stop and search persons or vehicles for stolen or prohibited articles on the basis of reasonable suspicion. In cases where reasonable suspicion exists, an officer retains discretion as to whether to use the power of stop and search or not. The circumstances in which that discretion may, or should, be exercised has been the subject of a number of detailed, critical, academic studies. The Review of PACE seeks to address concerns that the power is not always used in a proportionate way, pointing to research that has shown stop-and-search to be most effective "when used in a targeted and intelligence led way" (General Findings, para.7), and that "searches based on solid grounds, drawing on up-to-date and accurate intelligence, are most likely to be effective, lawful, and secure public confidence" (Ch.2, para.12). Critics may not be convinced that the Review adequately addresses issues as to (1) how police officers make "targeting" decisions, or (2) how police officers exercise their discretion to use the power to stop-and-search, or (3) why particular groups appear to be targeted more than others (General Findings, para.8). The Review of PACE noted, "there was significant police support during the Review for extending stop and search powers to situations where an officer reasonably suspects that articles intended for use in causing criminal damage are being carried. Graffiti was highlighted as an increasingly serious social nuisance during the Review. Extending relevant search powers to cover articles intended to be used in causing criminal damage would enable police to search for paint spray cans and other relevant equipment." (Ch.2, para.10).

Section 1(2)(a) PACE empowers a police officer to stop ("detain") and search any person or vehicle for (among other things) "prohibited articles" where he has reasonable grounds for suspecting he will find such articles (s.1(3) PACE). By s.1(7)(b)(i), an article is prohibited if it is "made or adapted for use in the course of or in connection with an offence to which this sub-paragraph applies", or by s.1(7)(b)(ii) it is "intended by the person having it with him for such use by him or some other person". The relevant offences are specified in s.1(8) PACE and include burglary and theft. Section 1(2) of the Criminal Justice Act 2003 (c.44) ("the 2003 Act") adds the offence of criminal damage to s.1(8) PACE. The measure is intended to tackle unlawful graffiti (*e.g.* a person carrying a can of spray paint). A tin of paint would not ordinarily be a "prohibited" article for the purposes of s.1 PACE, unless it was held by a person with the intention of using it to cause criminal damage. Similarly, a hammer, or a knife, carried with the intention of damaging a work of art, would also be "prohibited" articles. A brick transported in a car, to be thrown through a window, would be a "prohibited" article. A can of spray paint fitted with a nozzle to facilitate unlawful graffiti would be a "prohibited" article because the article had been adapted for use in connection with an offence.

2   Warrants to enter and search

In section 16 of the 1984 Act (execution of warrants), after subsection (2) there is inserted—

  "(2A) A person so authorised has the same powers as the constable whom he accompanies in respect of—
      (a) the execution of the warrant, and
      (b) the seizure of anything to which the warrant relates.
  (2B) But he may exercise those powers only in the company, and under the supervision, of a constable."

DEFINITIONS
   "the 1984 Act": s.1(1)

GENERAL NOTE
   This short provision is of significant practical importance and concerns the use of civilians who accompany police officers when executing a search warrant. Section 2 has been enacted having regard to the findings of the Government's Review of PACE (Ch.2 para.20 issue 9). The section should be read mindful of s.12 and Sch.1 to the 2003 Act.
   Section 16(1) PACE states that a warrant to enter and search premises may be executed "by any constable". Section 16(2) PACE provides that the warrant may authorise "persons to accompany any constable who is executing it". Thus, officers executing a warrant to enter and search premises for the unlawful production of a controlled drug, might wish persons other than constables to attend the scene (for example forensic chemists, photographers, or financial investigators). The investigation of serious fraud poses particular difficulties with regard to the examination of perhaps thousands of business records held at business premises. The presence of a computer expert, or an accountant, might be highly productive. Experts are able to assist police decide which items are relevant to an inquiry, and which items should be preserved for further examination or analysis. It is not unknown for a lawyer, in independent private practice, to assist police during the course of the search if it is believed that documents subject to legal professional privilege might be kept there.
   Before the enactment of this provision, the power of persons other than constables to assist in a search was uncertain. It was not clear to what extent such persons were entitled to sift through material during the course of a search, and to make decisions as to property that they were entitled to inspect or to seize. If a constable was so heavily dependent on the advice, of the expert, was it the constable or the civilian/expert who effectively "executed" the warrant for the purposes of s.16 PACE (as originally drafted)? Human rights issues are involved, because everyone has the right to respect for his private life and correspondence, subject to interference by a public authority in accordance with the law (Art.8 of Sch.1 to the Human Rights Act 1998 (c.42), and note Art.1 of the First Protocol of the European Convention on Human Rights and see *Funke v France* [1993] 16 E.H.R.R. 297).
   The purpose of s.2 of the 2003 Act is to make the legal position clear by vesting persons authorised by the section with almost the same powers as a constable in respect of the execution of the warrant, and in respect of the seizure of anything relevant to the offence under investigation. A civilian endorsed on the warrant would not be entitled to use force to gain entry to premises (see the Police Reform Act 2002 (c.30); and note the statements of the Parliamentary Under Secretary of State for the Home Department, Hilary Benn, Standing Committee B, December 17, 2002, col.39). Note that Sch.4 to the Police Reform Act 2002 (powers exercisable by police civilians) is amended by Sch.1 to the 2003 Act (see paras 16–18 inclusive).
   By s.16(2B) PACE, civilians may exercise powers only in the company, and under the supervision, of a constable. This probably does not mean that immediate supervision is required, *i.e.* that actions taken by an authorised person must be witnessed by a constable (see Standing Committee B, December 17, 2002, col.42).

3   Arrestable offences

(1) Schedule 1A to the 1984 Act (specific offences which are arrestable offences) is amended as follows.

(2) After paragraph 2 there is inserted—

> "*Criminal Justice Act 1925*
> 2ZA   An offence under section 36 of the Criminal Justice Act 1925 (untrue statement for procuring a passport)."

(3) After paragraph 6 there is inserted—

> "*Misuse of Drugs Act 1971*
> 6A   An offence under section 5(2) of the Misuse of Drugs Act 1971 (having possession of a controlled drug) in respect of cannabis or cannabis resin (within the meaning of that Act)."

(4) After paragraph 17 there is inserted—
> "17A   An offence under section 174 of the Road Traffic Act 1988 (false statements and withholding material information)."

DEFINITIONS
"arrestable offence": s.24 PACE
"controlled drug": s.2 and s.37 Misuse of Drugs Act 1971 (c.38)
"the 1984 Act": s.1(1)

GENERAL NOTE
Of all the measures that s.3 introduces, subs.(3) (formerly clause 9 of the Bill) remains a highly controversial provision that was the subject of lengthy debate when the Bill was examined in Standing Committee B on January 7, 2003 (col.127, *et seq.*) and later.

Simon Hughes MP led much of the critical discussion both in Standing Committee B and in the House of Commons. In July 2002 the Home Secretary announced his intention to bring forward proposals to Parliament to re-classify cannabis from Class B to Class C for the purposes of the Misuse of Drugs Act 1971. The proposals came in the wake of findings and recommendations of the *Independent Inquiry Into The Misuse of Drugs Act 1971* (chairman: Viscountess Runciman DBE, Ch.7) of which this author was a member; the findings of the House of Lords Select Committee on Science and Technology, "*Cannabis the Scientific and Medical Evidence*" (HL, paper 151, November 1998), the British Medical Association Report, "*Therapeutic Uses of Cannabis*" 1997, the Report of the Advisory Council On The Misuse Of Drugs "*The Classification of Cannabis Under the Misuse Of Drugs Act 1971*" (March 2002) "*Cannabis, A Review*" (Professor D. J. Nutt and Dr J. Nash, March 2002), and the recommendations of the Home Affairs Select Committee. A motion that the draft of the Misuse of Drugs Act 1971 (Modification) (No. 2) Order 2003 (SI 2003/3201), laid before the House of Commons on September 11, 2003, be approved, was debated on October 29, 2003 (*Hansard*, HC Vo. 412, col.329 (October 29, 2003)).

Prior to the enactment of ss.3(3), 284 and Sch.28 para.1 (penalties for some drug trafficking offences) of the 2003 Act, the effect of moving any controlled drug from Class B to Class C, was (1) that the simple possession of the drug (*i.e.* not intending to supply it) ceased to be an "arrestable offence" for the purpose of s.24 of PACE (the possession of any Class C drug carried a maximum penalty on indictment of two years' imprisonment), and (2) the trafficking of any Class C drug carried a maximum penalty of five years' imprisonment. The Runciman Independent Inquiry recommended that the simple possession of cannabis should not be an arrestable offence (in effect concluding that there should be no change in the law regarding the power to arrest for possession of any Class C drug), but that the penalty for dealing/trafficking in a Class C drug should be increased from five years to seven years' imprisonment (see Ch.7, para.77). Ten years earlier, the Justice Report "*Drugs and The Law*" also recommended that cannabis should be downgraded, but that it should be placed in a Class unique to that drug, and that the simple possession of cannabis should continue to be an arrestable offence. This was based on representations made by the police service that the power to arrest for possession of cannabis was a useful policing tool. These representations were further examined by the Independent Inquiry and rejected in the light of ten years further experience of the Misuse of Drugs Act 1971 following the publication of the Justice Report. The Independent Inquiry noted that for the thirty years since the Misuse of Drugs Act 1971 was enacted, the fact that possession of a Class C drug was not an arrestable offence had not created any reported difficulties for the police enforcing the Act. (Simon Hughes MP made this point during Parliamentary debates in Standing Committee B, *Hansard*, Vol.397, col.128 (January 7, 2003)). Views within the police service have been divided as to the desirability, or need, for a power of arrest for the possession cannabis as a Class C drug. However, the view that prevailed was that the power to arrest for the simple possession of cannabis should be retained (see, for example, "*Policing cannabis reclassification — easy as A B C*", Detective Sergeant Geoff Monaghan, DrugLink).

On December 3, 2002, the Government signalled its intention to re-classify cannabis from Class B to Class C as part of its "updated drugs strategy 2002", but it also said that the police "will retain the power of arrest to be used where there are aggravating factors, such as flagrantly disregarding the law". This left open questions as to who would draft the guidelines, what form they would take, and whether the guidelines would have the force of law or be largely informal. Although in early 2003, there was talk of guidelines being drafted by the Association of Chief Police Officers ("ACPO"), by May 2003 it became clear that no national guidelines were likely to be drawn up. However, the position changed: guidelines have now been published by ACPO. Frontline officers will have discretion whether to arrest for possession of cannabis or not, but the exercise of that discretion is likely to be determined in part by the guidelines and partly by local considerations (including policing priorities).

The timing of the inclusion of what was then clause 9 (now s.3(3)) in the Bill was unfortunate. The Bill was published on November 21, 2002 but the Explanatory Notes were not published until November 29, 2002. The Home Secretary did not publicly announced his proposals regarding cannabis until the December 3, 2002 by which time lawyers (such as the present author) had read the Bill, and challenged the Government about its intentions and plans regarding cannabis. For almost one year, it seemed as if the Government was determined to adhere to its proposal that the simple possession of any Class C drug would be an arrestable offence. That changed in November 2003, when at a very late stage in the history of the Bill, the Government introduced amendments (in the House of Lords) with the effect of limiting the power of arrest under s.3(3) of the 2003 Act to the simple possession of cannabis and cannabis resin (*Hansard*, Vol. 413, col.1774 (November 17, 2003)). It follows, that from January 29, 2004, the only drugs of Class C, for which there is a power of arrest for simple possession, is cannabis, cannabis resin, cannabinol, and cannabinol derivatives.

What then, makes the simple possession of cannabis as a Class C drug, deserving of a power of arrest? One view is that such a power is a useful policing tool: for example, crowd control, or (as stated by Detective Sergeant Monaghan), the ability of the police to obtain DNA samples from cannabis offenders: "Policing cannabis reclassification — easy as A B C". Quite apart from the issue as to whether a power of arrest should be used in this way (*i.e.* for purposes not related to the offence under investigation), the usefulness of the power of arrest seems to be linked (ironically) to the fact that cannabis is the most popular controlled drug illicitly acquired and consumed, and thus it is the substance most likely to be encountered by police. In the absence of a significant causal link between cannabis use and crime, the possession of cannabis is often coincidental, and incidental, to the matter under investigation by the police. During the debates in Committee, the Parliamentary Under-Secretary for the Home Department argued that the power of arrest might be needed in respect of Class C drugs other than cannabis (for example, in circumstances where a doctor has not prescribed a particular Class C drug): see Standing Committee B, col.139. This speculative basis for widening arrestability for the possession of any Class C drug has been abandoned.

The twists and turns in the history of United Kingdom drug laws regarding cannabis has resulted in a spate of complaints that the new measures are confusing the public (see "*New Drug Law Confuses the Public*" (The Times, January 16, 2004), summarising the views of Sir John Stevens, the Commissioner of the Metropolitan Police).

Note the increase in maximum penalties for drug trafficking offences in connection with Class C drugs: s.284, Sch.28 para.1. The effect of the amendments is to increase the penalty for drug trafficking in any Class C drug from five years' to 14 years' imprisonment. This is primarily to deal with the fact that cannabis and cannabis resin — as well as Cannabinol, Cannabinol derivatives — have (from the January 29, 2004) been reclassified from Class B to a Class C drug: see The Misuse of Drugs Act 1971 (Modification) (No. 2) Order 2003.

4   Bail elsewhere than at police station

(1) Section 30 of the 1984 Act (arrest elsewhere than at police station) is amended as follows.

(2) For subsection (1) there is substituted—

> "(1) Subsection (1A) applies where a person is, at any place other than a police station—
>> (a) arrested by a constable for an offence, or
>> (b) taken into custody by a constable after being arrested for an offence by a person other than a constable.
>
> (1A) The person must be taken by a constable to a police station as soon as practicable after the arrest.
>
> (1B) Subsection (1A) has effect subject to section 30A (release on bail) and subsection (7) (release without bail)."

(3) In subsection (2) for "subsection (1)" there is substituted "subsection (1A)".

(4) For subsection (7) there is substituted—

> "(7) A person arrested by a constable at any place other than a police station must be released without bail if the condition in subsection (7A) is satisfied.
>
> (7A) The condition is that, at any time before the person arrested reaches a police station, a constable is satisfied that there are no grounds for keeping him under arrest or releasing him on bail under section 30A."

(5) For subsections (10) and (11) there is substituted—

"(10) Nothing in subsection (1A) or in section 30A prevents a constable delaying taking a person to a police station or releasing him on bail if the condition in subsection (10A) is satisfied.

(10A) The condition is that the presence of the person at a place (other than a police station) is necessary in order to carry out such investigations as it is reasonable to carry out immediately.

(11) Where there is any such delay the reasons for the delay must be recorded when the person first arrives at the police station or (as the case may be) is released on bail."

(6) In subsection (12) for "subsection (1)" there is substituted "subsection (1A) or section 30A".

(7) After section 30 there is inserted—

"30A Bail elsewhere than at police station

(1) A constable may release on bail a person who is arrested or taken into custody in the circumstances mentioned in section 30(1).

(2) A person may be released on bail under subsection (1) at any time before he arrives at a police station.

(3) A person released on bail under subsection (1) must be required to attend a police station.

(4) No other requirement may be imposed on the person as a condition of bail.

(5) The police station which the person is required to attend may be any police station.

30B Bail under section 30A: notices

(1) Where a constable grants bail to a person under section 30A, he must give that person a notice in writing before he is released.

(2) The notice must state—
 (a) the offence for which he was arrested, and
 (b) the ground on which he was arrested.

(3) The notice must inform him that he is required to attend a police station.

(4) It may also specify the police station which he is required to attend and the time when he is required to attend.

(5) If the notice does not include the information mentioned in subsection (4), the person must subsequently be given a further notice in writing which contains that information.

(6) The person may be required to attend a different police station from that specified in the notice under subsection (1) or (5) or to attend at a different time.

(7) He must be given notice in writing of any such change as is mentioned in subsection (6) but more than one such notice may be given to him.

30C Bail under section 30A: supplemental

(1) A person who has been required to attend a police station is not required to do so if he is given notice in writing that his attendance is no longer required.

(2) If a person is required to attend a police station which is not a designated police station he must be—
 (a) released, or
 (b) taken to a designated police station,
not more than six hours after his arrival.

(3) Nothing in the Bail Act 1976 applies in relation to bail under section 30A.

(4) Nothing in section 30A or 30B or in this section prevents the re-arrest without a warrant of a person released on bail under section 30A if new evidence justifying a further arrest has come to light since his release.

30D Failure to answer to bail under section 30A

(1) A constable may arrest without a warrant a person who—
  (a) has been released on bail under section 30A subject to a requirement to attend a specified police station, but
  (b) fails to attend the police station at the specified time.

(2) A person arrested under subsection (1) must be taken to a police station (which may be the specified police station or any other police station) as soon as practicable after the arrest.

(3) In subsection (1), "specified" means specified in a notice under subsection (1) or (5) of section 30B or, if notice of change has been given under subsection (7) of that section, in that notice.

(4) For the purposes of—
  (a) section 30 (subject to the obligation in subsection (2)), and
  (b) section 31, an arrest under this section is to be treated as an arrest for an offence."

DEFINITIONS
  "the 1984 Act": s.1(1)

GENERAL NOTE
  This section deals with what is sometimes styled "street bail". Before the section was enacted, a constable who took into custody a person arrested at a place other than a police station, was required to take that person to a police station (usually a "designated police station") as soon as practicable after the arrest. When an arrested person is taken to a non-designated police station, he/she should either be released or transferred to a "designated" police station after no longer than six hours. The significance of a police station being "designated" is that the greatest protections exist in that environment for the arrestee, and for the police. There was one situation in which the arrested person could be released, before arriving at the police station, namely, if a constable was satisfied that there were no grounds for keeping him under arrest. There was no power for a constable to release a suspect on unconditional, or conditional, bail at the place of arrest no matter how minor the alleged infringement. Section 4 of the 2003 Act amends s.30 PACE so that in a typical case, the arrested person will, normally, be taken to a designated police station as soon as practicable, but the constable may (for various reasons) release him on bail at any time before he arrives there.

  Bail will always be subject to one condition (and one only) namely to attend any police station (whether designated or not): see ss.30A(1)–(5) inserted by s.4(7) of the 2003 Act. The officer has no power to impose a condition of residence, or to produce documents, or not to go into certain areas or places. If before reaching the police station, the officer is satisfied that there are no grounds for keeping the person under arrest, or that there are no grounds for releasing him on bail subject to the condition that he attends any police station, the officer must release that person without further ado: s.30(7) and s.30(7A) inserted by s.4(4) of the 2003 Act.

  It will be seen that the new power to release on bail under s.30A of PACE gives no guidance to constables at all as to when, or how, the discretion to grant bail shall be exercised. Would it be permissible for a constable to release on bail a person who pleaded extenuating domestic circumstances (for example, that he was the principal carer of his disabled wife)? It would seem that the Government proposes to address this issue by way of providing guidance to officers (see Standing Committee B, col.70, December 17, 2002). A decision to not release on bail amounts to a decision to continue detaining the suspect (see Standing Committee B, col.68, December 17, 2002).

  The criteria, by which officers decide to grant, or refuse bail, are clearly important. Much controversy has arisen concerning the application of s.3(3) of the 2003 Act, in respect of the extended power to arrest persons in possession of the Class C controlled drugs cannabis and cannabis resin (now that those substances have been transferred from Class B to Class C of Sch.2 to the Misuse of Drugs Act 1971). Government thinking maybe that the new "street bail" provisions will be of great practical importance in relation to such arrests. The arresting officer might decide to release the suspect on bail (under s.30A PACE) with a direction to attend a named police station as soon as the substance has been analysed, or subsequent to a decision to prosecute (or not to do so), or to deal with the case in some other way — for example by way of a caution, warning, or referral to another agency.

What is to be the procedure for removing property from a suspect in the context of an officer making a decision whether to grant street-bail or not, for example, taking a substance suspected of being a controlled drug for analysis? Should that be done at a police station and in the presence of the arrested person? An officer might believe that to remove property at the scene, and to grant "street bail" might expose him to false complaints of misconduct (*e.g.* that a substance had been planted or switched). At least one Member of Parliament sought clarification of the position in cases where the arrested person sought the return of property seized by police at the time street bail was granted (Standing Committee B, col.69, December 17, 2002). At that stage, the arrested person would be unlikely to have the benefit of legal advice or assistance. The Government's position again appears to be that all such concerns can be met by providing guidance to constables as to how the new powers should be exercised.

Subsection 5 — delay in taking a suspect to a police station

Section 3(5) of the 2003 Act, substitutes ss.30(10), 30(10A) and 30(11) for the old subss.(10) and (11) of PACE.

As originally drafted, s.30(1) imposed a mandatory requirement that the arrested person be conveyed to a police station "as soon as practicable". The police voiced concern that those words may not introduce sufficient flexibility to enable them to carry out investigations that ought to be made immediately notwithstanding that the consequence would be that the arrested person's arrival at a police station would be delayed. However, the purpose of the restriction is to protect the interests of both the arrested person and the police, so that the rights and duties are overseen and appropriately managed at a police station. It is there that a suspect should be interviewed (tape-recorded), that the facts and circumstances of detention are recorded and monitored; that legal and medical assistance can be provided. It has been suggested that a typical arrest can keep the arresting officer "off the beat" for some three-and-a-half hours (PA Consulting Group, Police Research Series Paper 149, November 2001, p.vi; and see Research Paper 02/72, HC, p.28). On the other hand, there may be circumstances when it would be preferable for the arresting officer to immediately make inquiries following an arrest (for example, the suspect claims that he discarded a firearm in a field five miles from the scene of the arrest).

Section 4 of the 2003 Act amends s.30 PACE by retaining the general rule that an arrested person must be taken to a police station as soon as practicable, but new ss.30(10), 30(10A), and 30(11) empower a constable to delay taking the arrested person to a police station, or releasing him on street bail, if — and only if — the presence of the arrested person at a place other than a police station "is necessary in order to carry out such investigations as it is reasonable to carry out immediately" (s.30(10a)). Paragraph 110 of the Explanatory Notes (December 2003), indicates that the power may be exercised if "necessary for immediate investigative purposes". This would seem to mean that an officer is able to investigate an offence straight away. Thus, an officer might execute a s.18 PACE search before the suspect is taken to the police station. It will be noted that no limit is placed on the period of delay caused by the exercise of the power, and this is deliberate (see Standing Committee B, col.53, December 17, 2002). The power does not seem to include cases where the police received information in connection with an unrelated matter or incident that ought to be investigated immediately.

Despite the existence of the new powers, the police must heed the warning of the Court Appeal that use of the powers must not circumvent the PACE Codes of Practice, for otherwise evidence thus obtained might be excluded under s.78 of PACE: see *R. v Khan* [1993] Crim. L.R. 54 and *R. v Raphaie (Daniel)* [1996] Crim. L.R. 812.

5   Drug testing for under-eighteens

(1) The 1984 Act is amended as follows.

(2) In section 38 (duties of custody officer after charge)—

    (a) in subsection (1)—

        (i) for sub-paragraph (iiia) of paragraph (a) there is substituted—

            "(iiia) except in a case where (by virtue of subsection (9) of section 63B below) that section does not apply, the custody officer has reasonable grounds for believing that the detention of the person is necessary to enable a sample to be taken from him under that section;",

(ii) in sub-paragraph (i) of paragraph (b), after "satisfied" there is inserted "(but, in the case of paragraph (a)(iiia) above, only if the arrested juvenile has attained the minimum age)",

(b) in subsection (6A), after the definition of "local authority accommodation" there is inserted—

""minimum age" means the age specified in section 63B(3) below;".

(3) In section 63B (testing for presence of Class A drugs)—

(a) in subsection (3), for "18" there is substituted "14",

(b) after subsection (5) there is inserted—

"(5A) In the case of a person who has not attained the age of 17—

(a) the making of the request under subsection (4) above;

(b) the giving of the warning and (where applicable) the information under subsection (5) above; and

(c) the taking of the sample,

may not take place except in the presence of an appropriate adult.",

(c) after subsection (6) there is inserted—

"(6A) The Secretary of State may by order made by statutory instrument amend subsection (3) above by substituting for the age for the time being specified a different age specified in the order.

(6B) A statutory instrument containing an order under subsection (6A) above shall not be made unless a draft of the instrument has been laid before, and approved by a resolution of, each House of Parliament.",

(d) after subsection (8) there is inserted—

"(9) In relation to a person who has not attained the age of 18, this section applies only where—

(a) the relevant chief officer has been notified by the Secretary of State that arrangements for the taking of samples under this section from persons who have not attained the age of 18 have been made for the police area as a whole, or for the particular police station, in which the person is in police detention; and

(b) the notice has not been withdrawn.

(10) In this section—

"appropriate adult", in relation to a person who has not attained the age of 17, means—

(a) his parent or guardian or, if he is in the care of a local authority or voluntary organisation, a person representing that authority or organisation; or

(b) a social worker of a local authority social services department; or

(c) if no person falling within paragraph (a) or (b) is available, any responsible person aged 18 or over who is not a police officer or a person employed by the police;

"relevant chief officer" means—

(a) in relation to a police area, the chief officer of police of the police force for that police area; or

(b) in relation to a police station, the chief officer of police of the police force for the police area in which the police station is situated."

GENERAL NOTE

Paragraphs 119 and 120 of the Explanatory Notes (December 2003) explain the purpose of s.5 as follows:

"119. Section 57 of the Criminal Justice and Court Services Act 2000 inserted new provisions in the Police and Criminal Evidence Act 1984 (PACE), enabling custody officers after charge, to detain a person to enable a sample to be taken to test for the presence of any specified class A drug, subject to the conditions detailed in section 63B of PACE. The conditions include that the person concerned has attained the age of 18. The provisions currently apply only within certain police areas where section 57 has been brought into force.

120. Section 5 amends these provisions in PACE (in respect of section 63B and section 38) to enable persons under the age of 18 to be tested for specified Class A drugs and for custody officers to detain a person after charge to enable a sample to be taken for that purpose. The person concerned must have attained the age of 14. The section also makes provision for an appropriate adult to be present during the testing procedure in the case of a person who is under 17 years old. The Secretary of State is given power by order (under the draft affirmative procedure) to change the minimum age."

Accordingly, the minimum age for testing for the presence of a Class A drug is now 14 years of age (s.63B(3) PACE) that might be varied by an order made by Statutory Instrument: and see s.63B(6A) inserted by s.5(3)(c) of the 2003 Act.

When this provision was being examined in Standing Committee, concern was expressed as to the appropriateness of carrying out drug tests on those aged 17 and under, within the criminal justice system (Standing Committee B, col.154, December 17, 2002). Further concerns related to the exercise of the power and facilities for dealing with those aged under 18 who have drug related problems. The Parliamentary Under Secretary of State for the Home Department stressed that the age groups identified in the legislation for drug testing, are consistent with the provisions of the Children and Young Persons Act 1933 (c.66) as amended by Sch.8 to the Criminal Justice Act 1991 (c.53) (Standing Committee B, col.162, January 7, 2003). However, it would appear that the Government's decision to set the minimum age at 14 years, was in part influenced by the results of a lifestyle survey carried out by the Department of Health and the Youth Justice Board in respect of 11–15 year-olds, which showed that Class A drug use was "very rare". Thus, the "testing for Class A drugs in those under the age of 14 would not be an effective use of resources" (Standing Committee B, col.162, Parliamentary Under Secretary of State For The Home Department).

Those aged between 10 and 13 who commit a "trigger offence" (see s.63B PACE) will be referred to a Youth Offending Team either at the point of charging the suspect/offender, or under the final warning scheme. Section 63B(7) sets out instances where a sample taken under the section may be disclosed *e.g.* for the purpose of sentencing the defendant. The subsection makes no express provision for disclosure of the results of the sample as evidence in the trial of an offence. The categories permitting disclosure under ss.63B(7)(a)–(d) may be closed, but the courts have yet to decide whether a positive result might be admissible to rebut the defendant's evidence (or account in interview) that he/she had not ingested the Class A drug in question. However the Parliamentary Under Secretary for the Home Department had this to say about the matter (Standing Committee B, col.166, January 7, 2003):

"It is not intended that the test results will be used as additional evidence in support of offences with which the detainee has been charged or for the purposes of other investigations or as an aggravating factor when sentencing. The testing is a screening tool; it is intended to identify those who have misused specified class A drugs and who may need treatment and to encourage them to get treatment for their drug misuse. It might be helpful if I remind the Committee that the legislation sets out the purpose for which the information obtained through drug testing after charge may be disclosed. It provides for appropriate disclosure under the criminal justice system in order to inform decisions on bail and sentencing, and decisions on the supervision of the person concerned throughout the criminal justice process, and to ensure that appropriate advice and treatment are made available to the person concerned.

The legislation also ensures that the sensitive nature of the information is respected and that the individual's rights are preserved. Those are the provisions that apply to the testing of adults in the pilot areas; they would be replicated when operating the clause."

6   Use of telephones for review of police detention

For section 40A(1) and (2) of the 1984 Act (use of telephone for review under s.40) there is substituted—

"(1) A review under section 40(1)(b) may be carried out by means of a discussion, conducted by telephone, with one or more persons at the police station where the arrested person is held.

(2) But subsection (1) does not apply if—

(a) the review is of a kind authorised by regulations under section 45A to be carried out using video-conferencing facilities; and

(b) it is reasonably practicable to carry it out in accordance with those regulations."

GENERAL NOTE

At the time this provision was being considered in Parliament, there seemed to have been a great deal of confusion about its scope and purpose. By s.40(1) PACE, reviews of the detention of a person at a police station in connection with the investigation of an offence, shall be carried out periodically, and (in the case of a person arrested but not charged) shall be carried out by an officer of at least the rank of inspector who has not been directly involved in the investigation (s.40(1)(b) PACE). The authors of *Research Paper 02/72* (December 2, 2002, p.31) appear to suggest that the purpose of the amendments is to remove the need for an officer of at least the rank of inspector to carry out the review, but this is not the view of the Government (see Standing Committee B, col.73, December 17, 2002). The Parliamentary Under-Secretary of State for the Home Department said, "I point out that all reviews of detention without charge, including telephone reviews, must be carried out by an officer of at least the rank of inspector. That is unchanged."

Section 40A, as originally drafted, was inserted into PACE by s.73(1) and s.73(2) of the Criminal Justice and Police Act 2001 (c.16), but not brought into force. The intention then was that reviews can be carried out by telephone if it was not reasonably practicable for an officer of at least the rank of inspector to be present in a police station, and the use of video — conference facilities is either not an option or not reasonably practicable.

Section 4 of the 2003 Act, amends ss.40A(1) and (2), so that a Review under s.40(1)(b) PACE may be carried out by use of a telephone whether it is reasonably practicable for an officer of at least the rank of inspector to be present or not. In practice, the Review will be carried out by an officer of such rank because although the revised version of s.40A(1) is silent on that point, s.40(1)(b) PACE is explicit. If the inspector cannot carry out the review in person at the police station, he may conduct a telephone review, and now under substituted s.40A(1) PACE, the review may be carried out by him in consultation with others at the police station, usually the custody officer and perhaps the suspect's legal adviser.

7   Limits on period of detention without charge

In section 42(1) of the 1984 Act (conditions to be satisfied before detention without charge may be extended from 24 to 36 hours), for paragraph (b) there is substituted—

"(b) an offence for which he is under arrest is an arrestable offence; and".

DEFINITIONS

"serious arrestable offence": s.116 PACE 1984

GENERAL NOTE

This short, but important section, empowers an officer of at least the rank of superintendent, to authorise keeping a suspect in police detention for a period up to 36 hours if the offence for which he is arrested is an "arrestable offence" and the remaining conditions of s.42(1) PACE, are met. Previously, the power applied where the offence was a "serious arrestable offence".

The justification for extending the power in this way is expressed in the Explanatory Notes as follows (para.125):

> "(to) assist the police in dealing effectively with a range of offences, for example robbery, where it will sometimes be extremely difficult or impossible to complete the necessary investigatory process within 24 hours."

The concept of the "serious arrestable offence" was introduced into the law by PACE in order to give the police greater powers in relation to road checks (s.4(b) PACE), searching premises (s.8(1) PACE), inspection of material (s.9 and Sch.1 to PACE), detention (ss.42, 43 and 44 PACE), access to a legal adviser (s.58 PACE), and the taking of samples (ss.62 and 63 PACE). A "serious arrestable offence" is defined by s.116 PACE. Some arrestable offences are "always serious" for example, murder and rape (see Pt 1 of Sch.5 to PACE). Other arrestable offences are "serious" by reference to consequences (intended or actual) flowing from the commission of the offences, as described in s.116(6) PACE. By contrast, an "arrestable offence" is a very much broader concept (see s.24 PACE, as amended) being mainly offences that carry a sentence of five years' imprisonment or more (s.24(1) PACE), but include offences listed in Sch.1A to PACE (and see s.24(1)(c) PACE).

The Government anticipates that the power of extended detention will be used in only a small number of cases. For the year 2001–2002, those detained for longer than 24 hours and released without charge, numbered 697 out of a total of 1.25 million detentions, but apparently no figures were kept of those detained for longer than 24 hours and then charged. The then Parliamentary Under Secretary of State for the Home Department suggested that the figure was "unlikely to be large".

Concern was expressed by a number of Members of Parliament, that the amendment to PACE introduced by s.7 of the 2003 Act, might have the effect of empowering police to detain persons in excess of 24 hours for stealing a Mars bar, or being in possession of a controlled drug. The Government successfully resisted an amendment to limit the reach of the new power to arrestable offences "punishable by more than 10 years' imprisonment" (Standing Committee B, cols.81–90, December 19, 2002). Attempts to delete what was then clause 5 from the Bill were also defeated. The challenge was mounted on the ground that one object of PACE was to bring detention within the control of that statute, to ensure that detention was for as short a period as possible and that people would know that there are rules about the likely duration of detention (Simon Hughes MP, Standing Committee B, col.90).

The Government pointed out that the statistical evidence shows that the average length of detention was about five and a quarter hours (*ibid.* col.101).

8   Property of detained persons

(1) In subsection (1) of section 54 of the 1984 Act (which requires the custody officer at a police station to ascertain and record everything which a detained person has with him), there is omitted "and record or cause to be recorded".

(2) For subsection (2) of that section (record of arrested person to be made as part of custody record) there is substituted—

> "(2) The custody officer may record or cause to be recorded all or any of the things which he ascertains under subsection (1).
>
> (2A) In the case of an arrested person, any such record may be made as part of his custody record."

DEFINITIONS
  "the 1984 Act": s.1(1)

GENERAL NOTE
  Section 54 PACE requires the custody officer at a police station to ascertain and to record everything that a detained person has with him or her. This has always been regarded as a very important safeguard for both the detained person and for the police, against complaints that property has been stolen, or "planted". The presence of cash, or other financial documents, found on a suspect and carefully recorded on a custody record, has been of evidential value in many criminal trials.
  Section 8 of the 2003 Act removes the requirement on the custody officer to "record or cause to be recorded" everything which a detained person has with him, yet it shall be his task to "ascertain everything which a person has with him" when entering the police station. What is recorded is thus entirely at the discretion of the custody officer. How that discretion should be exercised will presumably be a matter of training and experience.

Section 8 of the 2003 Act has its origins in the Review of PACE (para.34). The Government noted complaints from the police that the burden of making a list on the custody record of a detained persons property, was time-consuming "and not always necessary". The Review said nothing about removing the burden on the custody officer to record "everything", but merely recommended "Modifying the requirement so that the custody officer must secure all a detained person's property in that person's presence and make whatever supporting records he considers necessary. Any subsequent accessing of the property would again be in the detained person's presence. This would allow for the use of sealable property bags and have the potential to save resources without compromising protections." The Government has indicated that "guidance will make it clear that money and articles of significant value should continue to be recorded" (Standing Committee B, col.106, December 19, 2003). The Explanatory Notes say that it will be open to the police to make judgments about how to balance the need for recording items found in the possession of the detained person "against the amount of administrative work involved" (para.126).

9   Taking fingerprints without consent

(1) Section 61 of the 1984 Act (fingerprinting) is amended as follows.

(2) For subsections (3) and (4) (taking of fingerprints without appropriate consent) there is substituted—

> "(3) The fingerprints of a person detained at a police station may be taken without the appropriate consent if—
>> (a) he is detained in consequence of his arrest for a recordable offence; and
>> (b) he has not had his fingerprints taken in the course of the investigation of the offence by the police.
>
> (4) The fingerprints of a person detained at a police station may be taken without the appropriate consent if—
>> (a) he has been charged with a recordable offence or informed that he will be reported for such an offence; and
>> (b) he has not had his fingerprints taken in the course of the investigation of the offence by the police."

(3) In subsection (3A) (disregard of incomplete or unsatisfactory fingerprints) for the words from the beginning to "subsection (3) above" there is substituted "Where a person mentioned in paragraph (a) of subsection (3) or (4) has already had his fingerprints taken in the course of the investigation of the offence by the police".

(4) In subsection (5) (authorisation to be given or confirmed in writing) for "subsection (3)(a) or (4A)" there is substituted "subsection (4A)".

(5) In subsection (7) (reasons for taking of fingerprints without consent) for "subsection (3) or (6)" there is substituted "subsection (3), (4) or (6)".

GENERAL NOTE

Section 9 applies to persons arrested for a recordable offence and who are being held in a police station. The section provides further powers to take a suspect's fingerprints without his/her consent (see s.61 PACE). The Explanatory Notes summarise the powers as follows:

"130. Subsection (2) replaces the existing provisions about the taking of fingerprints on the authority of an Inspector with a wider power to take fingerprints from any person detained in consequence of his arrest for a recordable offence.

131. The existing requirement to give a person whose fingerprints are taken without consent reasons for doing so and for recording the reason as soon as practical applies to the new power (see subsection (5) of section 9).

132. This amendment to section 61 of PACE will prevent persons who come into police custody and who may be wanted on a warrant or for questioning on other matters from avoiding detection by giving the police a false name and address. Using Livescan technology, which enables the police to take fingerprints electronically and which is linked to the national fingerprint database (NAFIS), the police will be able to confirm a person's identity whilst he is still in police detention if his fingerprints have been taken previously. It

will also assist in enabling vulnerable or violent people to be identified more quickly and dealt with more effectively. A speculative search of the fingerprint crime scene database will also reveal if the person may have been involved in other crimes."

10   Taking non-intimate samples without consent

(1) Section 63 of the 1984 Act (other samples) is amended as follows.

(2) After subsection (2) (consent to be given in writing) there is inserted—

> "(2A) A non-intimate sample may be taken from a person without the appropriate consent if two conditions are satisfied.
>
> (2B) The first is that the person is in police detention in consequence of his arrest for a recordable offence.
>
> (2C) The second is that—
>
> > (a) he has not had a non-intimate sample of the same type and from the same part of the body taken in the course of the investigation of the offence by the police, or
> >
> > (b) he has had such a sample taken but it proved insufficient."

(3) In subsection (3)(a) (taking of samples without appropriate consent) the words "is in police detention or" are omitted.

(4) In subsection (3A) (taking of samples without appropriate consent after charge) for "(whether or not he falls within subsection (3)(a) above)" there is substituted "(whether or not he is in police detention or held in custody by the police on the authority of a court)".

(5) In subsection (8A) (reasons for taking of samples without consent) for "subsection (3A)" there is substituted "subsection (2A), (3A)".

GENERAL NOTE

By virtue of this section the police are given further powers (see s.63 PACE) to take a non-intimate sample from a suspect arrested for a recordable offence and who is being held at a police station. The Explanatory Notes concisely explain the changes as follows:

> "135. In relation to a person in police detention, subsections (2) and (3) replace the existing provisions about the taking of a non-intimate sample on the authority of an inspector with a wider power to take a non-intimate sample from any person in police detention in consequence of his arrest for a recordable offence. This is conditional on him not having had a sample of the same type and from the same part of the body taken already in the course of the investigation or if one has that it proved insufficient for the analysis.
>
> 136. The new power is available whether or not the sample is required for the investigation of an offence in which the person is suspected of being involved. But of course the police will be able to use the new power to obtain samples in cases where under the present law an inspector's authorisation would be given (for example, in a rape investigation, to obtain a foot impression, a hair sample and a mouth swab).
>
> 137. The existing requirement to give a person from whom a non-intimate sample is taken without consent the reason for doing so and for recording the reason as soon as practicable applies to the new power. (see subsection (5) of Section 10).
>
> 138. The amendments do not affect the existing powers to take samples from persons held in custody by the police on the authority of a court.
>
> 139. DNA profiles extracted from non-intimate samples taken from arrested persons will be added to the samples already held on the National DNA Database and checked for matches with DNA taken from crime scenes."

11   Codes of practice

(1) In section 67 of the 1984 Act (supplementary provisions about codes), for subsections (1) to (7C) there is substituted—

> "(1) In this section, "code" means a code of practice under section 60, 60A or 66.
>
> (2) The Secretary of State may at any time revise the whole or any part of a code.
>
> (3) A code may be made, or revised, so as to—
>
> > (a) apply only in relation to one or more specified areas,

(b) have effect only for a specified period,
(c) apply only in relation to specified offences or descriptions of offender.

(4) Before issuing a code, or any revision of a code, the Secretary of State must consult—
(a) persons whom he considers to represent the interests of police authorities,
(b) persons whom he considers to represent the interests of chief officers of police,
(c) the General Council of the Bar,
(d) the Law Society of England and Wales,
(e) the Institute of Legal Executives, and
(f) such other persons as he thinks fit.

(5) A code, or a revision of a code, does not come into operation until the Secretary of State by order so provides.

(6) The power conferred by subsection (5) is exercisable by statutory instrument.

(7) An order bringing a code into operation may not be made unless a draft of the order has been laid before Parliament and approved by a resolution of each House.

(7A) An order bringing a revision of a code into operation must be laid before Parliament if the order has been made without a draft having been so laid and approved by a resolution of each House.

(7B) When an order or draft of an order is laid, the code or revision of a code to which it relates must also be laid.

(7C) No order or draft of an order may be laid until the consultation required by subsection (4) has taken place.

(7D) An order bringing a code, or a revision of a code, into operation may include transitional or saving provisions."

(2) Section 113 of the 1984 Act (application of Act to armed forces) is amended as follows.

(3) After subsection (3) there is inserted—

"(3A) In subsections (4) to (10), "code" means a code of practice under subsection (3)."

(4) For subsections (5) to (7) there is substituted—

"(5) The Secretary of State may at any time revise the whole or any part of a code.

(6) A code may be made, or revised, so as to—
(a) apply only in relation to one or more specified areas,
(b) have effect only for a specified period,
(c) apply only in relation to specified offences or descriptions of offender.

(7) The Secretary of State must lay a code, or any revision of a code, before Parliament."

DEFINITIONS
"code": s.67(1) PACE as amended by s.7 of the 2003 Act
"the 1984 Act": s.1(1)

GENERAL NOTE
The Explanatory Notes (para.140) say that the purpose of the section is to make "fundamental changes to the process for establishing and amending codes of practice under PACE". The notes say very little about the extent of the changes, or their practical effect.

By s.66 PACE, the Secretary of State is required to issue Codes of Practice in connection with various aspects of the treatment of suspects by the police and other law enforcement agencies. Section 67(1) as originally drafted, required the Secretary of State to "prepare and publish a draft of that code" and to consider representations made to him. He was then empowered to "modify the draft accordingly". No order, bringing in the Code into force, could be made by Statutory Instrument unless approved by resolution of each House of Parliament. The Codes of Practice have been reviewed and updated under this procedure on several occasions, but the PACE Review states that updating the Codes is a "long and complicated process" resulting in considerable delays to changes to primary legislation. The Review also states that the Codes would benefit from a "greater degree of clarity in their structure and content" (Ch.2, para.2). Section 11 of the 2003 Act addresses the first of these complaints.

The Review makes no secret of the fact that the Government wishes to restrict the statutory requirement to consult on proposed revisions to the codes, and to replace the previous procedure with a "straightforward requirement to lay new (or changed) codes before Parliament".

It will be seen that s.67(4) of PACE in the form substituted by s.11(1) of the 2003 Act requires the Secretary of State to consult before issuing or revising a Code, but then gives him wide discretion to consult those persons "whom he considers to represent the interests of police authorities", or the interests of "chief officers of police", or such "other persons as he thinks fit". In the initial version of the Bill there was no requirement to consult other interested groups or parties. The Government pointed out that s.67, as originally enacted, did not expressly require the Secretary of State to consult at all (Standing Committee B, col.121, January 7, 2003) merely to "consider representations made to him". It argued that there was provision for parliamentary scrutiny of any revision to the Codes, and that it would be "almost inconceivable that there would be circumstances in which the Bar Council and the Law Society would not be consulted". The Parliamentary Under-Secretary of State for the Home Department pointed out that "it is generally not a good idea to include in primary legislation names of particular organisations, because those organisations sometimes cease to exist" and that "other organisations ask why their names have not been included in the list" (Standing Committee B, col.122, January 7, 2003). The second point arguably has greater force. In the light of assurances given by the Government that it would consult agencies other than the police, the original draft of the revised version of s.67(4) PACE (see s.11(1) of the 2003 Act), survived the debates in Standing Committee B, but it will be noted that s.11 does now include the General Council of the Bar (of England and Wales), the Law Society of England and Wales, and the Institute of Legal Executives.

12   Amendments related to Part 1

Schedule 1 (which makes amendments related to the provisions of this Part) has effect.

GENERAL NOTE

This section makes a number of amendments by virtue of Sch.1 to Part 1 of the 2003 Act. The Parliamentary Under-Secretary of State for the Home Department explained its purpose as follows (Standing Committee B, col.126, January 7, 2003):

"(The section) introduces schedule 1, which makes amendments that are related to part 1. Paragraphs 1 to 10 are necessary to make various amendments that are consequential on the specific modifications and extensions to powers set out in part 1. Paragraphs 11 to 13 are needed to allow certain persons accompanying constables in executing warrants under section 2 of the Criminal Justice Act 1987 (c.38) — which deals with cases of serious fraud — to exercise relevant powers of a constable. That effectively allows the same flexibility for warrants relating to the work of the Serious Fraud Office as (section 2) allows for search warrants in general.

Paragraph 15 is necessary to provide military police with the same stop and search powers relating to articles made, adapted or intended for use in causing criminal damage as clause 1 provides more generally.

Paragraphs 16 to 19 amend schedule 4 to the Police Reform Act 2002, which allows certain police powers to be exercised by designated civilian members of staff. The amendments are necessary to ensure that the provisions are consistent with the amendments to PACE powers set out in the Bill."

PART 2

BAIL

13   Grant and conditions of bail

(1) In section 3(6) of the 1976 Act (which sets out cases where bail conditions may be imposed)—

    (a) the words "to secure that" are omitted,
    (b) the words "to secure that" are inserted at the beginning of each of paragraphs (a) to (e),
    (c) after paragraph (c) there is inserted—
      "(ca) for his own protection or, if he is a child or young person, for his own welfare or in his own interests,",

    (d) for "or (c)" there is substituted ", (c) or (ca)".
  (2) In section 3A(5) of the 1976 Act (no conditions may be imposed under section 3(4), (5), (6) or (7) unless necessary for certain purposes)—
    (a) the words "for the purpose of preventing that person from" are omitted,
    (b) the words "for the purpose of preventing that person from" are inserted at the beginning of each of paragraphs (a) to (c),
    (c) after paragraph (c) there is inserted "or
    (d) for that person's own protection or, if he is a child or young person, for his own welfare or in his own interests."

  (3) In paragraph 8(1) of Part 1 of Schedule 1 to the 1976 Act (no conditions may be imposed under section 3(4) to (7) unless necessary to do so for certain purposes) for the words from "that it is necessary to do so" onwards there is substituted "that it is necessary to do so—
    (a) for the purpose of preventing the occurrence of any of the events mentioned in paragraph 2(1) of this Part of this Schedule, or
    (b) for the defendant's own protection or, if he is a child or young person, for his own welfare or in his own interests."

  (4) For paragraph 5 of Part 2 of that Schedule (defendant need not be granted bail if having been released on bail he has been arrested in pursuance of section 7) there is substituted—

    "5 The defendant need not be granted bail if—
    (a) having been released on bail in or in connection with the proceedings for the offence, he has been arrested in pursuance of section 7 of this Act; and
    (b) the court is satisfied that there are substantial grounds for believing that the defendant, if released on bail (whether subject to conditions or not) would fail to surrender to custody, commit an offence on bail or interfere with witnesses or otherwise obstruct the course of justice (whether in relation to himself or any other person)."

GENERAL NOTE

  The purposes of Pt 2 of the Act is to amend the Bail Act 1976 (c.63) ("the 1976 Act") in order to ensure that the 1976 Act complies with the terms of the Human Rights Act 1998, and the European Convention on Human Rights. The amendments are intended to give effect to recommendations of the Law Commission regarding the 1976 Act (see Law Commission Report 269 and see Explanatory Notes and see Standing Committee B, col.170, January 7, 2003).

  Article 3 of the United Nations Convention On The Right The Child, makes the interest of the child the paramount consideration. The 1976 Act empowers the court to refuse bail to a defendant for his own protection, or in the case of a juvenile, for this welfare. That might lead to a defendant being remanded in custody whereas release on conditional bail would have been appropriate. Similarly, by s.38(1)(b)(ii) PACE, a custody officer at a police station may decline to release an arrested juvenile from police detention if the officer "has reasonable grounds for believing that he ought to be detained in his own interests". Subject to ss.38(6)(a) and (b) PACE, an arrested juvenile charged with an offence, but refused bail by a custody officer, should be transferred to local authority accommodcation. However, power in the hands of a custody officer to grant stringent conditions of bail, might enable the arrested juvenile to be released. It will be noted the s.3A of the 1976 Act states that s.3 of that Act applies in relation to bail granted by a custody officer. Accordingly, and subject to s.3A(2), the custody officer may impose conditions for the purposes set out in s.3(6).

Section 13(1) amends s.3(6) of the 1976 Act to include subparagraph(ca), so that conditional bail may be granted to an adult by a court "for his own protection", or if he is a child or young person "for his own welfare"; and conditional bail may be granted by a custody officer in respect of an "arrested juvenile" if conditions are necessary "in his own interests" (adopting the phrase in s.38(1)(b)(ii) PACE). The fact that the conditions must be "necessary" for any of those purposes is reinforced by s.3A(5) 1976 Act as amended by s.13(2)(c) of the 2003 Act. Note that s.13(3) amends para.8(1) of Pt 1 to Sch.1 to the 1976 Act, to make that part consistent with the above changes.

Subsection (4)

The Explanatory Notes summarise the position as follows (para.146);

"Subsection (4) amends paragraph 5 of Part 2 of Schedule 1 to the Bail Act 1976 so that, where a defendant charged with a non-imprisonable offence is arrested under section 7, bail may be refused only if the court is satisfied that there are substantial grounds for believing that if released on bail (where subject to conditions or not) he or she would fail to surrender to custody, commit an offence whilst on bail, or interfere with witnesses or otherwise obstruct the course of justice."

14   Offences committed on bail

(1) For paragraph 2A of Part 1 of Schedule 1 to the 1976 Act (defendant need not be granted bail where he was on bail on date of offence) there is substituted—

"2A   (1) If the defendant falls within this paragraph he may not be granted bail unless the court is satisfied that there is no significant risk of his committing an offence while on bail (whether subject to conditions or not).
(2) The defendant falls within this paragraph if—
(a) he is aged 18 or over, and
(b) it appears to the court that he was on bail in criminal proceedings on the date of the offence."

(2) After paragraph 9 of that Part there is inserted—

"9AA   (1) This paragraph applies if—
(a) the defendant is under the age of 18, and
(b) it appears to the court that he was on bail in criminal proceedings on the date of the offence.
(2) In deciding for the purposes of paragraph 2(1) of this Part of this Schedule whether it is satisfied that there are substantial grounds for believing that the defendant, if released on bail (whether subject to conditions or not), would commit an offence while on bail, the court shall give particular weight to the fact that the defendant was on bail in criminal proceedings on the date of the offence."

GENERAL NOTE

Paragraph 2A of Pt 1 of Sch.1 to the 1976 Act (as originally drafted) empowered the court not to grant bail where a defendant charged with an indictable, or an indictable only, offence was already on bail. Subsection (1) replaces para.2A of Pt 1 of Sch.1 to the 1976 Act. If a defendant is aged 18 or over, and he was on bail on the date the current offence was allegedly committed, then he may not be granted bail unless the court is satisfied that there is no significant risk of his committing an offence whilst on bail.

Paragraph 9AA to Pt 1 is added to Pt 1 of Sch.1 to the 1976 Act by s.14(2) of the 2003 Act. This paragraph applies in cases where the defendant is under 18 years of age and on bail for another alleged offence. This provision does not create a presumption against bail being granted, but when the court is considering whether there are substantial grounds for believing that the defendant would commit further offences if granted bail, the court can give "particular weight" to the fact that he was already on bail.

15   **Absconding by persons released on bail**

(1) For paragraph 6 of Part 1 of Schedule 1 to the 1976 Act (defendant need not be granted bail if having been released on bail he has been arrested in pursuance of section 7) there is substituted—

> "6   (1) If the defendant falls within this paragraph, he may not be granted bail unless the court is satisfied that there is no significant risk that, if released on bail (whether subject to conditions or not), he would fail to surrender to custody.
>
> (2) Subject to sub-paragraph (3) below, the defendant falls within this paragraph if—
>
> (a) he is aged 18 or over, and
>
> (b) it appears to the court that, having been released on bail in or in connection with the proceedings for the offence, he failed to surrender to custody.
>
> (3) Where it appears to the court that the defendant had reasonable cause for his failure to surrender to custody, he does not fall within this paragraph unless it also appears to the court that he failed to surrender to custody at the appointed place as soon as reasonably practicable after the appointed time.
>
> (4) For the purposes of sub-paragraph (3) above, a failure to give to the defendant a copy of the record of the decision to grant him bail shall not constitute a reasonable cause for his failure to surrender to custody."

(2) After paragraph 9AA of that Part (inserted by section 14(2)) there is inserted—

> "9AB   (1) Subject to sub-paragraph (2) below, this paragraph applies if—
>
> (a) the defendant is under the age of 18, and
>
> (b) it appears to the court that, having been released on bail in or in connection with the proceedings for the offence, he failed to surrender to custody.
>
> (2) Where it appears to the court that the defendant had reasonable cause for his failure to surrender to custody, this paragraph does not apply unless it also appears to the court that he failed to surrender to custody at the appointed place as soon as reasonably practicable after the appointed time.
>
> (3) In deciding for the purposes of paragraph 2(1) of this Part of this Schedule whether it is satisfied that there are substantial grounds for believing that the defendant, if released on bail (whether subject to conditions or not), would fail to surrender to custody, the court shall give particular weight to—
>
> (a) where the defendant did not have reasonable cause for his failure to surrender to custody, the fact that he failed to surrender to custody, or
>
> (b) where he did have reasonable cause for his failure to surrender to custody, the fact that he failed to surrender to custody at the appointed place as soon as reasonably practicable after the appointed time.
>
> (4) For the purposes of this paragraph, a failure to give to the defendant a copy of the record of the decision to grant him bail shall not constitute a reasonable cause for his failure to surrender to custody."

(3) In section 6 of the 1976 Act (offence of absconding by person released on bail) after subsection (9) there is inserted—

"(10) Section 127 of the Magistrates' Courts Act 1980 shall not apply in relation to an offence under subsection (1) or (2) above.

(11) Where a person has been released on bail in criminal proceedings and that bail was granted by a constable, a magistrates' court shall not try that person for an offence under subsection (1) or (2) above in relation to that bail (the "relevant offence") unless either or both of subsections (12) and (13) below applies.

(12) This subsection applies if an information is laid for the relevant offence within 6 months from the time of the commission of the relevant offence.

(13) This subsection applies if an information is laid for the relevant offence no later than 3 months from the time of the occurrence of the first of the events mentioned in subsection (14) below to occur after the commission of the relevant offence.

(14) Those events are—
   (a) the person surrenders to custody at the appointed place;
   (b) the person is arrested, or attends at a police station, in connection with the relevant offence or the offence for which he was granted bail;
   (c) the person appears or is brought before a court in connection with the relevant offence or the offence for which he was granted bail."

GENERAL NOTE

A defendant aged 18 or over, who (without reasonable excuse) failed to answer to bail in current proceedings will be refused bail unless the court is satisfied that there is no significant risk that he will not abscond again.

The test is slightly different in connection with a defendant aged under 18, namely, that the court shall give particular weight to the fact that he failed to surrender to custody (if he did not have reasonable cause for his failure to surrender), or to the fact that he failed to surrender to custody at the appointed place as soon as reasonably practicable after the appointed time (if the defendant did have reasonable cause for his failure to surrender to custody).

Subsection (3)

The Explanatory Notes summarise this provision in the following terms:

"151. Subsection (3) disapplies section 127 of the Magistrates' Courts Act 1980 (which prevents summary proceedings from being instituted more than 6 months after the commission of an offence) in respect of offences under section 6 of the Bail Act, and instead provides that such an offence may not be tried unless an information is laid either within 6 months of the commission of the offence, or within three months of the defendant's surrender to custody, arrest or court appearance in respect of that offence. This will ensure that a defendant cannot escape being prosecuted for the Bail Act offence merely by succeeding in absconding for more than six months."

16   Appeal to Crown Court

(1) This section applies where a magistrates' court grants bail to a person ("the person concerned") on adjourning a case under—
   (a) section 10 of the Magistrates' Courts Act 1980 (c. 43) (adjournment of trial),
   (b) section 17C of that Act (intention as to plea: adjournment),
   (c) section 18 of that Act (initial procedure on information against adult for offence triable either way),
   (d) section 24C of that Act (intention as to plea by child or young person: adjournment),
   (e) section 52(5) of the Crime and Disorder Act 1998 (c. 37) (adjournment of proceedings under section 51 etc), or

      (f) section 11 of the Powers of Criminal Courts (Sentencing) Act 2000 (c. 6) (remand for medical examination).

(2) Subject to the following provisions of this section, the person concerned may appeal to the Crown Court against any condition of bail falling within subsection (3).

(3) A condition of bail falls within this subsection if it is a requirement—
    (a) that the person concerned resides away from a particular place or area,
    (b) that the person concerned resides at a particular place other than a bail hostel,
    (c) for the provision of a surety or sureties or the giving of a security,
    (d) that the person concerned remains indoors between certain hours,
    (e) imposed under section 3(6ZAA) of the 1976 Act (requirements with respect to electronic monitoring), or
    (f) that the person concerned makes no contact with another person.

(4) An appeal under this section may not be brought unless subsection (5) or (6) applies.

(5) This subsection applies if an application to the magistrates' court under section 3(8)(a) of the 1976 Act (application by or on behalf of person granted bail) was made and determined before the appeal was brought.

(6) This subsection applies if an application to the magistrates' court—
    (a) under section 3(8)(b) of the 1976 Act (application by constable or prosecutor), or
    (b) under section 5B(1) of that Act (application by prosecutor), was made and determined before the appeal was brought.

(7) On an appeal under this section the Crown Court may vary the conditions of bail.

(8) Where the Crown Court determines an appeal under this section, the person concerned may not bring any further appeal under this section in respect of the conditions of bail unless an application or a further application to the magistrates' court under section 3(8)(a) of the 1976 Act is made and determined after the appeal.

DEFINITIONS
    "bail": s.21
    "vary": s.21

GENERAL NOTE

The procedure by which bail determinations are made by the court was considered as part of the Review of PACE conducted by Lord Justice Auld (Ch.10 paras 60–90).

Sections 16, 17, and 18 of the 2003 Act arise out of observations and recommendations made in the Review concerning appeals from bail decisions. As for appeals to the Crown Court, and applications to a High Court judge, the processes were "all a bit of a muddle" and a "wasteful duplication" (Review of PACE, Ch.10 para.85). If magistrates' refused bail, the defendant had a right of appeal to the Crown Court, but no such right existed in respect of conditions attached to the granting of bail by magistrates. There was, however, a discreet process by which defendants were able to apply to a High Court judge for bail, following a decisions of the magistrates' to refuse bail, or against the imposition of conditions in the grant of bail. Lord Justice Auld recommended "the removal of the right of application to a High Court judge for bail after determination by any criminal court exercising its original or appellate jurisdiction, and the substitution therefore of a right of appeal from the District Division or Crown Division (Crown Court) on a point of law only" (para.87).

The Review also recommended that defendants should have a right of appeal from the magistrates court to the Crown Court in respect of conditions imposed as to residence away from home, and/or the provision of sureties, or the giving of security. It was recommended that the prosecution should have a right of appeal to the Crown Court against a decision of a magistrates' court to grant bail in respect of all offences that would, on conviction, be punishable by a custodial, or partly custodial, sentence (para.90).

Section 16 of the 2003 Act gives defendants, who are granted conditional bail by a magistrates' court, the right to appeal any requirement particularised in s.16(3) of the Act. The Crown Court is empowered to vary the conditions of bail: s.16(7). The list of conditions that can be challenged on appeal is deliberately limited in order to avoid what Lord Justice Auld described as "endless wrangling over conditions that in most cases should be manageable for the defendant" (*Review of the Criminal Courts of England and Wales*, Ch.10, para.88). The Bar Council agreed with Lord Justice Auld that the right of appeal should be restricted, but considered that the right of appeal should extend to curfews that represent a "clear restriction of liberty", as well as tagging. The Government agreed, but rejected the Bar Council's further submission that a condition, not to enter a certain area, should also be capable of challenge on appeal.

A High Court judge also has a separate power to grant bail before and after a case was committed or sent to the Crown Court.

17   Appeals to High Court

(1) In section 22(1) of the Criminal Justice Act 1967 (c. 80) (extension of power of High Court to grant, or vary conditions of, bail)—
  (a) after "Where" there is inserted "(a)", and
  (b) after "proceedings,", in the second place where it occurs, there is inserted "and
  (b) it does so where an application to the court to state a case for the opinion of the High Court is made,".

(2) The inherent power of the High Court to entertain an application in relation to bail where a magistrates' court—
  (a) has granted or withheld bail, or
  (b) has varied the conditions of bail,
  is abolished.

(3) The inherent power of the High Court to entertain an application in relation to bail where the Crown Court has determined—
  (a) an application under section 3(8) of the 1976 Act, or
  (b) an application under section 81(1)(a), (b), (c) or (g) of the Supreme Court Act 1981 (c. 54),
  is abolished.

(4) The High Court is to have no power to entertain an application in relation to bail where the Crown Court has determined an appeal under section 16 of this Act.

(5) The High Court is to have no power to entertain an application in relation to bail where the Crown Court has granted or withheld bail under section 88 or 89 of this Act.

(6) Nothing in this section affects—
  (a) any other power of the High Court to grant or withhold bail or to vary the conditions of bail, or
  (b) any right of a person to apply for a writ of habeas corpus or any other prerogative remedy.

(7) Any reference in this section to an application in relation to bail is to be read as including—
  (a) an application for bail to be granted,
  (b) an application for bail to be withheld,
  (c) an application for the conditions of bail to be varied.

(8) Any reference in this section to the withholding of bail is to be read as including a reference to the revocation of bail.

DEFINITIONS
  "the 1976 Act": s.21
  "vary": s.21

GENERAL NOTE
  Read the General Note to s.16 above. Section 17 gives effect to the recommendations of Lord Justice Auld in his *Review of the Criminal Courts of England and Wales* (Ch.10, paras 83–87).

Section 17 abolishes the jurisdiction of the High Court in respect of bail in as much as that jurisdiction duplicated the jurisdiction of the Crown Court. Section 17(5) was inserted by amendment No.42 which deals with cases where the Crown Court makes bail decisions under new powers to order a retrial for serious offences notwithstanding the acquittal of the defendants under Pt 10 of the 2003 Act (note ss.88 and 89 of the 2003 Act) (see Standing Committee B, col.179, January 9, 2003).

18   Appeal by prosecution

(1) Section 1 of the Bail (Amendment) Act 1993 (c. 26) (prosecution right of appeal) is amended as follows.

(2) For subsection (1) (prosecution may appeal to Crown Court judge against bail in case of offence punishable by imprisonment for five years or more etc) there is substituted—

"(1) Where a magistrates' court grants bail to a person who is charged with, or convicted of, an offence punishable by imprisonment, the prosecution may appeal to a judge of the Crown Court against the granting of bail."

(3) In subsection (10)(a) for "punishable by a term of imprisonment" there is substituted "punishable by imprisonment".

DEFINITIONS
"bail": s.21

GENERAL NOTE
Section 18 amends s.1 of the Bail (Amendment) Act 1993 (c.26) so that the prosecution's right of appeal to the Crown Court in respect of a decision of the magistrates' to admit a defendant to bail, embraces all imprisonable offences. Previously, s.1(1) of the Bail (Amendment) Act 1993 was confined to offences punishable by a term of imprisonment or five years or more, or an offence under s.12 or s.12A of Theft Act 1968 (c.60). A probing amendment to limit the right of appeal to cases where the relevant offence is punishable by imprisonment for a period of two years or more, was withdrawn following a statement by the Parliamentary Under Secretary for the Home Department that it "would not be usual for the prosecution to appeal against the grant of bail for a defendant charged with a minor offence" (Standing Committee B, col.181, January 9, 2003). It seems likely that the internal guidance given to lawyers of the Crown Prosecution Service regarding appeals will be revised to take account of amendments made by the 2003 Act. The practical effect of the prosecution orally declaring an intention to appeal a bail decision (s.1(4) of the Bail (Amendment) Act 1993) is to act as a stay until the determination of the appeal (s.1(6) of the Bail (Amendment) Act 1993), but the appeal must be heard within 48 hours excluding days set out in s.1(8) of the Bail (Amendment) Act 1993.

19   Drug users: restriction on bail

(1) The 1976 Act is amended as follows.

(2) In section 3 (general provisions), after subsection (6B) there is inserted—

"(6C) Subsection (6D) below applies where—

(a) the court has been notified by the Secretary of State that arrangements for conducting a relevant assessment or, as the case may be, providing relevant follow-up have been made for the petty sessions area in which it appears to the court that the person referred to in subsection (6D) would reside if granted bail; and

(b) the notice has not been withdrawn.

(6D) In the case of a person ("P")—

(a) in relation to whom paragraphs (a) to (c) of paragraph 6B(1) of Part 1 of Schedule 1 to this Act apply;

(b) who, after analysis of the sample referred to in paragraph (b) of that paragraph, has been offered a relevant assessment or, if a relevant assessment has been carried out, has had relevant follow-up proposed to him; and

(c) who has agreed to undergo the relevant assessment or, as the case may be, to participate in the relevant follow-up,

the court, if it grants bail, shall impose as a condition of bail that P both undergo the relevant assessment and participate in any relevant follow-up proposed to him or, if a relevant assessment has been carried out, that P participate in the relevant follow-up.

(6E) In subsections (6C) and (6D) above—

(a) "relevant assessment" means an assessment conducted by a suitably qualified person of whether P is dependent upon or has a propensity to misuse any specified Class A drugs;

(b) "relevant follow-up" means, in a case where the person who conducted the relevant assessment believes P to have such a dependency or propensity, such further assessment, and such assistance or treatment (or both) in connection with the dependency or propensity, as the person who conducted the relevant assessment (or conducts any later assessment) considers to be appropriate in P's case,

and in paragraph (a) above "Class A drug" and "misuse" have the same meaning as in the Misuse of Drugs Act 1971, and "specified" (in relation to a Class A drug) has the same meaning as in Part 3 of the Criminal Justice and Court Services Act 2000.

(6F) In subsection (6E)(a) above, "suitably qualified person" means a person who has such qualifications or experience as are from time to time specified by the Secretary of State for the purposes of this subsection."

(3) In section 3A(3) (conditions of bail in case of police bail), for ", (6A) and (6B)" there is substituted "and (6A) to (6F)".

(4) In Schedule 1 (which contains supplementary provisions about bail), in Part 1 (imprisonable offences)—

(a) after paragraph 6 there is inserted—

"Exception applicable to drug users in certain areas

6A Subject to paragraph 6C below, a defendant who falls within paragraph 6B below may not be granted bail unless the court is satisfied that there is no significant risk of his committing an offence while on bail (whether subject to conditions or not).

6B (1) A defendant falls within this paragraph if—

(a) he is aged 18 or over;

(b) a sample taken—

(i) under section 63B of the Police and Criminal Evidence Act 1984 (testing for presence of Class A drugs) in connection with the offence; or

(ii) under section 161 of the Criminal Justice Act 2003 (drug testing after conviction of an offence but before sentence),

has revealed the presence in his body of a specified Class A drug;

(c) either the offence is one under section 5(2) or (3) of the Misuse of Drugs Act 1971 and relates to a specified Class A drug, or the court is satisfied that there are substantial grounds for believing—

(i) that misuse by him of any specified Class A drug caused or contributed to the offence; or

        (ii) (even if it did not) that the offence was motivated wholly or partly by his intended misuse of such a drug; and

    (d) the condition set out in sub-paragraph (2) below is satisfied or (if the court is considering on a second or subsequent occasion whether or not to grant bail) has been, and continues to be, satisfied.

(2) The condition referred to is that after the taking and analysis of the sample—

    (a) a relevant assessment has been offered to the defendant but he does not agree to undergo it; or

    (b) he has undergone a relevant assessment, and relevant follow-up has been proposed to him, but he does not agree to participate in it.

(3) In this paragraph and paragraph 6C below—

    (a) "Class A drug" and "misuse" have the same meaning as in the Misuse of Drugs Act 1971;

    (b) "relevant assessment" and "relevant follow-up" have the meaning given by section 3(6E) of this Act;

    (c) "specified" (in relation to a Class A drug) has the same meaning as in Part 3 of the Criminal Justice and Court Services Act 2000.

6C Paragraph 6A above does not apply unless—

    (a) the court has been notified by the Secretary of State that arrangements for conducting a relevant assessment or, as the case may be, providing relevant follow-up have been made for the petty sessions area in which it appears to the court that the defendant would reside if granted bail; and

    (b) the notice has not been withdrawn.",

    (b) in paragraph 8(1), for "(4) to (7)" there is substituted "(4) to (6B) or (7)".

DEFINITIONS
  "the 1976 Act": s.21

GENERAL NOTE
  In cases where there is a causal link between problematic drug use of one or more specified Class A drugs, and the commission of crime (particularly acquisitive crime to fund habitual drug use), the Government has introduced a package of measures designed to break that link. Section 19 is one such measure.

  Under the 1976 Act there is a general right to bail unless one of the statutory exceptions apply: see s.4 of the 1976 Act. Exceptions are provided in Schedule 1 to the Act. It will be seen that s.19(4) of the 2003 Act amends Sch.1 to the 1976 Act by inserting three new paragraphs (namely paras 6A, 6B, and 6C). Section 19(2) also adds three new subsections to s.3 of the 1976 Act (namely ss.3(6C), 3(6D) and 3(6E)).

  Broadly stated, the general rule is that certain users of specified Class A drugs will not be granted bail unless the court is satisfied that there is no significant risk of offences being committed by them whilst on bail (see para.6A to Sch.1 to the 1976 Act inserted by s.19(4) of the 2003 Act). Defendants/users subject to the rule in para.6A are identified in para.6B of Sch.1. The defendant must be 18 or over. A sample taken from him must be positive for the presence in his body of a "specified Class A drug" (para.6B(1)(b)): the sample may be obtained under s.63B PACE, or under s.161 of the 2003 Act. The offence must be simple possession of, or possession with intent to supply, a specified Class A drug. Alternatively, the court must be satisfied that there are substantial grounds for believing that the specified drug caused or contributed to the offence, or that the offence was motivated (even if partly) by his intended misuse of the drug. The defendant must also refuse to consent to undergo an assessment as to his dependency upon, or propensity to misuse, specified Class A drugs — or he has undergone such an assessment but he does not wish to take part in "relevant follow-up" offered (paras 6B(1)(d) and 6B(2)).

  If a defendant-user of a specified Class A controlled drug does agree to "relevant assessment" or "relevant follow up" (as defined by s.3(6E) of the 1976 Act, inserted by s.19(2) of the 2003

Act), he may be granted bail but on condition that he complies with the assessment or follow-up programme (s.3(6D) of the 1976 Act).

The above mentioned measures apply if the court has been notified by the Secretary of State that arrangements are in place to carry out assessment, and/or follow-up (see s.3(6C) of the 1976 inserted by s.19(2) of the 2003 Act).

As was pointed out by the Parliamentary Under-Secretary of State for the Home Department during the course of debates in Standing Committee (Standing Committee B, col.184, January 9, 2003) "assessment does not involve the provision of treatment" but that "it is designed to identify the offender's needs and develop a comprehensive core plan". The Government believes the measure to be Human Rights Act 1998/European Convention on Human Rights compliant because "the court retains the discretion to grant bail if satisfied that the offender will not commit offences whilst on bail" and that "the clause contains a proportionate response to what is clearly a significant problem" (see col.191). At least one MP (Simon Hughes) has expressed concern about the validity of the Government's argument on this point (col.192). Note the views of the Home Affairs Select Committee Report with regard to what was then clause 16 of the Criminal Justice Bill 2002.

20   Supplementary amendments to the Bail Act 1976

(1) In Part 1 of Schedule 1 to the 1976 Act (supplementary provisions relating to bail of defendant accused or convicted of imprisonable offence) the existing text of paragraph 2 is to be sub-paragraph (1) of that paragraph, and after that sub-paragraph (as so re-numbered) there is inserted—

"(2) Where the defendant falls within one or more of paragraphs 2A, 6 and 6B of this Part of this Schedule, this paragraph shall not apply unless—
(a) where the defendant falls within paragraph 2A, the court is satisfied as mentioned in sub-paragraph (1) of that paragraph;
(b) where the defendant falls within paragraph 6, the court is satisfied as mentioned in sub-paragraph (1) of that paragraph;
(c) where the defendant falls within paragraph 6B, the court is satisfied as mentioned in paragraph 6A of this Part of this Schedule or paragraph 6A does not apply by virtue of paragraph 6C of this Part of this Schedule."

(2) In paragraph 9 of that Part (matters to be taken into account in making decisions under paragraph 2 or 2A of that Part) for "2 or 2A" there is substituted "2(1), or in deciding whether it is satisfied as mentioned in paragraph 2A(1), 6(1) or 6A,".

21   Interpretation of Part 2

In this Part—
"bail" means bail in criminal proceedings (within the meaning of the 1976 Act),
"bail hostel" has the meaning given by section 2(2) of the 1976 Act,
"the 1976 Act" means the Bail Act 1976 (c. 63),
"vary" has the same meaning as in the 1976 Act.

PART 3

CONDITIONAL CAUTIONS

22   Conditional cautions

(1) An authorised person may give a conditional caution to a person aged 18 or over ("the offender") if each of the five requirements in section 23 is satisfied.

(2) In this Part "conditional caution" means a caution which is given in respect of an offence committed by the offender and which has conditions attached to it with which the offender must comply.

(3) The conditions which may be attached to such a caution are those which have either or both of the following objects—
  (a) facilitating the rehabilitation of the offender,
  (b) ensuring that he makes reparation for the offence.

(4) In this Part "authorised person" means—
  (a) a constable,
  (b) an investigating officer, or
  (c) a person authorised by a relevant prosecutor for the purposes of this section.

DEFINITIONS

"authorised person": ss.22(4), 27
"conditional caution": ss.22(2), 27
"investigating officer": ss.22(3), 27
"offender": ss.22(1), 27

GENERAL NOTE

The Government's White Paper "*Justice For All*", Cm.5563 (2003) proposed a number of powers that would have the effect of diverting persons who committed a minor offence away from the criminal trial process: *e.g.* increased use of fixed penalty notices (para.4.9), conditional cautions (para.4.10), and deferred cautioning (para.4.16). The White Paper says nothing about the history of cautioning, and barely explains the context in which conditional and deferred cautioning would operate. It is perhaps surprising that this important topic has not been the subject of greater academic research and comment. However, the Police Foundation *Independent Inquiry into the Misuse of Drugs Act 1971* (Chairman: Viscountess Runciman DBE) did examine cautioning, and other diversionary schemes, in the context of case disposal of some drug offences (see Ch.6, paras 17–38; Ch.8, paras 16–21).

The cautioning of adults by the police in the United Kingdom and in Australia was considered by the Queensland's Criminal-Justice Commission (*Police Cautioning of Adults: Drug and Other Offences — A Briefing Paper* (April 1999)). For other interesting papers concerning this subject, see "*Entry Into The Criminal-Justice System: A Survey of Police Arrests and Outcomes*" Coretta Phillips *et al*, "*Entry into the criminal justice system: a survey of police arrests and outcomes*", Home Office Research Study 185; "*Police Cautioning In The 1990s*", Home Office Research findings No. 52; Evans and Ellis; "*Cautioning: Counting the Cost of Retrenchment*" Ellis, [1994] Crim. L.R. 566; "*The Legal Effect on a Police Caution*", Richard May, [1997] Crim. L.R. 491; Runciman *Royal Commission on Criminal Justice 1993* (Cm.2263, Ch.5, para.57).

The practice of cautioning persons who commit offences (including indictable offences) has been established in the United Kingdom for well over 30 years. It is an out-of-court disposal that until 1998, was unregulated by statute. The Crime and Disorder Act 1998 (c.37) abolished cautions for persons under 18 years of age, and introduced a new system of "reprimands" and "warnings" (see ss.65 and 66 of the Crime and Disorder Act 1998). Both can only be administered if the offender admits the offence, but a warning is more onerous than a caution because a warning results in the offender being referred to a Youth Offending Team. A warning may also be repeated — but only once — and even then, only if more than two years have passed since the previous warning.

In England and Wales, a simple caution may be administered at a police station to a person aged 18 or over. The offender must admit the offence, but once administered, no further action is taken against the offender. In Scotland there is no equivalent of the "caution", but the Procurator Fiscal may write a "warning letter" to the accused: no admission of guilt is necessary (see *Drugs And The Law*, Police Foundation, March 2000, Ch.6 para.27). Over the last 10 years, England and Wales has seen the emergence of "caution plus" schemes. These are not statutory schemes. The offender agrees to be cautioned, on the basis that he/she will seek treatment and/or counselling, or instruction. There is no power to enforce the agreement, or to stay the caution pending compliance with the proposed programme. The police must be very careful not to breach the requirements of PACE, and the Codes of Practice made under that Act, regarding the treatment of suspects, including the questioning of suspects. Similar problems exist in relation to the "arrest referral schemes" (see "Drugs And The Law" Ch.8, paras 20–21).

It is against this background that the Government has introduced "conditional cautions". The offender must comply with conditions attached to such a caution (s.22(2) of the 2003 Act). It can only be administered if the offender is 18 or over, and the five requirements set out in s.23 are complied with. If the offender fails to comply with the conditions of the caution (or any of them) he/she is at risk of the caution ceasing to have effect (s.24(3)) and a prosecution may result (s.24(1)). A code of practice must be prepared in relation to conditional cautions (s.25) and laid before Parliament (s.25(4)). As to the range of conditions that might be attached, the code will "illustrate as clearly as possible what we're trying to do ... But we do not want to inhibit people at local level if ... they can think of a condition that we have not thought of" (the Solicitor-General, Standing Committee B, col.204, January 9, 2003). Admissions made in respect of a conditional caution might be admissible in evidence in the event that proceedings are initiated for the offence. It is submitted that such admissions might be admissible in other proceedings. It is anticipated that the Code of Practice will require persons to have the benefit of legal advice if a conditional caution is being considered. The Government is also considering whether a conditional caution would be the decision of the Crown Prosecution Service, or of the police.

23   The five requirements

(1) The first requirement is that the authorised person has evidence that the offender has committed an offence.
(2) The second requirement is that a relevant prosecutor decides—
   (a) that there is sufficient evidence to charge the offender with the offence, and
   (b) that a conditional caution should be given to the offender in respect of the offence.
(3) The third requirement is that the offender admits to the authorised person that he committed the offence.
(4) The fourth requirement is that the authorised person explains the effect of the conditional caution to the offender and warns him that failure to comply with any of the conditions attached to the caution may result in his being prosecuted for the offence.
(5) The fifth requirement is that the offender signs a document which contains—
   (a) details of the offence,
   (b) an admission by him that he committed the offence,
   (c) his consent to being given the conditional caution, and
   (d) the conditions attached to the caution.

24   Failure to comply with conditions

(1) If the offender fails, without reasonable excuse, to comply with any of the conditions attached to the conditional caution, criminal proceedings may be instituted against the person for the offence in question.
(2) The document mentioned in section 23(5) is to be admissible in such proceedings.
(3) Where such proceedings are instituted, the conditional caution is to cease to have effect.

25   Code of practice

(1) The Secretary of State must prepare a code of practice in relation to conditional cautions.
(2) The code may, in particular, include provision as to—
   (a) the circumstances in which conditional cautions may be given,
   (b) the procedure to be followed in connection with the giving of such cautions,
   (c) the conditions which may be attached to such cautions and the time for which they may have effect,
   (d) the category of constable or investigating officer by whom such cautions may be given,
   (e) the persons who may be authorised by a relevant prosecutor for the purposes of section 22,

(f) the form which such cautions are to take and the manner in which they are to be given and recorded,

(g) the places where such cautions may be given, and

(h) the monitoring of compliance with conditions attached to such cautions.

(3) After preparing a draft of the code the Secretary of State—

(a) must publish the draft,

(b) must consider any representations made to him about the draft, and

(c) may amend the draft accordingly,

but he may not publish or amend the draft without the consent of the Attorney General.

(4) After the Secretary of State has proceeded under subsection (3) he must lay the code before each House of Parliament.

(5) When he has done so he may bring the code into force by order.

(6) The Secretary of State may from time to time revise a code of practice brought into force under this section.

(7) Subsections (3) to (6) are to apply (with appropriate modifications) to a revised code as they apply to an original code.

26 Assistance of National Probation Service

(1) Section 1 of the Criminal Justice and Court Services Act 2000 (c. 43) (purposes of Chapter 1) is amended as follows.

(2) After subsection (1) there is inserted—

"(1A) This Chapter also has effect for the purposes of providing for—

(a) authorised persons to be given assistance in determining whether conditional cautions should be given and which conditions to attach to conditional cautions, and

(b) the supervision and rehabilitation of persons to whom conditional cautions are given."

(3) After subsection (3) there is inserted—

"(4) In this section "authorised person" and "conditional caution" have the same meaning as in Part 3 of the Criminal Justice Act 2003."

27 Interpretation of Part 3

In this Part—

"authorised person" has the meaning given by section 22(4),

"conditional caution" has the meaning given by section 22(2),

"investigating officer" means a person designated as an investigating officer under section 38 of the Police Reform Act 2002 (c. 30),

"the offender" has the meaning given by section 22(1),

"relevant prosecutor" means—

(a) the Attorney General,

(b) the Director of the Serious Fraud Office,

(c) the Director of Public Prosecutions,

(d) a Secretary of State,

(e) the Commissioners of Inland Revenue,

(f) the Commissioners of Customs and Excise, or

(g) a person who is specified in an order made by the Secretary of State as being a relevant prosecutor for the purposes of this Part.

PART 4

CHARGING ETC

28   Charging or release of persons in police detention

Schedule 2 (which makes provision in relation to the charging or release of persons in police detention) shall have effect.

DEFINITIONS
"public prosecutor": s.29

GENERAL NOTE

The Government's Explanatory Note of December 3, 2003 describes the purpose of the section in conjunction with Sch.2 to the 2003 Act (the contents of that Schedule were heavily amended in Standing Committee, col.211) as follows:

"167. Section 28 introduces Schedule 2 which makes additional provision for the charging or release of people in police detention. It amends section 37 of the Police and Criminal Evidence Act 1984 and inserts new sections 37A–37D. New section 37A enables the Director of Public Prosecutions to issue guidance to which custody officers are to have regard in deciding whether, in cases where they consider that there is sufficient evidence to charge a suspect, they should release the suspect without charge but on bail, release him or her without charge and without bail, or charge him.

168. It is envisaged that the DPP's guidance will set out the circumstances in which it will be appropriate for the police to charge or otherwise deal with a suspect without reference to the Crown Prosecution Service; this is likely to include minor cases (such as the majority of road traffic offences), cases where there is an admission by the suspect and which could be disposed of by the magistrates' court, and cases where there is a need to bring the suspect before a court with a view to seeking a remand in custody. In other cases it will be appropriate for the police to release the suspect without charge but on bail while (as required by section 37B) the case is referred to the CPS. 169. Section 37B provides that, if a suspect is released without charge but on bail, it is then for the CPS to determine, if they agree that the evidence is sufficient, whether the suspect should be charged, and if so with what offence; or whether he should be given a caution (and if so in respect of what offence). The suspect is then to be charged, cautioned, or informed in writing that he is not to be prosecuted.

170. Section 37C makes provision for dealing with breach of any conditions attached to police bail granted pending the CPS decision as to charge. Paragraph 5 of Schedule 2 amends section 46A of the Police and Criminal Evidence Act 1984 to confer a power of arrest on reasonable suspicion that bail conditions have been broken. Paragraph 6(3) of that Schedule amends section 47(1A) of that Act to enable conditions to be imposed where a person is released on bail pending consultation with the CPS."

29   New method of instituting proceedings

(1) A public prosecutor may institute criminal proceedings against a person by issuing a document (a "written charge") which charges the person with an offence.

(2) Where a public prosecutor issues a written charge, it must at the same time issue a document (a "requisition") which requires the person to appear before a magistrates' court to answer the written charge.

(3) The written charge and requisition must be served on the person concerned, and a copy of both must be served on the court named in the requisition.

(4) In consequence of subsections (1) to (3), a public prosecutor is not to have the power to lay an information for the purpose of obtaining the issue of a summons under section 1 of the Magistrates' Courts Act 1980 (c. 43).

(5) In this section "public prosecutor" means—

(a) a police force or a person authorised by a police force to institute criminal proceedings,

(b) the Director of the Serious Fraud Office or a person authorised by him to institute criminal proceedings,

   (c) the Director of Public Prosecutions or a person authorised by him to institute criminal proceedings,

   (d) the Attorney General or a person authorised by him to institute criminal proceedings,

   (e) a Secretary of State or a person authorised by a Secretary of State to institute criminal proceedings,

   (f) the Commissioners of Inland Revenue or a person authorised by them to institute criminal proceedings,

   (g) the Commissioners of Customs and Excise or a person authorised by them to institute criminal proceedings, or

   (h) a person specified in an order made by the Secretary of State for the purposes of this section or a person authorised by such a person to institute criminal proceedings.

  (6) In subsection (5) "police force" has the meaning given by section 3(3) of the Prosecution of Offences Act 1985 (c. 23).

DEFINITIONS

"police force": ss.29(6) and 3(3) Prosecution of offences Act 1985 (c.23)
"public prosecutor": s.29(5)
"requisition": s.29(2)
"written charge": s.29(1)

GENERAL NOTE

This section provides an alternative method of launching criminal proceedings with the least number of formal requirements attaching to them. The method is available to all "public prosecutor's" — (defined by s.29(5)) entailing no more than (i) the issuing of a "written charge" (s.29(1)) that describes the offence, and (ii) serving a document styled a "requisition", requiring the accused to appear before a magistrates' court to answer the written charge: s.29(2). The form, content, recording, authentication, and method of serving both documents will be a matter of rules made under s.144 of the Magistrates' Courts Act 1980 (c.43) (s.30 of the 2003 Act).

Nothing in s.29 of the 2003 Act affects the power of a "public prosecutor" to lay an information before a magistrate for the purpose of obtaining the issue of a warrant under s.1 of the Magistrates' Courts Act 1980 for the arrest of any person in connection with an offence (s.30(4)(a)). Again, nothing in s.29 affects the power of a person who is not a public prosecutor to lay an information before a magistrate in order to obtain the issuing of a summons pursuant to s.1 of the Magistrates' Courts Act 1980 (see s.30(4)(b)).

Nothing in s.29 affects the power to charge a person with an offence whilst he is in custody (s.30(4)(c)). However, the process of laying an information has been simplified by removing the requirement of substantiating the information on oath in respect of warrants issued under s.1 of the Magistrates' Courts Act 1980, and similarly in respect of warrants issued following the non-appearance of a defendant under s.13 of the Magistrates' Courts Act 1980 (see s.31(2) of the 2003 Act).

Part 4 was ordered to stand part of the Criminal Justice Bill without any oral challenge or complaint by the Standing Committee (see col.211, January 9, 2003). At first sight, the lack of any judicial supervision before a "requisition" is issued with the "written charge" might be disquieting, but the answer is that as a matter of routine, cases have been initiated by "charging" individuals with an offence, normally at a police station — yet, this is not a judicial act. The issuing of a summons to a person requiring him/her to attend a magistrates' court to answer an information has also been widely used by police (54 per cent of all prosecutions in 1999; see Lord Justice Auld, *Review of the Criminal Courts of England and Wales*, Ch.10, para.53). As Lord Justice Auld points out, the decision whether to issue a summons is judicial, but the magistrate's "consideration of each information or batch of them is necessarily perfunctory" (para.53). The practice of "charging" suspects, without the permission of the court, occurs in respect of the most serious cases, whereas it is the less serious offences that are prosecuted using the summons procedure. Lord Justice Auld suggested that "the time has come up to introduce a common form for the commencement of Public Prosecutions" (Ch.55 para.55). Part 4 of the 2003 Act give statutory effect to that viewpoint. However, the context in which Lord Justice Auld expressed his conclusion was wider than merely the historical mechanisms for initiating prosecutions.

Lord Justice Auld also identified problems associated with the fact that the police, not the Crown Prosecution Service, initiates prosecutions that not infrequently results in "overcharging" — something that the Crown Prosecution Service fails to remedy at an early stage (Ch.10

para.35), contributing to delays in defendants entering pleas of guilty, or delays in identifying issues for trial. Those concerns are not expressed in the Government's White Paper "*Justice For All*" but an altogether more general view is included in para.4.41 namely that "many in the system believe that defendants' delayed guilty pleas are a tactic employed in the hope that witnesses will lose patience and decide not to testify". Lord Justice Auld said that "consideration should be given to a move towards early and more influential involvement of the Crown Prosecution Service in the process, to the point where, in all but minor routine cases, or where there is a need for a holding charge, it should determine the charge and initiate a prosecution" (Ch.10 para.44). There is, however, nothing in the 2003 Act that gives effect to this part of Lord Justice Auld's Review. Lord Justice Auld also noted that the police and the Crown Prosecution Service have different tests for charging (see para.16.1 of Code C, PACE regarding charging; and see para.43 of the Review, Ch.10).

30   Further provision about new method

(1) Rules under section 144 of the Magistrates' Courts Act 1980 may make—
   (a) provision as to the form, content, recording, authentication and service of written charges or requisitions, and
   (b) such other provision in relation to written charges or requisitions as appears to the Lord Chancellor to be necessary or expedient.
(2) Without limiting subsection (1), the provision which may be made by virtue of that subsection includes provision—
   (a) which applies (with or without modifications), or which disapplies, the provision of any enactment relating to the service of documents,
   (b) for or in connection with the issue of further requisitions.
(3) Nothing in subsection (1) or (2) is to be taken as affecting the generality of section 144(1) of that Act.
(4) Nothing in section 29 affects—
   (a) the power of a public prosecutor to lay an information for the purpose of obtaining the issue of a warrant under section 1 of the Magistrates' Courts Act 1980 (c. 43),
   (b) the power of a person who is not a public prosecutor to lay an information for the purpose of obtaining the issue of a summons or warrant under section 1 of that Act, or
   (c) any power to charge a person with an offence whilst he is in custody.
(5) Except where the context otherwise requires, in any enactment contained in an Act passed before this Act—
   (a) any reference (however expressed) which is or includes a reference to an information within the meaning of section 1 of the Magistrates' Courts Act 1980 (c.43) (or to the laying of such an information) is to be read as including a reference to a written charge (or to the issue of a written charge),
   (b) any reference (however expressed) which is or includes a reference to a summons under section 1 of the Magistrates' Courts Act 1980 (or to a justice of the peace issuing such a summons) is to be read as including a reference to a requisition (or to a public prosecutor issuing a requisition).
(6) Subsection (5) does not apply to section 1 of the Magistrates' Courts Act 1980.
(7) The reference in subsection (5) to an enactment contained in an Act passed before this Act includes a reference to an enactment contained

in that Act as a result of an amendment to that Act made by this Act or by any other Act passed in the same Session as this Act.

(8) In this section "public prosecutor", "requisition" and "written charge" have the same meaning as in section 29.

GENERAL NOTE
See the General Note to s.29 above.

31   Removal of requirement to substantiate information on oath

(1) In section 1(3) of the Magistrates' Courts Act 1980 (warrant may not be issued unless information substantiated on oath) the words "and substantiated on oath" are omitted.

(2) In section 13 of that Act (non-appearance of defendant: issue of warrant) in subsection (3)(a) the words "the information has been substantiated on oath and" are omitted.

(3) For subsection (3A)(a) of that section there is substituted—

"(a) the offence to which the warrant relates is punishable, in the case of a person who has attained the age of 18, with imprisonment, or".

GENERAL NOTE
The process of laying an information has been simplified by removing the requirement of substantiating the information on oath in respect of warrants issued under s.1 of the Magistrates' Courts Act 1980, and similarly in respect of warrants issued following the non-appearance of a defendant under s.13 of the Magistrates' Courts Act 1980 (and see the General Note to s.29 above).

PART 5

DISCLOSURE

GENERAL NOTE
Disclosure and the "search for truth"
The Government's White Paper "*Justice For All*" advocates a "trial system that works" based on "the presumption of innocence before proof of guilt, whilst making the role of victims and witnesses easier" and requiring "everyone involved in the running of the court to do the most effective and satisfying job" (para.4.69 and 4.70). Those statements are unremarkable. However, the White Paper has a message for defendants: that "the accused who wants to contest the charge will know that the trial and its preparation will focus on the search for the truth" (para.4.4). The use of the trial process as a means of focusing on the "search for the truth" is (understandably) a popular notion. In the Review, Lord Justice Auld wrote:
"a criminal trial is not a game under which a guilty defendant should be provided with a sporting chance. It is a search for truth in accordance with the twin principles that the prosecution must prove its case and that a defendant is not obliged to inculpate himself, the object being to convict the guilty and acquit the innocent" (Ch.10 para.154, *Review of the Criminal Courts of England and Wales*).
With respect, this is a somewhat oversimplified, albeit popular, claim: it is perhaps more in the nature of an ideal. The "search for truth" is indeed significantly circumscribed by the "twin principles" identified by Lord Justice Auld, but this is enough to indicate that the object of the trial process in England and Wales is to answer a single question, namely, "is the accused guilty of the offence charged?", which means "has the prosecution proved its case to the requisite standard of proof?". There is no need to search for the truth of a defendant's innocence when that much is usually presumed. The court's function is to test the evidence put before it. Traditionally, it has not been the function of the trial process to investigate a case, neither has it been a "the job of the defendant to be helpful to the prosecution or to the system" (see Professor Zander, "*Note of Dissent*", Runciman Royal Commission Report, p.221, paras 1 and 2). The "search for truth" in a criminal trial is therefore a rather limited inquiry. On the other hand, concerns that the presumption of innocence might be unjustly exploited by defendants who "ambush" the prosecution at trial with testimony, or with a defence which could not be adequately investigated (short of considerably delaying the trial or aborting it), has resulted in rules being enacted to prevent that happening.

Pre-trial defence disclosure of an alibi has been a statutory requirement since 1967 (s.11 of the Criminal Justice Act 1967 (c.80), now superseded by requirements of the Criminal Procedure and Investigations Act 1996 (c.25) ("the 1996 Act")). See also s.81 of PACE, and the Crown Court (Advance Notice Of Expert Evidence) Rules 1987 (SI 1987/716), in relation to the proposed use of experts in criminal proceedings. The 1996 Act replaced most of the common law rules of prosecution disclosure (but note s.21(3) of the 1996 Act), and introduced the statutory steps of primary disclosure, defence disclosure of issues, and secondary disclosure (coupled with power to apply to the court for further disclosure, under s.8 of the 1996 Act).

The extent to which the prosecution and the defence should be required to disclose material to each other has been the subject of intense debate since the early 1960s and the subject of examination by the Philips Royal Commission, the Runciman Royal Commission, and again most recently by Lord Justice Auld as part of his *Review of the Criminal Courts of England and Wales* (Ch.10 paras 115–197). The latter reviewed the arguments, and literature, regarding this difficult topic. Lord Justice Auld concluded (1) that the police should be properly resourced and trained to gather and schedule unused material, (2) that prosecuting lawyers should exist in sufficient number, and have sufficient time to examine material and to make informed, appropriate, disclosure decisions, and (3) that the police and lawyers should be assisted in their task with information technology systems (see Ch.10 para.130 of the Review). Lord Justice Auld further concluded that certain categories of documents (*e.g.* incident report books) might be routinely disclosed at the primary stage, and that other categories of material should be disclosed by reference to a common test, perhaps "material which in the prosecutor's opinion, might reasonably have weakened the prosecution case or assist that of the defence" (see Ch.10 para.171). For additional information see Justice, *"Briefing for the Second Reading and Committee Stages in the House of Lords"*, June 2003 http://www.justice.org.uk/images/pdfs/cjbparts1to11.pdf

Prosecution Disclosure

It will be noted that Parliament, in s.32 of the 2003 Act, amends s.3 of the 1996 Act by substituting the words "might reasonably be considered capable of undermining" (the prosecution case), and "or of assisting the case of the accused", for the original wording. It will also be noted that s.37 of the 2003 Act inserts s.7A into the 1996 Act, requiring the prosecutor to keep disclosure under review applying the test stated above (as recommended by Lord Justice Auld; see new s.7A(2)(a) of the 1996 Act) and "at any time" — but particularly following service of a Defence Statement (again, as recommended by Lord Justice Auld, see s.37 of the 2003 Act, inserting s.7A of the 1996 Act: see Ch.10 para.171, noting Lord Justice Auld's words "coupled with a defence statement identifying those issues to the extent that they are not otherwise apparent to the prosecutor at the outset").

Defence Disclosure

As for defence disclosure, and what should be contained in a "Defence Statement", Lord Justice Auld did not recommend the imposition of statutory requirements beyond those originally enacted under the 1996 Act, partly because "many would find them objectionable as going beyond definition of the issues", and partly because "they would be difficult to enforce" (para.180). Lord Justice Auld recommended that the original requirement to s.5 of the 1996 Act should be made more effective (Ch.10 para.183 of the Review):

"There are other and better avenues to making the defence statement requirement effective. Though even they are limited in this imperfect field of criminal litigation, with many defendants incapable or unwilling to co-operate with the system and whose hard pressed lawyers often have difficulty in obtaining instructions and, where publicly funded, are inadequately paid for preparatory work.

The first, as I have urged, is to provide full and timely prosecution disclosure, aided with modern communications technology.

The second, as I have also urged, is to pay publicly funded defence lawyers a proper and discrete fee for preparatory work, including taking instructions from the defendant whether in custody or on bail, and the drafting of a defence statement. This may sound a basic requirement, but, for the reasons I have given, is not the case today.

The third is to make defendants on remand in custody more accessible to their lawyers than they are now. As I have shown earlier, the limited visiting times are often difficult for busy criminal advocates and the visiting periods too short for taking adequate instructions, a product largely of Prison Service budgetary constraints taking priority over the needs of the criminal justice system as a whole. Much could be done to meet this problem by the introduction of lawyer to prison video conferencing facilities.

The fourth is for the prosecuting advocate, routinely, to advise on the adequacy of the defence statement and, where he considers it is inadequate, to request particulars of it, seeking a direction from the court if necessary.

The fifth is, through professional conduct rules and guidance, training and, in the rare cases where it might be appropriate, discipline, to inculcate in criminal defence practitioners and, through them, their clients the principle that a defendant's right of silence is not a right to conceal in advance of trial the issues he is going to take at it. Its purpose is to protect the innocent from wrongly incriminating themselves, not to enable the guilty, by fouling up the criminal process, to make it as procedurally difficult as possible for the prosecution to prove their guilt regardless of cost and disruption to others involved.

The requirements that Parliament has actually imposed on the defence are set out in s.33(2) and s.33(3) and ss.34, 35, and 36 of the 2003 Act, which amend the 1996 Act. These provisions are likely to generate much case-law as practitioners and judges endeavour to ascertain the amount of information the defendant must provide in order to comply with the overriding obligation to set out "the nature" of his defence (new s.6A(1)(a) of the 1996 Act, inserted by s.33(2) of the 2003 Act) and/or the "matters of fact on which he takes issue with the prosecution" (new s.6A(1)(b) of the 1996 Act). Is it enough to generalise, or must each and every disputed fact be particularised in that statement?

It is true that neither the new s.6C of the 1996 Act (see s.34 2003 Act), nor the new s.6D (s.35 of the 2003 Act), require detailed disclosure of a defence witness's proposed testimony, but it will not be difficult in many cases for the prosecution to anticipate the issue to which the witness's testimony is likely to relate. Only experience will show the extent to which the prosecution will interview defence witnesses pre-trial, and the extent to which defendants refused to comply with s.6C on the grounds that their witnesses might otherwise be "scared off", or that the prosecution might choose to shift the way it intended to present its case (see for example, concerns raised during the debates in Standing Committee B, col.215).

32 Initial duty of disclosure by prosecutor

In the Criminal Procedure and Investigations Act 1996 (c. 25) (in this Part referred to as "the 1996 Act"), in subsection (1)(a) of section 3 (primary disclosure by prosecutor)—

    (a) for "in the prosecutor's opinion might undermine" there is substituted "might reasonably be considered capable of undermining";

    (b) after "against the accused" there is inserted "or of assisting the case for the accused".

GENERAL NOTE

There has been much criticism that the original test for primary disclosure in s.3(1)(a) of the 1996 Act was seriously flawed because (a) the words "in the prosecutor's opinion might undermine (the prosecution case)" invited disclosure only of material that might have a fundamental effect on the prosecution case (see the Review Ch.10 para.161) and (b) the test was subjective. Parliament has modified the test in s.3 of the 1996 Act to an objective one, requiring the prosecutor to disclose material at a primary stage if it "might reasonably be considered capable of undermining the case for the prosecution against the accused, or of assisting the case for the accused". Disclosure under the latter limb will depend on the extent to which the prosecution is aware of the nature of the defendant's case. The defence is likely to be less obvious where, for example, the defendant gives a "no comment" interview. The changes introduced by s.32 were broadly welcomed by members of the Standing Committee (see Standing Committee B, cols.215–219, January 9, 2003)).

33 Defence disclosure

  (1) In section 5 of the 1996 Act (compulsory disclosure by accused), after subsection (5) there is inserted—

    "(5A) Where there are other accused in the proceedings and the court so orders, the accused must also give a defence statement to each other accused specified by the court.

    (5B) The court may make an order under subsection (5A) either of its own motion or on the application of any party.

    (5C) A defence statement that has to be given to the court and the prosecutor (under subsection (5)) must be given during the period which, by virtue of section 12, is the relevant period for this section.

(5D) A defence statement that has to be given to a co-accused (under subsection (5A)) must be given within such period as the court may specify."

(2) After section 6 of that Act there is inserted—

"6A Contents of defence statement

(1) For the purposes of this Part a defence statement is a written statement—

    (a) setting out the nature of the accused's defence, including any particular defences on which he intends to rely,

    (b) indicating the matters of fact on which he takes issue with the prosecution,

    (c) setting out, in the case of each such matter, why he takes issue with the prosecution, and

    (d) indicating any point of law (including any point as to the admissibility of evidence or an abuse of process) which he wishes to take, and any authority on which he intends to rely for that purpose.

(2) A defence statement that discloses an alibi must give particulars of it, including—

    (a) the name, address and date of birth of any witness the accused believes is able to give evidence in support of the alibi, or as many of those details as are known to the accused when the statement is given;

    (b) any information in the accused's possession which might be of material assistance in identifying or finding any such witness in whose case any of the details mentioned in paragraph (a) are not known to the accused when the statement is given.

(3) For the purposes of this section evidence in support of an alibi is evidence tending to show that by reason of the presence of the accused at a particular place or in a particular area at a particular time he was not, or was unlikely to have been, at the place where the offence is alleged to have been committed at the time of its alleged commission.

(4) The Secretary of State may by regulations make provision as to the details of the matters that, by virtue of subsection (1), are to be included in defence statements."

(3) After section 6A of that Act (inserted by subsection (2) above) there is inserted—

"6B Updated disclosure by accused

(1) Where the accused has, before the beginning of the relevant period for this section, given a defence statement under section 5 or 6, he must during that period give to the court and the prosecutor either—

    (a) a defence statement under this section (an "updated defence statement"), or

    (b) a statement of the kind mentioned in subsection (4).

(2) The relevant period for this section is determined under section 12.

(3) An updated defence statement must comply with the requirements imposed by or under section 6A by reference to the state of affairs at the time when the statement is given.

(4) Instead of an updated defence statement, the accused may give a written statement stating that he has no changes to make to the defence statement which was given under section 5 or 6.

(5) Where there are other accused in the proceedings and the court so orders, the accused must also give either an updated defence statement or a statement of the kind mentioned in subsection (4), within such period as may be specified by the court, to each other accused so specified.

(6) The court may make an order under subsection (5) either of its own motion or on the application of any party."

GENERAL NOTE
Subsection (1)

There has been some uncertainty as to the status of a defence statement served under s.5 of the 1996 Act. Is it a privileged legal document notwithstanding that it has been served on the prosecution and on the court? Even if it is not a document to which legal professional privilege attaches, is it a document that the prosecution should disclose to other defendants in the proceedings (whether jointly charged in respect of all relevant offences on the indictment or not)? There is authority for the proposition that where one defendant (D1) intends to pursue a "cut throat" defence against another, the latter is entitled to a copy of D1's Defence Statement: *R. v Cairns (Alison Louise)* [2003] 1 Cr. App. R. 38.

Section 33 (1) of the 2003 Act amends s.5 of the 1996 Act by putting disclosure of a co-defendant's Defence Statement on a statutory basis. Section 33(1) adds subss.(5A)–(5D) to s.5 of the 1996 Act. When read together, it is implicit that, in the ordinary way, a defendant is not entitled to a copy of a co-defendant's Defence Statement. However, the court may of its own motion, or on the application of any party to the proceedings, order one accused to give a copy of his Defence Statement to each other co-accused specified in the order. An amendment was tabled in respect of the new s.5(5B), but later withdrawn (amendment No.185), requiring representations be heard from all parties before the court makes such an order (see Standing Committee B, col.219). The amendment was considered unnecessary because the courts "will inevitably consider representations from all parties before making an order for the cross-service of Defence Statements" (Parliamentary Under Secretary for the Home Department, Standing Committee B, col.231, January 9, 2003).

Subsection (2) — content of a Defence Statement

This subsection adds s.6A to the 1996 Act. It replaces ss.5(6)–(9) of the 1996 Act (which subsections are repealed).

Section 6A defines a "Defence Statement" for the purposes of the 1996 Act, and specifies matters that such statements must contain.

Section 5(6)(a) of the 1996 Act required an accused to set out "in general terms the nature of the accused's defence", but s.6A(1)(a) omits the words 'general terms' and now requires the accused to set out the nature of his defence including "any particular defences on which he intends to rely". This would appear to mean that the accused should set out recognised defences (for example, 'self-defence'), and also matters of fact or circumstances, which (if true) are likely to be fatal to the prosecution case or which significantly undermine it (for example, that a drug is not controlled, or that a complainant's injuries were self-inflicted).

During the examination of this provision in Standing Committee, concern was expressed as to whether new s.6A(1)(b) ("indicating matters of fact on which he takes issue with the prosecution") would require the defence to provide a detailed pleading in respect of all disputed issues. As originally drafted, s.5(6)(b) of the 1996 Act required the defendant to disclose "matters on which he takes issue with the prosecution", whereas s.6A(1)(b) goes further requiring "matters of fact on which he takes issue with the prosecution" to be pleaded. The Government suggests that this means "main facts" and not a requirement to rebut "point by point, everything in every witness statement" (Standing Committee B, col.234, January 9, 2003). Resolution of this issue might not be found in judicial opinions, but in Regulations that the Secretary of State is empowered to make under new s.6A(4) as to the "details of the matters" that are to be included in Defence Statements.

Section 6A(3) reproduces the definition of "evidence in support of an alibi" as it appears in s.11(8) of the Criminal Justice Act 1967.

Subsection (3)

This subsection inserts s.6B into the 1996 Act. While this provision gives the defence further opportunity to clarify, rectify, or expand on matters not contained in the initial defence statement, it may also provide the prosecution with further material with which to attack the credibility of the defence case — particularly if the defendant gives evidence and is cross-examined. The section appears to envisage one update and no more. If an accused has nothing further to add to the Defence Statement then he 'may' give a written statement confirming that fact (s.6B(4) of the 1996 Act).

34   Notification of intention to call defence witnesses

After section 6B of the 1996 Act (inserted by section 33 above) there is inserted—

"6C Notification of intention to call defence witnesses

(1) The accused must give to the court and the prosecutor a notice indicating whether he intends to call any persons (other than himself) as witnesses at his trial and, if so—

    (a) giving the name, address and date of birth of each such proposed witness, or as many of those details as are known to the accused when the notice is given;

    (b) providing any information in the accused's possession which might be of material assistance in identifying or finding any such proposed witness in whose case any of the details mentioned in paragraph (a) are not known to the accused when the notice is given.

(2) Details do not have to be given under this section to the extent that they have already been given under section 6A(2).

(3) The accused must give a notice under this section during the period which, by virtue of section 12, is the relevant period for this section.

(4) If, following the giving of a notice under this section, the accused—

    (a) decides to call a person (other than himself) who is not included in the notice as a proposed witness, or decides not to call a person who is so included, or

    (b) discovers any information which, under subsection (1), he would have had to include in the notice if he had been aware of it when giving the notice,

he must give an appropriately amended notice to the court and the prosecutor."

GENERAL NOTE

Section 34 of the 2003 Act adds s.6C to the 1996 Act. Where the accused proposes calling witnesses other than himself, he must serve on the prosecution a notice (styled a "witness notice" for the purposes of s.39 of the 2003 Act (see s.39(12))). The notice must set out the matters referred to in new ss.6C(1)(a), and (b) of the 1996 Act. Section 6C represents something of a departure from the conclusions of Lord Justice Auld who, whilst recognising that requirements of the sort set out in s.6C of the 1996 Act might have much to commend them "as a matter of efficiency", they would nevertheless be difficult to enforce, and be objectionable to many as going beyond the definition of issues as well as imposing on the defendant an obligation to set out pre-trial, an affirmative case (see Review, Ch.10 para.180). It is important to note that the section does not require the defence to identify the issue to which the witness relates, still less does it require the defence to disclose the evidence the witness will give.

Concern was expressed in Parliament that this provision might deter witnesses from coming forward, or attending court. The Government's position was expressed by the Parliamentary Under-Secretary of State for the Home Department (Standing Committee B, col.247, January 9, 2003):

"The advantages to the measure are that it deters surprise witness and ambush defences in so far as that remains a problem, helps to weed out incomplete, inadequate or false defences — indeed, it enables the police to make criminal records checks on defence witnesses, thus helping the jury to assess their credibility — and allows the police to interview defence witnesses before the trial, if necessary, and to make further inquiries."

35 Notification of names of experts instructed by defendant

After section 6C of the 1996 Act (inserted by section 34 above) there is inserted—

"6D Notification of names of experts instructed by accused

(1) If the accused instructs a person with a view to his providing any expert opinion for possible use as evidence at the trial of the accused, he must give to the court and the prosecutor a notice specifying the person's name and address.

(2) A notice does not have to be given under this section specifying the name and address of a person whose name and address have already been given under section 6C.

(3) A notice under this section must be given during the period which, by virtue of section 12, is the relevant period for this section."

GENERAL NOTE

This section is designed to put the prosecution, and the court, on notice of the fact that the defence intend to instruct an expert to provide an opinion for possible use in evidence during criminal proceedings. It frequently happens that the defence seek an independent opinion to verify the conclusions of a prosecution expert. Occasionally, the defence will seek the assistance of an expert even if the prosecution has not done so. At a pre-trial hearing, the defence often disclose the fact that an expert has been instructed, but rarely divulge to the court, or to the prosecutor the identity of the expert in question. Accordingly, if the defence choose not to call their expert, the prosecution would not know who to contact with a view to interviewing, and perhaps calling, that witness itself. In any event, although there is no property in a witness, objection is sometimes taken to an expert divulging to another party material that is said to be the subject of legal professional privilege. Sections 6D of the 1996 Act does not alter the rules of legal professional privilege in any way, but gives the prosecution an opportunity to interview the expert pre-trial (whether to be called by the defence or not), and to obtain information from him/her (see Standing Committee B, col.255, January 9, 2003).

This provision will enable fact-finders to receive relevant admissible expert evidence that the defence chooses not to call. However, it is also likely to attract criticism that the prosecution is able to capitalise on information gained somewhat parasitically in circumstances where the defence took the initiative to seek expert assistance whereas the prosecution agencies did not. Although s.39 of the 2003 Act amends s.11 of the 1996 Act (faults in disclosure by the accused) it would seem that no statutory power exists to permit either the court, or any party to the proceedings, to comment adversely on the failure of the defendant to call an expert. The Government considered making it a requirement for the defence to disclose unused experts reports, and having sought views on that proposal, considered that this was not a good idea (Standing Committee B, col.254).

36 Further provisions about defence disclosure

After section 6D of the 1996 Act (inserted by section 35 above) there is inserted—

"6E Disclosure by accused: further provisions

(1) Where an accused's solicitor purports to give on behalf of the accused—
  (a) a defence statement under section 5, 6 or 6B, or
  (b) a statement of the kind mentioned in section 6B(4), the statement shall, unless the contrary is proved, be deemed to be given with the authority of the accused.

(2) If it appears to the judge at a pre-trial hearing that an accused has failed to comply fully with section 5, 6B or 6C, so that there is a possibility of comment being made or

inferences drawn under section 11(5), he shall warn the accused accordingly.
(3) In subsection (2) "pre-trial hearing" has the same meaning as in Part 4 (see section 39).
(4) The judge in a trial before a judge and jury—
    (a) may direct that the jury be given a copy of any defence statement, and
    (b) if he does so, may direct that it be edited so as not to include references to matters evidence of which would be inadmissible.
(5) A direction under subsection (4)—
    (a) may be made either of the judge's own motion or on the application of any party;
    (b) may be made only if the judge is of the opinion that seeing a copy of the defence statement would help the jury to understand the case or to resolve any issue in the case.
(6) The reference in subsection (4) to a defence statement is a reference—
    (a) where the accused has given only an initial defence statement (that is, a defence statement given under section 5 or 6), to that statement;
    (b) where he has given both an initial defence statement and an updated defence statement (that is, a defence statement given under section 6B), to the updated defence statement;
    (c) where he has given both an initial defence statement and a statement of the kind mentioned in section 6B(4), to the initial defence statement."

GENERAL NOTE

Section 36 adds a new s.6E to the 1996 Act. The provisions are short but of practical importance. Section 6E(1) demonstrates the point that a defence statement (or an updated notice) is a formal document that is not be treated lightly. Whether the document is signed by the defendant or not, service of it will be deemed to be given with the authority of the defendant — unless the contrary is proved, presumably on a *voire dire*. Defence lawyers would therefore be well advised to ensure that a defence statement, or updated statement, or a notice, served under ss.5, 6, 6B, 6B(4) or 6C of the 1996 Act, is signed and dated by the defendant. Best practice might be to draw the accused's attention to s.6E of the 1996 Act and require him to endorse that he has read and understood its terms.

By s.6E(4) the judge is empowered to direct that the jury be given a copy of a defence statement, but it is not clear at what stage this might be done. Notwithstanding that the court may act of its own motion (s.6E(5)(a)), in practice, the court will only give such a direction after hearing representations from all parties to the proceedings. Section 6E(5)(a) permits any party to make an application for a direction under the section, but this assumes that the party has seen a copy of a defence statement (or a statement mentioned in s.6B(4)) served by another party. This seems only to be permitted (in the absence of voluntary disclosure) if the court makes an order for cross-service of a defence statement under s.5(5A) of the 1996 Act, inserted by s.33 of the 2003 Act.

37   Continuing duty of disclosure by prosecutor

Before section 8 of the 1996 Act there is inserted—

"7A Continuing duty of prosecutor to disclose
    (1) This section applies at all times—
        (a) after the prosecutor has complied with section 3 or purported to comply with it, and
        (b) before the accused is acquitted or convicted or the prosecutor decides not to proceed with the case concerned.

(2) The prosecutor must keep under review the question whether at any given time (and, in particular, following the giving of a defence statement) there is prosecution material which—

    (a) might reasonably be considered capable of under-mining the case for the prosecution against the accused or of assisting the case for the accused, and

    (b) has not been disclosed to the accused.

(3) If at any time there is any such material as is mentioned in subsection (2) the prosecutor must disclose it to the accused as soon as is reasonably practicable (or within the period mentioned in subsection (5)(a), where that applies).

(4) In applying subsection (2) by reference to any given time the state of affairs at that time (including the case for the prosecution as it stands at that time) must be taken into account.

(5) Where the accused gives a defence statement under section 5, 6 or 6B—

    (a) if as a result of that statement the prosecutor is required by this section to make any disclosure, or further disclosure, he must do so during the period which, by virtue of section 12, is the relevant period for this section;

    (b) if the prosecutor considers that he is not so required, he must during that period give to the accused a written statement to that effect.

(6) For the purposes of this section prosecution material is material—

    (a) which is in the prosecutor's possession and came into his possession in connection with the case for the prosecution against the accused, or

    (b) which, in pursuance of a code operative under Part 2, he has inspected in connection with the case for the prosecution against the accused.

(7) Subsections (3) to (5) of section 3 (method by which prosecutor discloses) apply for the purposes of this section as they apply for the purposes of that.

(8) Material must not be disclosed under this section to the extent that the court, on an application by the prosecutor, concludes it is not in the public interest to disclose it and orders accordingly.

(9) Material must not be disclosed under this section to the extent that it is material the disclosure of which is prohibited by section 17 of the Regulation of Investigatory Powers Act 2000 (c. 23)."

GENERAL NOTE

See the General Note to Pt 5 above. The topic of disclosure, continuing disclosure, public interest immunity, and the proper test to be applied at the relevant stages of disclosure, was examined by Lord Justice Auld as part of his Review (Ch.10 paras 115–197). Section 37 adds s.7A to the 1996 Act, and by doing so, largely gives effect to Lord Justice Auld recommendations. Section 7A should be read in conjunction with amendments made to s.3 of the 1996 Act by s.32 of the 2003 Act.

Service of a Defence Statement may assist the prosecutor in the exercise of his duty regarding disclosure, but whether a defence statement has been served or not, the test be applied is as stated in s.7A(2) and s.3 of the 1996 Act.

Rules regarding the disclosure of sensitive matters subject to public interest immunity remain largely unchanged. The recommendation of Lord Justice Auld that there should be introduced "a scheme for instruction by the Court of special independent counsel to represent the interests of the defendant in those cases at first instance, and on appeal, where the court now considers prosecution applications in the absence of the defence in respect of the non-disclosure of sensitive material", has not been given statutory support: and see *Edwards v United Kingdom* 15 B.H.R.C. 189; *R. v C* [2003] EWCA Crim 2847.

38   Application by defence for disclosure

In section 8 of the 1996 Act (application by accused for disclosure), for subsections (1) and (2) there is substituted—

"(1)   This section applies where the accused has given a defence statement under section 5, 6 or 6B and the prosecutor has complied with section 7A(5) or has purported to comply with it or has failed to comply with it.

(2)   If the accused has at any time reasonable cause to believe that there is prosecution material which is required by section 7A to be disclosed to him and has not been, he may apply to the court for an order requiring the prosecutor to disclose it to him."

GENERAL NOTE

   This section amends s.8 of the 1996 Act in a way that makes the application of that section less restrictive than hitherto. What seems to matter is the fact that the accused has served a Defence Statement rather than the terms in which the defence is expressed. Even if the defence, or defences, actually advanced during the trial stray beyond the defence as pleaded in the Defence Statement, s.8 (as now amended) seems to permit the defence to apply for further disclosure. That said, it is obviously the case that the task of the prosecutor, and the task of the court, is made easier if the issues in dispute at trial that impact on the prosecutor's duty to disclose, are set out in a defence statement.

39   Faults in defence disclosure

For section 11 of the 1996 Act there is substituted—

"11 Faults in disclosure by accused

(1)   This section applies in the three cases set out in subsections (2), (3) and (4).

(2)   The first case is where section 5 applies and the accused—

(a)   fails to give an initial defence statement,

(b)   gives an initial defence statement but does so after the end of the period which, by virtue of section 12, is the relevant period for section 5,

(c)   is required by section 6B to give either an updated defence statement or a statement of the kind mentioned in subsection (4) of that section but fails to do so,

(d)   gives an updated defence statement or a statement of the kind mentioned in section 6B(4) but does so after the end of the period which, by virtue of section 12, is the relevant period for section 6B,

(e)   sets out inconsistent defences in his defence statement, or

(f)   at his trial—

(i)   puts forward a defence which was not mentioned in his defence statement or is different from any defence set out in that statement,

(ii)   relies on a matter which, in breach of the requirements imposed by or under section 6A, was not mentioned in his defence statement,

         (iii) adduces evidence in support of an alibi without having given particulars of the alibi in his defence statement, or

         (iv) calls a witness to give evidence in support of an alibi without having complied with section 6A(2)(a) or (b) as regards the witness in his defence statement.

(3) The second case is where section 6 applies, the accused gives an initial defence statement, and the accused—

    (a) gives the initial defence statement after the end of the period which, by virtue of section 12, is the relevant period for section 6, or

    (b) does any of the things mentioned in paragraphs (c) to (f) of subsection (2).

(4) The third case is where the accused—

    (a) gives a witness notice but does so after the end of the period which, by virtue of section 12, is the relevant period for section 6C, or

    (b) at his trial calls a witness (other than himself) not included, or not adequately identified, in a witness notice.

(5) Where this section applies—

    (a) the court or any other party may make such comment as appears appropriate;

    (b) the court or jury may draw such inferences as appear proper in deciding whether the accused is guilty of the offence concerned.

(6) Where—

    (a) this section applies by virtue of subsection (2)(f)(ii) (including that provision as it applies by virtue of subsection (3)(b)), and

    (b) the matter which was not mentioned is a point of law (including any point as to the admissibility of evidence or an abuse of process) or an authority,

comment by another party under subsection (5)(a) may be made only with the leave of the court.

(7) Where this section applies by virtue of subsection (4), comment by another party under subsection (5)(a) may be made only with the leave of the court.

(8) Where the accused puts forward a defence which is different from any defence set out in his defence statement, in doing anything under subsection (5) or in deciding whether to do anything under it the court shall have regard—

    (a) to the extent of the differences in the defences, and

    (b) to whether there is any justification for it.

(9) Where the accused calls a witness whom he has failed to include, or to identify adequately, in a witness notice, in doing anything under subsection (5) or in deciding whether to do anything under it the court shall have regard to whether there is any justification for the failure.

(10) A person shall not be convicted of an offence solely on an inference drawn under subsection (5).

(11) Where the accused has given a statement of the kind mentioned in section 6B(4), then, for the purposes of subsections (2)(f)(ii) and (iv), the question as to whether there has been a breach of the requirements imposed by or under section 6A or a failure to comply with section 6A(2)(a) or (b) shall be determined—

  (a) by reference to the state of affairs at the time when that statement was given, and

  (b) as if the defence statement was given at the same time as that statement.

(12) In this section—

  (a) "initial defence statement" means a defence statement given under section 5 or 6;

  (b) "updated defence statement" means a defence statement given under section 6B;

  (c) a reference simply to an accused's "defence statement" is a reference—

    (i) where he has given only an initial defence statement, to that statement;

    (ii) where he has given both an initial and an updated defence statement, to the updated defence statement;

    (iii) where he has given both an initial defence statement and a statement of the kind mentioned in section 6B(4), to the initial defence statement;

  (d) a reference to evidence in support of an alibi shall be construed in accordance with section 6A(3);

  (e) "witness notice" means a notice given under section 6C."

DEFINITIONS
"initial defence statement": s.39(12)
"updated defence statement": s.39(12)
"witness notice": s.39(12)

GENERAL NOTE
Section 39 makes substantial changes to the content of s.11 of the 1996 Act. These changes were the subject of little discussion by the Standing Committee (see Standing Committee B, col.263, January 9, 2003). By s.11(5) of the 1996 Act, as amended, both the court and any party to the proceedings may comment as appropriate, and the court may draw proper inferences, if the defendant does any of the things mentioned in the new s.11(2) or s.11(3). However, it seems that a defendant is only at risk of adverse comment, or inferences, if he gives a witness notice outside the relevant period (s.11(4)(a)), or calls a witness who is not named, or not adequately identified in a witness notice (s.11(4)(b), and only then if the leave of the court has been obtained (s.11(6)) and the court has taken into account the matters set out in s.11(8). It would appear that the defendant is not at risk of adverse comment, or adverse inferences, if he fails to call a witness named in the notice, or fails to call an expert named in the notice. The reason for this may be the such a direction would usually be meaningless, and unfair, because it was always open to the prosecutor to interview a witness named, and to call him/her. Note that there is no statutory provision for a copy of a notice served under the new s.6C or s.6D, to be served on a co-defendant.

40   **Code of practice for police interviews of witnesses notified by accused**

In Part 1 of the 1996 Act after section 21 there is inserted—

"21A Code of practice for police interviews of witnesses notified by accused

  (1) The Secretary of State shall prepare a code of practice which gives guidance to police officers, and other persons

charged with the duty of investigating offences, in relation to the arranging and conducting of interviews of persons—
   (a) particulars of whom are given in a defence statement in accordance with section 6A(2), or
   (b) who are included as proposed witnesses in a notice given under section 6C.

(2) The code must include (in particular) guidance in relation to—
   (a) information that should be provided to the interviewee and the accused in relation to such an interview;
   (b) the notification of the accused's solicitor of such an interview;
   (c) the attendance of the interviewee's solicitor at such an interview;
   (d) the attendance of the accused's solicitor at such an interview;
   (e) the attendance of any other appropriate person at such an interview taking into account the interviewee's age or any disability of the interviewee.

(3) Any police officer or other person charged with the duty of investigating offences who arranges or conducts such an interview shall have regard to the code.

(4) In preparing the code, the Secretary of State shall consult—
   (a) to the extent the code applies to England and Wales—
      (i) any person who he considers to represent the interests of chief officers of police;
      (ii) the General Council of the Bar;
      (iii) the Law Society of England and Wales;
      (iv) the Institute of Legal Executives;
   (b) to the extent the code applies to Northern Ireland—
      (i) the Chief Constable of the Police Service of Northern Ireland;
      (ii) the General Council of the Bar of Northern Ireland;
      (iii) the Law Society of Northern Ireland;
   (c) such other persons as he thinks fit.

(5) The code shall not come into operation until the Secretary of State by order so provides.

(6) The Secretary of State may from time to time revise the code and subsections (4) and (5) shall apply to a revised code as they apply to the code as first prepared.

(7) An order bringing the code into operation may not be made unless a draft of the order has been laid before each House of Parliament and approved by a resolution of each House.

(8) An order bringing a revised code into operation shall be laid before each House of Parliament if the order has been made without a draft having been so laid and approved by a resolution of each House.

(9) When an order or a draft of an order is laid in accordance with subsection (7) or (8), the code to which it relates shall also be laid.

(10) No order or draft of an order may be laid until the consultation required by subsection (4) has taken place.

(11) A failure by a person mentioned in subsection (3) to have regard to any provision of a code for the time being in operation by virtue of an order under this section shall not in itself render him liable to any criminal or civil proceedings.

(12) In all criminal and civil proceedings a code in operation at any time by virtue of an order under this section shall be admissible in evidence.

(13) If it appears to a court or tribunal conducting criminal or civil proceedings that—

(a) any provision of a code in operation at any time by virtue of an order under this section, or

(b) any failure mentioned in subsection (11),

is relevant to any question arising in the proceedings, the provision or failure shall be taken into account in deciding the question."

PART 6

ALLOCATION AND SENDING OF OFFENCES

41   Allocation of offences triable either way, and sending cases to Crown Court

Schedule 3 (which makes provision in relation to the allocation and other treatment of offences triable either way, and the sending of cases to the Crown Court) shall have effect.

GENERAL NOTE

Important changes to practice and procedure, relating to mode of trial determinations in the magistrates' court, are introduced by s.41 in conjunction with Sch.3 to the 2003 Act. These changes are briefly described in the Explanatory Notes but the changes were not extensively debated during committee (see Standing Committee B, cols.1082–1098, February 25, 2003).

The lack of debate is perhaps somewhat surprising given that the allocation of business between the magistrates' court and the Crown Court has been, at times, a highly contentious issue. True it is that the 2003 Act does not give statutory effect to a number of conclusions and recommendations of Lord Justice Auld in his *Review of the Criminal Courts of England and Wales*, and which were likely to be strenuously fought over had they formed part of an intended legislative scheme. Thus, the Government declined to create a "unified criminal court" structure, or the creation of an "intermediate tier court" to try a number of cases now tried on indictment (see "*Justice For All*", para.4.19). The Government's position is that the benefits of unification that Lord Justice Auld identified can be obtained by a "closer alignment" of the business of the magistrates' court and the Crown Courts: see "*Justice For All*", para.4.6. Some measures introduced by Sch.3 to the 2003 Act, are steps on the way to bringing about that closer alignment (see the Explanatory Notes, paras 230–245).

The 2003 Act does not redistribute business as between the Crown Court and the magistrates' court. It does however, seek to reduce the number of either way cases going to the Crown Court, by filtering out those cases that are more suitable for summary trial, as well as cases likely to "crack" before the Crown Court by the defendant pleading guilty. Lord Justice Auld recommended that with regards to all either-way cases, the magistrates' court — and not the defendant — should determine mode of trial (see the *Review of the Criminal Courts in England and Wales*, para.172). This was rejected by the Government (see "*Justice For All*", para.4.22) recognising "the issues of principle that arise over it, and that the number of defendants who elect jury trial are a small and diminishing proportion of those who could do so" (para.4.25).

The Government will keep the matter under review, but for the moment, the strategy is to (a) commit cases to the Crown Court that meet statutory criteria; and (b) in all other cases, to encourage the defendant to accept the opinion of a magistrates' court that the case is more suitable for summary trial — and to achieve the result by minimising uncertainties about the likely sentence if the defendant pleads guilty or not guilty. Thus, some cases will automatically be sent to the Crown Court *e.g.* indictable only offences (see s.51(2)(a) of the Crime and Disorder Act 1998 and para.18 of Sch.3 to the 2003 Act), or where notices given to the court by a "designated authority" of "serious or complex fraud" or "certain cases involving children" should be taken over by the Crown Court (see new s.51B and new s.51C of the Crime and Disorder Act 1998 (inserted by para.18 of Sch.3 to the 2003 Act), and s.51 Crime and Disorder

Act 1998 (as amended by that paragraph)). Sections 51B and 51C therefore take in the transfer provisions previously found in s.4 of the Criminal Justice Act 1987 (Serious Fraud), and s.53 Criminal Justice Act 1991 (child cases).

In respect of either way cases, an adult defendant will (as before), be invited to indicate his plea before venue (s.17A of the Magistrates' Courts Act 1980, as amended by paras 1 and 2 of Sch.3 to the 2003 Act), but he will be warned that in the event that he pleads guilty, the magistrates' will have power to commit him to the Crown Court for sentence if the offences are "so serious" the Crown Court should deal with him (s.3 of the Powers of The Criminal Courts (Sentencing) Act 2000 (c.6), as amended by para.22 of Sch.3 to the 2003 Act) or — and this is new — if the court forms a view that he is a "dangerous offender" (see Ch.5 of the 2003 Act) who must therefore be committed to the Crown Court for sentence under s.3A Powers of The Criminal Court (Sentencing) Act 2000 (inserted by para.23 of Sch.3 of the 2003 Act). There is also a similar plea before venue scheme in respect of children and young persons (see s.24 of the Magistrates' Courts Act 1980, and note amendments made by para.23 to the 2003 Act). It will be seen that para.10 of Sch.3 to the 2003 Act adds new ss.24A–24D to the Magistrates' Courts Act 1980 and which broadly mirror the procedure relating to adults under new ss.17A–17C Magistrates' Courts Act 1980.

In cases where the defendant indicates that he would plead guilty, the court proceeds as if it exercised summary trial of the charge from the beginning: s.17A(6) of the Magistrates' Courts Act 1980. In other words, once a defendant indicates a plea of guilty he has no right to elect trial in the Crown Court: see *Review of the Criminal Courts*, para.129, p.185. In other cases the court will consider (as before) mode of trial under s.19 of the Magistrates' Courts Act 1980 (in its amended form: see para.5 of Sch.3 to the 2003 Act). At this stage, the court must have regard to s.22 of the Magistrates' Courts Act 1980 which makes certain offences summary only if the value involved is below the "relevant sum".

Due to a technical error in the drafting of s.17A(6) of the Magistrates' Courts Act 1980, it was unclear whether a defendant who indicated a guilty plea before venue could be committed to the Crown Court for sentence for that offence notwithstanding that the amount was small so that s.22 of the Magistrates' Courts Act 1980 would have been engaged if had he pleaded "not guilty": see *R. v Kelly (Robert Joseph)* [2001] R.T.R. 5. New s.17D of the Magistrates' Courts Act 1980 (inserted by para.3 of Sch.3 to the 2003 Act) appears to deal with that situation and limits the maximum penalty to three months, or find no greater than level for on the standard scale, and s.3 powers the Criminal Courts (Sentencing) Act 2000 (as amended) shall not apply.

Character relevant to mode of trial

The court will determine mode of trial under s.19 of the Magistrates' Courts Act 1980 (see the substituted wording, para.5 of Sch.3 to the 2003 Act). Since at least 1980, the court deciding mode of trial was not informed of the defendant's criminal record or personal circumstances, and the *National Mode of Trial Guidelines (1990)* issued by the then Lord Chief Justice, described those matters as irrelevant to the decision. As Lord Justice Auld has pointed out, the history of either way offences tells us that the character and antecedents of the accused had been included in the mode of trial criteria for the purposes of the Summary Jurisdiction Act 1879 (c.49), and the Criminal Justice Act 1925 (c.86) (see *Review of the Criminal Courts*, para.123–127). The lack of legal certainty is removed by s.19(2)(a) of the Magistrates' Courts Act 1980 (as amended by para.5 of Sch.3 to the 2003 Act), so that the court making a decision as to mode of trial "shall give the prosecution an opportunity to inform the court of the accused's previous convictions (if any)" (and see *"Justice For All"*, para.4.23; see also Permanent Under Secretary for the Home Department, Hilary Benn, Standing Committee B, col.1085, February 25, 2003). The court will be required to have regard to allocation guidelines that may be issued by the Sentencing Guidelines Council under s.167. Although this provision is likely to attract criticism that evidence of bad character might discriminate in favour of those of good character (note the Auld Review, para.148, p.192), this has to be balanced against s.20 of the Magistrates' Courts Act 1980 (as it is now worded, para.6 of Sch.3 to the 2003 Act) which permits the defendant to request an indication from the court as to whether a custodial or non custodial sentence would be likely to be imposed were he to be tried summarily for the offence and to plead guilty to it: s.20(3) of the Magistrates' Courts Act 1980.

Indication of Sentence

The court need not give an indication under s.20 Magistrates' Courts Act 1980 (s.20(4)) but if an indication is given, the defendant will be asked if he wishes to reconsider his plea: s.20(5). The court will be in a stronger position to give an indication (and perhaps be more prepared to do so) if it knows the antecedents of the defendant.

Although the defendant may only make such a request after the court has expressed an opinion that summary trial is more suitable, the defendant retains the right to elect trial by jury if he maintains a plea of not guilty: see s.20(9) Magistrates' Courts Act 1980.

Where a defendant pleads guilty (following a decision by the court that the case is suitable for summary trial) no court may impose a custodial sentence for the offence unless such a sentence was disclosed to the defendant as part of the "indication of sentence" procedure (s.20A(1), Magistrates' Courts Act 1980, inserted by para.6 of Sch.3 to the 2003 Act), and the offender is not "dangerous" (see Ch.5 of the 2003 Act, and s.28(2) of the Magistrates' Courts Act 1980; and see s.3A(4) Powers of The Criminal Courts (Sentencing) Act 2000, inserted by s.41, para.23 of Sch.3 to the 2003 Act). A "dangerous offender" is one convicted of a "specified violent" or a "specified sexual" offence, and where other conditions are met: see ss.224–236 of the 2003 Act. This might seem to be empowering the court to be able to renege on an indication if the offender meets the criteria of a "dangerous offender" for the purposes of Ch.5 of the 2003 Act. The Parliamentary Under-Secretary for the Home Department provided two examples in support of the existence of the power. First, the power may be invoked if it becomes apparent following the preparation of reports that the imposition of a sentence on a "dangerous offender" is required. Secondly, facts emerge at any other stage to show that such a sentence is warranted (Standing Committee B, col.1089, February 25, 2003). However, the committee did not give detailed consideration of the likely application of s.229(3) regarding the assessment of dangerousness.

It follows that once a magistrates' court decides that a case is suitable for summary trial, and the defendant pleads guilty following an indication as to sentence (which the defendant accepts), he will know that he will not then be committed to the Crown Court for sentence unless he falls within Ch.5 of the 2003 Act ("dangerous offenders"). The court is not bound by the indication if the defendant accepts summary trial and is convicted, but in such a case (or in a case where the defendant receives no indication of sentence, or does not ask for one) he knows that the sentence will not exceed the statutory maximum the magistrates' have power to impose.

Where the defendant elects trial on indictment, the matter will be transferred to the Crown Court under the revised version of s.51 of the Crime and Disorder Act 1998 (see para.18 of Sch.3 to the 2003 Act). Note that the previous power to switch between summary trial and committal proceedings has been removed (para.11 of Sch.3 to the 2003 Act amending s.25 of the Magistrates' Courts Act 1980) and a new power enacted to enable the prosecution to apply to the magistrates' for an either way case to be tried on indictment.

It is regrettable that neither the 2003 Act, nor the Explanatory Notes, make the revised procedures much clearer as to their purpose and practical effect. For an interesting perspective of the history of trial by jury, and mode of trial determinations by Magistrates' Courts, the reader is encouraged to read "*Trial of Cases on Indictment Without a Jury, Review of the Criminal Courts of England and Wales*", Sir Robin Auld, pp.177–200; see also "*The Jury Under Attack*" Findlay and Duff, Butterworths, 1988.

42   Mode of trial for certain firearms offences: transitory arrangements

(1) The Magistrates' Courts Act 1980 is amended as follows.
(2) In section 24 (summary trial of information against child or young person for indictable offence)—
   (a) in subsection (1), for "homicide" there is substituted "one falling within subsection (1B) below",
   (b) in subsection (1A)(a), for "of homicide" there is substituted "falling within subsection (1B) below",
   (c) after subsection (1A), there is inserted—
      "(1B) An offence falls within this subsection if—
      (a) it is an offence of homicide; or
      (b) each of the requirements of section 51A(1) of the Firearms Act 1968 would be satisfied with respect to—
        (i) the offence; and

        (ii) the person charged with it,
      if he were convicted of the offence."

(3) In section 25 (power to change from summary trial to committal proceedings and vice versa), in subsection (5), for "homicide" there is substituted "one falling within section 24(1B) above".

PART 7

TRIALS ON INDICTMENT WITHOUT A JURY

GENERAL NOTE

Although Pt 7 of the 2003 Act might be described as creating exceptions to the general rule that cases on indictment are tried by judge and jury, it is possible to view this Part as something of a test bed on which the future shape, and structure, of the criminal trial process is likely to be shaped. The Government, in its White Paper *"Justice For All"* indicated that it would not be implementing Lord Justice Auld's proposals for a unified criminal court, on the grounds that "the benefits from unification can be realised through a closer alignment of the magistrates' court and the Crown Courts, without a complete reordering of the court system" (para.4.6). The Government therefore pledged to bring those courts closer together so that collectively they will be known as "the criminal courts". How then will this "alignment" be achieved? A partial answer is to improve, and to integrate, the management of those two courts, but there is no doubt that greater alignment would be achieved if cases (whether tried summarily or on indictment) were broadly subject to the same process by which legal and factual issues were resolved.

The Government was adamant that changes proposed in the White Paper and in the original version of the Bill as printed on the November 21, 2002, do not represent the "thin edge of the wedge" and that jury trial will continue to be the norm (Standing Committee B, col.276, January 14, 2003). However, note the views of the Bar Council and the Criminal Bar Association (see Standing Committee B, col.296, January 14, 2003). Nevertheless, rules of evidence in criminal cases (formulated to safeguard defendants from unwarranted conclusions drawn by fact-finders) are revised, so as to place more material before the courts: weight being a matter for fact-finders. Part 11 changes the rules of evidence relating to bad character and hearsay and these will apply whether a defendant is tried by jury or by judge alone: it might be said that the process of closer alignment has already begun.

Part 7 goes further than the recommendations of Lord Justice Auld in that the latter proposed empowering a judge to direct trial "by himself sitting with lay members, or where the defendant has opted for trial by jury, judge alone, by himself alone". Trial by judge and lay members was an option supported by the majority of the Roskill Committee (Fraud trials Committee Report, 1986, HMSO), but as Lord Justice Auld noted, this option harbours potential difficulties concerning the process by which lay members are selected for a particular case, and the fact that a long trial might be as burdensome for lay member as for jurors. The Government has rejected the idea of trial by judge and lay members, or by a panel of judges. The choice is between jury trial, and by judge alone. The same process applies to cases of all types and not just complex or serious fraud.

Lord Justice Auld recommended that there should be a staged approach to reform based on experience, so that "in the first instance" serious or complex fraud might be tried without a jury (*Review the Criminal Courts of England Wales*; Ch.5, para.202). Lord Justice Auld noted the argument that it might be difficult to justify putting one defendant in charge of a jury, and another in front of some other form of tribunal when the difference between the cases is not complexity, but the type of offence. The Government sought views as to whether the power to direct trial by judge alone should apply to all cases that are particularly complex or likely to be so long as to be excessively burdensome on a jury (para.4.31, *"Justice For All"*).

The Criminal Justice Bill, Pt 7 (as printed on the November 21, 2002) went much further than is the case now. It exceeded the staged approach to reform recommended by Lord Justice Auld. The original idea was that the prosecution should be empowered to apply to the judge of the Crown Court for a trial — irrespective of the allegation — to be conducted without a jury on the grounds of the complexity or the length of the trial (or both) (clause 37). It was further provided that even if the prosecution did not make such an application, a defendant could apply for his trial be conducted without a jury (clause 36). Such a measure was contemplated by Lord Justice Auld (Review, Ch.5, para.194). It is a feature of the jurisdictions of Canada, New Zealand, and the USA (Standing Committee B, col.276, January 14, 2003).

In the event, clause 36 of the original version of the CJB — application by the defendant for trial to be conducted without a jury — has gone. What was clause 37 (now s.43) has been substantially revised so that applications by the prosecution for trials of complexity to be conducted without a jury, are now limited to "certain fraud cases" (s.43) — in effect, where notice has been given under s.51B of the Crime and Disorder Act 1998 in serious or complex fraud cases. The 2003 Act also empowers the prosecution to apply for trial without a jury where there is a "real and present danger" of jury tampering (s.44), or where jury tampering has occurred and that jury has been discharged (s.46).

Section 45 relates to the procedure to be followed in cases where the prosecution apply for a trial to be conducted without a jury. The defendant may appeal to the Court Appeal (Criminal Division) against a decision of a judge of the Crown Court ordering trial without a jury, or an order to continue a trial in the absence of a jury, or to order that a trial be conducted without a jury on the grounds of a real and present danger of jury tampering (see ss.45 and 47).

These are landmark reforms. They have already been questioned as having the potential to undermine the criminal justice system by creating a "two types of justice in the higher court" (Simon Hughes MP, Standing Committee B, col.293, January 14, 2003), but others point to the existence of both types of process under pre-existing law (in civil and criminal law) (Paul Stinchcombe, Standing Committee B, col.295, January 14, 2003).

43   Applications by prosecution for certain fraud cases to be conducted without a jury

(1) This section applies where—
   (a) one or more defendants are to be tried on indictment for one or more offences, and
   (b) notice has been given under section 51B of the Crime and Disorder Act 1998 (c. 37) (notices in serious or complex fraud cases) in respect of that offence or those offences.
(2) The prosecution may apply to a judge of the Crown Court for the trial to be conducted without a jury.
(3) If an application under subsection (2) is made and the judge is satisfied that the condition in subsection (5) is fulfilled, he may make an order that the trial is to be conducted without a jury; but if he is not so satisfied he must refuse the application.
(4) The judge may not make such an order without the approval of the Lord Chief Justice or a judge nominated by him.
(5) The condition is that the complexity of the trial or the length of the trial (or both) is likely to make the trial so burdensome to the members of a jury hearing the trial that the interests of justice require that serious consideration should be given to the question of whether the trial should be conducted without a jury.
(6) In deciding whether or not he is satisfied that that condition is fulfilled, the judge must have regard to any steps which might reasonably be taken to reduce the complexity or length of the trial.
(7) But a step is not to be regarded as reasonable if it would significantly disadvantage the prosecution.

GENERAL NOTE

This section applies to certain fraud cases, that is to say, where notice has been given under s.51B of the Crime and Disorder Act 1998 in respect of serious or complex fraud (s.43). The test to be applied is whether the complexity of the trial and/or its length, "is likely to make the trial so burdensome to members of the jury... that the interests of justice require that... the trial should be conducted without a jury" (s.43(5)). It will be seen from the terms of s.43(6) that the trial judge must have regard "to any steps which might reasonably be taken to reduce the complexity or length of the trial". The judge may not make an order under s.43 without the approval of the Lord Chief Justice or a judge nominated by him (s.43(4)).

The issues as to whether, how, in what circumstances, a defendant might be tried without a jury, have been debated for many years, and the arguments comprehensively reviewed by Lord Justice Auld in his Review of the criminal courts (Ch.5, paras 173–206). It is not without interest that some key words, and expressions, found in s.43 appear in the Review — *e.g.* "burdensome", "complexity" (para.183), and that the overriding criteria should be expressed as "the interests of justice" (para.203). Lord Justice Auld supported the option of trial without a jury on grounds that include cases which "by reason of their length, complexity, and speciality, now demand much more of the traditional English jury than that it is equipped to provide... That juries have not kept pace with modern requirements of the criminal-justice system" (para.183). Other reasons include concerns that jurors in long cases may not be truly representative of society, and the burdens that will be placed on jurors in very long, arduous, cases.

Inasmuch as s.8 of the Juries Act 1974 (c.23) limits research as to whether juries do, or do not, understand complex cases, Lord Justice Auld pointed to the "wealth of research work on juries throughout the common law world", and he remarked that the preponderance of it emphasises "the need to simplify their task" and which "only underlines what is already obvious, the more complicated the issue the more difficult it is for them" (Review, Ch.5, para.198). Sensible, experienced, judges also like their task to be simplified, with the assistance of schedules and technological aids. It is not clear to what extent the public would prefer experienced judges to try complex cases.

It is not easy to predict how often this provision is likely to be invoked — if it ever comes into force. What factors or circumstances would the trial judge be entitled to take into account when deciding whether the test is satisfied? If a trial is expected to last so long that attempts to find 12 jurors to try it repeatedly fail, or the panel of jurors able to hear a long case is demonstrably unlikely to be representative of society, a judge might conclude that the case ought to be tried by judge alone. But on what basis might a judge properly conclude that the combined intellectual ability of 12 jurors selected to try the case is such that its complexity will make the trial so burdensome to the jury, that a judge alone should try it? As for the 'interests of justice' component, what are these interests, and what rank should each interest attract? How important is public participation in the trial process? Unfortunately, the task of the judge is made more difficult by the fact that an application under s.43 must be determined at a preparatory hearing (s.45(2)). The judge cannot wait until the selection process is underway before making a determination under s.43. He will have to anticipate the burdens likely to be experienced by jurors, and to rule accordingly.

The judge is required by s.43(6) to have regard to any steps which might reasonably be taken to reduce the complexity, or length, of the trial without placing the prosecution at a disadvantage (see s.43(7)).

The Government is keen to ensure that "the full case is heard and the full extent of the alleged criminality is exposed to the trial's consideration without excessively burdening juries" (Hilary Benn, Standing Committee B, col.321. The Government's position appears to be that s.48 is not about whether a jury can understand a complex trial, but whether the trial is manageable (Hilary Benn, Standing Committee B, col.355, January 16, 2003).

An application must be made at a preparatory hearing (s.39). The defendant or prosecutor may appeal a decision made under s.43 (see ss.45(5) and s.45(9)).

44   Application by prosecution for trial to be conducted without a jury where danger of jury tampering

(1) This section applies where one or more defendants are to be tried on indictment for one or more offences.

(2) The prosecution may apply to a judge of the Crown Court for the trial to be conducted without a jury.

(3) If an application under subsection (2) is made and the judge is satisfied that both of the following two conditions are fulfilled, he must make an order that the trial is to be conducted without a jury; but if he is not so satisfied he must refuse the application.

(4) The first condition is that there is evidence of a real and present danger that jury tampering would take place.

(5) The second condition is that, notwithstanding any steps (including the provision of police protection) which might reasonably be taken to prevent jury tampering, the likelihood that it would take place would be so substantial as to make it necessary in the interests of justice for the trial to be conducted without a jury.

(6) The following are examples of cases where there may be evidence of a real and present danger that jury tampering would take place—

(a) a case where the trial is a retrial and the jury in the previous trial was discharged because jury tampering had taken place,

(b) a case where jury tampering has taken place in previous criminal proceedings involving the defendant or any of the defendants,

(c) a case where there has been intimidation, or attempted intimidation, of any person who is likely to be a witness in the trial.

GENERAL NOTE

See the General Note to this part of the Act. The court has no power under this section to make an order of its own motion. There must be a real and present danger that tampering would take place (s.44(4)) and (notwithstanding steps that might be taken to prevent jury tampering) the likelihood that it would take place would be so substantial as to make it necessary in the interests of justice for the trial to be conducted without a jury (s.44(5)).

Section 44(6) helpfully provides examples where the section might be invoked. An application under s.44 must be made at a preparatory hearing (s.45(2)) and the parties must be given an opportunity to make representations with respect to the application (s.45(3)). This prevents the prosecution making an application under s.44 *ex parte*, but it is not clear to what extent the court is entitled to act on information that is sensitive, and which would not normally be in the public interest to disclose to the defence or third parties.

An appeal is available to the prosecutor, or to the defence, under ss45(5) or (9) depending on whether the preparatory hearing was directed under the Criminal Justice Act 1987, or the 1996 Act. Jury tampering, and how to deal with it, was not the subject of detailed consideration by Lord Justice Auld as part of the Review. What was then clause 38, was extensively debated in Standing Committee, but the Government did not respond fully to the criticisms made of this provision (Standing Committee B, cols.337–354, January 14, 2003). Section 46 has been described as the companion to s.44 (col.351), but s.46 actually deals with a different situation, namely, where tampering "appears to have taken place". The safeguards to the defence in s.46(2), against "whispering" and idle talk, do not apply in relation to pre-trial determinations made under s.45.

45 Procedure for applications under sections 43 and 44

(1) This section applies—
   (a) to an application under section 43, and
   (b) to an application under section 44.

(2) An application to which this section applies must be determined at a preparatory hearing (within the meaning of the 1987 Act or Part 3 of the 1996 Act).

(3) The parties to a preparatory hearing at which an application to which this section applies is to be determined must be given an opportunity to make representations with respect to the application.

(4) In section 7(1) of the 1987 Act (which sets out the purposes of preparatory hearings) for paragraphs (a) to (c) there is substituted—

   "(a) identifying issues which arc likely to be material to the determinations and findings which are likely to be required during the trial,
   (b) if there is to be a jury, assisting their comprehension of those issues and expediting the proceedings before them,
   (c) determining an application to which section 45 of the Criminal Justice Act 2003 applies,".

(5) In section 9(11) of that Act (appeal to Court of Appeal) after "above," there is inserted "from the refusal by a judge of an application to which section 45 of the Criminal Justice Act 2003 applies or from an order of a judge under section 43 or 44 of that Act which is made on the determination of such an application,".

(6) In section 29 of the 1996 Act (power to order preparatory hearing) after subsection (1) there is inserted—

   "(1A) A judge of the Crown Court may also order that a preparatory hearing shall be held if an application to which section 45 of the Criminal Justice Act 2003 applies (application for trial without jury) is made."

(7) In subsection (2) of that section (which sets out the purposes of preparatory hearings) for paragraphs (a) to (c) there is substituted—

   "(a) identifying issues which are likely to be material to the determinations and findings which are likely to be required during the trial,

        (b) if there is to be a jury, assisting their comprehension of those issues and expediting the proceedings before them,

        (c) determining an application to which section 45 of the Criminal Justice Act 2003 applies,".

(8) In subsections (3) and (4) of that section for "subsection (1)" there is substituted "this section".

(9) In section 35(1) of that Act (appeal to Court of Appeal) after "31(3)," there is inserted "from the refusal by a judge of an application to which section 45 of the Criminal Justice Act 2003 applies or from an order of a judge under section 43 or 44 of that Act which is made on the determination of such an application,".

(10) In this section—

    "the 1987 Act" means the Criminal Justice Act 1987 (c. 38),

    "the 1996 Act" means the Criminal Procedure and Investigations Act 1996 (c. 25).

DEFINITIONS

  "the 1987 Act": s.45(10)
  "the 1996 Act": s.45(10)

GENERAL NOTE

Where an application is made by the prosecutor (ss.43 and 44) for an order that the trial be conducted without a jury, the proper course is for the application to be determined at a preparatory hearing (s.45(2)). Preparatory hearings may be ordered in respect of fraud of "seriousness or complexity" under s.7 of the Criminal Justice Act 1987, or in any other case that is complex or lengthy (s.34 of the 1996 Act). However, it will be seen that s.45(6) of the 2003 Act adds s.34(1A) to the 1996 Act, the effect of which is to empower a judge to order a preparatory hearing to determine an application under ss.43 or 44 of the 2003 Act in any case other than cases of serious fraud (in which instance the procedure under s.7 of the Criminal Justice Act 1987, as amended by s.45(4) of the 2003 Act, should be followed). Sections 45(5) and (9) provide both the defendant and the prosecutor a right of appeal to the Court of Appeal (Criminal Division) in respect of a determination made in connection with an application made pursuant to ss.43 or 44.

46   Discharge of jury because of jury tampering

(1) This section applies where—

    (a) a judge is minded during a trial on indictment to discharge the jury, and

    (b) he is so minded because jury tampering appears to have taken place.

(2) Before taking any steps to discharge the jury, the judge must—

    (a) inform the parties that he is minded to discharge the jury,

    (b) inform the parties of the grounds on which he is so minded, and

    (c) allow the parties an opportunity to make representations.

(3) Where the judge, after considering any such representations, discharges the jury, he may make an order that the trial is to continue without a jury if, but only if, he is satisfied—

    (a) that jury tampering has taken place, and

    (b) that to continue the trial without a jury would be fair to the defendant or defendants;

    but this is subject to subsection (4).

(4) If the judge considers that it is necessary in the interests of justice for the trial to be terminated, he must terminate the trial.

(5) Where the judge terminates the trial under subsection (4), he may make an order that any new trial which is to take place must be conducted without a jury if he is satisfied in respect of the new trial that both of the conditions set out in section 44 are likely to be fulfilled.

(6) Subsection (5) is without prejudice to any other power that the judge may have on terminating the trial.

(7) Subject to subsection (5), nothing in this section affects the application of section 43 or 44 in relation to any new trial which takes place following the termination of the trial.

GENERAL NOTE

See the General Note to Pt 7 of this Act. This section should be read in conjunction with s.47 that provides a right of appeal to the Court of Appeal (Criminal Division) from an order made under s.46(3) (order to continue with the trial without a jury), or made under s.46(5) (new trial ordered to be conducted without a jury).

Section 46 should be contrasted with s.44. The latter relates to a pre-trial situation if there is a "real and present danger" that jury tampering would take place (s.44(4)). Section 46 applies if jury tampering has occurred. The language of s.46(1) is mildly misleading. The section applies if a judge is minded to discharge the jury because jury tampering "appears to have taken place" (s.46(1)(b)). It might have been preferable for that subparagraph to have read "he is satisfied that jury tampering has taken place" — which is precisely what s.46(3)(a) requires to be established. The phrase "appears to have taken place" existed in the Bill, as originally printed on the November 21, 2002, at a time when the measure was intended to apply in cases where jury tampering "has, or appears to have, occurred" (Explanatory Notes, November 29, 2002, para.212). Subsections (3)(a) and (b) were added late in the day to remove ambiguities that then existed as to the scope of the section (see *Hansard*, HL, Vol. 413, col.2066 (November 20, 2003); HC Amendment No.36D–36G). Even in its present form, nothing is said in s.46 as to the standard of proof the trial judge must apply for the purpose of determining whether jury tampering "has taken place". The judge must give the parties to the proceedings notice of his intention to discharge the jury, and to provide reasons, and to afford the parties the opportunity to make representations (s.40(2)).

Note that s.46 is engaged only if a judge is minded to discharge the jury. It does not address what the judge should do when he/she first learns of an allegation of jury tampering.

47   Appeals

(1) An appeal shall lie to the Court of Appeal from an order under section 46(3) or (5).

(2) Such an appeal may be brought only with the leave of the judge or the Court of Appeal.

(3) An order from which an appeal under this section lies is not to take effect—

   (a) before the expiration of the period for bringing an appeal under this section, or

   (b) if such an appeal is brought, before the appeal is finally disposed of or abandoned.

(4) On the termination of the hearing of an appeal under this section, the Court of Appeal may confirm or revoke the order.

(5) Subject to rules of court made under section 53(1) of the Supreme Court Act 1981 (c. 54) (power by rules to distribute business of Court of Appeal between its civil and criminal divisions)—

   (a) the jurisdiction of the Court of Appeal under this section is to be exercised by the criminal division of that court, and

   (b) references in this section to the Court of Appeal are to be construed as references to that division.

(6) In section 33(1) of the Criminal Appeal Act 1968 (c. 19) (right of appeal to House of Lords) after "1996" there is inserted "or section 47 of the Criminal Justice Act 2003".

(7) In section 36 of that Act (bail on appeal by defendant) after "hearings)" there is inserted "or section 47 of the Criminal Justice Act 2003".

(8) The Secretary of State may make an order containing provision, in relation to proceedings before the Court of Appeal under this section, which corresponds to any provision, in relation to appeals or other

proceedings before that court, which is contained in the Criminal Appeal Act 1968 (subject to any specified modifications).

48   Further provision about trials without a jury

(1) The effect of an order under section 43, 44 or 46(5) is that the trial to which the order relates is to be conducted without a jury.

(2) The effect of an order under section 46(3) is that the trial to which the order relates is to be continued without a jury.

(3) Where a trial is conducted or continued without a jury, the court is to have all the powers, authorities and jurisdiction which the court would have had if the trial had been conducted or continued with a jury (including power to determine any question and to make any finding which would be required to be determined or made by a jury).

(4) Except where the context otherwise requires, any reference in an enactment to a jury, the verdict of a jury or the finding of a jury is to be read, in relation to a trial conducted or continued without a jury, as a reference to the court, the verdict of the court or the finding of the court.

(5) Where a trial is conducted or continued without a jury and the court convicts a defendant—

    (a) the court must give a judgment which states the reasons for the conviction at, or as soon as reasonably practicable after, the time of the conviction, and

    (b) the reference in section 18(2) of the Criminal Appeal Act 1968 (c. 19) (notice of appeal or of application for leave to appeal to be given within 28 days from date of conviction etc) to the date of the conviction is to be read as a reference to the date of the judgment mentioned in paragraph (a).

(6) Nothing in this Part affects—

    (a) the requirement under section 4 of the Criminal Procedure (Insanity) Act 1964 (c. 84) that a question of fitness to be tried be determined by a jury, or

    (b) the requirement under section 4A of that Act that any question, finding or verdict mentioned in that section be determined, made or returned by a jury.

49   Rules of court

(1) Rules of court may make such provision as appears to the authority making them to be necessary or expedient for the purposes of this Part.

(2) Without limiting subsection (1), rules of court may in particular make provision for time limits within which applications under this Part must be made or within which other things in connection with this Part must be done.

(3) Nothing in this section is to be taken as affecting the generality of any enactment conferring powers to make rules of court.

50   Application of Part 7 to Northern Ireland

(1) In its application to Northern Ireland this Part is to have effect—
    (a) subject to subsection (2), and
    (b) subject to the modifications in subsections (3) to (16).

(2) This Part does not apply in relation to a trial to which section 75 of the Terrorism Act 2000 (c. 11) (trial without jury for certain offences) applies.

(3) For section 45 substitute—

"45   Procedure for applications under sections 43 and 44

(1) This section applies—
  (a) to an application under section 43, and
  (b) to an application under section 44.
(2) An application to which this section applies must be determined—
  (a) at a preparatory hearing (within the meaning of the 1988 Order), or
  (b) at a hearing specified in, or for which provision is made by, Crown Court rules.
(3) The parties to a hearing mentioned in subsection (2) at which an application to which this section applies is to be determined must be given an opportunity to make representations with respect to the application.
(4) In Article 6(1) of the 1988 Order (which sets out the purposes of preparatory hearings) for sub-paragraphs (a) to (c) there is substituted—
  "(a) identifying issues which are likely to be material to the determinations and findings which are likely to be required during the trial;
  (b) if there is to be a jury, assisting their comprehension of those issues and expediting the proceedings before them;
  (c) determining an application to which section 45 of the Criminal Justice Act 2003 applies; or".
(5) In Article 8(11) of the 1988 Order (appeal to Court of Appeal) after "(3)," there is inserted "from the refusal by a judge of an application to which section 45 of the Criminal Justice Act 2003 applies or from an order of a judge under section 43 or 44 of that Act which is made on the determination of such an application,".
(6) In this section "the 1988 Order" means the Criminal Justice (Serious Fraud) (Northern Ireland) Order 1988."
(4) For section 47(1) substitute—
  "(1) An appeal shall lie to the Court of Appeal—
  (a) from the refusal by a judge at a hearing mentioned in section 45(2)(b) of an application to which section 45 applies or from an order of a judge at such a hearing under section 43 or 44 which is made on the determination of such an application,
  (b) from an order under section 46(3) or (5)."
(5) In section 47(3) after "order" insert "or a refusal of an application".
(6) In section 47(4) for "confirm or revoke the order" substitute—
  "(a) where the appeal is from an order, confirm or revoke the order, or
  (b) where the appeal is from a refusal of an application, confirm the refusal or make the order which is the subject of the application".
(7) Omit section 47(5).
(8) For section 47(6) substitute—
  "(6) In section 31(1) of the Criminal Appeal (Northern Ireland) Act 1980 (right of appeal to House of Lords) after "1988" there is inserted "or section 47 of the Criminal Justice Act 2003"."
(9) For section 47(7) substitute—
  "(7) In section 35 of that Act (bail) after "hearings)" there is inserted "or section 47 of the Criminal Justice Act 2003"."
(10) In section 47(8) for "Criminal Appeal Act 1968" substitute "Criminal Appeal (Northern Ireland) Act 1980".

(11) In section 48(4) after "enactment" insert "(including any provision of Northern Ireland legislation)".

(12) For section 48(5)(b) substitute—

"(b) the reference in section 16(1) of the Criminal Appeal (Northern Ireland) Act 1980 (c. 47) (notice of appeal or application for leave) to the date of the conviction is to be read as a reference to the date of the judgment mentioned in paragraph (a)."

(13) In section 48(6)—

(a) for "section 4 of the Criminal Procedure (Insanity) Act 1964 (c. 84)" substitute "Article 49 of the Mental Health (Northern Ireland) Order 1986",

(b) for "section 4A of that Act" substitute "Article 49A of that Order", and

(c) for "that section" substitute "that Article".

(14) After section 48 insert—

"48A Reporting restrictions

(1) Sections 41 and 42 of the Criminal Procedure and Investigations Act 1996 (c. 25) are to apply in relation to—

(a) a hearing of the kind mentioned in section 45(2)(b), and

(b) any appeal or application for leave to appeal relating to such a hearing,

as they apply in relation to a ruling under section 40 of that Act, but subject to the following modifications.

(2) Section 41(2) of that Act is to have effect as if for paragraphs (a) to (d) there were substituted—

"(a) a hearing of the kind mentioned in section 45(2)(b) of the Criminal Justice Act 2003;

(b) any appeal or application for leave to appeal relating to such a hearing."

(3) Section 41(3) of that Act is to have effect as if—

(a) for "(2)" there were substituted "(2)(a) or an application to that judge for leave to appeal to the Court of Appeal", and

(b) after "matter" in the second place where it occurs there were inserted "or application".

(4) Section 41 of that Act is to have effect as if after subsection (3) there were inserted—

"(3A) The Court of Appeal may order that subsection (1) shall not apply, or shall not apply to a specified extent, to a report of—

(a) an appeal to that Court, or

(b) an application to that Court for leave to appeal.

(3B) The House of Lords may order that subsection (1) shall not apply, or shall not apply to a specified extent, to a report of—

(a) an appeal to that House, or

(b) an application to that House for leave to appeal."

(5) Section 41(4) of that Act is to have effect as if for "(3) the judge" there were substituted "(3), (3A) or (3B), the judge, the Court of Appeal or the House of Lords".

(6) Section 41(5) of that Act is to have effect as if for "(3) the judge" there were substituted "(3), (3A) or (3B), the judge, the Court of Appeal or the House of Lords"."

(15) For section 49(2) substitute—

"(2) Without limiting subsection (1), rules of court may in particular make provision—

    (a) for time limits within which applications under this Part must be made or within which other things in connection with this Part must be done;

    (b) in relation to hearings of the kind mentioned in section 45(2)(b) and appeals under section 47."

(16) In section 49(3)—

    (a) after "section" insert "or section 45(2)(b)", and

    (b) after "enactment" insert "(including any provision of Northern Ireland legislation)".

PART 8

LIVE LINKS

GENERAL NOTE

This part of the 2003 Act concerns the use of information technology to enable witnesses — other than the defendant — to give evidence in real time by electronic means. A "live link" is defined by s.56(2) of the 2003 Act, but the relevant feature is the ability of the relevant parties, at the place where the proceedings are being held, to hear and see each other. This might be by way of a "live television link" (s.56(2)), or by "other arrangement". A "witness" is defined by s.56(1) as a person "called, or proposed to be called, to give evidence in the proceedings". It is s.51(1) that restricts a defendant giving evidence through live link: that is perhaps unfortunate in cases where the defendant with good reason is unable to travel yet he would be prepared to give evidence on his own behalf through a live link.

Part 8 is based (in part) on the recommendations of Lord Justice Auld as part of his *Review of the Criminal Courts in England and Wales*. The law as it then existed did provide use of a live link in a limited range of circumstances (for example, in respect of young, disabled, vulnerable, or intimidated witnesses: see the Youth Justice and Criminal Evidence Act 1999 (c.23)). It is submitted that Lord Justice Auld envisaged the use of live link technology on a greater scale than that enacted under Part 8, namely, (i) that it should be used to "link courts and lawyers on both sides, and defendants, in or out of custody" (Ch.10, para.9, and see Ch.7, para.115); (ii) that its use should enable prisoners to give instructions to the lawyers (Ch.10, para.215), to enable defendants in custody (and with their consent) to participate in pre-trial hearings (Ch.10, para.224), including the taking of pleas, applications for bail (Ch.10, paras 295–261); (iii) to enable the courts to receive evidence, in a more flexible way, from children and other vulnerable witnesses (Ch.11, paras 121–128), and (iv) to enable persons pre-trial to give instructions to, and confer with, experts (Ch.11, para.148). Part 8 does not give statutory effect to all of those recommendations.

A witness may give evidence through a live link in respect of trials and appeals, if the court gives a direction for that course to be adopted (s.51(1)), and only if it is satisfied that it would be in the interests of the "efficient or effective administration of justice" to do so (s.51(4)(a)) having regard to all the circumstances of the case (s.51(6)), including any of the matters set out in s.51(7).

A direction given under s.51 of the 2003 Act may be rescinded under s.52(3) either of the court's own motion (s.52(5)(b)), or on the application of any party to the proceedings (s.52(5)(a)) but only if the party shows a material change of circumstances since the direction was given (s.52 (6)). The court must not rescind the direction if it is not in the interests of justice to do so (s.52(3)). There is provision for an order made under s.51, but then rescinded, to be restored (s.52(4)): presumably a statutory safeguard in the event that the court acts in error, or in haste, in rescinding an order under s.51.

The procedure to be followed for making an application for a direction under s.51, and arrangements, or safeguards to be put in place regarding the use of live links, will be the subject of rules of court made under s.55. Note that if evidence is given through live link, it is open to the judge to give appropriate directions to a jury (if there is one) regarding the weight to be attached to the evidence: see s.54.

51   Live links in criminal proceedings

(1) A witness (other than the defendant) may, if the court so directs, give evidence through a live link in the following criminal proceedings.

(2) They are—

(a) a summary trial,
(b) an appeal to the Crown Court arising out of such a trial,
(c) a trial on indictment,
(d) an appeal to the criminal division of the Court of Appeal,
(e) the hearing of a reference under section 9 or 11 of the Criminal Appeal Act 1995 (c. 35),
(f) a hearing before a magistrates' court or the Crown Court which is held after the defendant has entered a plea of guilty, and
(g) a hearing before the Court of Appeal under section 80 of this Act.

(3) A direction may be given under this section—
(a) on an application by a party to the proceedings, or
(b) of the court's own motion.

(4) But a direction may not be given under this section unless—
(a) the court is satisfied that it is in the interests of the efficient or effective administration of justice for the person concerned to give evidence in the proceedings through a live link,
(b) it has been notified by the Secretary of State that suitable facilities for receiving evidence through a live link are available in the area in which it appears to the court that the proceedings will take placc, and
(c) that notification has not been withdrawn.

(5) The withdrawal of such a notification is not to affect a direction given under this section before that withdrawal.

(6) In deciding whether to give a direction under this section the court must consider all the circumstances of the case.

(7) Those circumstances include in particular—
(a) the availability of the witness,
(b) the need for the witness to attend in person,
(c) the importance of the witness's evidence to the proceedings,
(d) the views of the witness,
(e) the suitability of the facilities at the place where the witness would give evidence through a live link,
(f) whether a direction might tend to inhibit any party to the proceedings from effectively testing the witness's evidence.

(8) The court must state in open court its reasons for refusing an application for a direction under this section and, if it is a magistrates' court, must cause them to be entered in the register of its proceedings.

GENERAL NOTE
See the General Note to Pt 8 above.

52   Effect of, and rescission of, direction

(1) Subsection (2) applies where the court gives a direction under section 51 for a person to give evidence through a live link in particular proceedings.

(2) The person concerned may not give evidence in those proceedings after the direction is given otherwise than through a live link (but this is subject to the following provisions of this section).

(3) The court may rescind a direction under section 51 if it appears to the court to be in the interests of justice to do so.

(4) Where it does so, the person concerned shall cease to be able to give evidence in the proceedings through a live link, but this does not prevent the court from giving a further direction under section 51 in relation to him.

(5) A direction under section 51 may be rescinded under subsection (3)—
(a) on an application by a party to the proceedings, or
(b) of the court's own motion.

(6) But an application may not be made under subsection (5)(a) unless there has been a material change of circumstances since the direction was given.

(7) The court must state in open court its reasons—
    (a) for rescinding a direction under section 51, or
    (b) for refusing an application to rescind such a direction,
        and, if it is a magistrates' court, must cause them to be entered in the register of its proceedings.

GENERAL NOTE

See the General Note to Pt 8 above.

53   Magistrates' courts permitted to sit at other locations

(1) This section applies where—
    (a) a magistrates' court is minded to give a direction under section 51 for evidence to be given through a live link in proceedings before the court, and
    (b) suitable facilities for receiving such evidence are not available at any petty-sessional court-house in which the court can (apart from subsection (2)) lawfully sit.

(2) The court may sit for the purposes of the whole or any part of the proceedings at any place at which such facilities are available and which has been appointed for the purposes of this section by the justices acting for the petty sessions area for which the court acts.

(3) A place appointed under subsection (2) may be outside the petty sessions area for which it is appointed; but (if so) it shall be deemed to be in that area for the purpose of the jurisdiction of the justices acting for that area.

GENERAL NOTE

See the General Note to Pt 8 above.

54   Warning to jury

(1) This section applies where, as a result of a direction under section 51, evidence has been given through a live link in proceedings before the Crown Court.

(2) The judge may give the jury (if there is one) such direction as he thinks necessary to ensure that the jury gives the same weight to the evidence as if it had been given by the witness in the courtroom or other place where the proceedings are held.

GENERAL NOTE

See the General Note to Pt 8 above.

55   Rules of court

(1) Rules of court may make such provision as appears to the authority making them to be necessary or expedient for the purposes of this Part.

(2) Rules of court may in particular make provision—
    (a) as to the procedure to be followed in connection with applications under section 51 or 52, and
    (b) as to the arrangements or safeguards to be put in place in connection with the operation of live links.

(3) The provision which may be made by virtue of subsection (2)(a) includes provision—

(a) for uncontested applications to be determined by the court without a hearing,

(b) for preventing the renewal of an unsuccessful application under section 51 unless there has been a material change of circumstances,

(c) for the manner in which confidential or sensitive information is to be treated in connection with an application under section 51 or 52 and in particular as to its being disclosed to, or withheld from, a party to the proceedings.

(4) Nothing in this section is to be taken as affecting the generality of any enactment conferring power to make rules of court.

GENERAL NOTE
See the General Note to Pt 8 above.

56   Interpretation of Part 8

(1) In this Part—

"legal representative" means an authorised advocate or authorised litigator (as defined by section 119(1) of the Courts and Legal Services Act 1990 (c. 41)),

"petty-sessional court-house" has the same meaning as in the Magistrates' Courts Act 1980 (c. 43),

"petty sessions area" has the same meaning as in the Justices of the Peace Act 1997 (c. 25),

"rules of court" means Magistrates' Courts Rules, Crown Court Rules or Criminal Appeal Rules,

"witness", in relation to any criminal proceedings, means a person called, or proposed to be called, to give evidence in the proceedings.

(2) In this Part "live link" means a live television link or other arrangement by which a witness, while at a place in the United Kingdom which is outside the building where the proceedings are being held, is able to see and hear a person at the place where the proceedings are being held and to be seen and heard by the following persons.

(3) They are—

(a) the defendant or defendants,

(b) the judge or justices (or both) and the jury (if there is one),

(c) legal representatives acting in the proceedings, and

(d) any interpreter or other person appointed by the court to assist the witness.

(4) The extent (if any) to which a person is unable to see or hear by reason of any impairment of eyesight or hearing is to be disregarded for the purposes of subsection (2).

(5) Nothing in this Part is to be regarded as affecting any power of a court—

(a) to make an order, give directions or give leave of any description in relation to any witness (including the defendant or defendants), or

(b) to exclude evidence at its discretion (whether by preventing questions being put or otherwise).

PART 9

PROSECUTION APPEALS

Introduction

57   **Introduction**

(1) In relation to a trial on indictment, the prosecution is to have the rights of appeal for which provision is made by this Part.

(2) But the prosecution is to have no right of appeal under this Part in respect of—

    (a) a ruling that a jury be discharged, or

    (b) a ruling from which an appeal lies to the Court of Appeal by virtue of any other enactment.

(3) An appeal under this Part is to lie to the Court of Appeal.

(4) Such an appeal may be brought only with the leave of the judge or the Court of Appeal.

GENERAL NOTE

Introduction

This part of the Act underwent a number of significant changes during its passage in Parliament as a Bill. The issues as to whether, and to what extent, the prosecution should be empowered to appeal against rulings made by a judge at first instance, have been the subject of intense discussion and consultation for several years, usually as part of a wider discussion concerning the principle against double jeopardy: see "*Double Jeopardy*" (M Friedland, 1969); the "*Report of the Royal Commission on Criminal Justice*, Ch.10: the Law Commission "*Prosecution Appeals Against Judges' Rulings*" Cm.158 (2002); the Law Commission for Report on a "*Double Jeopardy and Prosecution Appeals*", Pt VII; and the *Review of the Criminal Court of England and Wales* (the Auld Review), Ch.12. In February 2001, the Government expressed its interest in extending the ability of the prosecution to appeal against acquittals and terminating rulings: see "*The Way Ahead*", para.3.53.

It is desirable that ss.58–61 and Pt 10 of the 2003 Act be read together.

Part 10 (retrial for serious offences) gives the prosecution power to apply to the Court Appeal for orders quashing an acquittal, and ordering a retrial, in respect of "qualifying offences" (defined by s.75(8)) where there is a "new and compelling evidence", and it is in the public interest for the application to be made.

By contrast, ss.58–91 are primarily concerned with cases in respect of which, as a consequence of rulings made by a court, the trial of the accused in respect of any offence tried on indictment, will come to an end (either by way of an acquittal, or by reason of a stay, or by an order that the charge be "left on the file"). The Government's Explanatory Notes (December 2003, para.276) state that s.58 covers rulings that are "formally terminating and those that are de facto terminating in the sense that they are so fatal to the prosecution case that, in the absence of a right of appeal, the prosecution would offer no, or no further evidence". Although s.58 does not say as much, the practical effect of the section will be as stated in the Explanatory Notes because should leave to appeal be refused, or the appeal is abandoned, the defendant is to be acquitted (see ss.58(8) and 58(12)). Section 58, sensibly, does not seek to distinguish between rulings that are "formally terminating" or "de facto terminating". When the Bill was first printed in November 2002, Pt 9 did attempt to distinguish between "terminating rulings" and other rulings, but this soon gave rise to drafting problems as well as foreseeable problems of applying the distinction in practice. However, given the number of cases that do collapse at the end of the prosecution case — or are stayed — applications under s.58 are likely to be made quite often (albeit not routinely).

Sections 62–67 give the prosecution rights to appeal "evidential rulings". An unsuccessful appeal will not necessarily be fatal to the prosecution case. However, the right of appeal is confined to rulings made before the case for the defence begins, and only in respect of "qualifying offences" tried on indictment (see ss.62(2), 62(3) and 62(9), and Sch.4).

In this discussion it is important to note that prior to the enactment of the 2003 Act, the prosecution already had statutory powers to appeal decisions adverse to it with regard to rulings of law, or as to the admissibility of evidence in preparatory hearings in some serious, complex, or long cases (s.9(11) of the Criminal Justice Act 1987; s.35(1) of the 1996 Act), or in cases where an acquittal is tainted through the intimidation of a witness or juror (ss.54–57 of the 1996 Act), or on a Attorney-General's reference where a sentence is unduly lenient (s.36 of the Criminal Justice Act 1988 (c.33), or on an Attorney-General's reference on a point of law (s.36 of the Criminal Justice Act 1972 (c.71). There are also statutory powers enabling the prosecution to appeal determinations made by judge in connection with the making of a confiscation order under the Proceeds of Crime Act 2002 (c.29), or against the decision of a judge not to make a confiscation order at all: s.32(2) of the Proceeds of Crime Act 2002.

Outline of new scheme

The right of appeal exists only in connection with trials on indictment. The scheme of ss.58–61 of the 2003 Act is to empower the prosecution to appeal rulings made by the trial judge at any time before the start of the judge's summing up to the jury (s.58(13)). In respect of offences on an indictment that are not the subject of an appeal, the trial judge may continue with the proceedings (s.60). It is also open to the judge to continue with proceedings as against co-defendants who are not directly affected by the appeal (see s.74(5))

Restrictions are placed on the reporting of appeal proceedings initiated under Pt 9 of the 2003 Act: see s.71.

In respect of a number of key areas, Pt 9 does not follow all of the recommendations of the Law Commission in its final Report (*Double Jeopardy and Prosecution Appeals*). Thus, whereas the Law Commission made no recommendation for a prosecution right of appeal against a non terminating ruling made during the course of the trial (para.7.39), s.62 of the 2003 Act does give such a right.

Again, s.58 empowers the prosecution to appeal a ruling of "no case to answer" (whether under the first, or second, limb of *R. v Galbraith (George Charles)* [1981] 1 W.L.R. 1039, or presumably in a "fleeting glimpse" case, see *R. v Turnbull (Raymond)* [1976] 3 W.L.R. 445). The Law Commission, by contrast, recommended that the right be confined to the first limb of *Galbraith* only (see paras 7–74 of the final Report).

Thirdly, the Law Commission recommended that a right of the prosecution to appeal terminating rulings should be available only if the offence is of a type that gives the Attorney-General power to refer an unduly lenient sentence to the Court of Appeal (para.7.85). There is no such limitation under Part 9. The only limitation is that the appeal relates to a trial on indictment. Part 9 gives the prosecution no power to appeal a ruling made in a magistrates' court.

Fourthly, Pt 9 does not lay down a procedural timetable, or impose time limits, in connection with the granting of adjournments to the prosecution to consider whether to appeal, or as to the hearing of the appeal, or after the resumption/institution of proceedings in the Crown Court (see, by contrast, the Law Commission, para.7.114). However, such matters are likely to be the subject of Rules of Court made under s.73 of the 2003 Act.

Fifthly, the Law Commission recommended a custody time limit of two months from the conclusion of the trial until the conclusion of the appeal before the Court of Appeal (subject to a power to extend that period), whereas Part 9 makes no such provision (see Law Commission Report, para.7.129, and see s.70).

The Government estimate is that the annual total number of appeals will be between 100 and 150, of which 80 to 120 would not involve expedited hearings. According to the Solicitor-General, "the interlocutory appeal was developed at the instigation of the senior judiciary and in consultation with them. This is not an ivory-tower job" (Standing Committee B, col.1128).

General right of appeal in respect of rulings

58   General right of appeal in respect of rulings

  (1) This section applies where a judge makes a ruling in relation to a trial on indictment at an applicable time and the ruling relates to one or more offences included in the indictment.

  (2) The prosecution may appeal in respect of the ruling in accordance with this section.

  (3) The ruling is to have no effect whilst the prosecution is able to take any steps under subsection (4).

  (4) The prosecution may not appeal in respect of the ruling unless—

    (a) following the making of the ruling, it—

      (i) informs the court that it intends to appeal, or

      (ii) requests an adjournment to consider whether to appeal, and

    (b) if such an adjournment is granted, it informs the court following the adjournment that it intends to appeal.

  (5) If the prosecution requests an adjournment under subsection (4)(a)(ii), the judge may grant such an adjournment.

  (6) Where the ruling relates to two or more offences—

    (a) any one or more of those offences may be the subject of the appeal, and

    (b) if the prosecution informs the court in accordance with subsection (4) that it intends to appeal, it must at the same time inform the court of the offence or offences which are the subject of the appeal.

(7) Where—

(a) the ruling is a ruling that there is no case to answer, and

(b) the prosecution, at the same time that it informs the court in accordance with subsection (4) that it intends to appeal, nominates one or more other rulings which have been made by a judge in relation to the trial on indictment at an applicable time and which relate to the offence or offences which are the subject of the appeal,

that other ruling, or those other rulings, are also to be treated as the subject of the appeal.

(8) The prosecution may not inform the court in accordance with subsection (4) that it intends to appeal, unless, at or before that time, it informs the court that it agrees that, in respect of the offence or each offence which is the subject of the appeal, the defendant in relation to that offence should be acquitted of that offence if either of the conditions mentioned in subsection (9) is fulfilled.

(9) Those conditions are—

(a) that leave to appeal to the Court of Appeal is not obtained, and

(b) that the appeal is abandoned before it is determined by the Court of Appeal.

(10) If the prosecution informs the court in accordance with subsection (4) that it intends to appeal, the ruling mentioned in subsection (1) is to continue to have no effect in relation to the offence or offences which are the subject of the appeal whilst the appeal is pursued.

(11) If and to the extent that a ruling has no effect in accordance with this section—

(a) any consequences of the ruling are also to have no effect,

(b) the judge may not take any steps in consequence of the ruling, and

(c) if he does so, any such steps are also to have no effect.

(12) Where the prosecution has informed the court of its agreement under subsection (8) and either of the conditions mentioned in subsection (9) is fulfilled, the judge or the Court of Appeal must order that the defendant in relation to the offence or each offence concerned be acquitted of that offence.

(13) In this section "applicable time", in relation to a trial on indictment, means any time (whether before or after the commencement of the trial) before the start of the judge's summing-up to the jury.

DEFINITIONS

"applicable time": s.58(13)

GENERAL NOTE

For all practical purposes, s.58 applies to what are sometimes styled "terminating rulings" (see Law Commission Report No.267). These are rulings that will have the effect of bringing proceedings for the offence charged to an end, for example, following a submission of no case to answer, or a stay of proceedings. The appeal must relate to a trial on indictment, but the type of offence, or the actual gravity of the offence does not restrict or qualify the right of appeal.

Where an indictment alleges several offences and the appeal relates to one or more offences/counts, the proceedings may nevertheless continue in connection with those counts not the subject of an appeal (s.60). Similarly, where defendants are jointly charged with an offence, but the ruling affects one defendant, and not another, proceedings may continue in respect of the latter (s.74(5)).

The prosecution must inform the court that it intends to appeal, or it may request an adjournment to consider whether to appeal (s.58(4)) The judge is not bound to grant the adjournment (s.58(5)). Rules of Court are likely to stipulate the period of any adjournment (Explanatory Notes, December 2003, para.277).

Although the prosecution may usually only appeal a single ruling, there is a statutory exception in respect of a ruling that the defendant has "no case to answer": the prosecutor may nominate one or more other rulings which are to be the subject of appeal (s.58(7)). The prosecution may only appeal if it agrees that the defendant is to be acquitted if leave to the Court of Appeal is refused or the appeal is abandoned (ss.58(8), 58(9) and 58(12)).

59 Expedited and non-expedited appeals

(1) Where the prosecution informs the court in accordance with section 58(4) that it intends to appeal, the judge must decide whether or not the appeal should be expedited.

(2) If the judge decides that the appeal should be expedited, he may order an adjournment.

(3) If the judge decides that the appeal should not be expedited, he may—
   (a) order an adjournment, or
   (b) discharge the jury (if one has been sworn).

(4) If he decides that the appeal should be expedited, he or the Court of Appeal may subsequently reverse that decision and, if it is reversed, the judge may act as mentioned in subsection (3)(a) or (b).

GENERAL NOTE

This section is summarised by the Explanatory Notes (December 2003, para.281) as follows: "This section provides two alternative appeal routes, an expedited (fast) route and a non-expedited (slower) route. The judge must determine which route the appeal will follow (subsection (1)). In the case of an expedited appeal the trial may be adjourned (subsection (2)). If the judge decides that the appeal should follow the non-expedited route he may either adjourn the proceedings or discharge the jury, if one has been sworn (subsection (3)). Subsection (4) gives both the judge and the Court of Appeal power to reverse a decision to expedite an appeal, thus transferring the case to the slower non-expedited route. If a decision is reversed under this subsection, the jury may be discharged."

Whether the appeal is expedited or not, the court "may" order an adjournment. An adjournment enables the case to remain in the list, to keep the parties together, to retain the jury (if there is one), to prevent defendants in custody having to return to court weeks or months later for a retrial, and save costs thrown away by an aborted trial. The usual course will be for a trial judge to order an adjournment but ss.59(2), and (3)(a), indicate that he is not obliged to do so. By virtue of s.60, proceedings may be continued in respect of any offence not the subject of an appeal. In a complex case involving multiple charges, and where the defendants are represented by two counsel, proceedings may be conducted in the Court of Appeal by one lawyer, whilst the trial continues in the presence of the other lawyer.

In committee, the Solicitor-General repeatedly referred to a "chart" that detailed the procedure a court was likely to follow. Unhappily this chart has not been appended to the Explanatory Notes (see Standing Committee B, February 25, 2003, cols.1105 and 1131). However, the Government was anxious to ensure that s.59 could be applied in a flexible way, and that details will appear in rules of court, and "if necessary, in practice directions, and other guidance issued by the Court of Appeal".

60 Continuation of proceedings for offences not affected by ruling

(1) This section applies where the prosecution informs the court in accordance with section 58(4) that it intends to appeal.

(2) Proceedings may be continued in respect of any offence which is not the subject of the appeal.

GENERAL NOTE

See the General Note to Pt 9, ss.58–59.

61 Determination of appeal by Court of Appeal

(1) On an appeal under section 58, the Court of Appeal may confirm, reverse or vary any ruling to which the appeal relates.

(2) Subsections (3) to (5) apply where the appeal relates to a single ruling.

(3) Where the Court of Appeal confirms the ruling, it must, in respect of the offence or each offence which is the subject of the appeal, order

that the defendant in relation to that offence be acquitted of that offence.

(4) Where the Court of Appeal reverses or varies the ruling, it must, in respect of the offence or each offence which is the subject of the appeal, do any of the following—

    (a) order that proceedings for that offence may be resumed in the Crown Court,

    (b) order that a fresh trial may take place in the Crown Court for that offence,

    (c) order that the defendant in relation to that offence be acquitted of that offence.

(5) But the Court of Appeal may not make an order under subsection (4)(a) or (b) in respect of an offence unless it considers it necessary in the interests of justice to do so.

(6) Subsections (7) and (8) apply where the appeal relates to a ruling that there is no case to answer and one or more other rulings.

(7) Where the Court of Appeal confirms the ruling that there is no case to answer, it must, in respect of the offence or each offence which is the subject of the appeal, order that the defendant in relation to that offence be acquitted of that offence.

(8) Where the Court of Appeal reverses or varies the ruling that there is no case to answer, it must in respect of the offence or each offence which is the subject of the appeal, make any of the orders mentioned in subsection (4)(a) to (c) (but subject to subsection (5)).

GENERAL NOTE

This section was revised in Standing Committee (Standing Committee B, col.1135). The provision enables the Court of Appeal to uphold, or to reverse, or vary the ruling (s.61(4)), but in all cases the court has power to direct that the defendant be acquitted (ss.61(3) 61(4)(c)). In cases where a ruling is either reversed, or varied, the Court Appeal may (in the interests of justice, s.61(5)) order the defendant to be retried, or for the trial to be resumed if proceedings in the Crown Court have been adjourned (ss.61(4)(a) and (b)). Even if the prosecution succeeds on appeal, a retrial might not be ordered if, for example, where the defendant was very ill.

Right of appeal in respect of evidentiary rulings

62   Right of appeal in respect of evidentiary rulings

(1) The prosecution may, in accordance with this section and section 63, appeal in respect of—

    (a) a single qualifying evidentiary ruling, or

    (b) two or more qualifying evidentiary rulings.

(2) A "qualifying evidentiary ruling" is an evidentiary ruling of a judge in relation to a trial on indictment which is made at any time (whether before or after the commencement of the trial) before the opening of the case for the defence.

(3) The prosecution may not appeal in respect of a single qualifying evidentiary ruling unless the ruling relates to one or more qualifying offences (whether or not it relates to any other offence).

(4) The prosecution may not appeal in respect of two or more qualifying evidentiary rulings unless each ruling relates to one or more qualifying offences (whether or not it relates to any other offence).

(5) If the prosecution intends to appeal under this section, it must before the opening of the case for the defence inform the court—

    (a) of its intention to do so, and

    (b) of the ruling or rulings to which the appeal relates.

(6) In respect of the ruling, or each ruling, to which the appeal relates—

    (a) the qualifying offence, or at least one of the qualifying offences, to which the ruling relates must be the subject of the appeal, and

(b) any other offence to which the ruling relates may, but need not, be the subject of the appeal.

(7) The prosecution must, at the same time that it informs the court in accordance with subsection (5), inform the court of the offence or offences which are the subject of the appeal.

(8) For the purposes of this section, the case for the defence opens when, after the conclusion of the prosecution evidence, the earliest of the following events occurs—

(a) evidence begins to be adduced by or on behalf of a defendant,

(b) it is indicated to the court that no evidence will be adduced by or on behalf of a defendant,

(c) a defendant's case is opened, as permitted by section 2 of the Criminal Procedure Act 1865 (c. 18).

(9) In this section—

"evidentiary ruling" means a ruling which relates to the admissibility or exclusion of any prosecution evidence,

"qualifying offence" means an offence described in Part 1 of Schedule 4.

(10) The Secretary of State may by order amend that Part by doing any one or more of the following—

(a) adding a description of offence,

(b) removing a description of offence for the time being included,

(c) modifying a description of offence for the time being included.

(11) Nothing in this section affects the right of the prosecution to appeal in respect of an evidentiary ruling under section 58.

DEFINITIONS
"evidentiary ruling": s.62(9)
"qualifying offence": s.62(9)

GENERAL NOTE
The origin of this section is Amendment No.111, which was mentioned, but not moved, in the House of Lords on the October 30, 2003 (*Hansard*, HL, Vol. 654, col.458). The current wording of s.62 was inserted into the Bill by Amendment No.39 moved in the House of Lords on behalf of the Government on the November 17, 2003 (*Hansard*, HL, Vol. 654 col.1785). The object of the measure, and the reasoning behind it, was broadly explained by Lord Goldsmith as follows:

"...we have introduced a range of measures here to limit the number of appeals that there may be. I wish to identify them.

First, an appeal against an evidentiary ruling or rulings in a series will be allowed only where the ruling or rulings are made before the defence case opens. That timing is more restrictive than that now applicable to appeals against a single terminating ruling.

Secondly, an appeal against an evidentiary ruling will be available only in relation to a qualifying offence as set out in the schedule. That schedule has intentionally been constructed so as to include only serious offences.

Thirdly, the prosecution must obtain leave to appeal from either the judge or the Court of Appeal before it can appeal.

Fourthly, that leave may be granted only if the relevant condition is met. That relevant condition is that the evidentiary ruling or rulings, 'significantly weakens the prosecution case'.

Fifthly, I anticipate that the guidance which the Director of Public Prosecutions will issue to prosecutors on the operation of the prosecution appeals regime as a whole will include specific guidance on evidentiary appeals.

Finally — this matter arises from detailed discussions with the senior judiciary in the Court of Appeal — the evidentiary appeal regime will be implemented later than, and separately from, the terminating rulings appeals. That will give an opportunity to see how the terminating appeal works in practice and give us advance warning of any unexpected resource implications of the evidentiary regime.

I hope that your Lordships will agree that, taken together, those amendments represent a formidable battery of safeguards." (*Hansard*, HL, Vol. 413, col.1787 (November 17, 2003)

The prosecution may appeal one or more "qualifying evidential rulings" being a ruling that relates to the admissibility or exclusion of any prosecution evidence (s.62(9)), and which must relate to at least one "qualifying offence" — *i.e.* an offence listed in Pt 1 of Sch.4 to the 2003 Act (see ss.62(3), (4) and (9)). The distinction between a "single qualifying evidential ruling" and "two or more qualifying evidential rulings" seems to be relevant only in the context of s.63 — that is to say, that leave to appeal will not be given unless a single ruling or the combined effect of two or more rulings "significantly weaken the prosecution's case in relation to the offence or offences which are the subject of the appeal".

63   Condition that evidentiary ruling significantly weakens prosecution case

(1) Leave to appeal may not be given in relation to an appeal under section 62 unless the judge or, as the case may be, the Court of Appeal is satisfied that the relevant condition is fulfilled.

(2) In relation to an appeal in respect of a single qualifying evidentiary ruling, the relevant condition is that the ruling significantly weakens the prosecution's case in relation to the offence or offences which are the subject of the appeal.

(3) In relation to an appeal in respect of two or more qualifying evidentiary rulings, the relevant condition is that the rulings taken together significantly weaken the prosecution's case in relation to the offence or offences which are the subject of the appeal.

DEFINITIONS
"qualifying evidentiary ruling": s.74(1)
"ruling": s.74(1)

GENERAL NOTE
See the General Note to s.62 above.

64   Expedited and non-expedited appeals

(1) Where the prosecution informs the court in accordance with section 62(5), the judge must decide whether or not the appeal should be expedited.

(2) If the judge decides that the appeal should be expedited, he may order an adjournment.

(3) If the judge decides that the appeal should not be expedited, he may—
   (a) order an adjournment, or
   (b) discharge the jury (if one has been sworn).

(4) If he decides that the appeal should be expedited, he or the Court of Appeal may subsequently reverse that decision and, if it is reversed, the judge may act as mentioned in subsection (3)(a) or (b).

GENERAL NOTE
See the General Note to s.59 above.

65   Continuation of proceedings for offences not affected by ruling

(1) This section applies where the prosecution informs the court in accordance with section 62(5).

(2) Proceedings may be continued in respect of any offence which is not the subject of the appeal.

66   Determination of appeal by Court of Appeal

(1) On an appeal under section 62, the Court of Appeal may confirm, reverse or vary any ruling to which the appeal relates.

(2) In addition, the Court of Appeal must, in respect of the offence or each offence which is the subject of the appeal, do any of the following—

(a) order that proceedings for that offence be resumed in the Crown Court,

(b) order that a fresh trial may take place in the Crown Court for that offence,

(c) order that the defendant in relation to that offence be acquitted of that offence.

(3) But no order may be made under subsection (2)(c) in respect of an offence unless the prosecution has indicated that it does not intend to continue with the prosecution of that offence.

67   Reversal of rulings

The Court of Appeal may not reverse a ruling on an appeal under this Part unless it is satisfied—

(a) that the ruling was wrong in law,

(b) that the ruling involved an error of law or principle, or

(c) that the ruling was a ruling that it was not reasonable for the judge to have made.

Miscellaneous and supplemental

68   Appeals to the House of Lords

(1) In section 33(1) of the 1968 Act (right of appeal to House of Lords) after "this Act" there is inserted "or Part 9 of the Criminal Justice Act 2003".

(2) In section 36 of the 1968 Act (bail on appeal by defendant) after "under" there is inserted "Part 9 of the Criminal Justice Act 2003 or".

(3) In this Part "the 1968 Act" means the Criminal Appeal Act 1968 (c. 19).

DEFINITIONS
  "the 1968 Act": s.68(3) and s.74(1)

GENERAL NOTE
  Provision is made for the rare instance that a decision of the Court of Appeal on a point of law is taken by either the prosecution or the defence, to the House of Lords.

69   Costs

(1) The Prosecution of Offences Act 1985 (c. 23) is amended as follows.

(2) In section 16(4A) (defence costs on an appeal under section 9(11) of Criminal Justice Act 1987 may be met out of central funds) after "hearings)" there is inserted "or under Part 9 of the Criminal Justice Act 2003".

(3) In section 18 (award of costs against accused) after subsection (2) there is inserted—

"(2A) Where the Court of Appeal reverses or varies a ruling on an appeal under Part 9 of the Criminal Justice Act 2003, it may make such order as to the costs to be paid by the accused, to such person as may be named in the order, as it considers just and reasonable."

(4) In subsection (6) after "subsection (2)" there is inserted "or (2A)".

70   Effect on time limits in relation to preliminary stages

(1) Section 22 of the Prosecution of Offences Act 1985 (c. 23) (power of Secretary of State to set time limits in relation to preliminary stages of criminal proceedings) is amended as follows.

(2) After subsection (6A) there is inserted—

"(6B) Any period during which proceedings for an offence are adjourned pending the determination of an appeal under Part 9 of the Criminal Justice Act 2003 shall be disregarded, so far as the offence is concerned, for the purposes of the overall time limit and the custody time limit which applies to the stage which the proceedings have reached when they are adjourned."

GENERAL NOTE

This provision deals with the situation where the prosecution appeals a ruling of the judge before the commencement of the trial. In such cases, the provision suspends the usual custody time limits under s.22 of the Prosecution of Offences Act 1985 pending the determination of the appeal (see Standing Committee B, February 25, 2003, col.1138). Part 9 makes no provision adopting the recommendation of the Law Commission that there should be a custody time limit of two months, or that the Court Appeal should have power to extend that time limit if (a) the prosecution has exercised due diligence in promoting the hearing of the appeal, and (b) that there is good and sufficient reason to extend a time limit in the interests of justice (Report, *Double Jeopardy and Prosecution Appeals*, para.7.129).

There is no overall time limit, stated in the 2003 Act, within which all prosecution appeals must be heard whether the defendant is in custody or not but time limits will form part of the Rules of Court made under s.73 of the 2003 Act (see para.7.135 of the Law Commission Report).

71   Restrictions on reporting

(1) Except as provided by this section no publication shall include a report of—
  (a) anything done under section 58, 59, 62, 63 or 64,
  (b) an appeal under this Part,
  (c) an appeal under Part 2 of the 1968 Act in relation to an appeal under this Part, or
  (d) an application for leave to appeal in relation to an appeal mentioned in paragraph (b) or (c).
(2) The judge may order that subsection (1) is not to apply, or is not to apply to a specified extent, to a report of—
  (a) anything done under section 58, 59, 62, 63 or 64, or
  (b) an application to the judge for leave to appeal to the Court of Appeal under this Part.
(3) The Court of Appeal may order that subsection (1) is not to apply, or is not to apply to a specified extent, to a report of—
  (a) an appeal to the Court of Appeal under this Part,
  (b) an application to that Court for leave to appeal to it under this Part, or
  (c) an application to that Court for leave to appeal to the House of Lords under Part 2 of the 1968 Act.
(4) The House of Lords may order that subsection (1) is not to apply, or is not to apply to a specified extent, to a report of—
  (a) an appeal to that House under Part 2 of the 1968 Act, or
  (b) an application to that House for leave to appeal to it under Part 2 of that Act.
(5) Where there is only one defendant and he objects to the making of an order under subsection (2), (3) or (4)—
  (a) the judge, the Court of Appeal or the House of Lords are to make the order if (and only if) satisfied, after hearing the representations of the defendant, that it is in the interests of justice to do so, and
  (b) the order (if made) is not to apply to the extent that a report deals with any such objection or representations.
(6) Where there are two or more defendants and one or more of them object to the making of an order under subsection (2), (3) or (4)—

(a) the judge, the Court of Appeal or the House of Lords are to make the order if (and only if) satisfied, after hearing the representations of each of the defendants, that it is in the interests of justice to do so, and

(b) the order (if made) is not to apply to the extent that a report deals with any such objection or representations.

(7) Subsection (1) does not apply to the inclusion in a publication of a report of—

(a) anything done under section 58, 59, 62, 63 or 64,

(b) an appeal under this Part,

(c) an appeal under Part 2 of the 1968 Act in relation to an appeal under this Part, or

(d) an application for leave to appeal in relation to an appeal mentioned in paragraph (b) or (c),

at the conclusion of the trial of the defendant or the last of the defendants to be tried.

(8) Subsection (1) does not apply to a report which contains only one or more of the following matters—

(a) the identity of the court and the name of the judge,

(b) the names, ages, home addresses and occupations of the defendant or defendants and witnesses,

(c) the offence or offences, or a summary of them, with which the defendant or defendants are charged,

(d) the names of counsel and solicitors in the proceedings,

(e) where the proceedings are adjourned, the date and place to which they are adjourned,

(f) any arrangements as to bail,

(g) whether a right to representation funded by the Legal Services Commission as part of the Criminal Defence Service was granted to the defendant or any of the defendants.

(9) The addresses that may be included in a report by virtue of subsection (8) are addresses—

(a) at any relevant time, and

(b) at the time of their inclusion in the publication.

(10) Nothing in this section affects any prohibition or restriction by virtue of any other enactment on the inclusion of any matter in a publication.

(11) In this section—

"programme service" has the same meaning as in the Broadcasting Act 1990 (c. 42),

"publication" includes any speech, writing, relevant programme or other communication in whatever form, which is addressed to the public at large or any section of the public (and for this purpose every relevant programme is to be taken to be so addressed), but does not include an indictment or other document prepared for use in particular legal proceedings,

"relevant time" means a time when events giving rise to the charges to which the proceedings relate are alleged to have occurred,

"relevant programme" means a programme included in a programme service.

DEFINITIONS
"publication": s.71(11) and s.74(1)
"relevant time": s.71(11) and s.74(1)
"the 1968 Act ": s.74(1)

GENERAL NOTE
The issue as to whether, or to what extent, the reporting of an appeal should be permitted, was considered by the Law Commission both in its consultation paper (Cm.158), and in its final

Report (*Double Jeopardy and Prosecution Appeals*, para.7.140). The Law Commission recommended an automatic ban on the reporting of an appeal until the hearing of the appeal, and any retrial, had been concluded, but subject to a decision of the Court of Appeal and the House of Lords, to lift or to vary the order (ss.71(2)–(4)). The Law Commission was confident that such a proposal would not violate Article 10 of the ECHR in the light of the decision of the European Commission of Human Rights in *BBC Scotland v United Kingdom* (1998) 25 E.H.R.R. CD179.

Section 71 introduces a more flexible scheme that requires the court to balance a number of interests. The reporting of matters listed in s.71(8)(a) may be reported (*e.g.* the identity of the court, or arrangements as to bail) including (surprisingly perhaps) the "names, ages, home addresses" of defence witnesses (see s.71(8)(b)).

Beyond those matters, there is an automatic ban in respect of the reporting of an application for leave to appeal, or the fact that the prosecution is considering an appeal, as well as reporting steps taken under ss.58, 59, 62, 63, or 64 of the 2003 Act. The order may be varied, and some reporting permitted, but only to the extent that it is in the interest of justice to do so, and that the order "deals with any such objection or representations" voiced by a defendant or co-defendant: see ss.71(5) and (6).

72   Offences in connection with reporting

(1) This section applies if a publication includes a report in contravention of section 71.

(2) Where the publication is a newspaper or periodical, any proprietor, editor or publisher of the newspaper or periodical is guilty of an offence.

(3) Where the publication is a relevant programme—
  (a) any body corporate or Scottish partnership engaged in providing the programme service in which the programme is included, and
  (b) any person having functions in relation to the programme corresponding to those of an editor of a newspaper,
  is guilty of an offence.

(4) In the case of any other publication, any person publishing it is guilty of an offence.

(5) If an offence under this section committed by a body corporate is proved—
  (a) to have been committed with the consent or connivance of, or
  (b) to be attributable to any neglect on the part of,
  an officer, the officer as well as the body corporate is guilty of the offence and liable to be proceeded against and punished accordingly.

(6) In subsection (5), "officer" means a director, manager, secretary or other similar officer of the body, or a person purporting to act in any such capacity.

(7) If the affairs of a body corporate are managed by its members, "director" in subsection (6) means a member of that body.

(8) Where an offence under this section is committed by a Scottish partnership and is proved to have been committed with the consent or connivance of a partner, he as well as the partnership shall be guilty of the offence and shall be liable to be proceeded against and punished accordingly.

(9) A person guilty of an offence under this section is liable on summary conviction to a fine not exceeding level 5 on the standard scale.

(10) Proceedings for an offence under this section may not be instituted—
  (a) in England and Wales otherwise than by or with the consent of the Attorney General, or
  (b) in Northern Ireland otherwise than by or with the consent of—
    (i) before the relevant date, the Attorney General for Northern Ireland, or
    (ii) on or after the relevant date, the Director of Public Prosecutions for Northern Ireland.

(11) In subsection (10) "the relevant date" means the date on which section 22(1) of the Justice (Northern Ireland) Act 2002 (c. 26) comes into force.

DEFINITIONS
"officer": s.72(6)
"programme service": ss.71(11) and 74(1)
"publication": s.71(11) and s.74(1)

GENERAL NOTE
Summary offences are created pursuant to s.72 in connection with a breach of the restrictions imposed by s.71. The penalty is as stated in s.72(9). Criminal proceedings may only be initiated in England and Wales by or with the consent of the Attorney General (s.72(10)(a) or, where instituted in Northern Ireland, by or with the consent of the Attorney General for Northern Ireland or, after the Justice (Northern Ireland) Act 2002 (c.26) comes into force, the Director of Public Prosecutions for Northern Ireland (s.72(10)(b)).

73   Rules of court

(1) Rules of court may make such provision as appears to the authority making them to be necessary or expedient for the purposes of this Part.
(2) Without limiting subsection (1), rules of court may in particular make provision—
  (a) for time limits which are to apply in connection with any provisions of this Part,
  (b) as to procedures to be applied in connection with this Part,
  (c) enabling a single judge of the Court of Appeal to give leave to appeal under this Part or to exercise the power of the Court of Appeal under section 58(12).
(3) Nothing in this section is to be taken as affecting the generality of any enactment conferring powers to make rules of court.

74   Interpretation of Part 9

(1) In this Part—
    "programme service" has the meaning given by section 71(11),
    "publication" has the meaning given by section 71(11),
    "qualifying evidentiary ruling" is to be construed in accordance with section 62(2),
    "the relevant condition" is to be construed in accordance with section 63(2) and (3),
    "relevant programme" has the meaning given by section 71(11),
    "ruling" includes a decision, determination, direction, finding, notice, order, refusal, rejection or requirement,
    "the 1968 Act" means the Criminal Appeal Act 1968 (c. 19).
(2) Any reference in this Part (other than section 73(2)(c)) to a judge is a reference to a judge of the Crown Court.
(3) There is to be no right of appeal under this Part in respect of a ruling in relation to which the prosecution has previously informed the court of its intention to appeal under either section 58(4) or 62(5).
(4) Where a ruling relates to two or more offences but not all of those offences are the subject of an appeal under this Part, nothing in this Part is to be regarded as affecting the ruling so far as it relates to any offence which is not the subject of the appeal.
(5) Where two or more defendants are charged jointly with the same offence, the provisions of this Part are to apply as if the offence, so far as relating to each defendant, were a separate offence (so that, for example, any reference in this Part to a ruling which relates to one or more offences includes a ruling which relates to one or more of those separate offences).

(6) Subject to rules of court made under section 53(1) of the Supreme Court Act 1981 (c. 54) (power by rules to distribute business of Court of Appeal between its civil and criminal divisions)—

    (a) the jurisdiction of the Court of Appeal under this Part is to be exercised by the criminal division of that court, and

    (b) references in this Part to the Court of Appeal are to be construed as references to that division.

PART 10

RETRIAL FOR SERIOUS OFFENCES

GENERAL NOTE

This part of the 2003 Act is concerned with one highly contentious aspect of the double jeopardy rule, namely, the retrial of a person previously acquitted by a court of competent jurisdiction, in respect of whom the decision of the court would ordinarily be regarded in law as "final". By "final", we mean that all ordinary procedures, in the jurisdiction that originally tried that person, have been exhausted including appeals. Put shortly, a defendant who has been acquitted (or convicted) may not be tried again for the same offence. In English law, this is known as the "*autrefois rule*", but in other systems, the principle is better understood as "*ne bis in idem*".

The justification for the existence of the rule has been variously stated, but frequently on the grounds that there should be finality in criminal proceedings so that all should know where they stand: that a defendant should be entitled to build a future that is not put in jeopardy by the risk of renewed proceedings; that a defendant should not be harassed by the threat of renewed proceedings; that law enforcement agencies and the criminal trial process should be encouraged to "get it right the first time"; that the principle of double jeopardy is a "significant strand of the limits on a State's moral authority to censure and punish through criminal law" (*per* Paul Roberts, "*Acquitted Misconduct Evidence and Double Jeopardy Principles from Sambasivam to Z*" [2000] Crim. L.R. 952).

As against those views, others have been voiced, notably the complaint that the reputation of the law is damaged when the law is powerless to prevent persons previously acquitted of serious crime from exploiting that fact, either by escaping sanction if new compelling evidence of their guilt comes to light, or by reason of high financial rewards received by them notwithstanding that evidence emerges of their guilt (for example, proceeds from a book in which a detailed confession is laid out).

The Runciman Royal Commission on Criminal Justice made no recommendation for a general right of appeals against acquittals. The Law Commission did recommend a limited power to reopen an acquittal if new evidence emerged in all cases in which the sentence for the offence would be at least three years' imprisonment ("*Double Jeopardy*", Law Commission; Consultation Paper 156, 1999). The Home Affairs Committee of the House of Commons, Third Report ("*Double Jeopardy*", session 1999–2000) also recommended a change in the law to relax the rule, in cases where the offence charged carried a statutory maximum of life imprisonment. The Law Commission, in its final Report (2001, Law, Commission No.267) revised its opinions and recommended that the Court of Appeal should have power to quash an acquittal and order a retrial, in cases of murder, genocide (discounting 'reckless killing') (Pt VIII, para.1) in which there was new, reliable, and compelling, evidence of the guilt of the accused. Confining the power only to murder was strongly criticised by Lord Justice Auld in his *Review of the Criminal Courts of England and Wales* (see Ch.12, paras 58–63).

In its White Paper "*Justice For All*" (2002, para.4.63) the Government made it clear that its reforms would go "wider than the proposal that change would be limited to murder and certain allied offences". The Government did not adopt the recommendation of the Law Commission that the personal consent of the Director of Public Prosecutions should be obtained before applying to the Court of Appeal for an acquittal to be quashed on the grounds of new evidence, in cases where "an application is in the public interest and a retrial is fully justified" (see Law Commission 267, para.4.98).

The response to the Law Commission Consultation Paper 156, suggest that members of the public, the legal profession, and the judiciary, were divided on the issue as to whether there should be an exception to the *autrefois acquit* rule on the grounds of new evidence (see para.4.6, Final Report, Law Commission 267). Police and prosecuting authorities were in favour. Academic legal opinion was also divided: see for example, "*Rethinking Double Jeopardy*", Professor Ian Dennis [2000] Crim. L.R. 933; "*Acquitted Misconduct Evidence and Double*

Jeopardy Principles", Paul Roberts [2000] Crim. L.R. 952; "*Reform of The Double Jeopardy Law*", Professor Adrian Keene, The Times, May 20, 2003.

It is against that background that the Government has a enacted Part 10 in keeping with proposals in its white paper "*Justice For All*". Part 10 is only concerned with the re-investigation and retrial of final acquittals. The Act applies to any "qualifying offence" (listed in Pt 1 of Sch.5, s.75(8)) and includes murder, manslaughter, rape, attempted rape, the trafficking in class A controlled drugs, specified war crimes, and acts of terrorism. Cases that may be retried are thus determined by the offence in question, and not by the maximum penalty that may be imposed.

Territorial jurisdiction and acquittals in foreign courts

Part 10 applies to England and Wales (and with some modifications to Northern Ireland: see s.96), but not as yet to Scotland. Part 10 will be of retrospective application: s.75(6). It will also apply in respect of an acquittal in proceedings heard in a foreign jurisdiction if the conduct relied on would have amounted to, or included, the commission of a Sch.5 offence in the United Kingdom (see ss.75(4) and (5)).

The Law Commission, in its Final Report, noted that Art.20(3) of the "Rome statute of the International Criminal Court" permits a second trial albeit on the same facts, where the first trial was "designed to shield a suspect from prosecution elsewhere, or was not independent, impartial, or consistent with an intent to bring the perpetrator to justice" (para.6.14). The Law Commission therefore thought it appropriate to adopt a similar criteria in English law. It also recommended that an acquittal by a foreign court should not be regarded as subject to the *autrefois acquit* rule if the result was based solely on the fact that the alleged offence was committed outside the territorial jurisdiction of that court (para.6.20). It will be seen that Part 10 of the Act does not specifically give statutory effect to these recommendations: s.75 (4) is more open-ended. Presumably, the thinking is that in respect of a foreign acquittal neither the Director of Public Prosecutions nor the Court Appeal, would be party to the quashing of an acquittal, and the ordering of a retrial, without at least having regard to the factors the Law Commission took into account in support of its recommendations.

Without the benefit of s.76(4)(c) the Government would have been exposed to criticism that its failure to specify in the Act the basis on which a foreign acquittal might be quashed, and a retrial ordered, proved to be something of a political handicap in its negotiations with foreign powers regarding proposals for closer co-operation on law-enforcement issues, and the mutual recognition of decisions and judgments in criminal matters. The *ne bis in idem* principle is hallowed in many jurisdictions as a significant safeguard against excessive action by one State to reach out and punish nationals of another State. *Ne bis in idem* is likely to be the subject of legislative measures across the European Union. Central to many international instruments are the twin components of mutual trust, and confidence, in the legal systems of States to which the instruments relate. Invariably, those two components are analysed in the context of minimum procedural safeguards and standards that must exist in each participating State. It is therefore rare that *ne bis in idem* does not feature in the analysis. There remains some risk that s.75(4) will be analysed as incorporating too few limitations. On the other hand, it may be said that Pt 10 is European Convention on Human Rights compliant, in that Art.4(2) of Protocol 7 does not prevent "the reopening of the case in accordance with the law and penal procedure of the State concerned, if there is evidence of new or newly discovered facts, or if there has been a fundamental defect in the previous proceedings". Thus Pt 10 provides a legal route by which earlier proceedings might be reopened but does not empower prosecuting authorities to launch fresh proceedings without limitation. Similarly, it might be said that Pt 10 does not offend Art.14(7) of the *United Nations International Convention on Civil And Political Rights* if that Article permits a "resumption" of criminal proceedings (*General Comment, 13/21, of The UN Human Rights Committee*; see para.3.6, Law Commission 267).

As indicated earlier, the real difficulty about ss.75(4) and (5), may be in the politics of a statutory approach that appears to allow the Court of Appeal to overturn an acquittal of a foreign court on grounds wider than the Law Commission recommended, and which lacks international comity. In practice it will surely be exceedingly rare for a court to overturn an acquittal of a foreign court. Under the 2003 Act there might be circumstances in which it might be easier to reopen an acquittal of a foreign court than an acquittal obtained in an English Court. What would be the position if the Court Appeal were to find that a foreign court did not take into account material held in England, that (for whatever reason) was not passed on to investigators in the other State? Although the reason maybe a relevant matter for the Court of

Appeal to consider when deciding whether it would be "in the interests of justice" for a case to be reopened, the absence of any statutory factors which the court is directed to consider in determining where the interests of justice lie, leaves the "interests of justice" requirement exceedingly ambiguous.

Role of the DPP in connection with foreign acquittals

It will be noted that s.76(4)(c) requires the Director of Public Prosecutions to give his consent only if satisfied that any trial pursuant to an order under Pt 10 would not be inconsistent with obligations of the United Kingdom under Arts 31 and 34 of the Treaty of the European Union relating to the principle of ne bis in idem. However, EU States are not alone in applying this principle. Treaty obligations concerning ne bis in idem should surely also be relevant when the Court of Appeal is considering an application made to it under Pt 10 of the Act.

Limit of autrefois acquit/convict

It is important to have regard to the limits of the *autrefois acquit/convict* (or *ne bis in idem*) principle. In English law, the plea is available when the offence "embraces both the facts which constitute the crime and the legal characteristics which make it an offence. For the doctrine to apply, it must be the same offence both in fact and in law" (Lord Devlin, *Connelly v DPP* [1964] A.C. 1254), although it seems that the facts need only be substantially the same: see *R. v Beedie (Thomas Sim)* [1998] Q.B. 356, and see Law Commission 267, Pt 2.

An acquittal, or conviction, does not become *res judicata* until all ordinary domestic legal proceedings, and remedies, have been exhausted. Accordingly, an order for a retrial following the quashing of a conviction, or remitting a case to the magistrates' court and the quashing of an acquittal, is currently permitted in English law. An acquittal tainted by the proven intimidation of a witness, or juror, may also result in the acquittal being quashed and a retrial ordered.

Cases that may be retried

75   Cases that may be retried

(1) This Part applies where a person has been acquitted of a qualifying offence in proceedings—
    (a) on indictment in England and Wales,
    (b) on appeal against a conviction, verdict or finding in proceedings on indictment in England and Wales, or
    (c) on appeal from a decision on such an appeal.

(2) A person acquitted of an offence in proceedings mentioned in subsection (1) is treated for the purposes of that subsection as also acquitted of any qualifying offence of which he could have been convicted in the proceedings because of the first-mentioned offence being charged in the indictment, except an offence—
    (a) of which he has been convicted,
    (b) of which he has been found not guilty by reason of insanity, or
    (c) in respect of which, in proceedings where he has been found to be under a disability (as defined by section 4 of the Criminal Procedure (Insanity) Act 1964 (c. 84)), a finding has been made that he did the act or made the omission charged against him.

(3) References in subsections (1) and (2) to a qualifying offence do not include references to an offence which, at the time of the acquittal, was the subject of an order under section 77(1) or (3).

(4) This Part also applies where a person has been acquitted, in proceedings elsewhere than in the United Kingdom, of an offence under the law of the place where the proceedings were held, if the commission of the offence as alleged would have amounted to or included the commission (in the United Kingdom or elsewhere) of a qualifying offence.

(5) Conduct punishable under the law in force elsewhere than in the United Kingdom is an offence under that law for the purposes of subsection (4), however it is described in that law.

(6) This Part applies whether the acquittal was before or after the passing of this Act.

(7) References in this Part to acquittal are to acquittal in circumstances within subsection (1) or (4).

(8) In this Part "qualifying offence" means an offence listed in Part 1 of Schedule 5.

DEFINITIONS
"acquitted": ss.75(7) and 95(1)
"qualifying offence": ss.75(8) and 95(1)

GENERAL NOTE
See the General Note to Pt 10. This section specifies the circumstances that must exist before Pt 10 is engaged at all. By subs.(1), the acquittal must be the result of a trial on indictment. Acquittals in magistrates' court do not fall within Pt 10. The acquittal must be in respect of a "qualifying offence" listed in Pt 1 of Sch.5 (s.75(8)), and includes what are sometimes styled "implied acquittals" — that is to say, offences properly regarded as alternatives to the offence in respect to which the defendant was acquitted (see Explanatory Notes, para.311; and note the exceptions in ss.75(2)(a)–(c)).

Where a defendant has been retried under the Part 10 procedure, and acquitted, his acquittal cannot be the subject of further proceedings under Pt 10 of the 2003 Act. This is the effect of s.75(3) that deems a retried offence as not constituting a "qualifying offence" in those circumstances.

Part 10 is engaged if the acquittal relates to proceedings for a qualifying offence in England and Wales (s.75(1)) or "elsewhere than in the United Kingdom" if the commission of the offence would have amounted to, or included, the commission in the United Kingdom of a qualifying offence (s.75(4)). Note that acquittals relating to proceedings in Scotland cannot be reopened under Pt 10. This is deliberate — Pt 10 does not yet apply to Scotland. The wording of s.75(4) makes it plain that for the purposes of Pt 10, an acquittal in Scotland is not be regarded as relating to proceedings in a foreign jurisdiction (and see Explanatory Notes, para.313). Note that for the purposes of s.75(4), a matter tried in a foreign jurisdiction will still be an "offence" however it is described there (*e.g.* an administrative violation). Whether the offence is a "qualifying" one depends on the conduct and facts complained of.

Application for retrial

76   Application to Court of Appeal

(1) A prosecutor may apply to the Court of Appeal for an order—
   (a) quashing a person's acquittal in proceedings within section 75(1), and
   (b) ordering him to be retried for the qualifying offence.

(2) A prosecutor may apply to the Court of Appeal, in the case of a person acquitted elsewhere than in the United Kingdom, for—
   (a) a determination whether the acquittal is a bar to the person being tried in England and Wales for the qualifying offence, and
   (b) if it is, an order that the acquittal is not to be a bar.

(3) A prosecutor may make an application under subsection (1) or (2) only with the written consent of the Director of Public Prosecutions.

(4) The Director of Public Prosecutions may give his consent only if satisfied that—
   (a) there is evidence as respects which the requirements of section 78 appear to be met,
   (b) it is in the public interest for the application to proceed, and
   (c) any trial pursuant to an order on the application would not be inconsistent with obligations of the United Kingdom under

Article 31 or 34 of the Treaty on European Union relating to the principle of *ne bis in idem.*

(5) Not more than one application may be made under subsection (1) or (2) in relation to an acquittal.

DEFINITIONS
"of prosecutor": s.95(1)
"acquittal": s.95(1)
"of qualifying offence": s.95(1)

GENERAL NOTE

Read the General Note to Pt 10. In respect of acquittals for a "qualifying offence" arising out of proceedings conducted in England and Wales, the prosecutor may apply to the Court of Appeal for two orders: the first, quashing a defendant's acquittal, and the second, ordering him to be retried for the qualifying offence (ss.76(1)(a) and (b)). In all cases the prosecutor must have the written personal consent of the Director of Public Prosecutions to make such an application (s.76(3)), and not more than one application may be made in relation to an acquittal (s.76(5)). For his part, the Director of Public Prosecutions must comply with s.76(4).

The procedure in relation to foreign acquittals is somewhat different. Note that Pt 10 does not apply to Scotland, or to acquittals in proceedings there (see the General Note to s.75).

It may be that the facts of a case reveal that an acquittal in a foreign jurisdiction does not prevent a fresh prosecution being initiated against a defendant in England, Wales, or Northern Ireland, for the reason that the matter is neither *res judicata* in those jurisdictions, nor subject to the *autrefois acquit/ne bis in idem* principle. Such cases do not require the foreign acquittal to be quashed before launching a fresh prosecution. However, under s.76 it is for the Court Appeal to decide that issue, and therefore the prosecutor should follow the Pt 10 procedure. By virtue of s.76(3) the prosecutor must obtain the consent of the Director of Public Prosecutions to make an application under s.76(2)(a) for a determination whether the acquittal is a bar to the person being tried in England, Wales (or Northern Ireland) for the qualifying offence. If the answer to that question is "no", the court must make a declaration to that effect (s.77(4)), and a fresh prosecution may be brought. If the answer is that the acquittal is (or, but for Pt 10, would be) a bar to fresh proceedings, the prosecutor must seek an order under s.76(2)(b) that the acquittal is "not to be a bar" to fresh proceedings.

77 Determination by Court of Appeal

(1) On an application under section 76(1), the Court of Appeal—
  (a) if satisfied that the requirements of sections 78 and 79 are met, must make the order applied for;
  (b) otherwise, must dismiss the application.
(2) Subsections (3) and (4) apply to an application under section 76(2).
(3) Where the Court of Appeal determines that the acquittal is a bar to the person being tried for the qualifying offence, the court—
  (a) if satisfied that the requirements of sections 78 and 79 are met, must make the order applied for;
  (b) otherwise, must make a declaration to the effect that the acquittal is a bar to the person being tried for the offence.
(4) Where the Court of Appeal determines that the acquittal is not a bar to the person being tried for the qualifying offence, it must make a declaration to that effect.

DEFINITIONS
"acquittal": s.95(1)
"qualifying offence": s.95(1)

GENERAL NOTE

The approach to be taken by the Court of Appeal will depend on whether the acquittal relates to an acquittal for a qualifying offence arising out of proceedings in England, Wales, or Northern Ireland, or in respect of a foreign acquittal. If the former, then s.77(1) is applicable. If the latter, then ss.77(2)–(4) are to be applied because the prosecution must apply under s.76(2) of the Act for a determination as to whether the acquittal is a bar to the person being tried in England and Wales for the "qualifying offence". In either situation, s.77 must be read in conjunction with ss.78 and 79 (*i.e.* a new compelling evidence, and interest of justice considerations). In respect of a foreign acquittal, the Court of Appeal must first decide whether the acquittal (but for Pt 10) is *autrefois acquit*. If it is not, then the court moves to s.77(4) and makes a declaration to that effect. If the acquittal is *autrefois acquit*, then the court must see if the conditions in ss.78 and 79 are met. If they are met, the court must make an order that there is now no bar to a fresh proceedings being initiated (s.77(3)(a)). If the conditions are not met, the bar remains and the court must make a declaration to that effect (s.77(3)(b)).

78 New and compelling evidence

(1) The requirements of this section are met if there is new and compelling evidence against the acquitted person in relation to the qualifying offence.

(2) Evidence is new if it was not adduced in the proceedings in which the person was acquitted (nor, if those were appeal proceedings, in earlier proceedings to which the appeal related).

(3) Evidence is compelling if—
   (a) it is reliable,
   (b) it is substantial, and
   (c) in the context of the outstanding issues, it appears highly probative of the case against the acquitted person.

(4) The outstanding issues are the issues in dispute in the proceedings in which the person was acquitted and, if those were appeal proceedings, any other issues remaining in dispute from earlier proceedings to which the appeal related.

(5) For the purposes of this section, it is irrelevant whether any evidence would have been admissible in earlier proceedings against the acquitted person.

DEFINITIONS
   "evidence is new": ss.78(2) and 95(1)
   "prosecutor": ss.65(6) and 95(1)
   "officer": s.95(1)
   "qualifying offence": s.95(1)
   "acquittal": s.95(1)
   "compelling evidence": s.78(3)
   "outstanding issues": s.78(4)

GENERAL NOTE
   See the General Note to Pt 10. This section concerns one of two requirements that must be met before the Court of Appeal is required to make orders under ss.76 and 77. The requirement here is that there exists "new and compelling evidence" that the acquitted person is guilty of the qualifying offence. Despite the phrase "is guilty" in s.78(1), it seems that the actual test is that found in s.78(3)(c) namely, that "in the context of the outstanding issues, it appears highly probative of the case against the acquitted person". This differs from the test as it first appeared in (what was then) clause 65(3)(c) of the Bill as printed on the November 21, 2002, namely, that it is "highly probable that the person is guilty of the offence". Even if the evidence is compelling, it must also be "new" as defined by s.78(2). Whether the evidence is "compelling" depends on what was in issue in the original trial. There is no merit in an application for a retrial under Pt 10 if the new compelling evidence merely relates to a point that was admitted by the parties at trial. The new material must therefore relate to issues that were in dispute at trial, or during an appeal against conviction. Section 78(3)(c), and s.78(4), appear to have their origin in the proposals of the Law Commission in its final Report (Law Commission 267, para.4.63). Note that it is irrelevant whether the new evidence would have been inadmissible at the time the original proceedings took place (s.78(5)).

79 Interests of justice

(1) The requirements of this section are met if in all the circumstances it is in the interests of justice for the court to make the order under section 77.

(2) That question is to be determined having regard in particular to—
  (a) whether existing circumstances make a fair trial unlikely;
  (b) for the purposes of that question and otherwise, the length of time since the qualifying offence was allegedly committed;
  (c) whether it is likely that the new evidence would have been adduced in the earlier proceedings against the acquitted person but for a failure by an officer or by a prosecutor to act with due diligence or expedition;
  (d) whether, since those proceedings or, if later, since the commencement of this Part, any officer or prosecutor has failed to act with due diligence or expedition.

(3) In subsection (2) references to an officer or prosecutor include references to a person charged with corresponding duties under the law in force elsewhere than in England and Wales.

(4) Where the earlier prosecution was conducted by a person other than a prosecutor, subsection (2)(c) applies in relation to that person as well as in relation to a prosecutor.

DEFINITIONS
  "qualifying offence": s.95(1)
  "officer": s.95(1)
  "prosecutor": s.95(1)
  "new evidence": ss.95(1) and 78(2)

GENERAL NOTE
  See the General Note to Pt 10, and the notes to ss.77 and 78. The court will be able to take into account factors such as adverse publicity and its likely effect on a jury.

80   Procedure and evidence

(1) A prosecutor who wishes to make an application under section 76(1) or (2) must give notice of the application to the Court of Appeal.

(2) Within two days beginning with the day on which any such notice is given, notice of the application must be served by the prosecutor on the person to whom the application relates, charging him with the offence to which it relates or, if he has been charged with it in accordance with section 87(4), stating that he has been so charged.

(3) Subsection (2) applies whether the person to whom the application relates is in the United Kingdom or elsewhere, but the Court of Appeal may, on application by the prosecutor, extend the time for service under that subsection if it considers it necessary to do so because of that person's absence from the United Kingdom.

(4) The Court of Appeal must consider the application at a hearing.

(5) The person to whom the application relates—
  (a) is entitled to be present at the hearing, although he may be in custody, unless he is in custody elsewhere than in England and Wales or Northern Ireland, and
  (b) is entitled to be represented at the hearing, whether he is present or not.

(6) For the purposes of the application, the Court of Appeal may, if it thinks it necessary or expedient in the interests of justice—
  (a) order the production of any document, exhibit or other thing, the production of which appears to the court to be necessary for the determination of the application, and
  (b) order any witness who would be a compellable witness in proceedings pursuant to an order or declaration made on the application to attend for examination and be examined before the court.

(7) The Court of Appeal may at one hearing consider more than one application (whether or not relating to the same person), but only if the offences concerned could be tried on the same indictment.

DEFINITIONS
"prosecutor": s.95(1)

GENERAL NOTE
This short section harbours a number of interesting issues. Express provision is made for the defendant to attend the hearing if he wishes to be there (s.80(5)(a)). Section 12(2) of the Access to Justice Act 1999 (c.22) will ensure that the defendant will receive adequate legal assistance for the application hearing and a retrial (if there is one).

Section 80(6) empowers the Court of Appeal to receive evidence "for the determination of the application". This might be evidence of a technical, scientific, or statistical, nature the validity of which is challenged by the defence. There seems to be no reason why the court should not hear the evidence in order to satisfy itself that the evidence is compelling for the purposes of s.78(3). There is also no reason why the evidence should be limited to expert evidence and may include confession evidence — *e.g.* the defendant allegedly 'confessed' to a murder in the presence and hearing of a number of his friends at a party. It is submitted that it is not the intended purpose of s.80(6) that either the prosecution and/or the defence should be able to fully explore the strengths and weaknesses of the evidence in anticipation of a possible, or likely retrial.

Section 80(7) appears to indicate that the prosecution must make a separate application in respect of each offence that it intends to reopen. The court may therefore hear more than one application, "but only if the offences concerned could be tried on the same indictment". Note that the prosecutor may serve notice of the Application for an order pursuant to ss.76(1) or (2) of the 2003 Act (s.80(1)). A notice must also be served on the acquitted person that charges him with the offence to which the application relates unless he has already been charged by police under s.87(4) of the Act (s.80(2)).

81   Appeals

(1) The Criminal Appeal Act 1968 (c. 19) is amended as follows.

(2) In section 33 (right of appeal to House of Lords), after subsection (1A) there is inserted—

"(1B) An appeal lies to the House of Lords, at the instance of the acquitted person or the prosecutor, from any decision of the Court of Appeal on an application under section 76(1) or (2) of the Criminal Justice Act 2003 (retrial for serious offences)."

(3) At the end of that section there is inserted—

"(4) In relation to an appeal under subsection (1B), references in this Part to a defendant are references to the acquitted person."

(4) In section 34(2) (extension of time for leave to appeal), after "defendant" there is inserted "or, in the case of an appeal under section 33(1B), by the prosecutor".

(5) In section 38 (presence of defendant at hearing), for "has been convicted of an offence and" substitute "has been convicted of an offence, or in whose case an order under section 77 of the Criminal Justice Act 2003 or a declaration under section 77(4) of that Act has been made, and who".

DEFINITIONS
"acquitted": ss.75(7) and 95(1)
"prosecutor": ss.65(6) and 95(1)

GENERAL NOTE
The Government has made it clear that the prosecution and the defence has a right of appeal to the House of Lords on a point of law in respect of decisions made by the Court of Appeal

regarding applications made under Pt 10 of the 2003 Act. What is not entirely clear is whether the Court of Appeal must first certify that a point of law of general public importance is involved.

82   Restrictions on publication in the interests of justice

(1) Where it appears to the Court of Appeal that the inclusion of any matter in a publication would give rise to a substantial risk of prejudice to the administration of justice in a retrial, the court may order that the matter is not to be included in any publication while the order has effect.

(2) In subsection (1) "retrial" means the trial of an acquitted person for a qualifying offence pursuant to any order made or that may be made under section 77.

(3) The court may make an order under this section only if it appears to it necessary in the interests of justice to do so.

(4) An order under this section may apply to a matter which has been included in a publication published before the order takes effect, but such an order—
   (a) applies only to the later inclusion of the matter in a publication (whether directly or by inclusion of the earlier publication), and
   (b) does not otherwise affect the earlier publication.

(5) After notice of an application has been given under section 80(1) relating to the acquitted person and the qualifying offence, the court may make an order under this section only—
   (a) of its own motion, or
   (b) on the application of the Director of Public Prosecutions.

(6) Before such notice has been given, an order under this section—
   (a) may be made only on the application of the Director of Public Prosecutions, and
   (b) may not be made unless, since the acquittal concerned, an investigation of the commission by the acquitted person of the qualifying offence has been commenced by officers.

(7) The court may at any time, of its own motion or on an application made by the Director of Public Prosecutions or the acquitted person, vary or revoke an order under this section.

(8) Any order made under this section before notice of an application has been given under section 80(1) relating to the acquitted person and the qualifying offence must specify the time when it ceases to have effect.

(9) An order under this section which is made or has effect after such notice has been given ceases to have effect, unless it specifies an earlier time—
   (a) when there is no longer any step that could be taken which would lead to the acquitted person being tried pursuant to an order made on the application, or
   (b) if he is tried pursuant to such an order, at the conclusion of the trial.

(10) Nothing in this section affects any prohibition or restriction by virtue of any other enactment on the inclusion of any matter in a publication or any power, under an enactment or otherwise, to impose such a prohibition or restriction.

(11) In this section—
   "programme service" has the same meaning as in the Broadcasting Act 1990 (c. 42),
   "publication" includes any speech, writing, relevant programme or other communication in whatever form, which is addressed to the public at large or any section of the public (and for this purpose every relevant programme is to be taken to be so

addressed), but does not include an indictment or other document prepared for use in particular legal proceedings,

"relevant programme" means a programme included in a programme service.

DEFINITIONS

"publication": s.82(11)

"acquitted person": s.95(1)

"programme service": s.82(11)

"relevant programme": s.82(11)

GENERAL NOTE

Sections 82 and 83 apply to Scotland and Northern Ireland (s.337(2)) and therefore reporting restrictions cover the whole of the United Kingdom. It will be more difficult to control information available over the Internet. The section applies to both the application, and to anything done in connection with it — including the making of the application (Standing Committee B, col.486; January 21, 2003). Restrictions may be imposed by s.69(1) against the reporting of matters that would "give rise to a substantial risk of prejudice to the administration of justice in a retrial". The purpose of this section is summarised in the Explanatory Notes (para.326) as follows:

"These provisions are aimed at ensuring that a fair trial can take place by limiting the extent to which the media can report on the proceedings under this Part of the Act, to ensure that any potential jury is not influenced by these developments. Reporting restrictions may be sought only by the Director of Public Prosecutions or made by the Court of its own motion and may be imposed by order of the Court of Appeal at any stage after a new investigation into the acquitted person has commenced. The restrictions may apply to any information in respect of the investigation and to the republication of matters previously published. The Court will decide whether such restrictions are required, and their content and duration, according to what is necessary in the interests of justice."

83   Offences in connection with publication restrictions

(1) This section applies if—

    (a) an order under section 82 is made, whether in England and Wales or Northern Ireland, and

    (b) while the order has effect, any matter is included in a publication, in any part of the United Kingdom, in contravention of the order.

(2) Where the publication is a newspaper or periodical, any proprietor, editor or publisher of the newspaper or periodical is guilty of an offence.

(3) Where the publication is a relevant programme—

    (a) any body corporate or Scottish partnership engaged in providing the programme service in which the programme is included, and

    (b) any person having functions in relation to the programme corresponding to those of an editor of a newspaper,

    is guilty of an offence.

(4) In the case of any other publication, any person publishing it is guilty of an offence.

(5) If an offence under this section committed by a body corporate is proved—

    (a) to have been committed with the consent or connivance of, or

    (b) to be attributable to any neglect on the part of,

    an officer, the officer as well as the body corporate is guilty of the offence and liable to be proceeded against and punished accordingly.

(6) In subsection (5), "officer" means a director, manager, secretary or other similar officer of the body, or a person purporting to act in any such capacity.

(7) If the affairs of a body corporate are managed by its members, "director" in subsection (6) means a member of that body.

(8) Where an offence under this section is committed by a Scottish partnership and is proved to have been committed with the consent or connivance of a partner, he as well as the partnership shall be guilty of the offence and shall be liable to be proceeded against and punished accordingly.

(9) A person guilty of an offence under this section is liable on summary conviction to a fine not exceeding level 5 on the standard scale.

(10) Proceedings for an offence under this section may not be instituted—
   (a) in England and Wales otherwise than by or with the consent of the Attorney General, or
   (b) in Northern Ireland otherwise than by or with the consent of—
      (i) before the relevant date, the Attorney General for Northern Ireland, or
      (ii) on or after the relevant date, the Director of Public Prosecutions for Northern Ireland.

(11) In subsection (10) "the relevant date" means the date on which section 22(1) of the Justice (Northern Ireland) Act 2002 (c. 26) comes into force.

DEFINITIONS
   "director": s.83(7)
   "officer": s.83(6)
   "programme service": s.82(11)
   "publication":s.82(11)
   "relevant programme": s.82(11)

GENERAL NOTE
   Section 83 sets creates summary offences arising out of reporting restrictions imposed under s.82 (see ss.83(2), (3), (4), and (5)). The statutory penalty is set out in s.83(9) of the Act. Proceedings may not be initiated in England and Wales without the consent of the Attorney General (s.83(10)(a)), or (in Northern Ireland) with the consent of the Attorney General for Northern Ireland (s.83(10)(b)(i), or the Director of Public Prosecutions for Northern Ireland after s.22(1) of the Justice (Northern Ireland) Act 2002 comes into force (s.83(10)(b)(ii)).

Retrial

84   Retrial

(1) Where a person—
   (a) is tried pursuant to an order under section 77(1), or
   (b) is tried on indictment pursuant to an order under section 77(3),
   the trial must be on an indictment preferred by direction of the Court of Appeal.

(2) After the end of 2 months after the date of the order, the person may not be arraigned on an indictment preferred in pursuance of such a direction unless the Court of Appeal gives leave.

(3) The Court of Appeal must not give leave unless satisfied that—
   (a) the prosecutor has acted with due expedition, and
   (b) there is a good and sufficient cause for trial despite the lapse of time since the order under section 77.

(4) Where the person may not be arraigned without leave, he may apply to the Court of Appeal to set aside the order and—
   (a) for any direction required for restoring an earlier judgment and verdict of acquittal of the qualifying offence, or
   (b) in the case of a person acquitted elsewhere than in the United Kingdom, for a declaration to the effect that the acquittal is a bar to his being tried for the qualifying offence.

(5) An indictment under subsection (1) may relate to more than one offence, or more than one person, and may relate to an offence which,

or a person who, is not the subject of an order or declaration under section 77.

(6) Evidence given at a trial pursuant to an order under section 77(1) or (3) must be given orally if it was given orally at the original trial, unless—

    (a) all the parties to the trial agree otherwise,

    (b) section 116 applies, or

    (c) the witness is unavailable to give evidence, otherwise than as mentioned in subsection (2) of that section, and section 114(1)(d) applies.

(7) At a trial pursuant to an order under section 77(1), paragraph 5 of Schedule 3 to the Crime and Disorder Act 1998 (c. 37) (use of depositions) does not apply to a deposition read as evidence at the original trial.

DEFINITIONS
"acquittal": s.95(1)
"qualifying offence": s.95(1)

GENERAL NOTE
This section gives the prosecution two months to prepare its case, and to arraign the defendant on the new indictment. The defendant may not be arraigned outside that period unless the Court of Appeal gives leave (s.84(2)). Note that there seems to be no time limit beyond which the prosecution cannot seek leave from the Court of Appeal. If the prosecution miss the deadline for arrangement, it is not automatic that the defendant will be acquitted. By s.84(4) it is open to the defendant to apply to the Court of Appeal to set aside the order quashing his acquittal and directing a retrial, but there seems to be no statutory bar that prevents the prosecution resisting the application as well as seeking leave under s.84(2) to arraign the defendant out of time. In the unlikely event that the prosecution allowed the case to lapse, there would be no formal acquittal until the defendant secured a direction restoring the acquittal under s.84(4)(a), or (in the case of a foreign national) that the "acquittal is a bar to his being tried for the qualifying offence" (s.84(4)(b)). It is not clear what power the Court has to restore an acquittal if the defendant died before making an application under the section. As far as foreign acquittals are concerned, it will be seen that s.77(3)(a) requires the court to "make the order applied for". By s.77(2)(b) the "order applied for" should be "an order that the acquittal is not to be a bar (to the person being tried in England and Wales)". Yet, s.84(4)(b) enables a defendant to apply for a declaration to the effect that the acquittal is a bar to his being tried for the qualifying offence". Would it not have been preferable for s.84(4)(b) merely to require the court for appeal to set aside its earlier order that the acquittal is not to be a bar?

Where a defendant makes an application under s.84(4), in circumstances where leave to arraign out of time has been refused, the likely outcome is that the Court of Appeal would restore the defendant to his original position. However, there seems to be no statutory obligation to do so. Might a court be justified in declining to restore an acquittal if there was new compelling evidence that it was highly probable that the defendant is guilty of the offence, but leave under s.84(2) has been refused?

Investigations

85   Authorisation of investigations

(1) This section applies to the investigation of the commission of a qualifying offence by a person—

    (a) acquitted in proceedings within section 75(1) of the qualifying offence, or

    (b) acquitted elsewhere than in the United Kingdom of an offence the commission of which as alleged would have amounted to or included the commission (in the United Kingdom or elsewhere) of the qualifying offence.

(2) Subject to section 86, an officer may not do anything within subsection (3) for the purposes of such an investigation unless the Director of Public Prosecutions—

      (a) has certified that in his opinion the acquittal would not be a bar to the trial of the acquitted person in England and Wales for the qualifying offence, or

      (b) has given his written consent to the investigation (whether before or after the start of the investigation).

(3) The officer may not, either with or without the consent of the acquitted person—

      (a) arrest or question him,

      (b) search him or premises owned or occupied by him,

      (c) search a vehicle owned by him or anything in or on such a vehicle,

      (d) seize anything in his possession, or

      (e) take his fingerprints or take a sample from him.

(4) The Director of Public Prosecutions may only give his consent on a written application, and such an application may be made only by an officer who—

      (a) if he is an officer of the metropolitan police force or the City of London police force, is of the rank of commander or above, or

      (b) in any other case, is of the rank of assistant chief constable or above.

(5) An officer may make an application under subsection (4) only if—

      (a) he is satisfied that new evidence has been obtained which would be relevant to an application under section 76(1) or (2) in respect of the qualifying offence to which the investigation relates, or

      (b) he has reasonable grounds for believing that such new evidence is likely to be obtained as a result of the investigation.

(6) The Director of Public Prosecutions may not give his consent unless satisfied that—

      (a) there is, or there is likely as a result of the investigation to be, sufficient new evidence to warrant the conduct of the investigation, and

      (b) it is in the public interest for the investigation to proceed.

(7) In giving his consent, the Director of Public Prosecutions may recommend that the investigation be conducted otherwise than by officers of a specified police force or specified team of customs and excise officers.

Definitions

"acquitted": s.95(1)
"new evidence": ss.95(1) and 78(2)
"officer": s.95(1)
"qualifying offence": s.95(1)

General Note

Following the acquittal of a person for an offence, there is nothing in law to prevent the police investigating the offence even if it relates to the acquitted person. The powers of the police in connection with such an investigation are limited. The effect of s.85(2) is to prohibit an officer who is investigating the commission of a qualifying offence, performing any of the actions set out in s.85(3) of the 2003 Act concerning the acquitted person without the personal, written, consent of the Director of Public Prosecutions. This prohibition applies whether the acquitted person gives his consent to any of the activities set out in s.85(3) or not. The reason is to avoid the police "leaning on the acquitted person to co-operate" (*per* Hilary Benn, the Permanent Under Secretary for the Home Department, Standing Committee B, col.501, January 21, 2003).

It seems to be immaterial whether in the light of the new evidence the officer has reasonable grounds for suspecting the acquitted person to be guilty of the offence or not. An "officer" for these purposes means an officer of at least the rank of Commander (in the Metropolitan, or City of London, police force), or at least the rank of Assistant Chief Constable (s.85(4)). The application must be in writing (s.85(4)). The officer must only make such an application if "new evidence" in respect of the qualifying offence is available or known to him, or he has reasonable grounds for believing that such new evidence is likely to become available as a result of the investigation (s.85(5)). The Director of Public Prosecutions may not give his consent unless he is satisfied that the investigation is in the public interest, and that there is, or will be, sufficient new evidence to justify the investigation. Section 85(6)(a) may therefore require the Director of Public Prosecutions to form a view about the reliability of the intelligence available to police as to the existence and quality of evidence that might become available. The Director of Public Prosecutions must also comply with s.85(2). A failure to comply with s.85 presumably renders the acts of the officer unlawful, and any evidence obtained as a result of those acts would be liable to be excluded under s.78 PACE. What is not entirely clear from the language of s.85 is whether any new police powers are created for the purposes of Part 10, or whether s.85 merely places a restraint on the exercise of existing powers by an officer. It is submitted that the answer is the latter. Note that neither the officer at nor the Director of Public Prosecutions has to be satisfied that the evidence is likely to be "compelling" (as defined by s.78(3) of the 2003 Act.

86   Urgent investigative steps

(1) Section 85 does not prevent an officer from taking any action for the purposes of an investigation if—
  (a) the action is necessary as a matter of urgency to prevent the investigation being substantially and irrevocably prejudiced,
  (b) the requirements of subsection (2) are met, and
  (c) either—
    (i) the action is authorised under subsection (3), or
    (ii) the requirements of subsection (5) are met.
(2) The requirements of this subsection are met if—
  (a) there has been no undue delay in applying for consent under section 85(2),
  (b) that consent has not been refused, and
  (c) taking into account the urgency of the situation, it is not reasonably practicable to obtain that consent before taking the action.
(3) An officer of the rank of superintendent or above may authorise the action if—
  (a) he is satisfied that new evidence has been obtained which would be relevant to an application under section 76(1) or (2) in respect of the qualifying offence to which the investigation relates, or
  (b) he has reasonable grounds for believing that such new evidence is likely to be obtained as a result of the investigation.
(4) An authorisation under subsection (3) must—
  (a) if reasonably practicable, be given in writing;
  (b) otherwise, be recorded in writing by the officer giving it as soon as is reasonably practicable.
(5) The requirements of this subsection are met if—
  (a) there has been no undue delay in applying for authorisation under subsection (3),
  (b) that authorisation has not been refused, and
  (c) taking into account the urgency of the situation, it is not reasonably practicable to obtain that authorisation before taking the action.
(6) Where the requirements of subsection (5) are met, the action is nevertheless to be treated as having been unlawful unless, as soon as reasonably practicable after the action is taken, an officer of the rank of superintendent or above certifies in writing that he is satisfied that, when the action was taken—
  (a) new evidence had been obtained which would be relevant to an application under section 76(1) or (2) in respect of the qualifying offence to which the investigation relates, or
  (b) the officer who took the action had reasonable grounds for believing that such new evidence was likely to be obtained as a result of the investigation.

DEFINITIONS
    "new evidence" and: ss.78(2) and s.95(1)
    "officer": s.95(1)
    "qualifying offence": s.95(1)

GENERAL NOTE
    Section 76 compliments s.85 and applies if, as a matter of urgency, it is necessary for action to be taken to prevent the investigation being "substantially and irrevocably prejudiced" (see s.85(1)). The action must be authorised by an officer of at least the rank of Superintendent) s.86(3)), and there must have been no undue delay obtaining the consent of the Director of Public Prosecutions, or alternatively, it is not reasonably practicable to obtain that consent before taking action (ss.86(1) and (2)). Section 86 might be invoked if for example information was given to police concerning the existence of an item suspected to be the murder weapon, at an address owned and occupied by the acquitted person, and that there was reason to believe the acquitted person was contemplating selling the house and moving overseas. It is not the intention of the Government that the use of s.86 should be the norm rather than using the procedure under s.85 — on the contrary (see Standing Committee B, January 21, 2003, col.503).

Arrest, custody and bail

87   Arrest and charge

(1) Where section 85 applies to the investigation of the commission of an offence by any person and no certification has been given under subsection (2) of that section—

   (a) a justice of the peace may issue a warrant to arrest that person for that offence only if satisfied by written information that new evidence has been obtained which would be relevant to an application under section 76(1) or (2) in respect of the commission by that person of that offence, and

   (b) that person may not be arrested for that offence except under a warrant so issued.

(2) Subsection (1) does not affect section 89(3)(b) or 91(3), or any other power to arrest a person, or to issue a warrant for the arrest of a person, otherwise than for an offence.

(3) Part 4 of the 1984 Act (detention) applies as follows where a person—

   (a) is arrested for an offence under a warrant issued in accordance with subsection (1)(a), or

   (b) having been so arrested, is subsequently treated under section 34(7) of that Act as arrested for that offence.

(4) For the purposes of that Part there is sufficient evidence to charge the person with the offence for which he has been arrested if, and only if, an officer of the rank of superintendent or above (who has not been directly involved in the investigation) is of the opinion that the evidence available or known to him is sufficient for the case to be referred to a prosecutor to consider whether consent should be sought for an application in respect of that person under section 76.

(5) For the purposes of that Part it is the duty of the custody officer at each police station where the person is detained to make available or known to an officer at that police station of the rank of superintendent or above any evidence which it appears to him may be relevant to an application under section 76(1) or (2) in respect of the offence for which the person has been arrested, and to do so as soon as practicable—

   (a) after the evidence becomes available or known to him, or

   (b) if later, after he forms that view.

(6) Section 37 of that Act (including any provision of that section as applied by section 40(8) of that Act) has effect subject to the following modifications—

   (a) in subsection (1)—

         (i) for "determine whether he has before him" there is substituted "request an officer of the rank of superintendent or above (who has not been directly involved in the investigation) to determine, in accordance with section 87(4) of the Criminal Justice Act 2003, whether there is";

         (ii) for "him to do so" there is substituted "that determination to be made";

    (b) in subsection (2)—

         (i) for the words from "custody officer determines" to "before him" there is substituted "officer determines that there is not such sufficient evidence";

         (ii) the word "custody" is omitted from the second place where it occurs;

    (c) in subsection (3)—

         (i) the word "custody" is omitted;

         (ii) after "may" there is inserted "direct the custody officer to";

    (d) in subsection (7) for the words from "the custody officer" to the end of that subsection there is substituted "an officer of the rank of superintendent or above (who has not been directly involved in the investigation) determines, in accordance with section 87(4) of the Criminal Justice Act 2003, that there is sufficient evidence to charge the person arrested with the offence for which he was arrested, the person arrested shall be charged.";

    (e) subsections (7A), (7B) and (8) do not apply;

    (f) after subsection (10) there is inserted—

        "(10A) The officer who is requested by the custody officer to make a determination under subsection (1) above shall make that determination as soon as practicable after the request is made.".

  (7) Section 40 of that Act has effect as if in subsections (8) and (9) of that section after "(6)" there were inserted "and (10A)".

  (8) Section 42 of that Act has effect as if in subsection (1) of that section for the words from "who" to "detained" there were substituted "(who has not been directly involved in the investigation)".

DEFINITIONS
    "new evidence" ss.78(2) and 95(1)
    "officer": s.95(1)
    "qualifying offence": s.95(1)

GENERAL NOTE
    It is important to note that s.87 applies in circumstances where the Director of Public Prosecutions has not certified that in his opinion the acquittal would not be a bar to the trial of the acquitted person in England and Wales for the qualifying offence (see ss.85(2) and 87(1)). The Explanatory Notes summarise the effect of this section as follows (para.338):

      Section 87 allows for the arrest of a person in respect of a qualifying offence by warrant, if the DPP's consent has not previously been obtained and the police are acting under the urgent procedures. A justice of the peace may issue a warrant where he is satisfied that new evidence against the acquitted person has been obtained. This does not affect his arrest in respect of any matter other than the qualifying offence. Where a person is arrested, the Section provides that he may be charged with the offence for which he has been arrested in accordance with the provisions of the Police and Criminal Evidence Act 1984 (PACE), if an officer of the rank of Superintendent or above, who has not been involved with the investigation, considers that there is sufficient evidence available for the case to be referred to a prosecutor in order to consider making an application for the acquittal to be quashed in accordance with this Part of the Act. This is the equivalent stage to bringing a criminal charge under PACE in normal proceedings, but provides the additional safeguard that the evidence must be considered at Superintendent level or above.

    Note that if a person has been charged under s.87 he must be brought before a Crown Court not more then 24 hours after being charged (see s.88(2)). There appears to be no power for the police to grant bail, or for that matter, a magistrates' court to do so. This seems to be deliberate "in recognition of the nature of the offences and the provisions" (see Standing Committee B, *per* Hilary Benn, col.520). However, note that by s.88, the Crown Court has power to admit the acquitted person to bail.

Note that there is no provision under Part 10 for compensation to be paid to a defendant in the event that he/she is acquitted after a retrial, or if the consent of the Director of Public Prosecutions to make an application under Part 10 for a retrial, is refused, or if the application is dismissed. That omission is deliberate (see Standing Committee B, col.518).

88   Bail and custody before application

(1) In relation to a person charged in accordance with section 87(4)—
   (a) section 38 of the 1984 Act (including any provision of that section as applied by section 40(10) of that Act) has effect as if, in subsection (1), for "either on bail or without bail" there were substituted "on bail",
   (b) section 47(3) of that Act does not apply and references in section 38 of that Act to bail are references to bail subject to a duty to appear before the Crown Court at such place as the custody officer may appoint and at such time, not later than 24 hours after the person is released, as that officer may appoint, and
   (c) section 43B of the Magistrates' Courts Act 1980 (c. 43) does not apply.
(2) Where such a person is, after being charged—
   (a) kept in police detention, or
   (b) detained by a local authority in pursuance of arrangements made under section 38(6) of the 1984 Act,
   he must be brought before the Crown Court as soon as practicable and, in any event, not more than 24 hours after he is charged, and section 46 of the 1984 Act does not apply.
(3) For the purpose of calculating the period referred to in subsection (1) or (2), the following are to be disregarded—
   (a) Sunday,
   (b) Christmas Day,
   (c) Good Friday, and
   (d) any day which is a bank holiday under the Banking and Financial Dealings Act 1971 (c. 80) in the part of the United Kingdom where the person is to appear before the Crown Court as mentioned in subsection (1) or, where subsection (2) applies, is for the time being detained.
(4) Where a person appears or is brought before the Crown Court in accordance with subsection (1) or (2), the Crown Court may either—
   (a) grant bail for the person to appear, if notice of an application is served on him under section 80(2), before the Court of Appeal at the hearing of that application, or
   (b) remand the person in custody to be brought before the Crown Court under section 89(2).
(5) If the Crown Court grants bail under subsection (4), it may revoke bail and remand the person in custody as referred to in subsection (4)(b).
(6) In subsection (7) the "relevant period", in relation to a person granted bail or remanded in custody under subsection (4), means—
   (a) the period of 42 days beginning with the day on which he is granted bail or remanded in custody under that subsection, or
   (b) that period as extended or further extended under subsection (8).
(7) If at the end of the relevant period no notice of an application under section 76(1) or (2) in relation to the person has been given under section 80(1), the person—
   (a) if on bail subject to a duty to appear as mentioned in subsection (4)(a), ceases to be subject to that duty and to any conditions of that bail, and

    (b) if in custody on remand under subsection (4)(b) or (5), must be released immediately without bail.

  (8) The Crown Court may, on the application of a prosecutor, extend or further extend the period mentioned in subsection (6)(a) until a specified date, but only if satisfied that—

    (a) the need for the extension is due to some good and sufficient cause, and

    (b) the prosecutor has acted with all due diligence and expedition.

DEFINITIONS
"relevant period": s.88(6)
"the 1984 Act": s.95(1)

GENERAL NOTE
See the General Note to s.87 above.

89   Bail and custody before hearing

  (1) This section applies where notice of an application is given under section 80(1).

  (2) If the person to whom the application relates is in custody under section 88(4)(b) or (5), he must be brought before the Crown Court as soon as practicable and, in any event, within 48 hours after the notice is given.

  (3) If that person is not in custody under section 88(4)(b) or (5), the Crown Court may, on application by the prosecutor—

    (a) issue a summons requiring the person to appear before the Court of Appeal at the hearing of the application, or

    (b) issue a warrant for the person's arrest,
        and a warrant under paragraph (b) may be issued at any time even though a summons has previously been issued.

  (4) Where a summons is issued under subsection (3)(a), the time and place at which the person must appear may be specified either—

    (a) in the summons, or

    (b) in a subsequent direction of the Crown Court.

  (5) The time or place specified may be varied from time to time by a direction of the Crown Court.

  (6) A person arrested under a warrant under subsection (3)(b) must be brought before the Crown Court as soon as practicable and in any event within 48 hours after his arrest, and section 81(5) of the Supreme Court Act 1981 (c. 54) does not apply.

  (7) If a person is brought before the Crown Court under subsection (2) or (6) the court must either—

    (a) remand him in custody to be brought before the Court of Appeal at the hearing of the application, or

    (b) grant bail for him to appear before the Court of Appeal at the hearing.

  (8) If bail is granted under subsection (7)(b), the Crown Court may revoke the bail and remand the person in custody as referred to in subsection (7)(a).

  (9) For the purpose of calculating the period referred to in subsection (2) or (6), the following are to be disregarded—

    (a) Sunday,

    (b) Christmas Day,

    (c) Good Friday, and

    (d) any day which is a bank holiday under the Banking and Financial Dealings Act 1971 (c. 80) in the part of the United Kingdom where the person is for the time being detained.

GENERAL NOTE
  Section 89 applies only if a notice of an application for an order is given to the Court of Appeal under ss.76(1) or (2) of the Act. It is submitted that the person will by then have been charged with the offence in accordance with s.80(2) or s.87(4), and he has either been remanded into custody or granted bail by the Crown Court (see s.88). If the defendant is in custody at the time notice is given to the Court of Appeal, he must be brought before the Crown Court once again for the purpose of directing his appearance before the Court of Appeal (s.89(7)). The Crown Court must review the bail/custody position at that stage (see s.89(7)). If the defendant is on bail, his attendance before the Court of Appeal may be secured in one of two ways. The usual option will be for the prosecutor to ask the Crown Court to issue a summons requiring the defendant to attend the Court of Appeal (s.89(3)(a)). The warrant may specify the time, date and place of the hearing. Alternatively, those details may be given by way of a direction of the Crown Court.
  The second method of securing the defendant's appearance at the Court of Appeal, is by way of a warrant of arrest issued by the Crown Court on the application of the prosecutor (s.89(3)(b)). In this instance, the defendant must first be brought before the Crown Court, and the question of bail will be dealt with there (s.89(6) and (7)).

90   Bail and custody during and after hearing

(1) The Court of Appeal may, at any adjournment of the hearing of an application under section 76(1) or (2)—
    (a) remand the person to whom the application relates on bail, or
    (b) remand him in custody.
(2) At a hearing at which the Court of Appeal—
    (a) makes an order under section 77,
    (b) makes a declaration under subsection (4) of that section, or
    (c) dismisses the application or makes a declaration under subsection (3) of that section, if it also gives the prosecutor leave to appeal against its decision or the prosecutor gives notice that he intends to apply for such leave,
    the court may make such order as it sees fit for the custody or bail of the acquitted person pending trial pursuant to the order or declaration, or pending determination of the appeal.
(3) For the purpose of subsection (2), the determination of an appeal is pending—
    (a) until any application for leave to appeal is disposed of, or the time within which it must be made expires;
    (b) if leave to appeal is granted, until the appeal is disposed of.
(4) Section 4 of the Bail Act 1976 (c. 63) applies in relation to the grant of bail under this section as if in subsection (2) the reference to the Crown Court included a reference to the Court of Appeal.
(5) The court may at any time, as it sees fit—
    (a) revoke bail granted under this section and remand the person in custody, or
    (b) vary an order under subsection (2).

GENERAL NOTE
  The Explanatory Notes (para.343) summarise the position as follows:
  "Section 90 makes similar provision for bail or remand in custody during and after the Court of Appeal hearing. At this stage decisions on bail or remand will be made by the Court of Appeal, which will need to take into account its own decision in relation to the application. The Court may decide either to bail the person or remand him in custody until a retrial can be held, or until any appeal against the Court's ruling is determined."

91   Revocation of bail

(1) Where—

    (a) a court revokes a person's bail under this Part, and

    (b) that person is not before the court when his bail is revoked,
the court must order him to surrender himself forthwith to the custody of the court.

(2) Where a person surrenders himself into the custody of the court in compliance with an order under subsection (1), the court must remand him in custody.

(3) A person who has been ordered to surrender to custody under subsection (1) may be arrested without a warrant by an officer if he fails without reasonable cause to surrender to custody in accordance with the order.

(4) A person arrested under subsection (3) must be brought as soon as practicable, and, in any event, not more than 24 hours after he is arrested, before the court and the court must remand him in custody.

(5) For the purpose of calculating the period referred to in subsection (4), the following are to be disregarded—

    (a) Sunday,

    (b) Christmas Day,

    (c) Good Friday,

    (d) any day which is a bank holiday under the Banking and Financial Dealings Act 1971 (c. 80) in the part of the United Kingdom where the person is for the time being detained.

Part 10: supplementary

92   Functions of the DPP

(1) Section 1(7) of the Prosecution of Offences Act 1985 (c. 23) (DPP's functions exercisable by Crown Prosecutor) does not apply to the provisions of this Part other than section 85(2)(a).

(2) In the absence of the Director of Public Prosecutions, his functions under those provisions may be exercised by a person authorised by him.

(3) An authorisation under subsection (2)—

    (a) may relate to a specified person or to persons of a specified description, and

    (b) may be general or relate to a specified function or specified circumstances.

93   Rules of court

(1) Rules of court may make such provision as appears to the authority making them to be necessary or expedient for the purposes of this Part.

(2) Without limiting subsection (1), rules of court may in particular make provision as to procedures to be applied in connection with sections 76 to 82, 84 and 88 to 90.

(3) Nothing in this section is to be taken as affecting the generality of any enactment conferring power to make rules of court.

94   Armed Forces: Part 10

(1) Section 31 of the Armed Forces Act 2001 (c. 19) (provision in consequence of enactments relating to criminal justice) applies to an enactment contained in this Part so far as relating to matters not specified in subsection (2) of that section as it applies to a criminal justice enactment.

(2) The power under that section to make provision equivalent to that made in relation to qualifying offences by an enactment contained in this Part (with or without modifications) includes power to make such

provision in relation to such service offences as the Secretary of State thinks fit.

(3) In subsection (2) "service offence" means an offence under the Army Act 1955 (3 & 4 Eliz. 2 c. 18), the Air Force Act 1955 (3 & 4 Eliz. 2 c. 19) or the Naval Discipline Act 1957 (c. 53).

95   Interpretation of Part 10

(1) In this Part—

"the 1984 Act" means the Police and Criminal Evidence Act 1984 (c. 60),

"acquittal" and related expressions are to be read in accordance with section 75(7),

"customs and excise officer" means an officer as defined by section 1(1) of the Customs and Excise Management Act 1979 (c. 2), or a person to whom section 8(2) of that Act applies,

"new evidence" is to be read in accordance with section 78(2),

"officer", except in section 83, means an officer of a police force or a customs and excise officer,

"police force" has the meaning given by section 3(3) of the Prosecution of Offences Act 1985 (c. 23),

"prosecutor" means an individual or body charged with duties to conduct criminal prosecutions,

"qualifying offence" has the meaning given by section 75(8).

(2) Subject to rules of court made under section 53(1) of the Supreme Court Act 1981 (c. 54) (power by rules to distribute business of Court of Appeal between its civil and criminal divisions)—

(a) the jurisdiction of the Court of Appeal under this Part is to be exercised by the criminal division of that court, and

(b) references in this Part to the Court of Appeal are to be construed as references to that division.

(3) References in this Part to an officer of a specified rank or above are, in the case of a customs and excise officer, references to an officer of such description as—

(a) appears to the Commissioners of Customs and Excise to comprise officers of equivalent rank or above, and

(b) is specified by the Commissioners for the purposes of the provision concerned.

96   Application of Part 10 to Northern Ireland

(1) In its application to Northern Ireland this Part is to have effect subject to the modifications in this section.

(2) In sections 75(1)(a) and (b), 76(2)(a), 79(3) and 85(2)(a) for "England and Wales" substitute "Northern Ireland".

(3) For section 75(2)(c) substitute—

"(c) in respect of which, in proceedings where he has been found to be unfit to be tried in accordance with Article 49 of the Mental Health (Northern Ireland) Order 1986 (S.I. 1986/595 (N.I. 4)), a finding has been made that he did the act or made the omission charged against him."

(4) In section 75(8) for "Part 1" substitute "Part 2".

(5) In section 81(1) for "Criminal Appeal Act 1968 (c. 19)" substitute "Criminal Appeal (Northern Ireland) Act 1980 (c. 47)".

(6) In section 81(2)—

(a) for "33" substitute "31", and

(b) for "An" substitute "Subject to the provisions of this Part of this Act, an".

(7) In section 81(4)—

(a) for "34(2)" substitute "32(2)", and

(b) for "33(1B)" substitute "31(1B)".

(8) In section 82(10) after "enactment" in each place insert "(including any provision of Northern Ireland legislation)".

(9) In section 84(1) and (2) for "preferred" substitute "presented".

(10) Section 84(6) has effect—

(a) as if any reference to a provision of Part 11 were a reference to any corresponding provision contained in an Order in Council to which section 334(1) applies, at any time when such corresponding provision is in force;

(b) at any other time, with the omission of paragraphs (b) and (c).

(11) After section 84(6) insert—

"(6A) Article 29 of the Legal Aid, Advice and Assistance (Northern Ireland) Order 1981 (S.I. 1981/228 (N.I. 8)) applies in the case of a person who is to be tried in accordance with subsection (1) as if—

(a) he had been returned for trial for the offence in question, and

(b) the reference in paragraph (2)(a) of that Article to a magistrates' court included a reference to the Court of Appeal."

(12) In section 87—

(a) in subsection (3), for "Part 4 of the 1984 Act" substitute "Part 5 of the Police and Criminal Evidence (Northern Ireland) Order 1989 (S.I. 1989/1341 (N.I. 12)) ("the 1989 Order")",

(b) in paragraph (b) of that subsection, for "section 34(7) of that Act" substitute "Article 35(8) of that Order",

(c) in subsection (6)—

(i) for the words from the beginning to "40(8) of that Act)" substitute "Article 38 of that Order (including any provision of that Article as applied by Article 41(8) of that Order)",

(ii) for "subsection" in each place substitute "paragraph",

(iii) in paragraph (e), for "subsections (7A), (7B) and (8)" substitute "paragraph (8)", and

(iv) in paragraph (f), in the inserted paragraph (10A) omit "above",

(d) for subsection (7) substitute—

"(7) Article 41 of that Order has effect as if in paragraphs (8) and (9) of that Article after "(6)" there were inserted "and (10A)".",

(e) in subsection (8)—

(i) for "Section 42 of that Act" substitute "Article 43 of that Order", and

(ii) for "subsection (1) of that section" substitute "paragraph (1) of that Article".

(13) For section 88(1) substitute—

"(1) In relation to a person charged in accordance with section 87(4)—

(a) Article 39 of the 1989 Order (including any provision of that Article as applied by Article 41(10) of that Order) has effect as if, in paragraph (1), for "either on bail or without bail" there were substituted "on bail",

      (b) Article 48 of that Order has effect as if for paragraphs (1) to (11) there were substituted—

> "(1) A person who is released on bail shall be subject to a duty to appear before the Crown Court at such place as the custody officer may appoint and at such time, not later than 24 hours after the person is released, as that officer may appoint.
>
> (2) The custody officer may require a person who is to be released on bail to enter into a recognisance conditioned upon his subsequent appearance before the Crown Court in accordance with paragraph (1).
>
> (3) A recognisance under paragraph (2) may be taken before the custody officer.", and

      (c) Article 132A of the Magistrates' Courts (Northern Ireland) Order 1981 (S.I. 1981/1675 (N.I. 26)) does not apply."

(14) In section 88(2)—

      (a) for paragraph (b) substitute—

> "(b) detained in a place of safety in pursuance of arrangements made under Article 39(6) of the 1989 Order,", and

      (b) for "section 46 of the 1984 Act" substitute "Article 47 of the 1989 Order".

(15) In section 89(6) for "section 81(5) of the Supreme Court Act 1981 (c. 54)" substitute "section 51(8) of the Judicature (Northern Ireland) Act 1978 (c. 23)".

(16) For section 90(4) substitute—

> "(4) The court may at any time, as it sees fit, vary the conditions of bail granted under this section."

(17) In section 92(1) for the words from the beginning to "does" substitute "Sections 30(4) and 36 of the Justice (Northern Ireland) Act 2002 (c. 26) do".

(18) Until the coming into force of section 36 of that Act of 2002 the reference to that section in subsection (17) is to be read as a reference to Article 4(8) of the Prosecution of Offences (Northern Ireland) Order 1972 (S.I. 1972/538 (N.I. 1)).

(19) In section 93(2) for "the Criminal Appeal Rules and the Crown Court Rules" substitute "rules under section 55 of the Judicature (Northern Ireland) Act 1978 and Crown Court Rules".

(20) In section 93(3) after "enactment" insert "(including any provision of Northern Ireland legislation)".

(21) In section 95(1) for the definition of "police force" substitute—

> "police force" means—
>
>   (a) the Police Service of Northern Ireland or the Police Service of Northern Ireland Reserve,
>
>   (b) the Ministry of Defence Police,
>
>   (c) any body of constables appointed under Article 19 of the Airports (Northern Ireland) Order 1994 (S.I. 1994/426 (N.I. 1)), or
>
>   (d) any body of special constables appointed in Northern Ireland under section 79 of the Harbours, Docks and Piers Clauses Act 1847 (c. 27) or section 57 of the Civil Aviation Act 1982 (c. 16),".

(22) Omit section 95(2).

97 Application of Criminal Appeal Acts to proceedings under Part 10

Subject to the provisions of this Part, the Secretary of State may make an order containing provision, in relation to proceedings before the Court of Appeal under this Part, which corresponds to any provision, in relation to appeals or other proceedings before that court, which is contained in the Criminal Appeal Act 1968 (c. 19) or the Criminal Appeal (Northern Ireland) Act 1980 (c. 47) (subject to any specified modifications).

PART 11

EVIDENCE

CHAPTER 1

EVIDENCE OF BAD CHARACTER

GENERAL NOTE

There is one overarching principle for determining the admissibility of evidence, namely, that all relevant evidence is *prima facie* admissible (see Law Commission Consultation Paper 141 para.2.2; *The Review of the Criminal Courts of England and Wales*, conducted by Lord Justice Auld, Ch.11, para.112; Tapper, *"Evidence"* 9th ed., p.339). To this principle there existed a long-standing common law exception: evidence of the defendant's "bad character", other than that directly relating to the offence charged, is inadmissible: *Makin v Attorney General of New South Wales* [1894] A.C. 57. The rule at common law was therefore exclusionary "which prevents the prosecution generally from producing evidence in a trial of a defendant's previous misconduct" (Explanatory Notes, December 2003, para.44). This was so even if it could be shown that the defendant had a propensity to act in a particular way, and notwithstanding that his propensity was relevant to the offence charged. This rule was not absolute. In cases where the evidence was not only relevant, but possessed probative force "sufficiently great to make it just to admit the evidence, notwithstanding that it is prejudicial to the accused in tending to show that he was guilty of another crime", then that evidence was capable of being adduced (see *DPP v P* [1991] 2 A.C. 447, *per* Lord Mackay LC). This was the so-called "similar fact rule" that encompassed evidence of misconduct whether proved by virtue of a conviction or otherwise, as well as evidence of a propensity to act in a particular way. There remains force in Lord Hailsham's analysis in *Boardman v DPP* [1975] A.C. 241, that the evidence must have probative purpose beyond "the forbidden type of reasoning" — sometimes styled "reasoning prejudice". There were other circumstances (at common law and under statute) in which fact finders might learn of a defendant's "bad character" for example, by operation of s.1(3) of the Criminal Evidence Act 1898 (c.36) (now repealed: s.332, Sch.37, Pt 5); s.27(3) of the Theft Act 1968 (not repealed); or where misconduct is an element of an offence, or under the *res gestae* principle.

The law developed in a piecemeal way both at common law and at the hands of the Legislature. Most rules of evidence consist of criteria for the admissibility of information having regard to its purpose and relevance –but subject to judicial discretion in jury trials to exclude evidence if its "prejudicial effect" outweighs it's "probative value". Some rules — mainly exclusionary — are rooted in policy "to safeguard the fairness of the criminal process" (Law Commission, Consultation Paper No. 141, para.7.1). These rules give fact finders only the information they need to determine a disputed fact. Such rules aim to avoid the risk that fact finders may speculate, or make unwarranted assumptions, or act on moral or reasoning prejudice.

Evidence and the trial process

Criticisms of rules of evidence are often related to complaints about the criminal trial process itself. A common complaint is that rules of evidence are of general application regardless of the mode of trial. This is based on the fact that most common law rules of evidence are the product of decisions of the Court of Appeal (Criminal Division), or the House of Lords, concerning trials on indictment by judge and jury whereas the majority of trials are dealt with summarily. A long-standing complaint is that rules of evidence have been built on an unjustified lack of trust in the competence of lay fact finders to evaluate information appropriately. The measures in Pt 11 are predicated on a high level of trust in fact finders to correctly evaluate evidence. There has also been criticism that rules of evidence (before the 2003 Act) created an unjustified imbalance in the way witnesses were liable to be treated during the course of a criminal trial. Except for complainants in respect of some sexual offences, non-defendant witnesses might have their character impugned by a defendant using evidence that was admitted subject to a requirement of bare relevance. Defendants, on the other hand, were largely shielded from attacks on their character and this was so whether they gave evidence or not. The oldest and most frequently voiced complaint, is that this area of law was highly complex and often difficult to apply in practice. If the hope is that the statutory scheme under this chapter, will lessen those burdens, the result is likely to be a disappointment.

In his *Review of the Criminal Courts of England and Wales*, Lord Justice Auld recommended that "the English law of criminal evidence should in general, move away from technical rules of inadmissibility to trusting judicial and lay fact finders to give relevant evidence the weight it deserves" (para.78, the Review). Lord Justice Auld supported a comprehensive review of "the whole law of criminal evidence to make it a simple and effective agent for ensuring that all criminal courts are told all and only what they need to know". Such a review has much to commend it but whether a court needs evidence of a particular type or quality, depends on the question the court is required to answer, and the magnitude of risk society is prepared to accept of the answer being wrong. Frequently, the question in an adversarial criminal trial is whether the fact finder is sure of the defendant's guilt after applying the presumption of innocence. Lord Justice Auld states that relevance should be "a threshold of admissibility" and "fairness as a criterion for admission" (para.77). The Government's thinking behind Pt 11 of the Act is broadly in line with the sentiments expressed in the Review. The Permanent Under Secretary of State for the Home Department, Hilary Benn, said "(at) the heart of our proposals is the concept that the criminal justice system should be more trusting of fact finders to assess the relevant evidence, and that requires the new inclusive framework" (Standing Committee B, col.588). At one stage and the Government seemed to favour a single test for the admissibility of evidence, namely, relevance — subject to the discretion of the court to exclude evidence if its prejudicial effect outweighs its probative value (see "*The Way Ahead*"). The test appears to have been revised in the Government's White Paper "*Justice For All*" so that "relevant evidence, including criminal convictions should be admissible unless there are good reasons to the contrary, such as jeopardising the right to a fair trial" (p.16).

Rules of evidence; the trial process and "searching for truth"

Proposals intended to loosen rules of evidence are usually justified as being necessary to enable a court to "search for the truth". In "*Justice For All*" (p.32) the Government wrote that, "trials should be a search for the truth in accordance with the twin principles that the prosecution must prove its case and that defendants are not obliged to incriminate themselves. The object must be to *convict the guilty and acquit the innocent*" (emphasis added). It will be seen that this statement mirrors almost word for word, a passage in the Auld Review (Ch.10, para.154; and see Ch.11, paras 78, 101 and 103). Understandably, such statements are likely to have mass appeal, but they are also likely to be misunderstood. The suggestion that the object of the criminal trial process is to "convict the guilty and acquit the innocent" is a questionable proposition: its true purpose is to answer a single question, "has the prosecution proved the guilt of the accused in respect of the offence charged, to the criminal standard of proof?". The question is to be answered objectively by fact finders who are not part of the investigative process. There is no need to search for that which is assumed. In many cases proof of innocence is as elusive as proof of guilt. In *Jones v the National Coal Board* (1957) 2 Q.B. 55, Denning LJ said:

> "a judge sits to hear to determine the issues raised by the parties, not to conduct an investigation or examination on behalf of society at large... However, a judge is not a mere umpire to answer the question 'How's that?' his object above all, is to find out the truth and do justice according to law..."

The role of the fact finder, in an adversarial system of criminal trials, is confined to the evaluation of evidence put before the court by the parties, and thereafter to reach a conclusion applying the presumption of innocence, displaced only by proof of guilt to the criminal standard of proof. In his Review, Lord Justice Auld remarked that "the boundaries between the adversarial and inquisitorial systems of trial are blurring; our judges and magistrates' are already assuming an increasingly active role in the preparation of cases for trial and becoming more interventionist in the course of it than has been traditional" (Review, Ch.11; para.104). To the extent that courts are exercising firmer control over the management of cases than hitherto, the remarks of Lord Justice Auld hold true. But whilst powers vested in a court to manage a trial may ease the task of fact finders to evaluate the evidence, those powers rarely empower fact finders to search for information. Criminal courts have limited authority to secure the production of the best available evidence (in the sense of asking for such evidence to be obtained), and the power of fact finders to call for evidence, or to call a witness that the parties are minded not to call, is also exceedingly limited. In instances where evidence gives rise to a "dilemma created by the clash of probative force and prejudicial effect", and which if admitted, is likely to present an unacceptable level of risk of a wrongful conviction, the tendency has been to devise rules that automatically exclude such evidence (note, Cross and Tapper *"Evidence"*, 9th ed., p.335). When it has been possible to devise exceptions to the exclusionary rule, the trial judge is usually charged with the task of determining whether the evidence is relevant at all, and if it is, of balancing its probative value against its prejudicial effect (if any) when deciding whether a piece of information is admissible or not: the weight of the evidence is a matter for the jury in the event that the evidence is admitted. This approach exists in order to avoid errors of reasoning that might occur on the part of fact finders if the only test for of admissibility were relevance.

The approach of the Law Commission

The Law Commission's Consultation Paper No.143 is a seminal study of the rules of evidence as they largely existed in England and Wales until the enactment of Pt 11 the 2003 Act. The reader will gain much by reading Pts 6 and 7 of the consultation paper. For present purposes it is sufficient to identify a number of key components explained in the paper. Evidence has "probative value" where it is both true and relevant (Pt 6, para.6.2). The likelihood of evidence being true is its "cogency" (para.6.3). "Relevance" means logical relevance, so that "evidence is relevant if it affects the probabilities of the existence or non-existence of material facts in the slightest degree" (para.6.8). According to Thayer "nothing is to be admitted which is not logically probative of some matter requiring to be proved", and "everything which is thus probative should come in, unless a clear ground of policy or law excludes it" (*"A Preliminary Treatise on Evidence at The Common Law"* (1898) p.530). The Law Commission evaluated "the psychological research" (paras 6.10–6.38; 6.49; 6.60–6.62, Consultation Paper No.141) and made the following "provisional conclusions":

6.86 Even if an individual has a specific character trait, its existence cannot be inferred with confidence from a single observation of a person's character.

6.87 Even if a character trait is known, it will not necessarily assist in predicting an instance of conduct in isolation.

6.88 True predictive value is dependent upon a number of instances of conduct and a degree of similarity between the situations.

6.89 The notion that "character" is indivisible is not supported by the research.

6.90 If fact finders hear that a person has acted in a particular way in one situation, they will make assumptions about how that person will act in a different situation, assuming that a character trait will persist across different situations, and that the kind of person who has one character trait will have other associated traits.

6.91 A blanket assumption that a criminal will lie on oath, irrespective of his or her particular criminal history, is not supported by the research. Previous convictions for dishonesty do not necessarily indicate a tendency to lie on oath.

6.92 Fact finders who are told of a defendant's similar previous convictions are more likely to convict. A direction that they should treat the convictions as relevant only to the defendant's credibility is likely to be ineffective, particularly where the convictions are of a similar nature to the charge. A conviction for a sexual assault on a child is likely to prejudice fact finders against a defendant, whether or not it is similar to the charge.

6.93 Past behaviour can be probative on the question whether the defendant is likely to have acted in the way alleged, but the probative value of a single previous instance can be easily over-estimated. The research supports the present approach, that past misbehaviour can be admitted where there are close and unusual similarities between the past and the present situations.

The research was reviewed in the Final Report (para.6.11 and see Appendix A to the Final Report (Dr Sally Lloyd-Bostock study; and see (2000) Crim. L.R. 734).

In Pt 7 of its consultation paper, the Law Commission discusses "reasoning prejudice", "moral prejudice", the effectiveness of a judicial direction in an attempt to counteract prejudice, and safeguarding the fairness of the criminal justice process. The "prejudicial effect" is said to be the effect the evidence is like to have rather than the value it ought to have (para.7.2; Law Commission 141; and 7.7). Unsurprisingly, this part of the discussion proved to be controversial (Final Report, 6.33–6.42).

In its Final Report, the main recommendations made by the Law Commission were:

1.12 Fundamental to the scheme we recommend is the idea that, in any given trial, there is a *central set of facts* about which any party should be free to adduce relevant evidence without constraint — even evidence of bad character. Evidence falls within this central set of facts if it has to do with the offence charged, or is of misconduct connected with the investigation or prosecution of that offence. We recommend that evidence of bad character which falls outside this category should only be admissible if the court gives leave for it to be adduced. (Footnote at this point reads, "Or all parties agree to its admission, or it is evidence of a *defendant's* bad character and it is that defendant who wishes to adduce it). 1.13 An important feature of our scheme is that this basic rule applies equally whether the evidence is of the bad character of a defendant or of anyone else. Thus witnesses, no less than the defendant, will be protected against allegations of misconduct extraneous to the events the subject of the trial, which have only marginal relevance to the facts of the case. For the purpose of deciding whether the evidence has sufficient enhanced relevance so that leave might be granted, the same criteria will apply to defendants and non-defendants. Defendants will have additional protection from the prejudicial impact of such evidence to reflect the fact that it is their liability to criminal sanction which is at stake.

1.14 Under our scheme, leave may be given to adduce evidence of the bad character of a *non-defendant* if it has substantial explanatory value, or it has substantial probative value in relation to a matter in issue in the proceedings which is of substantial importance in the context of the case as a whole.

1.15 Leave may be given to adduce evidence of the bad character of a *defendant* in four situations, the first two of which correspond to those in which evidence of the bad character of a non-defendant may be admitted.

1.16 First, leave may be given to any party if the evidence has the same degree of explanatory value as would be required in the case of a non-defendant, but in addition it is only admissible if the interests of justice *require* it to be admissible, even taking account of its potentially prejudicial effect.

1.17 Secondly, leave may be given *to the prosecution* if (1) the evidence has substantial probative value in relation to a matter in issue which is itself of substantial importance, and (2) the interests of justice require it to be admissible, even taking account of its potentially prejudicial effect. If it has probative value only in showing that the defendant has a propensity to be untruthful, leave may not be given unless, *in addition*, (3) the defendant has suggested that another person has a propensity to be untruthful, and (4) adduces evidence in support of that suggestion of that person's bad character which falls outside the central set of facts, and (5) without the evidence of the defendant's bad character the fact-finders would get a misleading impression of the defendant's propensity to be untruthful in comparison with that of the other person.

1.18 Thirdly, leave may be given *to the prosecution* if (1) the defendant is responsible for an assertion which creates a false or misleading impression about the defendant, (2) the evidence has substantial probative value in correcting that impression, and (3) the interests of justice require it to be admissible, even taking account of its potentially prejudicial effect.

1.19 Fourthly, leave may be given *to a co-defendant* (D2) to adduce evidence of the bad character of a defendant (D1) if the evidence has substantial probative value in relation to a matter in issue between D2 and D1 which is itself of substantial importance in the context of the case as a whole. If it has probative value only in showing that D1 has a propensity to be untruthful, leave may not be given unless, *in addition*, D1's case is such as to undermine that of D2.

The Law Commission recommended a two-staged approach to the admissibility of evidence. First, an automatic inclusionary rule in respect of evidence of bad character that has to do with the alleged facts of the offence charged, or is misconduct in connection with the investigation or prosecution of that offence (see ss.98(a) and (b) of the 2003 Act). This would include "incident conduct" such as breaking a window (criminal damage) in order to commit burglary (the offence charged). However, where evidence of bad character falls outside the central set of facts, such evidence would be prima facie excluded unless it came within statutory exceptions, and (in the absence of agreement) only then with the leave of the court, subject to an interests of justice test.

Note that the 2003 Act abolishes all common law rules governing the admissibility of evidence of bad character in criminal proceedings (s.99(1)) save and insofar as s.118(1) preserves the rule that a person's reputation is admissible for the purposes of proving bad character (s.118).

The Government's approach

In its policy document "*The Way Ahead*", the Government indicated its preference for a single test namely, relevance — subject to the discretion of the court to exclude evidence if its prejudicial effect outweighed its probative value. Uncertainty as to how this would translate in practice, became only marginally clearer when the Government published its white paper "*Justice For All*". In that document the Government stated that "relevant evidence, including criminal convictions should be admissible unless there are good reasons to the contrary, such as jeopardising the right to a fair trial" (p.16). Taken at face value, this statement appears to reject the Law Commission's recommendation for an exclusionary rule subject to exceptions, in favour of an automatic inclusionary rule. In its Explanatory Notes to the 2003 Act, the

Government claims that Ch.1 to Pt 11 does take an "inclusionary approach" (para.365). However, when Chapter 1 is stripped to its bare essentials, it will be seen that the structure of the new scheme is to place evidence of bad character below the threshold of admissibility unless the 2003 Act allows a party to the proceedings to cross the threshold with it.

For the Government, Baroness Scotland of Asthal informed the House of Lords that the Government's proposals had been drawn substantially on the Law Commission's work "although adopting a slightly different structure" (*Hansard*, HL, Vol. 654, col.737 (November 4, 2003)). As to similarities of approach, Baroness Scotland suggested that "both schemes apply a test that involves the weighing of the probative value of the evidence against its prejudicial effect in determining whether it should be admitted" — adding that "there is no dramatic change there". The Government pointed out that a number of recommendations made by the Law Commission have been adopted: (i) stopping the case where evidence is contaminated (see s.107), (ii) the assumption of truth when assessing relevance (see s.109), (iii) the court's duty to give reasons (see s.110), and (iv) the requirement for rules of court (s.111).

Baroness Scotland conceded that there are "substantial differences" between the Law Commission's proposals and the measures now enacted in Ch.1 to Pt 11 of the 2003 Act (*Hansard*, HL, Vol. 654, cols.737–738 (November 4, 2003)). The Government rejected the Law Commission's proposal that the defendant should "lose his shield" only in respect of certain attacks directed against the character of a witness. It will be noted that s.1(3) of the Criminal Evidence Act 1898 is repealed (Sch.37, Pt 5). The Government was also of the view that an exclusionary test as proposed by the commission "has no role to play, for example, in respect of explanatory evidence (s.101(1)(c)); or evidence to correct a false impression (s.101(f)), where we have adopted different safeguards" (*Hansard*, HL, Vol. 654, col.739 (November 4, 2003)). The Government suggest that the greatest difference is "in our general approach to admission", namely, that "we need to signal that there has been a change... one of inclusion that makes it clear that relevant evidence is admissible...We therefore stand firmly behind the inclusionary approach adopted by the Bill... We think that it is an important part of shifting the emphasis towards admitting evidence that is relevant unless it is not safe to do so."

Is the approach "exclusionary" or "inclusionary"

The above suggests that the answer is that the approach is "inclusionary", and this was the position taken by those in Parliament who voiced opposition to this part of the 2003 Act. During the course of an earlier debate, Baroness Scotland seemed to leave the point open, "Some say that there is a huge difference between the approach being inclusionary or exclusionary. We, the Government, do not say that this is so. We believe that it is an issue of emphasis, and we trust that the judiciary will be able to operate with the statutory framework in a way that will guarantee fairness and parity, as has been the case in the past" (*Hansard*, HL, Vol. 652, col.1085 (September 18, 2003)). It is submitted that this is a fair and appropriate explanation. In cases where evidence of bad character falls outside the central set of facts (*i.e.* it does not come within s.98(a) or (b)), such evidence — if relevant — may still be admissible under Ch.1 of Pt 11 of the Act, but it must not be admitted if it falls within s.101(3). There is no doubt that the Law Commission's proposals if enacted would have placed wider and tighter restrictions on the admissibility of bad character evidence.

On the other hand, Ch.1 to Pt 11 does not create a general presumptive rule in favour of the admissibility of bad character evidence: quite the contrary. This is apparent from the definition of "bad character" in s.98 — the revised wording of which appeared by way of an Amendment moved in the House of Lords as late at the November 19, 2003 (*Hansard*, HL, Vol. 654, col.1986). When considering s.98, note s.112(1) and the definition of "misconduct". The definition of "bad character" remains — as Baroness Scotland explained — a "wide definition", and necessarily so for "otherwise potentially prejudicial evidence will fall outside it and thus outside the rules and safeguards in the (Act)... Our intention is to ensure that a wide range of potentially prejudicial evidence is caught by the definition... the wording offers a tighter formulation for doing so." The Permanent Under Secretary of State for the Home Department (Hilary Benn) emphasised that the "scope of the definition is far reaching, in order to ensure that any evidence that is treated as bad character evidence at common law is also covered by the statutory regime" (Standing Committee B, col.545, January 23, 2003).

Evidence of bad character is not admissible unless it is permitted by the 2003 Act. Is the scheme therefore exclusionary or inclusionary, or is it a question of emphasis? It is submitted that the answer is that the 2003 Act adopts a staged approach towards admissibility. First, evidence of "bad character" (as defined by s.98) is not admissible unless it is permitted by the Act. Secondly, different rules apply in the case of defendants (s.101) and non-defendants (s.100). Whether, under the new scheme, bad character evidence will be admitted more often than not, is difficult to predict. It is a matter of personal preference whether the statutory scheme is described as "exclusionary" or "inclusionary". It will be noted that so far as non-defendants are concerned — whether they are witnesses in the proceedings or not — the presumption is that evidence as to their character is inadmissible, and it will only be admissible if one of the conditions set out in s.100(1) is satisfied. Even then, the evidence must not be given without the leave of the court unless the parties agree to the evidence being admitted (see s.100(4)). By contrast, leave of the court is not a precondition of admissibility with regards to evidence of the defendant's bad character if the conditions of s.101 are met. Note that s.101(3) applies in two situations, namely, s.101(1)(d) or (g) — on the defendant's application.

Definition of "bad character" — breadth of meaning

Because common law rules, governing the admissibility of evidence of bad character, are abolished by s.99 (subject to s.118(1)), and in order to give effect to Parliament's intention that evidence of bad character is to be admissible only under the 2003 Act, it was important to define "bad character" widely (*Hansard*, HL, Vol. 654, col.1986 (November 19, 2003)).

The Law Commission defined "bad character" as "... evidence which shows or tends to show that, (a) he has committed an offence, or (b) he has behaved, or is disposed to behave, in a way that, in the opinion of the court, might be viewed with disapproval by a reasonable person" (see clause 1, Draft Bill, Final Report No.273). That definition appeared and remained in the Criminal Justice Bill until the November 19, 2003, but during Parliamentary debates "concern was expressed that it was too vague and enabled evidence that was too remote to be admitted" (Baroness Scotland of Asthal, *Hansard*, HL, Vol. 654, col.1985 (November 19, 2003)).

The definition was reworked so that a person's bad character now means "evidence of, or of a disposition towards, misconduct on his part" — other than evidence which (a) "has to do with the alleged facts of the offence with which the defendant is charged, or (b) is evidence of misconduct in connection with the investigation or prosecution of that offence" (s.98).

In practice, there is perhaps little to choose between the two formulations because the definition of "misconduct" is "the commission of an offence or other reprehensible behaviour" (s.112(1)). The offence might be proved by a conviction but this need not be so. It is not clear whether the words "an offence" includes offences committed abroad, but even if the answer is in the negative, the same conduct may be evidence of bad character if it constitutes "other reprehensible behaviour". In any event, "offence" includes a "service offence" (s.112(1)). If evidence of misconduct, or reprehensible behaviour, forms part of the "central set of facts" (to use the language of the Law Commission) — that is to say, it comes within ss.98(a) or (b), the evidence falls outside the rules in Ch.1 to Pt 11 of the 2003 Act.

Before 1898, "character" meant "reputation" and not disposition: *Rowton* (1860) L&C 520. As Adrian Keane points out, for the purposes of the Criminal Evidence Act 1898, character evidence may now take the form of disposition and reputation ("*The Modern Law of Evidence*"). Section 98 of the 2003 Act expressly includes "disposition" — that is to say, "disposition towards misconduct" as "misconduct" is defined by s.112(1).

The structure of the 2003 Act, and its approach to bad character evidence, was not initially appreciated by some members of Standing Committee B who argued that the definition of bad character was too broad and too imprecise (cols.526–558). The error is understandable because it is not immediately apparent from the language of the statute whether the approach is fundamentally exclusionary or inclusionary.

Bad character and non-defendant witnesses

One of the objects of the 2003 Act (Ch.1 of Pt 11) is to address concerns of the Law Commission (and voiced by others) that "no person who is involved in a criminal trial should be subject to a gratuitous and irrelevant public attack on their character" (para.7.2, Final Report).

Until the 2003 Act, a defendant had an almost free rein to challenge the character and credibility of a witness. The Youth Justice and Criminal Evidence Act 1999 imposes limitations on the questions that a defendant may ask of a complainant in respect of an alleged "sexual offence" (as defined by s.62). The restrictions imposed by ss.41–43 of the 1999 Act forbid a defendant asking any question that has as its purpose (or main purpose), "impugning the credibility of a complainant as a witness" (see s.41(4) of the Youth Justice and Criminal Evidence Act 1999, but note *R v A (No.2)* [2001] 2 W.L.R. 1546. In other cases there is no similar limitation — just a requirement of bare relevance.

There is a distinction between cross-examination as to credit, and calling evidence as to credit. It has been open to the defendant to cross-examine a witness as to credit "to show that (he) might not be believed on oath" and thus "the matters about which he is questioned must relate to his likely standing after cross-examination with the tribunal which is trying him or listening to his evidence" (*R. v Sweet-Escott (Robin Patrick Bickham)* (1971) 55 Cr. App. R. 316; *R. v Funderburk (Roy)* (1990) 90 Cr. App. R. 466).

If a witness testified to the truth of an allegation put to him/her, then that admission formed part of the fund of evidence in the case, but if a witness denied an allegation, it was not usually open to the cross-examining party to call evidence to contradict the answer: in other words, answers as to credit were final and could not be impeached (*Cargill* (1913) 2 K.B. 271; *R. v*

Mendy (Eileen) (1977) 64 Cr. App. R. 4). Where allegations of misconduct have been put to a witness, it was not open to the party calling that witness to call good character evidence on his behalf: *Hamilton*, The Times, July 25, 1998; *Beard* [1998] Crim. L.R. 585.

However, a witness could testify to the general reputation of a non defendant witness (whether called by the prosecution or by a co-defendant) and the impeaching witness could testify that he would not believe the latter on his oath: *R. v Richardson (Charles William)* (1968) 52 Cr. App. R. 317. The impeaching witness was not permitted to give reasons for his belief, but he could be asked for them in cross-examination: *R. v Gunewardene (Sumatalage Reginald)* [1951] 2 K.B. 600. In this situation evidence can be adduced as to the good character of the impeached witness. These principles must now be reconsidered and the light of the provisions of Ch.1, Pt 11 of the 2003 Act.

The Law Commission Consultation Paper and the Final Report focus heavily on the law relating to the bad character of the defendant, but noted that "witnesses, no less than the defendants, will be protected against allegations of misconduct extraneous to the events the subject of the trial, which have only marginal relevance to the facts of the case" (Law Commission 273, para.1.12; and see para.7.4).

Accordingly s.100 now excludes all evidence of bad character of any person other than the defendant (whether a witness in the proceedings or not) — unless ("if and only if"), (1) it is important explanatory evidence, or (2) it has substantial probative value in relation to a matter in issue in the proceedings and is of substantial importance in the context of the case as a whole, or (3) the parties agreed to the evidence being admissible. Leave of the court to adduce such evidence is required: s.100 (4).

The Government say that s.100 offers "substantial new protection to witnesses against unnecessarily wide ranging and humiliating attacks on their character; and will ensure that only evidence that is clearly relevant it is admissible" (Hilary Benn, Standing Committee B, col.566, January 23, 2003). Evidence that a witness was bribed to testify, or had been paid money by a journalist to testify and had agreed to be interviewed for a news report, would meet the criteria (but leave of the court will be required). It seems plain that the cross-examiner cannot put to a non-defendant witness allegations that he/she is of bad character without first seeking the leave of the court to do so, on the grounds that any admission made by the witness to that effect would trigger the rules in s.100.

In practice, the effect of s.100 might be that s.100 is honoured more in the breach than it in its observance, or cross-examination as to credit will be largely confined to the witness's knowledge of facts, judgment, perception, and comprehension, but not as to his integrity, or veracity, or as to his lifestyle that might be styled "other reprehensible behaviour" (s.112(1)).

Defendant's bad character

Section 100 is to be contrasted with s.101. The Law Commission did not recommend equivalence as between defendants and non-defendants. It recommended that the criteria or for the admissibility of evidence of the bad character of a defendant be more stringent than that required in respect of non-defendants. In each of the four situations described by the Law Commission the leave of the court is required (paras 1.15–1.19; see Pt IV above). Leave is not a requirement of s.101. In three situations the Law Commission recommended the enactment of an "interests of justice" condition, *i.e.* that the interests of justice require the evidence to be admissible "even taken account of its potentially prejudicial effect". By contrast, s.101(3) gives the court discretion to exclude evidence of bad character if it appears to the court "that the admission of the evidence would have such an adverse effect on the fairness of the proceedings that the court ought not to admit it". However, this requires an application by the defendant to exclude the evidence. Section 101(3) does not expressly empower the court of his own motion to exclude the evidence, although it may of course enquire whether the defence is going to make such an application. The Government say that this protection is designed to reflect the existing position under the common law and under s.78 PACE.

Introductory

98   **"Bad character"**

> References in this Chapter to evidence of a person's "bad character" are to evidence of, or of a disposition towards, misconduct on his part, other than evidence which—
>
> (a) has to do with the alleged facts of the offence with which the defendant is charged, or
>
> (b) is evidence of misconduct in connection with the investigation or prosecution of that offence.

DEFINITIONS
    "bad character": ss.98 and 112(1)
    "defendant": s.112(1)
    "important explanatory evidence": s.102

GENERAL NOTE
    Section 98 must be read in conjunction with s.99. The latter abolishes the common law rules
concerning the admissibility of evidence of bad character in criminal proceedings save for those
specified in s.118(1). Note amendments and repeals to previous legislation: Part 5 of Sch.36, and
Pt 5 of Sch.37 respectively.
    The definition of "bad character" is widely drawn in order to avoid the result that material
previously subject to an exclusionary rule, would fall outside the current statutory scheme, and
thus become admissible (subject to any other enactments) (see Standing Committee B, col.545,
January 23, 2003). For the purposes of the statutory definition of "bad character", it is
immaterial whether the defendant has been convicted of an offence arising out of the conduct
complained of or not, or whether he has been acquitted of an offence or not (see *R. v Z (Prior
Acquittal)* [2000] 2 A.C. 483). The fact that a person has been charged with another offence, and
a trial is pending, is not an absolute bar to the use of the evidence relating to that charge in
current proceedings (see Standing Committee B, col.546, but note *Stirland v DPP* [1944] A.C.
315, at p.324, *per* Viscount Simon LC: and *Maxwell v DPP* (1935) A.C. 309).
    Note that evidence that falls within s.98(a) or (b) is not subject to the rules under Ch.1 to Pt 11
of the 2003 Act at all (note the words "other than"). It is therefore important to distinguish s.98
and the definition of "important explanatory evidence" for the purposes of ss.100 and 101(1)(c).
    As for ss.98(a) and (b), this is illustrated by the Explanatory Notes (para.357) as follows:
    "...if the defendant were charged with burglary, the prosecution's evidence on the facts of
    the offence — any witnesses to the crime, forensic evidence etc — would be admissible
    outside the terms of these provisions. So too would evidence of an assault that had been
    committed in the course of the burglary, as evidence to do with the facts of the offence.
    Evidence that the defendant had tried to intimidate prosecution witnesses would also be
    admissible outside this scheme as evidence of misconduct in connection with, as
    appropriate, the investigation or the prosecution of the offence, as would allegations by the
    defendant that evidence had been planted. However, evidence that the defendant had
    committed a burglary on another occasion or that a witness had previously lied on oath
    would not be evidence to do with the facts of the offence or its investigation or prosecution
    and would therefore be caught by the definition in section 98 and its admissibility would fall
    to be dealt with under the Act's provisions."
    However, this illustration does not reveal the full reach of s.98. Paragraphs (a) and (b) have
their origin in the Law Commission's recommendations in its Final Report (No.273, paras 1.12
and 10.4) The Paragraphs relate to evidence that is part of the narrative of the offence (Report
No.273, para.10.6). Thus, if during a burglary, the defendant is alleged to have smashed a
window to a house to gain entry, the fact that the defendant is not charged with criminal damage
does not prevent that evidence from being adduced on a charge of burglary. Similarly, evidence
that the defendant was in the unlawful possession of a firearm, at the moment he is alleged to
have stolen money from a bank, may be adduced to prove a charge of robbery despite the
absence of a specific count relating to the firearm.
    However, the fact that a person habitually, and unlawfully, carries a firearm in a public place,
might be relevant "important explanatory evidence", for the purposes of s.100, or s.101. It is
helpful to separate "important" from the concept of "explanatory evidence". As to the latter,
the evidence should explain other evidence. As to the former, the evidence is important if the
fact finder would find it difficult or impossible to understand the evidence in the case without it.
Paragraphs 360–361 of the Explanatory Note (December 2003) give some insight into what
Parliament has in mind:
    "360. The term "explanatory evidence" is used to describe evidence which, whilst not going
    to the question of whether the defendant is guilty, is necessary for the jury to have a proper
    understanding of other evidence being given in the case by putting it in its proper context.
    An example might be a case involving the abuse by one person of another over a long
    period of time. For the jury to understand properly the victim's account of the offending
    and why they did not seek help from, for example, a parent or other guardian, it might be
    necessary for evidence to be given of a wider pattern of abuse involving that other person.
    361. For evidence to be admissible as "important explanatory evidence", it must be such
    that, without it, the magistrates' or jury would find it impossible or difficult to understand
    other evidence in the case — section 100(2). If, therefore, the facts or account to which the
    bad character evidence relates are largely understandable without this additional
    explanation, then the evidence should not be admitted. The explanation must also give the

court some substantial assistance in understanding the case as a whole. In other words, it will not be enough for the evidence to assist the court to understand some trivial piece of evidence."

Note that the *res gestae* rule is preserved by s.118(1) para.4.

99   Abolition of common law rules

(1) The common law rules governing the admissibility of evidence of bad character in criminal proceedings are abolished.

(2) Subsection (1) is subject to section 118(1) in so far as it preserves the rule under which in criminal proceedings a person's reputation is admissible for the purposes of proving his bad character.

DEFINITIONS
"bad character": ss.98 and 112(1)
"defendant": s.112(1)
"important explanatory evidence": s.102

GENERAL NOTE
See the General Note to s.98. Note the extent to which a number of common law rules are preserved: s.112(1). Note the amendments made to previous enactments listed in Pt 5 of Sch.36; and the repeals listed in Pt 5 of Sch.37. The Government has made it clear that s.99(2) merely enables reputation evidence to be adduced to prove a person's bad character (Standing Committee B, col.561, January 23, 2003, *per* the Parliamentary Under-Secretary of State for the Home Department).

Persons other than defendants

100   Non-defendant's bad character

(1) In criminal proceedings evidence of the bad character of a person other than the defendant is admissible if and only if—

   (a) it is important explanatory evidence,

   (b) it has substantial probative value in relation to a matter which—

     (i) is a matter in issue in the proceedings, and

     (ii) is of substantial importance in the context of the case as a whole,

       or

   (c) all parties to the proceedings agree to the evidence being admissible.

(2) For the purposes of subsection (1)(a) evidence is important explanatory evidence if—

   (a) without it, the court or jury would find it impossible or difficult properly to understand other evidence in the case, and

   (b) its value for understanding the case as a whole is substantial.

(3) In assessing the probative value of evidence for the purposes of subsection (1)(b) the court must have regard to the following factors (and to any others it considers relevant)—

   (a) the nature and number of the events, or other things, to which the evidence relates;

   (b) when those events or things are alleged to have happened or existed;

   (c) where—

     (i) the evidence is evidence of a person's misconduct, and

     (ii) it is suggested that the evidence has probative value by reason of similarity between that misconduct and other alleged misconduct,

   the nature and extent of the similarities and the dissimilarities between each of the alleged instances of misconduct;

   (d) where—

     (i) the evidence is evidence of a person's misconduct,

         (ii) it is suggested that that person is also responsible for the misconduct charged, and

         (iii) the identity of the person responsible for the misconduct charged is disputed,

the extent to which the evidence shows or tends to show that the same person was responsible each time.

(4) Except where subsection (1)(c) applies, evidence of the bad character of a person other than the defendant must not be given without leave of the court.

DEFINITIONS

"bad character": s.98

"important explanatory evidence": s.102

"misconduct": s.112(1)

"probative value": s.112(1)

"the defendant": s.112(1)

GENERAL NOTE

The reader is invited to read the General Note to Ch.1 of Pt 11. The legislature's aim is that only evidence that will assist the court to reach an accurate finding of fact should be admissible. The cross-examination of witnesses in respect of conduct that might be viewed as "reprehensible" (s.112(1) of the 2003 Act), but which was barely relevant (or marginally relevant) to any issue the fact finder had to determine, was a familiar feature of criminal trials. The court has power to control cross-examination, including the power to disallow questions that are utterly irrelevant, vexatious, or that are intended to humiliate a witness for the personal gratification of the party cross-examining the witness. However, character and credibility, are often viewed as indivisible concepts. In their Final report, the Law Commission (Law Commission report No. 273) cited Professor Eaglestone, an Australian judge, who wrote:

> "as most witnesses will lie if the motive is strong enough, and many will lie merely to save lengthy explanations about matters that they think have nothing to do with the case, I do not regard the demonstration that a witness has lied about some irrelevant matter as affording much help in deciding whether he is telling the truth about the facts in issue" (see Report No. 273, para.9.14; R. Eaglestone *"Evidence, Proof and Probability"*, 2nd ed., (1983) p.77).

Nevertheless, judges tend to be reluctant to disallow questions that go to the credibility of a non-defendant witness. The true value of a point might not be apparent at the time a question is put in cross-examination, but in any event, whilst the value of a piece of bad character evidence — viewed in isolation — might be trivial, the cumulative effect of evidence relating to the credibility and the character of a witness, might be compelling. In jury trials, judges are careful not to usurp the function of the jury. A pointless cross-examination might also be telling as to where the truth of the matter really lies.

Section 100 radically alters the previous position. Judges will be required to ensure that evidence of the "bad character" of a non-defendant witness meets the statutory criteria for admissibility set out in s.100(1). Other than evidence admitted by agreement (s.100(1)(c)) the leave of the court must be obtained (s.100(4)). In its final report, the Law Commission recommended a rule of law, that where evidence of the bad character of a non-defendant is "barely or only minimally relevant, it should be excluded" (report No. 273; para.9.35). The object is to exclude evidence, and to disallow questions, that do not substantially advance the case of the party seeking to use evidence of bad character (see report No. 273, para.9.21), or which distorts the fact finders process (paragraph 9.22).

Subsection (1)(a)

Section 100(1) (a) is intended to deal with matters so closely linked with the central so facts that it would be a nonsense to exclude such evidence. Thus, the fact W unlawfully assaulted D may be relevant to D's defence that he acted in self-defence; or that he was entitled to resist arrest.

Subsection (1)(b)

See the Law Commission Final Report No.273, paras 9.38–9.43. This concerns evidence falling short of being "important explanatory evidence". A piece of information may have high probative value, be relevant, yet is of negligible importance in the context of the case as a whole. Such evidence would not satisfy s.100(1)(b). The Law Commission supported a test of "enhanced relevance", but made it clear that the object of doing so would be to exclude only bad character evidence which is of "trivial relevance" — not that it should exclude "as much bad character evidence as Art.6 will allow" (see Law Commission report 273; para.9.36).

Under the commission's proposals, the threshold for admissibility of bad character evidence, in respect of non-defendant witnesses, would therefore be set quite low. Although evidence of bad character might be highly relevant to an issue in the case, that evidence (seen in the context of the case as a whole) might be of marginal importance. The Law Commission concluded that the test of enhanced relevance should be "whether the evidence has substantial probative value in relation to a matter in issue which is itself of substantial importance in the context of the case as a whole" (para.9.39). Section 100(1)(b) substantially reproduces that wording. If the cross-examiner wishes to introduce evidence of an old conviction for dishonesty recorded against a witness in respect of whom it is alleged that his/her testimony is mistaken, such evidence is unlikely to meet the test of enhanced relevance. If the allegation is that the witness is lying, and not merely mistaken, the test of enhanced relevance is likely to be satisfied. For its part, the government supported the reasoning of the Law Commission stating that "it is important that a defendant should not be able to introduce trivial or irrelevant evidence of a non-defendant's bad character; and it is to protect non-defendants from such attacks that a test of enhanced relevance is proposed" (per Hilary Benn, Parliamentary Under Secretary of State for the Home Department, Standing Committee B, col.568, January 23, 2003). In assessing "probative value" the court must have regard to the matters set out in s.100(3) but it is obviously not limited to the factors there stated.

Section 100 is likely to generate much case-law until such time as practitioners are able to gauge from the authorities the limits within which they are able to introduce evidence of bad character. It seems likely that initially practitioners will stray, almost blindly, into the pit falls presented by s.100. The section also requires another layer of management in the presentation of cases, and (from a judge's perspective) in the way trials are managed. The cross-examiner may have several, or many, questions that he/she wishes to put to a non-defendant witness. Should the practitioner apply for leave on a question-by-question basis, or should he ask for a ruling in respect of the entire list? Best practice is likely to favour the latter, but in forensic life, matters are rarely clear-cut.

Section 100(4) gives no guidance as to the factors the court may properly take into account when granting, or refusing, leave.

Defendants

101   Defendant's bad character

(1) In criminal proceedings evidence of the defendant's bad character is admissible if, but only if—
    (a) all parties to the proceedings agree to the evidence being admissible,
    (b) the evidence is adduced by the defendant himself or is given in answer to a question asked by him in cross-examination and intended to elicit it,
    (c) it is important explanatory evidence,
    (d) it is relevant to an important matter in issue between the defendant and the prosecution,
    (e) it has substantial probative value in relation to an important matter in issue between the defendant and a co-defendant,
    (f) it is evidence to correct a false impression given by the defendant, or
    (g) the defendant has made an attack on another person's character.
(2) Sections 102 to 106 contain provision supplementing subsection (1).
(3) The court must not admit evidence under subsection (1)(d) or (g) if, on an application by the defendant to exclude it, it appears to the court that the admission of the evidence would have such an adverse effect on the fairness of the proceedings that the court ought not to admit it.
(4) On an application to exclude evidence under subsection (3) the court must have regard, in particular, to the length of time between the matters to which that evidence relates and the matters which form the subject of the offence charged.

DEFINITIONS
  "bad character": ss.98 and s.112(1)
  "criminal proceedings": s.112(1)
  "defendant": s.112(1)
  "evidence attacking the other person's character": s.106(2)
  "important explanatory evidence": s.102
  "imputation about the other person": s.106(2)
  "prosecution evidence": s.112(1)

GENERAL NOTE
  For a general discussion, see the General Note to Ch.1 of Pt 11 of this Act. For a brief discussion as to whether s.101 is an inclusionary or an exclusionary rule, see the General Note to Ch.1 of Pt 11 of this Act.
  This has been one of the most contentious areas of the Act. A series of amendments, tabled in the House of Lords, designed to delete this Chapter, and to insert into PACE an alternative scheme for admitting evidence of bad character, was accepted by a majority in that House, but rejected by the House of Commons (see *Hansard*, HL, Vol. 654, cols.719–744 (November 4, 2003)).
  Lord Alexander of Weedon adopted the criticisms of the Legal Action Group that s.101 would "allow evidence of the defendant's bad character to be admitted more readily" and that "fact finders will be heavily influenced by information about previous misconduct, and that the presumption of innocence will be undermined" (*Hansard*, HL, Vol. 654, col.731 (November 4, 2003)). Lord Kingsland was more forceful in his complaints describing the Government's approach to evidence relating to propensity as "profoundly pernicious" that makes "a complete mockery of the presumption of innocence" (*Hansard*, HL, Vol. 654, col.729 (November 4, 2003)). Later Lord Kingsland spoke of the provision being an "affront to the presumption of innocence" (col.741). The presumption of innocence is undermined if the process by which judgments are made are influenced by "reasoning prejudice", or "moral prejudice", rather than by a valid assessment of the probative cogency of the evidence. If the question is posed starkly, "why should fact finders not routinely hear evidence of a defendant's bad character?", the most candid answer is that even those of the highest intellect cannot be confident that they will not be guilty of either form of forbidden reasoning. The psychological research summarised in the Law Commission's consultation paper and Final Report is instructive.

Subsections 101(1)(a) and (b)
  Little difficulty is likely to be encountered in cases where the parties agree to evidence of bad character being adduced. Section 101(1)(b) reflects the pre-existing position. A defendant has long been entitled to volunteer the fact that he/she has a criminal record, or a bad reputation. The provision does not make admissible unsolicited disclosures by a witness of a defendant's bad character, or (it would seem) evidence of bad character elicited in cross-examination due to a carelessly framed question by the cross-examiner: note the words in s.101(1)(b) "intended to elicit it"

Subsection 101(1)(c)
  This provision must be read in conjunction with s.102 (the definition of "important explanatory evidence"). See the General Note to s.98 that discusses the difference between "important explanatory evidence" and evidence that is automatically admissible because it falls outside the definition of "bad character" in s.98.
  The Law Commission concluded that there were circumstances in which it would be appropriate for a jury to learn of a defendant's bad character if it had substantial explanatory value (a term that should not be confused with "substantial probative value") and the interests of justice require it to be admissible, even taking account of its potentially prejudicial effect (Law Commission report 273, paras 10.7–10.12; noting para.10.9). The definition of "important explanatory evidence" has been discussed in relation to s.100(2). However, unlike the Law Commission's proposal, ss.101(1)(c) and 102, do not require the prosecution to show that the interests of justice require the evidence to be admissible, or to obtain leave to adduce the evidence.

Subsection 101(1)(d)
  This provision should be read in conjunction with s.103 ("matter in issue between the defendant and the prosecution"), noting s.101(3). In its final report, the Law Commission recommended that leave may be given to the prosecution to adduce evidence of a defendant's bad character if "the evidence has substantial probative value in relation to a matter in issue (other than whether the defendant has a propensity to be untruthful) which is itself of a substantial importance in the context of the case as a whole" (Law Commission Report 273;

para.11.46). As for the meaning of "substantial probative value", see the commentary to s.100(1)(b).

Section 101(1)(d) differs from the Law Commission's recommendations in several notable respects. First, under s.101(1)(d) the prosecution is not required to obtain the leave of the court, although in practice the prosecution will usually only be able to adduce evidence under this provision following a ruling by the court. Secondly, the evidence must be relevant, and possess "substantial probative value", but unlike clause 5(2) and clause 8(4) of the Law Commission's draft Bill, the 2003 Act does not specify factors the court must take into account when assessing the probative value of the evidence (unless that is a matter dealt with by Rules of Court under s.111). Thirdly, the issue must be an "important matter" but not (as under s.100(1)(b)(ii)) of "substantial importance in the context of the case as a whole". Fourthly, s.103(1)(a) makes it clear that s.101(1)(d) includes questions as to whether the defendant has a propensity to commit offences of the kind charged where his propensity makes it more likely that he is guilty of the offence charged. This is a much more open-ended approach than recommended by the Law Commission (and consider the approach of the House of Lords in *DPP v P* [1991] 2 A.C. 447. Fifthly, s.103(1)(b) imports into s.101(1)(d) questions whether the defendant has a propensity to be untruthful. The Law Commission recommended that in cases where this is an issue, the prosecution may not adduce evidence of the defendant's bad character unless the defendant makes an attack on a person's character by suggesting, or to support a suggestion that the person has a propensity to be untruthful (see clause 9 of the Law Commission's draft Bill). Without evidence of the defendant's bad character, fact finders would get a misleading impression of the defendant's propensity to be untruthful in comparison with that of the other person (see Law Commission Report No.273, para.1.17). There are no such requirements in respect to s.101(1)(d). Finally, s.101(1)(d) does not expressly require the prosecution to satisfy an "interests of justice" test.

Subsection 101(1)(e)

This provision must be read in conjunction with s.104. The provision broadly follows the recommendations of the Law Commission (Law Commission 273; para.1.19) but unlike the scheme proposed by the Law Commission, it is not necessary for a co-defendant to apply for leave to adduce bad character evidence of another defendant. This provision is not subject to s.101(3).

Subsection 101(1)(f)

This relates to what the Law Commission's styled "the corrective exception" (see Law Commission 273, Pt 13). This provision — which is not subject to s.101(3) — must be read in conjunction with s.105. By s.105(1) the defendant may give a false impression as to his/her character expressly or by implication. Traditionally, criminal courts have been generous to defendants in not allowing evidence of their bad character to be adduced to correct a false impression — usually preferring to deal with the matter in some other way. Much of course depends on the facts of a given case. A defendant of bad character, who appears in court dressed in the robes of a priest, would be putting his character in issue under pre-existing rules, but he would normally only risk losing his shield under the Criminal Evidence Act 1898 if the testified whilst wearing such robes and had "cloaked" his testimony with a false impression of good character.

In its consultation paper, the Law Commission stated five instances where the shield should be lost by a defendant who gives a false impression about his character, and these have been incorporated into the provisions of s.105(2) (see Law Commission 273, paras 13.3 and 13.7, and see Law Commission No.141; para.11.39). Evidence to correct a false impression need not be adduced if the defendant withdraws the assertion creating a false impression, or he disassociate himself from it (s.105(3)). Note that where a defendant gives a false impression as to his good character by means of misconduct, "conduct" includes appearance or dress (s.105(5)).

Subsection 101(1)(g)

This provision must be read together with s.106 ("attack on another person's character"), noting s.101(3). A defendant, charged with an offence, who testified on his own behalf, lost his shield under s.1(3)(ii) of the Criminal Evidence Act 1898 if he attacked the character of a prosecution witness by the nature or conduct of his defence, such as to involve imputations on the character of the prosecutor, or the character of a witness for the prosecution, or the deceased victim of the alleged crime. Section 1(3)(ii)) of the Criminal Evidence Act 1898 was only engaged if the defendant gave evidence. This provision has been described as permitting cross-examination on a "tit for tat" basis.

To address these issues, the Law Commission recommended the enactment of a very different scheme (see Law Commission 273, Pt 12). It is not a scheme that has entirely found its way into s.101 of the 2003 Act. First, where an accused's defence involves attacking another person's character by way of adducing evidence, or by way of cross-examination as to that person's alleged bad character (falling outside the central set of facts), the defendant must obtain the leave of the court to do so: see s.100(4). On an application for leave, the court will be clear as to the purpose of the defendant's proposed attack (para.12.5). The judge might be in a position to form a preliminary view as to whether the proposed attack might result in the defendant's character (or as much of it as is relevant) being received in evidence. In the light of that indication, the defendant is able to consider whether it is in his interests to pursue, or to abandon, the proposed attack. There is nothing in the 2003 Act that requires the judge to consider giving such an indication. If the prosecution tenders evidence of a defendant's bad character, the court must take account of the risk of prejudice in deciding whether to admit the evidence (para.12.9). Section 101(3) puts the onus on the defendant to raise that issue. Under the Law Commission's proposals, the evidence must also have substantial probative value in relation to a matter in issue, which is itself of substantial importance and the court must apply an interests of justice test taking into account of the risk of prejudice (para.12.9). No such mandatory requirements exist in s.101.

The Law Commission accepted that there would be occasions when bad character evidence, would have probative value in demonstrating only a defendant's propensity to be untruthful and which might be admissible (in addition to the evidence having substantial probative value in showing that the defendant has such a propensity) if:
  (1) the defendant has suggested that another person has such a propensity;
  (2) the evidence in support of that suggestion falls outside the central set of facts of the case;
  (3) without the evidence of the defendants bad character, the fact finders would get a misleading impression of the defendant's propensity to be untruthful in comparison with that of the person in question, and;
  (4) that the interests of justice require the evidence to be admissible even taking account of its potentially prejudicial effect (see report No. 273, paras 1.17 and 12.13).

For the purpose of s.101, evidence of a defendant's "bad character" is not confined to offences committed, but includes facts relevant to a charge in respect of which the defendant was acquitted. This probably goes no further than the current law: see *Sambasivam v Public Prosecutor, Malaya* [1950] A.C. 458; and *R. v Z (Prior Acquittal)* [2000] 2 A.C. 483; see also Law Commission Report 273, Pt 11, para.11.2). See also the General Note to s.106.

Effect of s.101
In the past, evidence of a defendant's bad character received under s.1(3)(ii) of the Criminal Evidence Act 1898 went to the credit of the defendant. It remains to be seen whether the courts adopt a similar approach in connection with evidence adduced under ss.101(f) and (g). Trial judges will need to tailor directions to a jury having regard the purpose for which the evidence is admitted, and the statutory provision that permitted it admission.

102 "Important explanatory evidence"

For the purposes of section 101(1)(c) evidence is important explanatory evidence if—
  (a) without it, the court or jury would find it impossible or difficult properly to understand other evidence in the case, and
  (b) its value for understanding the case as a whole is substantial.

DEFINITIONS
"bad character": s.98
"defendant": s.112(1)
"important explanatory evidence": s.102

GENERAL NOTE
See the General Note to s.101 and s.101(1)(c). "Important explanatory evidence" is intended to deal with matters so closely linked with the central so facts that it would be a nonsense to exclude such evidence. Thus, the fact W unlawfully assaulted D may be relevant to D's defence that he acted in self-defence; or that he was entitled to resist arrest. See the General Note to s.98 that discusses the difference between "important explanatory evidence" and evidence that is automatically admissible because it falls outside the definition of "bad character" in s.98.

103 "Matter in issue between the defendant and the prosecution"

  (1) For the purposes of section 101(1)(d) the matters in issue between the defendant and the prosecution include—

(a) the question whether the defendant has a propensity to commit offences of the kind with which he is charged, except where his having such a propensity makes it no more likely that he is guilty of the offence;

(b) the question whether the defendant has a propensity to be untruthful, except where it is not suggested that the defendant's case is untruthful in any respect.

(2) Where subsection (1)(a) applies, a defendant's propensity to commit offences of the kind with which he is charged may (without prejudice to any other way of doing so) be established by evidence that he has been convicted of—

(a) an offence of the same description as the one with which he is charged, or

(b) an offence of the same category as the one with which he is charged.

(3) Subsection (2) does not apply in the case of a particular defendant if the court is satisfied, by reason of the length of time since the conviction or for any other reason, that it would be unjust for it to apply in his case.

(4) For the purposes of subsection (2)—

(a) two offences are of the same description as each other if the statement of the offence in a written charge or indictment would, in each case, be in the same terms;

(b) two offences are of the same category as each other if they belong to the same category of offences prescribed for the purposes of this section by an order made by the Secretary of State.

(5) A category prescribed by an order under subsection (4)(b) must consist of offences of the same type.

(6) Only prosecution evidence is admissible under section 101(1)(d).

DEFINITIONS

"bad character": ss.98 and 112(1)
"defendant": s.112(1)
"important explanatory evidence": s.102
"offences": s.112(1)
"prosecution evidence": s.112(1)

GENERAL NOTE

See the General Note to s.101 and s.101(1)(d).

Sections 103(2)–(4)

The history of subss.(2)-(4) begins with clause 84(1)(d) and clause 86 of the Bill, as printed on November 21, 2002. But for an Amendment moved, and agreed, in the House of Lords in November 2003, both clause 84(1)(d) and clause 86 would have been part of the scheme of the 2003 Act.

As originally worded, clause 84(1)(d) was part of the list of circumstances (now set out in s.101) in respect of which evidence of a defendant's bad character is admissible "if but only if"... (cl.84(d)) ... (d) it is evidence of the defendant's conviction for an offence of the same description, or of the same category, as the one with which he is charged".

Clause 86 read:

"86 Offences "of the same description" or "of the same category"

(1) For the purposes of s.84(1)(d)–

(a) two offences are of the same description as each other if the statement of the offence in an information or indictment would, in each case, be in the same terms;

(b) two offences are of the same category as each other if they belong to the same category of offences prescribed for the purposes of this section by an order made by the Secretary of State.

(2) A category prescribed by an order under this section must consist of offences of the same type.

(3) Only prosecution evidence is admissible under s.84(1)(d)"

It will be noted that the wording of clause 84(1)(d) is reflected in the wording of s.103(2). Clause 86(1)(a), (b), subs.(2) now appears in ss.103(4) and (5).

The original scheme was strongly criticised as on the grounds that it allowed "previous convictions to be put in merely because they exist. There is no requirement for relevance whatever" (Lord Kingsland, *Hansard*, HL, Vol. 654, col.1988 (November 19, 2003)). The Government stated that the provision was "intended to create a presumption that certain convictions will be relevant to a case and therefore should be admitted, unless their probative value is outweighed by their prejudicial effect" (*per* Baroness Scotland, *Hansard*, Vol. 653, col.742 (September 15, 2003)). Amendment 143 (later withdrawn, col.754) was designed to "leave out paragraph (d)"; (col.747). However, the Government defended its position drawing attention to s.101(3) that was "drawn directly from s.78 PACE ... to include the test in the common law under which probative value and prejudicial effect are weighed against each other" (Baroness Scotland, *Hansard*, HL, Vol. 654, col.752, (September 15, 2003)).

The Government relented on the November 20, 2003, stating that the "presumption that convictions for the same, or a similar, offence should be admissible", but that the Government would achieve that result "by bringing the presumption under the category of evidence relevant to the issues in the case. In doing so, we have created a closer link between that evidence and the question of propensity" (Baroness Scotland, *Hansard*, HL, Vol. 654, col.2080 (November 20, 2003)). In other words, a defendant's propensity to commit offences of a particular description, is not a discreet ground for admission (as it was under clause 84(1)(d)) but is now subject to the requirements of s.100(1)(d) of the 2003 Act.

The Explanatory Notes express the Government's view as to how ss.103(2)–(6) might operate:

"372. Where propensity is an issue, subsection (2) provides that this propensity may be established by evidence that the defendant has been convicted of an offence of the same description or category as the one with which he is charged. This is subject to subsection (3), which provides that the propensity may not be established in this way if the court is satisfied that due to the length of time since the previous conviction or for any other reason that would be unjust.

373. An offence of the same description is defined by reference to how the offence appears on an indictment or written charge. It therefore relates to the particular law that has been broken, rather than the circumstances in which it was committed. An offence will be of the same category as another if they both fall within a category drawn up by the Secretary of State in secondary legislation. An order establishing such categories will be subject to the affirmative procedure (see section 330(5)). The categories must contain offences that are of the same type (section 103(4)), for example, offences involving violence against the person or sexual offences.

374. Section 103(1)(b) makes it clear that evidence relating to whether the defendant has a propensity to be untruthful (in other words, is not to be regarded as a credible witness) can be admitted. This is intended to enable the admission of a limited range of evidence such as convictions for perjury or other offences involving deception (for example, obtaining property by deception), as opposed to the wider range of evidence that will be admissible where the defendant puts his character in issue by for example, attacking the character of another person. Evidence will not be admissible under this head where it is not suggested that the defendant's case is untruthful in any respect, for example, where the defendant and prosecution are agreed on the facts of the alleged offence and the question is whether all the elements of the offence have been made out."

It is not necessary for the earlier conviction to be described in terms identical to the statement of offence in respect of the offence charged for example "conspiracy to defraud", or "supplying a controlled drug". What matters is that the facts in support of the earlier conviction (that is to say the material being "evidence of the defendant's conviction") would be sufficient to support an offence charged in the same terms. Thus, on a charge of burglary, a conviction for theft committed on premises whilst the defendant was a trespasser, would on those facts, be in the same terms, namely, "burglary".

104　"Matter in issue between the defendant and a co-defendant"

(1) Evidence which is relevant to the question whether the defendant has a propensity to be untruthful is admissible on that basis under section 101(1)(e) only if the nature or conduct of his defence is such as to undermine the co-defendant's defence.

(2) Only evidence—
(a) which is to be (or has been) adduced by the co-defendant, or
(b) which a witness is to be invited to give (or has given) in cross-examination by the co-defendant,
　　is admissible under section 101(1)(e).

GENERAL NOTE
See the General Note to s.101 and s.101(1)(e).

105 "Evidence to correct a false impression"

(1) For the purposes of section 101(1)(f)—

  (a) the defendant gives a false impression if he is responsible for the making of an express or implied assertion which is apt to give the court or jury a false or misleading impression about the defendant;

  (b) evidence to correct such an impression is evidence which has probative value in correcting it.

(2) A defendant is treated as being responsible for the making of an assertion if—

  (a) the assertion is made by the defendant in the proceedings (whether or not in evidence given by him),

  (b) the assertion was made by the defendant—

    (i) on being questioned under caution, before charge, about the offence with which he is charged, or

    (ii) on being charged with the offence or officially informed that he might be prosecuted for it,
    and evidence of the assertion is given in the proceedings,

  (c) the assertion is made by a witness called by the defendant,

  (d) the assertion is made by any witness in cross-examination in response to a question asked by the defendant that is intended to elicit it, or is likely to do so, or

  (e) the assertion was made by any person out of court, and the defendant adduces evidence of it in the proceedings.

(3) A defendant who would otherwise be treated as responsible for the making of an assertion shall not be so treated if, or to the extent that, he withdraws it or disassociates himself from it.

(4) Where it appears to the court that a defendant, by means of his conduct (other than the giving of evidence) in the proceedings, is seeking to give the court or jury an impression about himself that is false or misleading, the court may if it appears just to do so treat the defendant as being responsible for the making of an assertion which is apt to give that impression.

(5) In subsection (4) "conduct" includes appearance or dress.

(6) Evidence is admissible under section 101(1)(f) only if it goes no further than is necessary to correct the false impression.

(7) Only prosecution evidence is admissible under section 101(1)(f).

DEFINITIONS
"bad character": ss.98 and s.112(1)
"conduct": s.105(5)
"defendant": s.112(1)
"important explanatory evidence": s.102
"prosecution evidence": s.112(1)

GENERAL NOTE
See the General Note to s.101 and s.101(1)(f).

106 "Attack on another person's character"

(1) For the purposes of section 101(1)(g) a defendant makes an attack on another person's character if—

  (a) he adduces evidence attacking the other person's character,

  (b) he (or any legal representative appointed under section 38(4) of the Youth Justice and Criminal Evidence Act 1999 (c. 23) to cross-examine a witness in his interests) asks questions in cross-examination that are intended to elicit such evidence, or are likely to do so, or

(c) evidence is given of an imputation about the other person made by the defendant—

    (i) on being questioned under caution, before charge, about the offence with which he is charged, or

    (ii) on being charged with the offence or officially informed that he might be prosecuted for it.

(2) In subsection (1) "evidence attacking the other person's character" means evidence to the effect that the other person—

(a) has committed an offence (whether a different offence from the one with which the defendant is charged or the same one), or

(b) has behaved, or is disposed to behave, in a reprehensible way; and "imputation about the other person" means an assertion to that effect.

(3) Only prosecution evidence is admissible under section 101(1)(g).

DEFINITIONS

"bad character": ss.98 and 112(1)
"conduct": s.105(5)
"defendant": s.112(1)
"evidence attacking the other person's character": s.106(2)
"important explanatory evidence": s.102
"imputation about the other person": s.106(2)
"prosecution evidence": s.112(1)

GENERAL NOTE

See the General Note to s.101 and s.101(1)(g).

107   Stopping the case where evidence contaminated

(1) If on a defendant's trial before a judge and jury for an offence—

(a) evidence of his bad character has been admitted under any of paragraphs (c) to (g) of section 101(1), and

(b) the court is satisfied at any time after the close of the case for the prosecution that—

    (i) the evidence is contaminated, and

    (ii) the contamination is such that, considering the importance of the evidence to the case against the defendant, his conviction of the offence would be unsafe,

    the court must either direct the jury to acquit the defendant of the offence or, if it considers that there ought to be a retrial, discharge the jury.

(2) Where—

(a) a jury is directed under subsection (1) to acquit a defendant of an offence, and

(b) the circumstances are such that, apart from this subsection, the defendant could if acquitted of that offence be found guilty of another offence,

the defendant may not be found guilty of that other offence if the court is satisfied as mentioned in subsection (1)(b) in respect of it.

(3) If—

(a) a jury is required to determine under section 4A(2) of the Criminal Procedure (Insanity) Act 1964 (c. 84) whether a person charged on an indictment with an offence did the act or made the omission charged,

(b) evidence of the person's bad character has been admitted under any of paragraphs (c) to (g) of section 101(1), and

(c) the court is satisfied at any time after the close of the case for the prosecution that—

          (i) the evidence is contaminated, and

         (ii) the contamination is such that, considering the importance of the evidence to the case against the person, a finding that he did the act or made the omission would be unsafe,

           the court must either direct the jury to acquit the defendant of the offence or, if it considers that there ought to be a rehearing, discharge the jury.

(4) This section does not prejudice any other power a court may have to direct a jury to acquit a person of an offence or to discharge a jury.

(5) For the purposes of this section a person's evidence is contaminated where—

    (a) as a result of an agreement or understanding between the person and one or more others, or

    (b) as a result of the person being aware of anything alleged by one or more others whose evidence may be, or has been, given in the proceedings,

    the evidence is false or misleading in any respect, or is different from what it would otherwise have been.

DEFINITIONS
    "bad character": ss.98 and 112(1)
    "defendant": s.112(1)
    "evidence is contaminated": s.107(5)

GENERAL NOTE
    Section 107 applies only in cases where evidence of the bad character of a defendant has been admitted under ss.101(1)(c)–(g). It therefore does not apply where all the parties agreed to the evidence being admitted (whether the parties were aware of the contamination or not), or where the evidence is adduced by the defendant himself, or in answer to a question put in cross-examination. The circumstances in which a person's evidence is contaminated are set out in s.107(5). Where evidence of bad character is false or misleading — in any respect — or is different from what it would otherwise have been, as a result of collusion, or innocent conversation between witnesses, or perhaps careless press reporting, that evidence is contaminated.

    At the close of the prosecution case, in addition to any other submission the defence might make (for example that there is "no case to answer"), the court may stop a case if the contamination is such that the defendant's conviction in respect of the offence charged (or an alternative offence: see s.107(2)) would be unsafe. The court may discharge the jury, and order a retrial, or direct the jury to acquit the defendant. In practice, if the evidence is such that the defendant's conviction would be unsafe, it is difficult to see how a judge would not uphold a defence submission of "no case to answer".

    Section 107 seems to empower a judge to seize the initiative and to stop the case whether the defence make a submission to that effect or not. The words "at any time after the close of the case for the prosecution" in s.107(1)(b) empower a judge to stop the case at any stage during the defence case — or even later. It will be noted that s.107 applies only to trials by judge and jury. The reasoning for this appears to be that fact finders other than juries will be sufficiently disciplined to evaluate the evidence correctly and to disregard the evidence if it is contaminated, and reach a finding on the basis of any other evidence that remains.

108 Offences committed by defendant when a child

(1) Section 16(2) and (3) of the Children and Young Persons Act 1963 (c. 37) (offences committed by person under 14 disregarded for purposes of evidence relating to previous convictions) shall cease to have effect.

(2) In proceedings for an offence committed or alleged to have been committed by the defendant when aged 21 or over, evidence of his conviction for an offence when under the age of 14 is not admissible unless—

    (a) both of the offences are triable only on indictment, and

    (b) the court is satisfied that the interests of justice require the evidence to be admissible.

(3) Subsection (2) applies in addition to section 101.

GENERAL NOTE
Section 16 (2) of the Children and Young Persons Act 1963 (c.37) imposed a complete embargo on any reference in criminal proceedings to any offence in respect which the defendant was found guilty while under the age of 14. Where a conviction was disclosed in breach of s.16 (2), the court had discretion whether the jury should be discharged: *R. v Dickerson* [1964] Crim. L.R. 821.

This provision, in conjunction with s.16(3) of the Children and Young Persons Act 1963 shall cease to have effect. Section 16(3) was inserted by the Crime (Sentences) Act 1997 (c.43), s.55 and Sch.4, para.4; as amended by the Power of the Criminal Courts (Sentencing) Act 2000 (c.6), s.165(1) and Sch.9, para.23. It will be noted that before the September 30, 1998 there was a rebuttable presumption of law that a child aged 10 or over is incapable of committing an offence. This presumption no longer applies in respect of anything done after that date: see s.34 of the Crime and Disorder Act 1998 and The Crime and Disorder Act 1998 (Commencement No. 2 and Transitional Provisions) Order 1998 (SI 1998/2327).

Section 92 was the subject of some discussion in the House of Lords when this provision was considered as part of the Bill (*Hansard*, HL, Vol. 652, col.1099 (September 18, 2003); and again at *Hansard*, HL, Vol. 654, col.744 (November 4, 2003)).

General

109   Assumption of truth in assessment of relevance or probative value

(1) Subject to subsection (2), a reference in this Chapter to the relevance or probative value of evidence is a reference to its relevance or probative value on the assumption that it is true.

(2) In assessing the relevance or probative value of an item of evidence for any purpose of this Chapter, a court need not assume that the evidence is true if it appears, on the basis of any material before the court (including any evidence it decides to hear on the matter), that no court or jury could reasonably find it to be true.

DEFINITIONS
"probative value": s.96(1)

GENERAL NOTE
Given that the common law rules relating to bad character have been abolished, this provision is perhaps best seen as merely confirming that the meaning of "relevance" and "probative value" — as those terms had been understood for decades — remains unchanged. Evidence has no probative value unless it is both relevant and true. When an issue arises as to the admissibility of evidence, the practice of the court has been to resolve the issue on the assumption that the evidence in question is true. The likelihood of the evidence being true — sometimes expressed as the "cogency of evidence" — is usually a matter for fact finders.

110   Court's duty to give reasons for rulings

(1) Where the court makes a relevant ruling—
   (a) it must state in open court (but in the absence of the jury, if there is one) its reasons for the ruling;
   (b) if it is a magistrates' court, it must cause the ruling and the reasons for it to be entered in the register of the court's proceedings.

(2) In this section "relevant ruling" means—
   (a) a ruling on whether an item of evidence is evidence of a person's bad character;
   (b) a ruling on whether an item of such evidence is admissible under section 100 or 101 (including a ruling on an application under section 101(3));
   (c) a ruling under section 107.

111   Rules of court

(1) Rules of court may make such provision as appears to the appropriate authority to be necessary or expedient for the purposes of this Act;

and the appropriate authority is the authority entitled to make the rules.

(2) The rules may, and, where the party in question is the prosecution, must, contain provision requiring a party who—
  (a) proposes to adduce evidence of a defendant's bad character, or
  (b) proposes to cross-examine a witness with a view to eliciting such evidence,
  to serve on the defendant such notice, and such particulars of or relating to the evidence, as may be prescribed.

(3) The rules may provide that the court or the defendant may, in such circumstances as may be prescribed, dispense with a requirement imposed by virtue of subsection (2).

(4) In considering the exercise of its powers with respect to costs, the court may take into account any failure by a party to comply with a requirement imposed by virtue of subsection (2) and not dispensed with by virtue of subsection (3).

(5) The rules may—
  (a) limit the application of any provision of the rules to prescribed circumstances;
  (b) subject any provision of the rules to prescribed exceptions;
  (c) make different provision for different cases or circumstances.

(6) Nothing in this section prejudices the generality of any enactment conferring power to make rules of court; and no particular provision of this section prejudices any general provision of it.

(7) In this section—
  "prescribed" means prescribed by rules of court;
  "rules of court" means—
  (a) Crown Court Rules;
  (b) Criminal Appeal Rules;
  (c) rules under section 144 of the Magistrates' Courts Act 1980 (c. 43).

112 Interpretation of Chapter 1

(1) In this Chapter—
  "bad character" is to be read in accordance with section 98;
  "criminal proceedings" means criminal proceedings in relation to which the strict rules of evidence apply;
  "defendant", in relation to criminal proceedings, means a person charged with an offence in those proceedings; and "co-defendant", in relation to a defendant, means a person charged with an offence in the same proceedings;
  "important matter" means a matter of substantial importance in the context of the case as a whole;
  "misconduct" means the commission of an offence or other reprehensible behaviour;
  "offence" includes a service offence;
  "probative value", and "relevant" (in relation to an item of evidence), are to be read in accordance with section 109;
  "prosecution evidence" means evidence which is to be (or has been) adduced by the prosecution, or which a witness is to be invited to give (or has given) in cross-examination by the prosecution;
  "service offence" means an offence under the Army Act 1955 (3 & 4 Eliz. 2 c. 18), the Air Force Act 1955 (3 & 4 Eliz. 2 c. 19) or the Naval Discipline Act 1957 (c. 53);

"written charge" has the same meaning as in section 29 and also includes an information.

(2) Where a defendant is charged with two or more offences in the same criminal proceedings, this Chapter (except section 101(3)) has effect as if each offence were charged in separate proceedings; and references to the offence with which the defendant is charged are to be read accordingly.

(3) Nothing in this Chapter affects the exclusion of evidence—

(a) under the rule in section 3 of the Criminal Procedure Act 1865 (c. 18) against a party impeaching the credit of his own witness by general evidence of bad character,

(b) under section 41 of the Youth Justice and Criminal Evidence Act 1999 (c. 23) (restriction on evidence or questions about complainant's sexual history), or

(c) on grounds other than the fact that it is evidence of a person's bad character.

113   Armed forces

Schedule 6 (armed forces) has effect.

CHAPTER 2

HEARSAY EVIDENCE

GENERAL NOTE

There is broad agreement that previous rules governing the admissibility of hearsay evidence were complex, difficult to understand, and difficult to apply in practice. The Government added its voice to "growing public concern that evidence relevant to the search for truth is being wrongly excluded" (*"Justice For All"*, White Paper; para.4.52). The expression "search for truth" is potentially misleading: the "search for truth" is limited to an evaluation of the evidence that the parties chose to place before the fact finders. Fact finders in criminal courts have very limited power to call for evidence, for example, to call a witness or to demand the production of documents.

The Government recommended that rules of evidence should be relaxed, and that it would be safe to do so because fact finders "should be trusted to give appropriate evidence the weight it deserves when they exercise their judgment" (*"Justice For All"*, White Paper; para.4.53). Chapter 1 to Pt 11 of the Act is also predicated on confidence that fact finders can be trusted to evaluate evidence correctly.

On Radio 4 the Today programme (November 22, 2003 at 8:30am) the Home Secretary remarked that it was a "sad thing" that critics of the (then) Criminal Justice Bill tended to debate "what was right within the process, not what the outcome should be ... (are) we really interested in process more than outcomes". Although the statement was said in the heat of a live radio interview, it does provide some insight as to the direction law reform is likely to take. The majority of debates have been about outcomes — convictions, acquittals, wrongful convictions, unwarranted acquittals: all have been examined, but legitimate differences of opinion exist as to how these outcomes come about.

It would be idle to pretend that the reforms introduced by the 2003 Act do not have potential constitutional implications. As part of his Review, Lord Justice Auld remarked that "the boundaries between adversarial and inquisitorial systems of trial are blurring; our judges and magistrates' are already assuming an increasingly active role in the preparation of cases for trial and becoming more interventionist in the course of it than has been traditional" (para.104, Ch.11). This statement, although accurate, must be kept in context. The trial process is distinctly adversarial. Although the judiciary is playing an increasingly active role in trial management, judges avoid entering the forensic arena, and they tend not to play any part in the process by which evidence is gathered by the parties. That said, it is appropriate to consider whether this state of affairs is about to change, albeit slowly, by a process of creeping incremental reform of which the 2003 Act is a part. The Government's White Paper *"Justice for All"*, suggests that the answer is "no" because the reforms are intended to "build on the best traditions of our justice system, and we are intended to strengthen and update it" (para.4.69). Similarly, Lord Justice Auld, remarked that "there is no persuasive case for a general move away from our adversarial process" (Ch.1; para.28; and see the *Report of the Royal Commission on Criminal Procedure*, para.1.8; and the *Report of the Royal Commission on Criminal Justice*, paras 11–14)".

Lord Justice Auld recommended moving away from technical rules of inadmissibility, to trusting fact finders to give relevant evidence "the weight it deserves" (Review, Ch.11, para.78). He added, "much, of course, depends on the quality of fact finders, who are mostly jurors, or magistrates. Many are of the view that both are already more competent than we give them credit for assessing the weight of the evidence, including hearsay evidence" (Ch.11; para.98).

With the above in mind, one might have expected the Review to press for either an all-inclusive approach to hearsay evidence (the Law Commission's option 2), or the adoption of the "best available principle" (option 3) in which no hearsay would be excluded as such, but each party would be obliged to produce material from the source closest to the original supplier of the information (Law Commission Report 245, para.6.23). In the event, Lord Justice Auld suggested that this area be looked again, but he made no secret of his preference for option 3 (see Ch.11, paras 101–104):

> "In my view, this difficult subject should be looked at again, I suggest by the body that I have recommended should be established to undertake the reform and codification of our law of criminal evidence. It would also have the benefit of the impressive Report in 1999 of New Zealand Law Commission and its Draft Code for criminal and civil evidence. That body took as its two main criteria the reliability of the proposed statement and the unavailability of the person who made it, adopting the following proposition of Lamer CJ: (*R. v Smith* [1992] 15 CR (4th) 133 SCC, at p.152):
>
> > '(H)earsay evidence of statements made by a person who is not available to give evidence at trial ought generally to be admissible, where the circumstances under which the statements were made satisfy the criteria of necessity and reliability ... and subject to the residual discretion of the trial judge to exclude the evidence when its probative value is slight and undue prejudice might extend to the accused. Properly cautioned by the trial judge, juries are perfectly capable of determining what weight ought to be attached to such evidence, and of drawing reasonable inferences therefrom.'"

The Law Commission of England and Wales was "troubled by the change of attitude that option 3 would require on the part of practitioners and judges. It would be necessary for them to change the habits of a lifetime and be re-educated". (Report No.245; para.6.31). For its part, the Review remarked that "resistance to a particular form of change should not hold sway if there is otherwise a compelling case for it".

The Government decided not to adopt option 3 probably because of the Law Commission found only a "significant, but very small, minority" in favour of this option (Report No.245, para.6.23). However, there was "wide support for the Law Commission's proposal for automatic admission for certain categories of evidence, with judicial discretion to admit other cogent and reliable evidence" (Parliamentary Under Secretary of State for the Home Department, Standing Committee B, col.601, January 28, 2003; and see Report No.245, para.6.52).

The debates in the House of Lords suggest that the judiciary (at least in the appellate courts) would have preferred a statutory measure giving judges in criminal trials a greater discretion as to hearsay evidence that ought to be received by fact finders. Lord Ackner drew their Lordships attention to paper written by the Lord Chief Justice, Lord Woolf (*Hansard*, HL, Vol. 654, cols.752–753 (November 4, 2003)):

> "I referred again to the paper by the noble and learned Lord, Lord Woolf, which is deposited in the Library and which bore the support of all the judges in the Court of Appeal criminal division. Paragraph 23 on page 7 states:
>
> > "What happens now in civil proceedings is that a judge has a general discretion to determine how matters are to be proved. The judge has to exercise the discretion in the interests of justice. He is assisted in doing this, because the probative value of the evidence depends upon its nature and source. If it is not first-hand evidence, then it has the disadvantage that it has not been tested by cross-examination. Whether this matters depends on the circumstances".
>
> I stress what follows:
>
> > "If we have got to the stage where it is considered that it is safe to allow juries to hear hearsay evidence, then we must be accepting that they can be trusted to use that evidence in accordance with the directions of the judge. Instead of the detailed and complex provisions which are contained in Chapter 2, what is needed is a simple rule putting the judge in charge of what evidence is admissible and giving him the responsibility of ensuring that the jury use the evidence in an appropriate manner"."

This was also the view of Lord Cooke of Thorndon who, on the September 18 2003, said (*Hansard*, HL, Vol. 652, col.1110):

> "Unfortunately, though, the Law Commission, after a meticulous review of the field, produced a highly elaborate set of proposed new rules in a pattern reflected in the present Bill. In complexity, it far outdoes the existing law. I would respectfully urge the Government to heed the advice of the noble and learned Lord, Lord Woolf, the Lord Chief Justice. In his background paper lodged in the Library, he puts it:
>
> > "What is needed is a simple rule putting the judge in charge of what evidence is admissible and giving him the responsibility of ensuring that the jury use the evidence in an appropriate manner".
>
> It seems to me that a similar rule should apply in summary proceedings, bearing in mind that any misapplication of it could be corrected on appeal or otherwise — by review, for instance."

A contrary argument was expressed by Lord Thomas of Gresford (*Hansard*, HL, Vol. 652, col.1108 (September 18, 2003)):

> "We now turn to the problem of hearsay evidence, which always relates to the difficulty of challenging it. When a person says that he has been told some information by a third party, two questions arise. First, did the third party actually say what the witness says that he said? Secondly, if he did say what the witness says that he said, is it true? The difficulties can be illustrated through the unfortunate circumstances of yesterday, when Mr Andrew Gilligan told the Hutton inquiry what he had been told by Dr Kelly, who unfortunately died. The issue was whether Mr Gilligan was actually told what he said he was told and whether it was true. That is a basic problem with hearsay evidence, and one approaches the clause with that in mind. We on these Benches find the whole clause objectionable, which is why the clause stand part debate is grouped with the amendment to which I am speaking."

Baroness Scotland explained why the Government was not yet minded to support the wide discretionary power advocated by the appellate judges:

> "... if Parliament were to decide not to codify those categories, the courts, in their appellate capacity, would be bound to develop rules on these issues. Practitioners would have to become familiar with relevant and possibly complicated case-law. That approach also assumes that there would be little conflict with the authorities in such cases. It is an assumption which we do not believe we could safely make, given the problematic way in which that area of law has evolved so far. Thus, there are arguments against the uncertainties of a wholly discretionary approach and in favour of a code which seeks to build on recognised categories in current law, but stating them in a comprehensive and coherent fashion, accessible to all and capable of straightforward application, seems to be one of the measures for which a number of people have been crying out for a long time."

There are two main objections to the receipt of hearsay evidence, (1) that hearsay evidence is liable to be inaccurate, and (2) hearsay evidence offends the principle of orality.

Reliability

Some hearsay evidence "may be almost as good as the first hand account would have been" (Consultation Paper No.138, para.6.5). When hearsay evidence is the best evidence (and not just the best available evidence) the rule against hearsay "operates irrationally to prevent its admission" (consultation paper 138, para.6.7).

Chapter 2 to Pt 11 ensures that such evidence is admissible. A much more difficult area concerns hearsay evidence that is the best available. When should that evidence be excluded? As to concerns that hearsay evidence might be concocted, or that there might exist "errors in transmission", the Law Commission concluded that "risks implicit in first hand hearsay from an identified person should not affect its admissibility but only its weight"; that such risks could be reduced to an acceptable level by empowering a party against whom hearsay evidence is directed, to adduce evidence that undermines the credibility of the original supplier of the information as if she/he had been present at court to testify. In the case of first hand hearsay, fact finders are capable of understanding and following judicial directions and warnings of the defects of such evidence (Report No. 245, para.3.28).

The Law Commission noted that the hearsay rule does not always protect the defendant and may occasionally create injustice in the presentation of his/her case (Report No.245, para.3.33; see *Sparks v Queen, The* [1964] A.C. 964; *R. v William Arnold Thomson* [1912] 7 Cri. App. R. 276; *R. v Blastland (Douglas)* [1986] A.C. 41; *Beckford and Daley* [1991] Crim. L.R. 833). The Law Commission agreed that it is desirable for witnesses to testify in the presence of the accused but that "there are other factors which may outweigh the need for this" (para.3.35).

In cases of multiple hearsay, or where the declarant cannot be identified, "it may be acceptable to admit the hearsay evidence if it is known what words the declarant used, or the risk of fabrication is low" (Law Commission Report 245, para.3.8). The Law Commission found no clear evidence that an oath or affirmation in itself encourages testimony to be truthful (para.3.14). Although the absence of cross-examination was found to be the most valid justification of the hearsay rule, the Law Commission concluded that this was not true for all hearsay and did not justify the hearsay rule as it existed before the 2003 Act (para.3.17).

Orality

There is broad agreement that "Oral evidence is preferable to hearsay" and that "first hand hearsay is preferable to multiple hearsay" (Report No.245, para.1.29). The obvious advantage of oral testimony is that communication between the supplier of the information, and the fact finder, is direct. Live witnesses may add to, qualify, or correct, earlier statements and representations. A witness's account may be tested by cross-examination. The value of "body language" or the "demeanour" of a witness as a basis for deciding whether the evidence of a witness is accurate or true, tends to be assumed rather than known (see *Review of the Criminal Courts of England and Wales*, Lord Justice Auld, Ch.11, para.79). The Law Commission was not persuaded that the significance of demeanour "is such as to justify the exclusion of hearsay, but we do believe that is a matter which merits as a judicial warning" (Report No.245, para.3.12).

The Law Commission's approach

The Law Commission recommended a general rule against hearsay, subject to specified exceptions, plus a limited inclusionary discretion (the "safety valve") (option 7; Report No.245; para.6.53, recommendation 1). Under this scheme, four categories of hearsay are automatically admissible, (1) where the witness is unavailable; (2) business documents; (3) confessions and admissions — subject to s.76 and s.78(1) PACE, (4) various pre-existing statutory and common law exceptions, e.g. *res gestae;* public documents. Two categories of hearsay evidence are admissible at the discretion of the court, namely, (i) where a witness is in fear, and (ii) a limited inclusionary discretion ("the safety valve") (see Pt 8, Law Commission Report 245). As an added safeguard, there would be a general discretion to exclude hearsay evidence (see s.126; report No.245, para.11.18).

The statutory approach

Chapter 2 gives statutory force to option 7 of the Law Commission's Final Report on hearsay (Report No.245, paras 2.48–6.54). Chapter 2 of Pt 11 is closely modelled on the Law Commission's recommendations in its Final Report, and indeed the majority of statutory provisions in Ch.2 mirror those of the draft Bill appended to the Final Report.

The definition of a hearsay evidence

It is advisable to consider ss.115 and 129 first. Both sections are relevant to the definition of hearsay for the purpose of Ch.2 of the Act. Section 115 it defines "statements" and "matters stated", while s.129 is concerned with representations made "other than by a person" that is to say representations produced by machines. Both provisions should be read mindful of the analysis of the Law Commission in Pt VII of its Final Report ("formulation of a rule against hearsay").

As for evidence gathered by machines, careful attention must be given as to whether the hearsay rule is in fact engaged at all. A video recording, a photograph, or the result of a test performed electronically is real evidence of a fact and does not infringe the hearsay rule: *R. v Cook (Christopher)* [1987] 1 All E.R. 1049: *The Statue of Liberty* [1968] 1 W.L.R. 739; *R. v Wood (Stanley William)* (1983) 76 Cr. App. R. 23; *Castle v Cross* [1985] 1 All E.R. 87. If a machine provides a statement that it is an assertion of a fact based on information imparted by any person, then the hearsay rule is engaged: *R. v Coventry Justices Ex p. Bullard* (1992) 95 Cr. App. R. 175. The distinction maybe a fine one, but the critical point is whether the statement is a representation of fact or opinion asserted (implanted) by a person albeit by means of a machine. If the answer is in the affirmative, the representation is hearsay, and it will be admissible only if it can be brought within a recognised exception to the hearsay rule.

Sections 115 and 129 mirror the wording of clauses 2 and 18 respectively of the Law Commission's draft Bill appended to its Final Report. For the purposes of Ch.2, a "representation" means an assertion that a fact or opinion is true. This appears to be modelled on Professor Cross's formulation that "an assertion [statement] other than one made by a person giving oral evidence in the proceedings is inadmissible as evidence of any fact or opinion asserted". A shorter formulation that omits the phrase "or opinion" was approved in *R. v Sharp (Colin)* [1988] 1 W.L.R. 7, and *R. v Kearley Kearley (Alan Robert)* [1992] 2 A.C. 228 (see Report No.245, para.2.2, footnote 4, and see Tapper "*Evidence*" p.530, 9th ed.). It is not clear why the words "or opinion" were dropped from an earlier edition of Professor Cross's original formulation, but the words are a feature of s.115(2).

The representation may be made by a person by "whatever means" including a sketch, photofit or other pictorial form. It is respectfully submitted that a court might need to reconsider the correctness of decisions of the Court of Appeal in *R. v Cook (Christopher)* [1987] 1 All E.R. 1049 (commentary [1987] Crim. L.R. 402); and in *R. v Constantinou (Richard)* (1990) 91 Cr. App. R. 74 (commentary [1989] Crim. L.R. 571). Both cases concerned photofit pictures. In each case, the court held that such pictures are in a class of their own to which the hearsay rule did not apply notwithstanding that the construction of the pictures required human input. The reasoning has been criticised by the late Professor Sir John Smith QC (see [1987] Crim L.R. 4 02; and *"Criminal Evidence"*, J. C. Smith, p.68, Sweet and Maxwell; and see *Percy Smith* [1976] Crim. L.R. 510. The argument is that a photofit picture, constructed under the direction of a witness, is analogous to a statement dictated by the witness to a police officer. A statement written by a witness is hearsay as to the truth of the matters stated in it. Given that s.115(2) defines a "statement" to include representations made in a sketch, photofit, or other pictorial form", such items will be admissible only if one of the statutory exceptions apply.

Section 115(3) — definition of a "matter stated"

Section 115(3) addresses two difficult but related issues concerning the limits of the hearsay rule, namely, (1) so-called "implied assertions" and (2) whether hearsay must always concern an assertion that is intended, or purposed, for example, negative assertions: see *R. v Harry (Deryck)* (1988) 86 Cr. App. R. 105 (note Final Report No.245, paras 7.17–7.23). The effect of the provision is that the decision of the House of Lords in *R. v Kearley (Alan Robert)* [1992] 2 A.C. 228, is overruled (see the statement of Baroness Scotland of Asthal, (*Hansard*, HL, Vol. 654, col.754 (November 4, 2003)).

The Law Commission identified two methods of proving a fact in issue: (1) circumstantially, "by proving some other fact which renders it more likely to be true", or (2) by means of a person's assertion that it is true (Law Commission Report 245, para.7.2). Professor Birch has said "somewhere there is a line between circumstantial evidence and implied assertions, but it is not entirely clear to me where it is" (commentary to *Kearley* [1992] Crim. L.R. 797, at p.798; and see Colin Tapper, *Hearsay In Criminal Cases, an Overview of the Law Commission Report No.245* [1997] Crim. L.R. 771). Professor Birch is not alone: see Law Commission Consultation Paper No.138, paras 2.20–2.25 and 7.58.

An implied assertion is an assertion of fact usually expressed in words, but sometimes by conduct (*Wright v Doe D Tatham* (1837) 112 E R 488) from which another fact can be inferred (consider *Teper v R.* [1952] A.C. 480: "your place burning and you going away from the fire!"). The House of Lords has held that evidence is hearsay if it is adduced to prove a fact inferred from words or conduct, irrespective as to whether the maker of the statement intended to assert some other fact, or did not intend to assert a fact at all (for example A hears B ask C "can you sell me a gram of heroin?" (*R. v Kearley (Alan Robert)* [1992] 2 A.C. 228)). The implication — whether intended or not by the maker of the statement — is that C is a heroin dealer. In Scotland, implied assertions are admissible: *Lord Advocate's Reference (No.1 of 1992)* 1992 S.L.T. 1010. This reinforced the Law Commission's view that such assertions should also be admissible in England and Wales, provided it was feasible to formulate a rule that distinguishes between assertions that convey an impression that is misleading or false, and assertions that are true. In order to do that, the Law Commission devised a model for admissible implied assertions (and analogous situations) that included a component, namely, that only if a person did not intend another person to believe that a statement was true "can it safely be inferred that he or she was not deliberately seeking to mislead" (Report No.245 para.7.25). The risk of fabrication or distortion that might otherwise exist is eliminated or reduced to an acceptable level.

The Law Commission refined that principle by focusing on the declarant's "purpose" in making a statement rather than his "intention". Purpose is a narrower than intention because the latter includes consequences that a person "knows to be an inevitable side-effect of the consequences that he or she desires" (7.36). The effect of all this is that if a person makes a statement from which an inference might properly be drawn, it is not hearsay if it is not the declarant's purpose to cause another to believe that the inference is true.

Section 115(3)(b) — to cause another person to act on the basis that a statement is true

The Law Commission recommended that a statement should be regarded as hearsay if it is made to cause another (or a machine) to act or to respond in a particular way. The assertion may or may not be true, but the declarant's purpose is that another should act as if it is true (para.7.33). This presumably includes the person who makes a "999" call and asks for the services of the police complaining that he was beaten up and injured by X. The assertion may or may not be true. The declarant intends that the operator should act on the assumption that it is true, and the operator does act on that basis (see Report No.245, para.7.33). Section 115(3)(b) brings such declarations within the scope of the hearsay rule.

Hearsay: main provisions

114   Admissibility of hearsay evidence

(1) In criminal proceedings a statement not made in oral evidence in the proceedings is admissible as evidence of any matter stated if, but only if—

    (a) any provision of this Chapter or any other statutory provision makes it admissible,

    (b) any rule of law preserved by section 118 makes it admissible,

    (c) all parties to the proceedings agree to it being admissible, or

    (d) the court is satisfied that it is in the interests of justice for it to be admissible.

(2) In deciding whether a statement not made in oral evidence should be admitted under subsection (1)(d), the court must have regard to the following factors (and to any others it considers relevant)—

    (a) how much probative value the statement has (assuming it to be true) in relation to a matter in issue in the proceedings, or how valuable it is for the understanding of other evidence in the case;

    (b) what other evidence has been, or can be, given on the matter or evidence mentioned in paragraph (a);

    (c) how important the matter or evidence mentioned in paragraph (a) is in the context of the case as a whole;

    (d) the circumstances in which the statement was made;

    (e) how reliable the maker of the statement appears to be;

    (f) how reliable the evidence of the making of the statement appears to be;

    (g) whether oral evidence of the matter stated can be given and, if not, why it cannot;

    (h) the amount of difficulty involved in challenging the statement;

        (i) the extent to which that difficulty would be likely to prejudice the party facing it.

(3) Nothing in this Chapter affects the exclusion of evidence of a statement on grounds other than the fact that it is a statement not made in oral evidence in the proceedings.

DEFINITIONS
   "matter stated": s.115(3)
   "statement": s.115(2)

GENERAL NOTE
   See the General Note to s.115, and the General Notes to Ch.2. Much in Ch.2 is modelled on the Law Commission's proposals for reform, and many of its provisions follow the wording of the draft Bill appended to the Law Commission's final Report No.245.

Section 114(1)(d) — and subs.(2) — the safety value
   This important provision is the inclusionary discretion recommended by the Law Commission, which is styled the "safety valve". The safety valve is an integral part of the Law Commission's preferred option for reform (Report No.245, para.8.133). Its purpose is to prevent injustice that might arise were hearsay to be excluded because it cannot be brought within any other exception to the hearsay rule. It is available to the prosecution and to the defence. Whilst recognising that judicial discretion induces a risk of inconsistency and unpredictability, the Law Commission was of the view that without the safety valve, the proposed reforms would be too rigid. The Law Commission envisaged and that the use of the safety valve would be exceptional, but will extend to multiple hearsay (paras 8.133 and 8.137). It

therefore proposed that the inclusionary discretion should extend to oral as well as to documentary hearsay, and to multiple as well as first hand hearsay (para.8.141). Section 114(1)(d) makes that possible subject to the factors set out in s.114(2).

Section 114(1)(d) is one of the relatively few provisions in this Chapter that was the subject of significant revision during its passage in Parliament as part of the Bill. Clause 9 of the Law Commission's draft Bill (see Final Report) read as follows:

"9. In criminal proceedings a statement not made in oral evidence in the proceedings is admissible as evidence of any matter stated if the court is satisfied that, despite the difficulties there may be in challenging the statement, its probative value is such that the interests of justice require it to be admissible."

The Law Commission commented that s.78(1) PACE, and the common law discretion to exclude prosecution evidence, or the statutory discretion to exclude under this Chapter (s.126) would add nothing to s.114(1)(d) and subs.(2) (Report No.245, para.8.145). This is because s.114(1)(d) already incorporates an "interests of justice" test. The Law Commission's draft Bill did not specify factors the court must consider, whereas s.114(2) of the 2003 Act does so.

Clause 98(1)(d) of the Criminal Justice Bill (as printed on the November 21, 2002) formulated the inclusionary discretion in these terms:

"(d) the court is satisfied that, despite the difficulties there may be in challenging the statement, it would not be contrary to the interests of justice for it to be admissible."

The last limb of that paragraph represented a marked shift of emphasis from the Law Commission's formulation. Clause 98(1)(d) was revised so that the wording as it now appears in s.114(1)(d) shifts the emphasis back to requiring the court to be satisfied that it is in the interest of justice for a hearsay statement to be admissible.

Probative value is one factor to be considered by the court in deciding whether hearsay evidence should be admitted (s.114(2)(a)). Probative value alone does not have to be such that the interests of justice require the statement to be admitted, but the court shall consider how important the evidence is "in the context of the case as a whole" (s.114(2)(c)). The Law Commission observed that the phrase "probative value" is designed to encourage the court to consider amongst other features, the factors set out in ss.114(2)(b)–(h), (para.8.142). The declarant need not have been competent at the time the statement or representation was made, and the declarant need not be identified (para.8.143). Where hearsay evidence is admitted under the inclusionary discretion, a judge should give the jury appropriate directions about its weaknesses, purpose, and other relevant matters.

The inclusionary discretion is available to all parties in the proceedings. The Government expect judges to give reasons for admitting or excluding evidence under s.114(1)(d) (Standing Committee B, col.619).

115   Statements and matters stated

(1) In this Chapter references to a statement or to a matter stated are to be read as follows.

(2) A statement is any representation of fact or opinion made by a person by whatever means; and it includes a representation made in a sketch, photofit or other pictorial form.

(3) A matter stated is one to which this Chapter applies if (and only if) the purpose, or one of the purposes, of the person making the statement appears to the court to have been—

(a) to cause another person to believe the matter, or

(b) to cause another person to act or a machine to operate on the basis that the matter is as stated.

DEFINITIONS
  "matters stated": s.115(3)
  "statement": s.115(2)

GENERAL NOTE
  See the General Note to Ch.2, "the definition of hearsay evidence".

Principal categories of admissibility

116   Cases where a witness is unavailable

(1) In criminal proceedings a statement not made in oral evidence in the proceedings is admissible as evidence of any matter stated if—

     (a) oral evidence given in the proceedings by the person who made the statement would be admissible as evidence of that matter,

     (b) the person who made the statement (the relevant person) is identified to the court's satisfaction, and

     (c) any of the five conditions mentioned in subsection (2) is satisfied.

(2) The conditions are—

     (a) that the relevant person is dead;

     (b) that the relevant person is unfit to be a witness because of his bodily or mental condition;

     (c) that the relevant person is outside the United Kingdom and it is not reasonably practicable to secure his attendance;

     (d) that the relevant person cannot be found although such steps as it is reasonably practicable to take to find him have been taken;

     (e) that through fear the relevant person does not give (or does not continue to give) oral evidence in the proceedings, either at all or in connection with the subject matter of the statement, and the court gives leave for the statement to be given in evidence.

(3) For the purposes of subsection (2)(e) "fear" is to be widely construed and (for example) includes fear of the death or injury of another person or of financial loss.

(4) Leave may be given under subsection (2)(e) only if the court considers that the statement ought to be admitted in the interests of justice, having regard—

     (a) to the statement's contents,

     (b) to any risk that its admission or exclusion will result in unfairness to any party to the proceedings (and in particular to how difficult it will be to challenge the statement if the relevant person does not give oral evidence),

     (c) in appropriate cases, to the fact that a direction under section 19 of the Youth Justice and Criminal Evidence Act 1999 (c. 23) (special measures for the giving of evidence by fearful witnesses etc) could be made in relation to the relevant person, and

     (d) to any other relevant circumstances.

(5) A condition set out in any paragraph of subsection (2) which is in fact satisfied is to be treated as not satisfied if it is shown that the circumstances described in that paragraph are caused—

     (a) by the person in support of whose case it is sought to give the statement in evidence, or

     (b) by a person acting on his behalf,

     in order to prevent the relevant person giving oral evidence in the proceedings (whether at all or in connection with the subject matter of the statement).

DEFINITIONS

"criminal proceedings": s.134(1)
"fear": s.116(3)
"statement": s.115(2)

GENERAL NOTE

This section — which is usually confined to first hand hearsay — should be read together with ss.121 (additional requirement for admissibility of multiple hearsay) and s.123 (capability to make statement). If multiple hearsay is involved, it is essential to read s.116 together with ss.121 and 123. Although the rules seem unduly complicated, the essential point to remember is that multiple hearsay is usually inadmissible, and will only be admitted in tightly prescribed circumstances *e.g.* in the case of a business document (admitted under s.117). This is to guard against inherently unreliable hearsay evidence being admitted. Note the statement of Baroness Scotland on this point (*Hansard*, HL, Vol. 654, col.760 (November 4, 2003)):

"(section 116) which allows evidence to be admitted where a witness is unavailable for good reason, will not operate to allow a chain of such statements to be admissible. However, where the hearsay is admissible in a reliable form, such as in a business document or in a previous statement of a witness who is in court to give evidence and can therefore be questioned on the statement, we consider that the evidence should be admissible."

It must also be stressed that the rules in s.116 may prevent evidence being automatically admitted, but in appropriate cases, hearsay (even multiple hearsay) might be admitted under the inclusionary discretion of s.114(1)(d) — *i.e.* the "safety valve" if its admission is in the interests of justice, and note s.121(1)(c).

In deciding whether to admit the evidence under s.116 the court must also be satisfied that any of the five conditions mentioned in s.116(2) is satisfied. Conditions (a) to (d) are relatively straightforward and build on the experience of the courts in applying s.23 of the Criminal Justice Act 1988 (see Report No.245, paras 8.35–8.47).

By s.23 of the Criminal Justice Act 1988, statements made by a person in a document, were admissible in criminal proceedings as evidence of any fact of which direct oral evidence by that person would have been admissible if he/she was unavailable for any of the reasons set out in s.23(2) or (3) (fear, or kept out of the way). Section 23 had several limitations of which the most significant is that the section was expressly limited to "documents" (although that term was given a wide construction by the courts: *R. v Duffy (Paula) (No.1)* [1999] 1 Cr. App. R. 307). The Law Commission recommended that the unavailability exception should extend to all hearsay (Law Commission Report 245; para.8.4), but only where the person who made the statement (the declarant) is identified to the satisfaction of the court (para.8.8; see s.116(1)(b)). This is to enable the opposing party to challenge the credibility or reliability of the declarant. The Law Commission was not prepared to go as far as allowing the admission of a statement "by a person about whose identity no, or no adequate, information was available" (para.8.5). Evidence adduced against a defendant by way of the statement made by an identified person whom the defence has had no chance to investigate or to cross-examine might breach Convention rights: *Doorson v Netherlands* (1996) 22 E.H.R.R. 330 (para.8.8).

The unavailability exception is separate from the business exception (s.117) in respect of which it is not a condition that the declarant should be identified. Accordingly the unavailability exception cannot reproduce the problem that arose in *Myers (James William) v DPP* [1965] A.C. 1001.

An underlying theme of the new statutory scheme is that the hearsay rule should allow hearsay statements to be received by a court if they are capable of being judged credible and reliable. It is not essential that "reliability be established with absolute certainty" (see Lamer CJ, *Smith* (1992) 94 D L R (4th) 590, 601, 604; Report No.245, para.8.139; David Ormerod "*The Hearsay Exception*" [1996] Crim. L.R. 16, at p.23).

Hearsay statements from an unidentified source may carry an unacceptably high level of risk of being unreliable. Even when the identity of the declarant is known, the risk of error of transmission is obviously greater if a statement is the product of multiple hearsay than first hand hearsay. For that reason s.23 of the Criminal Justice Act 1988 was limited to first hand hearsay (at least the shoulder note refers to "first hand hearsay") whereas s.24 of that Act (business documents) allows multiple hearsay to be received by a court at it's discretion: business documents can usually be assumed to be reliable. Accordingly, s.116 is usually limited to first hand hearsay.

By s.116(1)(a) a statement is admissible if oral evidence by the declarant "would be admissible as evidence of that matter". This excludes hearsay of facts that are not admissible at all, no matter who could give evidence about them (Report No.245, para.8.10), as well as facts that are capable of being admissible but the declarant is not able to give oral evidence of those facts (for example because the declarant was not competent at the time the statement was made (see s.123(1)), or he had no personal knowledge of the facts stated): see Report No.245, paras 8.10–8.12. The Law Commission concluded that in general, multiple hearsay is too unreliable to be admitted and the unavailability of the declarant is not a sufficient reason to justify an exception to that principle in this instance (para.8.17).

However, this seemingly straightforward approach is not without its drawbacks. This is particularly so where the original source of the information ("A") could have given oral evidence of the facts stated by reason of an exception to the hearsay rule, but neither he nor "B" (in whom "A" confided) are available to give oral evidence. To address this problem the Law Commission recommended that the unavailability exception should not apply "if the declarant's oral evidence of the facts stated would itself have been hearsay, and would have been admissible only under the unavailability exception (*i.e.* under s.116)", or under one of the common law exceptions preserved by the 2003 Act (Report No.245, para.8.23). That recommendation has been given statutory force by s.121 of the 2003 Act, (Report No.245 para.8.23).

Subsection 116(2)(e)

Section 23(3) of the Criminal Justice Act 1988 is of uncertain scope — what does "through fear" mean? Fear of whom? Fear of what? Section 116(3) states that "fear" is to be widely construed and includes fear of "financial loss". Parliament has enacted clause 5(7) of the Law Commission's draft Bill, no doubt mindful of the views of the Law Commission in its final Report (para.8.63–8.66). The Law Commission stated that the exception is designed to facilitate the reception of evidence from intimidated witnesses and from those "who were just scared of the process of giving evidence", but it would be quite wrong for it to be used where the witness was only afraid of being prosecuted (para.8.66). The commission said that it was unnecessary to make express provision for this situation "since no court would think it 'in the interests of justice' to allow a witness's statement to be read on this basis" (para.8.66). The Law Commission suggest that a court should look at matters through the eyes of a witness; that the "characteristics and circumstances of the witness clearly fall within the phrase 'other relevant circumstances'" (para.8.62; and see s.116(4)(e)).

Subsection 116(5)

This provision enacts recommendation 8 of the Law Commission Final Report, namely, that the unavailability exception should not apply where the unavailability of the declarant is caused by the person in support of whose case it is sought to give the statement in evidence, or by a person acting on his behalf (see Report No.245, para.8.30). The words "if it be shown" in subs.(5) suggest that the burden is on the party opposing the admission of the evidence to show that the subsection is applicable (see paras 8.31–32).

The Law Commission considered the position of the witness who attends court but refuses to be sworn, or if sworn, refuses to testify, or claims privilege against self-incrimination. It's provisional view was that hearsay evidence would be better than no evidence at all (para.8.44), but ultimately decided that the proposal was better omitted on the grounds that there was an unacceptable level of risk of statements being fabricated where the witness did not want to be cross-examined.

117   Business and other documents

(1) In criminal proceedings a statement contained in a document is admissible as evidence of any matter stated if—
  (a) oral evidence given in the proceedings would be admissible as evidence of that matter,
  (b) the requirements of subsection (2) are satisfied, and
  (c) the requirements of subsection (5) are satisfied, in a case where subsection (4) requires them to be.
(2) The requirements of this subsection are satisfied if—
  (a) the document or the part containing the statement was created or received by a person in the course of a trade, business, profession or other occupation, or as the holder of a paid or unpaid office,
  (b) the person who supplied the information contained in the statement (the relevant person) had or may reasonably be supposed to have had personal knowledge of the matters dealt with, and
  (c) each person (if any) through whom the information was supplied from the relevant person to the person mentioned in paragraph (a) received the information in the course of a trade, business, profession or other occupation, or as the holder of a paid or unpaid office.
(3) The persons mentioned in paragraphs (a) and (b) of subsection (2) may be the same person.
(4) The additional requirements of subsection (5) must be satisfied if the statement—
  (a) was prepared for the purposes of pending or contemplated criminal proceedings, or for a criminal investigation, but
  (b) was not obtained pursuant to a request under section 7 of the Crime (International Co-operation) Act 2003 (c. 32) or an order under paragraph 6 of Schedule 13 to the Criminal Justice Act 1988 (c. 33) (which relate to overseas evidence).
(5) The requirements of this subsection are satisfied if—
  (a) any of the five conditions mentioned in section 116(2) is satisfied (absence of relevant person etc), or

(b) the relevant person cannot reasonably be expected to have any recollection of the matters dealt with in the statement (having regard to the length of time since he supplied the information and all other circumstances).

(6) A statement is not admissible under this section if the court makes a direction to that effect under subsection (7).

(7) The court may make a direction under this subsection if satisfied that the statement's reliability as evidence for the purpose for which it is tendered is doubtful in view of—

(a) its contents,

(b) the source of the information contained in it,

(c) the way in which or the circumstances in which the information was supplied or received, or

(d) the way in which or the circumstances in which the document concerned was created or received.

DEFINITIONS
"criminal proceedings": s.134(1)
"documents": s.134(1)
"matter stated": s.115(3)
"oral evidence": s.134(1)
"statement": s.115(2)

GENERAL NOTE
The Government says that this section broadly corresponds to the pre-existing position for admitting business documents under s.24 of the Criminal Justice Act 1988 (Standing Committee B, col.638). There are, however, several key changes. First, most statements falling within this exception would be automatically admissible. The Law Commission initially proposed that the discretionary provisions of ss.24 and 25 should be repealed, leaving little room for the exercise of discretion to exclude business documents beyond s.78 PACE and the common law exception (and see s.82(3) PACE): see Report No.245, paras 8.71 and 8.72. However, the Law Commission recognised that although most business documents are inherently reliable, others are not. Section 117(6) and (7) vest the court with a new power to exclude documents if it is satisfied that the statements reliability is doubtful (see Report No.245, para.8.77). The thinking is that where there is no particular reason to doubt the reliability of a statement this power would not be available (para.8.76). It is far from certain that this will be obvious in practice. A court is unlikely to jump to conclusions without considering the factors set out in subs.(7).

Section 117 also rectifies what is generally regarded as a drafting error in the wording of s.24 (4) (b) (3) so that the person who must be unavailable, or unable to recollect the matters dealt with, is the person who supplied information (see Report No.245, paras 4.39 and 8.72: and see P. Plowden "*The Curate's Egg — Recollection and Hearsay*" (1995) 59 J Crim L.62; ss.23 and 24 of the Criminal Justice Act 1988: "some problems", Professor Sir John Smith QC [1994] Crim. L.R. 426; consultation paper para.7.26; *R v Derodra (Kishor)* [2000] 1 Cr. App. R. 41.

118   Preservation of certain common law categories of admissibility

(1) The following rules of law are preserved.

Public information etc
1 Any rule of law under which in criminal proceedings—

(a) published works dealing with matters of a public nature (such as histories, scientific works, dictionaries and maps) are admissible as evidence of facts of a public nature stated in them,

(b) public documents (such as public registers, and returns made under public authority with respect to matters of public interest) are admissible as evidence of facts stated in them,

(c) records (such as the records of certain courts, treaties, Crown grants, pardons and commissions) are admissible as evidence of facts stated in them, or

(d) evidence relating to a person's age or date or place of birth may be given by a person without personal knowledge of the matter.

Reputation as to character
2 Any rule of law under which in criminal proceedings evidence of a person's reputation is admissible for the purpose of proving his good or bad character.
Note
The rule is preserved only so far as it allows the court to treat such evidence as proving the matter concerned.

Reputation or family tradition
3 Any rule of law under which in criminal proceedings evidence of reputation or family tradition is admissible for the purpose of proving or disproving—
(a) pedigree or the existence of a marriage,
(b) the existence of any public or general right, or
(c) the identity of any person or thing.
Note
The rule is preserved only so far as it allows the court to treat such evidence as proving or disproving the matter concerned.

Res gestae
4 Any rule of law under which in criminal proceedings a statement is admissible as evidence of any matter stated if—
(a) the statement was made by a person so emotionally overpowered by an event that the possibility of concoction or distortion can be disregarded,
(b) the statement accompanied an act which can be properly evaluated as evidence only if considered in conjunction with the statement, or
(c) the statement relates to a physical sensation or a mental state (such as intention or emotion).

Confessions etc
5 Any rule of law relating to the admissibility of confessions or mixed statements in criminal proceedings.

Admissions by agents etc
6 Any rule of law under which in criminal proceedings—
(a) an admission made by an agent of a defendant is admissible against the defendant as evidence of any matter stated, or
(b) a statement made by a person to whom a defendant refers a person for information is admissible against the defendant as evidence of any matter stated.

Common enterprise
7 Any rule of law under which in criminal proceedings a statement made by a party to a common enterprise is admissible against another party to the enterprise as evidence of any matter stated.

Expert evidence
8 Any rule of law under which in criminal proceedings an expert witness may draw on the body of expertise relevant to his field.
(2) With the exception of the rules preserved by this section, the common law rules governing the admissibility of hearsay evidence in criminal proceedings are abolished.

DEFINITIONS
"bad character": s.98
"criminal proceedings": s.134(1)
"defendant": s.134(1)
"matters stated": s.115(3)
"statement": s.115(2)

GENERAL NOTE
Certain common law categories of admissibility have been retained following the recommendations of the Law Commission in its Final Report No.245 (paras 8.114–132). Exceptions relating to public information, reputation as to character, reputation or family tradition, informal admissions made by an agent, were all part of recommendation 27 (para.8.132). The *res gestae* principle has been retained (s.118(1) para.4). The Law Commission had been concerned about the admission of *res gestae* evidence because frequently the identity of the declarant is unknown. However, on consultation the Law Commission was "repeatedly reassured that nobody was aware of miscarriages of justice" caused by the operation of the *res gestae* principle (para.8.121). The wording of s.118(1) para.4(a), stresses the need to ensure that the probability of concoction or distortion can be disregarded. As for s.118(1) para.4 (b), there must be an essential connection between the relevant act and statement accompanying that act (Report No.245, para.8.122). A physical sensation, or a mental state, are typically matters within a person's knowledge, and usually cannot be proved other than by that person's own statements. Statements as to feelings of fear may thus be relevant to the application of s.116(3) (unavailability of a witness through fear): see Report No.245, paras 8.125–129. The rule in respect of acts and declarations in furtherance of a conspiracy or a joint enterprise has been retained (Report No.245, para.8.130; and see *R. v Blake* (1844) 6 QB 126; *Devonport* [1996] Crim. L.R. 255; *R. v Gray (David John)* [1995] 2 Cr. App. R. 100; *R. v Murray (Anthony John)* [1997] 2 Cr. App. R. 136.

The doctrine of recent complaint is not preserved under s.118 because s.120 enables such evidence to be admitted (see Standing Committee B, col.639, January 28, 2003).

Note that with the exception of rules preserved by s.118, all common law rules governing the admissibility of hearsay evidence in criminal proceedings are abolished: s.118(2).

119   Inconsistent statements

(1) If in criminal proceedings a person gives oral evidence and—
    (a) he admits making a previous inconsistent statement, or
    (b) a previous inconsistent statement made by him is proved by virtue of section 3, 4 or 5 of the Criminal Procedure Act 1865 (c. 18),
the statement is admissible as evidence of any matter stated of which oral evidence by him would be admissible.

(2) If in criminal proceedings evidence of an inconsistent statement by any person is given under section 124(2)(c), the statement is admissible as evidence of any matter stated in it of which oral evidence by that person would be admissible.

DEFINITIONS
"criminal proceedings": s.134(1)
"matter stated": s.115(3)

GENERAL NOTE
This is a short, but important provision that radically alters the previous position in a number of respects. Previous inconsistent statements may now serve as exceptions to the rule against hearsay and not just as tools to challenge the credibility of a witness. Witnesses are frequently cross-examined on oral, or written, out-of-court statements that are inconsistent with their testimony. The purpose is to undermine the credibility and reliability of the witness's testimony. If a witness accepted that the inconsistent statement is true, it became evidence in the case of the matters stated. If the witness denied that the statement is true, it was hearsay. Similarly, if a witness failed to come up to proof, and was treated "hostile", the content of an inconsistent statement was not evidence of the facts stated unless the witness testified that the statement is true.

Section 119 changes that state of affairs. It will be for the fact finders to decide whether a previous inconsistent statement represents the truth notwithstanding the denials of the witness. This provision is likely to produce some lively legal submissions. If a witness is cross-examined on part of an earlier statement does all of that statement become admissible? It is submitted that a pragmatic approach would be to receive in evidence only as much of the inconsistent statement as is necessary to resolve the issue in dispute. The Law Commission identified a number of practical consequences of this reform, which warrants reproducing here in full (Report No.245 para.10.98):

"The practical consequences of the reform that we recommend would be as follows.
    (1) A defendant could be convicted even where the complainant does not come up to

proof, because the fact-finders could accept the complainant's out-of-court statement as true (even though he or she does not confirm it in the witness box) (but see (4) below).

(2) When considering a submission of no case to answer, the court would have to take account of the contents of a previous inconsistent statement admitted in evidence.

(3) Where the previous statement was relied on by the prosecution, section 78 of PACE would apply.

(4) If the quality of the out-of-court statement were such that a conviction would be unsafe, the court would be under a duty to direct an acquittal (or, on summary trial, to dismiss the information).

(5) The judge would have to treat the previous statement as evidence in the summing up.

(6) Where a previous inconsistent statement was admitted in evidence although the witness maintained that it was untrue, a careful direction might be needed. Although the weight to be attached to the oral testimony and the out-of-court statement would be a matter for the fact-finders, it might help a jury if they were told that they are not obliged to accept either version of events as true, and if their attention were drawn to other items of evidence which might help them decide which parts of the evidence to believe and which to reject."

This provision may have the greatest impact in respective cases of alleged unlawful violence in which a complaint refuses to testify, or denies that an earlier inconsistent statement represents the truth (see Standing Committee B, cols.640–645, January 28, 2003).

120   Other previous statements of witnesses

(1) This section applies where a person (the witness) is called to give evidence in criminal proceedings.

(2) If a previous statement by the witness is admitted as evidence to rebut a suggestion that his oral evidence has been fabricated, that statement is admissible as evidence of any matter stated of which oral evidence by the witness would be admissible.

(3) A statement made by the witness in a document—
   (a) which is used by him to refresh his memory while giving evidence,
   (b) on which he is cross-examined, and
   (c) which as a consequence is received in evidence in the proceedings,
   is admissible as evidence of any matter stated of which oral evidence by him would be admissible.

(4) A previous statement by the witness is admissible as evidence of any matter stated of which oral evidence by him would be admissible, if—
   (a) any of the following three conditions is satisfied, and
   (b) while giving evidence the witness indicates that to the best of his belief he made the statement, and that to the best of his belief it states the truth.

(5) The first condition is that the statement identifies or describes a person, object or place.

(6) The second condition is that the statement was made by the witness when the matters stated were fresh in his memory but he does not remember them, and cannot reasonably be expected to remember them, well enough to give oral evidence of them in the proceedings.

(7) The third condition is that—
   (a) the witness claims to be a person against whom an offence has been committed,
   (b) the offence is one to which the proceedings relate,
   (c) the statement consists of a complaint made by the witness (whether to a person in authority or not) about conduct which would, if proved, constitute the offence or part of the offence,
   (d) the complaint was made as soon as could reasonably be expected after the alleged conduct,
   (e) the complaint was not made as a result of a threat or a promise, and

    (f) before the statement is adduced the witness gives oral evidence in connection with its subject matter.

(8) For the purposes of subsection (7) the fact that the complaint was elicited (for example, by a leading question) is irrelevant unless a threat or a promise was involved.

DEFINITIONS

"criminal proceedings": s.134(1)
"defendant": s.134(1)
"document": s.134(1)
"matter stated": s.115(3)
"oral evidence": s.134(1)
"statement": s.115(2)

GENERAL NOTE

As Lord Justice Buxton remarked, the "pervasive orality" and the "principle of testament by identified witnesses" are integral components of the English criminal trial: *R. v Derodra (Kishor)* [2000] 1 Cr. App. R. 41. Despite an increasing number of inroads being made into these components, the usual method of proving facts is by way of the oral testimony of witnesses. As Tapper points out, the position before the Evidence Act 1843 was that persons with an interest in the outcome of the proceedings were disqualified from testifying (*Evidence*, 9th ed., p.204). Even when witnesses are competent to testify, an elaborate set of rules exists governing the questioning of witnesses, and the evidence they are permitted to give. Rules were devised to restrict, or to forbid, the use in court of statements made out-of-court — irrespective as to whether statements of the latter kind were consistent or inconsistent with the testimony of the witness.

Tapper is right when he says that for all its apparent orality an examination in chief is rarely conducted "out of the blue" (*Evidence*, 9th ed., p.264). Witnesses are examined in chief on the strength of a witness statement, or on a proof of evidence. Much cross-examination is conducted on the strength of out-of-court statements made by the testifying witness. No matter how long, or how detailed the cross-examination, it is rare for jurors to have sight of written statements whether consistent or otherwise. The Government believes that the tradition that witnesses must give evidence in person is highly important "but so is the principle that relevant evidence should not be arbitrarily excluded in the search for truth". It said that "it would help witnesses to give better evidence if their earlier statements were made more widely admissible to supplement the evidence that they give at the trial" (Standing Committee B, col.646). Depending on how generously the courts construe and apply s.120, experience might show that previous consistent statements are routinely received in evidence and that oral testimony supplements previous statements made out of court. If s.120(4) applies, a witness might be asked in chief, to read the statement, and then be asked whether the statement is true.

Note that if a document or copy of it, is produced as an exhibit under s.120 (or s.119) it must not accompany the jury when they retire to consider their verdict unless the court considers that course appropriate or with the agreement of the parties to the proceedings: s.122.

An exception relates to statements made by an accused when questioned by an investigator about an offence. Transcripts of interviews may run to many pages, but whether the answers are incriminating, exculpatory, or mixed, they are put before the fact finder who may then read and analyse them as often as he or she wishes. This is usually done as part of the prosecution case — before it is known whether the accused person proposes to testify on his own behalf or not. Accusations put to a suspect in interview are not evidence of their truth, but it is the accused's reaction to them that may make the answers admissible (see consultation paper 3.12–3.15; *Sharpe* (1987) p.86, Report 274). The effect of ss.34–37 of the Criminal Justice and Public Order Act 1994 (c.33) is that most (if not all) of the accused reactions to questions are adduced and put before the court. This is partly out of fairness to the accused, but also because the court is often required to analyse the answers of an accused in the context of the case as a whole. The reaction of the accused, when first arrested, is usually adduced even if the evidence is entirely self-serving, but a carefully prepared exculpatory statement by the accused is inadmissible (*R. v McCarthy (Gerald Joseph)* (1980) 71 Cr. App. R. 142). Despite the existence of those rules, there seems to be a growing trend to deliver exculpatory statements at the beginning of an interview that is otherwise "no comment" — (perhaps in order to avoid engaging ss.34–37 of the Criminal Justice and Public Order Act 1994) and see *R. v Newsome (Kevin)* [1987] 71 Cr. App. R. 325; *Squire* [1990] Crim. L.R. 341. Confessions and admissions made against interest are admissible as to the truth of the facts stated and fall within a long-standing exception to the hearsay rule.

Out-of-court statements made by a witness are not usually evidence of the facts stated. A witness who testifies is not permitted to rely on an out-of-court statement to support, or to bolster, his or her oral evidence. This is sometimes described as the "rule against narrative." The rule exists for two reasons, (1) such statements are all too easy to manufacture, and (2) they are often unnecessary: court time is likely to be wasted exploring superfluous issues. There are five exceptions to the rule against the admission of previous consistent statements. Even when one of the exceptions applies, the statement is not evidence of the truth of facts asserted in it. The exceptions are, (1) recent complaint where the defendant is charged with a sexual offence, (2) identification of the accused by the witness out-of-court (*R. v Christie* [1914] AC 545), (3) to rebut an allegation of recent fabrication, (4) the reaction of the accused when confronted with an allegation, (5) a pre-recorded video interview with the child. Some of these exceptions are very limited in scope. Thus, in respect of (3) the consistent statement is admissible only in respect of the specific allegation of late invention of the story, but it does not enable a witness whose credibility has been impeached to use a previous consistent statement in order to regain lost credit: *Coll* (1889) 24 LR I R 522; and see *R. v Beattie (Alan James)* (1989) 89 Cr. App. R. 302; *R. v P* [1998] Crim. L.R. 663.

The Law Commission's approach
In its consultation paper, the Law Commission proposed that a previous statement should be admissible as evidence of the truth of its contents (a) to rebut recent invention or afterthought, (b) prove previous identification or description, (c) where the witness cannot remember details contained in a statement made when the details were fresh in the witness's mind, and the details are such that the witness cannot reasonably be expected to remember them (option 3; Paper No.138). The Law Commission included a 4th situation namely, statements made by a defendant following the making of an accusation, except in the case of prepared of self-serving statements (see consultation paper 138, para.13.55). Although this proposal was supported by a majority of respondents who commented on it, the Law Commission "experienced considerable difficulties in devising an alternative scheme which works fairly and sensibly and covers both the case where the defendant testifies and the case where he or she does not", and see the comments of Professor Birch [1997] Crim. L.R. 416.
The commission recommended that "the current law be preserved in respect of admissions, confessions, mixed statements, and evidence of reaction" (see Recommendation 18, Final Report 245, para.8.92).

The statutory approach
It will be seen that s.128 of the 2003 Act addresses confessions, but only in respect of confessions as evidence for a co-accused. Section 120 gives statutory force to option 3 in the Law Commission's Consultation Paper in respect of allegations of: (i) fabrication (see s.120(2); Report No.245, paras 10.41–10.45); (ii) previous identification of a person, object, or place (ss.120(4) and (5); Report No.245 paras 10.46–10.52); (iii) recent complaints (ss.120(4) and (7); Report No.245, paras 10.53– 10.62); (iv) previous statements the contents of which the witness cannot remember at the moment he/she testifies (ss.120(4) and (6); Report No.245, paras 10.73–10.80); and (v) documents on which the witness has been cross-examined (s.120(3); Report No.245, para.10.81–10.82).

Subsection (2)
See the Law Commission Report No.245, paras 10.41–10.45. Under pre-existing rules a witness might be cross-examined on an inconsistent statement, yet he he/she is prohibited from relying on a previous consistent statement (Consultation Paper No.138, para.13.36). The Law Commission pointed out that this is anomalous, and creates a paradox. Subsection (2) appears to be engaged even if the allegation is not one of recent fabrication. The earlier statement is admissible not just (1) on the issue of credibility, and (2) to prove the truth of the matters asserted.

Subsection (3) — witness can recall events after refreshing his memory
See the final Report 245, paras 10.81–10.82. Some witnesses may recall events after a refreshing their memory from a document. Note that in this instance subs.(3) refers to a statement made "in a document". The word "document" is to be widely construed (see s.134(1)). If the witness is cross-examined on it and as a consequence it is received in evidence, it becomes evidence of a matter stated of which oral evidence by him would be admissible. It is not clear whether this means the entire document is admissible or only that part of it that includes the matter on which the witness was cross-examined.

Subsection (5)
This provision should be read in conjunction with subs.(4). Witnesses have been permitted to testify to a previous identification for many years. The Law Commission recommended that statements relating to a previous identification should be admissible as to the matters stated,

and that the principle should be extended to the description of a person (*e.g.* where W describes the offender to X), as well as objects or places. Note that subs.(4) is not limited to statements in a document. Thus, where W indicates a car registration number to X who noted it in his diary, X will be able to testify to the number he/she noted (see Consultation Paper No.138, para.13.35). Note the position in Scotland where evidence of a prior description given by a witness is admissible there: *Frew v Jessop* 1989 S.C.C.R. 530.

Subsection (6) — witness cannot recall events and memory refreshing fails

Even when the witness reads the statement, he/she may still be unable to recall events, or he/she cannot reasonably be expected to do so well enough to give oral evidence. In such a case the previous statement may now be treated as admissible hearsay that goes to the truth of the matters asserted in it provided (i) oral evidence by him would be admissible, (ii) that to the best of his belief the statement made by him is true, and (iii) the statement was made by him when the matters were fresh in his memory. Note that under subs.(6), a statement may be proved in a number of ways including calling a witness who heard the statement and remembers it (see Report No.245, para.10.75; and note that subs.(6) does not refer to a "statement in a document"). Note that subs.(6) must be read together with subs.(4).

Subsection (7)

This provision must be read together with subsection(4). Note that a "statement" need not be contained in a document. The statement may be proved in several ways including an oral statement made to a witness who remembers it (see Report No.245, para.10.75). This provision gives statutory force to the recommendations of the Law Commission in its Final Report (paras 10.53–10.61). Evidence of recent complaint was confined to sexual offences, but this limitation has been removed (see s.120(7)(a)). The statement is not merely relevant to the credibility of the witness but admissible as evidence of any matter stated of which oral evidence by the witness would be admissible. The practical effect of this provision is that a party calling a complainant/victim will be able to adduce the previous statement in many — if not most — cases where there is an identifiable victim. It seems likely that s.120(7)(a) will be widely construed, but knowing where to draw the line between persons "against whom" an offence has been committed, and persons against whom it has not, might be difficult — particularly in cases of cross-border company frauds.

It is not necessary that the complaint was unassisted, and this is now a factor that goes to the weight of the evidence.

Note that the statement might nevertheless be excluded under s.78 PACE.

Supplementary

121   Additional requirement for admissibility of multiple hearsay

(1) A hearsay statement is not admissible to prove the fact that an earlier hearsay statement was made unless—

(a) either of the statements is admissible under section 117, 119 or 120,

(b) all parties to the proceedings so agree, or

(c) the court is satisfied that the value of the evidence in question, taking into account how reliable the statements appear to be, is so high that the interests of justice require the later statement to be admissible for that purpose.

(2) In this section "hearsay statement" means a statement, not made in oral evidence, that is relied on as evidence of a matter stated in it.

DEFINITIONS
    "oral evidence": s.134(1)
    "statements": s.115(2)

GENERAL NOTE

Multiple hearsay arises where the declarant has no personal knowledge of the matter stated by him, but derived his information from another source. Thus, where O observes a robbery and tells W about it, W will not be permitted to give oral testimony of O's account unless a hearsay exception applies. W's statement is multiple hearsay.

The Government has accepted that multiple hearsay is inherently more dangerous and more unreliable than first hand hearsay (Standing Committee B, col.650, January 28, 2003). This reflects the views of the Law Commission (Report No.245, para.8.17), who identified the following differences between first-hand and multiple hearsay including (1) room for distortion, (2) errors in transmission (Report No.245, para.3.5), (3) that it is impossible to challenge or question the original source of the information, and (4) the need to give juries much more complex directions for multiple hearsay than for first hand hearsay (Report No.245, para.8.16). However, not all not all hearsay is unreliable, and not all such hearsay is inherently unreliable.

Business records compiled from information that has passed through many hands may, or may not, be reliable. The Law Commission considered but rejected the proposition that if the only way material could be put before a court was by way of a statement that was multiple hearsay, then it should be received if the risk that it may be unreliable is outweighed by the fact that the maker of that statement is unavailable to testify (Report No.245, 8.18–8.23). The Law Commission concluded that "there comes a point where the need to exclude potentially unreliable evidence must come before the desirability of allowing the court to hear the best evidence available" (Report No.245, para.8.22).

If the purpose of the new rules is to make the hearsay rule less complex, and easier to understand, and easier to apply, the result is likely to be a disappointment. Many practitioners will find the relationship between a number of these deceptively short/simple provisions intricate, and difficult. This is true of ss.116 (witness unavailable) and 121 (multiple hearsay limitations). In cases where a witness is unavailable, a statement (although first hand hearsay) may be admitted as to the truth of its contents if — (in addition to other conditions) "oral evidence given in the proceedings by the person who made the statement would be admissible as evidence of that matter" (s.116(1)(a)). In such a case, the declarant does at least have personal knowledge of the matters stated. However, where the maker of the statement does not have personal knowledge of the event in question, but relies on what another person has told him, then he cannot give oral evidence about it. His statement is hearsay and the fact that he is now unavailable is irrelevant (see Report No.245, para.8.15). The Law Commission said at para.8.17 that "in general, multiple hearsay is too unreliable to be admitted; and we do not believe that the unavailability of the declarant is sufficient to justify an exception to this principle" (and see para.11.3). However, that is not to say that multiple hearsay is always inadmissible under s.116(1)(a) where the declarant is unavailable.

Note the statement of Baroness Scotland on this point (*Hansard*, HL, Vol. 654, col.760 (November 4, 2003)):

"(section 116) which allows evidence to be admitted where a witness is unavailable for good reason, will not operate to allow a chain of such statements to be admissible. However, where the hearsay is admissible in a reliable form, such as in a business document or in a previous statement of a witness who is in court to give evidence and can therefore be questioned on the statement, we consider that the evidence should be admissible."

By s.116(1)(a), an out-of-court statement is admissible as evidence of any matter stated if "oral evidence given ... by a person who made the statement would be admissible" if an exception to the hearsay rule applies, *e.g.* it is admissible under ss.116, 119 or 120. If W makes a statement that he was told by O that O saw X stab Y, O's out-of-court statement to W is hearsay, and W's statement is hearsay. But, if O testifies as to what he saw, and the defence allege that O's story is a fabrication, then W's statement might be admissible under s.120 and s.116(1) if W is unavailable to testify. Note the extension of the safety valve principle under s.121(1)(c).

122　Documents produced as exhibits

(1) This section applies if on a trial before a judge and jury for an offence—

　　(a) a statement made in a document is admitted in evidence under section 119 or 120, and

　　(b) the document or a copy of it is produced as an exhibit.

(2) The exhibit must not accompany the jury when they retire to consider their verdict unless—

　　(a) the court considers it appropriate, or

　　(b) all the parties to the proceedings agree that it should accompany the jury.

DEFINITIONS
　"copy": s.134(1)
　"document": s.134 (1)

GENERAL NOTE
　This section is largely self-explanatory, but see the Law Commission's final Report No.245, para.10.62 and see the General Note to s.120 of the 2003 Act.

123   Capability to make statement

(1) Nothing in section 116, 119 or 120 makes a statement admissible as evidence if it was made by a person who did not have the required capability at the time when he made the statement.

(2) Nothing in section 117 makes a statement admissible as evidence if any person who, in order for the requirements of section 117(2) to be satisfied, must at any time have supplied or received the information concerned or created or received the document or part concerned—

    (a) did not have the required capability at that time, or

    (b) cannot be identified but cannot reasonably be assumed to have had the required capability at that time.

(3) For the purposes of this section a person has the required capability if he is capable of—

    (a) understanding questions put to him about the matters stated, and

    (b) giving answers to such questions which can be understood.

(4) Where by reason of this section there is an issue as to whether a person had the required capability when he made a statement—

    (a) proceedings held for the determination of the issue must take place in the absence of the jury (if there is one);

    (b) in determining the issue the court may receive expert evidence and evidence from any person to whom the statement in question was made;

    (c) the burden of proof on the issue lies on the party seeking to adduce the statement, and the standard of proof is the balance of probabilities.

DEFINITIONS
"statement": s.115(2)

GENERAL NOTE
The exceptions to the hearsay rule under ss.116, 119, and 120 of the 2003 Act proceed on the basis that the maker of the statement or (as the case may be) the supplier of the information was competent (*i.e.* capable) to make the statement in question (see Law Commission final Report No.245, paras 8.13–8.14).

124   Credibility

(1) This section applies if in criminal proceedings—

    (a) a statement not made in oral evidence in the proceedings is admitted as evidence of a matter stated, and

    (b) the maker of the statement does not give oral evidence in connection with the subject matter of the statement.

(2) In such a case—

    (a) any evidence which (if he had given such evidence) would have been admissible as relevant to his credibility as a witness is so admissible in the proceedings;

    (b) evidence may with the court's leave be given of any matter which (if he had given such evidence) could have been put to him in cross-examination as relevant to his credibility as a witness but of which evidence could not have been adduced by the cross-examining party;

    (c) evidence tending to prove that he made (at whatever time) any other statement inconsistent with the statement admitted as evidence is admissible for the purpose of showing that he contradicted himself.

(3) If as a result of evidence admitted under this section an allegation is made against the maker of a statement, the court may permit a party to lead additional evidence of such description as the court may specify for the purposes of denying or answering the allegation.

(4) In the case of a statement in a document which is admitted as evidence under section 117 each person who, in order for the statement to be admissible, must have supplied or received the information concerned or created or received the document or part concerned is to be treated as the maker of the statement for the purposes of subsections (1) to (3) above.

"criminal proceedings": s.134(1)
"document": s.134(1)
"matter stated": s.115(3)
"oral evidence": s.134(1)
"statement": s.115(2)

GENERAL NOTE
By virtue of s.28(2), and Sch.2, para.1(c) to the Criminal Justice Act 1988 a defendant against whom hearsay evidence was directed, was entitled to adduce evidence to challenge the credibility of the maker of the statement as if he had given oral testimony. The provision for was considered in *R. v Derodra (Kishor)* [2000] 1 Cr. App. R. 41. It should also be noted that Ch.1 to Pt 11 of the 2003 Act has radically altered rules governing cross-examination, and evidence, relating to the bad character of defendants and non-defendants (and see Report No.245; paras 11.19–11.25). Section 124 (2) is intended to give parties affected by the statement the opportunity to adduce evidence relevant to the credibility of the declarant. In order to facilitate a balanced approach to all parties to the proceedings, a party may be given permission to call evidence to repair or bolster the credibility of the declarant by denying or answering an allegation made (see s.124 (3)).

125   Stopping the case where evidence is unconvincing

(1) If on a defendant's trial before a judge and jury for an offence the court is satisfied at any time after the close of the case for the prosecution that—
   (a) the case against the defendant is based wholly or partly on a statement not made in oral evidence in the proceedings, and
   (b) the evidence provided by the statement is so unconvincing that, considering its importance to the case against the defendant, his conviction of the offence would be unsafe,
    the court must either direct the jury to acquit the defendant of the offence or, if it considers that there ought to be a retrial, discharge the jury.

(2) Where—
   (a) a jury is directed under subsection (1) to acquit a defendant of an offence, and
   (b) the circumstances are such that, apart from this subsection, the defendant could if acquitted of that offence be found guilty of another offence,
    the defendant may not be found guilty of that other offence if the court is satisfied as mentioned in subsection (1) in respect of it.

(3) If—
   (a) a jury is required to determine under section 4A(2) of the Criminal Procedure (Insanity) Act 1964 (c. 84) whether a person charged on an indictment with an offence did the act or made the omission charged, and
   (b) the court is satisfied as mentioned in subsection (1) above at any time after the close of the case for the prosecution that—
      (i) the case against the defendant is based wholly or partly on a statement not made in oral evidence in the proceedings, and
      (ii) the evidence provided by the statement is so unconvincing that, considering its importance to the case against the

person, a finding that he did the act or made the omission would be unsafe,

the court must either direct the jury to acquit the defendant of the offence or, if it considers that there ought to be a rehearing, discharge the jury.

(4) This section does not prejudice any other power a court may have to direct a jury to acquit a person of an offence or to discharge a jury.

DEFINITIONS
"defendant": s.134(1)
"oral evidence": s.134(1)
"statement": s.115(2)

GENERAL NOTE

The wording of s.125 largely replicates clause 14 of the Law Commission's draft Bill appended to its Final Report No.245. The commission explained his reasons as follows:

11.30 The Royal Commission recommended that *Galbraith* be reversed, "so that a judge may stop any case if he or she takes the view that the prosecution evidence is demonstrably unsafe or unsatisfactory or too weak to be allowed to go to the jury". No final view has yet been reached about whether this recommendation will be acted upon by the Government. (At para.45 of Royal Commission on Criminal Justice: Final Government Response (1996) the Government said it was considering the recommendation, but saw some difficulties with the proposed formula and how it would differ from the ruling in *Galbraith*).

11.31 The justifications for creating exceptions to the rule in *Galbraith* is that the risk that the jury may act upon evidence which is not to be relied upon "may well be seen as serious enough to outweigh the general principle that the functions of the judge and jury must be kept apart". (*Daley v Queen, The* [1994] 1 A.C. 117, 129D, *per* Lord Mustill. In that case the Judicial Committee of the Privy Council examined the relationship between *Galbraith* and *Turnbull* (1977) QB 224. Their Lordships justified the approach adopted in the identification cases on the ground that "the case is withdrawn from the jury not because the judge considers that the witness is lying, but because the evidence even if taken to be honest has a base which is so slender that it is unreliable and therefore not sufficient to found a conviction": p.129F). Experience has shown that identification evidence, and confessions, can be unreliable. The same can be said of hearsay. It seems to us that a derogation from *Galbraith* may be justified in the case of hearsay evidence on the same basis: even though the (absent) declarant may be honest, his or her evidence, being hearsay, may be so poor that a conviction would be unsafe. (It is possible, for example, to envisage a case in which the defendant is charged with assault, and the evidence against him consists of the statement from the alleged victim (who is unavailable to testify at the trial) and medical evidence. The defence is self-defence. The medical evidence is consistent with both the prosecution and the defence version of events. At the trial, the defence adduces evidence that the alleged victim was so drunk at the time of the assault that it is likely that his perception of events at the time, and his recollection of them, were inaccurate. In such circumstances, the court would be likely to conclude that the alleged victim's statement is not to be relied upon, and that a conviction would be unsafe).

126   Court's general discretion to exclude evidence

(1) In criminal proceedings the court may refuse to admit a statement as evidence of a matter stated if—

   (a) the statement was made otherwise than in oral evidence in the proceedings, and

   (b) the court is satisfied that the case for excluding the statement, taking account of the danger that to admit it would result in undue waste of time, substantially outweighs the case for admitting it, taking account of the value of the evidence.

(2) Nothing in this Chapter prejudices—

   (a) any power of a court to exclude evidence under section 78 of the Police and Criminal Evidence Act 1984 (c. 60) (exclusion of unfair evidence), or

   (b) any other power of a court to exclude evidence at its discretion (whether by preventing questions from being put or otherwise).

DEFINITIONS
  "criminal proceedings": s.134(1)
  "matter stated": s.115(3)
  "oral evidence": s.134(1)
  "statement": s.115(2)

GENERAL NOTE
  This provision gives effect to the recommendations of the Law Commission that ss.25 and 26 of the Criminal Justice Act 1988 should be repealed. Section 78 of PACE applies across Ch.2 to Pt 11 of the 2003 Act. However, s.78 is not apt to deal with hearsay evidence that is either superfluous or where the probative value of the evidence is minimal. Section 126 has therefore been enacted to deal with such evidence. The view of the Law Commission is that the power will be appropriate "only in exceptional cases" (Report No.245, para.11.18). Experience may show that its use will be exceptional, but certainly not rare.

Miscellaneous

127   Expert evidence: preparatory work

(1) This section applies if—
    (a) a statement has been prepared for the purposes of criminal proceedings,
    (b) the person who prepared the statement had or may reasonably be supposed to have had personal knowledge of the matters stated,
    (c) notice is given under the appropriate rules that another person (the expert) will in evidence given in the proceedings orally or under section 9 of the Criminal Justice Act 1967 (c. 80) base an opinion or inference on the statement, and
    (d) the notice gives the name of the person who prepared the statement and the nature of the matters stated.
(2) In evidence given in the proceedings the expert may base an opinion or inference on the statement.
(3) If evidence based on the statement is given under subsection (2) the statement is to be treated as evidence of what it states.
(4) This section does not apply if the court, on an application by a party to the proceedings, orders that it is not in the interests of justice that it should apply.
(5) The matters to be considered by the court in deciding whether to make an order under subsection (4) include—
    (a) the expense of calling as a witness the person who prepared the statement;
    (b) whether relevant evidence could be given by that person which could not be given by the expert;
    (c) whether that person can reasonably be expected to remember the matters stated well enough to give oral evidence of them.
(6) Subsections (1) to (5) apply to a statement prepared for the purposes of a criminal investigation as they apply to a statement prepared for the purposes of criminal proceedings, and in such a case references to the proceedings are to criminal proceedings arising from the investigation.
(7) The appropriate rules are rules made—
    (a) under section 81 of the Police and Criminal Evidence Act 1984 (advance notice of expert evidence in Crown Court), or
    (b) under section 144 of the Magistrates' Courts Act 1980 (c. 43) by virtue of section 20(3) of the Criminal Procedure and Investigations Act 1996 (c. 25) (advance notice of expert evidence in magistrates' courts).

DEFINITIONS
"appropriate rules": s.127(7)
"criminal proceedings": s.134(1)
"matters stated": s.115(3)
"statement": s.115(2)

GENERAL NOTE

This section is concerned with hearsay issues arising in connection with preparatory work carried out by persons who would not ordinarily expect be called as witnesses in a criminal trial but act on behalf of an expert who in turn bases an opinion or inference on the strength of their work. The section does not address wider issues concerning the resolution of disputed matters with expert help carefully considered by Lord Justice Auld as part of his Review of the English criminal justice process.

The strict legal position is that an expert is not permitted to give an opinion in court based on scientific tests carried out by assistants unless those assistants are called to give supporting evidence (see the Report of the Royal Commission on Criminal Justice, Ch.9, para.78; *R. v Abadom (Steven)* (1983) 76 Cr. App. R. 48; Law Commission final Report No.245, para.9.1; consider *R. v Hodges (Kevin John)* [2003] EWCA Crim 290. Thus, where W expresses an expert opinion that a company was insolvent, based on schedules prepared by experienced accountants, W's opinion is hearsay if the primary facts are not proved by supporting evidence. The point is rarely taken by legal practitioners because, insisting on all the assistants being called to testify, would be a waste of time. There are cases where it is appropriate that the court should hear from persons who dealt with the primary facts, as well as from the expert who bases an opinion on those facts, and it is not the purpose of s.127 to prevent that happening.

The section is designed to prevent a technical point being taken that is devoid of merit. The Law Commission recommended — and the Government has accepted — a two-stage solution. First, tighter rules relating to disclosure, namely that the Crown Court (Advance Notice of Expert Evidence) Rules 1987 (SI 1987/716) (as amended), and the Magistrates' Court (Advance Notice of Expert Evidence) Rules 1997 (SI 1997/553) should be amended so as to require advance notice of the name of any person who has prepared a statement on which it is proposed that an expert witness should base any opinion or inference, and the nature of the matters stated (recommendation 33(1)). Secondly, in cases where such notice has been served, that the hearsay rule be revised by creating a new hearsay exception. The exception is set out in ss.127(1)–(3).

The new exception is not engaged if the court so orders (s.127(4)) following an application to that effect by a party to the proceedings. It would seem that the court cannot disapply the section of its own motion. The Law Commission envisaged that an application made under subs.(4) would be heard pre-trial (Report No.245, para.9.24), but there is nothing in the subsection to say that it must be made at that time. Section 30(4) of the Criminal Justice Act 1988 states that an expert's report when admitted under ss.30(1)–(3), "shall be evidence of any fact or opinion of which the person making it could have given oral evidence". This provision remains in force, but it does not deal with the hearsay issue that is the subject of s.127 of the 2003 Act: s.30 of the Criminal Justice Act 1988 permits first hand hearsay to be admitted, whereas s.127 permits experts to give evidence of facts and opinions stated by others.

Note that nothing in s.111 is intended to replace pre-existing rules in criminal proceedings that an expert may draw on the fund of knowledge that forms "part of the expert's professional expertise, although not acquired through person experience" (Report No.245, para.9.4). Section 118(1) para.4, expressly preserves those rules: and see *Milirrpum v Nobalco Property Ltd* (1971) 17 FLR 141; *Rowley v London and North West Railway* (1873) L R 8 Ex. 221; *Abadom* (1893) 76, Reports 48; *R. v Hodges (Kevin John)* [2003] EWCA Crim 290.

128   Confessions

(1) In the Police and Criminal Evidence Act 1984 (c. 60) the following section is inserted after section 76—

"76A   Confessions may be given in evidence for co-accused

(1) In any proceedings a confession made by an accused person may be given in evidence for another person charged in the same proceedings (a co-accused) in so far as it is relevant to any matter in issue in the proceedings and is not excluded by the court in pursuance of this section.

(2) If, in any proceedings where a co-accused proposes to give in evidence a confession made by an accused person, it is represented to the court that the confession was or may have been obtained—

(a) by oppression of the person who made it; or

(b) in consequence of anything said or done which was likely, in the circumstances existing at the time, to render unreliable any confession which might be made by him in consequence thereof,

the court shall not allow the confession to be given in evidence for the co-accused except in so far as it is proved to the court on the balance of probabilities that the confession (notwithstanding that it may be true) was not so obtained.

(3) Before allowing a confession made by an accused person to be given in evidence for a co-accused in any proceedings, the court may of its own motion require the fact that the confession was not obtained as mentioned in subsection (2) above to be proved in the proceedings on the balance of probabilities.

(4) The fact that a confession is wholly or partly excluded in pursuance of this section shall not affect the admissibility in evidence—

(a) of any facts discovered as a result of the confession; or

(b) where the confession is relevant as showing that the accused speaks, writes or expresses himself in a particular way, of so much of the confession as is necessary to show that he does so.

(5) Evidence that a fact to which this subsection applies was discovered as a result of a statement made by an accused person shall not be admissible unless evidence of how it was discovered is given by him or on his behalf.

(6) Subsection (5) above applies—

(a) to any fact discovered as a result of a confession which is wholly excluded in pursuance of this section; and

(b) to any fact discovered as a result of a confession which is partly so excluded, if the fact is discovered as a result of the excluded part of the confession.

(7) In this section 'oppression' includes torture, inhuman or degrading treatment, and the use or threat of violence (whether or not amounting to torture)."

(2) Subject to subsection (1), nothing in this Chapter makes a confession by a defendant admissible if it would not be admissible under section 76 of the Police and Criminal Evidence Act 1984 (c. 60).

(3) In subsection (2) "confession" has the meaning given by section 82 of that Act.

DEFINITIONS
 "confession": s.128(3)
 "oppression": s.128(1) inserting s.76A(7) of PACE

GENERAL NOTE
 At common law an out of court confession is admissible notwithstanding that it is hearsay, but the confession must be "perfectly voluntary" so that "any inducement in the nature of the promise or of a threat held out by a person in authority vitiates a confession".
 Confessions are now largely governed by statute, principally s.76 PACE which provides that a confession made by a "an accused person" is admissible against him if it is relevant to any

matter in issue in the proceedings and not excluded in pursuance of that section. Where the accused represents to the court that the confession was obtained by oppression (s.76(2)(a) PACE), or in consequence of anything said or done which was "likely in the circumstances existing at the time, to render unreliable any confession which might be made by him" (s.76(2)(b) PACE), the confession will be admissible unless the prosecutor proves beyond reasonable doubt that the confession — notwithstanding that it may be true — was not obtained in those circumstances. The court is concerned with potential unreliability and thus the fact the confession is true is irrelevant. Even an admissible confession might be excluded under s.78 PACE, or at common law, but these discretions come into play only if the prosecution seek to rely on the evidence.

There are circumstances in which an accused person would wish to rely on a confession made by a co-accused, or to rely on a confession made by a third party who has not been charged with the offence in question. The position of a co-accused, and that of a third party, needs to be kept separate.

The position at common law is that confessions by a third party, or by a co-accused, are inadmissible hearsay if adduced by an accused as evidence in his case: *Sussex Peerage Case* (1844) 11 CL and Fin 85. Documentary confessions were capable of being admissible under s.23 of the Criminal Justice Act 1988 subject to ss.25 and s.26 of that Act. However, where two defendants are jointly charged, s.76(1) PACE makes the confession of one accused admissible irrespective as to whether it is relied on by the prosecution, or by another party: see *R. v Campbell and Williams* [1993] Crim. L.R. 448, and *R. v Myers (Melanie)* [1998] A.C. 124, (and see Cross and Tapper, *Evidence*, pp.612–616, 9th ed.). Where the confession of one accused is adduced by a co-accused, and not by the prosecution, it cannot be excluded under s.78 PACE. If a confession might have been obtained by oppression, or might be unreliable in consequence of anything said or done, it should be excludable under s.76(2) PACE no matter which party seeks to rely on the confession.

To put the matter beyond doubt, and to put the matter on a statutory footing, the Law Commission recommended inserting s.76A to PACE (Recommendation 19) so that rules relating to confessions are the same whether adduced by the prosecution or by a co-accused. The one significant difference is that a co-accused shoulders the civil standard proof in respect of any of the matters he is required to prove under s.76A(2) whereas the burden on the prosecution is to the criminal standard of proof in respect of the corresponding matters set out in s.76(2) PACE.

Subsection 128(2) makes it clear that nothing in Ch.2 to Pt 11 of the 2003 Act makes a confession by a defendant admissible if it would be inadmissible under s.76 PACE. Thus, a confession of one other person charged with the offence would not be admissible under ss.116 or 117 if it would not be admissible under s.76 PACE. The embargo imposed by s.76A(2) seems a wide enough to exclude the application of the "safety valve" discretion that appears in s.114 of the 2003 Act.

Note that s.76A PACE is limited to statements by "an accused person". Section 128 of the 2003 Act makes no further provision for the use by an accused of a confession made by a third party who is neither before a court nor charged with the offence in question. This is because it was unnecessary for Parliament to do so. The accused has the option of calling the third party, or (if he/she is unavailable) to invoke s.116 or s.117 of the 2003 Act. Confessions of a third party admitted under those provisions would be automatically admissible provided oral testimony by the maker of the confession statement would be admissible.

129 Representations other than by a person

(1) Where a representation of any fact—
  (a) is made otherwise than by a person, but
  (b) depends for its accuracy on information supplied (directly or indirectly) by a person,
    the representation is not admissible in criminal proceedings as evidence of the fact unless it is proved that the information was accurate.
(2) Subsection (1) does not affect the operation of the presumption that a mechanical device has been properly set or calibrated.

GENERAL NOTE

This section should be read together with s.115.

Section 69 PACE has been repealed, and see the Law Commission Report No.245, Ch.13.

However, representations made by machines give rise to special problems as the process by which representations are made often require no human cerebral assistance for example a photograph, a tape recording, measurement printout: *Castle v Cross* [1984] 1 W.L.R. 1372; *R. v Wood (Stanley William)* [1983] 76 Cr. App. R. 23. Other results depend on information being "implanted" into the machine by a person so that if the information is not separately proved, the representations made by machine will be hearsay. The Law Commission regarded the distinction as "are well founded" (Report No.245, para.7.48) but if the data implanted is not proved to be accurate then it has no probative value at all, and the question of hearsay does not arise. It therefore recommended that the representation of any fact made otherwise than by a person, but depends for its accuracy on information supplied by a person, it should not be admissible as evidence of the fact unless proved to be accurate (recommendation 3; Report No.245, para.7.50). Section 129 therefore gives statutory effect to that recommendation (see Colin Tapper *"Hearsay in Criminal Cases: An Overview of Law Commission Report No. 245"* [1997] Crim. L.R. 784)

130   Depositions

In Schedule 3 to the Crime and Disorder Act 1998 (c. 37), sub-paragraph (4) of paragraph 5 is omitted (power of the court to overrule an objection to a deposition being read as evidence by virtue of that paragraph).

131   Evidence at retrial

For paragraphs 1 and 1A of Schedule 2 to the Criminal Appeal Act 1968 (c. 19) (oral evidence and use of transcripts etc at retrials under that Act) there is substituted—

"Evidence
1   (1) Evidence given at a retrial must be given orally if it was given orally at the original trial, unless—
  (a) all the parties to the retrial agree otherwise;
  (b) section 116 of the Criminal Justice Act 2003 applies (admissibility of hearsay evidence where a witness is unavailable); or
  (c) the witness is unavailable to give evidence, otherwise than as mentioned in subsection (2) of that section, and section 114(1)(d) of that Act applies (admission of hearsay evidence under residual discretion).
  (2) Paragraph 5 of Schedule 3 to the Crime and Disorder Act 1998 (use of depositions) does not apply at a retrial to a deposition read as evidence at the original trial."

General

132   Rules of court

(1) Rules of court may make such provision as appears to the appropriate authority to be necessary or expedient for the purposes of this Chapter; and the appropriate authority is the authority entitled to make the rules.
(2) The rules may make provision about the procedure to be followed and other conditions to be fulfilled by a party proposing to tender a statement in evidence under any provision of this Chapter.
(3) The rules may require a party proposing to tender the evidence to serve on each party to the proceedings such notice, and such particulars of or relating to the evidence, as may be prescribed.
(4) The rules may provide that the evidence is to be treated as admissible by agreement of the parties if—
  (a) a notice has been served in accordance with provision made under subsection (3), and

(b) no counter-notice in the prescribed form objecting to the admission of the evidence has been served by a party.
(5) If a party proposing to tender evidence fails to comply with a prescribed requirement applicable to it—
  (a) the evidence is not admissible except with the court's leave;
  (b) where leave is given the court or jury may draw such inferences from the failure as appear proper;
  (c) the failure may be taken into account by the court in considering the exercise of its powers with respect to costs.
(6) In considering whether or how to exercise any of its powers under subsection (5) the court shall have regard to whether there is any justification for the failure to comply with the requirement.
(7) A person shall not be convicted of an offence solely on an inference drawn under subsection (5)(b).
(8) Rules under this section may—
  (a) limit the application of any provision of the rules to prescribed circumstances;
  (b) subject any provision of the rules to prescribed exceptions;
  (c) make different provision for different cases or circumstances.
(9) Nothing in this section prejudices the generality of any enactment conferring power to make rules of court; and no particular provision of this section prejudices any general provision of it.
(10) In this section—
  "prescribed" means prescribed by rules of court;
  "rules of court" means—
    (a) Crown Court Rules;
    (b) Criminal Appeal Rules;
    (c) rules under section 144 of the Magistrates' Courts Act 1980 (c. 43).

133 Proof of statements in documents

Where a statement in a document is admissible as evidence in criminal proceedings, the statement may be proved by producing either—
(a) the document, or
(b) (whether or not the document exists) a copy of the document or of the material part of it,
authenticated in whatever way the court may approve.

134 Interpretation of Chapter 2

(1) In this Chapter—
  "copy", in relation to a document, means anything on to which information recorded in the document has been copied, by whatever means and whether directly or indirectly;
  "criminal proceedings" means criminal proceedings in relation to which the strict rules of evidence apply;
  "defendant", in relation to criminal proceedings, means a person charged with an offence in those proceedings;
  "document" means anything in which information of any description is recorded;
  "oral evidence" includes evidence which, by reason of any disability, disorder or other impairment, a person called as a witness gives in writing or by signs or by way of any device;
  "statutory provision" means any provision contained in, or in an instrument made under, this or any other Act, including any Act passed after this Act.
(2) Section 115 (statements and matters stated) contains other general interpretative provisions.

(3) Where a defendant is charged with two or more offences in the same criminal proceedings, this Chapter has effect as if each offence were charged in separate proceedings.

135 Armed forces

Schedule 7 (hearsay evidence: armed forces) has effect.

136 Repeals etc

In the Criminal Justice Act 1988 (c. 33), the following provisions (which are to some extent superseded by provisions of this Chapter) are repealed—

(a) Part 2 and Schedule 2 (which relate to documentary evidence);

(b) in Schedule 13, paragraphs 2 to 5 (which relate to documentary evidence in service courts etc).

CHAPTER 3

MISCELLANEOUS AND SUPPLEMENTAL

137 Evidence by video recording

(1) This section applies where—

(a) a person is called as a witness in proceedings for an offence triable only on indictment, or for a prescribed offence triable either way,

(b) the person claims to have witnessed (whether visually or in any other way)—

(i) events alleged by the prosecution to include conduct constituting the offence or part of the offence, or

(ii) events closely connected with such events,

(c) he has previously given an account of the events in question (whether in response to questions asked or otherwise),

(d) the account was given at a time when those events were fresh in the person's memory (or would have been, assuming the truth of the claim mentioned in paragraph (b)),

(e) a video recording was made of the account,

(f) the court has made a direction that the recording should be admitted as evidence in chief of the witness, and the direction has not been rescinded, and

(g) the recording is played in the proceedings in accordance with the direction.

(2) If, or to the extent that, the witness in his oral evidence in the proceedings asserts the truth of the statements made by him in the recorded account, they shall be treated as if made by him in that evidence.

(3) A direction under subsection (1)(f)—

(a) may not be made in relation to a recorded account given by the defendant;

(b) may be made only if it appears to the court that—

(i) the witness's recollection of the events in question is likely to have been significantly better when he gave the recorded account than it will be when he gives oral evidence in the proceedings, and

(ii) it is in the interests of justice for the recording to be admitted, having regard in particular to the matters mentioned in subsection (4).

(4) Those matters are—

(a) the interval between the time of the events in question and the time when the recorded account was made;

(b) any other factors that might affect the reliability of what the witness said in that account;

(c) the quality of the recording;

(d) any views of the witness as to whether his evidence in chief should be given orally or by means of the recording.

(5) For the purposes of subsection (2) it does not matter if the statements in the recorded account were not made on oath.

(6) In this section "prescribed" means of a description specified in an order made by the Secretary of State.

DEFINITIONS
"defendant": s.140
"prescribed": s.137(6)

GENERAL NOTE

The Government has said through its Permanent Under-Secretary of State for the Home Department that "video evidence is no different from any other evidence. It would be completely evident whether the witness had been led. The normal tests and safeguards would apply". It is beyond the scope of this commentary to discuss that proposition at length, but the Government clearly believes that video evidence does have several significant advantages over traditional testimony, namely that, (1) the giving of evidence is like to be less stressful for the witness, (2) the witness's recollection of events is likely to have been better when the recording was made, (3) the video recording can replace the witness's main evidence and, (4) the video serves as the transcript of the main part of the witness's evidence (Standing Committee B, col.672). This measure, in conjunction with s.139 (use of documents to refresh memory); and s.120 (other previous statements of witnesses), are all intended to help witnesses give their evidence to the best of their ability and thus provide the best evidence.

Note that s.137 applies to offences triable only on indictment, or for a "prescribed offence" triable either way (s.137(1)(a)). The provision is not limited to prosecution witnesses, but although defence witnesses may avail themselves of this facility the defendant himself cannot do so (s.137(3)(a)).

Note that the statements and representations made by the witness will be treated as made by him if, and only to the extent, that he asserts the truth of them in his oral evidence (subs.(2)). In practice, the witness will presumably be asked, in chief, to what extent the content of the recording represents the truth. For the purposes of subs.(2) it is immaterial that the recorded account was not made on oath (subs.(5)).

During the debates in Standing Committee, concern was expressed that it might be easier to "fiddle with digital evidence than with film" (col.677). This apparently, is true, but the Government says this is "incredibly difficult and enormously expensive". In any event, the witness can be asked in cross-examination about the content of the recording, and the manner it was recorded.

The effect of s.137(2) seems to be that the hearsay rule is not engaged (and a video recording is not treated as a previous out of court statement) because the content of the recording "shall be treated as if made by him in it that evidence". The effect of editing a video recording (to properly exclude prejudicial or irrelevant material), and the extent to which the witness may speak to matters dealt with in the recording, are the subject of s.138 of 2003 Act.

138   Video evidence: further provisions

(1) Where a video recording is admitted under section 137, the witness may not give evidence in chief otherwise than by means of the recording as to any matter which, in the opinion of the court, has been dealt with adequately in the recorded account.

(2) The reference in subsection (1)(f) of section 137 to the admission of a recording includes a reference to the admission of part of the recording; and references in that section and this one to the video recording or to the witness's recorded account shall, where appropriate, be read accordingly.

(3) In considering whether any part of a recording should be not admitted under section 137, the court must consider—

(a) whether admitting that part would carry a risk of prejudice to the defendant, and

(b) if so, whether the interests of justice nevertheless require it to be admitted in view of the desirability of showing the whole, or substantially the whole, of the recorded interview.

(4) A court may not make a direction under section 137(1)(f) in relation to any proceedings unless—

(a) the Secretary of State has notified the court that arrangements can be made, in the area in which it appears to the court that the proceedings will take place, for implementing directions under that section, and

(b) the notice has not been withdrawn.

(5) Nothing in section 137 affects the admissibility of any video recording which would be admissible apart from that section.

139   Use of documents to refresh memory

(1) A person giving oral evidence in criminal proceedings about any matter may, at any stage in the course of doing so, refresh his memory of it from a document made or verified by him at an earlier time if—

(a) he states in his oral evidence that the document records his recollection of the matter at that earlier time, and

(b) his recollection of the matter is likely to have been significantly better at that time than it is at the time of his oral evidence.

(2) Where—

(a) a person giving oral evidence in criminal proceedings about any matter has previously given an oral account, of which a sound recording was made, and he states in that evidence that the account represented his recollection of the matter at that time,

(b) his recollection of the matter is likely to have been significantly better at the time of the previous account than it is at the time of his oral evidence, and

(c) a transcript has been made of the sound recording,

he may, at any stage in the course of giving his evidence, refresh his memory of the matter from that transcript.

140   Interpretation of Chapter 3

In this Chapter—

"criminal proceedings" means criminal proceedings in relation to which the strict rules of evidence apply;

"defendant", in relation to criminal proceedings, means a person charged with an offence in those proceedings;

"document" means anything in which information of any description is recorded, but not including any recording of sounds or moving images;

"oral evidence" includes evidence which, by reason of any disability, disorder or other impairment, a person called as a witness gives in writing or by signs or by way of any device;

"video recording" means any recording, on any medium, from which a moving image may by any means be produced, and includes the accompanying sound-track.

141   Saving

No provision of this Part has effect in relation to criminal proceedings begun before the commencement of that provision.

PART 12

SENTENCING

CHAPTER 1

GENERAL PROVISIONS ABOUT SENTENCING

Matters to be taken into account in sentencing

142   Purposes of sentencing

(1) Any court dealing with an offender in respect of his offence must have regard to the following purposes of sentencing—

   (a) the punishment of offenders,

   (b) the reduction of crime (including its reduction by deterrence),

   (c) the reform and rehabilitation of offenders,

   (d) the protection of the public, and

   (e) the making of reparation by offenders to persons affected by their offences.

(2) Subsection (1) does not apply—

   (a) in relation to an offender who is aged under 18 at the time of conviction,

   (b) to an offence the sentence for which is fixed by law,

   (c) to an offence the sentence for which falls to be imposed under section 51A(2) of the Firearms Act 1968 (c. 27) (minimum sentence for certain firearms offences), under subsection (2) of section 110 or 111 of the Sentencing Act (required custodial sentences) or under any of sections 225 to 228 of this Act (dangerous offenders), or

   (d) in relation to the making under Part 3 of the Mental Health Act 1983 (c. 20) of a hospital order (with or without a restriction order), an interim hospital order, a hospital direction or a limitation direction.

(3) In this Chapter "sentence", in relation to an offence, includes any order made by a court when dealing with the offender in respect of his offence; and "sentencing" is to be construed accordingly.

GENERAL NOTE

Subsection (1) sets out a list of the purposes of sentencing to which a court dealing with an offender must have regard. The section does not indicate whether any purposes have priority over any other purposes. It appears that where, as will often be the case, different purposes point to different conclusions as to the appropriate sentence, the court has a free choice between those purposes.

Subsection (1) does not apply to offenders under the age of 18 at the time of conviction. Courts dealing with offenders below the age of 18 are required to have regard to the aims of the youth justice system as set out in the Crime and Disorder Act 1998, s.37. Section 37(1) provides that "it shall be the principal aim of the youth justice system to prevent offending by children and young persons". Courts dealing with offenders under the age of 18 must also still have regard to the Children and Young Persons Act 1933, s.44(1), which provides, "Every court in dealing with a child or young person who is brought before it, either as an offender or otherwise, shall have regard to the welfare of the child or young person and shall in a proper case take steps for removing him from undesirable surroundings, and for securing that proper provision is made for his education and training."

The obligation to have regard to the listed purposes of sentencing does not apply to offences where the sentence is fixed by law (at the present time, murder) and those offences or circumstances listed in subs.(2)(c) where a minimum sentence is required or the offender falls within the scope of the provisions for dangerous offenders. A court is not required to have regard to the listed purposes of sentencing when making a hospital order under the Mental Health Act 1983 (c.20).

143   Determining the seriousness of an offence

(1) In considering the seriousness of any offence, the court must consider the offender's culpability in committing the offence and any harm which the offence caused, was intended to cause or might forseeably have caused.

(2) In considering the seriousness of an offence ("the current offence") committed by an offender who has one or more previous convictions, the court must treat each previous conviction as an aggravating factor if (in the case of that conviction) the court considers that it can reasonably be so treated having regard, in particular, to—

    (a) the nature of the offence to which the conviction relates and its relevance to the current offence, and

    (b) the time that has elapsed since the conviction.

(3) In considering the seriousness of any offence committed while the offender was on bail, the court must treat the fact that it was committed in those circumstances as an aggravating factor.

(4) Any reference in subsection (2) to a previous conviction is to be read as a reference to—

    (a) a previous conviction by a court in the United Kingdom, or

    (b) a previous finding of guilt in service disciplinary proceedings.

(5) Subsections (2) and (4) do not prevent the court from treating a previous conviction by a court outside the United Kingdom as an aggravating factor in any case where the court considers it appropriate to do so.

General Note

This section sets out a number of matters which must be considered by a court considering the seriousness of an offence.

Subsection (1) may be considered to be a statement of the obvious.

Subsection (2) replaces s.151(1) of the Powers of Criminal Courts (Sentencing) Act 2000 which provides "In considering the seriousness of any offence, the court may take into account any previous convictions of the offender or any failure of his to respond to previous sentences." Unlike s.151(1), this subsection is mandatory, although subject to a broad discretionary qualification; a court is obliged to treat a previous conviction as an aggravating factor only if it considers "that it can reasonably be so treated" having regard to the nature of the previous offence, its relevance to the latest offence, and the time that has elapsed since the conviction. If the court considers that the previous conviction cannot reasonably be treated as an aggravating factor, it may refrain from so treating it.

"Previous conviction" is defined by subs.(4). This definition appears to exclude those convictions which are deemed not to be convictions by provisions dealing with discharges and probation orders. Under the Powers of Criminal Courts (Sentencing) Act 2000, s.14(1) a conviction which results in a discharge is deemed not to be a conviction, subject to the qualifications set out in subss.(2) and (3). A conviction before October 1, 1992 which led to a probation order, is also deemed not to have been a conviction (see the Powers of Criminal Courts Act 1973 (c.62), s.13). Such convictions do not fall within the scope of subs.(2), but the court appears to retain a general discretion to take them into account. Convictions by courts outside the United Kingdom are excluded from the operation of subs.(2), but the court may take them into account and treat them as aggravating factors if it considers it appropriate to do so (subs.(5)).

Subsection (3) reproduces the Powers of Criminal Courts (Sentencing) Act, s.151(2) but substitutes the word "must" for "shall" in that section.

144 Reduction in sentences for guilty pleas

(1) In determining what sentence to pass on an offender who has pleaded guilty to an offence in proceedings before that or another court, a court must take into account—

    (a) the stage in the proceedings for the offence at which the offender indicated his intention to plead guilty, and

    (b) the circumstances in which this indication was given.

(2) In the case of an offence the sentence for which falls to be imposed under subsection (2) of section 110 or 111 of the Sentencing Act, nothing in that subsection prevents the court, after taking into account any matter referred to in subsection (1) of this section, from imposing any sentence which is not less than 80 per cent of that specified in that subsection.

DEFINITIONS
"Sentencing": s.142(3)

GENERAL NOTE
This section substantially reproduces s.152 of the Powers of Criminal Courts (Sentencing) Act 2000, with minor changes in wording (substitution of "must" for "shall" in subs.(1) and "prevents" for "shall prevent" in subs.(2)).

It has been for many years the practice of the criminal courts to impose a lesser sentence on a defendant who has pleaded guilty than would have been imposed if he had been convicted of the same offences after a trial. This practice has been endorsed in numerous decisions of the Court of Appeal Criminal Division. Section 144 does not provide a statutory basis for this long established practice. The purpose of the section is to require the court to "take into account" the stage in the proceedings for the offence at which the offender indicated his intention to plead guilty and the circumstances in which the indication was given. The section does not in terms require the offender to be given credit for his plea (see *R. v Hussain (Altaf)* [2002] 2 Cr. App. R. (S.) 59 (at p.255)).

The purpose of the section as originally enacted was to encourage defendants to indicate their intention to plead guilty at an early stage of the proceedings, but the section is not limited to cases where the intention to plead guilty is indicated at an early stage. If the intention to plead guilty is indicated at a very late stage in the proceedings, perhaps after the trial has begun, the court must still take it into account and may give such credit as is appropriate. If the court imposes a punishment which is less severe than would otherwise have been imposed, as a result of taking into account the stage of the proceedings at which the offender indicated the intention to plead guilty and the circumstances in which the indication was given, it must state in open court that it has done so. The court is not required to state precisely what punishment would otherwise have been imposed, and what discount has been allowed in respect of the indication of the intention to plead guilty.

Subsection (3) deals with a case where the sentence falls to be imposed under the Powers of Criminal Courts (Sentencing) Act 2000, s.110 or s.111. Section 110 requires a court to impose a sentence of seven years on a person convicted on the third occasion of a class A drug dealing offence, and s.111 requires a court to impose a sentence of three years on an offender convicted on the third occasion of residential burglary. Where the offender has pleaded guilty, the court may take into account the stage in the proceedings at which he indicated the intention to plead guilty and the circumstances in which it was given; if it does so, it may impose a sentence which is not less than 80 per cent of the sentence which it would otherwise have been required to impose.

145 Increase in sentences for racial or religious aggravation

(1) This section applies where a court is considering the seriousness of an offence other than one under sections 29 to 32 of the Crime and Disorder Act 1998 (c. 37) (racially or religiously aggravated assaults, criminal damage, public order offences and harassment etc).

(2) If the offence was racially or religiously aggravated, the court—

(a) must treat that fact as an aggravating factor, and
(b) must state in open court that the offence was so aggravated.
(3) Section 28 of the Crime and Disorder Act 1998 (meaning of "racially or religiously aggravated") applies for the purposes of this section as it applies for the purposes of sections 29 to 32 of that Act.

DEFINITIONS
"Racially or religiously aggravated": s.28 of the Crime and Disorder Act 1998.

GENERAL NOTE
This section reproduces the Powers of Criminal Courts (Sentencing) Act 2000, s.153, (as amended by the Anti-terrorism, Crime and Security Act 2001 (c.24), s.39) with minor changes of wording (substitution of "must" for "shall" in subss.(2)(a) and (2)(B)).

This section applies to offences other than the racially aggravated offences created by ss.29 to 32 of the Crime and Disorder Act 1998. The section requires the court to treat the fact the offence was "racially or religiously aggravated" (as that expression is defined in s.28 of the Crime and Disorder Act 1998) as an aggravating factor of the offence. The sentencer is required to state in open court that the offence was so aggravated. It is not necessary for the sentencer to state how the fact that the offence was racially or religiously aggravated has affected the sentence. The fact that the offence was racially or religiously aggravated becomes one of the factors which the court has to consider in determining what sentence to pass in the particular case. It does not require the court to pass any particular form of sentence.

Section 153 lays down no procedure by which the question whether the offence was racially or religiously aggravated is to be determined. The section simply states that the fact that offence was racially or religiously aggravated must be treated as an aggravating factor. The section does not create distinct offences, and it is not necessary to include the allegation of racial or religious aggravation in the information or indictment (as it is in the case of an offence against ss.29–32 of the Crime and Disorder Act 1998).

146   Increase in sentences for aggravation related to disability or sexual orientation

(1) This section applies where the court is considering the seriousness of an offence committed in any of the circumstances mentioned in subsection (2).
(2) Those circumstances are—
(a) that, at the time of committing the offence, or immediately before or after doing so, the offender demonstrated towards the victim of the offence hostility based on—
(i) the sexual orientation (or presumed sexual orientation) of the victim, or
(ii) a disability (or presumed disability) of the victim, or
(b) that the offence is motivated (wholly or partly)—
(i) by hostility towards persons who are of a particular sexual orientation, or
(ii) by hostility towards persons who have a disability or a particular disability.
(3) The court—
(a) must treat the fact that the offence was committed in any of those circumstances as an aggravating factor, and
(b) must state in open court that the offence was committed in such circumstances.
(4) It is immaterial for the purposes of paragraph (a) or (b) of subsection (2) whether or not the offender's hostility is also based, to any extent, on any other factor not mentioned in that paragraph.
(5) In this section "disability" means any physical or mental impairment.

GENERAL NOTE
This section, which is new, requires a court to treat as an aggravating factor the fact that at the time of committing the offence, or immediately before or after committing the offence, the offender demonstrated hostility to the victim based on the victim's sexual orientation or

presumed sexual orientation, or disability or presumed disability, or the offence was motivated by hostility to persons who have a particular sexual orientation or disability. As in the case of racially or religiously aggravated crimes, the court must state in open court that the offence was so aggravated.

As in the case of s.145, no procedure is provided by which the question whether the offence was aggravated is to be determined. The section does not create distinct offences, and it is not necessary to include the allegation of aggravation in the information or indictment.

General restrictions on community sentences

147   Meaning of "community sentence" etc

(1) In this Part "community sentence" means a sentence which consists of or includes—

   (a) a community order (as defined by section 177), or

   (b) one or more youth community orders.

(2) In this Chapter "youth community order" means—

   (a) a curfew order as defined by section 163 of the Sentencing Act,

   (b) an exclusion order under section 40A(1) of that Act,

   (c) an attendance centre order as defined by section 163 of that Act,

   (d) a supervision order under section 63(1) of that Act, or

   (e) an action plan order under section 69(1) of that Act.

GENERAL NOTE

This section provides a definition of "community sentence" for the purposes of Pt 12 of the Act. It replaces the Powers of Criminal Courts (Sentencing) Act 2000, s.33, and reflects the new scheme of community sentences established by Ch.4 of Pt 12 of the Act, under which different forms of community orders are brought together as "community orders".

148   Restrictions on imposing community sentences

(1) A court must not pass a community sentence on an offender unless it is of the opinion that the offence, or the combination of the offence and one or more offences associated with it, was serious enough to warrant such a sentence.

(2) Where a court passes a community sentence which consists of or includes a community order—

   (a) the particular requirement or requirements forming part of the community order must be such as, in the opinion of the court, is, or taken together are, the most suitable for the offender, and

   (b) the restrictions on liberty imposed by the order must be such as in the opinion of the court are commensurate with the seriousness of the offence, or the combination of the offence and one or more offences associated with it.

(3) Where a court passes a community sentence which consists of or includes one or more youth community orders—

   (a) the particular order or orders forming part of the sentence must be such as, in the opinion of the court, is, or taken together are, the most suitable for the offender, and

   (b) the restrictions on liberty imposed by the order or orders must be such as in the opinion of the court are commensurate with the seriousness of the offence, or the combination of the offence and one or more offences associated with it.

(4) Subsections (1) and (2)(b) have effect subject to section 151(2).

DEFINITIONS

"Community sentence": s.147(1)

"Youth community order": s.147(2)

"Community order": s.177

GENERAL NOTE

This section substantially reproduces the Powers of Criminal Courts (Sentencing) Act 2000, s.35, with modifications appropriate to be new scheme of community orders established by the Act, and other minor verbal modifications.

This section lays down three criteria which must be satisfied before a court may pass a community order or youth community order as defined in s.147(2). The offence or the combination of the offence and one or more offences associated with the offence must be "serious enough to warrant such a sentence"; the particular community order or combination of community orders must be "the most suitable for the offender"; and the restrictions on liberty imposed by the order or orders must be "commensurate with the seriousness of the offence" or the combination of offences for which the sentence is imposed. In considering the seriousness of an offence or combination of offences, the court must have regard to the matters mentioned in s.143 (previous convictions and offending while on bail), s.144 (guilty plea), s.145 (racial or religious aggravation), and s.146 (aggravation based on victim's sexual orientation or disability).

149 Passing of community sentence on offender remanded in custody

(1) In determining the restrictions on liberty to be imposed by a community order or youth community order in respect of an offence, the court may have regard to any period for which the offender has been remanded in custody in connection with the offence or any other offence the charge for which was founded on the same facts or evidence.

(2) In subsection (1) "remanded in custody" has the meaning given by section 242(2).

DEFINITIONS

"Community order": s.177
"Youth community order": s.147(2)
"Remanded in custody": s.242(2)

GENERAL NOTE

This section, which is new, allows a court making a community order or youth community order to take into account the fact that the offender has been remanded in custody in the proceedings which have led to the making of the order. The section does not oblige the courts to take the time spent in custody on remand into account.

It has generally been the practice of the courts when imposing a custodial sentence following the revocation of a community order to take into account at that stage the fact that the defendant has spent custody time in custody on remand before the order was made (see *R. v Armstrong (Christopher Andrew)* [2002] 2 Cr. App. R. (S.) 87 (at p.396)). Such time in most cases did not count automatically against the sentence imposed, by virtue of the Criminal Justice Act 1967, s.67. This section does not have any apparent effect on that practice. It is in any event enacted in the context of the scheme for the treatment of time spent in custody on remand established by ss.240–242 of this Act.

150 Community sentence not available where sentence fixed by law etc.

The power to make a community order or youth community order is not exercisable in respect of an offence for which the sentence—
(a) is fixed by law,
(b) falls to be imposed under section 51A(2) of the Firearms Act 1968 (c. 27) (required custodial sentence for certain firearms offences),
(c) falls to be imposed under section 110(2) or 111(2) of the Sentencing Act (requirement to impose custodial sentences for certain repeated offences committed by offenders aged 18 or over), or
(d) falls to be imposed under any of sections 225 to 228 of this Act (requirement to impose custodial sentences for certain offences committed by offenders posing risk to public).

DEFINITIONS
"Community order": s.177
"Youth community order": s.147(2)
"Sentence": s.142(3)

GENERAL NOTE
This section excludes the power to make a community order or youth community order where the court is required by other provisions to impose a custodial sentence. The section as enacted assumes the repeal of the Powers of Criminal Courts (Sentencing) Act 2000, s.109, by s.303(d)(iv) of the 2003 Act and its replacement by the sentences of life imprisonment or imprisonment for public protection provided by ss.225–228 of this Act.

151   Community order for persistent offender previously fined

(1) Subsection (2) applies where—
   (a) a person aged 16 or over is convicted of an offence ("the current offence"),
   (b) on three or more previous occasions he has, on conviction by a court in the United Kingdom of any offence committed by him after attaining the age of 16, had passed on him a sentence consisting only of a fine, and
   (c) despite the effect of section 143(2), the court would not (apart from this section) regard the current offence, or the combination of the current offence and one or more offences associated with it, as being serious enough to warrant a community sentence.

(2) The court may make a community order in respect of the current offence instead of imposing a fine if it considers that, having regard to all the circumstances including the matters mentioned in subsection (3), it would be in the interests of justice to make such an order.

(3) The matters referred to in subsection (2) are—
   (a) the nature of the offences to which the previous convictions mentioned in subsection (1)(b) relate and their relevance to the current offence, and
   (b) the time that has elapsed since the offender's conviction of each of those offences.

(4) In subsection (1)(b), the reference to conviction by a court in the United Kingdom includes a reference to the finding of guilt in service disciplinary proceedings; and, in relation to any such finding of guilt, the reference to the sentence passed is a reference to the punishment awarded.

(5) For the purposes of subsection (1)(b), a compensation order does not form part of an offender's sentence.

(6) For the purposes of subsection (1)(b), it is immaterial whether on other previous occasions a court has passed on the offender a sentence not consisting only of a fine.

(7) This section does not limit the extent to which a court may, in accordance with section 143(2), treat any previous convictions of the offender as increasing the seriousness of an offence.

DEFINITIONS
"Sentence": s.142(3)

GENERAL NOTE
This section appears to be derived from the Powers of Criminal Courts (Sentencing) Act 2000, s.59, but with significant differences. Its main effect is to permit a court to impose a community sentence for an offence which would not normally be considered "serious enough" to warrant a community sentence (as required by s.148(1)) if the offender has a history of previous offences for which he has been fined. The most significant difference between this section and s.59, is that s.59 applied only if one or more of the fines had not been paid, and the offender's means would not be sufficient to pay a fine commensurate with the seriousness of the offence. This section is not concerned with the means of the offender; the power to make a

community order instead of imposing a fine may be exercised where all the previous fines have been paid. It appears to be aimed at an offender who is able to pay fines, and continues to offend in the knowledge that he can afford to do so. This is reflected in the requirement of subs.(1)(b) that the offender has on three previous occasions been dealt with by a sentence "consisting only of a fine" (or a fine and a compensation order, see subs.(5)). If these conditions are satisfied, the court may impose a community order instead of a fine if it concludes that it would be in the interests of justice to do so.

Subsection (1)(b) may lead to difficulties in some cases. The basic condition for the operation of section is that the offender should have had been sentenced to a sentence "consisting only of a fine" on the three or more previous applications. It is immaterial that on other occasions he has had other sentences, including presumably a custodial sentence or community order (see subs.(6)). A compensation order is to be disregarded when considering whether the previous sentences consisted only of a fine. In many cases to which the section might apply, the defendant may have been dealt with by a combination of a fine and other sentences, in particular disqualification from driving. It seems clear that if the defendant has previously been sentenced to a fine together with a period of disqualification from driving, the power to make an order under this section does not apply. This difficulty may be overcome by reliance on subs.(7), which allows the court to treat any previous convictions of the offender, whatever sentence was imposed, as increasing the seriousness of the offence, and thereby make a finding that the repetition of the offence makes the latest offence "serious enough" to warrant a community sentence. This prompts the question whether this section was necessarily at all. It also makes clear that a court imposing a community sentence for an offence which at first glance does not appear "serious enough" to warrant a community sentence should explain carefully whether it is exercising the power provided by this section or simply relying on the provisions of s.143 to assess the seriousness of the offence.

General restrictions on discretionary custodial sentences

152   General restrictions on imposing discretionary custodial sentences

(1) This section applies where a person is convicted of an offence punishable with a custodial sentence other than one—

   (a) fixed by law, or

   (b) falling to be imposed under section 51A(2) of the Firearms Act 1968 (c. 27), under 110(2) or 111(2) of the Sentencing Act or under any of sections 225 to 228 of this Act.

(2) The court must not pass a custodial sentence unless it is of the opinion that the offence, or the combination of the offence and one or more offences associated with it, was so serious that neither a fine alone nor a community sentence can be justified for the offence.

(3) Nothing in subsection (2) prevents the court from passing a custodial sentence on the offender if—

   (a) he fails to express his willingness to comply with a requirement which is proposed by the court to be included in a community order and which requires an expression of such willingness, or

   (b) he fails to comply with an order under section 161(2) (pre-sentence drug testing).

DEFINITIONS

   "Sentence": s.142(3)

   "Associated": Powers of Criminal Courts (Sentencing) Act 2000, s.161(1) (Note that this section is not repealed by this Act, but that the opening words of the section, which restrict the operation of the definition to "this Act" (the Powers of Criminal Courts (Sentencing) Act 2000) do not appear to have been amended.

GENERAL NOTE

   This section substantially reproduces the s.79 of the Powers of Criminal Courts (Sentencing) Act 2000 with minor modifications. It establishes the basic criterion for the imposition of a custodial sentence. The court must not pass a custodial sentence unless it is of the opinion that the offence or the combination of the offence and one or more offences associated with it was so serious that neither a fine alone nor a community sentence can be justified for the offence. The section reproduces the effect of s.79(3), permitting a custodial sentence for an offence which is not "so serious" if the offender fails to express his willingness to comply with a requirement of a community sentence, or fails to comply with an order for presentence drug testing. The section does not reproduce the Powers of Criminal Courts (Sentencing) Act 2000, s.79(2)(b), which allows a court to impose a custodial sentence for a sexual or violent offence if only such a sentence would be adequate to protect the public from serious harm from the offender. This provision is rendered obsolete by the new scheme for the sentencing of dangerous offenders provided in Ch.5 of this Part.

The section does not apply where the court is obliged to impose a custodial sentence by any of the provisions mentioned in subs.(1).

153   Length of discretionary custodial sentences: general provision

(1) This section applies where a court passes a custodial sentence other than one fixed by law or falling to be imposed under section 225 or 226.

(2) Subject to section 51A(2) of the Firearms Act 1968 (c. 27), sections 110(2) and 111(2) of the Sentencing Act and sections 227(2) and 228(2) of this Act, the custodial sentence must be for the shortest term (not exceeding the permitted maximum) that in the opinion of the court is commensurate with the seriousness of the offence, or the combination of the offence and one or more offences associated with it.

DEFINITIONS
"Sentence": s.142(3)
"Associated": Powers of Criminal Courts (Sentencing) Act 2000, s.161(1) (Note that this section is not repealed by this Act, but that the opening words of the section, which restrict the operation of the definition to "this Act" (the Powers of Criminal Courts (Sentencing) Act 2000) do not appear to have been amended.

GENERAL NOTE
This section substantially reproduces the effect of the Powers of Criminal Courts (Sentencing) Act 2000 s.80(2)(a), with some modifications. The general principle by reference to which the length of a custodial sentence is to be determined is expressed in subs.(2): the custodial sentence must be for the shortest term (not exceeding the permitted maximum) that in the opinion of the court is commensurate with the seriousness of the offence or the combination of the offence and the associated offences. By contrast, s.80 of the Powers of Criminal Courts (Sentencing) Act 2000 required that the sentence should be for "for such term" as in the opinion of the court was commensurate with the seriousness of the offence or offences.

The section does not reproduce the Powers of Criminal Courts (Sentencing) Act 2000, s.80(2)(b) (longer than commensurate sentences) which is replaced by the new provisions for dangerous offenders in ss.225–228. The section does not apply where the court is required by any of the statutory provisions mentioned in subs.(2) to impose a minimum sentence, or where the sentence is fixed by law.

General limit on magistrates' court's power to impose imprisonment

154   General limit on magistrates' court's power to impose imprisonment

(1) A magistrates' court does not have power to impose imprisonment for more than 12 months in respect of any one offence.

(2) Unless expressly excluded, subsection (1) applies even if the offence in question is one for which a person would otherwise be liable on summary conviction to imprisonment for more than 12 months.

(3) Subsection (1) is without prejudice to section 133 of the Magistrates' Courts Act 1980 (c. 43) (consecutive terms of imprisonment).

(4) Any power of a magistrates' court to impose a term of imprisonment for non-payment of a fine, or for want of sufficient distress to satisfy a fine, is not limited by virtue of subsection (1).

(5) In subsection (4) "fine" includes a pecuniary penalty but does not include a pecuniary forfeiture or pecuniary compensation.

(6) In this section "impose imprisonment" means pass a sentence of imprisonment or fix a term of imprisonment for failure to pay any sum

of money, or for want of sufficient distress to satisfy any sum of money, or for failure to do or abstain from doing anything required to be done or left undone.

(7) Section 132 of the Magistrates' Courts Act 1980 contains provisions about the minimum term of imprisonment which may be imposed by a magistrates' court.

DEFINITIONS

"Sentence": s.142(3)

GENERAL NOTE

This section substantially reproduces the Powers of Criminal Courts (Sentencing) Act 2000, s.78, with the substitution of "twelve months" for "six months" in subs.(1). It is unfortunate that it is not possible to make much sense of the section without reference to provisions of the Magistrates' Courts Act 1980.

Subsection (1) does not empower a magistrates' court to impose a sentence for any offence, it simply restricts the power to award imprisonment for any offence which a magistrates' court is capable of dealing with to a maximum of twelve months. If there existed a provision under which a magistrates' court was empowered to award a sentence in excess of twelve months for a single offence, this section would restrict that power. It does not appear that there is any such section. The power to award imprisonment on summary conviction for an either way offence is conferred on magistrates' courts by the Magistrates' Courts Act 1980, s.32(1). This section provides "On summary conviction of any of the offences triable either way listed in Sch.1 to the 2003 Act a person shall be liable to imprisonment for a term not exceeding six months." Section 154 is amended by s.282 of this Act so as to permit a sentence not exceeding twelve months. The amendment does not apply to any offence committed before the commencement of s.282.

The maximum term of imprisonment for any summary offence is that fixed by the statute creating the offence. The maximum terms of imprisonment for a large number of summary offences are increased by Sch.26 to 51 weeks.

155   Consecutive terms of imprisonment

(1) Section 133 of the Magistrates' Courts Act 1980 (consecutive terms of imprisonment) is amended as follows.

(2) In subsection (1), for "6 months" there is substituted "65 weeks".

(3) Subsection (2) is omitted.

(4) In subsection (3) for "the preceding subsections" there is substituted "subsection (1) above".

GENERAL NOTE

This section amends the Magistrates' Courts Act 1980, s.133 which restricts the powers of a magistrates' court to impose consecutive sentences. Section 133(1) provides that where a magistrates' court imposes two or more terms of imprisonment to run consecutively, the aggregate of such terms shall not exceed six months. This subsection applied in practice to cases where the offences concerned were summary offences, although there was no express limitation to this effect. Subsection (2) of this Act substitutes "65 weeks" for "six months," and thus allows consecutive terms amounting in aggregate to 65 weeks, whether the offences are summary or either way or a combination of both. Section 133(2) of the Magistrates' Courts Act 1980 provided for consecutive sentences for either way offences. It enabled magistrates' courts dealing with an offender for two or more either way offences to impose consecutive term with an aggregate of twelve months. As s.133(1) as amended now makes provision for this case, s.133(2) is redundant.

Procedural requirements for imposing community sentences and discretionary custodial sentences

156   Pre-sentence reports and other requirements

(1) In forming any such opinion as is mentioned in section 148(1), (2)(b) or (3)(b), section 152(2) or section 153(2), a court must take into account all such information as is available to it about the circumstances of the offence or (as the case may be) of the offence and the offence or offences associated with it, including any aggravating or mitigating factors.

(2) In forming any such opinion as is mentioned in section 148(2)(a) or (3)(a), the court may take into account any information about the offender which is before it.

(3) Subject to subsection (4), a court must obtain and consider a pre-sentence report before—

    (a) in the case of a custodial sentence, forming any such opinion as is mentioned in section 152(2), section 153(2), section 225(1)(b), section 226(1)(b), section 227(1)(b) or section 228(1)(b)(i), or

    (b) in the case of a community sentence, forming any such opinion as is mentioned in section 148(1), (2)(b) or (3)(b) or any opinion as to the suitability for the offender of the particular requirement or requirements to be imposed by the community order.

(4) Subsection (3) does not apply if, in the circumstances of the case, the court is of the opinion that it is unnecessary to obtain a pre-sentence report.

(5) In a case where the offender is aged under 18, the court must not form the opinion mentioned in subsection (4) unless—

    (a) there exists a previous pre-sentence report obtained in respect of the offender, and

    (b) the court has had regard to the information contained in that report, or, if there is more than one such report, the most recent report.

(6) No custodial sentence or community sentence is invalidated by the failure of a court to obtain and consider a pre-sentence report before forming an opinion referred to in subsection (3), but any court on an appeal against such a sentence—

    (a) must, subject to subsection (7), obtain a pre-sentence report if none was obtained by the court below, and

    (b) must consider any such report obtained by it or by that court.

(7) Subsection (6)(a) does not apply if the court is of the opinion—

    (a) that the court below was justified in forming an opinion that it was unnecessary to obtain a pre-sentence report, or

    (b) that, although the court below was not justified in forming that opinion, in the circumstances of the case at the time it is before the court, it is unnecessary to obtain a pre-sentence report.

(8) In a case where the offender is aged under 18, the court must not form the opinion mentioned in subsection (7) unless—

    (a) there exists a previous pre-sentence report obtained in respect of the offender, and

    (b) the court has had regard to the information contained in that report, or, if there is more than one such report, the most recent report.

DEFINITIONS

"Pre sentence report": s.158

"Sentence": s.142(3)

"Community sentence": s.147

GENERAL NOTE

This section reproduces the combined effect of the Powers of Criminal Courts (Sentencing) Act 2000, s.81 (custodial sentences) and s.36 (community sentences), modified to take account of the provisions of this Act.

Subsection (1) requires the court to take account of all available information about the circumstances of the offence when forming an opinion about the seriousness of the offence for the purpose of deciding whether the offence was "serious enough" to warrant a community order or youth community order, what restrictions on liberty are commensurate with the seriousness of the offence, whether an offence is so serious that a custodial sentence is necessary and what is the shortest term which is commensurate with the seriousness of the offence. By implication, when considering these questions the court is not entitled to have regard to information about the offender, except to the extent that such information relates to "aggravating or mitigating factors". This expression must include the offender's previous convictions, by virtue of s.143.

Subsection (2) permits information about the offender to be taken into account when a court is considering whether the requirements of a community order or youth community order are "the most suitable for the offender".

The remainder of the section deals with cases where a court is required to obtain a pre-sentence report before proceeding to a particular form of sentence. This part of the section reproduces the practical effect of ss.36 and 81 of the Powers of Criminal Courts (Sentencing) Act 2000 in this respect, with modifications required by the provisions of this Act. If a court proposes to impose a custodial sentence on any ground other than the failure of an offender to express his willingness to comply with one of the orders mentioned in s.152(3) it must "obtain and consider" a pre-sentence report unless it is of the opinion "that it is unnecessary" to do so. What appears to be a mandatory obligation in subs.(1) is negated by subs.(2), which gives the court a general discretion to proceed without a pre-sentence report if it chooses to do so.

In the case of a community sentence, a pre-sentence report is effectively mandatory in all cases, except where the court considers that it is unnecessary to obtain one.

In the case of an offender under the age of 18, a pre-sentence report is mandatory before the court imposes a custodial sentence (other than on the basis of a failure to express willingness under s.152(3)) or a youth community order unless there is an earlier pre-sentence report which the court considers. The exception in the Powers of Criminal Courts Act 1973, s.81 for cases where one of the offences for which the offender is to be sentenced is triable only on indictment is not repeated in this provision.

Subsections (6)–(8) deal with the consequences of a failure to obtain and consider a pre-sentence report, where one is required by this section. The failure does not affect the validity of the sentence or order of the court, but any appellate court dealing with the case is placed under similar obligations, subject to the same exceptions.

157   Additional requirements in case of mentally disordered offender

(1) Subject to subsection (2), in any case where the offender is or appears to be mentally disordered, the court must obtain and consider a medical report before passing a custodial sentence other than one fixed by law.

(2) Subsection (1) does not apply if, in the circumstances of the case, the court is of the opinion that it is unnecessary to obtain a medical report.

(3) Before passing a custodial sentence other than one fixed by law on an offender who is or appears to be mentally disordered, a court must consider—

    (a) any information before it which relates to his mental condition (whether given in a medical report, a pre-sentence report or otherwise), and

    (b) the likely effect of such a sentence on that condition and on any treatment which may be available for it.

(4) No custodial sentence which is passed in a case to which subsection (1) applies is invalidated by the failure of a court to comply with that subsection, but any court on an appeal against such a sentence—

    (a) must obtain a medical report if none was obtained by the court below, and

    (b) must consider any such report obtained by it or by that court.

(5) In this section "mentally disordered", in relation to any person, means suffering from a mental disorder within the meaning of the Mental Health Act 1983 (c. 20).

(6) In this section "medical report" means a report as to an offender's mental condition made or submitted orally or in writing by a registered medical practitioner who is approved for the purposes of section 12 of the Mental Health Act 1983 by the Secretary of State as

having special experience in the diagnosis or treatment of mental disorder.

(7) Nothing in this section is to be taken to limit the generality of section 156.

GENERAL NOTE

This section reproduces the Powers of Criminal Courts (Sentencing) Act 2000 s.82, with the deletion of references to s.109 of that Act (which is repealed by s.303(d)(iv) of the 2003 Act).

This section imposes a requirement on a court which proposes to pass a custodial sentence (other than a sentence fixed by law) on an offender who is or appears to be mentally disordered, to obtain and consider a medical report before doing so. The section applies to an offender who is liable to a prescribed minimum sentence under the Powers of Criminal Courts (Sentencing) Act 2000 ss.110 or 111, or the Firearms Act 1968 (c.27), s.51A. The requirement to obtain a medical report does not apply if the court considers it unnecessary to obtain a medical report. Subsection (3) imposes on the court a general requirement to consider information about the offender's mental condition, from whatever source, and the likely effect of the sentence on that condition and its treatment.

Subsection (4) provides for the consequences of a failure to obtain a medical report when one is required by subs.(1). Failure to obtain a report does not invalidate the custodial sentence, but any court dealing with an appeal against the sentence must obtain and consider a medical report. The duty of the appellate court is not subject to the qualification (as is the corresponding duty to obtain a pre-sentence report under s.81) that the appellate court may dispense with the report if it considers it unnecessary to obtain one. If the trial court considered a report necessary, but did not obtain one, the appellate court must obtain such a report, even though the appellate court considers the report unnecessary; but if the trial court considered a report unnecessary, s.82(1) does not apply and there is no obligation on the appellate court to obtain and consider a report.

158   Meaning of "pre-sentence report"

(1) In this Part "pre-sentence report" means a report which—

    (a) with a view to assisting the court in determining the most suitable method of dealing with an offender, is made or submitted by an appropriate officer, and

    (b) contains information as to such matters, presented in such manner, as may be prescribed by rules made by the Secretary of State.

(2) In subsection (1) "an appropriate officer" means—

    (a) where the offender is aged 18 or over, an officer of a local probation board, and

    (b) where the offender is aged under 18, an officer of a local probation board, a social worker of a local authority social services department or a member of a youth offending team.

GENERAL NOTE

This section reproduces the Powers of Criminal Courts (Sentencing) Act 2000, s.162, but omits the requirement in that section that the report should be in writing. The section appears to contemplate that an oral report may be sufficient to satisfy the requirements of s.156 and s.159 appears to confirm that an oral report given in open court may amount to a pre-sentence report.

Disclosure of pre-sentence reports etc

159   Disclosure of pre-sentence reports

(1) This section applies where the court obtains a pre-sentence report, other than a report given orally in open court.

(2) Subject to subsections (3) and (4), the court must give a copy of the report—

    (a) to the offender or his counsel or solicitor,

    (b) if the offender is aged under 18, to any parent or guardian of his who is present in court, and

    (c) to the prosecutor, that is to say, the person having the conduct of the proceedings in respect of the offence.

(3) If the offender is aged under 18 and it appears to the court that the disclosure to the offender or to any parent or guardian of his of any information contained in the report would be likely to create a risk of significant harm to the offender, a complete copy of the report need not be given to the offender or, as the case may be, to that parent or guardian.

(4) If the prosecutor is not of a description prescribed by order made by the Secretary of State, a copy of the report need not be given to the prosecutor if the court considers that it would be inappropriate for him to be given it.

(5) No information obtained by virtue of subsection (2)(c) may be used or disclosed otherwise than for the purpose of—

    (a) determining whether representations as to matters contained in the report need to be made to the court, or

    (b) making such representations to the court.

(6) In relation to an offender aged under 18 for whom a local authority have parental responsibility and who—

    (a) is in their care, or

    (b) is provided with accommodation by them in the exercise of any social services functions,

    references in this section to his parent or guardian are to be read as references to that authority.

(7) In this section and section 160—

    "harm" has the same meaning as in section 31 of the Children Act 1989 (c. 41);

    "local authority" and "parental responsibility" have the same meanings as in that Act;

    "social services functions", in relation to a local authority, has the meaning given by section 1A of the Local Authority Social Services Act 1970 (c. 42).

GENERAL NOTE

This section substantially reproduces the effect of the Powers of Criminal Courts (Sentencing) Act 2000 s.156, but with important modifications. In the case of an offender under the age of 18 who is represented by counsel or solicitor, the court must give a copy of the report to any parent or guardian of the offender who is present in court, even though a copy has been given to the offender or his counsel or solicitor. Under s.156(3), a copy was required to be given to the parent or guardian only if the young offender was not represented. This obligation is subject to the qualification stated in subs.(3), that if the disclosure to the offender or any parent or guardian of the information contained in the report would be likely to create a risk of significant harm to the offender a complete copy of the report need not be given to the offender or his parents or guardians. However it appears in such circumstances that a full copy of the report must be given to the offender's counsel or solicitor, who would be bound to disclose the complete contents of the report to the offender.

A copy of the report must be given to the prosecutor, provided that the prosecutor is of a description prescribed by order. (The order made in relation to the Powers of Criminal Courts (Sentencing) Act 2000 s.156, prescribes a crown prosecutor; any other person acting on behalf of the Crown Prosecution Service; or a person acting on behalf of the Commissioners of Customs and Excise, the Secretary of State for Social Security, the Commissioners of Inland Revenue or the Director of the Serious Fraud Office). If the prosecutor is not of such a description (such as a local authority or private prosecutor), a copy of the report need not be given to the prosecutor if court considers that it would be inappropriate for him to be given one.

160   Other reports of local probation boards and members of youth offending teams

(1) This section applies where—

    (a) a report by an officer of a local probation board or a member of a youth offending team is made to any court (other than a youth court) with a view to assisting the court in determining the most suitable method of dealing with any person in respect of an offence, and

(b) the report is not a pre-sentence report.

(2) Subject to subsection (3), the court must give a copy of the report—

(a) to the offender or his counsel or solicitor, and

(b) if the offender is aged under 18, to any parent or guardian of his who is present in court.

(3) If the offender is aged under 18 and it appears to the court that the disclosure to the offender or to any parent or guardian of his of any information contained in the report would be likely to create a risk of significant harm to the offender, a complete copy of the report need not be given to the offender, or as the case may be, to that parent or guardian.

(4) In relation to an offender aged under 18 for whom a local authority have parental responsibility and who—

(a) is in their care, or

(b) is provided with accommodation by them in the exercise of any social services functions,

references in this section to his parent or guardian are to be read as references to that authority.

DEFINITIONS

"Pre-sentence report": s.158

GENERAL NOTE

This section substantially reproduces the effect of the Powers of Criminal Courts (Sentencing) Act 2000 s.157, with modifications similar to those made in s.159 in relation to pre-sentence reports. The section applies to reports made to courts other than youth courts which are not "pre-sentence reports" within the meaning of s.158. The section does not apply to reports made with reference to the suitability of an offender for a particular sentence. The section does not apply to any report falling outside the scope of s.160(1) (such as a medical or psychiatric report prepared by order of the court).

Any parent or guardian of the offender who is present in court becomes entitled to be given a copy of the report, even though a copy of the report has been given to the offender or his counsel or solicitor, unless it appears to the court that the disclosure of information contained in a report to the parent or guardian would be likely to create a risk of significant harm to the offender. There is no duty on the court to provide a copy of a report to be a prosecutor.

Pre-sentence drug testing

161   Pre-sentence drug testing

(1) Where a person aged 14 or over is convicted of an offence and the court is considering passing a community sentence or a suspended sentence, it may make an order under subsection (2) for the purpose of ascertaining whether the offender has any specified Class A drug in his body.

(2) The order requires the offender to provide, in accordance with the order, samples of any description specified in the order.

(3) Where the offender has not attained the age of 17, the order must provide for the samples to be provided in the presence of an appropriate adult.

(4) If it is proved to the satisfaction of the court that the offender has, without reasonable excuse, failed to comply with the order it may impose on him a fine of an amount not exceeding level 4.

(5) In subsection (4) "level 4" means the amount which, in relation to a fine for a summary offence, is level 4 on the standard scale.

(6) The court may not make an order under subsection (2) unless it has been notified by the Secretary of State that the power to make such orders is exercisable by the court and the notice has not been withdrawn.

(7) The Secretary of State may by order amend subsection (1) by substituting for the age for the time being specified there a different age specified in the order.

(8) In this section—

"appropriate adult", in relation to a person under the age of 17, means—

(a) his parent or guardian or, if he is in the care of a local authority or voluntary organisation, a person representing that authority or organisation,

(b) a social worker of a local authority social services department, or

(c) if no person falling within paragraph (a) or (b) is available, any responsible person aged 18 or over who is not a police officer or a person employed by the police;

"specified Class A drug" has the same meaning as in Part 3 of the Criminal Justice and Court Services Act 2000 (c. 43).

DEFINITIONS

"Community sentence": s.147

"Suspended sentence": s.189(7)

"Specified class A drug": The Criminal Justice (Specified Class A Drugs) Order 2001 (SI 2001/1816)

GENERAL NOTE

This section replaces the confusing provisions of the Powers of Criminal Courts (Sentencing) Act 2000 s.36A (inserted by the Criminal Justice and Court Services Act 2000 (c.43), ss.48 and 52(4) which are repealed by the 2003 Act. The new provisions for "drug rehabilitation requirements", which replace drug treatment and testing orders, do not include a specific provision for pre-sentence drug testing such as was contained in s.52(4).

An order under this section may be made only where the court is considering passing a community sentence or suspended sentence, and for the purpose of determining whether the offender has any "specified Class A drug" in his body. "Specified Class A drug" is defined by reference to the Criminal Justice and Court Services Act 2000 Pt 3, which empowers the Secretary of State to specify Class A drugs for the purpose of the section. The drugs so specified by the Criminal Justice (Specified Class A Drugs) Order 2001 are (a) cocaine, its salts and any preparation or other product containing cocaine or its salts; and (b) diamorphine, its salts and any preparation or other product containing diamorphine or its salts. An order may not be made under this section for the purpose of ascertaining whether the offender has any other type of drug in his body, whether a Class A drug which is not a specified class A drug or any other drug such as amphetamine or cannabis.

The nature of the sample to be provided must be specified in the order.

It is not clear whether subs.(4) creates an offence, and if so, whether it is summary or either way. It appears that the court dealing with the offender for failure to comply with the order will be the court that made the original order. If the order is made by the Crown Court on conviction on indictment, as it may well be, it is uncertain what procedure should be followed in the Crown Court. Failure to comply with an order under this section may justify the imposition of a custodial sentence for the offence, even though the offence itself is not "so serious" that only a custodial sentence could be justified (see s.152(3)).

An order under this s.36A may be made only if the court has been notified that the power is exercisable by that court.

Fines

162 Powers to order statement as to offender's financial circumstances

(1) Where an individual has been convicted of an offence, the court may, before sentencing him, make a financial circumstances order with respect to him.

(2) Where a magistrates' court has been notified in accordance with section 12(4) of the Magistrates' Courts Act 1980 (c. 43) that an individual desires to plead guilty without appearing before the court, the court may make a financial circumstances order with respect to him.

(3) In this section "a financial circumstances order" means, in relation to any individual, an order requiring him to give to the court, within such period as may be specified in the order, such a statement of his financial circumstances as the court may require.

(4) An individual who without reasonable excuse fails to comply with a financial circumstances order is liable on summary conviction to a fine not exceeding level 3 on the standard scale.

(5) If an individual, in furnishing any statement in pursuance of a financial circumstances order—

(a) makes a statement which he knows to be false in a material particular,

(b) recklessly furnishes a statement which is false in a material particular, or

(c) knowingly fails to disclose any material fact,

he is liable on summary conviction to a fine not exceeding level 4 on the standard scale.

(6) Proceedings in respect of an offence under subsection (5) may, notwithstanding anything in section 127(1) of the Magistrates' Courts Act 1980 (c. 43) (limitation of time), be commenced at any time within two years from the date of the commission of the offence or within six months from its first discovery by the prosecutor, whichever period expires the earlier.

DEFINITIONS
"Sentencing": s.142(3)

GENERAL NOTE
This section exactly reproduces the Powers of Criminal Courts (Sentencing) Act 2000, s.126.

This section empowers a court to make a financial circumstances order in respect of an individual offender who has been convicted of an offence or who has notified a magistrates' court that he wishes to plead guilty without appearing before the court. The financial circumstances order requires the offender to give such a statement of his financial circumstances as the court may require. A person in respect of whom an order has been made who fails to comply with the order without reasonable excuse commits a summary offence punishable with a fine not exceeding Level 3 on the standard scale; a person who makes such a statement which he knows to be false or recklessly furnishes a statement which is false, or knowingly fails to disclose any material fact, commits a summary offence punishable with three months imprisonment or a fine not exceeding level 4 on the standard scale.

If an offender fails to comply with a financial circumstances order, the court dealing with him is empowered by s.164 to make such a determination in relation to his financial circumstances as it thinks fit.

A financial circumstances order may be made whatever form of sentence is in contemplation. Although the provision originated in the context of unit fines, it is clearly open to a court to make a financial circumstances order with a view to making a compensation order against an offender.

The Powers of Criminal Courts (Sentencing) Act 2000, s.136 provides a power to make a financial circumstances order against the parent or guardian of an offender under the age of 18.

163 General power of Crown Court to fine offender convicted on indictment

Where a person is convicted on indictment of any offence, other than an offence for which the sentence is fixed by law or falls to be imposed under section 110(2) or 111(2) of the Sentencing Act or under any of sections 225 to 228 of this Act, the court, if not precluded from sentencing an offender by its exercise of some other power, may impose a fine instead of or in addition to dealing with him in any other way in which the court has power to deal with him, subject however to any enactment requiring the offender to be dealt with in a particular way.

DEFINITIONS
   "Sentence": s.142(3)
   "Sentencing Act": s.305(1)

GENERAL NOTE
   This section substantially reproduces the Powers of Criminal Courts (Sentencing) Act 2000, s.127 with the substitution of references to ss.225–228 of this Act for references to s.109 of the Powers of Criminal Courts (Sentencing) Act 2000.
   This section confers on the Crown Court a general power to impose a fine on any person convicted on indictment, except in those cases which are excluded from the scope of the section. A fine may be imposed in addition to or instead of any other form of sentence. The power may be exercised in respect of an offender committed for sentence who falls to be sentenced as if convicted on indictment.
   The exercise of the power given by the section is subject to any enactment requiring the offender to be dealt with in a particular way. It does not apply where the offence of which the offender is convicted is either fixed by law or falls to be imposed under the Powers of Criminal Courts (Sentencing) Act 2000, ss.110–111 or ss.225–228 of the 2003 Act. (For the meaning of "falls to be imposed" see s.305(4)). The effect of the exclusion from the general power of offences for which sentences fall to be imposed under these sections appears to be that the Crown Court may not impose a fine in addition to the sentences required by these sections, but that if the conditions for not imposing the required sentence are present, the Crown Court may impose a fine, instead or in addition to any custodial sentence which may be imposed.

164   Fixing of fines

(1) Before fixing the amount of any fine to be imposed on an offender who is an individual, a court must inquire into his financial circumstances.

(2) The amount of any fine fixed by a court must be such as, in the opinion of the court, reflects the seriousness of the offence.

(3) In fixing the amount of any fine to be imposed on an offender (whether an individual or other person), a court must take into account the circumstances of the case including, among other things, the financial circumstances of the offender so far as they are known, or appear, to the court.

(4) Subsection (3) applies whether taking into account the financial circumstances of the offender has the effect of increasing or reducing the amount of the fine.

(5) Where—
   (a) an offender has been convicted in his absence in pursuance of section 11 or 12 of the Magistrates' Courts Act 1980 (c. 43) (non-appearance of accused), or
   (b) an offender—
      (i) has failed to furnish a statement of his financial circumstances in response to a request which is an official request for the purposes of section 20A of the Criminal Justice Act 1991 (c.53) (offence of making false statement as to financial circumstances),
      (ii) has failed to comply with an order under section 162(1), or
      (iii) has otherwise failed to co-operate with the court in its inquiry into his financial circumstances,
      and the court considers that it has insufficient information to make a proper determination of the financial circumstances of the offender, it may make such determination as it thinks fit.

DEFINITIONS
  "Seriousness": s.143

GENERAL NOTE
   This section substantially reproduces the Powers of Criminal Courts (Sentencing) Act 2000, s.128 with minor modifications (reference to official requests under the Criminal Justice Act 1991, s.20A).
   This section lays down a number of principles which should be followed by a court before determining the amount of any fine which is to be imposed. In the case of an individual offender, the court is placed under a duty to investigate the offender's financial circumstances. This does not apply in the case of an offender who is a corporation, although the court is required by subs.(3) to take into account the financial circumstances of the offender in both cases. Subsection (2) provides that the amount of any fine fixed by a court shall be such as in the opinion of the court reflects the seriousness of the offence. Subsection (3) provides that in fixing the amount of the fine the court shall take into account among other things the financial circumstances of the offender so far as they are known or appear to the court. It is the offender's duty to disclose his financial circumstances, if he wishes the court to take them into account. Subsection (4) provides that subs.(3) shall apply whether taking into account the financial circumstances of the offender leads the court to increase or reduce the amount of the fine. There is an obvious inconsistency between the principle stated in subs.(2) and that stated in subs.(3), as expanded by subs.(4).
   Subsection (5) makes further provision for an offender in whose case the court has not been provided with adequate information to make a proper determination of the financial circumstances. The court is empowered to make such determination at it thinks fit in this situation.

165   Remission of fines

(1) This section applies where a court has, in fixing the amount of a fine, determined the offender's financial circumstances under section 164(5).

(2) If, on subsequently inquiring into the offender's financial circumstances, the court is satisfied that had it had the results of that inquiry when sentencing the offender it would—
   (a) have fixed a smaller amount, or
   (b) not have fined him,
      it may remit the whole or part of the fine.

(3) Where under this section the court remits the whole or part of a fine after a term of imprisonment has been fixed under section 139 of the Sentencing Act (powers of Crown Court in relation to fines) or section 82(5) of the Magistrates' Courts Act 1980 (magistrates' powers in relation to default) it must reduce the term by the corresponding proportion.

(4) In calculating any reduction required by subsection (3), any fraction of a day is to be ignored.

GENERAL NOTE
   This section substantially reproduces the Powers of Criminal Courts (Sentencing) Act 2000, s.129 with the adaptation of references.
   The section provides for the case where a court in deciding the amount of a fine has determined the offender's financial circumstances in the absence of adequate information to make a proper determination under s.164. If on a subsequent inquiry the court is satisfied that if it had had the necessary information when sentencing the offender it would either have fixed a smaller amount or not fined him at all, it may remit the whole or part of the fine.
   The power under this section is conferred on the court which imposed the fine, and it may be exercised only where the original fine has been imposed on the basis of a determination under

s.164(5). This provision does not apply to cases where the offender's financial circumstances change after the fine has been imposed. Power to deal with an offender whose financial circumstances have changed is found in Magistrates' Courts Act 1980, s.85.

Savings for power to mitigate etc.

166   Savings for powers to mitigate sentences and deal appropriately with mentally disordered offenders

(1) Nothing in—
    (a) section 148 (imposing community sentences),
    (b) section 152, 153 or 157 (imposing custodial sentences),
    (c) section 156 (pre-sentence reports and other requirements),
    (d) section 164 (fixing of fines),
    prevents a court from mitigating an offender's sentence by taking into account any such matters as, in the opinion of the court, are relevant in mitigation of sentence.

(2) Section 152(2) does not prevent a court, after taking into account such matters, from passing a community sentence even though it is of the opinion that the offence, or the combination of the offence and one or more offences associated with it, was so serious that a community sentence could not normally be justified for the offence.

(3) Nothing in the sections mentioned in subsection (1)(a) to (d) prevents a court—
    (a) from mitigating any penalty included in an offender's sentence by taking into account any other penalty included in that sentence, and
    (b) in the case of an offender who is convicted of one or more other offences, from mitigating his sentence by applying any rule of law as to the totality of sentences.

(4) Subsections (2) and (3) are without prejudice to the generality of subsection (1).

(5) Nothing in the sections mentioned in subsection (1)(a) to (d) is to be taken—
    (a) as requiring a court to pass a custodial sentence, or any particular custodial sentence, on a mentally disordered offender, or
    (b) as restricting any power (whether under the Mental Health Act 1983 (c. 20) or otherwise) which enables a court to deal with such an offender in the manner it considers to be most appropriate in all the circumstances.

(6) In subsection (5) "mentally disordered", in relation to a person, means suffering from a mental disorder within the meaning of the Mental Health Act 1983.

DEFINITIONS
  "Community sentence": s.177
  "Sentence": s.142(3)
  "The Sentencing Act": s.305(1)

GENERAL NOTE
    This section substantially reproduces the the Powers of Criminal Courts (Sentencing) Act 2000, s.158 with minor changes in wording and the addition of subs.(2). The section preserves the power of the court to mitigate a sentence, notwithstanding the fact that the offence is either "so serious that neither a fine alone nor a sentence can be justified" (s.152(2)) or "serious enough to warrant" a community sentence (s.148). The section also qualifies s.164 (amount of fine to reflect the seriousness of the offence in respect of which it is imposed). The section does not qualify the duty of the court to impose a required custodial sentence under the Powers of Criminal Courts (Sentencing) Act 2000, ss.110 and 111, or the Firearms Act 1968, s.51A.
    Subsection (2) expresses what was the accepted interpretation of the previous section, namely that the existence of mitigating factors may justify a court in imposing a community sentence even though the seriousness of the offence or offences concerned was such that a

custodial sentence would normally be required (see *R. v Cox (David Geoffrey)* (1993) 14 Cr. App. R. (S.) 479). There might be an argument that this express provision in favour of community sentences means that the court may not use mitigating factors as a justification for imposing a fine alone where the seriousness of an offence would justify a custodial sentence under s.152(2).

Sentencing and allocation guidelines

167   The Sentencing Guidelines Council

(1) There shall be a Sentencing Guidelines Council (in this Chapter referred to as the Council) consisting of—
  (a) the Lord Chief Justice, who is to be chairman of the Council,
  (b) seven members (in this section and section 168 referred to as "judicial members") appointed by the Lord Chancellor after consultation with the Secretary of State and the Lord Chief Justice, and
  (c) four members (in this section and section 168 referred to as "non-judicial members") appointed by the Secretary of State after consultation with the Lord Chancellor and the Lord Chief Justice.

(2) A person is eligible to be appointed as a judicial member if he is—
  (a) a Lord Justice of Appeal,
  (b) a judge of the High Court,
  (c) a Circuit judge,
  (d) a District Judge (Magistrates' Courts), or
  (e) a lay justice.

(3) The judicial members must include a Circuit judge, a District Judge (Magistrates' Courts) and a lay justice.

(4) A person is eligible for appointment as a non-judicial member if he appears to the Secretary of State to have experience in one or more of the following areas—
  (a) policing,
  (b) criminal prosecution,
  (c) criminal defence, and
  (d) the promotion of the welfare of victims of crime.

(5) The persons eligible for appointment as a non-judicial member by virtue of experience of criminal prosecution include the Director of Public Prosecutions.

(6) The non-judicial members must include at least one person appearing to the Secretary of State to have experience in each area.

(7) The Lord Chief Justice must appoint one of the judicial members or non-judicial members to be deputy chairman of the Council.

(8) In relation to any meeting of the Council from which the Lord Chief Justice is to be absent, he may nominate any person eligible for appointment as a judicial member to act as a member on his behalf at the meeting.

(9) The Secretary of State may appoint a person appearing to him to have experience of sentencing policy and the administration of sentences to attend and speak at any meeting of the Council.

(10) In this section and section 168 "lay justice" means a justice of the peace who is not a District Judge (Magistrates' Courts).

DEFINITIONS
  "Sentencing": s.142(3)

GENERAL NOTE
  This section, and the sections which follow it, establish a system for the development of sentencing guidelines which is probably more convoluted than any to be found in the English speaking world. The system, when it is fully in operation, will effectively involve a minimum of

three stages. A guideline will be proposed by the Sentencing Advisory Panel, or if proposed by the Council itself will be considered by the Sentencing Advisory Panel. The Panel will advise the Sentencing Guidelines Council and the Sentencing Guidelines Council, taking that advice into account, will publish a draft guideline. The Council must then consult on these draft guidelines the Secretary of State and such other persons as either the Lord Chancellor or the Council consider appropriate. Although the statute it does not so provide, it is understood that the draft guidelines will be considered by the House of Commons Select Committee on Home Affairs.

After this process of consultation is complete, the Council may issue the guidelines as definitive guidelines, but only after making any amendments to the draft guidelines which it considers appropriate. Once "definitive guidelines" have been issued, every court must "have regard to" any guidelines which are relevant to the case in hand.

One consequence of the new legislation is the repeal of the Crime and Disorder Act 1998, ss.80 and 81 which among other things required the Court of Appeal, if it contemplated framing or revising sentencing guidelines, to notify the Sentencing Advisory Panel and take into account the views communicated to the court by the Sentencing Advisory Panel. That restriction is removed from the Court of Appeal and under this legislation the court is free to formulate such non-statutory guidelines as it considers appropriate.

One question which will doubtless trouble the courts when definitive guidelines are in effect under this legislation is whether such guidelines can have a retrospective effect, or whether Art.7 of the European Convention on Human Rights prevents them from doing so. On one view, the publication of a definitive guideline of this kind does not increase the penalty which is applicable to the offence, as it will not affect the maximum penalty available to the sentencing court. On the other hand it might be argued that a definitive guideline issued under these provisions is different in kind from a change in judicial sentencing practice operating within established statutory parameters and that Art.7 requires them to be applied prospectively only.

This section provides for the constitution of the Council. When the Bill was originally introduced, the Council was to consist only of members of the judiciary. The clause was amended eventually to extend membership to include four "non-judicial members". Under the section has finally enacted the judicial members of the Council will always outnumber the non-judicial members by two to one. If the Lord Chief Justice is prevented from attending a meeting of the Council, he is empowered by subs.(8) to nominate any person eligible for appointment as a judicial member to act as a member on his behalf at that meeting; such person need not be an existing member of the Council. The four non-judicial members must be qualified in accordance with subs.(4)), with experience of policing, criminal prosecution, criminal defence or the promotion of the welfare of victims of crime. As the non-judicial members must include at least one person appearing to have experience in each area, it seems likely that the four members will each represent one of those areas of experience, although it may be possible that some non-judicial members will have experience in m ore than one area. Subsection (9) permits the Secretary of State to appoint a person to attend and speak at a meeting of the Council, but not to be a member and to vote. It is understood that this provision is intended to permit a civil servant to take part in the proceedings of the Council to the extent permitted by the subsection.

168　　Sentencing Guidelines Council: supplementary provisions

(1) In relation to the Council, the Lord Chancellor may by order make provision—
   (a) as to the term of office, resignation and re-appointment of judicial members and non-judicial members,
   (b) enabling the appropriate Minister to remove a judicial member or non-judicial member from office on grounds of incapacity or misbehaviour, and
   (c) as to the proceedings of the Council.
(2) In subsection (1)(b) "the appropriate Minister" means—
   (a) in relation to a judicial member, the Lord Chancellor, and
   (b) in relation to a non-judicial member, the Secretary of State.
(3) The validity of anything done by the Council is not affected by any vacancy among its members, by any defect in the appointment of a member or by any failure to comply with section 167(3), (6) or (7).
(4) The Lord Chancellor may pay—
   (a) to any judicial member who is appointed by virtue of being a lay justice, such remuneration or expenses as he may determine, and

(b) to any other judicial member or the Lord Chief Justice, such expenses as he may determine.

(5) The Secretary of State may pay to any non-judicial member such remuneration or expenses as he may determine.

GENERAL NOTE

This section makes provision for the appointment of members of the Council and their removal on the grounds of incapacity or misbehaviour. The section also makes general provision empowering the Lord Chancellor or the Secretary of State to make provision for remuneration and the payment of expenses.

169   The Sentencing Advisory Panel

(1) There shall continue to be a Sentencing Advisory Panel (in this Chapter referred to as "the Panel") constituted by the Lord Chancellor after consultation with the Secretary of State and the Lord Chief Justice.

(2) The Lord Chancellor must, after consultation with the Secretary of State and the Lord Chief Justice, appoint one of the members of the Panel to be its chairman.

(3) The Lord Chancellor may pay to any member of the Panel such remuneration or expenses as he may determine.

GENERAL NOTE

This section provides for the preservation of the Sentencing Advisory Panel created by the Crime and Disorder Act 1998, s.81. Section 81 is repealed by this Act, and the necessary powers of appointment are granted in general terms by this section. The size and membership of the Sentencing Advisory Panel, unlike that of the Sentencing Guidelines Council, appears to be at the discretion of the Lord Chancellor, after consulting the Secretary of State and the Lord Chief Justice.

170   Guidelines relating to sentencing and allocation

(1) In this Chapter—
  (a) "sentencing guidelines" means guidelines relating to the sentencing of offenders, which may be general in nature or limited to a particular category of offence or offender, and
  (b) "allocation guidelines" means guidelines relating to decisions by a magistrates' court under section 19 of the Magistrates' Courts Act 1980 (c. 43) as to whether an offence is more suitable for summary trial or trial on indictment.

(2) The Secretary of State may at any time propose to the Council—
  (a) that sentencing guidelines be framed or revised by the Council—
    (i) in respect of offences or offenders of a particular category, or
    (ii) in respect of a particular matter affecting sentencing, or
  (b) that allocation guidelines be framed or revised by the Council.

(3) The Council may from time to time consider whether to frame sentencing guidelines or allocation guidelines and, if it receives—
  (a) a proposal under section 171(2) from the Panel, or
  (b) a proposal under subsection (2) from the Secretary of State,
  must consider whether to do so.

(4) Where sentencing guidelines or allocation guidelines have been issued by the Council as definitive guidelines, the Council must from time to time (and, in particular, if it receives a proposal under section 171(2) from the Panel or under subsection (2) from the Secretary of State) consider whether to revise them.

(5) Where the Council decides to frame or revise sentencing guidelines, the matters to which the Council must have regard include—

(a) the need to promote consistency in sentencing,

(b) the sentences imposed by courts in England and Wales for offences to which the guidelines relate,

(c) the cost of different sentences and their relative effectiveness in preventing re-offending,

(d) the need to promote public confidence in the criminal justice system, and

(e) the views communicated to the Council, in accordance with section 171(3)(b), by the Panel.

(6) Where the Council decides to frame or revise allocation guidelines, the matters to which the Council must have regard include—

(a) the need to promote consistency in decisions under section 19 of the Magistrates' Courts Act 1980 (c. 43), and

(b) the views communicated to the Council, in accordance with section 171(3)(b), by the Panel.

(7) Sentencing guidelines in respect of an offence or category of offences must include criteria for determining the seriousness of the offence or offences, including (where appropriate) criteria for determining the weight to be given to any previous convictions of offenders.

(8) Where the Council has prepared or revised any sentencing guidelines or allocation guidelines, it must—

(a) publish them as draft guidelines, and

(b) consult about the draft guidelines—

(i) the Secretary of State,

(ii) such persons as the Lord Chancellor, after consultation with the Secretary of State, may direct, and

(iii) such other persons as the Council considers appropriate.

(9) The Council may, after making any amendment of the draft guidelines which it considers appropriate, issue the guidelines as definitive guidelines.

GENERAL NOTE

This section lays down the duties of the Sentencing Guidelines Council. The Council will produce "sentencing guidelines" and "allocation guidelines" which will relate to decisions on the mode of trial of an offence under the Magistrates' Courts Act 1980, s.19.

The process of developing a new guideline may begin in a variety of ways. The Council may on its own initiative decide to proceed with a view to framing a guideline. Alternatively it may be stimulated into action by a proposal made by the Secretary of State under subs.(2) or a proposal from the Sentencing Advisory Panel made under s.171(2). If a proposal for a guideline is received from either source, the Council must consider "whether to" frame a sentencing or allocation guideline (subs.(3)). The clear implication of subs.(3) is that while the Council has a duty to consider whether to frame sentencing guidelines or allocation guidelines on receipt of such a proposal, it is empowered to decide not to do so. If the Council decides not to proceed with the framing of a guidelines, no further steps can be taken.

If the Council decides on its own initiative to frame or revise any sentencing or allocation guidelines, otherwise than in response to a proposal from the Sentencing Advisory Panel, the Council must notify the panel. This duty applies when the Secretary of State has initiated the process by a proposal to the Council. It is implied by subs.(5) that the Council must wait for the Sentencing Advisory Panel to communicate its views to the Council, after completing the process established by s.171. When the Council has received the views of the Panel, the Council must prepare its draft guidelines, taking into account the matters set out in subss.(5) or (6). Draft sentencing guidelines must include criteria for determining the seriousness of the offence or offences, including where appropriate criteria for determining the weight to be given to any previous convictions of offenders.

When the draft guidelines have been prepared, they must be published as "draft guidelines." Presumably in this context "publish" means "publish to the world at large". The Council must also consult the Secretary of State, and any other persons nominated by the Lord Chancellor, and such other persons as Council considers appropriate. After this process of consultation is complete, the Council may issue guidelines as "definitive guidelines" after making any amendments of the draft guidelines which it considers appropriate.

171   Functions of Sentencing Advisory Panel in relation to guidelines

(1) Where the Council decides to frame or revise any sentencing guidelines or allocation guidelines, otherwise than in response to a proposal from the Panel under subsection (2), the Council must notify the Panel.

(2) The Panel may at any time propose to the Council—
   (a) that sentencing guidelines be framed or revised by the Council—
      (i) in respect of offences or offenders of a particular category, or
      (ii) in respect of a particular matter affecting sentencing, or
   (b) that allocation guidelines be framed or revised by the Council.

(3) Where the Panel receives a notification under subsection (1) or makes a proposal under subsection (2), the Panel must—
   (a) obtain and consider the views on the matters in issue of such persons or bodies as may be determined, after consultation with the Secretary of State and the Lord Chancellor, by the Council, and
   (b) formulate its own views on those matters and communicate them to the Council.

(4) Paragraph (a) of subsection (3) does not apply where the Council notifies the Panel of the Council's view that the urgency of the case makes it impracticable for the Panel to comply with that paragraph.

DEFINITIONS
  "Sentencing": s.142(3)

GENERAL NOTE
  This section, derived from the Crime and Disorder Act 1998, s.81, lays down the functions of the Sentencing Advisory Panel. The original purpose of the Sentencing Advisory Panel was to provide advice to the Court of Appeal, Criminal Division in connection with the framing of guidelines by the court. Under the new scheme, the Panel will instead to give advice to the Sentencing Guidelines Council, and its scope is extended to include "allocation guidelines".

  As under the earlier legislation, the Panel may on its own initiative propose that sentencing or allocation guidelines should be framed or revised, or may act on a notification from the Council communicated to it in accordance with subs.(1). Where the Panel proposes that a guideline should be framed or revised, or receives a notification from the Council, it must carry out the process of consultation required by subs.(3) and formulate its own views on the matter in the light of that consultation. Subsection (4), which allows the Panel to dispense with the process of external consultation where the Council notifies the Panel that the urgency of the case makes it impractical to consult, is a new provision.

172   Duty of court to have regard to sentencing guidelines

(1) Every court must—
   (a) in sentencing an offender, have regard to any guidelines which are relevant to the offender's case, and
   (b) in exercising any other function relating to the sentencing of offenders, have regard to any guidelines which are relevant to the exercise of the function.

(2) In subsection (1) "guidelines" means sentencing guidelines issued by the Council under section 170(9) as definitive guidelines, as revised by subsequent guidelines so issued.

DEFINITIONS
   "Sentencing": s.142(3)

GENERAL NOTE
   This section, which is new, establishes the duty of sentencing courts in relation to guidelines which are published as "definitive guidelines" under s.170(9) of the 2003 Act, at the conclusion of the process established in the preceding sections. The principal duty of the court is to "have regard to" any guidelines which are relevant to the case. In addition, under s.174(2)(a), if the court decides that the appropriate sentence in a particular case is not one which is indicated by a relevant guideline, the court must state its reasons for deciding that the appropriate sentence is of a different kind or outside the range of sentences indicated by the guideline. Where the court imposes a sentence which is consistent with a "definitive guideline," the general duty imposed by s.174(1)(a) to state the reasons for deciding on the sentence passed appears to include by implication a duty to refer to the guideline to which the court has had regard.
   The question to which this section will undoubtedly give rise is the meaning of "have regard to". There is nothing in the section which compels courts to follow a "definitive guideline" without regard to the detailed circumstances of the individual case. What seems to be contemplated is that the court has a discretion to depart from a guideline in any case where it considers it to be appropriate or just to do so, provided that the court can give reasons for the departure.

173   Annual report by Council

(1) The Council must as soon as practicable after the end of each financial year make to the Ministers a report on the exercise of the Council's functions during the year.
(2) If section 167 comes into force after the beginning of a financial year, the first report may relate to a period beginning with the day on which that section comes into force and ending with the end of the next financial year.
(3) The Ministers must lay a copy of the report before each House of Parliament.
(4) The Council must publish the report once the copy has been so laid.
(5) In this section—
   "financial year" means a period of 12 months ending with 31st March;
   "the Ministers" means the Secretary of State and the Lord Chancellor.

GENERAL NOTE
   This section provides for the provision by the Council of annual reports on the exercise of the Council's functions, and the publication of the report once a copy of the report has been laid before each House of Parliament by the Secretary of State and the Lord Chancellor.

Duty of court to explain sentence

174   Duty to give reasons for, and explain effect of, sentence

(1) Subject to subsections (3) and (4), any court passing sentence on an offender—
   (a) must state in open court, in ordinary language and in general terms, its reasons for deciding on the sentence passed, and
   (b) must explain to the offender in ordinary language—
      (i) the effect of the sentence,

(ii) where the offender is required to comply with any order of the court forming part of the sentence, the effects of non-compliance with the order,

(iii) any power of the court, on the application of the offender or any other person, to vary or review any order of the court forming part of the sentence, and

(iv) where the sentence consists of or includes a fine, the effects of failure to pay the fine.

(2) In complying with subsection (1)(a), the court must—

(a) where guidelines indicate that a sentence of a particular kind, or within a particular range, would normally be appropriate for the offence and the sentence is of a different kind, or is outside that range, state the court's reasons for deciding on a sentence of a different kind or outside that range,

(b) where the sentence is a custodial sentence and the duty in subsection (2) of section 152 is not excluded by subsection (1)(a) or (b) or (3) of that section, state that it is of the opinion referred to in section 152(2) and why it is of that opinion,

(c) where the sentence is a community sentence and the case does not fall within section 151(2), state that it is of the opinion that section 148(1) applies and why it is of that opinion,

(d) where as a result of taking into account any matter referred to in section 144(1), the court imposes a punishment on the offender which is less severe than the punishment it would otherwise have imposed, state that fact, and

(e) in any case, mention any aggravating or mitigating factors which the court has regarded as being of particular importance.

(3) Subsection (1)(a) does not apply—

(a) to an offence the sentence for which is fixed by law (provision relating to sentencing for such an offence being made by section 270), or

(b) to an offence the sentence for which falls to be imposed under section 51A(2) of the Firearms Act 1968 (c. 27) or under subsection (2) of section 110 or 111 of the Sentencing Act (required custodial sentences).

(4) The Secretary of State may by order—

(a) prescribe cases in which subsection (1)(a) or (b) does not apply, and

(b) prescribe cases in which the statement referred to in subsection (1)(a) or the explanation referred to in subsection (1)(b) may be made in the absence of the offender, or may be provided in written form.

(5) Where a magistrates' court passes a custodial sentence, it must cause any reason stated by virtue of subsection (2)(b) to be specified in the warrant of commitment and entered on the register.

(6) In this section—

"guidelines" has the same meaning as in section 172;

"the register" has the meaning given by section 163 of the Sentencing Act.

DEFINITIONS
"Sentence": s.142(3)
"Community sentence": s.177

GENERAL NOTE
This section, which is a compilation of a number of different sections of the Powers of Criminal Courts (Sentencing) Act 2000, with the addition of some new provisions, is an attempt to bring it into one place all the matters which the court must state when imposing sentence. The

list is not comprehensive and there are various other statutory obligations which apply in particular cases which are not included in this list.

Subsection (1) is derived from the Powers of Criminal Courts (Sentencing) Act 2000, s.79(4) which applied to custodial sentences. The obligation imposed by subs.(1)(b) to explain the effect the sentence is derived from various provisions of that Act relating to community orders (*e.g.* s.41(7) relating to community service orders). Its application to custodial sentences is new. It appears to give statutory effect of the practice of requiring judges to explain the practical effect of a sentence. The requirement imposed by subs.(1)(b)(iv) to explain the effect of failure to pay a fine is new.

Subsection (2) imposes on the court which decides on a sentence which falls outside the range or kind of sentence indicated by a guideline published by the Sentencing Guidelines Council under s.170(9), to state the court's reasons for deciding on that sentence. The subsection appears to imply that where the court passes a sentence in accordance with a guideline, it should identify the guideline as part of the reasons for the sentence.

Subsection (2)(b) requires the court to state why it is of the opinion that the offence or offences were so serious that neither of fine alone or a community sentence can be justified for the offence when imposing a custodial sentence. This obligation does not apply where the sentence is fixed by law or is a required minimum sentence, or is imposed in the light of the offender's expression of unwillingness to comply with a requirement of a community order. Under subs.1(2)(c) a court imposing a community sentence must normally say why it is of the opinion that the offence is "serious enough" to warrant a community sentence.

Subsection (2)(d) requires the court to indicate that it has reduced the sentence as result of taking into account the stage of the proceedings at which the defendant indicated his intention to plead guilty to the offence.

Subsection (3) excludes from the operation of subs.(1)(a) offences for which the sentence is fixed by law. However a court imposing a mandatory life sentence on a conviction for murder (the only case in which the sentence is fixed by law) must in accordance with s.270 give reasons for deciding on the order made relation to the early release provisions (fixing of the minimum term to be served by the offender). Similarly, the general duty to explain the reasons for the sentence for under subs.(1)(a) does not apply to a required minimum sentence under the Firearms Act 1968, s.51A or the Powers of Criminal Courts (Sentencing) Act 2000, s.110 or s.111. The exclusion of subs.(1)(a) in these case does not relieve court of the duties imposed under subs.(1)(b), to explain to the offender the effect of the sentence.

Other statutory duties to explain why a sentence of a particular kind has or has not been imposed are created by the Powers of Criminal Courts (Sentencing) Act 2000, s.130 (failure to make a compensation order where the court has power to do so), s.150 (failure to bind over parent or guardian of offender under 16), the Football Spectators Act 1989 (c.37), s.14E (why the court has not made a banning order under the Football Spectators Act 1989 where it had power to do so), and the Criminal Justice and Court Services Act 2000, ss.28(6) and 29(5) (why the court has not made a disqualification order in respect of an adult offender convicted of an offence against a child).

There are other obligations to make statements (as under the Sexual Offenders Act 1997 (c.51), s.5 where an offender has been convicted of an offence to which the Act applies, and the Powers of Criminal Courts (Sentencing) Act 2000, s.113).

Publication of information by Secretary of State

## 175	Duty to publish information about sentencing

In section 95 of the Criminal Justice Act 1991 (c. 53) (information for financial and other purposes) in subsection (1) before the "or" at the end of paragraph (a) there is inserted—

"(aa) enabling such persons to become aware of the relative effectiveness of different sentences—
  (i) in preventing re-offending, and
  (ii) in promoting public confidence in the criminal justice system;".

GENERAL NOTE

The Criminal Justice Act 1991, s.95 imposes on the Secretary of State a duty to publish annually such information "as he considers expedient" for the purposes of enabling persons engaged in the administration of criminal justice to become aware of the financial implications of their decisions or facilitating the performance by such persons of their duty to avoid discriminating against any persons on the ground of race or sex or any other improper ground. This section adds a further purpose in relation to which the Secretary of State is obliged to publish such information.

Interpretation of Chapter

176   Interpretation of Chapter 1

In this Chapter—
"allocation guidelines" has the meaning given by section 170(1)(b);
"the Council" means the Sentencing Guidelines Council;
"the Panel" means the Sentencing Advisory Panel;
"sentence" and "sentencing" are to be read in accordance with section 142(3);
"sentencing guidelines" has the meaning given by section 170(1)(a);
"youth community order" has the meaning given by section 147(2).

GENERAL NOTE
This section provides a set of definitions of some of the expressions used in Ch.1 of Pt 12.

CHAPTER 2

COMMUNITY ORDERS: OFFENDERS AGED 16 OR OVER

177   Community orders

(1) Where a person aged 16 or over is convicted of an offence, the court by or before which he is convicted may make an order (in this Part referred to as a "community order") imposing on him any one or more of the following requirements—
    (a) an unpaid work requirement (as defined by section 199),
    (b) an activity requirement (as defined by section 201),
    (c) a programme requirement (as defined by section 202),
    (d) a prohibited activity requirement (as defined by section 203),
    (e) a curfew requirement (as defined by section 204),
    (f) an exclusion requirement (as defined by section 205),
    (g) a residence requirement (as defined by section 206),
    (h) a mental health treatment requirement (as defined by section 207),
    (i) a drug rehabilitation requirement (as defined by section 209),
    (j) an alcohol treatment requirement (as defined by section 212),
    (k) a supervision requirement (as defined by section 213), and
    (l) in a case where the offender is aged under 25, an attendance centre requirement (as defined by section 214).
(2) Subsection (1) has effect subject to sections 150 and 218 and to the following provisions of Chapter 4 relating to particular requirements—
    (a) section 199(3) (unpaid work requirement),
    (b) section 201(3) and (4) (activity requirement),
    (c) section 202(4) and (5) (programme requirement),
    (d) section 203(2) (prohibited activity requirement),
    (e) section 207(3) (mental health treatment requirement),
    (f) section 209(2) (drug rehabilitation requirement), and
    (g) section 212(2) and (3) (alcohol treatment requirement).
(3) Where the court makes a community order imposing a curfew requirement or an exclusion requirement, the court must also impose an electronic monitoring requirement (as defined by section 215) unless—
    (a) it is prevented from doing so by section 215(2) or 218(4), or

      (b) in the particular circumstances of the case, it considers it inappropriate to do so.

  (4) Where the court makes a community order imposing an unpaid work requirement, an activity requirement, a programme requirement, a prohibited activity requirement, a residence requirement, a mental health treatment requirement, a drug rehabilitation requirement, an alcohol treatment requirement, a supervision requirement or an attendance centre requirement, the court may also impose an electronic monitoring requirement unless prevented from doing so by section 215(2) or 218(4).

  (5) A community order must specify a date, not more than three years after the date of the order, by which all the requirements in it must have been complied with; and a community order which imposes two or more different requirements falling within subsection (1) may also specify an earlier date or dates in relation to compliance with any one or more of them.

  (6) Before making a community order imposing two or more different requirements falling within subsection (1), the court must consider whether, in the circumstances of the case, the requirements are compatible with each other.

GENERAL NOTE

This section introduces the new scheme for community orders in respect of offenders aged 16 or over. Under the new scheme, community orders which were previously distinct, such as community rehabilitation orders, community punishment orders, drug treatment and testing orders, curfew orders and others will be brought within the framework and of a single order, to be known as a "community order" and the requirements which would arise under the previous order will be attached to the new "community order". What would previously have been known as a community punishment order will in practice become a community order with an unpaid work requirement. A curfew order will become a community order with a curfew requirement, a drug treatment and testing order will become a community order with a drug rehabilitation requirement, and a community rehabilitation order will become a community order with a supervision requirement, and such other requirements as may be attached to the order. The circumstances in which the various types of requirement may be imposed are themselves set out in ss.199–214 of the 2003 Act.

One effect of the new scheme is to allow a court to impose a single order with an a combination of any requirements, previously capable of being imposed only in the context of one or other of the particular orders. Before taking advantage of this facility, subs.(6) requires the court to "consider whether in the circumstances of the case the requirements are compatible with each other".

178   Power to provide for court review of community orders

  (1) The Secretary of State may by order—

      (a) enable or require a court making a community order to provide for the community order to be reviewed periodically by that or another court,

      (b) enable a court to amend a community order so as to include or remove a provision for review by a court, and

      (c) make provision as to the timing and conduct of reviews and as to the powers of the court on a review.

  (2) An order under this section may, in particular, make provision in relation to community orders corresponding to any provision made by sections 191 and 192 in relation to suspended sentence orders.

  (3) An order under this section may repeal or amend any provision of this Part.

GENERAL NOTE

This section empowers the Secretary of State by order to make provision for the periodical review of community orders by the court which made the order or another court. Under previous legislation, such reviews were possible only in relation to drug treatment and testing orders. The provisions for such reviews are carried forward, with some modification, in s.210 of the Act, in relation to what will be drug rehabilitation requirements.

179　Breach, revocation or amendment of community order

Schedule 8 (which relates to failures to comply with the requirements of community orders and to the revocation or amendment of such orders) shall have effect.

GENERAL NOTE

This section gives effect to Sch.8 to the 2003 Act, which provides for failure to comply with the requirement of community orders, and for the revocation of such orders.

Schedule 8 is substantially based on the Powers of Criminal Courts (Sentencing) Act 2000, Sch.3 (as amended by the Criminal Justice and Court Services Act 2000) but with many minor amendments of detail and one major amendment of principle.

The major amendment, by comparison with Sch.3 to the Powers of Criminal Courts (Sentencing) Act 2000, is that a person subject to a community order who is convicted by a magistrates' court of an offence, becomes liable to the revocation of the order and to being resentenced by the court for the original offence in respect of which the community order was made (para.21). Similarly a person subject to a community order made by the Crown Court who is convicted of an offence by a magistrates' court, may be committed to the Crown Court with a view to the revocation of the community order. These provisions in effect revive the scheme of the Powers of Criminal Courts Act 1973, s.8 which was abandoned in the Criminal Justice Act 1991.

Some of the amendments to the Powers of Criminal Courts (Sentencing) Act 2000, Sch.3 which were made by the Criminal Justice and Court Services Act 2000, s.53 are carried forward into the new schedule (such as the duty of the responsible officer to institute breach proceedings after a failure to comply with an order after a warning has been given (paras 5 and 6) but the amendments made by the Criminal Justice and Court Services Act 2000, s.53(4) which would have required the court to impose a sentence of imprisonment on a person found to be in breach of a community order, are not carried forward into the new schedule. They were never brought into force in relation to Sch.3 of the Powers of Criminal Courts (Sentencing) Act 2000.

180　Transfer of community orders to Scotland or Northern Ireland

Schedule 9 (transfer of community orders to Scotland or Northern Ireland) shall have effect.

GENERAL NOTE

This section gives effect to Sch.9, which provides for the transfer of community order to Scotland or Northern Ireland, where a court in England and Wales makes a community order in respect of an offender who normally resides in one or the other of those jurisdictions.

CHAPTER 3

PRISON SENTENCES OF LESS THAN 12 MONTHS

Prison sentences of less than twelve months

181　Prison sentences of less than 12 months

(1) Any power of a court to impose a sentence of imprisonment for a term of less than 12 months on an offender may be exercised only in accordance with the following provisions of this section unless the court makes an intermittent custody order (as defined by section 183).

(2) The term of the sentence—
　(a) must be expressed in weeks,
　(b) must be at least 28 weeks,

    (c) must not be more than 51 weeks in respect of any one offence, and

    (d) must not exceed the maximum term permitted for the offence.

(3) The court, when passing sentence, must—

    (a) specify a period (in this Chapter referred to as "the custodial period") at the end of which the offender is to be released on a licence, and

    (b) by order require the licence to be granted subject to conditions requiring the offender's compliance during the remainder of the term (in this Chapter referred to as "the licence period") or any part of it with one or more requirements falling within section 182(1) and specified in the order.

(4) In this Part "custody plus order" means an order under subsection (3)(b).

(5) The custodial period—

    (a) must be at least 2 weeks, and

    (b) in respect of any one offence, must not be more than 13 weeks.

(6) In determining the term of the sentence and the length of the custodial period, the court must ensure that the licence period is at least 26 weeks in length.

(7) Where a court imposes two or more terms of imprisonment in accordance with this section to be served consecutively—

    (a) the aggregate length of the terms of imprisonment must not be more than 65 weeks, and

    (b) the aggregate length of the custodial periods must not be more than 26 weeks.

(8) A custody plus order which specifies two or more requirements may, in relation to any requirement, refer to compliance within such part of the licence period as is specified in the order.

(9) Subsection (3)(b) does not apply where the sentence is a suspended sentence.

DEFINITIONS

"Sentence": s.142(3)
"Custodial period": s.195
"Licence period": s.195

GENERAL NOTE

This section provides for a completely new system for dealing with sentences of imprisonment for a term of less than 12 months. The term of the sentence must be expressed in weeks (rather than in months as under the previous practice), must not be less than 28 weeks, and must not be more than 51 weeks in respect of any one offence. When passing such a sentence, the court must specify the period (the "custodial period") after which the offender is to be released on licence, and by order require the licence to be granted on condition that the offender complies during the remainder of term or any part of it with such requirements as the court may specify. The requirements which may be a specified are listed in s.182 and are substantially similar to the requirements which may be made in connection with a community order, although some of the requirements which may be made under a community order may not be made by virtue of an order under this section (these are a residence requirement, a mental health requirement, a drug rehabilitation requirement and an alcohol treatment requirement). A sentence in this form is to be known as a "custody plus order".

The form of a "custody plus order" will be more complex than that of a conventional sentence of imprisonment. An example might be in the following form: "you are sentenced to a term of imprisonment of forty weeks. The custodial period of the sentence will be twelve weeks and the licence period will be twenty eight weeks. During the fist six weeks of the licence period, you will be subject to a curfew requirement and during the whole of the licence period you will be subject to an exclusion requirement".

The court will be required to give the explanations required by s.174.

There is some uncertainty in the application of the section to cases where consecutive sentences are imposed. The uncertainty arises out of the use of the expression "term". There is no definition of this expression in either s.195 or s.305. Does "term" refer to the term imposed for an individual offence, or to the aggregate of terms imposed for a number of different offences? Does s.181 apply to two sentences, each of nine months imprisonment, ordered to run as consecutively, and resulting in aggregate of eighteen months imprisonment? If "term" in subs.(1) refers to the individual term, then the obligations imposed by section would apply to each individual sentence, and the aggregate sentence would be subject to subs.(7). If however in subs.(1) "term" refers to the aggregate sentence, then the section has no application. "Term" in subs.(2) could be read in either sense. Subsection (2)(c) appears to indicate that "term" means the aggregate term, but subs.(2)(d) appears to suggest that it is the term imposed for the individual offence.

Subsection (7) appears to indicate that "term" applies to the individual sentence rather than the aggregate. The section appears to require that if a court imposes two consecutive terms, each of less than 12 months, it must comply with the requirements of subs.(2), (3), (5) and (6), and in addition ensure that the total nominal aggregate term does not exceed 65 weeks, and that the total aggregate custodial period does not exceed 26 weeks.

182 Licence conditions

(1) The requirements falling within this subsection are—
  (a) an unpaid work requirement (as defined by section 199),
  (b) an activity requirement (as defined by section 201),
  (c) a programme requirement (as defined by section 202),
  (d) a prohibited activity requirement (as defined by section 203),
  (e) a curfew requirement (as defined by section 204),
  (f) an exclusion requirement (as defined by section 205),
  (g) a supervision requirement (as defined by section 213), and
  (h) in a case where the offender is aged under 25, an attendance centre requirement (as defined by section 214).
(2) The power under section 181(3)(b) to determine the conditions of the licence has effect subject to section 218 and to the following provisions of Chapter 4 relating to particular requirements—
  (a) section 199(3) (unpaid work requirement),
  (b) section 201(3) and (4) (activity requirement),
  (c) section 202(4) and (5) (programme requirement), and
  (d) section 203(2) (prohibited activity requirement).
(3) Where the court makes a custody plus order requiring a licence to contain a curfew requirement or an exclusion requirement, the court must also require the licence to contain an electronic monitoring requirement (as defined by section 215) unless—
  (a) the court is prevented from doing so by section 215(2) or 218(4), or
  (b) in the particular circumstances of the case, it considers it inappropriate to do so.
(4) Where the court makes a custody plus order requiring a licence to contain an unpaid work requirement, an activity requirement, a programme requirement, a prohibited activity requirement, a supervision requirement or an attendance centre requirement, the court may also require the licence to contain an electronic monitoring requirement unless the court is prevented from doing so by section 215(2) or 218(4).
(5) Before making a custody plus order requiring a licence to contain two or more different requirements falling within subsection (1), the court must consider whether, in the circumstances of the case, the requirements are compatible with each other.

GENERAL NOTE
This section lists the requirements which may be imposed on an offender as a condition of his licence under a "custody plus order" under s.181. The power to impose such requirement is subject to the general restrictions on the use of such requirements to areas where appropriate arrangements are in effect (s.218) and to the conditions relating to the imposition of such requirements under the community orders. Where a court contemplates making a custody plus

order requiring two or more different requirements, the court must consider whether the requirements are compatible with each other in the circumstances of the case.

Intermittent custody

183 Intermittent custody

(1) A court may, when passing a sentence of imprisonment for a term complying with subsection (4)—
  (a) specify the number of days that the offender must serve in prison under the sentence before being released on licence for the remainder of the term, and
  (b) by order—
    (i) specify periods during which the offender is to be released temporarily on licence before he has served that number of days in prison, and
    (ii) require any licence to be granted subject to conditions requiring the offender's compliance during the licence periods with one or more requirements falling within section 182(1) and specified in the order.

(2) In this Part "intermittent custody order" means an order under subsection (1)(b).

(3) In this Chapter—
  "licence period", in relation to a term of imprisonment to which an intermittent custody order relates, means any period during which the offender is released on licence by virtue of subsection (1)(a) or (b)(i);
  "the number of custodial days", in relation to a term of imprisonment to which an intermittent custody order relates, means the number of days specified under subsection (1)(a).

(4) The term of the sentence—
  (a) must be expressed in weeks,
  (b) must be at least 28 weeks,
  (c) must not be more than 51 weeks in respect of any one offence, and
  (d) must not exceed the maximum term permitted for the offence.

(5) The number of custodial days—
  (a) must be at least 14, and
  (b) in respect of any one offence, must not be more than 90.

(6) A court may not exercise its powers under subsection (1) unless the offender has expressed his willingness to serve the custodial part of the proposed sentence intermittently, during the parts of the sentence that are not to be licence periods.

(7) Where a court exercises its powers under subsection (1) in respect of two or more terms of imprisonment that are to be served consecutively—
  (a) the aggregate length of the terms of imprisonment must not be more than 65 weeks, and
  (b) the aggregate of the numbers of custodial days must not be more than 180.

(8) The Secretary of State may by order require a court, in specifying licence periods under subsection (1)(b)(i), to specify only—
  (a) periods of a prescribed duration,
  (b) periods beginning or ending at prescribed times, or
  (c) periods including, or not including, specified parts of the week.

(9) An intermittent custody order which specifies two or more requirements may, in relation to any requirement, refer to compliance within such licence period or periods, or part of a licence period, as is specified in the order.

GENERAL NOTE
This section provides a new power under which a court passing a sentence of imprisonment for a term of not more than 51 weeks in respect of any one offence may order that the offender be released temporarily on licence before he has served the whole number of days which he is required to serve in custody. An order made under this section is known as an "intermittent custody order". In order for the power to be available to the court, the term of sentence must be at least 28 weeks and must not be more than 51 weeks in respect of any one offence. There is the same unfortunate ambiguity in the use of the word "term" in this section as there is in s.181.

If the term of the sentence is within the limits specified in subs.(4) and the number of custodial days is between 14 and 90 in respect of any one offence, the court may make an order under the section, subject to s.184. A sentence of imprisonment passed in conjunction with an intermittent custody order will require the court first to identify the term of the sentence in accordance with subs.(4), then to specify the number of custodial days in accordance with subs.(5) and then to specified the periods during which the offender is to be released temporarily on licence during that period. The court must then specify the conditions of offender's licence during those periods. These may include compliance with any of the requirements set out in s.182. The court may not exercise this power unless the offender has expressed his willingness to serve the custodial part of the sentence intermittently. The court may specify requirements with which the offender must comply after his final release on licence, having served the custodial days specified under subs.(1)(a), as in the case of a "custody plus" order under s.181.

If the court passes one or more terms of imprisonment that are ordered to run consecutively, the power may be exercised only where the aggregate length of the terms of imprisonment is not more than 65 weeks, and the aggregate number of custodial days is not more than 180.

184   Restrictions on power to make intermittent custody order

(1) A court may not make an intermittent custody order unless it has been notified by the Secretary of State that arrangements for implementing such orders are available in the area proposed to be specified in the intermittent custody order and the notice has not been withdrawn.

(2) The court may not make an intermittent custody order in respect of any offender unless—
   (a) it has consulted an officer of a local probation board,
   (b) it has received from the Secretary of State notification that suitable prison accommodation is available for the offender during the custodial periods, and
   (c) it appears to the court that the offender will have suitable accommodation available to him during the licence periods.

(3) In this section "custodial period", in relation to a sentence to which an intermittent custody order relates, means any part of the sentence that is not a licence period.

GENERAL NOTE
A section lays down a number of conditions which must be satisfied before the court exercises the power under s.183 to make an "intermittent custody order" in conjunction with a sentence of imprisonment. The court must have been notified by the Secretary of State that arrangements for making such orders are available in the relevant area. In respect of the individual offender, the court may not make an intermittent custody order unless it has consulted an officer of a local probation board, received notification that suitable prison accommodation is available for the offender during the custodial periods of the sentence, and is satisfied that suitable accommodation appears to be available to the offender during the licence periods.

185   Intermittent custody: licence conditions

(1) Section 183(1)(b) has effect subject to section 218 and to the following provisions of Chapter 4 limiting the power to require the licence to contain particular requirements—
   (a) section 199(3) (unpaid work requirement),
   (b) section 201(3) and (4) (activity requirement),
   (c) section 202(4) and (5) (programme requirement), and

(d) section 203(2) (prohibited activity requirement).

(2) Subsections (3) to (5) of section 182 have effect in relation to an intermittent custody order as they have effect in relation to a custody plus order.

GENERAL NOTE

This section limits the power of the court when making an intermittent custody order to specify particular requirements to be included in the offender's licence. The court must comply with the general restrictions on imposing such requirements that are set out in the statutory provisions mentioned in the section. Some requirements may be imposed only where appropriate arrangements are in effect (s.218) and some are subject to specific requirements.

Subsection (2) applies subss.(3)–(5) of s.182 to intermittent custody orders. In particular, subs.(5) requires that where a court contemplates making a custody plus order requiring two or more different requirements, the court must consider whether the requirements are compatible with each other in the circumstances of the case.

186 Further provisions relating to intermittent custody

(1) Section 21 of the 1952 Act (expenses of conveyance to prison) does not apply in relation to the conveyance to prison at the end of any licence period of an offender to whom an intermittent custody order relates.

(2) The Secretary of State may pay to any offender to whom an intermittent custody order relates the whole or part of any expenses incurred by the offender in travelling to and from prison during licence periods.

(3) In section 49 of the 1952 Act (persons unlawfully at large) after subsection (4) there is inserted—

"(4A) For the purposes of this section a person shall also be deemed to be unlawfully at large if, having been temporarily released in pursuance of an intermittent custody order made under section 183 of the Criminal Justice Act 2003, he remains at large at a time when, by reason of the expiry of the period for which he was temporarily released, he is liable to be detained in pursuance of his sentence."

(4) In section 23 of the Criminal Justice Act 1961 (c. 39) (prison rules), in subsection (3) for "The days" there is substituted "Subject to subsection (3A), the days" and after subsection (3) there is inserted—

"(3A) In relation to a prisoner to whom an intermittent custody order under section 183 of the Criminal Justice Act 2003 relates, the only days to which subsection (3) applies are Christmas Day, Good Friday and any day which under the Banking and Financial Dealings Act 1971 is a bank holiday in England and Wales."

(5) In section 1 of the Prisoners (Return to Custody) Act 1995 (c. 16) (remaining at large after temporary release) after subsection (1) there is inserted—

"(1A) A person who has been temporarily released in pursuance of an intermittent custody order made under section 183 of the Criminal Justice Act 2003 is guilty of an offence if, without reasonable excuse, he remains unlawfully at large at any time after becoming so at large by virtue of the expiry of the period for which he was temporarily released."

(6) In this section "the 1952 Act" means the Prison Act 1952 (c. 52).

GENERAL NOTE

This section makes detailed provision for the administration of intermittent custody orders. In particular, its effect is that a person who is required to return to prison at the end of any licence period during an intermittent custody order must make his own way there, but the Secretary of State may pay the whole or part of his travelling expenses. If such a person fails to return to custody at the expiration of the temporary licence period, he is unlawfully at large and may be arrested under the Prison Act 1952 (c.52), s.49. A person who remains unlawfully at large at the end of a temporary licence period commits an offence under the Prisoners (Return to Custody) Act 1995 (c.16) if he does so without reasonable excuse.

Further provision about custody plus orders and intermittent custody orders

187 Revocation or amendment of order

Schedule 10 (which contains provisions relating to the revocation or amendment of custody plus orders and the amendment of intermittent custody orders) shall have effect.

GENERAL NOTE

This section gives effect to Sch.10, which relates to the revocation or amendment of custody plus orders and intermittent custody orders. The Schedule provides that the officer responsible for the offender or the offender may apply to the appropriate court for the order to be revoked. The revocation of a custody plus order does not affect the sentence of imprisonment except in relation to the conditions of the licence. In the case of an intermittent custody order, the court may revoke the conditions of the sentence requiring compliance with requirements during periods of release on licence (temporary or otherwise).

188 Transfer of custody plus orders and intermittent custody orders to Scotland or Northern Ireland

Schedule 11 (transfer of custody plus orders and intermittent custody orders to Scotland or Northern Ireland) shall have effect.

Suspended sentences

189 Suspended sentences of imprisonment

(1) A court which passes a sentence of imprisonment for a term of at least 28 weeks but not more than 51 weeks in accordance with section 181 may—

    (a) order the offender to comply during a period specified for the purposes of this paragraph in the order (in this Chapter referred to as "the supervision period") with one or more requirements falling within section 190(1) and specified in the order, and

    (b) order that the sentence of imprisonment is not to take effect unless either—

        (i) during the supervision period the offender fails to comply with a requirement imposed under paragraph (a), or

        (ii) during a period specified in the order for the purposes of this sub-paragraph (in this Chapter referred to as "the operational period") the offender commits in the United Kingdom another offence (whether or not punishable with imprisonment),

and (in either case) a court having power to do so subsequently orders under paragraph 8 of Schedule 12 that the original sentence is to take effect.

(2) Where two or more sentences imposed on the same occasion are to be served consecutively, the power conferred by subsection (1) is not exercisable in relation to any of them unless the aggregate of the terms of the sentences does not exceed 65 weeks.

(3) The supervision period and the operational period must each be a period of not less than six months and not more than two years beginning with the date of the order.

(4) The supervision period must not end later than the operational period.

(5) A court which passes a suspended sentence on any person for an offence may not impose a community sentence in his case in respect of that offence or any other offence of which he is convicted by or before the court or for which he is dealt with by the court.

(6) Subject to any provision to the contrary contained in the Criminal Justice Act 1967 (c. 80), the Sentencing Act or any other enactment passed or instrument made under any enactment after 31st December 1967, a suspended sentence which has not taken effect under paragraph 8 of Schedule 12 is to be treated as a sentence of imprisonment for the purposes of all enactments and instruments made under enactments.

(7) In this Part—
   (a) "suspended sentence order" means an order under subsection (1),
   (b) "suspended sentence" means a sentence to which a suspended sentence order relates, and
   (c) "community requirement", in relation to a suspended sentence order, means a requirement imposed under subsection (1)(a).

GENERAL NOTE

This section and ss.190–194 of the 2003 Act replace ss.118–125 of the Powers of Criminal Courts (Sentencing) Act 2000 and introduce a new form of suspended sentence.

Under the new system a court which passes a sentence of imprisonment for a term of at least 28 weeks but not more than 51 weeks may order that the sentence of imprisonment is not to take effect unless either the offender fails to comply with a requirement imposed by the court or commits another offence during the period specified in the order. A sentence which is capable of being a suspended is also subject to s.181 ("custody plus order") and the court is required to pass the sentence "in accordance with s.181". This appears to mean that before suspending such a sentence, the court must make the various orders required by s.181, which will take effect if the sentence is eventually ordered to be served. In addition the court must order the offender to comply with such requirements as may be specified during the "supervision period", and fix the "operational period" period. If the offender commits an offence during this period, he will be liable to serve the sentence, subject to the "custody plus" provisions.

The supervision and operational periods must each be at least six months and not more than two years; the supervision period may not extend beyond the operational period, but it appears that the operational period may extend beyond the end of the supervision period. If the court passes a suspended sentence, it may not impose a community sentence in respect of that offence or any other offence for which the offender is sentenced by the court.

If a court imposes two sentences to be served consecutively, the power to suspend the sentence is available only the aggregate term does not exceed 65 weeks.

When the court makes a suspended sentence order, it must explain the effect of the sentence, including the "custody plus" requirements, in accordance with s.174.

190   Imposition of requirements by suspended sentence order

(1) The requirements falling within this subsection are—
   (a) an unpaid work requirement (as defined by section 199),
   (b) an activity requirement (as defined by section 201),
   (c) a programme requirement (as defined by section 202),
   (d) a prohibited activity requirement (as defined by section 203),
   (e) a curfew requirement (as defined by section 204),
   (f) an exclusion requirement (as defined by section 205),
   (g) a residence requirement (as defined by section 206),
   (h) a mental health treatment requirement (as defined by section 207),
   (i) a drug rehabilitation requirement (as defined by section 209),
   (j) an alcohol treatment requirement (as defined by section 212),
   (k) a supervision requirement (as defined by section 213), and

(l) in a case where the offender is aged under 25, an attendance centre requirement (as defined by section 214).

(2) Section 189(1)(a) has effect subject to section 218 and to the following provisions of Chapter 4 relating to particular requirements—

  (a) section 199(3) (unpaid work requirement),

  (b) section 201(3) and (4) (activity requirement),

  (c) section 202(4) and (5) (programme requirement),

  (d) section 203(2) (prohibited activity requirement),

  (e) section 207(3) (mental health treatment requirement),

  (f) section 209(2) (drug rehabilitation requirement), and

  (g) section 212(2) and (3) (alcohol treatment requirement).

(3) Where the court makes a suspended sentence order imposing a curfew requirement or an exclusion requirement, it must also impose an electronic monitoring requirement (as defined by section 215) unless—

  (a) the court is prevented from doing so by section 215(2) or 218(4), or

  (b) in the particular circumstances of the case, it considers it inappropriate to do so.

(4) Where the court makes a suspended sentence order imposing an unpaid work requirement, an activity requirement, a programme requirement, a prohibited activity requirement, a residence requirement, a mental health treatment requirement, a drug rehabilitation requirement, an alcohol treatment requirement, a supervision requirement or an attendance centre requirement, the court may also impose an electronic monitoring requirement unless the court is prevented from doing so by section 215(2) or 218(4).

(5) Before making a suspended sentence order imposing two or more different requirements falling within subsection (1), the court must consider whether, in the circumstances of the case, the requirements are compatible with each other.

GENERAL NOTE

This section lists the various requirements which may be included in a suspended sentence order. They are the same requirements which may be included in a community order under s.177. Detailed provisions regulating each of the requirements are set out in the sections of the Act dealing with those requirements in particular. In specifying any requirement, and the court must comply with the general restrictions on imposing requirements, which relate in particular to the availability of the requirement to court concerned (s.218), and any specific provisions relating to the particular requirement. Before making a suspended order imposing two or more different requirements, the court must consider whether the requirement and their compatibility with each other.

191 Power to provide for review of suspended sentence order

(1) A suspended sentence order may—

  (a) provide for the order to be reviewed periodically at specified intervals,

  (b) provide for each review to be made, subject to section 192(4), at a hearing held for the purpose by the court responsible for the order (a "review hearing"),

  (c) require the offender to attend each review hearing, and

  (d) provide for the responsible officer to make to the court responsible for the order, before each review, a report on the offender's progress in complying with the community requirements of the order.

(2) Subsection (1) does not apply in the case of an order imposing a drug rehabilitation requirement (provision for such a requirement to be subject to review being made by section 210).

(3) In this section references to the court responsible for a suspended sentence order are references—

    (a) where a court is specified in the order in accordance with subsection (4), to that court;

    (b) in any other case, to the court by which the order is made.

(4) Where the area specified in a suspended sentence order made by a magistrates' court is not the area for which the court acts, the court may, if it thinks fit, include in the order provision specifying for the purpose of subsection (3) a magistrates' court which acts for the area specified in the order.

(5) Where a suspended sentence order has been made on an appeal brought from the Crown Court or from the criminal division of the Court of Appeal, it is to be taken for the purposes of subsection (3)(b) to have been made by the Crown Court.

GENERAL NOTE

This section allows a court making a suspended sentence order to provide, if it wishes to do so, for periodic reviews of the order at specified interval. The order may provide for the review to be made at a hearing held by the court responsible for the order and require the offender to attend each review hearing. At the hearing the responsible officer may be required to report on the offender's progress in complying with the community requirements of the order.

This provision does not apply where the suspended sentence order imposes a drug rehabilitation requirement, which will contain its own review provisions.

192 Periodic reviews of suspended sentence order

(1) At a review hearing (within the meaning of subsection (1) of section 191) the court may, after considering the responsible officer's report referred to in that subsection, amend the community requirements of the suspended sentence order, or any provision of the order which relates to those requirements.

(2) The court—

    (a) may not amend the community requirements of the order so as to impose a requirement of a different kind unless the offender expresses his willingness to comply with that requirement,

    (b) may not amend a mental health treatment requirement, a drug rehabilitation requirement or an alcohol treatment requirement unless the offender expresses his willingness to comply with the requirement as amended,

    (c) may amend the supervision period only if the period as amended complies with section 189(3) and (4),

    (d) may not amend the operational period of the suspended sentence, and

    (e) except with the consent of the offender, may not amend the order while an appeal against the order is pending.

(3) For the purposes of subsection (2)(a)—

    (a) a community requirement falling within any paragraph of section 190(1) is of the same kind as any other community requirement falling within that paragraph, and

    (b) an electronic monitoring requirement is a community require- ment of the same kind as any requirement falling within section 190(1) to which it relates.

(4) If before a review hearing is held at any review the court, after considering the responsible officer's report, is of the opinion that the

offender's progress in complying with the community requirements of the order is satisfactory, it may order that no review hearing is to be held at that review; and if before a review hearing is held at any review, or at a review hearing, the court, after considering that report, is of that opinion, it may amend the suspended sentence order so as to provide for each subsequent review to be held without a hearing.

(5) If at a review held without a hearing the court, after considering the responsible officer's report, is of the opinion that the offender's progress under the order is no longer satisfactory, the court may require the offender to attend a hearing of the court at a specified time and place.

(6) If at a review hearing the court is of the opinion that the offender has without reasonable excuse failed to comply with any of the community requirements of the order, the court may adjourn the hearing for the purpose of dealing with the case under paragraph 8 of Schedule 12.

(7) At a review hearing the court may amend the suspended sentence order so as to vary the intervals specified under section 191(1).

(8) In this section any reference to the court, in relation to a review without a hearing, is to be read—

(a) in the case of the Crown Court, as a reference to a judge of the court, and

(b) in the case of a magistrates' court, as a reference to a justice of the peace acting for the commission area for which the court acts.

GENERAL NOTE

This section provides further details in connection with periodic reviews of suspended sentence orders. Subsection (2) limits the powers of the court to vary the requirements imposed as a condition of the order. The operational period of the sentence may not be amended, and the supervision period may not be altered so that it is reduced to less than six months or extended beyond two years from the date of the order, or so as to end later than the end of the operational of period.

If the court receives a report from the responsible officer before a review hearing that offender's progress is satisfactory, it may order that no review hearing is to be held and may amend the suspended sentence order so as to provide that subsequent reviews are to be held about hearing. If at a review held without a hearing, the court is of the opinion that the offender's progress is no longer satisfactory, the court may require the offender to attend a hearing for the purpose of a review. If at a review hearing the court is of the opinion that the offender has failed to comply with the community requirements of the order without reasonable excuse, it may adjourn with a view to proceedings for breach.

193   Breach, revocation or amendment of suspended sentence order, and effect of further conviction

Schedule 12 (which relates to the breach, revocation or amendment of the community requirements of suspended sentence orders, and to the effect of any further conviction) shall have effect.

GENERAL NOTE

This section gives effect to Sch.12, which provides for breach of the community requirements of a suspended sentence order and for the effect of a conviction for an offence committed during the operational period of the order. The follows the scheme of Schedule 8, suitably adapted. If after the appropriate procedure has been followed the court is satisfied that the offender has failed without reasonable excuse to comply with any of the community requirements of the suspended sentence order, the court may order the suspended sentence to take effect with the original term and custodial period unaltered, or order the sentence to take effect with either a lesser term or a lesser custodial period, each of which must comply with s.181 of the 2003 Act (custody plus order). Alternatively the court may impose a more onerous community requirement or extend the supervision period or the operational appeared, complying in each case with s.189. The court must normally order the sentence to take effect unless it would be unjust to do so in all the circumstances, which include the extent to which the offender has complied with the community requirements of the suspended sentence order.

The same provisions apply where the offender is convicted of an offence committed during the operational period of the sentence. It is not necessarily for the offence to be punishable with imprisonment, as was the case under the corresponding provisions of the Powers of Criminal Courts (Sentencing) Act 2000.

194   Transfer of suspended sentence orders to Scotland or Northern Ireland

Schedule 13 (transfer of suspended sentence orders to Scotland or Northern Ireland) shall have effect.

Interpretation of Chapter

195   Interpretation of Chapter 3

In this Chapter—
"custodial period", in relation to a term of imprisonment imposed in accordance with section 181, has the meaning given by subsection (3)(a) of that section;
"licence period"—
(a) in relation to a term of imprisonment imposed in accordance with section 181, has the meaning given by subsection (3)(b) of that section, and
(b) in relation to a term of imprisonment to which an intermittent custody order relates, has the meaning given by section 183(3);
"the number of custodial days", in relation to a term of imprisonment to which an intermittent custody order relates, has the meaning given by section 183(3);
"operational period" and "supervision period", in relation to a suspended sentence, are to be read in accordance with section 189(1);
"sentence of imprisonment" does not include a committal for contempt of court or any kindred offence.

GENERAL NOTE
This section lists a number of definitions which are found in the particular provisions mentioned in the section.

CHAPTER 4

FURTHER PROVISIONS ABOUT ORDERS UNDER CHAPTERS 2 AND 3

Introductory

196   Meaning of "relevant order"

(1) In this Chapter "relevant order" means—
(a) a community order,
(b) a custody plus order,
(c) a suspended sentence order, or
(d) an intermittent custody order.
(2) In this Chapter any reference to a requirement being imposed by, or included in, a relevant order is, in relation to a custody plus order or an intermittent custody order, a reference to compliance with the requirement being required by the order to be a condition of a licence.

GENERAL NOTE
Part 4 of the Act creates a new scheme of community orders, to replace the previous scheme of separate types of community order, such as a community rehabilitation order, a community

punishment order, a drug treatment and testing order and so forth. Under the new scheme there will be a single community order, to which the sentencing court may attach such requirements as may be appropriate from the list of requirements set out in the following provisions of the Act. The same requirements in general may be attached to a custody plus order under s.181, a suspended sentence order under s.189 or an intermittent custody order under s.183.

197   Meaning of "the responsible officer"

(1) For the purposes of this Part, "the responsible officer", in relation to an offender to whom a relevant order relates, means—
  (a) in a case where the order—
      (i) imposes a curfew requirement or an exclusion requirement but no other requirement mentioned in section 177(1) or, as the case requires, section 182(1) or 190(1), and
      (ii) imposes an electronic monitoring requirement,
      the person who under section 215(3) is responsible for the electronic monitoring required by the order;
  (b) in a case where the offender is aged 18 or over and the only requirement imposed by the order is an attendance centre requirement, the officer in charge of the attendance centre in question;
  (c) in any other case, the qualifying officer who, as respects the offender, is for the time being responsible for discharging the functions conferred by this Part on the responsible officer.
(2) The following are qualifying officers for the purposes of subsection (1)(c)—
  (a) in a case where the offender is aged under 18 at the time when the relevant order is made, an officer of a local probation board appointed for or assigned to the petty sessions area for the time being specified in the order or a member of a youth offending team established by a local authority for the time being specified in the order;
  (b) in any other case, an officer of a local probation board appointed for or assigned to the petty sessions area for the time being specified in the order.
(3) The Secretary of State may by order—
  (a) amend subsections (1) and (2), and
  (b) make any other amendments of this Part that appear to him to be necessary or expedient in consequence of any amendment made by virtue of paragraph (a).
(4) An order under subsection (3) may, in particular, provide for the court to determine which of two or more descriptions of "responsible officer" is to apply in relation to any relevant order.

GENERAL NOTE

This section defines the expression "the responsible officer" in relation to the various types of requirement which may be imposed under the following subsections. In most cases, the responsible officer will be an officer of a local probation or board (formerly known as a probation officer). In cases where the only requirements of an order are curfew requirements or exclusion requirements and there is in addition an electronic monitoring requirement, the responsible officer is the person responsible for the electronic monitoring. Where the requirement is that an offender attend an attendance centre, the officer in charge of the attendance centre will be the responsible officer.

198   Duties of responsible officer

(1) Where a relevant order has effect, it is the duty of the responsible officer—
  (a) to make any arrangements that are necessary in connection with the requirements imposed by the order,

   (b) to promote the offender's compliance with those requirements, and

   (c) where appropriate, to take steps to enforce those requirements.

(2) In this section "responsible officer" does not include a person falling within section 197(1)(a).

GENERAL NOTE

   This section prescribes the duty of the "responsible officer" in connection with the operation of requirements imposed under community orders, custody plus orders intermittent custody orders and suspended sentence orders. The general duties imposed by this section to not apply to officers whose responsibility is limited to electronic monitoring of curfew and exclusion orders.

Requirements available in case of all offenders

199   Unpaid work requirement

(1) In this Part "unpaid work requirement", in relation to a relevant order, means a requirement that the offender must perform unpaid work in accordance with section 200.

(2) The number of hours which a person may be required to work under an unpaid work requirement must be specified in the relevant order and must be in the aggregate—

   (a) not less than 40, and

   (b) not more than 300.

(3) A court may not impose an unpaid work requirement in respect of an offender unless after hearing (if the courts thinks necessary) an appropriate officer, the court is satisfied that the offender is a suitable person to perform work under such a requirement.

(4) In subsection (3) "an appropriate officer" means—

   (a) in the case of an offender aged 18 or over, an officer of a local probation board, and

   (b) in the case of an offender aged under 18, an officer of a local probation board, a social worker of a local authority social services department or a member of a youth offending team.

(5) Where the court makes relevant orders in respect of two or more offences of which the offender has been convicted on the same occasion and includes unpaid work requirements in each of them, the court may direct that the hours of work specified in any of those requirements is to be concurrent with or additional to those specified in any other of those orders, but so that the total number of hours which are not concurrent does not exceed the maximum specified in subsection (2)(b).

GENERAL NOTE

   This section replaces the provisions in the Powers of Criminal Courts (Sentencing) Act 2000, s.46 regulating what was previously known as a "community punishment order", or in earlier times a "community service order". The section is substantially based on the earlier legislation, with amendments, and modifications to conform to the new scheme of community orders. The main change is that the maximum number of hours of unpaid work which may be required under an unpaid work requirement is increased from the previous maximum of 240 to 300.

   The requirements of the earlier legislation relating to the duty of the court to explain the meaning of a community punishment order are now found in the general obligations of the court to explain the effect of a sentence in s.174. It is not necessary that the offender should consent to the imposition of an unpaid work

200   Obligations of person subject to unpaid work requirement

(1) An offender in respect of whom an unpaid work requirement of a relevant order is in force must perform for the number of hours specified in the order such work at such times as he may be instructed by the responsible officer.

(2) Subject to paragraph 20 of Schedule 8 and paragraph 18 of Schedule 12 (power to extend order), the work required to be performed under an unpaid work requirement of a community order or a suspended sentence order must be performed during a period of twelve months.

(3) Unless revoked, a community order imposing an unpaid work requirement remains in force until the offender has worked under it for the number of hours specified in it.

(4) Where an unpaid work requirement is imposed by a suspended sentence order, the supervision period as defined by section 189(1)(a) continues until the offender has worked under the order for the number of hours specified in the order, but does not continue beyond the end of the operational period as defined by section 189(1)(b)(ii).

GENERAL NOTE

This section sets out the obligations of an offender who is subject to an unpaid work requirement. He must perform the number of hours specified in the order as and when instructed by the responsible officer. In normal circumstances, the whole of the work must be completed within a period of 12 months. The order remains in force until the number of hours of work specified have been completed, except in the case of an unpaid work requirement imposed by a suspended sentence order. In this case the requirement does not continue beyond the end of the operational period of the suspended sentence, even though the offender has not completed the number of hours he is required to work.

201 Activity requirement

(1) In this Part "activity requirement", in relation to a relevant order, means a requirement that the offender must do either or both of the following—

   (a) present himself to a person or persons specified in the relevant order at a place or places so specified on such number of days as may be so specified;

   (b) participate in activities specified in the order on such number of days as may be so specified.

(2) The specified activities may consist of or include activities whose purpose is that of reparation, such as activities involving contact between offenders and persons affected by their offences.

(3) A court may not include an activity requirement in a relevant order unless—

   (a) it has consulted—

      (i) in the case of an offender aged 18 or over, an officer of a local probation board,

      (ii) in the case of an offender aged under 18, either an officer of a local probation board or a member of a youth offending team, and

   (b) it is satisfied that it is feasible to secure compliance with the requirement.

(4) A court may not include an activity requirement in a relevant order if compliance with that requirement would involve the co-operation of a person other than the offender and the offender's responsible officer, unless that other person consents to its inclusion.

(5) The aggregate of the number of days specified under subsection (1)(a) and (b) must not exceed 60.

(6) A requirement such as is mentioned in subsection (1)(a) operates to require the offender—

   (a) in accordance with instructions given by his responsible officer, to present himself at a place or places on the number of days specified in the order, and

   (b) while at any place, to comply with instructions given by, or under the authority of, the person in charge of that place.

(7) A place specified under subsection (1)(a) must be—

    (a) a community rehabilitation centre, or

    (b) a place that has been approved by the local probation board for the area in which the premises are situated as providing facilities suitable for persons subject to activity requirements.

  (8) Where the place specified under subsection (1)(a) is a community rehabilitation centre, the reference in subsection (6)(a) to the offender presenting himself at the specified place includes a reference to him presenting himself elsewhere than at the centre for the purpose of participating in activities in accordance with instructions given by, or under the authority of, the person in charge of the centre.

  (9) A requirement to participate in activities operates to require the offender—

    (a) in accordance with instructions given by his responsible officer, to participate in activities on the number of days specified in the order, and

    (b) while participating, to comply with instructions given by, or under the authority of, the person in charge of the activities.

(10) In this section "community rehabilitation centre" means premises—

    (a) at which non-residential facilities are provided for use in connection with the rehabilitation of offenders, and

    (b) which are for the time being approved by the Secretary of State as providing facilities suitable for persons subject to relevant orders.

GENERAL NOTE

These provisions are derived from the Powers of Criminal Courts (Sentencing) Act 2000 Sch.2, with minor modifications of detail.

202   Programme requirement

  (1) In this Part "programme requirement", in relation to a relevant order, means a requirement that the offender must participate in an accredited programme specified in the order at a place so specified on such number of days as may be so specified.

  (2) In this Part "accredited programme" means a programme that is for the time being accredited by the accreditation body.

  (3) In this section—

    (a) "programme" means a systematic set of activities, and

    (b) "the accreditation body" means such body as the Secretary of State may designate for the purposes of this section by order.

  (4) A court may not include a programme requirement in a relevant order unless—

    (a) the accredited programme which the court proposes to specify in the order has been recommended to the court as being suitable for the offender—

      (i) in the case of an offender aged 18 or over, by an officer of a local probation board, or

     (ii) in the case of an offender aged under 18, either by an officer of a local probation board or by a member of a youth offending team, and

    (b) the court is satisfied that the programme is (or, where the relevant order is a custody plus order or an intermittent custody order, will be) available at the place proposed to be specified.

  (5) A court may not include a programme requirement in a relevant order if compliance with that requirement would involve the co-operation of a person other than the offender and the offender's responsible officer, unless that other person consents to its inclusion.

  (6) A requirement to attend an accredited programme operates to require the offender—

(a) in accordance with instructions given by the responsible officer, to participate in the accredited programme at the place specified in the order on the number of days specified in the order, and

(b) while at that place, to comply with instructions given by, or under the authority of, the person in charge of the programme.

(7) A place specified in an order must be a place that has been approved by the local probation board for the area in which the premises are situated as providing facilities suitable for persons subject to programme requirements.

GENERAL NOTE

This section, which is new, provides for a programme requirement requiring the offender to take part in a set of activities which has been accredited by the accreditation body.

203   Prohibited activity requirement

(1) In this Part "prohibited activity requirement", in relation to a relevant order, means a requirement that the offender must refrain from participating in activities specified in the order—

(a) on a day or days so specified, or

(b) during a period so specified.

(2) A court may not include a prohibited activity requirement in a relevant order unless it has consulted—

(a) in the case of an offender aged 18 or over, an officer of a local probation board;

(b) in the case of an offender aged under 18, either an officer of a local probation board or a member of a youth offending team.

(3) The requirements that may by virtue of this section be included in a relevant order include a requirement that the offender does not possess, use or carry a firearm within the meaning of the Firearms Act 1968 (c. 27).

GENERAL NOTE

This section replaces the "negative requirement" of the community punishment order for which provision was made in the Powers of Criminal Courts (Sentencing) Act 2000, Sch.2, para.2 with a "prohibited activity requirement".

204   Curfew requirement

(1) In this Part "curfew requirement", in relation to a relevant order, means a requirement that the offender must remain, for periods specified in the relevant order, at a place so specified.

(2) A relevant order imposing a curfew requirement may specify different places or different periods for different days, but may not specify periods which amount to less than two hours or more than twelve hours in any day.

(3) A community order or suspended sentence order which imposes a curfew requirement may not specify periods which fall outside the period of six months beginning with the day on which it is made.

(4) A custody plus order which imposes a curfew requirement may not specify a period which falls outside the period of six months beginning with the first day of the licence period as defined by section 181(3)(b).

(5) An intermittent custody order which imposes a curfew requirement must not specify a period if to do so would cause the aggregate number of days on which the offender is subject to the requirement for any part of the day to exceed 182.

(6) Before making a relevant order imposing a curfew requirement, the court must obtain and consider information about the place proposed

to be specified in the order (including information as to the attitude of persons likely to be affected by the enforced presence there of the offender).

GENERAL NOTE

This section replaces the Powers of Criminal Courts (Sentencing) Act 2000, s.37 which provided for a curfew order. Some of the requirements of the previous legislation which specific to curfew orders, in particular those relating to electronic monitoring, are now found in general provisions of this Act dealing with requirements generally.

205 Exclusion requirement

(1) In this Part "exclusion requirement", in relation to a relevant order, means a provision prohibiting the offender from entering a place specified in the order for a period so specified.

(2) Where the relevant order is a community order, the period specified must not be more than two years.

(3) An exclusion requirement—
  (a) may provide for the prohibition to operate only during the periods specified in the order, and
  (b) may specify different places for different periods or days.

(4) In this section "place" includes an area.

GENERAL NOTE

This section replaces the Powers of Criminal Courts (Sentencing) Act 2000, s.40A, inserted into the Act by the Criminal Justice and Court Services Act 2000, s.46. Section 46 was never brought into force so the exclusion order contemplated by the amended section has never been in operation. This section is essentially similar in its effect to s.40A, but many of the specific provisions of that section, such as the duty of the court to explain the order in ordinary language, are replaced by general obligations such as those set out in s.174 of the 2003 Act.

206 Residence requirement

(1) In this Part, "residence requirement", in relation to a community order or a suspended sentence order, means a requirement that, during a period specified in the relevant order, the offender must reside at a place specified in the order.

(2) If the order so provides, a residence requirement does not prohibit the offender from residing, with the prior approval of the responsible officer, at a place other than that specified in the order.

(3) Before making a community order or suspended sentence order containing a residence requirement, the court must consider the home surroundings of the offender.

(4) A court may not specify a hostel or other institution as the place where an offender must reside, except on the recommendation of an officer of a local probation board.

GENERAL NOTE

This section replaces the Powers of Criminal Courts (Sentencing) Act 2000 Sch.2, para.1, which provided for residence requirements as requirements of community rehabilitation orders.

207 Mental health treatment requirement

(1) In this Part, "mental health treatment requirement", in relation to a community order or suspended sentence order, means a requirement that the offender must submit, during a period or periods specified in the order, to treatment by or under the direction of a registered medical practitioner or a chartered psychologist (or both, for different

periods) with a view to the improvement of the offender's mental condition.

(2) The treatment required must be such one of the following kinds of treatment as may be specified in the relevant order—

   (a) treatment as a resident patient in an independent hospital or care home within the meaning of the Care Standards Act 2000 (c. 14) or a hospital within the meaning of the Mental Health Act 1983 (c. 20), but not in hospital premises where high security psychiatric services within the meaning of that Act are provided;

   (b) treatment as a non-resident patient at such institution or place as may be specified in the order;

   (c) treatment by or under the direction of such registered medical practitioner or chartered psychologist (or both) as may be so specified;

   but the nature of the treatment is not to be specified in the order except as mentioned in paragraph (a), (b) or (c).

(3) A court may not by virtue of this section include a mental health treatment requirement in a relevant order unless—

   (a) the court is satisfied, on the evidence of a registered medical practitioner approved for the purposes of section 12 of the Mental Health Act 1983, that the mental condition of the offender—

      (i) is such as requires and may be susceptible to treatment, but

      (ii) is not such as to warrant the making of a hospital order or guardianship order within the meaning of that Act;

   (b) the court is also satisfied that arrangements have been or can be made for the treatment intended to be specified in the order (including arrangements for the reception of the offender where he is to be required to submit to treatment as a resident patient); and

   (c) the offender has expressed his willingness to comply with such a requirement.

(4) While the offender is under treatment as a resident patient in pursuance of a mental health requirement of a relevant order, his responsible officer shall carry out the supervision of the offender to such extent only as may be necessary for the purpose of the revocation or amendment of the order.

(5) Subsections (2) and (3) of section 54 of the Mental Health Act 1983 (c. 20) have effect with respect to proof for the purposes of subsection (3)(a) of an offender's mental condition as they have effect with respect to proof of an offender's mental condition for the purposes of section 37(2)(a) of that Act.

(6) In this section and section 208, "chartered psychologist" means a person for the time being listed in the British Psychological Society's Register of Chartered Psychologists.

GENERAL NOTE

This section replaces the Powers of Criminal Courts (Sentencing) Act 2000 Sch.2, para.(5), which provided for requirements as to psychiatric treatment in the context of community rehabilitation orders. The substance of the section is substantially similar to that of the previous legislation, or with some minor modifications relating to the nature of the hospitals or care homes within which the required treatment may be carried out.

As under the previous legislation, a mental health treatment requirement may not be imposed on an offender unless he expresses his willingness to comply with the requirement.

208 Mental health treatment at place other than that specified in order

(1) Where the medical practitioner or chartered psychologist by whom or under whose direction an offender is being treated for his mental

condition in pursuance of a mental health treatment requirement is of the opinion that part of the treatment can be better or more conveniently given in or at an institution or place which—

(a) is not specified in the relevant order, and

(b) is one in or at which the treatment of the offender will be given by or under the direction of a registered medical practitioner or chartered psychologist,

he may, with the consent of the offender, make arrangements for him to be treated accordingly.

(2) Such arrangements as are mentioned in subsection (1) may provide for the offender to receive part of his treatment as a resident patient in an institution or place notwithstanding that the institution or place is not one which could have been specified for that purpose in the relevant order.

(3) Where any such arrangements as are mentioned in subsection (1) are made for the treatment of an offender—

(a) the medical practitioner or chartered psychologist by whom the arrangements are made shall give notice in writing to the offender's responsible officer, specifying the institution or place in or at which the treatment is to be carried out; and

(b) the treatment provided for by the arrangements shall be deemed to be treatment to which he is required to submit in pursuance of the relevant order.

GENERAL NOTE

This section substantially reproduces the Powers of Criminal Courts (Sentencing) Act 2000 Sch.2 paras (5)(5)–(5)(8).

209   Drug rehabilitation requirement

(1) In this Part "drug rehabilitation requirement", in relation to a community order or suspended sentence order, means a requirement that during a period specified in the order ("the treatment and testing period") the offender—

(a) must submit to treatment by or under the direction of a specified person having the necessary qualifications or experience with a view to the reduction or elimination of the offender's dependency on or propensity to misuse drugs, and

(b) for the purpose of ascertaining whether he has any drug in his body during that period, must provide samples of such description as may be so determined, at such times or in such circumstances as may (subject to the provisions of the order) be determined by the responsible officer or by the person specified as the person by or under whose direction the treatment is to be provided.

(2) A court may not impose a drug rehabilitation requirement unless—

(a) it is satisfied—

(i) that the offender is dependent on, or has a propensity to misuse, drugs, and

(ii) that his dependency or propensity is such as requires and may be susceptible to treatment,

(b) it is also satisfied that arrangements have been or can be made for the treatment intended to be specified in the order (including arrangements for the reception of the offender where he is to be required to submit to treatment as a resident),

(c) the requirement has been recommended to the court as being suitable for the offender—

(i) in the case of an offender aged 18 or over, by an officer of a local probation board, or

      (ii) in the case of an offender aged under 18, either by an officer of a local probation board or by a member of a youth offending team, and

    (d) the offender expresses his willingness to comply with the requirement.

(3) The treatment and testing period must be at least six months.

(4) The required treatment for any particular period must be—

    (a) treatment as a resident in such institution or place as may be specified in the order, or

    (b) treatment as a non-resident in or at such institution or place, and at such intervals, as may be so specified;

    but the nature of the treatment is not to be specified in the order except as mentioned in paragraph (a) or (b) above.

(5) The function of making a determination as to the provision of samples under provision included in the community order or suspended sentence order by virtue of subsection (1)(b) is to be exercised in accordance with guidance given from time to time by the Secretary of State.

(6) A community order or suspended sentence order imposing a drug rehabilitation requirement must provide that the results of tests carried out on any samples provided by the offender in pursuance of the requirement to a person other than the responsible officer are to be communicated to the responsible officer.

(7) In this section "drug" means a controlled drug as defined by section 2 of the Misuse of Drugs Act 1971 (c. 38).

GENERAL NOTE

This section, together with ss.210 and 211 of the 2003 Act, replace the provisions ss.52–55 of the Powers of Criminal Courts (Sentencing) Act 2000 providing for drug treatment and testing orders. The effect of the sections is substantially similar to those of the previous legislation, although some of the specific provisions, such as those imposing a duty on the court to explain the effect of the sentence, are carried forward into general provisions of the 2003 Act, such as s.174.

210   Drug rehabilitation requirement: provision for review by court

(1) A community order or suspended sentence order imposing a drug rehabilitation requirement may (and must if the treatment and testing period is more than 12 months)—

    (a) provide for the requirement to be reviewed periodically at intervals of not less than one month,

    (b) provide for each review of the requirement to be made, subject to section 211(6), at a hearing held for the purpose by the court responsible for the order (a "review hearing"),

    (c) require the offender to attend each review hearing,

    (d) provide for the responsible officer to make to the court responsible for the order, before each review, a report in writing on the offender's progress under the requirement, and

    (e) provide for each such report to include the test results communicated to the responsible officer under section 209(6) or otherwise and the views of the treatment provider as to the treatment and testing of the offender.

(2) In this section references to the court responsible for a community order or suspended sentence order imposing a drug rehabilitation requirement are references—

    (a) where a court is specified in the order in accordance with subsection (3), to that court;

    (b) in any other case, to the court by which the order is made.

(3) Where the area specified in a community order or suspended sentence order which is made by a magistrates' court and imposes a drug rehabilitation requirement is not the area for which the court acts, the court may, if it thinks fit, include in the order provision specifying for the purposes of subsection (2) a magistrates' court which acts for the area specified in the order.

(4) Where a community order or suspended sentence order imposing a drug rehabilitation requirement has been made on an appeal brought from the Crown Court or from the criminal division of the Court of Appeal, for the purposes of subsection (2)(b) it shall be taken to have been made by the Crown Court.

GENERAL NOTE

This section substantially reproduces the Powers of Criminal Courts (Sentencing) Act 2000, ss.54(6)–54(9) dealing with the periodic review of drug rehabilitation requirements.

211   Periodic review of drug rehabilitation requirement

(1) At a review hearing (within the meaning given by subsection (1) of section 210) the court may, after considering the responsible officer's report referred to in that subsection, amend the community order or suspended sentence order, so far as it relates to the drug rehabilitation requirement.

(2) The court—

  (a) may not amend the drug rehabilitation requirement unless the offender expresses his willingness to comply with the requirement as amended,

  (b) may not amend any provision of the order so as to reduce the period for which the drug rehabilitation requirement has effect below the minimum specified in section 209(3), and

  (c) except with the consent of the offender, may not amend any requirement or provision of the order while an appeal against the order is pending.

(3) If the offender fails to express his willingness to comply with the drug rehabilitation requirement as proposed to be amended by the court, the court may—

  (a) revoke the community order, or the suspended sentence order and the suspended sentence to which it relates, and

  (b) deal with him, for the offence in respect of which the order was made, in any way in which he could have been dealt with for that offence by the court which made the order if the order had not been made.

(4) In dealing with the offender under subsection (3)(b), the court—

  (a) shall take into account the extent to which the offender has complied with the requirements of the order, and

  (b) may impose a custodial sentence (where the order was made in respect of an offence punishable with such a sentence) notwithstanding anything in section 152(2).

(5) Where the order is a community order made by a magistrates' court in the case of an offender under 18 years of age in respect of an offence triable only on indictment in the case of an adult, any powers exercisable under subsection (3)(b) in respect of the offender after he attains the age of 18 are powers to do either or both of the following—

  (a) to impose a fine not exceeding £5,000 for the offence in respect of which the order was made;

  (b) to deal with the offender for that offence in any way in which the court could deal with him if it had just convicted him of an offence punishable with imprisonment for a term not exceeding twelve months.

(6) If at a review hearing (as defined by section 210(1)(b)) the court, after considering the responsible officer's report, is of the opinion that the offender's progress under the requirement is satisfactory, the court may so amend the order as to provide for each subsequent review to be made by the court without a hearing.

(7) If at a review without a hearing the court, after considering the responsible officer's report, is of the opinion that the offender's progress under the requirement is no longer satisfactory, the court may require the offender to attend a hearing of the court at a specified time and place.

(8) At that hearing the court, after considering that report, may—

(a) exercise the powers conferred by this section as if the hearing were a review hearing, and

(b) so amend the order as to provide for each subsequent review to be made at a review hearing.

(9) In this section any reference to the court, in relation to a review without a hearing, is to be read—

(a) in the case of the Crown Court, as a reference to a judge of the court;

(b) in the case of a magistrates' court, as a reference to a justice of the peace acting for the commission area for which the court acts.

GENERAL NOTE

This section substantially reproduces the Powers of Criminal Courts (Sentencing) Act 2000, s.55 with minor amendments.

212 Alcohol treatment requirement

(1) In this Part "alcohol treatment requirement", in relation to a community order or suspended sentence order, means a requirement that the offender must submit during a period specified in the order to treatment by or under the direction of a specified person having the necessary qualifications or experience with a view to the reduction or elimination of the offender's dependency on alcohol.

(2) A court may not impose an alcohol treatment requirement in respect of an offender unless it is satisfied—

(a) that he is dependent on alcohol,

(b) that his dependency is such as requires and may be susceptible to treatment, and

(c) that arrangements have been or can be made for the treatment intended to be specified in the order (including arrangements for the reception of the offender where he is to be required to submit to treatment as a resident).

(3) A court may not impose an alcohol treatment requirement unless the offender expresses his willingness to comply with its requirements.

(4) The period for which the alcohol treatment requirement has effect must be not less than six months.

(5) The treatment required by an alcohol treatment requirement for any particular period must be—

(a) treatment as a resident in such institution or place as may be specified in the order,

(b) treatment as a non-resident in or at such institution or place, and at such intervals, as may be so specified, or

(c) treatment by or under the direction of such person having the necessary qualification or experience as may be so specified;

but the nature of the treatment shall not be specified in the order except as mentioned in paragraph (a), (b) or (c) above.

GENERAL NOTE

This section substantially reproduces the Powers of Criminal Courts (Sentencing) Act 2000, Sch.2, para.6 insofar as that paragraph relates to treatment for dependency on alcohol.

An alcohol treatment requirement may not be imposed unless the offender expresses his willingness to complying with the requirement.

213   Supervision requirement

(1) In this Part "supervision requirement", in relation to a relevant order, means a requirement that, during the relevant period, the offender must attend appointments with the responsible officer or another person determined by the responsible officer, at such time and place as may be determined by the officer.

(2) The purpose for which a supervision requirement may be imposed is that of promoting the offender's rehabilitation.

(3) In subsection (1) "the relevant period" means—

(a) in relation to a community order, the period for which the community order remains in force,

(b) in relation to a custody plus order, the licence period as defined by section 181(3)(b),

(c) in relation to an intermittent custody order, the licence periods as defined by section 183(3), and

(d) in relation to a suspended sentence order, the supervision period as defined by section 189(1)(a).

GENERAL NOTE

This section replaces the Powers of Criminal Courts (Sentencing) Act 2000, s.41 which empowered the court to make a community rehabilitation order which always included a supervision requirement in addition to such other requirements as might be specified in the particular case. Section 41 provided that such an order might be made if the court considered supervision "desirable in the interests of (a) securing his rehabilitation, or (b) protecting the public from harm from him or preventing the commission by him of further offences". The second and third of these objectives disappear from the provision.

Requirements available only in case of offenders aged under 25

214   Attendance centre requirement

(1) In this Part "attendance centre requirement", in relation to a relevant order, means a requirement that the offender must attend at an attendance centre specified in the relevant order for such number of hours as may be so specified.

(2) The aggregate number of hours for which the offender may be required to attend at an attendance centre must not be less than 12 or more than 36.

(3) The court may not impose an attendance centre requirement unless the court is satisfied that the attendance centre to be specified in it is reasonably accessible to the offender concerned, having regard to the means of access available to him and any other circumstances.

(4) The first time at which the offender is required to attend at the attendance centre is a time notified to the offender by the responsible officer.

(5) The subsequent hours are to be fixed by the officer in charge of the centre, having regard to the offender's circumstances.

(6) An offender may not be required under this section to attend at an attendance centre on more than one occasion on any day, or for more than three hours on any occasion.

<small>GENERAL NOTE</small>

This section replaces the provisions of the Powers of Criminal Courts (Sentencing) Act 2000, s.60 providing for attendance centre orders for offenders over the age of sixteen. The new legislation is not subject to maximum age limit, and an attendance centre requirement may be made for an offence which is not punishable with imprisonment. Otherwise, the legislation is substantially similar in its effect to the legislation it replaces.

Electronic monitoring

215   Electronic monitoring requirement

(1) In this Part "electronic monitoring requirement", in relation to a relevant order, means a requirement for securing the electronic monitoring of the offender's compliance with other requirements imposed by the order during a period specified in the order, or determined by the responsible officer in accordance with the relevant order.

(2) Where—
   (a) it is proposed to include in a relevant order a requirement for securing electronic monitoring in accordance with this section, but
   (b) there is a person (other than the offender) without whose co-operation it will not be practicable to secure the monitoring, the requirement may not be included in the order without that person's consent.

(3) A relevant order which includes an electronic monitoring requirement must include provision for making a person responsible for the monitoring; and a person who is made so responsible must be of a description specified in an order made by the Secretary of State.

(4) Where an electronic monitoring requirement is required to take effect during a period determined by the responsible officer in accordance with the relevant order, the responsible officer must, before the beginning of that period, notify—
   (a) the offender,
   (b) the person responsible for the monitoring, and
   (c) any person falling within subsection (2)(b),
   of the time when the period is to begin.

<small>GENERAL NOTE</small>

This section replaces the Powers of Criminal Courts (Sentencing) Act 2000, s.36B as inserted by the Criminal Justice and Court Services Act 2000, s.52 and never brought into force, and the monitoring provisions of s.37 of that Act, which related to curfew orders.

Provisions applying to relevant orders generally

216   Petty sessions area to be specified in relevant order

(1) A community order or suspended sentence order must specify the petty sessions area in which the offender resides or will reside.

(2) A custody plus order or an intermittent custody order must specify the petty sessions area in which the offender will reside—
   (a) in the case of a custody plus order, during the licence period as defined by section 181(3)(b), or

(b) in the case of an intermittent custody order, during the licence periods as defined by section 183(3).

GENERAL NOTE
This section reproduces the obligation of a court making a community rehabilitation order or a community punishment order to specify the petty sessional area in which the offender resides or will reside (see the Powers of Criminal Courts (Sentencing) Act 2000, ss.41(3) and 46(9)) and applies it to all community orders and suspended sentence orders, and to the licence period of custody plus orders and intermittent custody orders.

217 Requirement to avoid conflict with religious beliefs, etc.

(1) The court must ensure, as far as practicable, that any requirement imposed by a relevant order is such as to avoid—
  (a) any conflict with the offender's religious beliefs or with the requirements of any other relevant order to which he may be subject; and
  (b) any interference with the times, if any, at which he normally works or attends school or any other educational establishment.
(2) The responsible officer in relation to an offender to whom a relevant order relates must ensure, as far as practicable, that any instruction given or requirement imposed by him in pursuance of the order is such as to avoid the conflict or interference mentioned in subsection (1).
(3) The Secretary of State may by order provide that subsection (1) or (2) is to have effect with such additional restrictions as may be specified in the order.

GENERAL NOTE
This section reproduces as a general provision applicable to all requirements the provisions of the Powers of Criminal Courts (Sentencing) Act 2000, s.37 dealing with curfew orders.

218 Availability of arrangements in local area

(1) A court may not include an unpaid work requirement in a relevant order unless the court is satisfied that provision for the offender to work under such a requirement can be made under the arrangements for persons to perform work under such a requirement which exist in the petty sessions area in which he resides or will reside.
(2) A court may not include an activity requirement in a relevant order unless the court is satisfied that provision for the offender to participate in the activities proposed to be specified in the order can be made under the arrangements for persons to participate in such activities which exist in the petty sessions area in which he resides or will reside.
(3) A court may not include an attendance centre requirement in a relevant order in respect of an offender unless the court has been notified by the Secretary of State that an attendance centre is available for persons of his description.
(4) A court may not include an electronic monitoring requirement in a relevant order in respect of an offender unless the court—
  (a) has been notified by the Secretary of State that electronic monitoring arrangements are available in the relevant areas mentioned in subsections (5) to (7), and
  (b) is satisfied that the necessary provision can be made under those arrangements.
(5) In the case of a relevant order containing a curfew requirement or an exclusion requirement, the relevant area for the purposes of subsection (4) is the area in which the place proposed to be specified in the order is situated.

(6) In the case of a relevant order containing an attendance centre requirement, the relevant area for the purposes of subsection (4) is the area in which the attendance centre proposed to be specified in the order is situated.

(7) In the case of any other relevant order, the relevant area for the purposes of subsection (4) is the petty sessions area proposed to be specified in the order.

(8) In subsection (5) "place", in relation to an exclusion requirement, has the same meaning as in section 205.

GENERAL NOTE

This section brings together in one place a series of restrictions on the powers of a court to impose requirements of particular kinds. The various kinds of requirements specified in the section may not be made unless either appropriate arrangements for their administration exist, or in some cases the court has been notified by the Secretary of State that such arrangements are in effect. Similar provisions are found in the provisions relating to the specific community orders replaced by Ch.4 of this Act.

219   Provision of copies of relevant orders

(1) The court by which any relevant order is made must forthwith provide copies of the order—
   (a) to the offender,
   (b) if the offender is aged 18 or over, to an officer of a local probation board assigned to the court,
   (c) if the offender is aged 16 or 17, to an officer of a local probation board assigned to the court or to a member of a youth offending team assigned to the court, and
   (d) where the order specifies a petty sessions area for which the court making the order does not act, to the local probation board acting for that area.

(2) Where a relevant order imposes any requirement specified in the first column of Schedule 14, the court by which the order is made must also forthwith provide the person specified in relation to that requirement in the second column of that Schedule with a copy of so much of the order as relates to that requirement.

(3) Where a relevant order specifies a petty sessions area for which the court making the order does not act, the court making the order must provide to the magistrates's court acting for that area—
   (a) a copy of the order, and
   (b) such documents and information relating to the case as it considers likely to be of assistance to a court acting for that area in the exercise of its functions in relation to the order.

DEFINITIONS
   "Relevant order": s.196

GENERAL NOTE

Most of the provisions of the Powers of Criminal Courts (Sentencing) Act 2000 dealing with community orders require the court to give a copy of the order to the offender and others concerned with administration of the order as soon as it has been made (see ss.41(9) and 46(11)). This section makes a general provision to the same effect which applies to all "relevant orders" as defined in s.196.

220   Duty of offender to keep in touch with responsible officer

(1) An offender in respect of whom a community order or a suspended sentence order is in force—
   (a) must keep in touch with the responsible officer in accordance with such instructions as he may from time to time be given by that officer, and

(b) must notify him of any change of address.

(2) The obligation imposed by subsection (1) is enforceable as if it were a requirement imposed by the order.

An obligation to keep in touch with the responsible officer and to notify the officer of any change of address is found in the provisions of the Powers of Criminal Courts (Sentencing) Act 2000 governing separate community orders (see ss.41(11) and 47(1)). This section creates a general obligation which applies to all community orders and suspended sentences. Failure to comply with the obligation amounts in effect to a breach of a requirement of the order.

Powers of Secretary of State

221 Provision of attendance centres

(1) The Secretary of State may continue to provide attendance centres.
(2) In this Part "attendance centre" means a place at which offenders aged under 25 may be required to attend and be given under supervision appropriate occupation or instruction in pursuance of—
    (a) attendance centre requirements of relevant orders, or
    (b) attendance centre orders under section 60 of the Sentencing Act.
(3) For the purpose of providing attendance centres, the Secretary of State may make arrangements with any local authority or police authority for the use of premises of that authority.

GENERAL NOTE
This section replaces the Powers of Criminal Courts (Sentencing) Act 2000, s.62 authorising the Secretary of State to continue to provide attendance centres.

222 Rules

(1) The Secretary of State may make rules for regulating—
    (a) the supervision of persons who are subject to relevant orders,
    (b) without prejudice to the generality of paragraph (a), the functions of responsible officers in relation to offenders subject to relevant orders,
    (c) the arrangements to be made by local probation boards for persons subject to unpaid work requirements to perform work and the performance of such work,
    (d) the provision and carrying on of attendance centres and community rehabilitation centres,
    (e) the attendance of persons subject to activity requirements or attendance centre requirements at the places at which they are required to attend, including hours of attendance, reckoning days of attendance and the keeping of attendance records,
    (f) electronic monitoring in pursuance of an electronic monitoring requirement, and
    (g) without prejudice to the generality of paragraph (f), the functions of persons made responsible for securing electronic monitoring in pursuance of such a requirement.
(2) Rules under subsection (1)(c) may, in particular, make provision—
    (a) limiting the number of hours of work to be done by a person on any one day,
    (b) as to the reckoning of hours worked and the keeping of work records, and
    (c) for the payment of travelling and other expenses in connection with the performance of work.

GENERAL NOTE
This section confers upon the Secretary of State rule making powers in connection with the various matters specified in the section.

223 Power to amend limits

(1) The Secretary of State may by order amend—
    (a) subsection (2) of section 199 (unpaid work requirement), or
    (b) subsection (2) of section 204 (curfew requirement),
        by substituting, for the maximum number of hours for the time being specified in that subsection, such other number of hours as may be specified in the order.

(2) The Secretary of State may by order amend any of the provisions mentioned in subsection (3) by substituting, for any period for the time being specified in the provision, such other period as may be specified in the order.

(3) Those provisions are—
    (a) section 204(3) (curfew requirement);
    (b) section 205(2) (exclusion requirement);
    (c) section 209(3) (drug rehabilitation requirement);
    (d) section 212(4) (alcohol treatment requirement).

GENERAL NOTE

This section empowers the Secretary of State to make minor amendments of detail, as specified in the section, to the provisions relating to the requirements mentioned in the section.

CHAPTER 5

DANGEROUS OFFENDERS

224 Meaning of "specified offence" etc.

(1) An offence is a "specified offence" for the purposes of this Chapter if it is a specified violent offence or a specified sexual offence.

(2) An offence is a "serious offence" for the purposes of this Chapter if and only if—
    (a) it is a specified offence, and
    (b) it is, apart from section 225, punishable in the case of a person aged 18 or over by—
        (i) imprisonment for life, or
        (ii) imprisonment for a determinate period of ten years or more.

(3) In this Chapter—
    "relevant offence" has the meaning given by section 229(4);
    "serious harm" means death or serious personal injury, whether physical or psychological;
    "specified violent offence" means an offence specified in Part 1 of Schedule 15;
    "specified sexual offence" means an offence specified in Part 2 of that Schedule.

GENERAL NOTE

Chapter Five of Pt 12 of the 2003 Act establishes a new scheme of custodial sentences for dangerous offenders. None of the provisions apply to offences committed before the commencement date of the relevant sections, and presumably the previous law will continue in effect for the purpose of pre-commencement offences. The new scheme applies to offenders convicted of either a "serious offence" or a "specified offence". A "serious offence" is a "specified offence" which is punishable by life imprisonment, or imprisonment for a term of 10 years or more. An offence which is punishable by a term of imprisonment for 10 years or more but which is not listed as a "specified offence" does not qualify as a "serious offence". Burglary of a dwelling, which is punishable by 14 years imprisonment, is a "specified violent offence" only if it is committed with intent to inflict grievous bodily harm on a person or do unlawful damage to a building or anything in it; burglary with intent to rape is a "specified sexual offence". Burglary of a dwelling is thus a "serious offence" only if committed with one of those intents.

Under the scheme of this Chapter of the 2003 Act, life imprisonment will continue to be available where an offence is punishable by life imprisonment and the court considers "that the seriousness of the offence, or of the offence and one or more offences associated with it, is such as to justify the imposition of a sentence of imprisonment for life". It remains to be seen how this requirement will be interpreted by the courts. The traditional criteria for the imposition of a discretionary life sentence have always included a requirement that the offence be sufficiently serious as to justify a long custodial sentence, but it may be that the statutory provision goes further and requires that a life sentence be justifiable as a commensurate sentence. If this is so, the sentence of life imprisonment will become extremely rare, and will in practice be replaced by the new sentence of "imprisonment for public protection". This sentence will be available where an offender has been convicted of a "serious offence", the court is of the opinion that there is a significant risk to the public of serious harm being occasioned by the commission by him of further specified (but not necessarily "serious") offences, and the offence of which the offender has been convicted is either punishable with imprisonment for life, or with 10 years imprisonment or more.

The sentence of imprisonment for public protection is an indeterminate sentence and a court passing such a sentence must fix a "minimum term" in accordance with the Powers of Criminal Courts (Sentencing) Act 2000, s.82A.

Extended sentences, which take the form of a custodial sentence followed by an extended licence period, will be limited so far as adult offenders are concerned to offenders convicted of "specified offences" which are not "serious offences" (that is, are punishable by a sentence of the less than 10 years imprisonment). The "longer than commensurate" sentence introduced by the Criminal Justice Act 1991, s.2(2)(b) replaced by the Powers of Criminal Courts (Sentencing) Act 2000, s.80(2)(b) disappears.

This section provides the definitions which form the basis of the new scheme.

225 Life sentence or imprisonment for public protection for serious offences

(1) This section applies where—
    (a) a person aged 18 or over is convicted of a serious offence committed after the commencement of this section, and
    (b) the court is of the opinion that there is a significant risk to members of the public of serious harm occasioned by the commission by him of further specified offences.

(2) If—
    (a) the offence is one in respect of which the offender would apart from this section be liable to imprisonment for life, and
    (b) the court considers that the seriousness of the offence, or of the offence and one or more offences associated with it, is such as to justify the imposition of a sentence of imprisonment for life,
    the court must impose a sentence of imprisonment for life.

(3) In a case not falling within subsection (2), the court must impose a sentence of imprisonment for public protection.

(4) A sentence of imprisonment for public protection is a sentence of imprisonment for an indeterminate period, subject to the provisions of Chapter 2 of Part 2 of the Crime (Sentences) Act 1997 (c. 43) as to the release of prisoners and duration of licences.

(5) An offence the sentence for which is imposed under this section is not to be regarded as an offence the sentence for which is fixed by law.

GENERAL NOTE

This section empowers the courts to impose either a sentence of imprisonment for life, or a sentence or imprisonment for public protection, on a person aged 18 or over. Corresponding provisions relating to persons aged under 18 are set out in s.226. To qualify for a sentence of imprisonment for life, the offender must satisfy four conditions. He must have been convicted of a "serious offence" punishable with life imprisonment; the offence must have been committed after the commencement date of the section; the court must be of the opinion that there is a significant risk to members of the public of serious harm occasioned by the commission by him of further specified offences; and the court must consider that "the seriousness of the offence or of the offence and one or more offences associated with it is such as to justify the imposition of a sentence of imprisonment for life". If these conditions are satisfied, the court must pass a sentence of life imprisonment. On one view, the statutory provisions reflect the well established criteria for the imposition of a discretionary life sentence, but there must be some doubt as to the meaning of the fourth condition, that the seriousness of the offence justifies the imposition of a sentence of imprisonment for life. Case-law requires that the offence for which a discretionary life sentence is imposed should be sufficiently serious to justify it a "very severe" sentence, but this does not necessarily indicate that a determinate sentence equivalent to life imprisonment would be appropriate. It remains to be seen how the court will interpret this requirement. On one view the requirement is much stricter than the conventional requirement for a discretionary life sentence and if that is correct, the use of life imprisonment would become extremely uncommon. Most cases which would previously have been dealt with by means of a discretionary life sentence will fall to be dealt with by a sentence of imprisonment for public protection.

To qualify for sentence of imprisonment for public protection, the offender must have been convicted of a "serious offence", the offence must have been committed after the commencement date of the section, and the court must be of the opinion that there is a significant risk to members of the public of serious harm occasioned by the commission by him of further specified offences. If these conditions are satisfied, the court must impose a sentence of imprisonment for public protection even though the maximum sentence for the offence is 10 years imprisonment.

In imposing a sentence of life imprisonment under subs.(2)(a) the court must fix a "minimum term" to be served before the offender can be considered for parole, in accordance with the Powers of Criminal Courts (Sentencing) Act 2000, s.82A unless under s.82A(4) it considers that in view of the seriousness of the offence or of the combination of the offence and one or more offences associated with it, no order should be made under the section. If the narrow view of the new statutory criterion of seriousness for a life sentence is adopted, this will normally be the case.

In imposing a sentence of imprisonment for public protection, the court must fix a "minimum term" under s.82A, and may not decline to do so on the grounds of the seriousness of the offence. The offender will be released on the direction of the Parole Board, in accordance with the Crime (Sentences) Act 1997, s.28 (as amended). Nothing is said in the section about the relationship between the minimum term specified for the purpose of the Powers of Criminal Courts (Sentencing) Act 2000, s.82A as amended by the 2003 Act, and the maximum sentence for the offence. It is clear that an offender subject to a sentence of imprisonment imposed for a "serious offence" normally punishable with a determinate maximum sentence may be detained in custody for a period longer than that maximum, but is a court entitled to fix a minimum term under the Powers of Criminal Courts (Sentencing) Act 2000, s.82A which is longer than the maximum sentence permitted for the offence, or longer than the maximum period during which the offender would be liable to be detained under the maximum sentence for the offence (normally half of that term, if the new parole provisions of Ch.6 are brought into force).

An offender sentenced to a term of imprisonment for public protection will remain on licence on release for at least the qualifying period of 10 years (see Sch.18), after which he may apply to the Parole Board for an order directing that his licence should cease to have effect.

It is a matter of great regret that in setting out these new provisions for dangerous offenders, it was not considered it necessary to bring within this Chapter of the 2003 Act those provisions of the other statutes which govern the release of offenders sentenced to the new forms of sentence, which are at present scattered in different parts of the statute book and have been heavily amended. The basic provisions governing release are found in the Crime (Sentences) Act 1997, Pt 2, Ch.2. They are significantly amended by the 2003 Act (Sch.18). The Powers of Criminal Courts (Sentencing) Act 2000, s.82A which was itself inserted into that Act by the Criminal Justice and Court Services Act 2000, s.60 is itself further amended by this Act. It is impossible to see any reason why the relevant provisions, in the form in which they will apply to this legislation, could not have been set out as part of this Chapter so as to indicate clearly what the consequences of imposing the new sentences are, and what are the duties of the court in doing so.

226   Detention for life or detention for public protection for serious offences committed by those under 18

(1) This section applies where—
   (a) a person aged under 18 is convicted of a serious offence committed after the commencement of this section, and
   (b) the court is of the opinion that there is a significant risk to members of the public of serious harm occasioned by the commission by him of further specified offences.
(2) If—

    (a) the offence is one in respect of which the offender would apart from this section be liable to a sentence of detention for life under section 91 of the Sentencing Act, and

    (b) the court considers that the seriousness of the offence, or of the offence and one or more offences associated with it, is such as to justify the imposition of a sentence of detention for life,

    the court must impose a sentence of detention for life under that section.

(3) If, in a case not falling within subsection (2), the court considers that an extended sentence under section 228 would not be adequate for the purpose of protecting the public from serious harm occasioned by the commission by the offender of further specified offences, the court must impose a sentence of detention for public protection.

(4) A sentence of detention for public protection is a sentence of detention for an indeterminate period, subject to the provisions of Chapter 2 of Part 2 of the Crime (Sentences) Act 1997 (c. 43) as to the release of prisoners and duration of licences.

(5) An offence the sentence for which is imposed under this section is not to be regarded as an offence the sentence for which is fixcd by law.

GENERAL NOTE

This section makes provision for sentences of detention for life, or detention for public protection, in the case of offenders under the age of 18. The section broadly corresponds to s.225, except in one respect. In the case of an adult offender, if the offender would qualify for a sentence of imprisonment for public protection, the court must impose that sentence and is not permitted to impose an extended sentence under s.227, which is available for a "specified offence" which is not a "serious offence". In the case of an offender under the age of 18, the court under subs.(3) is effectively given the choice between an extended sentence under s.228 of the Act and a sentence of detention for public protection. On the assumption that a sentence of detention for life is not available, on the ground that the maximum penalty for the offence is not life imprisonment, or that the seriousness condition set out in subs.(2)(b) is not satisfied, the statute contemplates that the court should first consider whether an extended sentence under s.228 would be adequate for the purpose of protecting the public from serious harm from the offender; only if it considers that such a sentence would not be adequate to protect the public may the court pass a sentence of detention for public protection under this section.

The main difference between a sentence or detention for public protection and an extended sentence is that under an extended sentence, the custodial period and the period of extended licence may not exceed the maximum sentence for the offence, and the extension period must not exceed the periods mentioned in s.228(4).

227   Extended sentence for certain violent or sexual offences: persons 18 or over

(1) This section applies where—

    (a) a person aged 18 or over is convicted of a specified offence, other than a serious offence, committed after the commencement of this section, and

    (b) the court considers that there is a significant risk to members of the public of serious harm occasioned by the commission by the offender of further specified offences.

(2) The court must impose on the offender an extended sentence of imprisonment, that is to say, a sentence of imprisonment the term of which is equal to the aggregate of—

    (a) the appropriate custodial term, and

    (b) a further period ("the extension period") for which the offender is to be subject to a licence and which is of such length as the court considers necessary for the purpose of protecting members of the public from serious harm occasioned by the commission by him of further specified offences.

(3) In subsection (2) "the appropriate custodial term" means a term of imprisonment (not exceeding the maximum term permitted for the offence) which—

    (a) is the term that would (apart from this section) be imposed in compliance with section 153(2), or

    (b) where the term that would be so imposed is a term of less than 12 months, is a term of 12 months.

(4) The extension period must not exceed—

    (a) five years in the case of a specified violent offence, and

    (b) eight years in the case of a specified sexual offence.

(5) The term of an extended sentence of imprisonment passed under this section in respect of an offence must not exceed the maximum term permitted for the offence.

GENERAL NOTE

This section, derived from the Powers of Criminal Courts (Sentencing) Act 2000, s.85 provides for extended sentences for offenders over the age of 18. To qualify for such a sentence, the offender must be convicted of a "specified offence" which is not a "serious offence," that is say, a specified offence with a maximum sentence of less than 10 years imprisonment. If the court considers that there is a significant risk that serious harm will be occasioned to members of the public by further specified offences committed by the offender, the court may impose an "extended sentence". The sentence has two components, the "appropriate custodial term" and the "extension period". The appropriate custodial term is the term which would otherwise be imposed in the normal way as the shortest term which is commensurate with the seriousness of the offence, or 12 months, whichever is the greater. The custodial term must not be increased to provide greater protection for the public. The extension period, the period of licence which follows release from the sentence, must not exceed five years in the case of a violent offence or eight years in the case of a sexual offence. The aggregate length of appropriate custodial term and the extension period must not exceed the maximum term permitted for the offence.

Provisions for the release of prisoners serving extended sentences, whether under s.227 (those over 18 when convicted) or s.228 (those under 18 when convicted) are set out in s.247. An extended sentence prisoner will serve a minimum of one half of the "appropriate custodial term" and will then have remain in custody until the Parole Board has directed his release. The Parole Board may not give a direction for his release unless it is satisfied that it is no longer necessary for the protection of the public that he should be confined. As soon as he has served the whole of the appropriate custodial term, (on the assumption that he has not already been released on licence) he must be released on licence.

228   Extended sentence for certain violent or sexual offences: persons under 18

(1) This section applies where—

    (a) a person aged under 18 is convicted of a specified offence committed after the commencement of this section, and

    (b) the court considers—

        (i) that there is a significant risk to members of the public of serious harm occasioned by the commission by the offender of further specified offences, and

        (ii) where the specified offence is a serious offence, that the case is not one in which the court is required by section 226(2) to impose a sentence of detention for life under section 91 of the Sentencing Act or by section 226(3) to impose a sentence of detention for public protection.

(2) The court must impose on the offender an extended sentence of detention, that is to say, a sentence of detention the term of which is equal to the aggregate of—

(a) the appropriate custodial term, and

(b) a further period ("the extension period") for which the offender is to be subject to a licence and which is of such length as the court considers necessary for the purpose of protecting members of the public from serious harm occasioned by the commission by him of further specified offences.

(3) In subsection (2) "the appropriate custodial term" means such term as the court considers appropriate, which—

(a) must be at least 12 months, and

(b) must not exceed the maximum term of imprisonment permitted for the offence.

(4) The extension period must not exceed—

(a) five years in the case of a specified violent offence, and

(b) eight years in the case of a specified sexual offence.

(5) The term of an extended sentence of detention passed under this section in respect of an offence must not exceed the maximum term of imprisonment permitted for the offence.

(6) Any reference in this section to the maximum term of imprisonment permitted for an offence is a reference to the maximum term of imprisonment that is, apart from section 225, permitted for the offence in the case of a person aged 18 or over.

GENERAL NOTE

This section makes provision for extended sentences to be imposed on offenders under the age of 18 on the date of conviction. The section is substantially similar to s.227 except in two respects. In the case of an offender under the age of 18, the court is not prevented from imposing an extended sentence by the fact that the offender has been convicted of a "serious offence". If the offence is a "serious offence", the court may impose an extended sentence if it is not obliged to impose a sentence of detention for life or a sentence of detention for public protection under s.226. The other difference is in the meaning of "the appropriate custodial term". In s.227, this is defined by reference to s.153(2), and must therefore be the shortest term which would be commensurate with the seriousness of the offence, or 12 months, whichever is the less. In this section, the "appropriate custodial term" is "such term as the court considers appropriate", being not less than 12 months nor more than the maximum permitted for the offence. The implication appears to be that in the case of an offender under 18, the court may pass an extended sentence with a custodial term which is longer than the shortest term which would be commensurate with the seriousness of the offence or offences.

229   The assessment of dangerousness

(1) This section applies where—

(a) a person has been convicted of a specified offence, and

(b) it falls to a court to assess under any of sections 225 to 228 whether there is a significant risk to members of the public of serious harm occasioned by the commission by him of further such offences.

(2) If at the time when that offence was committed the offender had not been convicted in any part of the United Kingdom of any relevant offence or was aged under 18, the court in making the assessment referred to in subsection (1)(b)—

(a) must take into account all such information as is available to it about the nature and circumstances of the offence,

(b) may take into account any information which is before it about any pattern of behaviour of which the offence forms part, and

(c) may take into account any information about the offender which is before it.

(3) If at the time when that offence was committed the offender was aged 18 or over and had been convicted in any part of the United Kingdom of one or more relevant offences, the court must assume that there is such a risk as is mentioned in subsection (1)(b) unless, after taking into account—

    (a) all such information as is available to it about the nature and circumstances of each of the offences,

    (b) where appropriate, any information which is before it about any pattern of behaviour of which any of the offences forms part, and

    (c) any information about the offender which is before it,

the court considers that it would be unreasonable to conclude that there is such a risk.

(4) In this Chapter "relevant offence" means—

    (a) a specified offence,

    (b) an offence specified in Schedule 16 (offences under the law of Scotland), or

    (c) an offence specified in Schedule 17 (offences under the law of Northern Ireland).

DEFINITIONS

"Specified offence": s.224
"Serious harm": s.224

GENERAL NOTE

This section deals with the matters which may be considered by a court in assessing whether an offender convicted of a "specified offence" is to be treated as a dangerous offender for the purposes of life imprisonment for detention for life, imprisonment or detention for public protection, or extended sentences. Subsection (2) obliges of the court to take into account all information available to it about the nature and circumstances of the offence, and permits the court to take into account any other information relating to the pattern of behaviour of which the offence forms part and any other information about offender. Why it was considered necessary to enact such a provision, which does not do more than state the obvious, is not clear.

Subsection (3) contains the vestigial remains of the short-lived automatic life sentence, originally enacted under the Crime (Sentences) Act 1997, and subsequently re-enacted as the Powers of Criminal Courts (Sentencing) Act 2000, s.109. If an offender convicted of a "specified offence" had been convicted before the day on which that offence was committed of a "relevant offence", which means a "specified offence" or an equivalent offence under the law of Scotland or Northern Ireland, the court must assume there is a such of serious harm to the public, unless it considers in the light of all such information as it before it that it would be unreasonable to conclude that there is such a risk. If the court does conclude that there is such a risk, it must pass either a life sentence, a sentence of imprisonment for public protection, or an extended sentence in the case of an adult, or in the case of an offender under 18, a life sentence, a sentence of detention for public protection or an extended sentence of detention.

230 Imprisonment or detention for public protection: release on licence

Schedule 18 (release of prisoners serving sentences of imprisonment or detention for public protection) shall have effect.

GENERAL NOTE

This section gives effect to Sch.18, which deals with the release of prisoners serving sentences of imprisonment or detention for public protection. Unfortunately, Sch.18 does not itself set out the relevant provisions a comprehensible form. It simply consists of a number of amendments which to the existing provisions, which have already been heavily amended by other legislation.

231 Appeals where previous convictions set aside

(1) This section applies where—

    (a) a sentence has been imposed on any person under section 225 or 227, and

    (b) any previous conviction of his without which the court would not have been required to make the assumption mentioned in section 229(3) has been subsequently set aside on appeal.

(2) Notwithstanding anything in section 18 of the Criminal Appeal Act 1968 (c. 19), notice of appeal against the sentence may be given at any time within 28 days from the date on which the previous conviction was set aside.

GENERAL NOTE

This section, derived from the Powers of Criminal Courts (Sentencing) Act 2000, s.112 deals with the case where a court has imposed a sentence on an offender on of the assumption that he is dangerous, and the assumption is based, in accordance with s.229(3), on a previous conviction for a "relevant offence". If the previous conviction is subsequently set aside on appeal, the offender may appeal against the sentence, and is not restricted by the normal time limits for appeal in the Criminal Appeal Act 1968 (c.19).

232 Certificates of convictions for purposes of section 229

Where—

(a) on any date after the commencement of this section a person is convicted in England and Wales of a relevant offence, and

(b) the court by or before which he is so convicted states in open court that he has been convicted of such an offence on that date, and

(c) that court subsequently certifies that fact,

that certificate shall be evidence, for the purposes of section 229, that he was convicted of such an offence on that date.

GENERAL NOTE

This section, derived from the Powers of Criminal Courts (Sentencing) Act 2000, s.113 provides for a court to state in open court and then to certify that the offender has been convicted on a specified date of an offence which is a "relevant offence", (that is to say a "specified offence" or an equivalent offence under the law of Scotland or Northern Ireland). Such a certificate is evidence of the conviction for the purposes of making the assumption under s.229(3). The certificate is not conclusive proof of the conviction, and the failure to make the statement in open court does not prevent proof of the conviction by other means.

233 Offences under service law

Where—

(a) a person has at any time been convicted of an offence under section 70 of the Army Act 1955 (3 & 4 Eliz. 2 c. 18), section 70 of the Air Force Act 1955 (3 & 4 Eliz. 2 c. 19) or section 42 of the Naval Discipline Act 1957 (c. 53), and

(b) the corresponding civil offence (within the meaning of that Act) was a relevant offence,

section 229 shall have effect as if he had at that time been convicted in England and Wales of the corresponding civil offence.

DEFINITIONS

"Relevant offence": s.229

GENERAL NOTE

This section reproduces the effect of the Powers of Criminal Courts (Sentencing) Act 2000 s.114, with reference to the concept of "relevant offence" under this Chapter.

234 Determination of day when offence committed

Where an offence is found to have been committed over a period of two or more days, or at some time during a period of two or more days, it shall be taken for the purposes of section 229 to have been committed on the last of those days.

GENERAL NOTE

This section is included in the Act for the purposes of applying s.229(3). If an offender convicted of a "specified offence" has been convicted on a previous occasion of a "relevant offence", but the indictment on which he was convicted of the specified offence charged that the offence was committed over a period of two or more days, or at some time such during such a period, the offence must be taken to have been committed on the last of those days, for the purpose of determining whether he had been convicted of the earlier "relevant offence" before committing the later "specified offence". Provisions similar to this one are frequently found in criminal statutes, but normally provide the opposite of this section — the offence is taken to have been committed on the earliest of the days concerned.

235   Detention under sections 226 and 228

A person sentenced to be detained under section 226 or 228 is liable to be detained in such place, and under such conditions, as may be determined by the Secretary of State or by such other person as may be authorised by him for the purpose.

236   Conversion of sentences of detention into sentences of imprisonment

For section 99 of the Sentencing Act (conversion of sentence of detention and custody into sentence of imprisonment) there is substituted—

"Conversion of sentence of detention to sentence of imprisonment

99   Conversion of sentence of detention to sentence of imprisonment
   (1) Subject to the following provisions of this section, where an offender has been sentenced by a relevant sentence of detention to a term of detention and either—
       (a) he has attained the age of 21, or
       (b) he has attained the age of 18 and has been reported to the Secretary of State by the board of visitors of the institution in which he is detained as exercising a bad influence on the other inmates of the institution or as behaving in a disruptive manner to the detriment of those inmates,
       the Secretary of State may direct that he shall be treated as if he had been sentenced to imprisonment for the same term.
   (2) Where the Secretary of State gives a direction under subsection (1) above in relation to an offender, the portion of the term of detention imposed under the relevant sentence of detention which he has already served shall be deemed to have been a portion of a term of imprisonment.
   (3) Where the Secretary of State gives a direction under subsection (1) above in relation to an offender serving a sentence of detention for public protection under section 226 of the Criminal Justice Act 2003 the offender shall be treated as if he had been sentenced under section 225 of that Act; and where the Secretary of State gives such a direction in relation to an offender serving an extended sentence of detention under section 228 of that Act the offender shall be treated as if he had been sentenced under section 227 of that Act.
   (4) Rules under section 47 of the Prison Act 1952 may provide that any award for an offence against discipline made in respect of an offender serving a relevant sentence of detention shall continue to have effect after a direction under subsection (1) has been given in relation to him.
   (5) In this section "relevant sentence of detention" means—
       (a) a sentence of detention under section 90 or 91 above,
       (b) a sentence of detention for public protection under section 226 of the Criminal Justice Act 2003, or

(c) an extended sentence of detention under section 228 of that Act."

GENERAL NOTE

This section provides a replacement for the Powers of Criminal Courts (Sentencing) Act 2000, s.99 updating it to incorporate the new forms of sentence introduced by this Chapter. It is possible it see easily how the section applies to them. This section is an example of what might have been done in Sch.18.

CHAPTER 6

RELEASE ON LICENCE

Preliminary

237 Meaning of "fixed-term prisoner"

(1) In this Chapter "fixed-term prisoner" means—
 (a) a person serving a sentence of imprisonment for a determinate term, or
 (b) a person serving a determinate sentence of detention under section 91 of the Sentencing Act or under section 228 of this Act.
(2) In this Chapter, unless the context otherwise requires, "prisoner" includes a person serving a sentence falling within subsection (1)(b); and "prison" includes any place where a person serving such a sentence is liable to be detained.

GENERAL NOTE

Chapter 6 of Pt 12 of the Act establishes a new system governing the release on licence of fixed term prisoners serving determinate terms of imprisonment or detention. Offenders other than those sentenced to special forms of sentence for dangerous offenders, will serve half of the term imposed by the court and then become entitled to be released on licence. A court imposing a determinate sentence of 12 months or more is empowered to make a recommendation as to the particular conditions which should be included in any licence granted to an offender on his release. The Secretary of State is not bound to act on such a recommendation, but must take it into account.

A defendant who has been released on licence may have his licence revoked and be required to return to custody to continue to serve the sentence. The power of a court to order a defendant to serve a part of an earlier sentence, when he is convicted of an offence committed after his release from that sentence, previously found in the Powers of Criminal Courts (Sentencing) Act 2000 s.116, is not reproduced in this Chapter.

This section provides the basic definitions for the purpose of this chapter.

Power of court to recommend licence conditions

238 Power of court to recommend licence conditions for certain prisoners

(1) A court which sentences an offender to a term of imprisonment of twelve months or more in respect of any offence may, when passing sentence, recommend to the Secretary of State particular conditions which in its view should be included in any licence granted to the offender under this Chapter on his release from prison.
(2) In exercising his powers under section 250(4)(b) in respect of an offender, the Secretary of State must have regard to any recommendation under subsection (1).
(3) A recommendation under subsection (1) is not to be treated for any purpose as part of the sentence passed on the offender.
(4) This section does not apply in relation to a sentence of detention under section 91 of the Sentencing Act or section 228 of this Act.

GENERAL NOTE

This section empowers a court which imposes on an offender over the age of the 18 a term of imprisonment of 12 months or more in respect of any offence, to recommend particular conditions which should be included in any licence granted to the offender on his release from prison after serving half of the term imposed. It appears that the power is limited to a case where a term of 12 months is imposed in respect of a single offence, and it may be that it is not available were the court imposes an aggregate of two terms, each of less than 12 months, but amounting in total to more than 12 (for example, nine months and nine months consecutive). The power is not available in respect of an offender under the age of 18 sentenced to detention under the Powers of Criminal Courts (Sentencing) Act 2000, s.91 or and an offender under the age of 18 sentenced to an extended sentence under s.228 of the 2003 Act.

The Secretary of State is not bound to impose any condition recommended.

239   The Parole Board

(1) The Parole Board is to continue to be, by that name, a body corporate and as such is—
   (a) to be constituted in accordance with this Chapter, and
   (b) to have the functions conferred on it by this Chapter in respect of fixed-term prisoners and by Chapter 2 of Part 2 of the Crime (Sentences) Act 1997 (c. 43) (in this Chapter referred to as "the 1997 Act") in respect of life prisoners within the meaning of that Chapter.

(2) It is the duty of the Board to advise the Secretary of State with respect to any matter referred to it by him which is to do with the early release or recall of prisoners.

(3) The Board must, in dealing with cases as respects which it makes recommendations under this Chapter or under Chapter 2 of Part 2 of the 1997 Act, consider—
   (a) any documents given to it by the Secretary of State, and
   (b) any other oral or written information obtained by it;
   and if in any particular case the Board thinks it necessary to interview the person to whom the case relates before reaching a decision, the Board may authorise one of its members to interview him and must consider the report of the interview made by that member.

(4) The Board must deal with cases as respects which it gives directions under this Chapter or under Chapter 2 of Part 2 of the 1997 Act on consideration of all such evidence as may be adduced before it.

(5) Without prejudice to subsections (3) and (4), the Secretary of State may make rules with respect to the proceedings of the Board, including proceedings authorising cases to be dealt with by a prescribed number of its members or requiring cases to be dealt with at prescribed times.

(6) The Secretary of State may also give to the Board directions as to the matters to be taken into account by it in discharging any functions under this Chapter or under Chapter 2 of Part 2 of the 1997 Act; and in giving any such directions the Secretary of State must have regard to—
   (a) the need to protect the public from serious harm from offenders, and
   (b) the desirability of preventing the commission by them of further offences and of securing their rehabilitation.

(7) Schedule 19 shall have effect with respect to the Board.

GENERAL NOTE
This section provides for the continued existence of the Parole Board. The functions of the Parole Board will be those imposed by this Chapter in respect of fixed term prisoners and those imposed by the Crime (Sentences) Act 1997, Pt 2, Ch.2 with respect to life sentence prisoners (including those serving sentences of imprisonment for public protection). Under this legislation the Parole Board ceases to have any jurisdiction over the release of prisoners serving determinate sentences but it will be concerned with the revocation of licences in accordance

with s.254. The Board will be concerned in deciding on the release of offenders sentenced to extended sentences under ss.227 and 228 of the 2003 Act.

Effect of remand in custody

240 Crediting of periods of remand in custody: terms of imprisonment and detention

(1) This section applies where—
    (a) a court sentences an offender to imprisonment for a term in respect of an offence committed after the commencement of this section, and
    (b) the offender has been remanded in custody (within the meaning given by section 242) in connection with the offence or a related offence, that is to say, any other offence the charge for which was founded on the same facts or evidence.

(2) It is immaterial for that purpose whether the offender—
    (a) has also been remanded in custody in connection with other offences; or
    (b) has also been detained in connection with other matters.

(3) Subject to subsection (4), the court must direct that the number of days for which the offender was remanded in custody in connection with the offence or a related offence is to count as time served by him as part of the sentence.

(4) Subsection (3) does not apply if and to the extent that—
    (a) rules made by the Secretary of State so provide in the case of—
        (i) a remand in custody which is wholly or partly concurrent with a sentence of imprisonment, or
        (ii) sentences of imprisonment for consecutive terms or for terms which are wholly or partly concurrent, or
    (b) it is in the opinion of the court just in all the circumstances not to give a direction under that subsection.

(5) Where the court gives a direction under subsection (3), it shall state in open court—
    (a) the number of days for which the offender was remanded in custody, and
    (b) the number of days in relation to which the direction is given.

(6) Where the court does not give a direction under subsection (3), or gives such a direction in relation to a number of days less than that for which the offender was remanded in custody, it shall state in open court—
    (a) that its decision is in accordance with rules made under paragraph (a) of subsection (4), or
    (b) that it is of the opinion mentioned in paragraph (b) of that subsection and what the circumstances are.

(7) For the purposes of this section a suspended sentence—
    (a) is to be treated as a sentence of imprisonment when it takes effect under paragraph 8(2)(a) or (b) of Schedule 12, and
    (b) is to be treated as being imposed by the order under which it takes effect.

(8) For the purposes of the reference in subsection (3) to the term of imprisonment to which a person has been sentenced (that is to say, the reference to his "sentence"), consecutive terms and terms which are wholly or partly concurrent are to be treated as a single term if—
    (a) the sentences were passed on the same occasion, or
    (b) where they were passed on different occasions, the person has not been released under this Chapter at any time during the period beginning with the first and ending with the last of those occasions.

(9) Where an offence is found to have been committed over a period of two or more days, or at some time during a period of two or more days, it shall be taken for the purposes of subsection (1) to have been committed on the last of those days.

(10) This section applies to a determinate sentence of detention under section 91 of the Sentencing Act or section 228 of this Act as it applies to an equivalent sentence of imprisonment.

DEFINITIONS
"Remanded in custody": s.242(2)

GENERAL NOTE
This section was originally enacted as the Crime (Sentences) Act 1997, s.9 and was subsequently consolidated as the Powers of Criminal Courts (Sentencing) Act 2000, s.87. It has never been brought into force.

The effect of the section is to give to the sentencing court control over the extent to which any time spent in custody by an offender on the remand in connection with the offence for which he is to be sentenced, or in connection with related offences, shall count against the sentence which he is ordered to serve. If implemented, the section would remove many of the complex anomalies which have arisen under the earlier legislation, the Criminal Justice Act 1967, s.67.

In the normal case, the section requires a court sentencing an offender to a term of imprisonment to direct that all of the days which the offender has spent in custody on remand in connection with the offence or related offences are to count as time served by him as part of the sentence. The court may not give a direction in relation to a greater number of days than have actually been served on remand. If the court is of the opinion that it would be "just in all the circumstances" to do so, it may refrain from giving any direction under subs.(3) (in which event no time will count against the sentence) of give a direction under subs.(6), that a number of days less than the whole period during which the defendant was remanded in custody shall count against the sentence imposed. If the court gives no direction that days spent in custody on remand shall count, or gives a direction that a number of days less than the whole number shall count, it must state in open court either that it is of the opinion that making no direction, or a direction that less than the whole number of days should count, would be just in all circumstances, or that the decision has made in accordance with rules made by the Secretary of State under subs.(4)(a). If it gives a direction that any of the days are to count, it must in the direction specify the number of days during which the offender was remanded in custody and the number of days which are to count against his sentence.

In the case of a suspended sentence, the direction under this section is to be made by the court implementing the sentence, and not by the court imposing the sentence originally.

Where an offender is sentenced to a number of terms on the same occasion and the terms are consecutive or wholly or partly concurrent, they are to be treated as a single term. The same applies where an offender who is serving a sentence from which he has not been released is sentenced to a further term of imprisonment.

Separate provision is made for the treatment of extradited offenders by s.243. Days spent in custody abroad awaiting extradition are to be treated as if they were days spent in custody on remand for the purposes of this section.

241 Effect of direction under section 240 on release on licence

(1) In determining for the purposes of this Chapter or Chapter 3 (prison sentences of less than twelve months) whether a person to whom a direction under section 240 relates—

  (a) has served, or would (but for his release) have served, a particular proportion of his sentence, or

  (b) has served a particular period,
    the number of days specified in the direction are to be treated as having been served by him as part of that sentence or period.

(2) In determining for the purposes of section 183 (intermittent custody) whether any part of a sentence to which an intermittent custody order relates is a licence period, the number of custodial days, as defined by subsection (3) of that section, is to be taken to be reduced by the number of days specified in a direction under section 240.

GENERAL NOTE

This section provides for the effect of a direction given under s.240 relation to time spent in custody on remand. The effect of the direction is that the number of days specified are to be treated as having been served by the offender as part of the sentence for the purpose of determining the proportion of his sentence which the offender must serve, normally one half of the term imposed, before becoming entitled to be released. In the case of a "custody plus" order under s.181, the number of days are to be counted as having been served for the purpose of determining when the offender is entitled to be released on licence under s.181(3). In the case of an intermittent custody order, the number of custodial days is taken to be reduced by the number of days specified in the direction.

242   Interpretation of sections 240 and 241

(1) For the purposes of sections 240 and 241, the definition of "sentence of imprisonment" in section 305 applies as if for the words from the beginning of the definition to the end of paragraph (a) there were substituted—

""sentence of imprisonment" does not include a committal—

    (a) in default of payment of any sum of money, other than one adjudged to be paid on a conviction,";

and references in those sections to sentencing an offender to imprisonment, and to an offender's sentence, are to be read accordingly.

(2) References in sections 240 and 241 to an offender's being remanded in custody are references to his being—

    (a) remanded in or committed to custody by order of a court,

    (b) remanded or committed to local authority accommodation under section 23 of the Children and Young Persons Act 1969 (c. 54) and kept in secure accommodation or detained in a secure training centre pursuant to arrangements under subsection (7A) of that section, or

    (c) remanded, admitted or removed to hospital under section 35, 36, 38 or 48 of the Mental Health Act 1983 (c. 20).

(3) In subsection (2), "secure accommodation" has the same meaning as in section 23 of the Children and Young Persons Act 1969.

GENERAL NOTE

This section provides definitions for some of the terms used in Ch.6 of Pt 12, in particular "remanded in custody". It is noticeable that the concept of "remanded in custody" is narrower than the equivalent concept in the Criminal Justice Act 1967, s.67 as amended, as this section makes no reference to time spent in police detention. Time will be treated as having been spent in custody only were the offender has been remanded or committed to custody by a court, remanded to local authority accommodation and kept in secure accommodation or otherwise detained in a secure training centre, or admitted to hospital under one of the specified sections of the Mental Health Act 1983. The fact that an offender is in custody simultaneously for some other reason, such as that he has been detained in connection with his immigration status, or is serving a term of imprisonment for which he has been committed in default of payment of a sum of money, does not prevent the relevant time from counting for the purpose of this part of the 2003 Act (see s.240(2)(b)).

243   Persons extradited to the United Kingdom

(1) A fixed-term prisoner is an extradited prisoner for the purposes of this section if—

    (a) he was tried for the offence in respect of which his sentence was imposed—

        (i) after having been extradited to the United Kingdom, and

        (ii) without having first been restored or had an opportunity of leaving the United Kingdom, and

    (b) he was for any period kept in custody while awaiting his extradition to the United Kingdom as mentioned in paragraph (a).

(2) In the case of an extradited prisoner, section 240 has effect as if the days for which he was kept in custody while awaiting extradition were days for which he was remanded in custody in connection with the offence, or any other offence the charge for which was founded on the same facts or evidence.

(3) In this section—

"extradited to the United Kingdom" means returned to the United Kingdom—

  (a) in pursuance of extradition arrangements,

  (b) under any law of a designated Commonwealth country corresponding to the Extradition Act 1989 (c. 33),

  (c) under that Act as extended to a British overseas territory or under any corresponding law of a British overseas territory,

  (d) in pursuance of a warrant of arrest endorsed in the Republic of Ireland under the law of that country corresponding to the Backing of Warrants (Republic of Ireland) Act 1965 (c. 45), or

  (e) in pursuance of arrangements with a foreign state in respect of which an Order in Council under section 2 of the Extradition Act 1870 (c. 52) is in force;

"extradition arrangements" has the meaning given by section 3 of the Extradition Act 1989;

"designated Commonwealth country" has the meaning given by section 5(1) of that Act.

GENERAL NOTE

This section provides for the case of persons who are extradited to the United Kingdom under one of these arrangements mentioned in subs.(3). If such a person is sentenced to a determinate sentence after spending days in custody in a foreign jurisdiction while awaiting extradition, those days are to be treated as if they were days during which he was remanded in custody in connection with the offence of which he has been convicted. It follows that the court may give a direction under s.240 in respect of those days, in addition to a direction in respect of any days which the offender has spent in custody between his return to the United Kingdom and the date on which he was sentenced. Section 240(5) requires a court which makes such a direction to state the number of days for which the offender has been remanded in custody, and the number of days in relation to which the direction is given. It may be that a court dealing with an extradited prisoner should give the direction in two parts, so as to indicate how many days are days treated as days during which the offender was remanded in custody, by virtue of this section (the days spent in custody awaiting extradition), and how many days have been spent in custody following the offender's return to the United Kingdom. Under s.240(4) the court has a discretion not to give a direction if it considers it "just in all the circumstances" to take that course, or to give a direction that less than the whole number of days should be treated as having been served in custody on remand. In the case of an extradited prisoner, the decisions of the Court of Appeal indicate that in exercising the equivalent discretion under the previous legislation, the court may take into account the extent to which the offender has prolonged the period spent in foreign custody by his attempts to resist extradition.

Release on licence

244   Duty to release prisoners

(1) As soon as a fixed-term prisoner, other than a prisoner to whom section 247 applies, has served the requisite custodial period, it is the duty of the Secretary of State to release him on licence under this section.

(2) Subsection (1) is subject to section 245.

(3) In this section "the requisite custodial period" means—

  (a) in relation to a person serving a sentence of imprisonment for a term of twelve months or more or any determinate sentence of

　　　　　detention under section 91 of the Sentencing Act, one-half of his
　　　　　sentence,

(b) in relation to a person serving a sentence of imprisonment for a
term of less than twelve months (other than one to which an
intermittent custody order relates), the custodial period within
the meaning of section 181,

(c) in relation to a person serving a sentence of imprisonment to
which an intermittent custody order relates, any part of the term
which is not a licence period as defined by section 183(3), and

(d) in relation to a person serving two or more concurrent or
consecutive sentences, the period determined under sections
263(2) and 264(2).

GENERAL NOTE

This section provides for the release of prisoners sentenced to determinate sentences, other
than extended sentences. Any prisoner who is a fixed term prisoner, other than one serving an
extended sentence, must be released after he has served the "requisite custodial period", which
is normally one half of the sentence. Offenders sentenced to a "custody plus" order under s.181
are released at the end of the custodial period specified in the custody plus order. An offender
sentenced to an intermittent custody order is released after serving any part of the term which is
not a licence period as defined in s.183(3), that is, when he has served all of the custodial days.

The section introduces a major change in the parole system by comparison with that
established by the Criminal Justice Act 1991. Under the Criminal Justice Act 1991, prisoners
were divided into two categories, "short term prisoners" serving terms of less than four years
imprisonment, and "long term prisoners" serving terms of four years imprisonment or more.
Short term prisoners were entitled to be released after serving half of the sentence; long-term
prisoners became eligible for release at that stage, but did not become entitled to be released
until they had served two-thirds of the sentence. In either case the licence period ran until the
end of the third quarter of the sentence. The effect of this section is to apply to all prisoners the
entitlement to be released after serving half of the sentence imposed, but subject to a licence
which remains in effect, under s.249, for the whole of the remainder of the sentence, and not (as
under the previous legislation) until halfway through the second half of the sentence. Under this
legislation, a person sentenced to two years imprisonment will not find himself released any
earlier than he would have been under the old scheme, but will find that his licence lasts for
twice as long. A person sentenced to six years may be released earlier than he would otherwise
have been, as he will be entitled to be released after serving half of the sentence and not merely
be eligible for release at the discretion of the Parole Board, but this gain will be compensated by
an increase in the duration of his licence, which will now run until the end of six years from the
date of sentence, as opposed to four and a half years under the Criminal Justice Act 1991.

**245　Restrictions on operation of section 244(1) in relation to intermittent
　　　custody prisoners**

(1) Where an intermittent custody prisoner returns to custody after being
unlawfully at large within the meaning of section 49 of the Prison Act
1952 (c. 52) at any time during the currency of his sentence, section
244(1) does not apply until—

(a) the relevant time (as defined in subsection (2)), or

(b) if earlier, the date on which he has served in prison the number of
custodial days required by the intermittent custody order.

(2) In subsection (1)(a) "the relevant time" means—

(a) in a case where, within the period of 72 hours beginning with the
return to custody of the intermittent custody prisoner, the
Secretary of State or the responsible officer has applied to the
court for the amendment of the intermittent custody order under
paragraph 6(1)(b) of Schedule 10, the date on which the
application is withdrawn or determined, and

(b) in any other case, the end of that 72–hour period.

(3) Section 244(1) does not apply in relation to an intermittent custody
prisoner at any time after he has been recalled under section 254,

unless after his recall the Board has directed his further release on licence.

246   Power to release prisoners on licence before required to do so

(1) Subject to subsections (2) to (4), the Secretary of State may—
  (a) release on licence under this section a fixed-term prisoner, other than an intermittent custody prisoner, at any time during the period of 135 days ending with the day on which the prisoner will have served the requisite custodial period, and
  (b) release on licence under this section an intermittent custody prisoner when 135 or less of the required custodial days remain to be served.

(2) Subsection (1)(a) does not apply in relation to a prisoner unless—
  (a) the length of the requisite custodial period is at least 6 weeks,
  (b) he has served—
    (i) at least 4 weeks of his sentence, and
    (ii) at least one-half of the requisite custodial period.

(3) Subsection (1)(b) does not apply in relation to a prisoner unless—
  (a) the number of required custodial days is at least 42, and
  (b) the prisoner has served—
    (i) at least 28 of those days, and
    (ii) at least one-half of the total number of those days.

(4) Subsection (1) does not apply where—
  (a) the sentence is imposed under section 227 or 228,
  (b) the sentence is for an offence under section 1 of the Prisoners (Return to Custody) Act 1995 (c. 16),
  (c) the prisoner is subject to a hospital order, hospital direction or transfer direction under section 37, 45A or 47 of the Mental Health Act 1983 (c. 20),
  (d) the sentence was imposed by virtue of paragraph 9(1)(b) or (c) or 10(1)(b) or (c) of Schedule 8 in a case where the prisoner has failed to comply with a curfew requirement of a community order,
  (e) the prisoner is subject to the notification requirements of Part 2 of the Sexual Offences Act 2003 (c. 42),
  (f) the prisoner is liable to removal from the United Kingdom,
  (g) the prisoner has been released on licence under this section during the currency of the sentence, and has been recalled to prison under section 255(1)(a),
  (h) the prisoner has been released on licence under section 248 during the currency of the sentence, and has been recalled to prison under section 254, or
    (i) in the case of a prisoner to whom a direction under section 240 relates, the interval between the date on which the sentence was passed and the date on which the prisoner will have served the requisite custodial period is less than 14 days or, where the sentence is one of intermittent custody, the number of the required custodial days remaining to be served is less than 14.

(5) The Secretary of State may by order—
  (a) amend the number of days for the time being specified in subsection (1) (a) or (b), (3) or (4)(i),
  (b) amend the number of weeks for the time being specified in subsection (2)(a) or (b)(i), and
  (c) amend the fraction for the time being specified in subsection (2)(b)(ii) or (3)(b)(ii).

(6) In this section—

"the required custodial days", in relation to an intermittent custody prisoner, means—

(a) the number of custodial days specified under section 183, or

(b) in the case of two or more sentences of intermittent custody, the aggregate of the numbers so specified;

"the requisite custodial period" in relation to a person serving any sentence other than a sentence of intermittent custody, has the meaning given by paragraph (a), (b) or (d) of section 244(3);

"sentence of intermittent custody" means a sentence to which an intermittent custody order relates.

DEFINITIONS
"Fixed term prisoner": s.237
"Requisite custodial period": s.244

GENERAL NOTE
This section preserves the Home Detention Curfew scheme. The Home Detention Curfew scheme was introduced under the Crime and Disorder Act 1998, which inserted into the Criminal Justice Act 1991 a new s.34A. This section permitted the Secretary of State to release on licence short term prisoners (those sentenced to less than four years imprisonment) provided that they were 18 or over and serving a sentence of three months or more. Under the scheme, the Secretary of State was empowered to release the prisoner on licence before he had served half of the sentence and therefore entitled to release under s.33 of the Criminal Justice Act 1991. The maximum period by which the normal date of release could be brought forward in this way was set at 60 days (in the case of a sentence of eight months or more). Certain types of prisoners were excluded by statute from the scheme.

Anyone released under this scheme was required to comply with a curfew condition which was subject to electronic monitoring ("tagging"). The curfew was required to amount to at least nine hours in any one day, and would remain in force until the date on which the prisoner would have served one half of its entrance, and thus become entitled to release in the normal way.

The scope of the scheme was extended by a series of statutory instruments, the Release of Short-Term Prisoners on Licence (Amendment of Requisite Period) Order 2002 (SI 2002/2933) and the Release of Short-Term Prisoners on Licence (Amendment of Requisite Period) Order 2003 (SI 2003/1602). The effect of these changes was to increase substantially the length of time during which a prisoner may be released subject to home detention curfew, and thereby substantially reduce the period of the sentence which is required to be served in custody.

The scheme, expanded as a desperate measure in the face of a rapidly increasing prison population, is objectionable in principle on many grounds. First, it reduces or eliminates the differential between sentences imposed by the courts, particularly at the lower end of the scale. Second, the scheme effectively transfers to the prison governors a sentencing function performed in secret, without appropriate procedural safeguards of any kind or any publicly declared criteria. Third, the scheme operates arbitrarily with regard to different categories of offenders. Fourth, the scheme operates in a manner which is wholly lacking transparency. It is an elementary requirement that sentencing should take place in public view. Little or nothing can be easily discovered about the working of the scheme in practice.

This section preserves the essential features of the scheme, adapted to the new legislation. An apparently absolute discretion is conferred on the Secretary of State, and nothing is said in relation to procedures to be followed before the discretion is exercised. A prisoner released under this section must, by virtue of s.253, be subject to curfew conditions which must be electronically monitored. A prisoner will qualify for discretionary release under this section for a period of up to 135 days before the date on which he would become entitled to be released under s.244, so long as the nominal term of the sentence is at least twelve weeks, so as to produce a "requisite custodial period" of six weeks, and he has served at least four weeks of his sentence and one half of the requisite custodial period. A prisoner may not be released on home detention curfew under this section unless there remain at least 14 days of the requisite custodial period.

A prisoner sentenced to eighteen months' imprisonment will have a requisite custodial period of nine months, and will become eligible for release under this section after serving four and a half months. The scheme is modified to take account of the new provisions introduced by this Act in a manner which corresponds to the earlier scheme. Offenders subject to extended sentences under ss.227 and 228 are excluded (as were prisoners subject to extended sentences under the Powers of Criminal Courts (Sentencing) Act 2000, s.85).

247   Release on licence of prisoner serving extended sentence under section 227 or 228

(1) This section applies to a prisoner who is serving an extended sentence imposed under section 227 or 228.

(2) As soon as—

    (a) a prisoner to whom this section applies has served one-half of the appropriate custodial term, and

    (b) the Parole Board has directed his release under this section,

    it is the duty of the Secretary of State to release him on licence.

(3) The Parole Board may not give a direction under subsection (2) unless the Board is satisfied that it is no longer necessary for the protection of the public that the prisoner should be confined.

(4) As soon as a prisoner to whom this section applies has served the appropriate custodial term, it is the duty of the Secretary of State to release him on licence unless the prisoner has previously been recalled under section 254.

(5) Where a prisoner to whom this section applies is released on a licence, the Secretary of State may not by virtue of section 250(4)(b) include, or subsequently insert, a condition in the licence, or vary or cancel a condition in the licence, except after consultation with the Board.

(6) For the purposes of subsection (5), the Secretary of State is to be treated as having consulted the Board about a proposal to include, insert, vary or cancel a condition in any case if he has consulted the Board about the implementation of proposals of that description generally or in that class of case.

(7) In this section "the appropriate custodial term" means the period determined by the court as the appropriate custodial term under section 227 or 228.

GENERAL NOTE

This section provides for the release of offenders sentenced to extended sentences of imprisonment under s.227 or detention under s.228. An extended sentence consists of an "appropriate custodial term" and an extension period, during which the offender will remain on licence. Under this section, offenders subject to extended sentences will be required to serve at least half of the appropriate custodial term, as in the case of offenders sentenced to normal determinate sentences, but they will not then be entitled to be released unless the Parole Board directs their release. The Parole Board may not direct the release of an extended sentence prisoner unless it is satisfied that it is no longer necessary for the protection to the public that he should be detained. If he is not released on such a direction before the end of the appropriate custodial term specified by the court, the prisoner subject to an extended sentence must be released when he has served the whole of the appropriate custodial term.

The licence period will begin on the date on which the defendant is released from custody under the appropriate custodial term, rather than at the end of the appropriate custodial term itself. This is a difference from an extended sentence under the Powers of Criminal Courts (Sentencing) Act 2000, s.85 under which the extended licence period begins at the end of the period which would have been the normal licence period if the custodial term of that sentence had been a normal custodial sentence.

248   Power to release prisoners on compassionate grounds

(1) The Secretary of State may at any time release a fixed-term prisoner on licence if he is satisfied that exceptional circumstances exist which justify the prisoner's release on compassionate grounds.

(2) Before releasing under this section a prisoner to whom section 247 applies, the Secretary of State must consult the Board, unless the circumstances are such as to render such consultation impracticable.

GENERAL NOTE

This section, derived from the Criminal Justice Act 1991, s.36 provides for the release of a prisoner on licence before he has served the "requisite custodial period" of a determinate sentence, or one half of the "appropriate custodial term" of an extended sentence, if there are exceptional circumstances justifying his release on compassionate grounds. The Parole Board must be consulted before a prisoner is released under this section, unless the circumstances are such that such consultation is impractical, and the prisoner remains on licence while he is released.

249   Duration of licence

(1) Subject to subsections (2) and (3), where a fixed-term prisoner is released on licence, the licence shall, subject to any revocation under section 254 or 255, remain in force for the remainder of his sentence.

(2) Where an intermittent custody prisoner is released on licence under section 244, the licence shall, subject to any revocation under section 254, remain in force—

   (a) until the time when he is required to return to prison at the beginning of the next custodial period of the sentence, or

   (b) where it is granted at the end of the last custodial period, for the remainder of his sentence.

(3) Subsection (1) has effect subject to sections 263(2) (concurrent terms) and 264(3) and (4) (consecutive terms).

(4) In subsection (2) "custodial period", in relation to a sentence to which an intermittent custody order relates, means any period which is not a licence period as defined by 183(3).

GENERAL NOTE

This section provides for the licence period following the release of a fixed term of prisoner. In the normal case, a prisoner released at the end of the "requisite custodial period" under s.244 will remain on licence until the end of the sentence as pronounced by the court. In effect, in normal circumstances he will serve half of the sentence in custody and be on licence for the second half of the sentence. This represents a significant change in the parole system. Under the scheme introduced by the Criminal Justice Act 1991, licences in the case of prisoners sentenced to fixed terms normally began on the date of release, and expired at the end of the third quarter of the sentence. Prisoners subject to the new scheme set up by this Act will in all cases be required to be on licence for a significantly longer period than would otherwise have been the case.

In the case of intermittent custody prisoners serving sentences of intermittent custody under s.183, there will be a series of licence periods, the earlier ones terminating when the offender is required to return to custody and the final period beginning on his release after serving the last of the custodial days and ending at the end of the term of the sentence.

250   Licence conditions

(1) In this section—

   (a) "the standard conditions" means such conditions as may be prescribed for the purposes of this section as standard conditions, and

   (b) "prescribed" means prescribed by the Secretary of State by order.

(2) Subject to subsection (6) and section 251, any licence under this Chapter in respect of a prisoner serving one or more sentences of imprisonment of less than twelve months and no sentence of twelve months or more—

   (a) must include—

     (i) the conditions required by the relevant court order, and

     (ii) so far as not inconsistent with them, the standard conditions, and

   (b) may also include—

     (i) any condition which is authorised by section 62 of the Criminal Justice and Court Services Act 2000 (c. 43) (electronic monitoring) or section 64 of that Act (drug testing requirements) and which is compatible with the conditions required by the relevant court order, and

      (ii) such other conditions of a kind prescribed for the purposes of this paragraph as the Secretary of State may for the time being consider to be necessary for the protection of the public and specify in the licence.

(3) For the purposes of subsection (2)(a)(i), any reference in the relevant court order to the licence period specified in the order is, in relation to a prohibited activity requirement, exclusion requirement, residence requirement or supervision requirement, to be taken to include a reference to any other period during which the prisoner is released on licence under section 246 or 248.

(4) Any licence under this Chapter in respect of a prisoner serving a sentence of imprisonment for a term of twelve months or more (including such a sentence imposed under section 227) or any sentence of detention under section 91 of the Sentencing Act or section 228 of this Act—

  (a) must include the standard conditions, and

  (b) may include—

      (i) any condition authorised by section 62 or 64 of the Criminal Justice and Court Services Act 2000, and

      (ii) such other conditions of a kind prescribed by the Secretary of State for the purposes of this paragraph as the Secretary of State may for the time being specify in the licence.

(5) A licence under section 246 must also include a curfew condition complying with section 253.

(6) Where—

  (a) a licence under section 246 is granted to a prisoner serving one or more sentences of imprisonment of less than 12 months and no sentence of 12 months or more, and

  (b) the relevant court order requires the licence to be granted subject to a condition requiring his compliance with a curfew requirement (as defined by section 204),

    that condition is not to be included in the licence at any time while a curfew condition required by section 253 is in force.

(7) The preceding provisions of this section have effect subject to section 263(3) (concurrent terms) and section 264(3) and (4) (consecutive terms).

(8) In exercising his powers to prescribe standard conditions or the other conditions referred to in subsection (4)(b)(ii), the Secretary of State must have regard to the following purposes of the supervision of offenders while on licence under this Chapter—

  (a) the protection of the public,

  (b) the prevention of re-offending, and

  (c) securing the successful re-integration of the prisoner into the community.

GENERAL NOTE

This section provides for the conditions which are to be included in the licences of prisoners released from custody under the provisions of this Part of the Act. The section assumes that standard conditions will be prescribed by the Secretary of State by order for all prisoners. In addition, the licences of prisoners released under "custody plus orders" made under s.181 must contain the conditions required by the "custody plus order". In addition, conditions relating to electronic monitoring or drug testing may be included in the licence.

In the case of prisoners released from sentences of 12 months or more (excluding an extended sentence imposed on an adult under s.227), the licence must include the standard conditions, and may include conditions relating to electronic monitoring and the testing, and any other conditions which may be specified in a licence, taken from a list of conditions to be described by the Secretary of State.

In the case of a prisoner released under s.246 (home detention curfew), the licence must contain a curfew condition. Where a prisoner is released from a custody plus sentence, in respect of which the court has ordered compliance with a curfew requirement during the licence period of the sentence, that requirement is not to be included in the licence while the curfew required by s.253 is in effect. The reason for this provision is presumably to prevent the defendant being subject to two different curfew requirements at the same time. If he is released on home detention curfew, he will be subject to the curfew requirements imposed by virtue of s.253 until he has reached the end of the "requisite custodial period" (half of the custodial period of his sentence); at this stage the curfew requirement imposed by virtue of s.181 as part of the custody plus order will come into force and replace the curfew requirement imposed by s.253.

251 Licence conditions on re-release of prisoner serving sentence of less than 12 months

(1) In relation to any licence under this Chapter which is granted to a prisoner serving one or more sentences of imprisonment of less than twelve months and no sentence of twelve months or more on his release in pursuance of a decision of the Board under section 254 or 256, subsections (2) and (3) apply instead of section 250(2).

(2) The licence—

  (a) must include the standard conditions, and

  (b) may include—

    (i) any condition authorised by section 62 or 64 of the Criminal Justice and Court Services Act 2000 (c. 43), and

    (ii) such other conditions of a kind prescribed by the Secretary of State for the purposes of section 250(4)(b)(ii) as the Secretary of State may for the time being specify in the licence.

(3) In exercising his powers under subsection (2)(b)(ii), the Secretary of State must have regard to the terms of the relevant court order.

(4) In this section "the standard conditions" has the same meaning as in section 250.

GENERAL NOTE

This section makes provision for the case of a prisoner sentenced to a "custody plus order" under s.181, who has been released from that sentence after serving the "requisite custodial period", that is half of the "custodial period" of the sentence, and who has been recalled to prison following the revocation of his licence by the Secretary of State. If the Parole Board, considering his case after the revocation, orders his immediate release under s.254(4), or his release at future date under s.256(1), the Secretary of State may include in his licence the conditions specified in subs.(2). The licence must contain the standard conditions and such conditions as may be specified; it need not contain the requirements required by the custody plus order.

252 Duty to comply with licence conditions

A person subject to a licence under this Chapter must comply with such conditions as may for the time being be specified in the licence.

GENERAL NOTE

This section imposes on a prisoner who has been released subject to a licence under this Chapter of the Act a duty to comply with such conditions as may be specified in the licence. It is not immediately obvious what the effect of non-compliance with the duty is to be. It does not appear that failure to comply with a condition of a licence is a criminal offence, and it is not a necessary condition for revocation of the licence under s.254.

253 Curfew condition to be included in licence under section 246

(1) For the purposes of this Chapter, a curfew condition is a condition which—

(a) requires the released person to remain, for periods for the time being specified in the condition, at a place for the time being so specified (which may be premises approved by the Secretary of State under section 9 of the Criminal Justice and Court Services Act 2000 (c. 43)), and

(b) includes requirements for securing the electronic monitoring of his whereabouts during the periods for the time being so specified.

(2) The curfew condition may specify different places or different periods for different days, but may not specify periods which amount to less than 9 hours in any one day (excluding for this purpose the first and last days of the period for which the condition is in force).

(3) The curfew condition is to remain in force until the date when the released person would (but for his release) fall to be released on licence under section 244.

(4) Subsection (3) does not apply in relation to a released person to whom an intermittent custody order relates; and in relation to such a person the curfew condition is to remain in force until the number of days during which it has been in force is equal to the number of the required custodial days, as defined in section 246(6), that remained to be served at the time when he was released under section 246.

(5) The curfew condition must include provision for making a person responsible for monitoring the released person's whereabouts during the periods for the time being specified in the condition; and a person who is made so responsible shall be of a description specified in an order made by the Secretary of State.

(6) Nothing in this section is to be taken to require the Secretary of State to ensure that arrangements are made for the electronic monitoring of released persons' whereabouts in any particular part of England and Wales.

Recall after release

254   Recall of prisoners while on licence

(1) The Secretary of State may, in the case of any prisoner who has been released on licence under this Chapter, revoke his licence and recall him to prison.

(2) A person recalled to prison under subsection (1)—
(a) may make representations in writing with respect to his recall, and
(b) on his return to prison, must be informed of the reasons for his recall and of his right to make representations.

(3) The Secretary of State must refer to the Board the case of a person recalled under subsection (1).

(4) Where on a reference under subsection (3) relating to any person the Board recommends his immediate release on licence under this Chapter, the Secretary of State must give effect to the recommendation.

(5) In the case of an intermittent custody prisoner who has not yet served in prison the number of custodial days specified in the intermittent custody order, any recommendation by the Board as to immediate release on licence is to be a recommendation as to his release on licence until the end of one of the licence periods specified by virtue of section 183(1)(b) in the intermittent custody order.

(6) On the revocation of the licence of any person under this section, he shall be liable to be detained in pursuance of his sentence and, if at large, is to be treated as being unlawfully at large.

(7) Nothing in subsections (2) to (6) applies in relation to a person recalled under section 255.

GENERAL NOTE

This section provides for the revocation of the licence of a prisoner who has been released on licence under this Chapter and for his return to prison. The section confers a broad discretion on the Secretary of State, which is not subject to any particular conditions. It is not necessary that the prisoner should be in breach of any requirement of his licence, or to have committed any offence during the licence period, before this power may be exercised.

A prisoner whose licence is revoked may make written representations in respect of his recall. On return to person he must be informed of the reasons for his recall and of his right to make representations. His case must be referred to the Parole Board. The Parole Board made at its discretion recommend his immediate release on licence or his release at a later date under s.256.

255   Recall of prisoners released early under section 246

(1) If it appears to the Secretary of State, as regards a person released on licence under section 246—
   (a) that he has failed to comply with any condition included in his licence, or
   (b) that his whereabouts can no longer be electronically monitored at the place for the time being specified in the curfew condition included in his licence,
   the Secretary of State may, if the curfew condition is still in force, revoke the licence and recall the person to prison under this section.

(2) A person whose licence under section 246 is revoked under this section—
   (a) may make representations in writing with respect to the revocation, and
   (b) on his return to prison, must be informed of the reasons for the revocation and of his right to make representations.

(3) The Secretary of State, after considering any representations under subsection (2)(b) or any other matters, may cancel a revocation under this section.

(4) Where the revocation of a person's licence is cancelled under subsection (3), the person is to be treated for the purposes of section 246 as if he had not been recalled to prison under this section.

(5) On the revocation of a person's licence under section 246, he is liable to be detained in pursuance of his sentence and, if at large, is to be treated as being unlawfully at large.

GENERAL NOTE

This section makes provision for the recall of prisoners released under the "home detention curfew scheme" established by s.246, during the period immediately before they would otherwise become entitled to be released under s.244. A person released under this section may have his licence revoked if it appears to the Secretary of State that he has failed to comply with any condition of the licence, or that his whereabouts can no longer be electronically monitored during the periods specified in the curfew condition which is a necessary condition of the licence. A person whose licence is revoked under this section may make written representations, and must be informed of the reasons for the revocation of his licence on his return to prison, but his case need not be referred to the Parole Board as in the case of a person whose licence is revoked under s.254. The Secretary of State may however reconsider his decision in the light of the representations, and may cancel the revocation of the licence.

It does not appear that this section excludes the power to recall under s.254 in the case of a prisoner released subject to home detention curfew, if it appears appropriate to revoke his licence on grounds other than a failure for comply with the conditions of the licence, or the inability to monitor his whereabouts

256   Further release after recall

(1) Where on a reference under section 254(3) in relation to any person, the Board does not recommend his immediate release on licence under this Chapter, the Board must either—
  (a) fix a date for the person's release on licence, or
  (b) fix a date as the date for the next review of the person's case by the Board.
(2) Any date fixed under subsection (1)(a) or (b) must not be later than the first anniversary of the date on which the decision is taken.
(3) The Board need not fix a date under subsection (1)(a) or (b) if the prisoner will fall to be released unconditionally at any time within the next 12 months.
(4) Where the Board has fixed a date under subsection (1)(a), it is the duty of the Secretary of State to release him on licence on that date.
(5) On a review required by subsection (1)(b) in relation to any person, the Board may—
  (a) recommend his immediate release on licence, or
  (b) fix a date under subsection (1)(a) or (b).

GENERAL NOTE

This section provides for the powers of the Parole Board when dealing with the case of a person which has been referred to the Board under s.254(3) following the revocation of his licence by the Secretary of State. If the Board does not recommend his immediate release on licence under s.254(4), it must either fix a date for the person's release on licence at some time in future, or fix a date for the next review of the person's case by the Board. The date fixed, whether for release or further review of the case, must be not later than one-year after the date on which the review takes place. No date need be fixed if the prisoner will be released unconditionally at any time within the following twelve months, normally at the end of the full term of the sentence as pronounced by the court. On a further review of the case, the Board may recommend immediate release, fix a future date for release or fix a date for a further review.

Additional days

257   Additional days for disciplinary offences

(1) Prison rules, that is to say, rules made under section 47 of the Prison Act 1952 (c. 52), may include provision for the award of additional days—
  (a) to fixed-term prisoners, or
  (b) conditionally on their subsequently becoming such prisoners, to persons on remand,
    who (in either case) are guilty of disciplinary offences.
(2) Where additional days are awarded to a fixed-term prisoner, or to a person on remand who subsequently becomes such a prisoner, and are not remitted in accordance with prison rules—
  (a) any period which he must serve before becoming entitled to or eligible for release under this Chapter,
  (b) any period which he must serve before he can be removed from prison under section 260, and
  (c) any period for which a licence granted to him under this Chapter remains in force,

is extended by the aggregate of those additional days.

DEFINITIONS
   "fixed term prisoner": s.237

GENERAL NOTE
   This section provides for prison rules to be made under the Prison Act 1952 to make provision for the award of additional day to prisoners who are guilty of disciplinary offences. Awards may be made to fixed term prisoners or to remand prisoners, but remand prisoners may not be required to serve the additional days unless they are convicted and sentenced to custodial sentences by reason of which they become fixed term prisoners. Where a prisoner is required to serve additional day, those days must be served before the prisoner becomes entitled to release under s.244; they are in effect added to the "requisite custodial period"; in addition they do not count as part of the licence period.

Fine defaulters and contemnors

258   Early release of fine defaulters and contemnors

(1) This section applies in relation to a person committed to prison—
   (a) in default of payment of a sum adjudged to be paid by a conviction, or
   (b) for contempt of court or any kindred offence.

(2) As soon as a person to whom this section applies has served one-half of the term for which he was committed, it is the duty of the Secretary of State to release him unconditionally.

(3) Where a person to whom this section applies is also serving one or more sentences of imprisonment, nothing in this section requires the Secretary of State to release him until he is also required to release him in respect of that sentence or each of those sentences.

(4) The Secretary of State may at any time release unconditionally a person to whom this section applies if he is satisfied that exceptional circumstances exist which justify the person's release on compassionate grounds.

GENERAL NOTE
   This section provides for the release of persons committed to prison in default of payment or for contempt of court. Such persons are not treated as serving a sentence of imprisonment for the purposes of this chapter (see s.242). The effect of the section is that as soon as such a person has served half of the term for which he was committed, he is entitled to be released absolutely without licence. (Under the previous legislation, as person serving more than twelve months' imprisonment in default was required to serve two thirds of the term). He may be detained in custody only if he is also serving one or more sentences of imprisonment in respect of which he has not yet served the requisite custodial period or half of the appropriate custodial term as the case may be. A person serving a term of imprisonment in default or for contempt may be released unconditionally under subs.(4)(a), if there are exceptional circumstances which justify his release on compassionate grounds. There is no obligation to consult the Parole Board in this context, and no power to require him to comply with any licence. When it is considered that a default sentence may be as long as ten years, this seems to be a generous concession.

Persons liable to removal from the United Kingdom

259   Persons liable to removal from the United Kingdom

For the purposes of this Chapter a person is liable to removal from the United Kingdom if—
   (a) he is liable to deportation under section 3(5) of the Immigration Act 1971 (c. 77) and has been notified of a decision to make a deportation order against him,
   (b) he is liable to deportation under section 3(6) of that Act,
   (c) he has been notified of a decision to refuse him leave to enter the United Kingdom,

(d) he is an illegal entrant within the meaning of section 33(1) of that Act, or

(e) he is liable to removal under section 10 of the Immigration and Asylum Act 1999 (c. 33).

GENERAL NOTE
   Sections 260, 261 and 262 make provision for the release of prisoners serving sentences who are liable to be removed from the United Kingdom, normally because they are liable to deportation or are otherwise not entitled to be in the United Kingdom. This section provides the definitions of the persons to whom the following sections apply.

260 Early removal of prisoners liable to removal from United Kingdom

(1) Subject to subsections (2) and (3), where a fixed-term prisoner is liable to removal from the United Kingdom, the Secretary of State may remove him from prison under this section at any time during the period of 135 days ending with the day on which the prisoner will have served the requisite custodial period.

(2) Subsection (1) does not apply in relation to a prisoner unless—
   (a) the length of the requisite custodial period is at least 6 weeks, and
   (b) he has served—
      (i) at least 4 weeks of his sentence, and
      (ii) at least one-half of the requisite custodial period.

(3) Subsection (1) does not apply where—
   (a) the sentence is imposed under section 227 or 228,
   (b) the sentence is for an offence under section 1 of the Prisoners (Return to Custody) Act 1995 (c. 16),
   (c) the prisoner is subject to a hospital order, hospital direction or transfer direction under section 37, 45A or 47 of the Mental Health Act 1983 (c. 20),
   (d) the prisoner is subject to the notification requirements of Part 2 of the Sexual Offences Act 2003 (c. 42), or
   (e) in the case of a prisoner to whom a direction under section 240 relates, the interval between the date on which the sentence was passed and the date on which the prisoner will have served the requisite custodial period is less than 14 days.

(4) A prisoner removed from prison under this section—
   (a) is so removed only for the purpose of enabling the Secretary of State to remove him from the United Kingdom under powers conferred by—
      (i) Schedule 2 or 3 to the Immigration Act 1971, or
      (ii) section 10 of the Immigration and Asylum Act 1999 (c. 33), and
   (b) so long as remaining in the United Kingdom, remains liable to be detained in pursuance of his sentence until he has served the requisite custodial period.

(5) So long as a prisoner removed from prison under this section remains in the United Kingdom but has not been returned to prison, any duty or power of the Secretary of State under section 244 or 248 is exercisable in relation to him as if he were in prison.

(6) The Secretary of State may by order—
   (a) amend the number of days for the time being specified in subsection (1) or (3)(e),
   (b) amend the number of weeks for the time being specified in subsection (2)(a) or (b)(i), and
   (c) amend the fraction for the time being specified in subsection (2)(b)(ii).

(7) In this section "the requisite custodial period" has the meaning given by paragraph (a), (b) or (d) of section 244(3).

GENERAL NOTE
   The section provides for the early release of fixed term prisoners who are liable to be removed from the United Kingdom at the end of their sentences. The effect of the section is to permit the Secretary of State to remove such a prisoner from prison before he has completely served the "requisite custodial period" under s.244 (half of the term of the sentence) under conditions which are broadly comparable to those which apply to home detention curfew under s.246. Such a prisoner may be removed from prison up to 135 days before the end of the "requisite custodial period", provided he has served at least four weeks of the sentence and at least one half of the requisite custodial period. He may be removed only for the purpose of enabling him to be deported or otherwise dealt with under the Immigration Act 1971 or the Immigration and Asylum Act 1999 (c.33), s.10. If he is still in the United Kingdom but has not been returned to prison when the requisite custodial period of his sentence expires, he must be released on licence.

261   Re-entry into United Kingdom of offender removed from prison early

   (1) This section applies in relation to a person who, after being removed from prison under section 260, has been removed from the United Kingdom before he has served the requisite custodial period.
   (2) If a person to whom this section applies enters the United Kingdom at any time before his sentence expiry date, he is liable to be detained in pursuance of his sentence from the time of his entry into the United Kingdom until whichever is the earlier of the following—
        (a) the end of a period ("the further custodial period") beginning with that time and equal in length to the outstanding custodial period, and
        (b) his sentence expiry date.
   (3) A person who is liable to be detained by virtue of subsection (2) is, if at large, to be taken for the purposes of section 49 of the Prison Act 1952 (c. 52) (persons unlawfully at large) to be unlawfully at large.
   (4) Subsection (2) does not prevent the further removal from the United Kingdom of a person falling within that subsection.
   (5) Where, in the case of a person returned to prison by virtue of subsection (2), the further custodial period ends before the sentence expiry date, section 244 has effect in relation to him as if the reference to the requisite custodial period were a reference to the further custodial period.
   (6) In this section—
        "further custodial period" has the meaning given by subsection (2)(a);
        "outstanding custodial period", in relation to a person to whom this section applies, means the period beginning with the date of his removal from the United Kingdom and ending with the date on which he would, but for his removal, have served the requisite custodial period;
        "requisite custodial period" has the meaning given by paragraph (a), (b) or (d) of section 244(3);
        "sentence expiry date", in relation to a person to whom this section applies, means the date on which, but for his removal from the United Kingdom, he would have ceased to be subject to a licence.

DEFINITIONS
   "Requisite custodial period": s.244

GENERAL NOTE
   This section provides for the case of a person who has been removed from prison under s.260 before he has served the "requisite custodial period" of his sentence and deported or otherwise removed from the United Kingdom. If he enters the United Kingdom at any time before the date on which the term of the sentence pronounced by the court would expire, he may be a

detained at any time following his re-entry into United Kingdom until the end of a period equal to the period of the "requisite custodial period" which remained when he was removed from the United Kingdom, or his sentence expiry date if that is earlier. He must in effect serve a period equal to the period he was relieved from serving by his removal from prison under s.260, unless the sentence expires before the end of that period is reached. If the period which he is required to serve ends before the expiry date of the sentence, he must be released on licence under s.244.

262 Prisoners liable to removal from United Kingdom: modifications of Criminal Justice Act 1991

Part 2 of the Criminal Justice Act 1991 (c. 53) (early release of prisoners) shall (until the coming into force of its repeal by this Act) have effect subject to the modifications set out in Schedule 20 (which relate to persons liable to removal from the United Kingdom).

GENERAL NOTE

Schedule 20 amends the Criminal Justice Act 1991, Pt 2 so as to introduce provisions broadly similar in their effect to ss.260 and 261.

Consecutive or concurrent terms

263 Concurrent terms

(1) This section applies where—
    (a) a person ("the offender") has been sentenced by any court to two or more terms of imprisonment which are wholly or partly concurrent, and
    (b) the sentences were passed on the same occasion or, where they were passed on different occasions, the person has not been released under this Chapter at any time during the period beginning with the first and ending with the last of those occasions.

(2) Where this section applies—
    (a) nothing in this Chapter requires the Secretary of State to release the offender in respect of any of the terms unless and until he is required to release him in respect of each of the others,
    (b) section 244 does not authorise the Secretary of State to release him on licence under that section in respect of any of the terms unless and until that section authorises the Secretary of State to do so in respect of each of the others,
    (c) on and after his release under this Chapter the offender is to be on licence for so long, and subject to such conditions, as is required by this Chapter in respect of any of the sentences.

(3) Where the sentences include one or more sentences of twelve months or more and one or more sentences of less than twelve months, the terms of the licence may be determined by the Secretary of State in accordance with section 250(4)(b), without regard to the requirements of any custody plus order or intermittent custody order.

(4) In this section "term of imprisonment" includes a determinate sentence of detention under section 91 of the Sentencing Act or under section 228 of this Act.

GENERAL NOTE

This section provides for the application of the provisions of this Chapter to an offender who is serving a number of sentences which are wholly or partly concurrent. The section applies whether the sentences were passed on the same occasion, or the later sentence was passed before the offender had been released from custody under the earlier sentence or sentences. The broad effect of the section is that if the sentences were imposed on the same occasion, the offender is not to be released until he has served the requisite period of the longest of the sentences. If the sentences were imposed on different occasions, the prisoner is not to be released until he has served the requisite period which will expire last. A prisoner who is sentenced to concurrent terms of three years, two years and eighteen months on the same occasion, will be required to serve eighteen months before release — the requisite custodial period of the three year sentence. If a prisoner who has already served twelve months of a three year sentence, and thus has six months of the requisite custodial period of that sentence to serve, is sentenced to a further sentence of two years concurrent with the three years, he will be required to serve a further twelve months, until he has served the requisite custodial period of the two year sentence. If a prisoner who has served twelve months of a five year sentence, and who thus has a further eighteen months of that sentence to serve before serving the requisite custodial period, is sentenced to a term of two years concurrent with the five years, his release date will not be affected; he will be released when he has served the requisite custodial period of the five year sentence, which will be reached after he has completed the requisite custodial period of the two year sentence.

His licence will expire when the last of the sentences to expire has done so.

264   Consecutive terms

(1) This section applies where—
   (a) a person ("the offender") has been sentenced to two or more terms of imprisonment which are to be served consecutively on each other, and
   (b) the sentences were passed on the same occasion or, where they were passed on different occasions, the person has not been released under this Chapter at any time during the period beginning with the first and ending with the last of those occasions.

(2) Nothing in this Chapter requires the Secretary of State to release the offender on licence until he has served a period equal in length to the aggregate of the length of the custodial periods in relation to each of the terms of imprisonment.

(3) Where any of the terms of imprisonment is a term of twelve months or more, the offender is, on and after his release under this Chapter, to be on licence—
   (a) until he would, but for his release, have served a term equal in length to the aggregate length of the terms of imprisonment, and
   (b) subject to such conditions as are required by this Chapter in respect of each of those terms of imprisonment.

(4) Where each of the terms of imprisonment is a term of less than twelve months, the offender is, on and after his release under this Chapter, to be on licence until the relevant time, and subject to such conditions as are required by this Chapter in respect of any of the terms of imprisonment, and none of the terms is to be regarded for any purpose as continuing after the relevant time.

(5) In subsection (4) "the relevant time" means the time when the offender would, but for his release, have served a term equal in length to the aggregate of—
   (a) all the custodial periods in relation to the terms of imprisonment, and
   (b) the longest of the licence periods in relation to those terms.

(6) In this section—
   (a) "custodial period"—
      (i) in relation to an extended sentence imposed under section 227 or 228, means the appropriate custodial term determined under that section,
      (ii) in relation to a term of twelve months or more, means one-half of the term, and

     (iii) in relation to a term of less than twelve months complying with section 181, means the custodial period as defined by subsection (3)(a) of that section;

   (b) "licence period", in relation to a term of less than twelve months complying with section 181, has the meaning given by subsection (3)(b) of that section.

(7) This section applies to a determinate sentence of detention under section 91 of the Sentencing Act or under section 228 of this Act as it applies to a term of imprisonment of 12 months or more.

GENERAL NOTE

This section provides for the application of Ch.6 of Pt 12 to persons serving consecutive sentences, whether the sentences have been passed on the same occasion, or the second sentence has been passed on a later occasion while the person was still in custody under the first sentence. The section does not apply to a sentence passed after the offender has been released from the first of the sentences.

The broad principle of the section in relation to normal fixed term sentences is that the consecutive terms are treated as an aggregate term, and the offender does not become entitled to be released until he has served a period equal to the aggregate of the requisite custodial periods in relation to each of the terms of imprisonment. The licence imposed on the offender on his release will continue in effect until he would have served a term equal to the aggregate length of the terms of imprisonment.

In the case of an extended sentence passed under s.227 or s.228, the period to be served before the offender becomes entitled to be released is the aggregate of the whole of the appropriate periods fixed by the court. It is not clear whether the Parole Board may exercise the power to direct the prisoner's release after he has served a period equal to half of the aggregate of the appropriate custodial terms.

In the case of consecutive sentences each of less than 12 months, which are subject to the "custody plus" provisions of s.181, the offender will remain on licence until the conclusion of a period which is equal in length to the aggregate of all of the custodial periods of the sentences, and the longest of the licence periods.

Restriction on consecutive sentences for released prisoners

265 Restriction on consecutive sentences for released prisoners

(1) A court sentencing a person to a term of imprisonment may not order or direct that the term is to commence on the expiry of any other sentence of imprisonment from which he has been released early under this Chapter.

(2) In this section "sentence of imprisonment" includes a sentence of detention under section 91 of the Sentencing Act or section 228 of this Act, and "term of imprisonment" is to be read accordingly.

GENERAL NOTE

This section is derived from the Crime and Disorder Act 1998, s.102 which was replaced by the Powers of Criminal Courts (Sentencing) Act 2000, s.84.

The practical effect of the section is to prohibit a court which passes a sentence on an offender who has been released from an existing custodial sentence from ordering the sentence to run consecutively to that sentence. It appears to be intended to apply to the case of an offender who has been released on licence from a custodial sentence and then recalled under s.254 to continue serving that sentence. If such an offender appears before the court for sentence while he is still serving the balance of the licence period of the original sentence, any new sentence must not be ordered to begin at the expiration of that sentence. The sentence must normally be ordered to begin at once and run concurrently with the original sentence.

Drug testing requirements

266 Release on licence etc: drug testing requirements

(1) Section 64 of the Criminal Justice and Court Services Act 2000 (c. 43) (release on licence etc: drug testing requirements) is amended as follows.

(2) In subsection (1) for paragraph (a) there is substituted—

"(a) the Secretary of State releases from prison a person aged 14 or over on whom a sentence of imprisonment has been imposed,

(aa) a responsible officer is of the opinion—

(i) that the offender has a propensity to misuse specified Class A drugs, and

(ii) that the misuse by the offender of any specified Class A drug caused or contributed to any offence of which he has been convicted, or is likely to cause or contribute to the commission of further offences, and".

(3) After subsection (4) there is inserted—

"(4A) A person under the age of 17 years may not be required by virtue of this section to provide a sample otherwise than in the presence of an appropriate adult."

(4) In subsection (5), after paragraph (e) there is inserted "and

(f) a sentence of detention under section 226 or 228 of the Criminal Justice Act 2003,".

(5) After subsection (5) there is inserted—

"(6) In this section—

"appropriate adult", in relation to a person aged under 17, means—

(a) his parent or guardian or, if he is in the care of a local authority or voluntary organisation, a person representing that authority or organisation,

(b) a social worker of a local authority social services department, or

(c) if no person falling within paragraph (a) or (b) is available, any responsible person aged 18 or over who is not a police officer or a person employed by the police;

"responsible officer" means—

(a) in relation to an offender aged under 18, an officer of a local probation board or a member of a youth offending team;

(b) in relation to an offender aged 18 or over, an officer of a local probation board."

GENERAL NOTE

The Criminal Justice and Court Services Act 2000, s.64 section empowers the Secretary of State to include in the licence (or other conditions of release) of any person released from a custodial sentence a requirement that the person concerned should provide a sample for the purpose of determining whether he has any specified Class A drug in his body. The power applied only to those persons who had been sentenced for a "trigger offence", that is say one of the offences listed in Sch.6 to the Act in connection with drug abstinence orders. The provision applied to a person released from a detention and training order under supervision.

The effect of the amendments made by this section to s.64 is that the minimum age for drug testing is lowered to fourteen, and the restriction on the power to those convicted of a "trigger offence" within the meaning of that Act is removed. This condition is replaced by the requirements of new subs.(1)(aa) that a "responsible officer" thinks that the offender has a propensity to misuse specified class A drugs and that such misuse has either caused or contributed to his previous offending, or may cause or contribute to future offending.

It is unfortunate that the amended version of s.64 could not have been included in Ch.6 of Pt 12, so that its effect could have been seen in the context of the Chapter as a whole, which otherwise provides a comprehensive set of provisions governing the release of prisoners. The only reason for not incorporating the section, as amended, into the Chapter, seems to be that the section relies on the definition of a "specified Class A drug", but this could have been incorporated easily by reference.

Supplemental

267 Alteration by order of relevant proportion of sentence

The Secretary of State may by order provide that any reference in section 244(3)(a), section 247(2) or section 264(6)(a)(ii) to a particular proportion of a prisoner's sentence is to be read as a reference to such other proportion of a prisoner's sentence as may be specified in the order.

GENERAL NOTE

This section empowers the Secretary of State to change the proportion of a fixed term sentence which must be served before the prisoner becomes entitled to be released (s.244(3)(a)), the proportion of the "appropriate custodial period" of an extended sentence which must be served before the Parole Board can direct his release (s.247(2)) or the proportion of a sentence which is one of a number of consecutive terms which must be served (s.264(6)(a)(ii)).

268 Interpretation of Chapter 6

In this Chapter—
"the 1997 Act" means the Crime (Sentences) Act 1997 (c. 43);
"the Board" means the Parole Board;
"fixed-term prisoner" has the meaning given by section 237(1);
"intermittent custody prisoner" means a prisoner serving a sentence of imprisonment to which an intermittent custody order relates;
"prison" and "prisoner" are to be read in accordance with section 237(2);
"release", in relation to a prisoner serving a sentence of imprisonment to which an intermittent custody order relates, includes temporary release;
"relevant court order", in relation to a person serving a sentence of imprisonment to which a custody plus order or intermittent custody order relates, means that order.

CHAPTER 7

EFFECT OF LIFE SENTENCE

269 Determination of minimum term in relation to mandatory life sentence

(1) This section applies where after the commencement of this section a court passes a life sentence in circumstances where the sentence is fixed by law.

(2) The court must, unless it makes an order under subsection (4), order that the provisions of section 28(5) to (8) of the Crime (Sentences) Act 1997 (referred to in this Chapter as "the early release provisions") are to apply to the offender as soon as he has served the part of his sentence which is specified in the order.

(3) The part of his sentence is to be such as the court considers appropriate taking into account—
 (a) the seriousness of the offence, or of the combination of the offence and any one or more offences associated with it, and
 (b) the effect of any direction which it would have given under section 240 (crediting periods of remand in custody) if it had sentenced him to a term of imprisonment.

(4) If the offender was 21 or over when he committed the offence and the court is of the opinion that, because of the seriousness of the offence,

or of the combination of the offence and one or more offences associated with it, no order should be made under subsection (2), the court must order that the early release provisions are not to apply to the offender.

(5) In considering under subsection (3) or (4) the seriousness of an offence (or of the combination of an offence and one or more offences associated with it), the court must have regard to—

    (a) the general principles set out in Schedule 21, and

    (b) any guidelines relating to offences in general which are relevant to the case and are not incompatible with the provisions of Schedule 21.

(6) The Secretary of State may by order amend Schedule 21.

(7) Before making an order under subsection (6), the Secretary of State shall consult the Sentencing Guidelines Council.

DEFINITIONS
    "Guidelines": s.171
    "Life sentence": s.277

GENERAL NOTE

Chapter 7 of the Act establishes a completely new system governing the release of persons convicted of murder and sentenced to a mandatory life sentence. Under this system, the court which imposes the life sentence will in addition fix the minimum term which the offender must serve before he can be considered for release on licence by the Parole Board. In fixing of the minimum term, the court must have regard to a set of detailed principles set out in Sch.21 of the Act. Once the offender has served the minimum term fixed by the court in accordance with these principles, his released will be considered by the Parole Board under the amended version of the Crime (Sentences) Act 1997, s.28. If the Parole Board decides that it is appropriate that the offender should be released, the Secretary of State must release the offender on licence. The Secretary of State will no longer play any part in determining either the minimum term which a mandatory life sentence prisoner must serve in custody or whether it is appropriate to release him on licence.

This section sets out the basic framework within which the court must determine the specified minimum period. Subsection (2) requires the court to make an order that the "the early release provisions" of the Crime (Sentences) Act 1997, s.28, will apply to the offender as soon as he has served the part of the sentence which is specified in the order. That part is such as the court considers appropriate taking into account the seriousness of the offence or offences concerned, and the effect of any direction which it would have given in relation to days spent in custody under s.240, if the offender had been sentenced to a determinate sentence. If the offender was 21 or over, the court need not order that the early release provisions should apply to the offender, if it considers that because of the seriousness of the offence or offences no order can be made under subs.(2), in other words that the offence is so serious that the offender should remain in custody for the whole of his life.

In considering the seriousness of the offences for the purposes of making an order under this section, the court must have regard to the detailed principles set out in Schedule 21, and any guide lines relating to offences in general which are relevant and which are not incompatible with those provisions. Schedule 21 sets out a framework for the purpose of identifying the appropriate minimum term, with the starting points at different levels according to the circumstances of the case, and identifying various aggravating or mitigating features. The Schedule does not restrict the application of the general principles of sentencing set out in the Act in ss.143 and 144 relating to previous convictions, offending while on bail, and guilty pleas. Schedule 21 of the Act replies to persons convicted of murder committed on or after the relevant commencement date, December 18, 2003. In the case of a person convicted of murder committed before that date but after the offender has attained the age of eighteen, the court must have regard to Sch.22, paras 9 and 10. The effect of these paragraphs is that the court may not make an order under s.269 specifying a part of the sentence which appears to be greater than the part which would have been notified to the offender under the practice followed by the Secretary of State before December 2002.

In the case of a person convicted of murder committed while under the age of eighteen, who will be sentenced to be detained during Her Majesty's pleasure, whatever his age on the date of conviction, the court must apply Sch.21, whether the offence was committed before December 18, 2003 or otherwise (see Sch.22, para.(1)) which excludes detention during Her Majesty's pleasure from the scope of the Schedule).

270   Duty to give reasons

(1) Any court making an order under subsection (2) or (4) of section 269 must state in open court, in ordinary language, its reasons for deciding on the order made.

(2) In stating its reasons the court must, in particular—

  (a) state which of the starting points in Schedule 21 it has chosen and its reasons for doing so, and

  (b) state its reasons for any departure from that starting point.

GENERAL NOTE

This section imposes on a court making an order fixing the minimum term of a mandatory life sentence a duty to state in open court the reasons for deciding on the order made, identifying which of the statutory starting points has been chosen and why, and stating the reasons for any departure from that starting point.

The general obligation to give reasons for sentence set out in s.174 does not apply in the case of a mandatory life sentence for murder (see s.174(3)(a)).

271   Appeals

(1) In section 9 of the Criminal Appeal Act 1968 (c. 19) (appeal against sentence following conviction on indictment), after subsection (1) there is inserted—

  "(1A) In subsection (1) of this section, the reference to a sentence fixed by law does not include a reference to an order made under subsection (2) or (4) of section 269 of the Criminal Justice Act 2003 in relation to a life sentence (as defined in section 277 of that Act) that is fixed by law.".

(2) In section 8 of the Courts-Martial (Appeals) Act 1968 (c. 20) (right of appeal from court-martial to Courts-Martial Appeal Court) after subsection (1) there is inserted—

  "(1ZA) In subsection (1) above, the reference to a sentence fixed by law does not include a reference to an order made under subsection (2) or (4) of section 269 of the Criminal Justice Act 2003 in relation to a life sentence (as defined in section 277 of that Act) that is fixed by law.".

GENERAL NOTE

The Criminal Appeal Act 1968, s.9(1) provides that "A person who has been convicted of an offence on indictment may appeal to the Court of Appeal against any sentence (not being a sentence fixed by law) passed on him for the offence, whether passed on his conviction or in subsequent proceedings." The effect of the new subsection inserted into that section by this section is that an order specifying the minimum term of a sentence, or failing to do so, made under s.269, is not to be treated as a sentence fixed by law. The practical effect is that an offender sentenced to a mandatory life sentence may not appeal against the life sentence but may appeal against the order made under s.269.

Subsection (2) makes an equivalent amendment to the Courts-Martial (Appeals) Act 1968 (c.20), s.8.

272   Review of minimum term on a reference by Attorney General

(1) In section 36 of the Criminal Justice Act 1988 (c. 33) (reviews of sentencing) after subsection (3) there is inserted—

  "(3A) Where a reference under this section relates to an order under subsection (2) of section 269 of the Criminal Justice Act 2003 (determination of minimum term in relation to mandatory life sentence), the Court of Appeal shall not, in deciding what order under that section is appropriate for the case, make any allowance for the fact that the person to whom it relates is being sentenced for a second time.".

(2) Each of the following sections (which relate to the review by the Courts-Martial Appeal Court of sentences passed by courts-martial)—

  (a) section 113C of the Army Act 1955 (3 & 4 Eliz. 2 c. 18),

  (b) section 113C of the Air Force Act 1955 (3 & 4 Eliz. 2 c. 19), and

  (c) section 71AC of the Naval Discipline Act 1957 (c. 53),

is amended as follows.

(3) After subsection (3) there is inserted—

"(3A) Where a reference under this section relates to an order under subsection (2) of section 269 of the Criminal Justice Act 2003 (determination of minimum term in relation to mandatory life sentence), the Courts-Martial Appeal Court shall not, in deciding what order under that section is appropriate for the case, make any allowance for the fact that the person to whom it relates is being sentenced for a second time.".

GENERAL NOTE

The Criminal Justice Act 1988 s.36 provides for the Attorney General to refer to the Court of Appeal, Criminal Division for review a sentence which he consider to be unduly lenient. An order under s.269 is a "sentence" for the purpose of this provision, by virtue of the Criminal Appeal Act 1968, s.50 which defines "sentence" to include "any order made by a court when dealing with an offender." It is the normal practice of the Court of Appeal, Criminal Division when substituting on such a reference a more severe sentence than the sentence imposed in the Crown Court, to substitute a sentence which is less severe than the sentence which in the view of the court should have been imposed in the Crown Court. This is usually known as the "double jeopardy element", a concession which recognises that the offender has been required to undergo the process of being sentenced twice. The effect of the new subsection inserted into s.36 is to prohibit the court from making any such allowance when substituting for an order made under s.269 an order specifying a longer period.

Corresponding amendments are made in the legislation relating to the review of sentences by the Courts-Martial Appeal Court.

273   Life prisoners transferred to England and Wales

(1) The Secretary of State must refer the case of any transferred life prisoner to the High Court for the making of one or more relevant orders.

(2) In subsection (1) "transferred life prisoner" means a person—

  (a) on whom a court in a country or territory outside the British Islands has imposed one or more sentences of imprisonment or detention for an indeterminate period, and

  (b) who has been transferred to England and Wales after the commencement of this section in pursuance of—

    (i) an order made by the Secretary of State under section 2 of the Colonial Prisoners Removal Act 1884 (c. 31), or

    (ii) a warrant issued by the Secretary of State under the Repatriation of Prisoners Act 1984 (c. 47),

  there to serve his sentence or sentences or the remainder of his sentence or sentences.

(3) In subsection (1) "a relevant order" means—

  (a) in the case of an offence which appears to the court to be an offence for which, if it had been committed in England and Wales, the sentence would have been fixed by law, an order under subsection (2) or (4) of section 269, and

  (b) in any other case, an order under subsection (2) or (4) of section 82A of the Sentencing Act.

(4) In section 34(1) of the Crime (Sentences) Act 1997 (c. 43) (meaning of "life prisoner" in Chapter 2 of Part 2 of that Act) at the end there is inserted "and includes a transferred life prisoner as defined by section 273 of the Criminal Justice Act 2003".

This section provides for prisoners who have been sentenced outside the British Islands to a sentence of imprisonment or detention for an indeterminate period, and who have been transferred to England and Wales under one of the statutes mentioned in subs.(2)(b). The case of any such transferred life prisoner must be referred to the High Court, to enable the High Court to make an order fixing the minimum term to be served in accordance with s.269 (in the case of a conviction for murder), or the Powers of Criminal Courts (Sentencing) Act 2000, s.82A if the offence was not subject to a mandatory life sentence.

274 Further provisions about references relating to transferred life prisoners

(1) A reference to the High Court under section 273 is to be determined by a single judge of that court without an oral hearing.

(2) In relation to a reference under that section, any reference to "the court" in subsections (2) to (5) of section 269, in Schedule 21 or in section 82A(2) to (4) of the Sentencing Act is to be read as a reference to the High Court.

(3) A person in respect of whom a reference has been made under section 273 may with the leave of the Court of Appeal appeal to the Court of Appeal against the decision of the High Court on the reference.

(4) Section 1(1) of the Administration of Justice Act 1960 (c. 65) (appeal to House of Lords from decision of High Court in a criminal cause or matter) and section 18(1)(a) of the Supreme Court Act 1981 (c. 54) (exclusion of appeal from High Court to Court of Appeal in a criminal cause or matter) do not apply in relation to a decision to which subsection (3) applies.

(5) The jurisdiction conferred on the Court of Appeal by subsection (3) is to be exercised by the criminal division of that court.

(6) Section 33(3) of the Criminal Appeal Act 1968 (c. 19) (limitation on appeal from criminal division of Court of Appeal) does not prevent an appeal to the House of Lords under this section.

(7) In relation to appeals to the Court of Appeal or the House of Lords under this section, the Secretary of State may make an order containing provision corresponding to any provision in the Criminal Appeal Act 1968 (subject to any specified modifications).

This section provides for the procedure to the followed in the High Court in respect of a transferred life prisoner whose case has been referred to the High Court under s.273. Such a reference is to be determined by a single judge of the court without an oral hearing, but the person concerned may appeal to the Court of Appeal (Criminal Division) against the decision of the High Court. There appears to be no corresponding provision for a reference to the made by the Attorney General on the ground that the period fixed is an unduly lenient.

275 Duty to release certain life prisoners

(1) Section 28 of the Crime (Sentences) Act 1997 (c. 43) (duty to release certain life prisoners) is amended as follows.

(2) For subsection (1A) there is substituted—

"(1A) This section applies to a life prisoner in respect of whom a minimum term order has been made; and any reference in this section to the relevant part of such a prisoner's sentence is a reference to the part of the sentence specified in the order."

(3) In subsection (1B)(a)—
   (a) for the words from the beginning to "applies" there is substituted "this section does not apply to him", and
   (b) for the words from "such an order" to "appropriate stage" there is substituted "a minimum term order has been made in respect of each of those sentences".

(4) After subsection (8) there is inserted—

"(8A) In this section "minimum term order" means an order under—

    (a) subsection (2) of section 82A of the Powers of Criminal Courts (Sentencing) Act 2000 (determination of minimum term in respect of life sentence that is not fixed by law), or

    (b) subsection (2) of section 269 of the Criminal Justice Act 2003 (determination of minimum term in respect of mandatory life sentence).".

GENERAL NOTE

This section makes amendments to the Crime (Sentences) Act 1997, s.28 which prescribes the procedure to be followed when the release of a life sentence prisoner is under consideration. The section has already been heavily amended. The section, as amended by this section, will read as follows:

(1A) This section applies to a life prisoner in respect of whom a minimum term order has been made; and any reference in this section to the relevant part of such a prisoner's sentence is a reference to the part of the sentence specified in the order.

(1B) But if a prisoner is serving two or more life sentences — (a) this section does not apply to him unless a minimum term order has been made in respect of each of those sentences and (b) the provisions of subsections (5) to (8) below do not apply in relation to him until he has served the relevant part of each of them.

(5) As soon as—

(a) a life prisoner to whom this section applies has served the relevant part of his sentence, and

(b) the Parole Board has directed his release under this section, it shall be the duty of the Secretary of State to release him on licence.

(6) The Parole Board shall not give a direction under subsection (5) above with respect to a life prisoner to whom this section applies unless—

(a) the Secretary of State has referred the prisoner's case to the Board; and

(b) the Board is satisfied that it is no longer necessary for the protection of the public that the prisoner should be confined.

(7) A life prisoner to whom this section applies may require the Secretary of State to refer his case to the Parole Board at any time—

(a) after he has served the relevant part of his sentence; and

(b) where there has been a previous reference of his case to the Board, after the end of the period of two years beginning with the disposal of that reference; and

(c) where he is also serving a sentence of imprisonment or detention for a term, after he has served one-half of that sentence; and in this subsection "previous reference" means a reference under subsection (6) above or section 32(4) below.

(8) In determining for the purpose of subsection (5) or(7) above whether a life prisoner to whom this section applies has served the relevant part of his sentence, no account shall be taken of any time during which he was unlawfully at large within the meaning of section 49 of the Prison Act 1952.

(8A) In this section "minimum term order" means an order under—

(a) subsection (2) of section 82A of the Powers of Criminal Courts (Sentencing) Act 2000 (determination of minimum term in respect of life sentence that is not fixed by law), or

(b) subsection (2) of section 269 of the Criminal Justice Act 2003 (determination of minimum term in respect of mandatory life sentence)

The effect of the amendments made to the section to is apply the procedure under s.28 to mandatory life sentences and thereby to exclude the Secretary of State from any involvement in the decision whether a particular offender who has served the minimum term prescribed by the court should be released. The Crime (Sentences) Act 1997, s.29 which previously permitted the Secretary of State to decide on the release of mandatory life sentence prisoners, is repealed by Sch.37, Pt 8 of the Act.

276   Mandatory life sentences: transitional cases

Schedule 22 (which relates to the effect in transitional cases of mandatory life sentences) shall have effect.

Schedule 22 provides for those sentenced to mandatory life for offences committed before December 18, 2003. The greater part of the schedule deals with procedures for the re-fixing by the High Court of minimum periods fixed by the Secretary of State under the former practice.

In relation to persons falling to be sentenced to a mandatory life sentence on or after December 18, 2003 for an offence committed before that date, para.10 provides that the court may not make a "minimum term order" under s.269 specifying a part of the sentence which in the opinion of the court is greater than the part which would have been specified by the Secretary of State under the earlier practice.

277   Interpretation of Chapter 7

In this Chapter—
"court" includes a court-martial;
"guidelines" has the same meaning as in section 172(1);
"life sentence" means—
  (a) a sentence of imprisonment for life,
  (b) a sentence of detention during Her Majesty's pleasure, or
  (c) a sentence of custody for life passed before the commencement of section 61(1) of the Criminal Justice and Court Services Act 2000 (c. 43) (which abolishes that sentence).

CHAPTER 8

OTHER PROVISIONS ABOUT SENTENCING

Deferment of sentence

278   Deferment of sentence

Schedule 23 (deferment of sentence) shall have effect.

Schedule 23 provides replacement sections for the Powers of Criminal Courts (Sentencing) Act 2000, ss.1 and 2, dealing with deferment of sentence. The principal changes made by the new sections are to enable a court which defers sentence to require the offender to undertake to comply with any requirements which the court considers appropriate to impose during the period of deferment. These requirements may include a requirement as to the residence of the offender during the whole or any part of the period of deferment. An officer of a local probation board or some other person may be appointed to act as a supervisor in relation to the offender. Provision is made for the court to deal with the offender before the end of the period of defefrrment if he is brought before the court and the court is satisfied that he has failed to comply with one or more requirements imposed in connection with the deferment. A court may also deal with the offender before the end of the period of deferment if he is convicted of an offence.

Power to include drug treatment and testing requirement in certain orders in respect of young offenders

279   Drug treatment and testing requirement in action plan order or supervision order

Schedule 24 (which enables a requirement as to drug treatment and testing to be included in an action plan order or a supervision order) shall have effect.

Schedule 24 amends the Powers of Criminal Court (Sentencing) Act 2000, s.70 and Sch.6 so as to allow drug treatment and testing requirements to be included in action plan orders or supervision orders.

Alteration of penalties for offences

280   Alteration of penalties for specified summary offences

(1) The summary offences listed in Schedule 25 are no longer punishable with imprisonment.

(2) Schedule 26 (which contains amendments increasing the maximum term of imprisonment for certain summary offences from 4 months or less to 51 weeks) shall have effect.

(3) This section does not affect the penalty for any offence committed before the commencement of this section.

GENERAL NOTE

Section 25 contains a long list of offences which cease to be punishable with imprisonment under this Act. Section 26 contains a list of summary offences for which the maximum term of imprisonment is increased, in accordance with s.154, to a maximum of 51.

281   Alteration of penalties for other summary offences

(1) Subsection (2) applies to any summary offence which—
   (a) is an offence under a relevant enactment,
   (b) is punishable with a maximum term of imprisonment of five months or less, and
   (c) is not listed in Schedule 25 or Schedule 26.

(2) The Secretary of State may by order amend any relevant enactment so as to—
   (a) provide that any summary offence to which this subsection applies is no longer punishable with imprisonment, or
   (b) increase to 51 weeks the maximum term of imprisonment to which a person is liable on conviction of the offence.

(3) An order under subsection (2) may make such supplementary, incidental or consequential provision as the Secretary of State considers necessary or expedient, including provision amending any relevant enactment.

(4) Subsection (5) applies to any summary offence which—
   (a) is an offence under a relevant enactment, and
   (b) is punishable with a maximum term of imprisonment of six months.

(5) The maximum term of imprisonment to which a person is liable on conviction of an offence to which this subsection applies is, by virtue of this subsection, 51 weeks (and the relevant enactment in question is to be read as if it had been amended accordingly).

(6) Neither of the following—
   (a) an order under subsection (2), or
   (b) subsection (5),
      affects the penalty for any offence committed before the commencement of that order or subsection (as the case may be).

(7) In this section and section 282 "relevant enactment" means any enactment contained in—
   (a) an Act passed before or in the same Session as this Act, or
   (b) any subordinate legislation made before the passing of this Act.

(8) In subsection (7) "subordinate legislation" has the same meaning as in the Interpretation Act 1978 (c. 30).

GENERAL NOTE

This section confers wide powers on the Secretary of State to vary the maximum terms of imprisonment for any summary offences which are at present punishable with imprisonment and which are not listed in either Sch.25 or Sch.26. If the offence is currently punishable with a maximum term of five months imprisonment or less, the Secretary of State may either provide that the offence should no longer be punishable with imprisonment at all, or increase the maximum term of imprisonment to 51 weeks. If the maximum term of imprisonment for the summary offence is six months, the Secretary of State may not change the status of the offence so that it is no longer punishable with imprisonment, but he may increase the maximum term of imprisonment to 51 weeks. No change made under these powers may affect the penalty for any offence committed before the commencement of the order or the section.

282 Increase in maximum term that may be imposed on summary conviction of offence triable either way

(1) In section 32 of the Magistrates' Courts Act 1980 (c. 43) (penalties on summary conviction for offences triable either way) in subsection (1) (offences listed in Schedule 1 to that Act) for "not exceeding 6 months" there is substituted "not exceeding 12 months".

(2) Subsection (3) applies to any offence triable either way which—
   (a) is an offence under a relevant enactment,
   (b) is punishable with imprisonment on summary conviction, and
   (c) is not listed in Schedule 1 to the Magistrates' Courts Act 1980.

(3) The maximum term of imprisonment to which a person is liable on summary conviction of an offence to which this subsection applies is by virtue of this subsection 12 months (and the relevant enactment in question is to be read as if it had been amended accordingly).

(4) Nothing in this section affects the penalty for any offence committed before the commencement of this section.

GENERAL NOTE

Consistently with s.154 of the Act, which raises the general limit on the powers of a magistrates' court to impose imprisonment to 12 months, this section increases the maximum term which may be imposed on summary conviction for an either way offence to a total of 12 months. The change applies to any either way offence which is listed in Sch.1 to the Magistrates' Courts Act 1980, or is treated as an either way offence by the statute which creates the offence. The increase does not apply to an either way offence which is not punishable with imprisonment on summary conviction, but is punishable with imprisonment on conviction on indictment.

283 Enabling powers: power to alter maximum penalties

(1) The Secretary of State may by order, in accordance with subsection (2) or (3), amend any relevant enactment which confers a power (however framed or worded) by subordinate legislation to make a person—
   (a) as regards a summary offence, liable on conviction to a term of imprisonment;
   (b) as regards an offence triable either way, liable on summary conviction to a term of imprisonment.

(2) An order made by virtue of paragraph (a) of subsection (1) may amend the relevant enactment in question so as to—
   (a) restrict the power so that a person may no longer be made liable on conviction of a summary offence to a term of imprisonment, or
   (b) increase to 51 weeks the maximum term of imprisonment to which a person may be made liable on conviction of a summary offence under the power.

(3) An order made by virtue of paragraph (b) of that subsection may amend the relevant enactment in question so as to increase the maximum term of imprisonment to which a person may be made liable on summary conviction of an offence under the power to 12 months.

(4) Schedule 27 (which amends the maximum penalties which may be imposed by virtue of certain enabling powers) shall have effect.

(5) The power conferred by subsection (1) shall not apply to the enactments amended under Schedule 27.

(6) An order under subsection (1) may make such supplementary, incidental or consequential provision as the Secretary of State considers necessary or expedient, including provision amending any relevant enactment.

(7) None of the following—

(a) an order under subsection (1), or

(b) Schedule 27,

affects the penalty for any offence committed before the commencement of that order or Schedule (as the case may be).

(8) In subsection (1) "subordinate legislation" has the same meaning as in the Interpretation Act 1978 (c. 30).

(9) In this section "relevant enactment" means any enactment contained in an Act passed before or in the same Session as this Act.

GENERAL NOTE

This section confers broad general powers on the Secretary of State to vary the maximum penalties for summary offences created by subordinate legislation. The Secretary of State is empowered either to provide that the offence is no longer punishable by imprisonment on summary conviction, or to increase the maximum term of imprisonment to 51 weeks.

284 Increase in penalties for drug-related offences

(1) Schedule 28 (increase in penalties for certain drug-related offences) shall have effect.

(2) That Schedule does not affect the penalty for any offence committed before the commencement of that Schedule.

GENERAL NOTE

This section amends Sch.4 to the Misuse of Drugs Act 1971 as a consequence of the re-grading of cannabis from the status of a Class B drug to a Class C drug. The effect of the amendments is to ensure that the maximum sentence for producing, supplying or being in possession of cannabis with intent to supply remains at 14 years, the level appropriate to a Class B drug, rather than being reduced to the level fixed by the Act for Class C drugs, five years. The effect of the changes is to increase the maximum sentence for supplying etc. other Class C drugs to fourteen years. The offences concerned are those under ss.4(2), 4(3) and 5(3) of producing, being concerned in the production, supplying, offering to supply or having possession of a Class C drug with intent supply it to another. The maximum penalties for being concerned in the management of premises at which class C drugs are used and other offences under ss.12 and 13 are also fixed at 14 years imprisonment where the drug concerned is a Class C drug. Corresponding amendments are made to the Customs and Excise Management Act 1979 (c.2), Sch.1 and the Criminal Justice (International Co-operation) Act 1990 (c.5).

285 Increase in penalties for certain driving-related offences

(1) In section 12A of the Theft Act 1968 (c. 60) (aggravated vehicle-taking), in subsection (4), for "five years" there is substituted "fourteen years".

(2) Part 1 of Schedule 2 to the Road Traffic Offenders Act 1988 (c. 53) (prosecution and punishment of offences) is amended in accordance with subsections (3) and (4).

(3) In the entry relating to section 1 of the Road Traffic Act 1988 (c. 52) (causing death by dangerous driving), in column 4, for "10 years" there is substituted "14 years".

(4) In the entry relating to section 3A of that Act (causing death by careless driving when under influence of drink or drugs), in column 4, for "10 years" there is substituted "14 years".

(5) Part I of Schedule 1 to the Road Traffic Offenders (Northern Ireland) Order 1996 (S.I. 1996/1320 (N.I. 10)) (prosecution and punishment of offences) is amended in accordance with subsections (6) and (7).

(6) In the entry relating to Article 9 of the Road Traffic (Northern Ireland) Order 1995 (S.I. 1995/2994 (N.I. 18)) (causing death or

grievous bodily injury by dangerous driving), in column 4, for "10 years" there is substituted "14 years".

(7) In the entry relating to Article 14 of that Order (causing death or grievous bodily injury by careless driving when under the influence of drink or drugs), in column 4, for "10 years" there is substituted "14 years".

(8) This section does not affect the penalty for any offence committed before the commencement of this section.

GENERAL NOTE
This section makes a number of amendments to the Road Traffic Offenders Act 1988 (c.53) and the Theft Act 1968, s.12A. The effect of the amendments is to increase to 14 years the maximum sentences for the offences of causing death by dangerous driving, causing death by careless driving when under the influence of drink or drugs, and aggravated vehicle taking when death results. Corresponding changes are made to the equivalent legislation in Northern Ireland.

286 Increase in penalties for offences under section 174 of Road Traffic Act 1988

(1) In Part 1 of Schedule 2 to the Road Traffic Offenders Act 1988 (c. 53) (prosecution and punishment of offences), in the entry relating to section 174 of the Road Traffic Act 1988 (c. 52) (false statements and withholding material information), for columns (3) and (4) there is substituted—

"(a) Summarily

(a) 6 months or the statutory maximum or both

(b) On indictment

(b) 2 years or a fine or both".

(2) Section 282(3) (increase in maximum term that may be imposed on summary conviction of offence triable either way) has effect in relation to the entry amended by subsection (1) as it has effect in relation to any other enactment contained in an Act passed before this Act.

(3) This section does not apply in relation to any offence committed before the commencement of this section.

Firearms offences

287 Minimum sentence for certain firearms offences

After section 51 of the Firearms Act 1968 (c. 27) there is inserted the following section—

"51A Minimum sentence for certain offences under s. 5

(1) This section applies where—
(a) an individual is convicted of—
(i) an offence under section 5(1)(a), (ab), (aba), (ac), (ad), (ae), (af) or (c) of this Act, or
(ii) an offence under section 5(1A)(a) of this Act, and
(b) the offence was committed after the commencement of this section and at a time when he was aged 16 or over.

(2) The court shall impose an appropriate custodial sentence (or order for detention) for a term of at least the required minimum term (with or without a fine) unless the court is of the opinion that there are exceptional circumstances relating to the offence or to the offender which justify its not doing so.

(3) Where an offence is found to have been committed over a period of two or more days, or at some time during a period of two or more days, it shall be taken for the purposes of this section to have been committed on the last of those days.

(4) In this section "appropriate custodial sentence (or order for detention)" means—

  (a) in relation to England and Wales—

    (i) in the case of an offender who is aged 18 or over when convicted, a sentence of imprisonment, and

    (ii) in the case of an offender who is aged under 18 at that time, a sentence of detention under section 91 of the Powers of Criminal Courts (Sentencing) Act 2000;

  (b) in relation to Scotland—

    (i) in the case of an offender who is aged 21 or over when convicted, a sentence of imprisonment,

    (ii) in the case of an offender who is aged under 21 at that time (not being an offender mentioned in sub-paragraph (iii)), a sentence of detention under section 207 of the Criminal Procedure (Scotland) Act 1995, and

    (iii) in the case of an offender who is aged under 18 at that time and is subject to a supervision requirement, an order for detention under section 44, or sentence of detention under section 208, of that Act.

(5) In this section "the required minimum term" means—

  (a) in relation to England and Wales—

    (i) in the case of an offender who was aged 18 or over when he committed the offence, five years, and

    (ii) in the case of an offender who was under 18 at that time, three years, and

  (b) in relation to Scotland—

    (i) in the case of an offender who was aged 21 or over when he committed the offence, five years, and

    (ii) in the case of an offender who was aged under 21 at that time, three years."

GENERAL NOTE

This section continues the regrettable trend towards the introduction of minimum sentences for particular offences, which began with the Crime (Sentences) Act 1997. The new s.51A of the Firearms Act 1968 requires the court to impose a custodial sentence of at least five years in the case of an offender for aged 18 or over when offence was committed, or three years if the offender was over 16 under the age of 18 when the offence was committed. The required minimum sentence applies to offences of possessing or otherwise dealing with a prohibited weapon other than a weapon designed to discharge liquid or gas. The minimum term must be imposed "unless the court is of the opinion that there are exceptional circumstances relating to the offence or to the offender which justify its not doing so". This ground for not imposing the required minimum term has been taken from the Powers of Criminal Courts (Sentencing) Act 2000, s.109 dealing with automatic life sentence, rather than s.110 or s.111 of that Act, dealing with convictions on third occasion for offences of trafficking in Class A drugs or domestic burglary, which allow a court not to impose the minimum term of imprisonment if it would be unjust to do so in all the circumstances.

288   Certain firearms offences to be triable only on indictment

In Part 1 of Schedule 6 to the Firearms Act 1968 (c. 27) (prosecution and punishment of offences) for the entries relating to offences under section 5(1) (possessing or distributing prohibited weapons or ammunition) and section 5(1A) (possessing or distributing other prohibited weapons) there is substituted—

"Section 5(1) (a), (ab), (aba), (ac), (ad), (ae), (af) or (c)	Possessing or distributing prohibited weapons or ammunition.	On indictment	10 years or a fine, or both.
Section 5(1)(b)	Possessing or distributing prohibited weapon designed for discharge of noxious liquid etc.	(a) Summary (b) On indictment	6 months or a fine of the statutory maximum, or both. 10 years or a fine or both.
Section 5(1A) (a)	Possessing or distributing firearm disguised as other object.	On indictment	10 years or a fine, or both.
Section 5(1A) (b), (c), (d), (e), (f) or (g)	Possessing or distributing other prohibited weapons.	(a) Summary (b) On indictment	6 months or a fine of the statutory maximum, or both. 10 years or a fine, or both."

GENERAL NOTE

As a consequence of s.287, which imposes a required minimum sentence of five years for certain offences connected with prohibited weapons under the Firearms Act 1968, s.5 this section alters the status of those offences by providing that they will be triable only on indictment.

289   Power to sentence young offender to detention in respect of certain firearms offences: England and Wales

(1) Section 91 of the Sentencing Act (offenders under 18 convicted of certain serious offences: power to detain for specified period) is amended as follows.

(2) After subsection (1) there is inserted—

"(1A) Subsection (3) below also applies where—
   (a) a person aged under 18 is convicted on indictment of an offence—
       (i) under subsection (1)(a), (ab), (aba), (ac), (ad), (ae), (af) or (c) of section 5 of the Firearms Act 1968 (prohibited weapons), or
       (ii) under subsection (1A)(a) of that section,
   (b) the offence was committed after the commencement of section 51A of that Act and at a time when he was aged 16 or over, and
   (c) the court is of the opinion mentioned in section 51A(2) of that Act (exceptional circumstances which justify its not imposing required custodial sentence)."

(3) After subsection (4) there is inserted—

"(5) Where subsection (2) of section 51A of the Firearms Act 1968 requires the imposition of a sentence of detention under this section for a term of at least the required minimum term (within the meaning of that section), the court shall sentence the offender to be detained for such period, of at least that term but not exceeding the maximum term of imprisonment with which the offence is punishable in the case of a person aged 18 or over, as may be specified in the sentence.".

GENERAL NOTE

As a consequence of s.287, which imposes on courts a duty to impose a required minimum sentence of three years on an offender under the age of eighteen who is convicted of certain offences in connection with the possession of prohibited weapons under the Firearms Act 1968 s.5, this section makes available for those offences the power to award detention to offenders under the age of eighteen under the Powers of Criminal Courts (Sentencing) Act 2000, s.91. The power is available only where the offender was aged 16 or over when the offence was committed. It appears that there may be a mistake in the new subs.(1A)(c), in that the word "not" may have been omitted. The section appears to mean "the court is [not] of the opinion" mentioned in s.51A(2).

290   Power to sentence young offender to detention in respect of certain firearms offences: Scotland

(1) The Criminal Procedure (Scotland) Act 1995 (c. 46) is amended as follows.

(2) In section 49(3) (children's hearing for purpose of obtaining advice as to treatment of child), at the end there is added "except that where the circumstances are such as are mentioned in paragraphs (a) and (b) of section 51A(1) of the Firearms Act 1968 it shall itself dispose of the case."

(3) In section 208 (detention of children convicted on indictment), the existing provisions become subsection (1); and after that subsection there is added—

    "(2) Subsection (1) does not apply where the circumstances are such as are mentioned in paragraphs (a) and (b) of section 51A(1) of the Firearms Act 1968.".

291   Power by order to exclude application of minimum sentence to those under 18

(1) The Secretary of State may by order—
    (a) amend section 51A(1)(b) of the Firearms Act 1968 (c. 27) by substituting for the word "16" the word "18",
    (b) repeal section 91(1A)(c) and (5) of the Sentencing Act,
    (c) amend subsection (3) of section 49 of the Criminal Procedure (Scotland) Act 1995 by repealing the exception to that subsection,
    (d) repeal section 208(2) of that Act, and
    (e) make such other provision as he considers necessary or expedient in consequence of, or in connection with, the provision made by virtue of paragraphs (a) to (d).

(2) The provision that may be made by virtue of subsection (1)(e) includes, in particular, provision amending or repealing any provision of an Act (whenever passed), including any provision of this Act.

GENERAL NOTE

This section empowers the Secretary of State to amend the new s.51A of the Firearms Act 1968 inserted into that Act by s.287, so as to restrict the application of the minimum sentence to offenders under the age of eighteen, and to make amendments consequential on that amendment.

292   Sentencing for firearms offences in Northern Ireland

Schedule 29 (which contains amendments of the Firearms (Northern Ireland) Order 1981 (S.I. 1981/155 (N.I. 2)) relating to sentencing) shall have effect.

293   Increase in penalty for offences relating to importation or exportation of certain firearms

(1) The Customs and Excise Management Act 1979 (c. 2) is amended as follows.

(2) In section 50 (penalty for improper importation of goods), for subsection (5A) there is substituted—

"(5A) In the case of—

   (a) an offence under subsection (2) or (3) above committed in Great Britain in connection with a prohibition or restriction on the importation of any weapon or ammunition that is of a kind mentioned in section 5(1)(a), (ab), (aba), (ac), (ad), (ae), (af) or (c) or (1A)(a) of the Firearms Act 1968,

   (b) any such offence committed in Northern Ireland in connection with a prohibition or restriction on the importation of any weapon or ammunition that is of a kind mentioned in Article 6(1)(a), (ab), (ac), (ad), (ae) or (c) or (1A)(a) of the Firearms (Northern Ireland) Order 1981, or

   (c) any such offence committed in connection with the prohibition contained in section 20 of the Forgery and Counterfeiting Act 1981,

subsection (4)(b) above shall have effect as if for the words "7 years" there were substituted the words "10 years"."

(3) In section 68 (offences in relation to exportation of prohibited or restricted goods) for subsection (4A) there is substituted—

"(4A) In the case of—

   (a) an offence under subsection (2) or (3) above committed in Great Britain in connection with a prohibition or restriction on the exportation of any weapon or ammunition that is of a kind mentioned in section 5(1)(a), (ab), (aba), (ac), (ad), (ae), (af) or (c) or (1A)(a) of the Firearms Act 1968,

   (b) any such offence committed in Northern Ireland in connection with a prohibition or restriction on the exportation of any weapon or ammunition that is of a kind mentioned in Article 6(1)(a), (ab), (ac), (ad), (ae) or (c) or (1A)(a) of the Firearms (Northern Ireland) Order 1981, or

   (c) any such offence committed in connection with the prohibition contained in section 21 of the Forgery and Counterfeiting Act 1981,

subsection (3)(b) above shall have effect as if for the words "7 years" there were substituted the words "10 years"."

(4) In section 170 (penalty for fraudulent evasion of duty, etc), for subsection (4A) there is substituted—

"(4A) In the case of—

   (a) an offence under subsection (2) or (3) above committed in Great Britain in connection with a prohibition or restriction on the importation or exportation of any weapon or ammunition that is of a kind mentioned in section 5(1)(a), (ab), (aba), (ac), (ad), (ae), (af) or (c) or (1A)(a) of the Firearms Act 1968,

(b) any such offence committed in Northern Ireland in connection with a prohibition or restriction on the importation or exportation of any weapon or ammunition that is of a kind mentioned in Article 6(1)(a), (ab), (ac), (ad), (ae) or (c) or (1A)(a) of the Firearms (Northern Ireland) Order 1981, or

(c) any such offence committed in connection with the prohibitions contained in sections 20 and 21 of the Forgery and Counterfeiting Act 1981,

subsection (3)(b) above shall have effect as if for the words "7 years" there were substituted the words "10 years"."

(5) This section does not affect the penalty for any offence committed before the commencement of this section.

GENERAL NOTE

The effect of these amendments is to increase the maximum sentence for the importation or exportation of prohibited firearms to which the mandatory minimum sentence imposed by the Firearms Act 1968 s.51A applies, from seven years to 10 years.

Offenders transferred to mental hospital

294 Duration of directions under Mental Health Act 1983 in relation to offenders

(1) Section 50 of the Mental Health Act 1983 (c. 20) (further provisions as to prisoners under sentence) is amended as follows.

(2) In subsection (1), for "the expiration of that person's sentence" there is substituted "his release date".

(3) For subsections (2) and (3) there is substituted—

"(2) A restriction direction in the case of a person serving a sentence of imprisonment shall cease to have effect, if it has not previously done so, on his release date.

(3) In this section, references to a person's release date are to the day (if any) on which he would be entitled to be released (whether unconditionally or on licence) from any prison or other institution in which he might have been detained if the transfer direction had not been given; and in determining that day there shall be disregarded—

(a) any powers that would be exercisable by the Parole Board if he were detained in such a prison or other institution, and

(b) any practice of the Secretary of State in relation to the early release under discretionary powers of persons detained in such a prison or other institution.".

GENERAL NOTE

The Mental Health Act 1983, s.50 deals with the position of offenders sentenced to imprisonment who are transferred to a mental hospital under s.36 of the Act. They are thereafter liable to be detained in hospital has is they had been made the subject of a hospital order with restriction under ss.37 and 41 of that Act. This provision amends s.50 to make it consistent with the new parole scheme established by Ch.6 of this Part of the Act. The effect of the amendment is that a person transferred to hospital under s.36 who is a subject to a "restriction direction" will cease to be subject to the restriction direction on the date on which he would have become entitled to be released from the sentence of imprisonment which he was serving at the time of the transfer, normally half way through the sentence. In determining the date on which he would be entitled to be released, the powers given by s.246 to release prisoners before they have served half of the sentence must be disregarded. In the case of a prisoner serving an extended sentence, it appears that the relevant date is the end of the "appropriate custodial sentence", rather than the date on which the Parole Board might otherwise direct his release under s.247.

295 Access to Parole Board for certain patients serving prison sentences

In section 74 of the Mental Health Act 1983 (restricted patients subject to restriction directions) after subsection (5) there is inserted—

"(5A) Where the tribunal have made a recommendation under subsection (1)(b) above in the case of a patient who is subject to a restriction direction or a limitation direction—

(a) the fact that the restriction direction or limitation direction remains in force does not prevent the making of any application or reference to the Parole Board by or in respect of him or the exercise by him of any power to require the Secretary of State to refer his case to the Parole Board, and

(b) if the Parole Board make a direction or recommendation by virtue of which the patient would become entitled to be released (whether unconditionally or on licence) from any prison or other institution in which he might have been detained if he had not been removed to hospital, the restriction direction or limitation direction shall cease to have effect at the time when he would become entitled to be so released."

296 Duration of directions under Mental Health (Northern Ireland) Order 1986 in relation to offenders

(1) Article 56 of the Mental Health (Northern Ireland) Order 1986 (S.I. 1986/ 595 (N.I. 4)) (further provisions as to prisoners under sentence) is amended as follows.

(2) In paragraph (1), for "the expiration of that person's sentence" there is substituted "his release date".

(3) For paragraphs (2) and (3) there is substituted—

"(2) A restriction direction in the case of a person serving a sentence of imprisonment shall cease to have effect, if it has not previously done so, on his release date.

(3) In this Article, references to a person's release date are to the day (if any) on which he would be entitled to be released (whether unconditionally or on licence) from any prison or juvenile justice centre in which he might have been detained if the transfer direction had not been given; and in determining that day any powers that would be exercisable by the Sentence Review Commissioners or the Life Sentence Review Commissioners if he were detained in such a prison or juvenile justice centre shall be disregarded."

297 Access to Sentence Review Commissioners and Life Sentence Review Commissioners for certain Northern Ireland patients

In Article 79 of the Mental Health (Northern Ireland) Order 1986 (restricted patients subject to restriction directions) after paragraph (5) there is inserted—

"(5A) Where the tribunal have made a recommendation under paragraph (1)(b) in the case of a patient who is subject to a restriction direction—

(a) the fact that the restriction direction remains in force does not prevent—

    (i) the making of any application or reference to the Life Sentence Review Commissioners by or in respect of him or the exercise by him of any power to require the Secretary of State to refer his case to those Commissioners, or

    (ii) the making of any application by him to the Sentence Review Commissioners, and

(b) if—

    (i) the Life Sentence Review Commissioners give a direction by virtue of which the patient would become entitled to be released (whether unconditionally or on licence) from any prison or juvenile justice centre in which he might have been detained if the transfer direction had not been given, or

    (ii) the Sentence Review Commissioners grant a declaration by virtue of which he would become so entitled,

the restriction direction shall cease to have effect at the time at which he would become so entitled.".

Term of detention and training order

298   Term of detention and training order

(1) Section 101 of the Sentencing Act (which relates to detention and training orders) is amended as follows.

(2) In subsection (1), for "subsection (2)" there is substituted "subsections (2) and (2A)".

(3) After subsection (2) there is inserted—

"(2A) Where—

    (a) the offence is a summary offence,

    (b) the maximum term of imprisonment that a court could (in the case of an offender aged 18 or over) impose for the offence is 51 weeks,

the term of a detention and training order may not exceed 6 months."

GENERAL NOTE

The Powers of Criminal Courts (Sentencing) Act 2000, s.101(2) provides that the term of a detention and training order may not exceed the maximum term of imprisonment that the Crown Court could impose for the offence. This new subsection deals with the power to award a detention and training order for a summary offence for which the maximum term of imprisonment, as a result of the changes made by the 2003 Act, is 51 weeks. The new subsection provides that in such a case the maximum term of a detention and training order may not exceed six months. The custody plus provisions of s.181 do not apply to a detention and training order.

Disqualification from working with children

299   Disqualification from working with children

Schedule 30 (which contains amendments of Part 2 of the Criminal Justice and Court Services Act 2000 (c. 43) relating to disqualification orders under that Part) shall have effect.

GENERAL NOTE

Scheduled 30 inserts into the Criminal Justice and Court Services Act 2000, two new sections dealing with disqualification orders. Under the Act as originally enacted, a court was required to make a disqualification order only when a "qualifying sentence", normally of 12 months imprisonment or detention, was imposed. The effect of the new s.29A is that a "senior court" (normally the Crown Court) is in addition given a discretionary power to make a disqualification order in respect of an offender convicted of an offence against a child within the meaning of the Act who is not sentenced to a "qualifying sentence". If the court makes such a discretionary order, it must state its reasons for doing so.

A new s.29B allows the prosecutor to apply to the court to make a disqualification order where the court has not made an order in circumstances where the court is obliged to make an order.

Fine defaulters

300　Power to impose unpaid work requirement or curfew requirement on fine defaulter

(1) Subsection (2) applies in any case where, in respect of a person aged 16 or over, a magistrates' court—

 (a) has power under Part 3 of the Magistrates' Courts Act 1980 (c. 43) to issue a warrant of commitment for default in paying a sum adjudged to be paid by a conviction (other than a sum ordered to be paid under section 6 of the Proceeds of Crime Act 2002 (c. 29)), or

 (b) would, but for section 89 of the Sentencing Act (restrictions on custodial sentences for persons under 18), have power to issue such a warrant for such default.

(2) The magistrates' court may, instead of issuing a warrant of commitment or, as the case may be, proceeding under section 81 of the Magistrates' Courts Act 1980 (enforcement of fines imposed on young offender), order the person in default to comply with—

 (a) an unpaid work requirement (as defined by section 199), or

 (b) a curfew requirement (as defined by section 204).

(3) In this Part "default order" means an order under subsection (2).

(4) Subsections (3) and (4) of section 177 (which relate to electronic monitoring) have effect in relation to a default order as they have effect in relation to a community order.

(5) Where a magistrates' court has power to make a default order, it may, if it thinks it expedient to do so, postpone the making of the order until such time and on such conditions (if any) as it thinks just.

(6) Schedule 8 (breach, revocation or amendment of community order), Schedule 9 (transfer of community orders to Scotland or Northern Ireland) and Chapter 4 (further provisions about orders under Chapters 2 and 3) have effect in relation to default orders as they have effect in relation to community orders, but subject to the modifications contained in Schedule 31.

(7) Where a default order has been made for default in paying any sum—

 (a) on payment of the whole sum to any person authorised to receive it, the order shall cease to have effect, and

 (b) on payment of a part of the sum to any such person, the total number of hours or days to which the order relates is to be taken to be reduced by a proportion corresponding to that which the part paid bears to the whole sum.

(8) In calculating any reduction required by subsection (7)(b), any fraction of a day or hour is to be disregarded.

GENERAL NOTE

 This section empowers a magistrates' court dealing with a person who has defaulted on the payment of a fine or other sum of money, other than a confiscation order made under the Proceeds of Crime Act 2002 (but not a confiscation order made under other provisions) to order the person to comply with an unpaid work requirement or a curfew requirement as an alternative to committing him to prison. The order may be suspended if the court considers it appropriate to do so. The order ceases to have effect if the whole of the sum payable is paid; if part of the sum is paid, the total number of hours or days is reduced proportionately.

301   Fine defaulters: driving disqualification

(1) Subsection (2) applies in any case where a magistrates' court—
(a) has power under Part 3 of the Magistrates' Courts Act 1980 (c. 43) to issue a warrant of commitment for default in paying a sum adjudged to be paid by a conviction (other than a sum ordered to be paid under section 6 of the Proceeds of Crime Act 2002 (c. 29)), or
(b) would, but for section 89 of the Sentencing Act (restrictions on custodial sentences for persons under 18), have power to issue such a warrant for such default.

(2) The magistrates' court may, instead of issuing a warrant of commitment or, as the case may be, proceeding under section 81 of the Magistrates' Courts Act 1980 (enforcement of fines imposed on young offenders), order the person in default to be disqualified, for such period not exceeding twelve months as it thinks fit, for holding or obtaining a driving licence.

(3) Where an order has been made under subsection (2) for default in paying any sum—
(a) on payment of the whole sum to any person authorised to receive it, the order shall cease to have effect, and
(b) on payment of part of the sum to any such person, the total number of weeks or months to which the order relates is to be taken to be reduced by a proportion corresponding to that which the part paid bears to the whole sum.

(4) In calculating any reduction required by subsection (3)(b) any fraction of a week or month is to be disregarded.

(5) The Secretary of State may by order amend subsection (2) by substituting, for the period there specified, such other period as may be specified in the order.

(6) A court which makes an order under this section disqualifying a person for holding or obtaining a driving licence shall require him to produce—
(a) any such licence held by him together with its counterpart; or
(b) in the case where he holds a Community licence (within the meaning of Part 3 of the Road Traffic Act 1988 (c. 52)), his Community licence and its counterpart (if any).

(7) In this section—
"driving licence" means a licence to drive a motor vehicle granted under Part 3 of the Road Traffic Act 1988;
"counterpart"—
(a) in relation to a driving licence, has the meaning given in relation to such a licence by section 108(1) of that Act; and
(b) in relation to a Community licence, has the meaning given by section 99B of that Act.

GENERAL NOTE

This section allows a magistrates' court dealing with a person who has defaulted on the payment of a fine or other sum of money, other than a confiscation order made under the Proceeds of Crime Act 2002, but not a confiscation order made under other legislation, to disqualify him from driving as an alternative to committing him to custody in default of payment. It is not necessary that the offence for which the fine or other payment was ordered to be made should be in any way connected with road traffic offences or motor vehicles. The period of disqualification must not exceed 12 months. If the whole of the outstanding amount is paid, the disqualification ceases to have effect; if part payment is made, the period is reduced proportionately.

CHAPTER 9

SUPPLEMENTARY

302   **Execution of process between England and Wales and Scotland**

Section 4 of the Summary Jurisdiction (Process) Act 1881 (c. 24) (execution of process of English and Welsh courts in Scotland) applies to any process issued by a magistrates' court under—
    paragraph 7(2) or (4), 13(6) or 25(1) of Schedule 8,
    paragraph 12 of Schedule 9,
    paragraph 8(1) of Schedule 10, or
    paragraph 6(2) or (4), 12(1) or 20(1) of Schedule 12,
    as it applies to process issued under the Magistrates' Courts Act 1980 by a magistrates' court.

303   **Sentencing: repeals**

The following enactments (which are superseded by the provisions of this Part) shall cease to have effect—
  (a) Part 2 of the Criminal Justice Act 1991 (c. 53) (early release of prisoners),
  (b) in the Crime (Sentences) Act 1997 (c. 43)—
    (i) section 29 (power of Secretary of State to release life prisoners to whom section 28 of that Act does not apply),
    (ii) section 33 (transferred prisoners), and
    (iii) sections 35 and 40 (fine defaulters),
  (c) sections 80 and 81 of the Crime and Disorder Act 1998 (c. 37) (sentencing guidelines), and
  (d) in the Sentencing Act—
    (i) Chapter 3 of Part 4 (community orders available only where offender 16 or over),
    (ii) section 85 (sexual or violent offences: extension of custodial term for licence purposes),
    (iii) sections 87 and 88 (remand in custody),
    (iv) section 109 (life sentence for second serious offence), and
    (v) Chapter 5 of Part 5 (suspended sentences).

304   **Amendments relating to sentencing**

Schedule 32 (which contains amendments related to the provisions of this Part) shall have effect.

305   **Interpretation of Part 12**

(1) In this Part, except where the contrary intention appears—
    "accredited programme" has the meaning given by section 202(2);
    "activity requirement", in relation to a community order, custody plus order, intermittent custody order or suspended sentence order, has the meaning given by section 201;
    "alcohol treatment requirement", in relation to a community order or suspended sentence order, has the meaning given by section 212;
    "the appropriate officer of the court" means, in relation to a magistrates' court, the clerk of the court;
    "associated", in relation to offences, is to be read in accordance with section 161(1) of the Sentencing Act;

"attendance centre" has the meaning given by section 221(2);

"attendance centre requirement", in relation to a community order, custody plus order, intermittent custody order or suspended sentence order, has the meaning given by section 214;

"community order" has the meaning given by section 177(1);

"community requirement", in relation to a suspended sentence order, has the meaning given by section 189(7);

"community sentence" has the meaning given by section 147(1);

"court" (without more), except in Chapter 7, does not include a service court;

"curfew requirement", in relation to a community order, custody plus order, intermittent custody order or suspended sentence order, has the meaning given by section 204;

"custodial sentence" has the meaning given by section 76 of the Sentencing Act;

"custody plus order" has the meaning given by section 181(4);

"default order" has the meaning given by section 300(3);

"drug rehabilitation requirement", in relation to a community order or suspended sentence order, has the meaning given by section 209;

"electronic monitoring requirement", in relation to a community order, custody plus order, intermittent custody order or suspended sentence order, has the meaning given by section 215;

"exclusion requirement", in relation to a community order, custody plus order, intermittent custody order or suspended sentence order, has the meaning given by section 205;

"guardian" has the same meaning as in the Children and Young Persons Act 1933 (c. 12);

"intermittent custody order" has the meaning given by section 183(2);

"licence" means a licence under Chapter 6;

"local probation board" means a local probation board established under section 4 of the Criminal Justice and Court Services Act 2000 (c. 43);

"mental health treatment requirement", in relation to a community order or suspended sentence order, has the meaning given by section 207;

"pre-sentence report" has the meaning given by section 158(1);

"programme requirement", in relation to a community order, custody plus order, intermittent custody order or suspended sentence order, has the meaning given by section 202;

"prohibited activity requirement", in relation to a community order, custody plus order, intermittent custody order or suspended sentence order, has the meaning given by section 203;

"residence requirement", in relation to a community order or suspended sentence order, has the meaning given by section 206;

"responsible officer", in relation to an offender to whom a community order, a custody plus order, an intermittent custody order or a suspended sentence order relates, has the meaning given by section 197;

"sentence of imprisonment" does not include a committal—

    (a) in default of payment of any sum of money,

    (b) for want of sufficient distress to satisfy any sum of money, or

(c) for failure to do or abstain from doing anything required to be done or left undone,

and references to sentencing an offender to imprisonment are to be read accordingly;

"the Sentencing Act" means the Powers of Criminal Courts (Sentencing) Act 2000 (c. 6);

"service court" means—

　(a) a court-martial constituted under the Army Act 1955 (3 & 4 Eliz. 2 c. 18), the Air Force Act 1955 (3 & 4 Eliz. 2 c. 19) or the Naval Discipline Act 1957 (c. 53);

　(b) a summary appeal court constituted under section 83ZA of the Army Act 1955, section 83ZA of the Air Force Act 1955 or section 52FF of the Naval Discipline Act 1957;

　(c) the Courts-Martial Appeal Court; or

　(d) a Standing Civilian Court;

"service disciplinary proceedings" means—

　(a) any proceedings under the Army Act 1955, the Air Force Act 1955 or the Naval Discipline Act 1957 (whether before a court-martial or any other court or person authorised under any of those Acts to award a punishment in respect of any offence), and

　(b) any proceedings before a Standing Civilian Court;

"supervision requirement", in relation to a community order, custody plus order, intermittent custody order or suspended sentence order, has the meaning given by section 213;

"suspended sentence" and "suspended sentence order" have the meaning given by section 189(7);

"unpaid work requirement", in relation to a community order, custody plus order, intermittent custody order or suspended sentence order, has the meaning given by section 199;

"youth offending team" means a team established under section 39 of the Crime and Disorder Act 1998 (c. 37).

(2) For the purposes of any provision of this Part which requires the determination of the age of a person by the court or the Secretary of State, his age is to be taken to be that which it appears to the court or (as the case may be) the Secretary of State to be after considering any available evidence.

(3) Any reference in this Part to an offence punishable with imprisonment is to be read without regard to any prohibition or restriction imposed by or under any Act on the imprisonment of young offenders.

(4) For the purposes of this Part—

　(a) a sentence falls to be imposed under subsection (2) of section 51A of the Firearms Act 1968 (c. 27) if it is required by that subsection and the court is not of the opinion there mentioned,

　(b) a sentence falls to be imposed under section 110(2) or 111(2) of the Sentencing Act if it is required by that provision and the court is not of the opinion there mentioned,

　(c) a sentence falls to be imposed under section 225 or 227 if, because the court is of the opinion mentioned in subsection (1)(b) of that section, the court is obliged to pass a sentence complying with that section,

(d) a sentence falls to be imposed under section 226 if, because the court is of the opinion mentioned in subsection (1)(b) of that section and considers that the case falls within subsection (2) or (3) of that section, the court is obliged to pass a sentence complying with that section, and

(e) a sentence falls to be imposed under section 228 if, because the court is of the opinion mentioned in subsection (1)(b)(i) and (ii) of that section, the court is obliged to pass a sentence complying with that section.

PART 13

MISCELLANEOUS

Detention of suspected terrorists

306 Limit on period of detention without charge of suspected terrorists

(1) Schedule 8 to the Terrorism Act 2000 (c. 11) (detention) is amended as follows.

(2) At the beginning of paragraph 29(3) (duration of warrants of further detention) there is inserted "Subject to paragraph 36(3A),".

(3) In sub-paragraph (3) of paragraph 36 (extension of warrants)—
  (a) at the beginning there is inserted "Subject to sub-paragraph (3A),", and
  (b) for the words from "beginning" onwards there is substituted "beginning with the relevant time".

(4) After that sub-paragraph there is inserted—
  "(3A) Where the period specified in a warrant of further detention—
    (a) ends at the end of the period of seven days beginning with the relevant time, or
    (b) by virtue of a previous extension (or further extension) under this sub-paragraph, ends after the end of that period,
        the specified period may, on an application under this paragraph, be extended or further extended to a period ending not later than the end of the period of fourteen days beginning with the relevant time.
  (3B) In this paragraph "the relevant time", in relation to a person, means—
    (a) the time of his arrest under section 41, or
    (b) if he was being detained under Schedule 7 when he was arrested under section 41, the time when his examination under that Schedule began."

GENERAL NOTE

This section concerns the detention of persons arrested as suspected terrorists pursuant to s.41 of the Terrorism Act 2000 (c.11). Schedule 8 to that Act is amended (s.306(1)(a)).

The amendments empower the "judicial authority" to extend the duration of a warrant for detention for a period up to 14 days from the "relevant time". The effect of these amendments are broadly explained in the Explanatory Notes as follows:

658. The judicial authority is only able to extend the period in the warrant for more than seven days if the warrant already authorises detention for the maximum seven days currently permitted. For example, the section does not allow the police to ask for ten more days' detention if the warrant only authorises detention for four days. At that stage the judicial authority would only be able extend the warrant for three more days. The section only permits an extension of detention for longer than seven days if the warrant already permits detention for the current maximum of seven days. Nevertheless, the Section does not prevent an application for an extension of the warrant for longer than seven days being made before the seven day period has expired so long as the warrant already authorises detention for seven

days. Accordingly, it is not possible for the fourteen days to be granted in one block no matter how compelling the reason.

659. The procedural requirements for making an application for extension to detention as stipulated in paragraphs 30(3) and 31 to 34 apply to extensions for up to 14 days just as they apply to other extensions of detention under paragraph 36.

Enforcement of legislation on endangered species

307 Enforcement of regulations implementing Community legislation on endangered species

(1) In this section—

"the 1972 Act" means the European Communities Act 1972 (c. 68);

"relevant Community instrument" means—

    (a) Council Regulation 338/97/EC on the protection of species of wild fauna and flora by regulating the trade therein, and

    (b) Commission Regulation 1808/01/EC on the implementation of the Council Regulation mentioned in paragraph (a).

(2) Regulations made under section 2(2) of the 1972 Act for the purpose of implementing any relevant Community instrument may, notwithstanding paragraph 1(1)(d) of Schedule 2 to the 1972 Act, create offences punishable on conviction on indictment with imprisonment for a term not exceeding five years.

(3) In relation to Scotland and Northern Ireland, regulations made under section 2(2) of the 1972 Act for the purpose of implementing any relevant Community instrument may, notwithstanding paragraph 1(1)(d) of Schedule 2 to the 1972 Act, create offences punishable on summary conviction with imprisonment for a term not exceeding six months.

(4) In Scotland, a constable may arrest without a warrant a person—

    (a) who has committed or attempted to commit an offence under regulations made under section 2(2) of the 1972 Act for the purpose of implementing any relevant Community instrument, or

    (b) whom he has reasonable grounds for suspecting to have committed or to have attempted to commit such an offence.

(5) Until the coming into force of paragraph 3 of Schedule 27 (which amends paragraph 1 of Schedule 2 to the 1972 Act), subsection (3) has effect—

    (a) with the omission of the words "in relation to Scotland and Northern Ireland", and

    (b) as if, in relation to England and Wales, the definition of "relevant Community instrument" also included Council Directive 92/43/EEC on the conservation of natural habitats and wild fauna and flora as amended by the Act of Accession to the European Union of Austria, Finland and Sweden and by Council Directive 97/62/EC.

(6) Any reference in this section to a Community instrument is to be read—

    (a) as a reference to that instrument as amended from time to time, and

    (b) where any provision of that instrument has been repealed, as including a reference to any instrument that re-enacts the repealed provision (with or without amendment).

GENERAL NOTE

See the EC Regulations 338/97/EC and 1808/01/EC. Subsection (2) is designed to ensure that offences committed contrary to Wildlife Trade Regulations as currently implemented by the

Control of Trade in Endangered Species (Enforcement) Regulations 1997 (SI 1997/1372) carry a maximum penalty on indictment of 5 years' imprisonment. In Scotland and Northern Ireland, the maximum penalty for the commission of such offences tried summarily is 6 months' imprisonment (subs.(3)).

In Scotland, a constable may arrest without warrant any person who commits wildlife trade offences (subs.(4)). The Explanatory Notes (para.662) point out that:

"Section 24 of the Police and Criminal Evidence Act 1984 and Article 26(1) of the Police and Criminal Evidence Order (NI) 1983, already provide that in other parts of the UK, offences which attract a maximum prison sentence of five years are automatically 'arrestable'. This subsection ensures that the arrest powers available to police officers throughout the UK are broadly consistent for these offences."

Subsection (5)

The effect of this subsection is concisely described by the Explanatory Notes as follows:

"661. Subsection (5) modifies subsection (3), by providing that the provisions of the 1972 Act are also disapplied, until the sentencing provisions in Part 12 of the Act are commenced, in relation to: Wildlife Trade Regulations offences in England and Wales; and offences arising from Council Directive 92/43/EEC on the conservation of natural habitats and wild fauna and flora ('the Habitats Directive") in England and Wales. The subsection supersedes and repeals sections 81(2) and (3) of the Countryside and Rights of Way Act 2000, which are repealed by the Act."

Miscellaneous provisions about criminal proceedings

308   Non-appearance of defendant: plea of guilty

In section 12 of the Magistrates' Courts Act 1980 (c. 43) (non-appearance of accused: plea of guilty) subsection (1)(a)(i) (which excludes offences punishable with imprisonment for term exceeding 3 months) is omitted.

GENERAL NOTE

This section empowers the magistrates' court to deal with a defendant who has pleaded guilty in his absence: the pre-existing bar in respect of cases punishable with a term of three months imprisonment or more, has been lifted.

309   Preparatory hearings for serious offences not involving fraud

In section 29 of the Criminal Procedure and Investigations Act 1996 (c. 25) (power to order preparatory hearings) in subsection (1) (preparatory hearing may be held in complex or lengthy trial) after "complexity" there is inserted "a case of such seriousness".

GENERAL NOTE

Section 29 of the Criminal Procedure and Investigations Act 1996 is amended so that statutory preparatory hearings may be conducted in non-fraud cases having regard to their "seriousness" — and not merely having regard to their "length" or "complexity".

310   Preparatory hearings to deal with severance and joinder of charges

(1) In section 7(1) of the Criminal Justice Act 1987 (c. 38) (which sets out the purposes of preparatory hearings in fraud cases) after paragraph (d) there is inserted "or

(e) considering questions as to the severance or joinder of charges".

(2) In section 9(3) of that Act (determinations as to the admissibility of evidence etc) after paragraph (c) there is inserted "and

(d) any question as to the severance or joinder of charges".

(3) In section 9(11) of that Act (appeals against orders or rulings under section 9(3)(b) or (c)) for "or (c)" there is substituted "(c) or (d)".

(4) In section 29(2) of the Criminal Procedure and Investigations Act 1996 (purposes of preparatory hearings in non-fraud cases) after paragraph (d) there is inserted—

"(e) considering questions as to the severance or joinder of charges,".

(5) In section 31(3) of that Act (rulings as to the admissibility of evidence etc) after paragraph (b) there is inserted—

"(c) any question as to the severance or joinder of charges".

GENERAL NOTE
Severance and joinder issues may be considered at statutory preparatory hearings ordered under either the Criminal Justice Act 1987 or the 1996 Act.

311   Reporting restrictions for preparatory hearings

(1) The Criminal Justice Act 1987 is amended as follows.

(2) In paragraphs (a) and (b) of section 11(1) (restrictions on reporting) for "Great Britain" there is substituted "the United Kingdom".

(3) In section 11A (offences in connection with reporting) after subsection (3) there is inserted—

"(3A) Proceedings for an offence under this section shall not be instituted in Northern Ireland otherwise than by or with the consent of the Attorney General for Northern Ireland."

(4) In section 17(3) (extent) after "sections 2 and 3;" there is inserted "sections 11 and 11A;".

(5) The Criminal Procedure and Investigations Act 1996 (c. 25) is amended as follows.

(6) In paragraphs (a) and (b) of section 37(1) (restrictions on reporting) for "Great Britain" there is substituted "the United Kingdom".

(7) In section 38 (offences in connection with reporting) after subsection (3) there is inserted—

"(3A) Proceedings for an offence under this section shall not be instituted in Northern Ireland otherwise than by or with the consent of the Attorney General for Northern Ireland."

(8) In paragraphs (a) and (b) of section 41(1) (restrictions on reporting) for "Great Britain" there is substituted "the United Kingdom".

(9) In section 79(3) (extent) after "Parts III" there is inserted "(other than sections 37 and 38)".

(10) In Schedule 4 (modifications for Northern Ireland) paragraph 16 is omitted.

GENERAL NOTE
Northern Ireland is brought within the scheme for imposing reporting restrictions in respect of preparatory hearings, and for dealing with breaches of the restrictions.

312   Awards of costs

(1) The Prosecution of Offences Act 1985 (c. 23) is amended as follows.

(2) In section 16(4A) (defence costs on an appeal under section 9(11) of Criminal Justice Act 1987 (c. 38) may be met out of central funds) after "1987" there is inserted "or section 35(1) of the Criminal Procedure and Investigations Act 1996".

(3) In section 18(2) (award of costs against accused in case of dismissal of appeal under section 9(11) of the Criminal Justice Act 1987 etc) after paragraph (c) there is inserted "or

(d) an appeal or application for leave to appeal under section 35(1) of the Criminal Procedure and Investigations Act 1996."

GENERAL NOTE
This section addresses a deficiency in pre-existing rules regarding the power of the Court of Appeal to award defence costs out of central funds (or to award costs against the defendant) in connection with appeals arising out of preparatory hearings in a non-fraud cases under the 1996 Act.

313 Extension of investigations by Criminal Cases Review Commission in England and Wales

(1) Section 23A of the Criminal Appeal Act 1968 (c. 19) (power to order investigations by Criminal Cases Review Commission) is amended as follows.

(2) In subsection (1) after "conviction" there is inserted "or an application for leave to appeal against conviction,".

(3) In paragraph (a) of that subsection—
  (a) at the beginning there is inserted "in the case of an appeal,", and
  (b) for "case", in both places where it occurs, there is substituted "appeal".

(4) After paragraph (a) of that subsection there is inserted—
  "(aa) in the case of an application for leave to appeal, the matter is relevant to the determination of the application and ought, if possible, to be resolved before the application is determined;".

(5) After that subsection there is inserted—
  "(1A) A direction under subsection (1) above may not be given by a single judge, notwithstanding that, in the case of an application for leave to appeal, the application may be determined by a single judge as provided for by section 31 of this Act."

(6) After subsection (4) there is inserted—
  "(5) In this section "respondent" includes a person who will be a respondent if leave to appeal is granted."

314 Extension of investigations by Criminal Cases Review Commission in Northern Ireland

(1) Section 25A of the Criminal Appeal (Northern Ireland) Act 1980 (c. 47) (power to order investigations by Criminal Cases Review Commission) is amended as follows.

(2) In subsection (1) after "conviction" there is inserted "or an application for leave to appeal against conviction,".

(3) In paragraph (a) of that subsection—
  (a) at the beginning there is inserted "in the case of an appeal,", and
  (b) for "case", in both places where it occurs, there is substituted "appeal".

(4) After paragraph (a) of that subsection there is inserted—
  "(aa) in the case of an application for leave to appeal, the matter is relevant to the determination of the application and ought, if possible, to be resolved before the application is determined;".

(5) After that subsection there is inserted—
  "(1A) A direction under subsection (1) above may not be given by a single judge, notwithstanding that, in the case of an application for leave to appeal, the application may be determined by a single judge as provided for by section 45 below."

(6) After subsection (4) there is inserted—
  "(5) In this section "respondent" includes a person who will be a respondent if leave to appeal is granted."

315 Appeals following reference by Criminal Cases Review Commission

(1) Section 14 of the Criminal Appeal Act 1995 (c. 35) (further provision about references by Criminal Cases Review Commission) is amended as follows.

(2) After subsection (4) there is inserted—
  "(4A) Subject to subsection (4B), where a reference under section 9 or 10 is treated as an appeal against any conviction, verdict,

finding or sentence, the appeal may not be on any ground which is not related to any reason given by the Commission for making the reference.

(4B) The Court of Appeal may give leave for an appeal mentioned in subsection (4A) to be on a ground relating to the conviction, verdict, finding or sentence which is not related to any reason given by the Commission for making the reference".

(3) In subsection (5) for "any of sections 9 to" there is substituted "section 11 or".

316 Power to substitute conviction of alternative offence on appeal in England and Wales

(1) The Criminal Appeal Act 1968 (c. 19) is amended as follows.
(2) In section 3 (power to substitute conviction of alternative offence) in subsection (1) after "an offence" there is inserted "to which he did not plead guilty".
(3) After section 3 there is inserted—

"3A Power to substitute conviction of alternative offence after guilty plea

(1) This section applies on an appeal against conviction where—
  (a) an appellant has been convicted of an offence to which he pleaded guilty,
  (b) if he had not so pleaded, he could on the indictment have pleaded, or been found, guilty of some other offence, and
  (c) it appears to the Court of Appeal that the plea of guilty indicates an admission by the appellant of facts which prove him guilty of the other offence.
(2) The Court of Appeal may, instead of allowing or dismissing the appeal, substitute for the appellant's plea of guilty a plea of guilty of the other offence and pass such sentence in substitution for the sentence passed at the trial as may be authorised by law for the other offence, not being a sentence of greater severity."

GENERAL NOTE

The Court of Appeal (Criminal Division) was previously empowered to quash a conviction, or to dismiss the appeal, or in some cases to order a retrial of the appellant. This section gives the Court a further power, namely, to substitute a conviction for an alternative offence. Note that the appeal must relate to a conviction in respect of which the appellant did not plead "guilty". However, in such a case s.316(3) adds s.3A to the Criminal Appeal Act 1968 (c.19) with the effect that the Court may substitute an alternative offence on facts that have been admitted by the appellant at the time he pleaded guilty.

317 Power to substitute conviction of alternative offence on appeal in Northern Ireland

(1) The Criminal Appeal (Northern Ireland) Act 1980 (c. 47) is amended as follows.
(2) In section 3 (power to substitute conviction of alternative offence) in subsection (1) after "an offence" there is inserted "to which he did not plead guilty".
(3) After section 3 there is inserted—

"3A Power to substitute conviction of alternative offence after guilty plea

(1) This section applies where—
  (a) an appellant has been convicted of an offence to which he pleaded guilty,

     (b) if he had not so pleaded, he could on the indictment have pleaded, or been found, guilty of some other offence, and

     (c) it appears to the Court of Appeal that the plea of guilty indicates an admission by the appellant of facts which prove him guilty of that other offence.

  (2) The Court may, instead of allowing or dismissing the appeal, substitute for the appellant's plea of guilty a plea of guilty of that other offence and pass such sentence in substitution for the sentence passed at the trial as may be warranted in law by the plea so substituted."

GENERAL NOTE
See the General Note to s.316.

318   Substitution of conviction on different charge on appeal from court-martial

  (1) The Courts-Martial (Appeals) Act 1968 (c. 20) is amended as follows.

  (2) In section 14 (substitution of conviction on different charge) in subsection (1) after "an offence" there is inserted "to which he did not plead guilty".

  (3) After section 14 there is inserted—

"14A Substitution of conviction on different charge after guilty plea

  (1) This section applies where—

     (a) an appellant has been convicted of an offence to which he pleaded guilty,

     (b) if he had not so pleaded, he could lawfully have pleaded, or been found, guilty of some other offence, and

     (c) it appears to the Appeal Court on an appeal against conviction that the plea of guilty indicates an admission by the appellant of facts which prove him guilty of that other offence.

  (2) The Appeal Court may, instead of allowing or dismissing the appeal, substitute for the appellant's plea of guilty a plea of guilty of the other offence, and may pass on the appellant, in substitution for the sentence passed on him by the court-martial, such sentence as they think proper, being a sentence warranted by the relevant Service Act for that other offence, but not a sentence of greater severity."

GENERAL NOTE
See the General Note to s.316

319   Appeals against sentences in England and Wales

  (1) The Criminal Appeal Act 1968 (c. 19) is amended as follows.

  (2) In section 10 (appeal against sentence in certain cases) for subsection (3) there is substituted—

    "(3) An offender dealt with for an offence before the Crown Court in a proceeding to which subsection (2) of this section applies may appeal to the Court of Appeal against any sentence passed on him for the offence by the Crown Court."

  (3) In section 11 (supplementary provisions as to appeal against sentence) after subsection (6) there is inserted—

    "(7) For the purposes of this section, any two or more sentences are to be treated as passed in the same proceeding if—

(a) they are passed on the same day; or
(b) they are passed on different days but the court in passing any one of them states that it is treating that one together with the other or others as substantially one sentence."

GENERAL NOTE
This section is described by the Explanatory Notes as follow (December 2003):
"676. Section 10(2) of the Criminal Appeal Act 1968 gives certain defendants who have not been tried in the Crown Court, but are sentenced there, a right of appeal to the Court of Appeal against the Crown Court's sentence. By virtue of section 10(3) of the 1968 Act, however, no appeal lies under section 10(2) where the offender is sentenced to less than six months imprisonment, unless he receives certain specified kinds of sentence described in section 10(3)(b), 10(3)(c) or 10(3)(cc) of the 1968 Act (for example, an order banning him from holding or obtaining a driving licence).
677. Section 319 simplifies section 10 of the 1968 Act by amending it to remove the six month limitation and various exceptions to that limitation. The overall effect of *section 319* is that anybody committed to the Crown Court for sentence in future, or dealt with by the Crown Court under the other circumstances set out in section 10(2) of the 1968 Act, will have a right of appeal to the Court of Appeal against the Crown Court's sentence."

Outraging public decency

320   Offence of outraging public decency triable either way

(1) After paragraph 1 of Schedule 1 to the Magistrates' Courts Act 1980 (c. 43) (offences triable either way by virtue of section 17) there is inserted—
"1A An offence at common law of outraging public decency."

(2) This section does not apply in relation to any offence committed before the commencement of this section.

GENERAL NOTE
The offence may now be tried summarily with a maximum penalty currently six months' imprisonment and/or a fine of £5,000 (see s.32(1) Magistrates' Courts Act 1980).

Jury service

321   Jury service

Schedule 33 (jury service) shall have effect.

GENERAL NOTE
See the content of Sch.33.

Individual support orders

322   Individual support orders

After section 1A of the Crime and Disorder Act 1998 (c. 37) there is inserted—

"1AA Individual support orders

(1) Where a court makes an anti-social behaviour order in respect of a defendant who is a child or young person when that order is made, it must consider whether the individual support conditions are fulfilled.
(2) If it is satisfied that those conditions are fulfilled, the court must make an order under this section ("an individual support order") which—
(a) requires the defendant to comply, for a period not exceeding six months, with such requirements as are specified in the order; and

    (b) requires the defendant to comply with any directions given by the responsible officer with a view to the implementation of the requirements under paragraph (a) above.

(3) The individual support conditions are—

    (a) that an individual support order would be desirable in the interests of preventing any repetition of the kind of behaviour which led to the making of the anti-social behaviour order;

    (b) that the defendant is not already subject to an individual support order; and

    (c) that the court has been notified by the Secretary of State that arrangements for implementing individual support orders are available in the area in which it appears to it that the defendant resides or will reside and the notice has not been withdrawn.

(4) If the court is not satisfied that the individual support conditions are fulfilled, it shall state in open court that it is not so satisfied and why it is not.

(5) The requirements that may be specified under subsection (2)(a) above are those that the court considers desirable in the interests of preventing any repetition of the kind of behaviour which led to the making of the anti-social behaviour order.

(6) Requirements included in an individual support order, or directions given under such an order by a responsible officer, may require the defendant to do all or any of the following things—

    (a) to participate in activities specified in the requirements or directions at a time or times so specified;

    (b) to present himself to a person or persons so specified at a place or places and at a time or times so specified;

    (c) to comply with any arrangements for his education so specified.

(7) But requirements included in, or directions given under, such an order may not require the defendant to attend (whether at the same place or at different places) on more than two days in any week; and "week" here means a period of seven days beginning with a Sunday.

(8) Requirements included in, and directions given under, an individual support order shall, as far as practicable, be such as to avoid—

    (a) any conflict with the defendant's religious beliefs; and

    (b) any interference with the times, if any, at which he normally works or attends school or any other educational establishment.

(9) Before making an individual support order, the court shall obtain from a social worker of a local authority social services department or a member of a youth offending team any information which it considers necessary in order—

    (a) to determine whether the individual support conditions are fulfilled, or

    (b) to determine what requirements should be imposed by an individual support order if made, and shall consider that information.

(10) In this section and section 1AB below "responsible officer", in relation to an individual support order, means one of the following who is specified in the order, namely—

(a) a social worker of a local authority social services department;

(b) a person nominated by a person appointed as chief education officer under section 532 of the Education Act 1996 (c. 56);

(c) a member of a youth offending team.

1AB Individual support orders: explanation, breach, amendment etc

(1) Before making an individual support order, the court shall explain to the defendant in ordinary language—

(a) the effect of the order and of the requirements proposed to be included in it;

(b) the consequences which may follow (under subsection (3) below) if he fails to comply with any of those requirements; and

(c) that the court has power (under subsection (6) below) to review the order on the application either of the defendant or of the responsible officer.

(2) The power of the Secretary of State under section 174(4) of the Criminal Justice Act 2003 includes power by order to—

(a) prescribe cases in which subsection (1) above does not apply; and

(b) prescribe cases in which the explanation referred to in that subsection may be made in the absence of the defendant, or may be provided in written form.

(3) If the person in respect of whom an individual support order is made fails without reasonable excuse to comply with any requirement included in the order, he is guilty of an offence and liable on summary conviction to a fine not exceeding—

(a) if he is aged 14 or over at the date of his conviction, £1,000;

(b) if he is aged under 14 then, £250.

(4) No referral order under section 16(2) or (3) of the Powers of Criminal Courts (Sentencing) Act 2000 (referral of young offenders to youth offender panels) may be made in respect of an offence under subsection (3) above.

(5) If the anti-social behaviour order as a result of which an individual support order was made ceases to have effect, the individual support order (if it has not previously ceased to have effect) ceases to have effect when the anti-social behaviour order does.

(6) On an application made by complaint by—

(a) the person subject to an individual support order, or

(b) the responsible officer,

the court which made the individual support order may vary or discharge it by a further order.

(7) If the anti-social behaviour order as a result of which an individual support order was made is varied, the court varying the anti-social behaviour order may by a further order vary or discharge the individual support order."

This makes important amendments to the Crime and Disorder Act 1998.

323 Individual support orders: consequential amendments

(1) The Crime and Disorder Act 1998 (c. 37) is amended as mentioned in subsections (2) to (5).

(2) In section 4 of that Act (appeals against orders)—
  (a) in subsection (1) after "an anti-social behaviour order" there is inserted ", an individual support order", and
  (b) in subsection (3) after "1(8)" there is inserted ", 1AB(6)".

(3) In section 18(1) of that Act (interpretation of Chapter 1)—
  (a) after the definition of "curfew notice" there is inserted—
      ""individual support order" has the meaning given by section 1AA(2) above;", and
  (b) in the definition of "responsible officer", before paragraph (a) there is inserted—
      "(za)in relation to an individual support order, has the meaning given by section 1AA(10) above;".

(4) In section 18(4) of that Act (cases where social worker or member of a youth offending team to give supervision or directions)—
  (a) after "directions under" there is inserted "an individual support order or", and
  (b) for "the child or, as the case may be, the parent" there is substituted "the child, defendant or parent, as the case may be,".

(5) In section 38 of that Act (local provision of youth justice services), in subsection (4)(f) after "in relation to" there is inserted "individual support orders,".

(6) In section 143(2) (provisions in which sums may be altered) of the Magistrates' Courts Act 1980 (c. 43), after paragraph (d) there is inserted—
  "(da) section 1AB(3) of the Crime and Disorder Act 1998 (failure to comply with individual support order);".

Parenting orders and referral orders

324 Parenting orders and referral orders

Schedule 34 (parenting orders and referral orders) shall have effect.

Assessing etc. risks posed by sexual or violent offenders

325 Arrangements for assessing etc risks posed by certain offenders

(1) In this section—
      "relevant sexual or violent offender" has the meaning given by section 327;
      "responsible authority", in relation to any area, means the chief officer of police, the local probation board for that area and the Minister of the Crown exercising functions in relation to prisons, acting jointly.

(2) The responsible authority for each area must establish arrangements for the purpose of assessing and managing the risks posed in that area by—
  (a) relevant sexual and violent offenders, and
  (b) other persons who, by reason of offences committed by them (wherever committed), are considered by the responsible authority to be persons who may cause serious harm to the public.

(3) In establishing those arrangements, the responsible authority must act in co-operation with the persons specified in subsection (6); and it

is the duty of those persons to co-operate in the establishment by the responsible authority of those arrangements, to the extent that such co-operation is compatible with the exercise by those persons of their functions under any other enactment.

(4) Co-operation under subsection (3) may include the exchange of information.

(5) The responsible authority for each area ("the relevant area") and the persons specified in subsection (6) must together draw up a memorandum setting out the ways in which they are to co-operate.

(6) The persons referred to in subsections (3) and (5) are—

  (a) every youth offending team established for an area any part of which falls within the relevant area,

  (b) the Ministers of the Crown exercising functions in relation to social security, child support, war pensions, employment and training,

  (c) every local education authority any part of whose area falls within the relevant area,

  (d) every local housing authority or social services authority any part of whose area falls within the relevant area,

  (e) every registered social landlord which provides or manages residential accommodation in the relevant area in which persons falling within subsection (2)(a) or (b) reside or may reside,

  (f) every Health Authority or Strategic Health Authority any part of whose area falls within the relevant area,

  (g) every Primary Care Trust or Local Health Board any part of whose area falls within the relevant area,

  (h) every NHS trust any part of whose area falls within the relevant area, and

    (i) every person who is designated by the Secretary of State by order for the purposes of this paragraph as a provider of electronic monitoring services.

(7) The Secretary of State may by order amend subsection (6) by adding or removing any person or description of person.

(8) The Secretary of State may issue guidance to responsible authorities on the discharge of the functions conferred by this section and section 326.

(9) In this section—

  "local education authority" has the same meaning as in the Education Act 1996 (c. 56);

  "local housing authority" has the same meaning as in the Housing Act 1985 (c. 68);

  "Minister of the Crown" has the same meaning as in the Ministers of the Crown Act 1975 (c. 26);

  "NHS trust" has the same meaning as in the National Health Service Act 1977 (c. 49);

  "prison" has the same meaning as in the Prison Act 1952 (c. 52);

  "registered social landlord" has the same meaning as in Part 1 of the Housing Act 1996 (c. 52);

  "social services authority" means a local authority for the purposes of the Local Authority Social Services Act 1970 (c. 42).

326　Review of arrangements

(1) The responsible authority for each area must keep the arrangements established by it under section 325 under review with a view to

monitoring their effectiveness and making any changes to them that appear necessary or expedient.

(2) The responsible authority for any area must exercise their functions under subsection (1) in consultation with persons appointed by the Secretary of State as lay advisers in relation to that authority.

(3) The Secretary of State must appoint two lay advisers under subsection (2) in relation to each responsible authority.

(4) The responsible authority must pay to or in respect of the persons so appointed such allowances as the Secretary of State may determine.

(5) As soon as practicable after the end of each period of 12 months beginning with 1st April, the responsible authority for each area must—
   (a) prepare a report on the discharge by it during that period of the functions conferred by section 325 and this section, and
   (b) publish the report in that area.

(6) The report must include—
   (a) details of the arrangements established by the responsible authority, and
   (b) information of such descriptions as the Secretary of State has notified to the responsible authority that he wishes to be included in the report.

327   Section 325: interpretation

(1) For the purposes of section 325, a person is a relevant sexual or violent offender if he falls within one or more of subsections (2) to (5).

(2) A person falls within this subsection if he is subject to the notification requirements of Part 2 of the Sexual Offences Act 2003 (c. 42).

(3) A person falls within this subsection if—
   (a) he is convicted by a court in England or Wales of murder or an offence specified in Schedule 15, and
   (b) one of the following sentences is imposed on him in respect of the conviction—
      (i) a sentence of imprisonment for a term of 12 months or more,
      (ii) a sentence of detention in a young offender institution for a term of 12 months or more,
      (iii) a sentence of detention during Her Majesty's pleasure,
      (iv) a sentence of detention for public protection under section 226,
      (v) a sentence of detention for a period of 12 months or more under section 91 of the Sentencing Act (offenders under 18 convicted of certain serious offences),
      (vi) a sentence of detention under section 228,
      (vii) a detention and training order for a term of 12 months or more, or
      (viii) a hospital or guardianship order within the meaning of the Mental Health Act 1983 (c. 20).

(4) A person falls within this subsection if—
   (a) he is found not guilty by a court in England and Wales of murder or an offence specified in Schedule 15 by reason of insanity or to be under a disability and to have done the act charged against him in respect of such an offence, and
   (b) one of the following orders is made in respect of the act charged against him as the offence—
      (i) an order that he be admitted to hospital, or
      (ii) a guardianship order within the meaning of the Mental Health Act 1983.

(5) A person falls within this subsection if—

  (a) the first condition set out in section 28(2) or 29(2) of the Criminal Justice and Court Services Act 2000 (c. 43) or the second condition set out in section 28(3) or 29(3) of that Act is satisfied in his case, or

  (b) an order under section 29A of that Act has been made in respect of him.

(6) In this section "court" does not include a service court, as defined by section 305(1).

Criminal record certificates

328 Criminal record certificates: amendments of Part 5 of Police Act 1997

Schedule 35 (which contains amendments of Part 5 of the Police Act 1997 (c. 50)) shall have effect.

Civil proceedings brought by offenders

329 Civil proceedings for trespass to the person brought by offender

(1) This section applies where—

  (a) a person ("the claimant") claims that another person ("the defendant") did an act amounting to trespass to the claimant's person, and

  (b) the claimant has been convicted in the United Kingdom of an imprisonable offence committed on the same occasion as that on which the act is alleged to have been done.

(2) Civil proceedings relating to the claim may be brought only with the permission of the court.

(3) The court may give permission for the proceedings to be brought only if there is evidence that either—

  (a) the condition in subsection (5) is not met, or

  (b) in all the circumstances, the defendant's act was grossly disproportionate.

(4) If the court gives permission and the proceedings are brought, it is a defence for the defendant to prove both—

  (a) that the condition in subsection (5) is met, and

  (b) that, in all the circumstances, his act was not grossly disproportionate.

(5) The condition referred to in subsection (3)(a) and (4)(a) is that the defendant did the act only because—

  (a) he believed that the claimant—

    (i) was about to commit an offence,

    (ii) was in the course of committing an offence, or

    (iii) had committed an offence immediately beforehand; and

  (b) he believed that the act was necessary to—

    (i) defend himself or another person,

    (ii) protect or recover property,

    (iii) prevent the commission or continuation of an offence, or

    (iv) apprehend, or secure the conviction, of the claimant after he had committed an offence;

  or was necessary to assist in achieving any of those things.

(6) Subsection (4) is without prejudice to any other defence.

(7) Where—

  (a) in service disciplinary proceedings, as defined by section 305(1), a person has been found guilty of an offence under section 70 of the Army Act 1955 (3 & 4 Eliz. 2 c. 18), section 70 of the Air Force Act 1955 (3 & 4 Eliz. 2 c. 19) or section 42 of the Naval Discipline Act 1957 (c. 53), and

(b) the corresponding civil offence (within the meaning of that Act) was an imprisonable offence,

he is to be treated for the purposes of this section as having been convicted in the United Kingdom of the corresponding civil offence.

(8) In this section—
   (a) the reference to trespass to the person is a reference to—
      (i) assault,
      (ii) battery, or
      (iii) false imprisonment;
   (b) references to a defendant's belief are to his honest belief, whether or not the belief was also reasonable;
   (c) "court" means the High Court or a county court; and
   (d) "imprisonable offence" means an offence which, in the case of a person aged 18 or over, is punishable by imprisonment.

PART 14

GENERAL

330 Orders and rules

(1) This section applies to—
   (a) any power conferred by this Act on the Secretary of State to make an order or rules;
   (b) the power conferred by section 168 on the Lord Chancellor to make an order.

(2) The power is exercisable by statutory instrument.

(3) The power—
   (a) may be exercised so as to make different provision for different purposes or different areas, and
   (b) may be exercised either for all the purposes to which the power extends, or for those purposes subject to specified exceptions, or only for specified purposes.

(4) The power includes power to make—
   (a) any supplementary, incidental or consequential provision, and
   (b) any transitory, transitional or saving provision,
      which the Minister making the instrument considers necessary or expedient.

(5) A statutory instrument containing—
   (a) an order under any of the following provisions—
      section 25(5),
      section 103,
      section 161(7),
      section 178,
      section 197(3),
      section 223,
      section 246(5),
      section 260,
      section 267,
      section 269(6),
      section 281(2),
      section 283(1),
      section 291,
      section 301(5),
      section 325(7), and
      paragraph 5 of Schedule 31,
   (b) an order under section 336(3) bringing section 43 into force,
   (c) an order making any provision by virtue of section 333(2)(b) which adds to, replaces or omits any part of the text of an Act, or

(d) rules under section 240(4)(a),

may only be made if a draft of the statutory instrument has been laid before, and approved by a resolution of, each House of Parliament.

(6) Any other statutory instrument made in the exercise of a power to which this section applies is subject to annulment in pursuance of a resolution of either House of Parliament.

(7) Subsection (6) does not apply to a statutory instrument containing only an order made under one or more of the following provisions—

section 202(3)(b),
section 215(3),
section 253(5),
section 325(6)(i), and
section 336.

GENERAL NOTE

Where a Minister is empowered by any provision of the 2003 Act to make Orders or Rules, he may do so by way of Statutory Instrument (subs.(2)). The power extends to making transitional and consequential provisions and savings in connection with a provision brought into force under this Act (subs.(4)).

331 Further minor and consequential amendments

Schedule 36 (further minor and consequential amendments) shall have effect.

GENERAL NOTE

This introduces Sch.36. Note the provisions relating to Evidence under Pt 5 of that Schedule, and see Pt 11 of the 2003 Act.

332 Repeals

Schedule 37 (repeals) shall have effect.

GENERAL NOTE

This introduces Sch.37. Note the provisions relating to Evidence under Pt 5 of that Schedule, and see Pt 11 of the 2003 Act.

333 Supplementary and consequential provision, etc.

(1) The Secretary of State may by order make—

(a) any supplementary, incidental or consequential provision, and

(b) any transitory, transitional or saving provision,

which he considers necessary or expedient for the purposes of, in consequence of, or for giving full effect to any provision of this Act.

(2) An order under subsection (1) may, in particular—

(a) provide for any provision of this Act which comes into force before another such provision has come into force to have effect, until that other provision has come into force, with such modifications as are specified in the order, and

(b) amend or repeal—

(i) any Act passed before, or in the same Session as, this Act, and

(ii) subordinate legislation made before the passing of this Act.

(3) Nothing in this section limits the power by virtue of section 330(4)(b) to include transitional or saving provision in an order under section 336.

(4) The amendments that may be made under subsection (2)(b) are in addition to those made by or under any other provision of this Act.

(5) In this section "subordinate legislation" has the same meaning as in the Interpretation Act 1978 (c. 30).

(6) Schedule 38 (which contains transitory and transitional provisions and savings) shall have effect.

GENERAL NOTE
Supplementary, incidental, transitional, or consequential provisions, or savings, may be made by the Secretary of State either by way of the negative resolution procedure (subs.(6)), or by affirmative resolution procedure if primary legislation is being amended (subs.(5)). This power — unlike s.330(4) — is not exercisable only if the Secretary of State has a commencement power under s.336. The Government has described it as being "…. necessary, particularly in respect of the sentencing provisions, to pick up any consequential amendments not identified before the Act's introduction or during its passage; and also to deal with long-term transitional arrangements created by the introduction of a new system which will gradually replace the existing arrangements" (Explanatory Notes para.737).

334 Provision for Northern Ireland

(1) An Order in Council under section 85 of the Northern Ireland Act 1998 (c. 47) (provision dealing with certain reserved matters) which contains a statement that it is made only for purposes corresponding to those of any provisions of this Act specified in subsection (2)—
  (a) shall not be subject to subsections (3) to (9) of that section (affirmative resolution of both Houses of Parliament), but
  (b) shall be subject to annulment in pursuance of a resolution of either House of Parliament.

(2) The provisions are—
  (a) in Part 1, sections 1, 3(3), 4, 7 to 10 and 12 and paragraphs 1, 2, 5 to 10 and 20 of Schedule 1, and
  (b) Parts 8, 9 and 11.

(3) In relation to any time when section 1 of the Northern Ireland Act 2000 (c. 1) is in force (suspension of devolved government in Northern Ireland)—
  (a) the reference in subsection (1) above to section 85 of the Northern Ireland Act 1998 shall be read as a reference to paragraph 1 of the Schedule to the Northern Ireland Act 2000 (legislation by Order in Council during suspension), and
  (b) the reference in subsection (1)(a) above to subsections (3) to (9) of that section shall be read as a reference to paragraph 2 of that Schedule.

(4) The reference in section 41(2) of the Justice (Northern Ireland) Act 2002 (c. 26) (transfer of certain functions to Director of Public Prosecutions for Northern Ireland) to any function of the Attorney General for Northern Ireland of consenting to the institution of criminal proceedings includes any such function which is conferred by an amendment made by this Act.

(5) Any reference to any provision of the Criminal Appeal (Northern Ireland) Act 1980 (c. 47) in the Access to Justice (Northern Ireland) Order 2003 (S.I. 2003/435 (N.I. 10)) is to be read as a reference to that provision as amended by this Act.

335 Expenses

There shall be paid out of money provided by Parliament—
  (a) any expenditure incurred by a Minister of the Crown by virtue of this Act, and
  (b) any increase attributable to this Act in the sums payable out of money so provided under any other enactment.

336 Commencement

(1) The following provisions of this Act come into force on the passing of this Act—

section 168(1) and (2),
section 183(8),
section 307(1) to (3), (5) and (6),
section 330,
section 333(1) to (5),
sections 334 and 335,
this section and sections 337, 338 and 339, and
the repeal in Part 9 of Schedule 37 of section 81(2) and (3) of the Countryside and Rights of Way Act 2000 (c. 37) (and section 332 so far as relating to that repeal), and
paragraphs 1 and 6 of Schedule 38 (and section 333(6) so far as relating to those paragraphs).

(2) The following provisions of this Act come into force at the end of the period of four weeks beginning with the day on which this Act is passed—
Chapter 7 of Part 12 (and Schedules 21 and 22);
section 303(b)(i) and (ii);
paragraphs 42, 43(3), 66, 83(1) to (3), 84 and 109(2), (3)(b), (4) and (5) of Schedule 32 (and section 304 so far as relating to those provisions);
Part 8 of Schedule 37 (and section 332 so far as relating to that Part of that Schedule).

(3) The remaining provisions of this Act come into force in accordance with provision made by the Secretary of State by order.

(4) Different provision may be made for different purposes and different areas.

337 Extent

(1) Subject to the following provisions of this section and to section 338, this Act extends to England and Wales only.

(2) The following provisions extend also to Scotland and Northern Ireland—
sections 71 and 72;
sections 82 and 83;
section 180 and Schedule 9;
section 188 and Schedule 11;
section 194 and Schedule 13;
section 293;
section 306
section 307;
section 311;
this Part, except sections 331, 332 and 334(5);
paragraphs 19, 70 and 71 of Schedule 3;
paragraph 12(3) of Schedule 12;
paragraphs 3, 6, 7 and 8 of Schedule 27;
paragraphs 6 to 8 of Schedule 31.

(3) The following provisions extend also to Scotland—
section 50(14);
section 286;
sections 287, 288, and 291;
section 302;
paragraph 2 of Schedule 23;
paragraphs 1, 2 and 5 of Schedule 27;
paragraph 7 of Schedule 38.

(4) Section 290 extends to Scotland only.

(5) The following provisions extend also to Northern Ireland—
Part 5;

Part 7;
sections 75 to 81;
sections 84 to 93;
sections 95 to 97;
section 315;
Schedule 5.

(6) The following provisions extend to Northern Ireland only—
section 292 and Schedule 29;
sections 296 and 297;
section 314;
section 317;
section 334(5).

(7) The amendment or repeal of any enactment by any provision of—
  (a) Part 1,
  (b) section 285,
  (c) Part 2 of Schedule 3 (except as mentioned in subsection (8)),
  (d) Schedule 27,
  (e) Schedule 28,
  (f) Part 1 of Schedule 32,
  (g) Parts 1 to 4 and 6 of Schedule 36, and
  (h) Parts 1 to 4, 6 to 8, 10 and 12 of Schedule 37 (except as mentioned in subsection (9)),
extends to the part or parts of the United Kingdom to which the enactment extends.

(8) Paragraphs 29, 30, 31, 39, 41, 50, 53 and 63 of Schedule 3 do not extend to Northern Ireland.

(9) The repeals in Part 4 of Schedule 37 relating to—
  (a) the Bankers' Books Evidence Act 1879 (c. 11),
  (b) the Explosive Substances Act 1883 (c. 3),
  (c) the Backing of Warrants (Republic of Ireland) Act 1965 (c. 45),
  (d) the Customs and Excise Management Act 1979 (c. 2), and
  (e) the Contempt of Court Act 1981 (c. 49),
do not extend to Northern Ireland.

(10) The provisions mentioned in subsection (11), so far as relating to proceedings before a particular service court, have the same extent as the Act under which the court is constituted.

(11) Those provisions are—
section 113 and Schedule 6;
section 135 and Schedule 7.

(12) Nothing in subsection (1) affects —
  (a) the extent of Chapter 7 of Part 12 so far as relating to sentences passed by a court-martial, or
  (b) the extent of section 299 and Schedule 30 so far as relating to the making of orders by, or orders made by, courts-martial or the Courts-Martial Appeal Court.

(13) Any provision of this Act which—
  (a) relates to any enactment contained in—
    (i) the Army Act 1955 (3 & 4 Eliz. 2 c. 18),
    (ii) the Air Force Act 1955 (3 & 4 Eliz. 2 c. 19),
    (iii) the Naval Discipline Act 1957 (c. 53),
    (iv) the Courts-Martial (Appeals) Act 1968 (c. 20),
    (v) the Armed Forces Act 1976 (c. 52),
    (vi) section 113 of the Police and Criminal Evidence Act 1984 (c. 60),
    (vii) the Reserve Forces Act 1996 (c. 14), or
    (viii) the Armed Forces Act 2001 (c. 19), and
  (b) is not itself contained in Schedule 25 or Part 9 of Schedule 37,
has the same extent as the enactment to which it relates.

338   Channel Islands and Isle of Man

(1) Subject to subsections (2) and (3), Her Majesty may by Order in Council extend any provision of this Act, with such modifications as appear to Her Majesty in Council to be appropriate, to any of the Channel Islands or the Isle of Man.

(2) Subsection (1) does not authorise the extension to any place of a provision of this Act so far as the provision amends an enactment that does not itself extend there and is not itself capable of being extended there in the exercise of a power conferred on Her Majesty in Council.

(3) Subsection (1) does not apply in relation to any provision that extends to the Channel Islands or the Isle of Man by virtue of any of subsections (10) to (13) of section 337.

(4) Subsection (4) of section 330 applies to the power to make an Order in Council under subsection (1) as it applies to any power of the Secretary of State to make an order under this Act, but as if references in that subsection to the Minister making the instrument were references to Her Majesty in Council.

339   Short title

This Act may be cited as the Criminal Justice Act 2003.

SCHEDULES

SCHEDULE 1   **Section 12**

AMENDMENTS RELATED TO PART 1

The 1984 Act

1   The 1984 Act is amended as follows.

2   In section 18 (entry and search after arrest), for subsection (5) there is substituted—
"(5) A constable may conduct a search under subsection (1)—
    (a) before the person is taken to a police station or released on bail under section 30A, and
    (b) without obtaining an authorisation under subsection (4),
if the condition in subsection (5A) is satisfied.
(5A) The condition is that the presence of the person at a place (other than a police station) is necessary for the effective investigation of the offence."

3   In section 21 (access and copying), at the end there is inserted—
"(9) The references to a constable in subsections (1), (2), (3)(a) and (5) include a person authorised under section 16(2) to accompany a constable executing a warrant."

4   In section 22 (retention), at the end there is inserted—
"(7) The reference in subsection (1) to anything seized by a constable includes anything seized by a person authorised under section 16(2) to accompany a constable executing a warrant."

5   In section 34 (limitation on police detention), for subsection (7) there is substituted—
"(7) For the purposes of this Part a person who—
    (a) attends a police station to answer to bail granted under section 30A,
    (b) returns to a police station to answer to bail granted under this Part, or
    (c) is arrested under section 30D or 46A,
is to be treated as arrested for an offence and that offence is the offence in connection with which he was granted bail."

6   In section 35(1) (designated police stations), for "section 30(3) and (5) above" there is substituted "sections 30(3) and (5), 30A(5) and 30D(2)".

7   In section 36 (custody officers at police stations), after subsection (7) there is inserted—
"(7A) Subject to subsection (7B), subsection (7) applies where a person attends a police station which is not a designated station to answer to bail granted under section 30A as it applies where a person is taken to such a station.
(7B) Where subsection (7) applies because of subsection (7A), the reference in subsection (7)(b) to the officer who took him to the station is to be read as a reference to the officer who granted him bail."

8   In section 41(2) (calculation of periods of time), after paragraph (c) there is inserted—
"(ca) in the case of a person who attends a police station to answer to bail granted under section 30A, the time when he arrives at the police station;".

9   In section 45A(2)(a) (functions which may be performed by video-conferencing), after "taken to" there is inserted ", or answering to bail at,".

10   In section 47 (bail after arrest)—
    (a) in subsection (6), after "granted bail" there is inserted "under this Part", and
    (b) in subsection (7), after "released on bail" there is inserted "under this Part".

Criminal Justice Act 1987 (c. 38)

11   In section 2 of the Criminal Justice Act 1987 (director's investigation powers), after subsection (6) there is inserted—
    "(6A) Where an appropriate person accompanies a constable, he may exercise the powers conferred by subsection (5) but only in the company, and under the supervision, of the constable."

12   In subsection (7) of that section (meaning of appropriate person), for "subsection (6) above" there is substituted "this section".

13   In subsection (8D) of that section (references to evidence obtained by Director), after "by a constable" there is inserted "or by an appropriate person".

Criminal Justice and Police Act 2001 (c. 16)

14   In section 56 of the Criminal Justice and Police Act 2001 (property seized by constables etc.), after subsection (4) there is inserted—
    "(4A) Subsection (1)(a) includes property seized on any premises—
        (a) by a person authorised under section 16(2) of the 1984 Act to accompany a constable executing a warrant, or
        (b) by a person accompanying a constable under section 2(6) of the Criminal Justice Act 1987 in the execution of a warrant under section 2(4) of that Act."

Armed Forces Act 2001 (c. 19)

15   In section 2(9) of the Armed Forces Act 2001 (offences for purpose of definition of prohibited article), at the end of paragraph (d) there is inserted "; and
    (e) offences under section 1 of the Criminal Damage Act 1971 (destroying or damaging property)."

Police Reform Act 2002 (c. 30)

16   Schedule 4 to the Police Reform Act 2002 (powers exercisable by police civilians) is amended as follows.

17   In paragraph 17 (access to excluded and special procedure material) after paragraph (b) there is inserted—
    "(bb) section 15 of that Act (safeguards) shall have effect in relation to the issue of any warrant under paragraph 12 of that Schedule to that person as it has effect in relation to the issue of a warrant under that paragraph to a constable;
    (bc) section 16 of that Act (execution of warrants) shall have effect in relation to any warrant to enter and search premises that is issued under paragraph 12 of that Schedule (whether to that person or to any other person) in respect of premises in the relevant police area as if references in that section to a constable included references to that person;".

18   In paragraph 20 (access and copying in case of things seized by constables) after "by a constable" there is inserted "or by a person authorised to accompany him under section 16(2) of that Act".

19   After paragraph 24 (extended powers of seizure) there is inserted—

"Persons accompanying investigating officers

    24A (1) This paragraph applies where a person ("an authorised person") is authorised by virtue of section 16(2) of the 1984 Act to accompany an investigating officer designated for the purposes of paragraph 16 (or 17) in the execution of a warrant.
        (2) The reference in paragraph 16(h) (or 17(e)) to the seizure of anything by a designated person in exercise of a particular power includes a reference to the seizure of anything by the authorised person in exercise of that power by virtue of section 16(2A) of the 1984 Act.

(3) In relation to any such seizure, paragraph 16(h) (or 17(e)) is to be read as if it provided for the references to a constable and to an officer in section 21(1) and (2) of the 1984 Act to include references to the authorised person.

(4) The reference in paragraph 16(i) (or 17(f)) to anything seized by a designated person in exercise of a particular power includes a reference to anything seized by the authorised person in exercise of that power by virtue of section 16(2A) of the 1984 Act.

(5) In relation to anything so seized, paragraph 16(i)(ii) (or 17(f)(ii)) is to be read as if it provided for—

(a) the references to the supervision of a constable in subsections (3) and (4) of section 21 of the 1984 Act to include references to the supervision of a person designated for the purposes of paragraph 16 (or paragraph 17), and

(b) the reference to a constable in subsection (5) of that section to include a reference to such a person or an authorised person accompanying him.

(6) Where an authorised person accompanies an investigating officer who is also designated for the purposes of paragraph 24, the references in sub-paragraphs (a) and (b) of that paragraph to the designated person include references to the authorised person."

20   In paragraph 34 (powers of escort officer to take arrested person to prison), in sub-paragraph (1)(a), for "subsection (1) of section 30" there is substituted "subsection (1A) of section 30".

SCHEDULE 2 **Section 28**

CHARGING OR RELEASE OF PERSONS IN POLICE DETENTION

1   The Police and Criminal Evidence Act 1984 (c. 60) is amended as follows.

2   (1) Section 37 (duties of custody officers before charge) is amended as follows.

(2) In subsection (7) for paragraphs (a) and (b) there is substituted—

"(a) shall be released without charge and on bail for the purpose of enabling the Director of Public Prosecutions to make a decision under section 37B below,

(b) shall be released without charge and on bail but not for that purpose,

(c) shall be released without charge and without bail, or

(d) shall be charged."

(3) After that subsection there is inserted—

"(7A) The decision as to how a person is to be dealt with under subsection (7) above shall be that of the custody officer.

(7B) Where a person is released under subsection (7)(a) above, it shall be the duty of the custody officer to inform him that he is being released to enable the Director of Public Prosecutions to make a decision under section 37B below."

(4) In subsection (8)(a) after "(7)(b)" there is inserted "or (c)".

3   After that section there is inserted—

"37A Guidance

(1) The Director of Public Prosecutions may issue guidance—

(a) for the purpose of enabling custody officers to decide how persons should be dealt with under section 37(7) above or 37C(2) below, and

(b) as to the information to be sent to the Director of Public Prosecutions under section 37B(1) below.

(2) The Director of Public Prosecutions may from time to time revise guidance issued under this section.

(3) Custody officers are to have regard to guidance under this section in deciding how persons should be dealt with under section 37(7) above or 37C(2) below.

(4) A report under section 9 of the Prosecution of Offences Act 1985 (report by DPP to Attorney General) must set out the provisions of any guidance issued, and any revisions to guidance made, in the year to which the report relates.

(5) The Director of Public Prosecutions must publish in such manner as he thinks fit—

(a) any guidance issued under this section, and

(b) any revisions made to such guidance.

(6) Guidance under this section may make different provision for different cases, circumstances or areas.

37B Consultation with the Director of Public Prosecutions

(1) Where a person is released on bail under section 37(7)(a) above, an officer involved in the investigation of the offence shall, as soon as is practicable, send to the Director of Public Prosecutions such information as may be specified in guidance under section 37A above.

(2) The Director of Public Prosecutions shall decide whether there is sufficient evidence to charge the person with an offence.

(3) If he decides that there is sufficient evidence to charge the person with an offence, he shall decide—

    (a) whether or not the person should be charged and, if so, the offence with which he should be charged, and

    (b) whether or not the person should be given a caution and, if so, the offence in respect of which he should be given a caution.

(4) The Director of Public Prosecutions shall give written notice of his decision to an officer involved in the investigation of the offence.

(5) If his decision is—

    (a) that there is not sufficient evidence to charge the person with an offence, or

    (b) that there is sufficient evidence to charge the person with an offence but that the person should not be charged with an offence or given a caution in respect of an offence,

a custody officer shall give the person notice in writing that he is not to be prosecuted.

(6) If the decision of the Director of Public Prosecutions is that the person should be charged with an offence, or given a caution in respect of an offence, the person shall be charged or cautioned accordingly.

(7) But if his decision is that the person should be given a caution in respect of the offence and it proves not to be possible to give the person such a caution, he shall instead be charged with the offence.

(8) For the purposes of this section, a person is to be charged with an offence either—

    (a) when he is in police detention after returning to a police station to answer bail or is otherwise in police detention at a police station, or

    (b) in accordance with section 29 of the Criminal Justice Act 2003.

(9) In this section "caution" includes—

    (a) a conditional caution within the meaning of Part 3 of the Criminal Justice Act 2003, and

    (b) a warning or reprimand under section 65 of the Crime and Disorder Act 1998.

37C Breach of bail following release under section 37(7)(a)

(1) This section applies where—

    (a) a person released on bail under section 37(7)(a) above or subsection (2)(b) below is arrested under section 46A below in respect of that bail, and

    (b) at the time of his detention following that arrest at the police station mentioned in section 46A(2) below, notice under section 37B(4) above has not been given.

(2) The person arrested—

    (a) shall be charged, or

    (b) shall be released without charge, either on bail or without bail.

(3) The decision as to how a person is to be dealt with under subsection (2) above shall be that of a custody officer.

(4) A person released on bail under subsection (2)(b) above shall be released on bail subject to the same conditions (if any) which applied immediately before his arrest.

37D Release under section 37(7)(a): further provision

(1) Where a person is released on bail under section 37(7)(a) or section 37C(2)(b) above, a custody officer may subsequently appoint a different time, or an additional time, at which the person is to attend at the police station to answer bail.

(2) The custody officer shall give the person notice in writing of the exercise of the power under subsection (1).

(3) The exercise of the power under subsection (1) shall not affect the conditions (if any) to which bail is subject.

(4) Where a person released on bail under section 37(7)(a) or 37C(2)(b) above returns to a police station to answer bail or is otherwise in police detention at a police station, he may be kept in police detention to enable him to be dealt with in accordance with section 37B or 37C above or to enable the power under subsection (1) above to be exercised.

     (5) If the person is not in a fit state to enable him to be so dealt with or to enable that power to be exercised, he may be kept in police detention until he is.

     (6) Where a person is kept in police detention by virtue of subsection (4) or (5) above, section 37(1) to (3) and (7) above (and section 40(8) below so far as it relates to section 37(1) to (3)) shall not apply to the offence in connection with which he was released on bail under section 37(7)(a) or 37C(2)(b) above."

4   In section 40 (review of police detention) in subsection (9) after "37(9)" there is inserted "or 37D(5)".

5   In section 46A (power of arrest for failure to answer police bail) after subsection (1) insert—

     "(1A) A person who has been released on bail under section 37(7)(a) or 37C(2)(b) above may be arrested without warrant by a constable if the constable has reasonable grounds for suspecting that the person has broken any of the conditions of bail."

6   (1) Section 47 (bail after arrest) is amended as follows.

     (2) In subsection (1) (release on bail under Part 4 shall be release on bail granted in accordance with certain provisions of the Bail Act 1976) for "Subject to subsection (2) below" there is substituted "Subject to the following provisions of this section".

     (3) In subsection (1A) (bail conditions may be imposed when a person is released under section 38(1)) after "section", in the first place where it occurs, there is inserted "37(7)(a) above or section".

     (4) After that subsection there is inserted—

     "(1B) No application may be made under section 5B of the Bail Act 1976 if a person is released on bail under section 37(7)(a) or 37C(2)(b) above.

     (1C) Subsections (1D) to (1F) below apply where a person released on bail under section 37(7)(a) or 37C(2)(b) above is on bail subject to conditions.

     (1D) The person shall not be entitled to make an application under section 43B of the Magistrates' Courts Act 1980.

     (1E) A magistrates' court may, on an application by or on behalf of the person, vary the conditions of bail; and in this subsection "vary" has the same meaning as in the Bail Act 1976.

     (1F) Where a magistrates' court varies the conditions of bail under subsection (1E) above, that bail shall not lapse but shall continue subject to the conditions as so varied."

SCHEDULE 3   **Section 41**

ALLOCATION OF CASES TRIABLE EITHER WAY, AND SENDING CASES TO THE CROWN COURT ETC

PART 1

PRINCIPAL AMENDMENTS

Magistrates' Courts Act 1980 (c. 43)

1   The Magistrates' Courts Act 1980 is amended as follows.

2   (1) Section 17A (initial indication as to plea) is amended as follows.

     (2) For paragraph (b) of subsection (4) there is substituted—

     "(b) he may (unless section 17D(2) below were to apply) be committed to the Crown Court under section 3 or (if applicable) 3A of the Powers of Criminal Courts (Sentencing) Act 2000 if the court is of such opinion as is mentioned in subsection (2) of the applicable section."

     (3) After subsection (9) there is inserted—

     "(10) If in respect of the offence the court receives a notice under section 51B or 51C of the Crime and Disorder Act 1998 (which relate to serious or complex fraud cases and to certain cases involving children respectively), the preceding provisions of this section and the provisions of section 17B below shall not apply, and the court shall proceed in relation to the offence in accordance with section 51 or, as the case may be, section 51A of that Act."

3   After section 17C there is inserted—

"17D Maximum penalty under section 17A(6) or 17B(2)(c) for certain offences

     (1) If—

     (a) the offence is a scheduled offence (as defined in section 22(1) below);

     (b) the court proceeds in relation to the offence in accordance with section 17A(6) or 17B(2)(c) above; and

    (c) the court convicts the accused of the offence,

the court shall consider whether, having regard to any representations made by him or by the prosecutor, the value involved (as defined in section 22(10) below) appears to the court to exceed the relevant sum (as specified for the purposes of section 22 below).

  (2) If it appears to the court clear that the value involved does not exceed the relevant sum, or it appears to the court for any reason not clear whether the value involved does or does not exceed the relevant sum—

    (a) subject to subsection (4) below, the court shall not have power to impose on the accused in respect of the offence a sentence in excess of the limits mentioned in section 33(1)(a) below; and

    (b) sections 3 and 4 of the Powers of Criminal Courts (Sentencing) Act 2000 shall not apply as regards that offence.

  (3) Subsections (9) to (12) of section 22 below shall apply for the purposes of this section as they apply for the purposes of that section (reading the reference to subsection (1) in section 22(9) as a reference to subsection (1) of this section).

  (4) Subsection (2)(a) above does not apply to an offence under section 12A of the Theft Act 1968 (aggravated vehicle-taking).

17E Functions under sections 17A to 17D capable of exercise by single justice

  (1) The functions of a magistrates' court under sections 17A to 17D above may be discharged by a single justice.

  (2) Subsection (1) above shall not be taken as authorising—

    (a) the summary trial of an information (otherwise than in accordance with section 17A(6) or 17B(2)(c) above); or

    (b) the imposition of a sentence,

by a magistrates' court composed of fewer than two justices."

4   In section 18 (initial procedure on information against adult for offence triable either way), for subsection (5) there is substituted—

    "(5) The functions of a magistrates' court under sections 19 to 23 below may be discharged by a single justice, but this subsection shall not be taken as authorising—

    (a) the summary trial of an information (otherwise than in accordance with section 20(7) below); or

    (b) the imposition of a sentence,

by a magistrates' court composed of fewer than two justices."

5   For section 19 (court to begin by considering which mode of trial appears more suitable) there is substituted—

"19 Decision as to allocation

  (1) The court shall decide whether the offence appears to it more suitable for summary trial or for trial on indictment.

  (2) Before making a decision under this section, the court—

    (a) shall give the prosecution an opportunity to inform the court of the accused's previous convictions (if any); and

    (b) shall give the prosecution and the accused an opportunity to make representations as to whether summary trial or trial on indictment would be more suitable.

  (3) In making a decision under this section, the court shall consider—

    (a) whether the sentence which a magistrates' court would have power to impose for the offence would be adequate; and

    (b) any representations made by the prosecution or the accused under subsection (2)(b) above,

and shall have regard to any allocation guidelines (or revised allocation guidelines) issued as definitive guidelines under section 170 of the Criminal Justice Act 2003.

  (4) Where—

    (a) the accused is charged with two or more offences; and

    (b) it appears to the court that the charges for the offences could be joined in the same indictment or that the offences arise out of the same or connected circumstances, subsection (3)(a) above shall have effect as if references to the sentence which a magistrates' court would have power to impose for the offence were a reference to the maximum aggregate sentence which a magistrates' court would have power to impose for all of the offences taken together.

(5) In this section any reference to a previous conviction is a reference to—

   (a) a previous conviction by a court in the United Kingdom; or

   (b) a previous finding of guilt in—

      (i) any proceedings under the Army Act 1955, the Air Force Act 1955 or the Naval Discipline Act 1957 (whether before a court-martial or any other court or person authorised under any of those Acts to award a punishment in respect of any offence); or

      (ii) any proceedings before a Standing Civilian Court.

(6) If, in respect of the offence, the court receives a notice under section 51B or 51C of the Crime and Disorder Act 1998 (which relate to serious or complex fraud cases and to certain cases involving children respectively), the preceding provisions of this section and sections 20, 20A and 21 below shall not apply, and the court shall proceed in relation to the offence in accordance with section 51(1) of that Act."

6   For section 20 (procedure where summary trial appears more suitable) there is substituted—

"20 Procedure where summary trial appears more suitable

(1) If the court decides under section 19 above that the offence appears to it more suitable for summary trial, the following provisions of this section shall apply (unless they are excluded by section 23 below).

(2) The court shall explain to the accused in ordinary language—

   (a) that it appears to the court more suitable for him to be tried summarily for the offence;

   (b) that he can either consent to be so tried or, if he wishes, be tried on indictment; and

   (c) in the case of a specified offence (within the meaning of section 224 of the Criminal Justice Act 2003), that if he is tried summarily and is convicted by the court, he may be committed for sentence to the Crown Court under section 3A of the Powers of Criminal Courts (Sentencing) Act 2000 if the committing court is of such opinion as is mentioned in subsection (2) of that section.

(3) The accused may then request an indication ("an indication of sentence") of whether a custodial sentence or non-custodial sentence would be more likely to be imposed if he were to be tried summarily for the offence and to plead guilty.

(4) If the accused requests an indication of sentence, the court may, but need not, give such an indication.

(5) If the accused requests and the court gives an indication of sentence, the court shall ask the accused whether he wishes, on the basis of the indication, to reconsider the indication of plea which was given, or is taken to have been given, under section 17A or 17B above.

(6) If the accused indicates that he wishes to reconsider the indication under section 17A or 17B above, the court shall ask the accused whether (if the offence were to proceed to trial) he would plead guilty or not guilty.

(7) If the accused indicates that he would plead guilty the court shall proceed as if—

   (a) the proceedings constituted from that time the summary trial of the information; and

   (b) section 9(1) above were complied with and he pleaded guilty under it.

(8) Subsection (9) below applies where—

   (a) the court does not give an indication of sentence (whether because the accused does not request one or because the court does not agree to give one);

   (b) the accused either—

      (i) does not indicate, in accordance with subsection (5) above, that he wishes; or

      (ii) indicates, in accordance with subsection (5) above, that he does not wish, to reconsider the indication of plea under section 17A or 17B above; or

(c) the accused does not indicate, in accordance with subsection (6) above, that he would plead guilty.

(9) The court shall ask the accused whether he consents to be tried summarily or wishes to be tried on indictment and—

(a) if he consents to be tried summarily, shall proceed to the summary trial of the information; and

(b) if he does not so consent, shall proceed in relation to the offence in accordance with section 51(1) of the Crime and Disorder Act 1998.

20A Procedure where summary trial appears more suitable: supplementary

(1) Where the case is dealt with in accordance with section 20(7) above, no court (whether a magistrates' court or not) may impose a custodial sentence for the offence unless such a sentence was indicated in the indication of sentence referred to in section 20 above.

(2) Subsection (1) above is subject to sections 3A(4), 4(8) and 5(3) of the Powers of Criminal Courts (Sentencing) Act 2000.

(3) Except as provided in subsection (1) above—

(a) an indication of sentence shall not be binding on any court (whether a magistrates' court or not); and

(b) no sentence may be challenged or be the subject of appeal in any court on the ground that it is not consistent with an indication of sentence.

(4) Subject to section 20(7) above, the following shall not for any purpose be taken to constitute the taking of a plea—

(a) asking the accused under section 20 above whether (if the offence were to proceed to trial) he would plead guilty or not guilty; or

(b) an indication by the accused under that section of how he would plead.

(5) Where the court gives an indication of sentence under section 20 above, it shall cause each such indication to be entered in the register.

(6) In this section and in section 20 above, references to a custodial sentence are to a custodial sentence within the meaning of section 76 of the Powers of Criminal Courts (Sentencing) Act 2000, and references to a non-custodial sentence shall be construed accordingly."

7   For section 21 (procedure where trial on indictment appears more suitable) there is substituted—

"21 Procedure where trial on indictment appears more suitable

If the court decides under section 19 above that the offence appears to it more suitable for trial on indictment, the court shall tell the accused that the court has decided that it is more suitable for him to be tried on indictment, and shall proceed in relation to the offence in accordance with section 51(1) of the Crime and Disorder Act 1998."

8   (1) Section 23 (power of court, with consent of legally represented accused, to proceed in his absence) is amended as follows.

(2) In subsection (4)—

(a) for the words preceding paragraph (a) there is substituted "If the court decides under section 19 above that the offence appears to it more suitable for trial on indictment then— ", and

(b) in paragraph (b), for the words from "to inquire" to the end there is substituted "in relation to the offence in accordance with section 51(1) of the Crime and Disorder Act 1998.".

(3) For subsection (5) there is substituted—

"(5) If the court decides under section 19 above that the offence appears to it more suitable for trial on indictment, section 21 above shall not apply and the court shall proceed in relation to the offence in accordance with section 51(1) of the Crime and Disorder Act 1998."

9   (1) Section 24 (summary trial of information against child or young persons for indictable offence), as amended by section 42 of this Act, is amended as follows.

(2) For subsection (1) there is substituted—

"(1) Where a person under the age of 18 years appears or is brought before a magistrates' court on an information charging him with an indictable offence he shall, subject to sections 51 and 51A of the Crime and Disorder Act 1998 and to sections 24A and 24B below, be tried summarily."

(3) Subsections (1A) and (2) are omitted.

10   After section 24 there is inserted—

"24A Child or young person to indicate intention as to plea in certain cases

(1) This section applies where—

    (a) a person under the age of 18 years appears or is brought before a magistrates' court on an information charging him with an offence other than one falling within section 51A(12) of the Crime and Disorder Act 1998 ("the 1998 Act"); and

    (b) but for the application of the following provisions of this section, the court would be required at that stage, by virtue of section 51(7) or (8) or 51A(3)(b), (4) or (5) of the 1998 Act to determine, in relation to the offence, whether to send the person to the Crown Court for trial (or to determine any matter, the effect of which would be to determine whether he is sent to the Crown Court for trial).

(2) Where this section applies, the court shall, before proceeding to make any such determination as is referred to in subsection (1)(b) above (the "relevant determination"), follow the procedure set out in this section.

(3) Everything that the court is required to do under the following provisions of this section must be done with the accused person in court.

(4) The court shall cause the charge to be written down, if this has not already been done, and to be read to the accused.

(5) The court shall then explain to the accused in ordinary language that he may indicate whether (if the offence were to proceed to trial) he would plead guilty or not guilty, and that if he indicates that he would plead guilty—

    (a) the court must proceed as mentioned in subsection (7) below; and

    (b) (in cases where the offence is one mentioned in section 91(1) of the Powers of Criminal Courts (Sentencing) Act 2000) he may be sent to the Crown Court for sentencing under section 3B or (if applicable) 3C of that Act if the court is of such opinion as is mentioned in subsection (2) of the applicable section.

(6) The court shall then ask the accused whether (if the offence were to proceed to trial) he would plead guilty or not guilty.

(7) If the accused indicates that he would plead guilty, the court shall proceed as if—

    (a) the proceedings constituted from the beginning the summary trial of the information; and

    (b) section 9(1) above was complied with and he pleaded guilty under it,

and, accordingly, the court shall not (and shall not be required to) proceed to make the relevant determination or to proceed further under section 51 or (as the case may be) section 51A of the 1998 Act in relation to the offence.

(8) If the accused indicates that he would plead not guilty, the court shall proceed to make the relevant determination and this section shall cease to apply.

(9) If the accused in fact fails to indicate how he would plead, for the purposes of this section he shall be taken to indicate that he would plead not guilty.

(10) Subject to subsection (7) above, the following shall not for any purpose be taken to constitute the taking of a plea—

    (a) asking the accused under this section whether (if the offence were to proceed to trial) he would plead guilty or not guilty;

    (b) an indication by the accused under this section of how he would plead.

24B Intention as to plea by child or young person: absence of accused

(1) This section shall have effect where—

    (a) a person under the age of 18 years appears or is brought before a magistrates' court on an information charging him with an offence other than one falling within section 51A(12) of the Crime and Disorder Act 1998;

    (b) but for the application of the following provisions of this section, the court would be required at that stage to make one of the determinations referred to in paragraph (b) of section 24A(1) above ("the relevant determination");

(c) the accused is represented by a legal representative;

(d) the court considers that by reason of the accused's disorderly conduct before the court it is not practicable for proceedings under section 24A above to be conducted in his presence; and

(e) the court considers that it should proceed in the absence of the accused.

(2) In such a case—

(a) the court shall cause the charge to be written down, if this has not already been done, and to be read to the representative;

(b) the court shall ask the representative whether (if the offence were to proceed to trial) the accused would plead guilty or not guilty;

(c) if the representative indicates that the accused would plead guilty the court shall proceed as if the proceedings constituted from the beginning the summary trial of the information, and as if section 9(1) above was complied with and the accused pleaded guilty under it;

(d) if the representative indicates that the accused would plead not guilty the court shall proceed to make the relevant determination and this section shall cease to apply.

(3) If the representative in fact fails to indicate how the accused would plead, for the purposes of this section he shall be taken to indicate that the accused would plead not guilty.

(4) Subject to subsection (2)(c) above, the following shall not for any purpose be taken to constitute the taking of a plea—

(a) asking the representative under this section whether (if the offence were to proceed to trial) the accused would plead guilty or not guilty;

(b) an indication by the representative under this section of how the accused would plead.

24C Intention as to plea by child or young person: adjournment

(1) A magistrates' court proceeding under section 24A or 24B above may adjourn the proceedings at any time, and on doing so on any occasion when the accused is present may remand the accused.

(2) Where the court remands the accused, the time fixed for the resumption of proceedings shall be that at which he is required to appear or be brought before the court in pursuance of the remand or would be required to be brought before the court but for section 128(3A) below.

24D Functions under sections 24A to 24C capable of exercise by single justice

(1) The functions of a magistrates' court under sections 24A to 24C above may be discharged by a single justice.

(2) Subsection (1) above shall not be taken as authorising—

(a) the summary trial of an information (other than a summary trial by virtue of section 24A(7) or 24B(2)(c) above); or

(b) the imposition of a sentence,

by a magistrates' court composed of fewer than two justices."

11 (1) Section 25 (power to change from summary trial to committal proceedings and vice versa), as amended by section 42 of this Act, is amended as follows.

(2) In subsection (1), for "(2) to (4)" there is substituted "(2) to (2D)".

(3) For subsection (2) there is substituted—

"(2) Where the court is required under section 20(9) above to proceed to the summary trial of the information, the prosecution may apply to the court for the offence to be tried on indictment instead.

(2A) An application under subsection (2) above—

(a) must be made before the summary trial begins; and

(b) must be dealt with by the court before any other application or issue in relation to the summary trial is dealt with.

(2B) The court may grant an application under subsection (2) above but only if it is satisfied that the sentence which a magistrates' court would have power to impose for the offence would be inadequate.

(2C) Where—

(a) the accused is charged on the same occasion with two or more offences; and

(b) it appears to the court that they constitute or form part of a series of two or more offences of the same or a similar character,

subsection (2B) above shall have effect as if references to the sentence which a magistrates' court would have power to impose for the offence were a reference to the maximum aggregate sentence which a magistrates' court would have power to impose for all of the offences taken together.

(2D) Where the court grants an application under subsection (2) above, it shall proceed in relation to the offence in accordance with section 51(1) of the Crime and Disorder Act 1998."

    (4) Subsections (3) to (8) are omitted.

12   For subsections (1) and (2) of section 26 (power to issue summons to accused in certain circumstances) there is substituted—

"(1) Where, in the circumstances mentioned in section 23(1)(a) above, the court is not satisfied that there is good reason for proceeding in the absence of the accused, the justice or any of the justices of which the court is composed may issue a summons directed to the accused requiring his presence before the court.

(2) In a case within subsection (1) above, if the accused is not present at the time and place appointed for the proceedings under section 19 or section 22(1) above, the court may issue a warrant for his arrest."

13   In section 33 (maximum penalties on summary conviction in pursuance of section 22), in subsection (1), paragraph (b) and the word "and" immediately preceding it are omitted.

14   Section 42 (restriction on justices sitting after dealing with bail) shall cease to have effect.

Crime and Disorder Act 1998 (c. 37)

15   The Crime and Disorder Act 1998 is amended as follows.

16   In section 50 (early administrative hearings), in subsection (1) (court may consist of single justice unless accused falls to be dealt with under section 51), the words "unless the accused falls to be dealt with under section 51 below" are omitted.

17   After section 50 there is inserted—

"50A Order of consideration for either-way offences

(1) Where an adult appears or is brought before a magistrates' court charged with an either-way offence (the "relevant offence"), the court shall proceed in the manner described in this section.

(2) If notice is given in respect of the relevant offence under section 51B or 51C below, the court shall deal with the offence as provided in section 51 below.

(3) Otherwise—

(a) if the adult (or another adult with whom the adult is charged jointly with the relevant offence) is or has been sent to the Crown Court for trial for an offence under section 51(2)(a) or 51(2)(c) below—

(i) the court shall first consider the relevant offence under subsection (3), (4), (5) or, as the case may be, (6) of section 51 below and, where applicable, deal with it under that subsection;

(ii) if the adult is not sent to the Crown Court for trial for the relevant offence by virtue of sub-paragraph (i) above, the court shall then proceed to deal with the relevant offence in accordance with sections 17A to 23 of the 1980 Act;

(b) in all other cases—

(i) the court shall first consider the relevant offence under sections 17A to 20 (excluding subsections (8) and (9) of section 20) of the 1980 Act;

(ii) if, by virtue of sub-paragraph (i) above, the court would be required to proceed in relation to the offence as mentioned in section 17A(6), 17B(2)(c) or 20(7) of that Act (indication of guilty plea), it shall proceed as so required (and, accordingly, shall not consider the offence under section 51 or 51A below);

(iii) if sub-paragraph (ii) above does not apply—

    (a) the court shall consider the relevant offence under sections 51 and 51A below and, where applicable, deal with it under the relevant section;

    (b) if the adult is not sent to the Crown Court for trial for the relevant offence by virtue of paragraph (a) of this sub-paragraph, the court shall then proceed to deal with the relevant offence as contemplated by section 20(9) or, as the case may be, section 21 of the 1980 Act.

  (4) Subsection (3) above is subject to any requirement to proceed as mentioned in subsections (2) or (6)(a) of section 22 of the 1980 Act (certain offences where value involved is small).

  (5) Nothing in this section shall prevent the court from committing the adult to the Crown Court for sentence pursuant to any enactment, if he is convicted of the relevant offence."

18   For section 51 (no committal proceedings for indictable-only offences) there is substituted—

"51 Sending cases to the Crown Court: adults

  (1) Where an adult appears or is brought before a magistrates' court ("the court") charged with an offence and any of the conditions mentioned in subsection (2) below is satisfied, the court shall send him forthwith to the Crown Court for trial for the offence.

  (2) Those conditions are—

    (a) that the offence is an offence triable only on indictment other than one in respect of which notice has been given under section 51B or 51C below;

    (b) that the offence is an either-way offence and the court is required under section 20(9)(b), 21, 23(4)(b) or (5) or 25(2D) of the Magistrates' Courts Act 1980 to proceed in relation to the offence in accordance with subsection (1) above;

    (c) that notice is given to the court under section 51B or 51C below in respect of the offence.

  (3) Where the court sends an adult for trial under subsection (1) above, it shall at the same time send him to the Crown Court for trial for any either-way or summary offence with which he is charged and which—

    (a) (if it is an either-way offence) appears to the court to be related to the offence mentioned in subsection (1) above; or

    (b) (if it is a summary offence) appears to the court to be related to the offence mentioned in subsection (1) above or to the either-way offence, and which fulfils the requisite condition (as defined in subsection (11) below).

  (4) Where an adult who has been sent for trial under subsection (1) above subsequently appears or is brought before a magistrates' court charged with an either-way or summary offence which—

    (a) appears to the court to be related to the offence mentioned in subsection (1) above; and

    (b) (in the case of a summary offence) fulfils the requisite condition,

the court may send him forthwith to the Crown Court for trial for the either-way or summary offence.

  (5) Where—

    (a) the court sends an adult ("A") for trial under subsection (1) or (3) above;

    (b) another adult appears or is brought before the court on the same or a subsequent occasion charged jointly with A with an either-way offence; and

    (c) that offence appears to the court to be related to an offence for which A was sent for trial under subsection (1) or (3) above,

the court shall where it is the same occasion, and may where it is a subsequent occasion, send the other adult forthwith to the Crown Court for trial for the either-way offence.

  (6) Where the court sends an adult for trial under subsection (5) above, it shall at the same time send him to the Crown Court for trial for any either-way or summary offence with which he is charged and which—

    (a) (if it is an either-way offence) appears to the court to be related to the offence for which he is sent for trial; and

    (b) (if it is a summary offence) appears to the court to be related to the offence for which he is sent for trial or to the either-way offence, and which fulfils the requisite condition.

  (7) Where—

    (a) the court sends an adult ("A") for trial under subsection (1), (3) or (5) above; and

(b) a child or young person appears or is brought before the court on the same or a subsequent occasion charged jointly with A with an indictable offence for which A is sent for trial under subsection (1), (3) or (5) above, or an indictable offence which appears to the court to be related to that offence,

the court shall, if it considers it necessary in the interests of justice to do so, send the child or young person forthwith to the Crown Court for trial for the indictable offence.

(8) Where the court sends a child or young person for trial under subsection (7) above, it may at the same time send him to the Crown Court for trial for any indictable or summary offence with which he is charged and which—

(a) (if it is an indictable offence) appears to the court to be related to the offence for which he is sent for trial; and

(b) (if it is a summary offence) appears to the court to be related to the offence for which he is sent for trial or to the indictable offence, and which fulfils the requisite condition.

(9) Subsections (7) and (8) above are subject to sections 24A and 24B of the Magistrates' Courts Act 1980 (which provide for certain cases involving children and young persons to be tried summarily).

(10) The trial of the information charging any summary offence for which a person is sent for trial under this section shall be treated as if the court had adjourned it under section 10 of the 1980 Act and had not fixed the time and place for its resumption.

(11) A summary offence fulfils the requisite condition if it is punishable with imprisonment or involves obligatory or discretionary disqualification from driving.

(12) In the case of an adult charged with an offence—

(a) if the offence satisfies paragraph (c) of subsection (2) above, the offence shall be dealt with under subsection (1) above and not under any other provision of this section or section 51A below;

(b) subject to paragraph (a) above, if the offence is one in respect of which the court is required to, or would decide to, send the adult to the Crown Court under—

(i) subsection (5) above; or

(ii) subsection (6) of section 51A below,

the offence shall be dealt with under that subsection and not under any other provision of this section or section 51A below.

(13) The functions of a magistrates' court under this section, and its related functions under section 51D below, may be discharged by a single justice.

51A Sending cases to the Crown Court: children and young persons

(1) This section is subject to sections 24A and 24B of the Magistrates' Courts Act 1980 (which provide for certain offences involving children or young persons to be tried summarily).

(2) Where a child or young person appears or is brought before a magistrates' court ("the court") charged with an offence and any of the conditions mentioned in subsection (3) below is satisfied, the court shall send him forthwith to the Crown Court for trial for the offence.

(3) Those conditions are—

(a) that the offence falls within subsection (12) below;

(b) that the offence is such as is mentioned in subsection (1) of section 91 of the Powers of Criminal Courts (Sentencing) Act 2000 (other than one mentioned in paragraph (d) below in relation to which it appears to the court as mentioned there) and the court considers that if he is found guilty of the offence it ought to be possible to sentence him in pursuance of subsection (3) of that section;

(c) that notice is given to the court under section 51B or 51C below in respect of the offence;

(d) that the offence is a specified offence (within the meaning of section 224 of the Criminal Justice Act 2003) and it appears to the court that if he is found guilty of the offence the criteria for the imposition of a sentence under section 226(3) or 228(2) of that Act would be met.

(4) Where the court sends a child or young person for trial under subsection (2) above, it may at the same time send him to the Crown Court for trial for any indictable or summary offence with which he is charged and which—

(a) (if it is an indictable offence) appears to the court to be related to the offence mentioned in subsection (2) above; or

(b) (if it is a summary offence) appears to the court to be related to the offence mentioned in subsection (2) above or to the indictable offence, and which fulfils the requisite condition (as defined in subsection (9) below).

(5) Where a child or young person who has been sent for trial under subsection (2) above subsequently appears or is brought before a magistrates' court charged with an indictable or summary offence which—

(a) appears to the court to be related to the offence mentioned in subsection (2) above; and

(b) (in the case of a summary offence) fulfils the requisite condition,

the court may send him forthwith to the Crown Court for trial for the indictable or summary offence.

(6) Where—

(a) the court sends a child or young person ("C") for trial under subsection (2) or (4) above; and

(b) an adult appears or is brought before the court on the same or a subsequent occasion charged jointly with C with an either-way offence for which C is sent for trial under subsection (2) or (4) above, or an either-way offence which appears to the court to be related to that offence,

the court shall where it is the same occasion, and may where it is a subsequent occasion, send the adult forthwith to the Crown Court for trial for the either-way offence.

(7) Where the court sends an adult for trial under subsection (6) above, it shall at the same time send him to the Crown Court for trial for any either-way or summary offence with which he is charged and which—

(a) (if it is an either-way offence) appears to the court to be related to the offence for which he was sent for trial; and

(b) (if it is a summary offence) appears to the court to be related to the offence for which he was sent for trial or to the either-way offence, and which fulfils the requisite condition.

(8) The trial of the information charging any summary offence for which a person is sent for trial under this section shall be treated as if the court had adjourned it under section 10 of the 1980 Act and had not fixed the time and place for its resumption.

(9) A summary offence fulfils the requisite condition if it is punishable with imprisonment or involves obligatory or discretionary disqualification from driving.

(10) In the case of a child or young person charged with an offence—

(a) if the offence satisfies any of the conditions in subsection (3) above, the offence shall be dealt with under subsection (2) above and not under any other provision of this section or section 51 above;

(b) subject to paragraph (a) above, if the offence is one in respect of which the requirements of subsection (7) of section 51 above for sending the child or young person to the Crown Court are satisfied, the offence shall be dealt with under that subsection and not under any other provision of this section or section 51 above.

(11) The functions of a magistrates' court under this section, and its related functions under section 51D below, may be discharged by a single justice.

(12) An offence falls within this subsection if—

(a) it is an offence of homicide; or

(b) each of the requirements of section 51A(1) of the Firearms Act 1968 would be satisfied with respect to—

(i) the offence; and

(ii) the person charged with it,

if he were convicted of the offence.

51B Notices in serious or complex fraud cases

(1) A notice may be given by a designated authority under this section in respect of an indictable offence if the authority is of the opinion that the evidence of the offence charged—

    (a) is sufficient for the person charged to be put on trial for the offence; and

    (b) reveals a case of fraud of such seriousness or complexity that it is appropriate that the management of the case should without delay be taken over by the Crown Court.

(2) That opinion must be certified by the designated authority in the notice.

(3) The notice must also specify the proposed place of trial, and in selecting that place the designated authority must have regard to the same matters as are specified in paragraphs (a) to (c) of section 51D(4) below.

(4) A notice under this section must be given to the magistrates' court at which the person charged appears or before which he is brought.

(5) Such a notice must be given to the magistrates' court before any summary trial begins.

(6) The effect of such a notice is that the functions of the magistrates' court cease in relation to the case, except—

    (a) for the purposes of section 51D below;

    (b) as provided by paragraph 2 of Schedule 3 to the Access to Justice Act 1999; and

    (c) as provided by section 52 below.

(7) The functions of a designated authority under this section may be exercised by an officer of the authority acting on behalf of the authority.

(8) A decision to give a notice under this section shall not be subject to appeal or liable to be questioned in any court (whether a magistrates' court or not).

(9) In this section "designated authority" means—

    (a) the Director of Public Prosecutions;

    (b) the Director of the Serious Fraud Office;

    (c) the Commissioners of the Inland Revenue;

    (d) the Commissioners of Customs and Excise; or

    (e) the Secretary of State.

51C Notices in certain cases involving children

(1) A notice may be given by the Director of Public Prosecutions under this section in respect of an offence falling within subsection (3) below if he is of the opinion—

    (a) that the evidence of the offence would be sufficient for the person charged to be put on trial for the offence;

    (b) that a child would be called as a witness at the trial; and

    (c) that, for the purpose of avoiding any prejudice to the welfare of the child, the case should be taken over and proceeded with without delay by the Crown Court.

(2) That opinion must be certified by the Director of Public Prosecutions in the notice.

(3) This subsection applies to an offence—

    (a) which involves an assault on, or injury or a threat of injury to, a person;

    (b) under section 1 of the Children and Young Persons Act 1933 (cruelty to persons under 16);

    (c) under the Sexual Offences Act 1956, the Protection of Children Act 1978 or the Sexual Offences Act 2003;

    (d) of kidnapping or false imprisonment, or an offence under section 1 or 2 of the Child Abduction Act 1984;

    (e) which consists of attempting or conspiring to commit, or of aiding, abetting, counselling, procuring or inciting the commission of, an offence falling within paragraph (a), (b), (c) or (d) above.

(4) Subsections (4), (5) and (6) of section 51B above apply for the purposes of this section as they apply for the purposes of that.

(5) The functions of the Director of Public Prosecutions under this section may be exercised by an officer acting on behalf of the Director.

(6) A decision to give a notice under this section shall not be subject to appeal or liable to be questioned in any court (whether a magistrates' court or not).

(7) In this section "child" means—

  (a) a person who is under the age of 17; or

  (b) any person of whom a video recording (as defined in section 63(1) of the Youth Justice and Criminal Evidence Act 1999) was made when he was under the age of 17 with a view to its admission as his evidence in chief in the trial referred to in subsection (1) above.

51D Notice of offence and place of trial

(1) The court shall specify in a notice—

  (a) the offence or offences for which a person is sent for trial under section 51 or 51A above; and

  (b) the place at which he is to be tried (which, if a notice has been given under section 51B above, must be the place specified in that notice).

(2) A copy of the notice shall be served on the accused and given to the Crown Court sitting at that place.

(3) In a case where a person is sent for trial under section 51 or 51A above for more than one offence, the court shall specify in that notice, for each offence—

  (a) the subsection under which the person is so sent; and

  (b) if applicable, the offence to which that offence appears to the court to be related.

(4) Where the court selects the place of trial for the purposes of subsection (1) above, it shall have regard to—

  (a) the convenience of the defence, the prosecution and the witnesses;

  (b) the desirability of expediting the trial; and

  (c) any direction given by or on behalf of the Lord Chief Justice with the concurrence of the Lord Chancellor under section 75(1) of the Supreme Court Act 1981.

51E Interpretation of sections 50A to 51D

For the purposes of sections 50A to 51D above—

  (a) "adult" means a person aged 18 or over, and references to an adult include a corporation;

  (b) "either-way offence" means an offence triable either way;

  (c) an either-way offence is related to an indictable offence if the charge for the either-way offence could be joined in the same indictment as the charge for the indictable offence;

  (d) a summary offence is related to an indictable offence if it arises out of circumstances which are the same as or connected with those giving rise to the indictable offence."

19 (1) After section 52 there is inserted—

"52A Restrictions on reporting

(1) Except as provided by this section, it shall not be lawful—

  (a) to publish in the United Kingdom a written report of any allocation or sending proceedings in England and Wales; or

  (b) to include in a relevant programme for reception in the United Kingdom a report of any such proceedings,

if (in either case) the report contains any matter other than that permitted by this section.

(2) Subject to subsections (3) and (4) below, a magistrates' court may, with reference to any allocation or sending proceedings, order that subsection (1) above shall not apply to reports of those proceedings.

(3) Where there is only one accused and he objects to the making of an order under subsection (2) above, the court shall make the order if, and only if, it is satisfied, after hearing the representations of the accused, that it is in the interests of justice to do so.

(4) Where in the case of two or more accused one of them objects to the making of an order under subsection (2) above, the court shall make the order if, and only if, it is satisfied, after hearing the representations of the accused, that it is in the interests of justice to do so.

(5) An order under subsection (2) above shall not apply to reports of proceedings under subsection (3) or (4) above, but any decision of the court to make or not to

make such an order may be contained in reports published or included in a relevant programme before the time authorised by subsection (6) below.

(6) It shall not be unlawful under this section to publish or include in a relevant programme a report of allocation or sending proceedings containing any matter other than that permitted by subsection (7) below—

  (a) where, in relation to the accused (or all of them, if there are more than one), the magistrates' court is required to proceed as mentioned in section 20(7) of the 1980 Act, after the court is so required;

  (b) where, in relation to the accused (or any of them, if there are more than one), the court proceeds other than as mentioned there, after conclusion of his trial or, as the case may be, the trial of the last to be tried.

(7) The following matters may be contained in a report of allocation or sending proceedings published or included in a relevant programme without an order under subsection (2) above before the time authorised by subsection (6) above—

  (a) the identity of the court and the name of the justice or justices;

  (b) the name, age, home address and occupation of the accused;

  (c) in the case of an accused charged with an offence in respect of which notice has been given to the court under section 51B above, any relevant business information;

  (d) the offence or offences, or a summary of them, with which the accused is or are charged;

  (e) the names of counsel and solicitors engaged in the proceedings;

  (f) where the proceedings are adjourned, the date and place to which they are adjourned;

  (g) the arrangements as to bail;

  (h) whether a right to representation funded by the Legal Services Commission as part of the Criminal Defence Service was granted to the accused or any of the accused.

(8) The addresses that may be published or included in a relevant programme under subsection (7) above are addresses—

  (a) at any relevant time; and

  (b) at the time of their publication or inclusion in a relevant programme.

(9) The following is relevant business information for the purposes of subsection (7) above—

  (a) any address used by the accused for carrying on a business on his own account;

  (b) the name of any business which he was carrying on on his own account at any relevant time;

  (c) the name of any firm in which he was a partner at any relevant time or by which he was engaged at any such time;

  (d) the address of any such firm;

  (e) the name of any company of which he was a director at any relevant time or by which he was otherwise engaged at any such time;

  (f) the address of the registered or principal office of any such company;

  (g) any working address of the accused in his capacity as a person engaged by any such company;

and here "engaged" means engaged under a contract of service or a contract for services.

(10) Subsection (1) above shall be in addition to, and not in derogation from, the provisions of any other enactment with respect to the publication of reports of court proceedings.

(11) In this section—

"allocation or sending proceedings" means, in relation to an information charging an indictable offence—

  (a) any proceedings in the magistrates' court at which matters are considered under any of the following provisions—

    (i) sections 19 to 23 of the 1980 Act;

    (ii) section 51, 51A or 52 above;

  (b) any proceedings in the magistrates' court before the court proceeds to consider any matter mentioned in paragraph (a) above; and

       (c) any proceedings in the magistrates' court at which an application under
           section 25(2) of the 1980 Act is considered;
   "publish", in relation to a report, means publish the report, either by itself or as
       part of a newspaper or periodical, for distribution to the public;
   "relevant programme" means a programme included in a programme service
       (within the meaning of the Broadcasting Act 1990);
   "relevant time" means a time when events giving rise to the charges to which the
       proceedings relate occurred.

52B Offences in connection with reporting

   (1) If a report is published or included in a relevant programme in contravention of
       section 52A above, each of the following persons is guilty of an offence—
       (a) in the case of a publication of a written report as part of a newspaper or
           periodical, any proprietor, editor or publisher of the newspaper or periodical;
       (b) in the case of a publication of a written report otherwise than as part of a
           newspaper or periodical, the person who publishes it;
       (c) in the case of the inclusion of a report in a relevant programme, any body
           corporate which is engaged in providing the service in which the programme
           is included and any person having functions in relation to the programme
           corresponding to those of the editor of a newspaper.
   (2) A person guilty of an offence under this section is liable on summary conviction to
       a fine not exceeding level 5 on the standard scale.
   (3) Proceedings for an offence under this section shall not, in England and Wales, be
       instituted otherwise than by or with the consent of the Attorney General.
   (4) Proceedings for an offence under this section shall not, in Northern Ireland, be
       instituted otherwise than by or with the consent of the Attorney General for
       Northern Ireland.
   (5) Subsection (11) of section 52A above applies for the purposes of this section as it
       applies for the purposes of that section.".

 (2) In section 121 (short title, commencement and extent)—
       (a) in subsection (6), after paragraph (b) there is inserted—
         "(bb) sections 52A and 52B;", and
       (b) in subsection (8), after "(5) above," there is inserted "sections 52A and 52B
         above,".

20 (1) Schedule 3 (procedure where persons are sent for trial under section 51 of the Crime
       and Disorder Act 1998) is amended as follows.
   (2) In paragraph 1(1)—
       (a) after "51" there is inserted "or 51A", and
       (b) in paragraph (b), for "subsection (7) of that section" there is substituted "section
         51D(1) of this Act".
   (3) In paragraph 2—
       (a) in sub-paragraph (1)—
         (i) after "51" there is inserted "or 51A", and
         (ii) for "subsection (7) of that section" there is substituted "section 51D(1) of this
           Act", and
       (b) sub-paragraphs (4) and (5) are omitted.
   (4) In paragraph 4, in sub-paragraph (1)(a), after "51" there is inserted "or 51A".
   (5) In paragraph 5, in sub-paragraph (2), after "51" there is inserted "or 51A".
   (6) Paragraph 6 is amended as follows—
       (a) in sub-paragraph (1), after "51" there is inserted "or 51A",
       (b) in sub-paragraph (2), for the words from the second "offence" to the end there is
         substituted "indictable offence for which he was sent for trial or, as the case may
         be, any of the indictable offences for which he was so sent", and
       (c) in sub-paragraph (9), for "indictable-only" there is substituted "indictable".
   (7) In paragraph 7—
       (a) in sub-paragraph (1)(a), after "51" there is inserted "or 51A",
       (b) in sub-paragraph (1)(b), for "offence that is triable only on indictment" there is
         substituted "main offence",
       (c) in sub-paragraph (3), after "each" there is inserted "remaining",
       (d) in sub-paragraph (7), for "consider" there is substituted "decide", and
       (e) after sub-paragraph (8) there is inserted—
         "(9) In this paragraph, a "main offence" is—
           (a) an offence for which the person has been sent to the Crown Court for
             trial under section 51(1) of this Act; or
           (b) an offence—

      (i) for which the person has been sent to the Crown Court for trial under subsection (5) of section 51 or subsection (6) of section 51A of this Act ("the applicable subsection"); and

      (ii) in respect of which the conditions for sending him to the Crown Court for trial under the applicable subsection (as set out in paragraphs (a) to (c) of section 51(5) or paragraphs (a) and (b) of section 51A(6)) continue to be satisfied."

(8) In paragraph 8—

  (a) in sub-paragraph (1)(a), after "51" there is inserted "or 51A",

  (b) in sub-paragraph (1)(b), for "offence that is triable only on indictment" there is substituted "main offence (within the meaning of paragraph 7 above)",

  (c) in sub-paragraph (2)(a), after "each" there is inserted "remaining", and

  (d) in sub-paragraph (2)(d), for "consider" there is substituted "decide".

(9) In paragraph 9—

  (a) in sub-paragraph (1), for "consider" there is substituted "decide", and

  (b) for sub-paragraphs (2) and (3), there is substituted-

"(2) Before deciding the question, the court—

  (a) shall give the prosecution an opportunity to inform the court of the accused's previous convictions (if any); and

  (b) shall give the prosecution and the accused an opportunity to make representations as to whether summary trial or trial on indictment would be more suitable.

(3) In deciding the question, the court shall consider—

  (a) whether the sentence which a magistrates' court would have power to impose for the offence would be adequate; and

  (b) any representations made by the prosecution or the accused under sub-paragraph (2)(b) above,

and shall have regard to any allocation guidelines (or revised allocation guidelines) issued as definitive guidelines under section 170 of the Criminal Justice Act 2003.

(4) Where—

  (a) the accused is charged on the same occasion with two or more offences; and

  (b) it appears to the court that they constitute or form part of a series of two or more offences of the same or a similar character;

sub-paragraph (3)(a) above shall have effect as if references to the sentence which a magistrates' court would have power to impose for the offence were a reference to the maximum aggregate sentence which a magistrates' court would have power to impose for all of the offences taken together.

(5) In this paragraph any reference to a previous conviction is a reference to—

  (a) a previous conviction by a court in the United Kingdom, or

  (b) a previous finding of guilt in—

      (i) any proceedings under the Army Act 1955, the Air Force Act 1955 or the Naval Discipline Act 1957 (whether before a court-martial or any other court or person authorised under any of those Acts to award a punishment in respect of any offence), or

      (ii) any proceedings before a Standing Civilian Court."

(10) In paragraph 10—

  (a) for sub-paragraph (2), there is substituted—

"(2) The court shall explain to the accused in ordinary language—

  (a) that it appears to the court more suitable for him to be tried summarily for the offence;

  (b) that he can either consent to be so tried or, if he wishes, be tried on indictment; and

  (c) in the case of a specified offence (within the meaning of section 224 of the Criminal Justice Act 2003), that if he is tried summarily and is convicted by the court, he may be committed for sentence to the Crown Court under section 3A of the Powers of Criminal Courts (Sentencing) Act 2000 if the committing court is of such opinion as is mentioned in subsection (2) of that section.", and

      (b) in sub-paragraph (3), for "by a jury" there is substituted "on indictment".

  (11) In paragraph 11, in sub-paragraph (a), for "by a jury" there is substituted "on indictment".

  (12) Paragraph 12 shall cease to have effect.

  (13) In paragraph 13—

      (a) in sub-paragraph (1)(a), after "51" there is inserted "or 51A",

      (b) in sub-paragraph (1)(b), for "offence that is triable only on indictment" there is substituted "main offence",

      (c) in sub-paragraph (2), the words from "unless" to the end are omitted, and

      (d) for sub-paragraph (3) there is substituted-

        "(3) In this paragraph, a "main offence" is—

          (a) an offence for which the child or young person has been sent to the Crown Court for trial under section 51A(2) of this Act; or

          (b) an offence—

            (i) for which the child or young person has been sent to the Crown Court for trial under subsection (7) of section 51 of this Act; and

            (ii) in respect of which the conditions for sending him to the Crown Court for trial under that subsection (as set out in paragraphs (a) and (b) of that subsection) continue to be satisfied."

  (14) In paragraph 15, in each of sub-paragraphs (3) and (4), for "considered" there is substituted "decided".

Powers of Criminal Courts (Sentencing) Act 2000 (c. 6)

21   The Powers of Criminal Courts (Sentencing) Act 2000 is amended as follows.

22   For section 3 (committal for sentence on summary trial of offence triable either way) there is substituted—

    "3 Committal for sentence on indication of guilty plea to serious offence triable either way

      (1) Subject to subsection (4) below, this section applies where—

        (a) a person aged 18 or over appears or is brought before a magistrates' court ("the court") on an information charging him with an offence triable either way ("the offence");

        (b) he or his representative indicates under section 17A or (as the case may be) 17B of the Magistrates' Courts Act 1980 (initial procedure: accused to indicate intention as to plea), but not section 20(7) of that Act, that he would plead guilty if the offence were to proceed to trial; and

        (c) proceeding as if section 9(1) of that Act were complied with and he pleaded guilty under it, the court convicts him of the offence.

      (2) If the court is of the opinion that—

        (a) the offence; or

        (b) the combination of the offence and one or more offences associated with it,

        was so serious that the Crown Court should, in the court's opinion, have the power to deal with the offender in any way it could deal with him if he had been convicted on indictment, the court may commit him in custody or on bail to the Crown Court for sentence in accordance with section 5(1) below.

      (3) Where the court commits a person under subsection (2) above, section 6 below (which enables a magistrates' court, where it commits a person under this section in respect of an offence, also to commit him to the Crown Court to be dealt with in respect of certain other offences) shall apply accordingly.

      (4) This section does not apply in relation to an offence as regards which this section is excluded by section 17D of the Magistrates' Courts Act 1980 (certain offences where value involved is small).

      (5) The preceding provisions of this section shall apply in relation to a corporation as if—

        (a) the corporation were an individual aged 18 or over; and

(b) in subsection (2) above, the words "in custody or on bail" were omitted."

23   After section 3 there is inserted—

"3A Committal for sentence of dangerous adult offenders

(1) This section applies where on the summary trial of a specified offence triable either way a person aged 18 or over is convicted of the offence.

(2) If, in relation to the offence, it appears to the court that the criteria for the imposition of a sentence under section 225(3) or 227(2) of the Criminal Justice Act 2003 would be met, the court must commit the offender in custody or on bail to the Crown Court for sentence in accordance with section 5(1) below.

(3) Where the court commits a person under subsection (2) above, section 6 below (which enables a magistrates' court, where it commits a person under this section in respect of an offence, also to commit him to the Crown Court to be dealt with in respect of certain other offences) shall apply accordingly.

(4) In reaching any decision under or taking any step contemplated by this section—

(a) the court shall not be bound by any indication of sentence given in respect of the offence under section 20 of the Magistrates' Courts Act 1980 (procedure where summary trial appears more suitable); and

(b) nothing the court does under this section may be challenged or be the subject of any appeal in any court on the ground that it is not consistent with an indication of sentence.

(5) Nothing in this section shall prevent the court from committing a specified offence to the Crown Court for sentence under section 3 above if the provisions of that section are satisfied.

(6) In this section, references to a specified offence are to a specified offence within the meaning of section 224 of the Criminal Justice Act 2003.

3B Committal for sentence on indication of guilty plea by child or young person

(1) This section applies where—

(a) a person aged under 18 appears or is brought before a magistrates' court ("the court") on an information charging him with an offence mentioned in subsection (1) of section 91 below ("the offence");

(b) he or his representative indicates under section 24A or (as the case may be) 24B of the Magistrates' Courts Act 1980 (child or young person to indicate intention as to plea in certain cases) that he would plead guilty if the offence were to proceed to trial; and

(c) proceeding as if section 9(1) of that Act were complied with and he pleaded guilty under it, the court convicts him of the offence.

(2) If the court is of the opinion that—

(a) the offence; or

(b) the combination of the offence and one or more offences associated with it,

was such that the Crown Court should, in the court's opinion, have power to deal with the offender as if the provisions of section 91(3) below applied, the court may commit him in custody or on bail to the Crown Court for sentence in accordance with section 5A(1) below.

(3) Where the court commits a person under subsection (2) above, section 6 below (which enables a magistrates' court, where it commits a person under this section in respect of an offence, also to commit him to the Crown Court to be dealt with in respect of certain other offences) shall apply accordingly.

3C Committal for sentence of dangerous young offenders

(1) This section applies where on the summary trial of a specified offence a person aged under 18 is convicted of the offence.

(2) If, in relation to the offence, it appears to the court that the criteria for the imposition of a sentence under section 226(3) or 228(2) of the Criminal Justice Act 2003 would be met, the court must commit the offender in custody or on bail to the Crown Court for sentence in accordance with section 5A(1) below.

(3) Where the court commits a person under subsection (2) above, section 6 below (which enables a magistrates' court, where it commits a person under

this section in respect of an offence, also to commit him to the Crown Court to be dealt with in respect of certain other offences) shall apply accordingly.

(4) Nothing in this section shall prevent the court from committing a specified offence to the Crown Court for sentence under section 3B above if the provisions of that section are satisfied.

(5) In this section, references to a specified offence are to a specified offence within the meaning of section 224 of the Criminal Justice Act 2003."

24 (1) Section 4 (committal for sentence on indication of guilty plea to offence triable either way) is amended as follows.

(2) For subsection (1)(b), there is substituted—

"(b) he or (where applicable) his representative indicates under section 17A, 17B or 20(7) of the Magistrates' Courts Act 1980 that he would plead guilty if the offence were to proceed to trial; and".

(3) In subsection (1)(c), for "the Magistrates' Courts Act 1980" there is substituted "that Act".

(4) After subsection (1) there is inserted—

"(1A) But this section does not apply to an offence as regards which this section is excluded by section 17D of that Act (certain offences where value involved is small)."

(5) For subsection (3), there is substituted—

"(3) If the power conferred by subsection (2) above is not exercisable but the court is still to determine to, or to determine whether to, send the offender to the Crown Court for trial under section 51 or 51A of the Crime and Disorder Act 1998 for one or more related offences—

(a) it shall adjourn the proceedings relating to the offence until after it has made those determinations; and

(b) if it sends the offender to the Crown Court for trial for one or more related offences, it may then exercise that power."

(6) In subsection (4)(b), after "section 3(2)" there is inserted "or, as the case may be, section 3A(2)".

(7) After subsection (7) there is inserted—

"(8) In reaching any decision under or taking any step contemplated by this section—

(a) the court shall not be bound by any indication of sentence given in respect of the offence under section 20 of the Magistrates' Courts Act 1980 (procedure where summary trial appears more suitable); and

(b) nothing the court does under this section may be challenged or be the subject of any appeal in any court on the ground that it is not consistent with an indication of sentence."

25   After section 4 there is inserted—

"4A Committal for sentence on indication of guilty plea by child or young person with related offences

(1) This section applies where—

(a) a person aged under 18 appears or brought before a magistrates' court ("the court") on an information charging him with an offence mentioned in subsection (1) of section 91 below ("the offence");

(b) he or his representative indicates under section 24A or (as the case may be) 24B of the Magistrates' Courts Act 1980 (child or young person to indicate intention as to plea in certain cases) that he would plead guilty if the offence were to proceed to trial; and

(c) proceeding as if section 9(1) of that Act were complied with and he pleaded guilty under it, the court convicts him of the offence.

(2) If the court has sent the offender to the Crown Court for trial for one or more related offences, that is to say one or more offences which, in its opinion, are related to the offence, it may commit him in custody or on bail to the Crown Court to be dealt with in respect of the offence in accordance with section 5A(1) below.

(3) If the power conferred by subsection (2) above is not exercisable but the court is still to determine to, or to determine whether to, send the offender to the Crown Court for trial under section 51 or 51A of the Crime and Disorder Act 1998 for one or more related offences—

(a) it shall adjourn the proceedings relating to the offence until after it has made those determinations; and

(b) if it sends the offender to the Crown Court for trial for one or more related offences, it may then exercise that power.

(4) Where the court—
(a) under subsection (2) above commits the offender to the Crown Court to be dealt with in respect of the offence; and
(b) does not state that, in its opinion, it also has power so to commit him under section 3B(2) or, as the case may be, section 3C(2) above,

section 5A(1) below shall not apply unless he is convicted before the Crown Court of one or more of the related offences.

(5) Where section 5A(1) below does not apply, the Crown Court may deal with the offender in respect of the offence in any way in which the magistrates' court could deal with him if it had just convicted him of the offence.

(6) Where the court commits a person under subsection (2) above, section 6 below (which enables a magistrates' court, where it commits a person under this section in respect of an offence, also to commit him to the Crown Court to be dealt with in respect of certain other offences) shall apply accordingly.

(7) Section 4(7) above applies for the purposes of this section as it applies for the purposes of that section."

26   For section 5 (power of Crown Court on committal for sentence under sections 3 and 4) there is substituted—

"5 Power of Crown Court on committal for sentence under sections 3, 3A and 4

(1) Where an offender is committed by a magistrates' court for sentence under section 3, 3A or 4 above, the Crown Court shall inquire into the circumstances of the case and may deal with the offender in any way in which it could deal with him if he had just been convicted of the offence on indictment before the court.

(2) In relation to committals under section 4 above, subsection (1) above has effect subject to section 4(4) and (5) above.

(3) Section 20A(1) of the Magistrates' Courts Act 1980 (which relates to the effect of an indication of sentence under section 20 of that Act) shall not apply in respect of any specified offence (within the meaning of section 224 of the Criminal Justice Act 2003)—
(a) in respect of which the offender is committed under section 3A(2) above; or
(b) in respect of which—
(i) the offender is committed under section 4(2) above; and
(ii) the court states under section 4(4) above that, in its opinion, it also has power to commit the offender under section 3A(2) above."

27   After section 5 there is inserted—

"5A Power of Crown Court on committal for sentence under sections 3B, 3C and 4A

(1) Where an offender is committed by a magistrates' court for sentence under section 3B, 3C or 4A above, the Crown Court shall inquire into the circumstances of the case and may deal with the offender in any way in which it could deal with him if he had just been convicted of the offence on indictment before the court.

(2) In relation to committals under section 4A above, subsection (1) above has effect subject to section 4A(4) and (5) above."

28   In section 6 (committal for sentence in certain cases where offender committed in respect of another offence), in subsection (4)(b), for "3 and 4" there is substituted "3 to 4A".

PART 2

MINOR AND CONSEQUENTIAL AMENDMENTS

Territorial Waters Jurisdiction Act 1878 (c. 73)

29   In section 4 of the Territorial Waters Jurisdiction Act 1878 (provisions as to procedure), in the paragraph beginning "Proceedings before a justice of the peace", for the words from the beginning to "his trial" there is substituted—

"Any stage of proceedings—
  (a) before the summary trial of the offence; or
  (b) before the offender has been sent for trial for the offence,".

Bankers' Books Evidence Act 1879 (c. 11)

30   (1) The Bankers' Books Evidence Act 1879 is amended as follows.
     (2) In section 4 (proof that book is a banker's book), the paragraph beginning "Where the proceedings" is omitted.
     (3) In section 5 (verification of copy), the paragraph beginning "Where the proceedings" is omitted.

Explosive Substances Act 1883 (c. 3)

31   In section 6 of the Explosive Substances Act 1883 (inquiry by Attorney-General, and apprehension of absconding witnesses), subsection (3) is omitted.

Criminal Justice Act 1925 (c. 86)

32   In section 49 of the Criminal Justice Act 1925 (interpretation, etc), subsection (2) is omitted.

Children and Young Persons Act 1933 (c. 12)

33   In section 42 of the Children and Young Persons Act 1933 (extension of power to take deposition of child or young person), in subsection (2)(a), for "committed" in both places there is substituted "sent".

Administration of Justice (Miscellaneous Provisions) Act 1933 (c. 36)

34   (1) Section 2 of the Administration of Justice (Miscellaneous Provisions) Act 1933 (procedure for indictment of offenders) is amended as follows.
     (2) In subsection (2)—
       (a) in paragraph (a), for "committed" there is substituted "sent",
       (b) paragraphs (aa) to (ac) are omitted,
       (c) for paragraph (i) there is substituted—
          "(i) where the person charged has been sent for trial, the bill of indictment against him may include, either in substitution for or in addition to any count charging an offence specified in the notice under section 57D(1) of the Crime and Disorder Act 1998, any counts founded on material which, in pursuance of regulations made under paragraph 1 of Schedule 3 to that Act, was served on the person charged, being counts which may lawfully be joined in the same indictment;",
       (d) paragraphs (iA) and (iB) are omitted,
       (e) in paragraph (ii), for "the committal" there is substituted "such notice", and
       (f) the words from "and in paragraph (iA)" to the end are omitted.
     (3) In subsection (3)(b), for "committed" there is substituted "sent".

Criminal Justice Act 1948 (c. 58)

35   (1) The Criminal Justice Act 1948 is amended as follows.
     (2) In section 27 (remand and committal of persons aged 17 to 20), in subsection (1), for "commits him for trial or" there is substituted "sends him to the Crown Court for trial or commits him there for".
     (3) In section 41 (evidence by certificate), subsection (5A) is omitted.
     (4) In section 80 (interpretation), the definition of "Court of summary jurisdiction" is omitted.

Prison Act 1952 (c. 52)

36   Until their repeal by (respectively) section 59 of, and paragraph 10(a)(ii) of Schedule 7 to, the Criminal Justice and Court Services Act 2000, paragraph (a) of subsection (1), and paragraphs (b) and (c) of subsection (2), of section 43 of the Prison Act 1952 (remand centres, detention centres and youth custody centres) are to have effect as if references to being committed for trial were references to being sent for trial.

Army Act 1955 (3 & 4 Eliz. 2 c. 18)

37   In section 187 of the Army Act 1955 (proceedings before a civil court where persons suspected of illegal absence), at the end of subsection (4) there is inserted—

"The references in this subsection to provisions of the Magistrates' Courts Act 1980 and to corresponding enactments are to be taken to refer to those provisions and enactments as if no amendment to them had been made by the Criminal Justice Act 2003."

Air Force Act 1955 (3 & 4 Eliz. 2 c. 19)

38   In section 187 of the Air Force Act 1955 (proceedings before a civil court where persons suspected of illegal absence), at the end of subsection (4) there is inserted—
        "The references in this subsection to provisions of the Magistrates' Courts Act 1980 and to corresponding enactments are to be taken to refer to those provisions and enactments as if no amendment to them had been made by the Criminal Justice Act 2003."

Geneva Conventions Act 1957 (c. 52)

39   In section 5 of the Geneva Conventions Act 1957 (reduction of sentence and custody of protected persons)—
        (a) in subsection (1), for "committal" there is substituted "having been sent",
        (b) in subsection (2), for "committal", where it first appears, there is substituted "having been sent".

Naval Discipline Act 1957 (c. 53)

40   In section 109 of the Naval Discipline Act 1957 (proceedings before summary courts), at the end of subsection (4) there is inserted—
        "The references in this subsection to provisions are to be taken to refer to those provisions as if no amendment to them had been made by the Criminal Justice Act 2003."

Backing of Warrants (Republic of Ireland) Act 1965 (c. 45)

41   In paragraph 4 of the Schedule to the Backing of Warrants (Republic of Ireland) Act 1965 (supplementary procedures as to proceedings under section 2)—
        (a) the words "and section 2 of the Poor Prisoners Defence Act 1930 (legal aid before examining justices)" are omitted, and
        (b) for "it had determined not to commit for trial" there is substituted "the offence were to be dealt with summarily and the court had dismissed the information".

Criminal Procedure (Attendance of Witnesses) Act 1965 (c. 69)

42   In section 2 of the Criminal Procedure (Attendance of Witnesses) Act 1965 (issue of witness summons on application to Crown Court)—
        (a) for subsection (4) there is substituted-
            "(4) Where a person has been sent for trial for any offence to which the proceedings concerned relate, an application must be made as soon as is reasonably practicable after service on that person, in pursuance of regulations made under paragraph 1 of Schedule 3 to the Crime and Disorder Act 1998, of the documents relevant to that offence.", and

        (b) subsection (5) is omitted.

Criminal Justice Act 1967 (c. 80)

43   (1) The Criminal Justice Act 1967 is amended as follows.
        (2) In section 9 (proof by written statement), in subsection (1), the words ", other than committal proceedings," are omitted.
        (3) In section 36 (interpretation), in subsection (1), the definition of "committal proceedings" is omitted.

Criminal Appeal Act 1968 (c. 19)

44   (1) The Criminal Appeal Act 1968 is amended as follows.
        (2) In section 1 (right of appeal), in subsection (3), for "committed him" there is substituted "sent him to the Crown Court".
        (3) In section 9 (appeal against sentence following conviction on indictment), in subsection (2), the words from "section 41" to "either way offence" are omitted.

Firearms Act 1968 (c. 27)

45   In Schedule 6 to the Firearms Act 1968 (prosecution and punishment of offences), in Part 2, paragraph 3 is omitted.

Theft Act 1968 (c. 60)

46   In section 27 of the Theft Act 1968 (evidence and procedure on charge of theft or handling stolen goods), subsection (4A) is omitted.

Criminal Justice Act 1972 (c. 71)

47   In section 46 of the Criminal Justice Act 1972 (admissibility of written statements outside England and Wales), subsections (1A) to (1C) are omitted.

Bail Act 1976 (c. 63)

48   (1) The Bail Act 1976 is amended as follows.
        (2) In section 3 (general provisions)—
            (a) in subsection (8)—
               (i) for "committed" there is substituted "sent", and
               (ii) after "for trial or" there is inserted "committed him on bail to the Crown Court", and
            (b) subsections (8A) and (8B), and the subsection (10) inserted by paragraph 12(b) of Schedule 9 to the Criminal Justice and Public Order Act 1994 (c. 33), are omitted.
        (3) In section 5 (supplementary provisions about decisions on bail)—
            (a) in subsection (6)(a), for "committing" there is substituted "sending", and
            (b) in subsection (6A)(a)—
               (i) after "under" there is inserted "section 52(5) of the Crime and Disorder Act 1998,",
               (ii) sub-paragraph (i) is omitted,
               (iii) after sub-paragraph (ii) there is inserted—
               "(iia) section 17C (intention as to plea: adjournment);", and
               (iv) at the end of sub-paragraph (iii) there is inserted "or
                  (iv) section 24C (intention as to plea by child or young person: adjournment),".
        (4) In section 6 (offence of absconding by person released on bail), in subsection (6)(b), for "commits" there is substituted "sends".
        (5) In section 9 (offence of agreeing to indemnify sureties in criminal proceedings), in subsection (3)(b), for "commits" there is substituted "sends".

Interpretation Act 1978 (c. 30)

49   In Schedule 1 to the Interpretation Act 1978 (words and expressions defined)—
            (a) in the definition of "Committed for trial", paragraph (a) is omitted,
            (b) after the entry for "Secretary of State" there is inserted—
            "Sent for trial" means, in relation to England and Wales, sent by a magistrates' court to the Crown Court for trial pursuant to section 51 or 51A of the Crime and Disorder Act 1998."

Customs and Excise Management Act 1979 (c. 2)

50   In section 147 of the Customs and Excise Management Act 1979 (proceedings for offences), subsection (2) is omitted.

Magistrates' Courts Act 1980 (c. 43)

51   (1) The Magistrates' Courts Act 1980 is amended as follows.
        (2) In section 2, as substituted by the Courts Act 2003 (trial of summary offences), in subsection (2), for "as examining justices over" there is substituted "under sections 51 and 51A of the Crime and Disorder Act 1998 in respect of".
        (3) Sections 4 to 8 (which relate to committal proceedings) shall cease to have effect and the cross-heading preceding section 4 is omitted.
        (4) In section 8B, as inserted by the Courts Act 2003 (effect of rulings at pre-trial hearing), in subsection (6), the words "commits or" are omitted.
        (5) In section 29 (power of magistrates' court to remit a person under 17 for trial to a juvenile court in certain circumstances), in subsection (2)(b)(i), for the words from

"proceeds" to the end there is substituted "sends him to the Crown Court for trial under section 51 or 51A of the Crime and Disorder Act 1998; and".

(6) The following sections shall cease to have effect—

    (a) section 97A (summons or warrant as to committal proceedings),

    (b) section 103 (evidence of persons under 14 in committal proceedings for assault, sexual offences etc), and

    (c) section 106 (false written statements tendered in evidence).

(7) In section 128 (remand in custody or on bail)—

    (a) in subsection (1)(b), the words "inquiring into or" are omitted,

    (b) in subsection (1A)(a)—

        (i) "5," is omitted, and

        (ii) for "or 18(4)" there is substituted ", 18(4) or 24C",

    (c) in subsection (3A)—

        (i) "5," is omitted, and

        (ii) for "or 18(4)" there is substituted ", 18(4) or 24C",

    (d) in subsection (3C)(a)—

        (i) "5," is omitted, and

        (ii) for "or 18(4)" there is substituted ", 18(4) or 24C", and

    (e) in subsection (3E)(a)—

        (i) "5," is omitted, and

        (ii) for "or 18(4)" there is substituted ", 18(4) or 24C".

(8) In section 129 (further remand), in subsection (4)—

    (a) for "commits a person" there is substituted "sends a person to the Crown Court", and

    (b) for "committed" there is substituted "sent".

(9) In section 130 (transfer of remand hearings), in subsection (1)—

    (a) "5," is omitted, and

    (b) for "or 18(4)" there is substituted ", 18(4) or 24C".

(10) In section 145 (rules: supplementary provisions), in subsection (1), paragraph (f) is omitted.

(11) In section 150 (interpretation of other terms), in subsection (1), the definition of "committal proceedings" is omitted.

(12) In section 155 (short title, extent and commencement), in subsection (2)(a), the words "8 (except subsection (9))" are omitted.

(13) In Schedule 3 (corporations)—

    (a) in paragraph 2, sub-paragraph (a) is omitted,

    (b) in paragraph 6, for "inquiry into, and trial of," there is substituted "trial of".

(14) In Schedule 5 (transfer of remand hearings)—

    (a) paragraph 2 is omitted, and

    (b) in paragraph 5, for "5, 10 or 18(4)" there is substituted "10, 17C, 18(4) or 24C".

Criminal Attempts Act 1981 (c. 47)

52   In section 2 of the Criminal Attempts Act 1981 (application of procedures and other provisions to offences under section 1), in subsection (2)(g), the words "or committed for trial" are omitted.

Contempt of Court Act 1981 (c. 49)

53   In section 4 of the Contempt of Court Act 1981 (contemporary reports of proceedings), in subsection (3), for paragraph (b) there is substituted—

    "(b) in the case of a report of allocation or sending proceedings of which publication is permitted by virtue only of subsection (6) of section 52A of the Crime and Disorder Act 1998 ("the 1998 Act"), if published as soon as practicable after publication is so permitted;

    (c) in the case of a report of an application of which publication is permitted by virtue only of sub-paragraph (5) or (7) of paragraph 3 of Schedule 3 to the 1998 Act, if published as soon as practicable after publication is so permitted."

Supreme Court Act 1981 (c. 54)

54   (1) The Supreme Court Act 1981 is amended as follows.

    (2) In section 76 (committal for trial: alteration of place of trial)—

      (a) in subsection (1), for the words from "varying" (where it first appears) to "to Crown Court)" there is substituted "substituting some other place for the place specified in a notice under section 51D(1) of the Crime and Disorder Act 1998 (a "section 51D notice"),

      (b) in subsection (3), for the words "fixed by the magistrates' court, as specified in a notice under a relevant transfer provision" there is substituted "specified in a section 51D notice",

      (c) subsection (5) is omitted, and

      (d) in the heading, for "**Committal**" there is substituted "**Sending**".

  (3) In section 77 (committal for trial: date of trial)—

      (a) in subsection (1), for "committal for trial or the giving of a notice of transfer under a relevant transfer provision" there is substituted "being sent for trial",

      (b) in subsection (2), for "committed by a magistrates' court or in respect of whom a notice of transfer under a relevant transfer provision has been given" there is substituted "sent for trial",

      (c) in subsection (3), for "of committal for trial or of a notice of transfer" there is substituted "when the defendant is sent for trial",

      (d) subsection (4) is omitted, and

      (e) in the heading, for "**Committal**" there is substituted "**Sending**".

  (4) In section 80 (process to compel appearance), in subsection (2), for "committed" there is substituted "sent".

  (5) In section 81—

      (a) in subsection (1)—

         (i) in paragraph (a)—

            (a) the words "who has been committed in custody for appearance before the Crown Court or in relation to whose case a notice of transfer has been given under a relevant transfer provision or" are omitted, and

            (b) after "51" there is inserted "or 51A",

         (ii) in paragraph (g), sub-paragraph (i) is omitted, and

      (b) subsection (7) is omitted.

Mental Health Act 1983 (c. 20)

55 (1) The Mental Health Act 1983 is amended as follows.

  (2) In section 43 (power of magistrates' court to commit for restriction order), for subsection (4) there is substituted—

    "(4) The powers of a magistrates' court under section 3 or 3B of the Powers of Criminal Courts (Sentencing) Act 2000 (which enable such a court to commit an offender to the Crown Court where the court is of the opinion, or it appears to the court, as mentioned in the section in question) shall also be exercisable by a magistrates' court where it is of that opinion (or it so appears to it) unless a hospital order is made in the offender's case with a restriction order."

  (3) In section 52 (further provisions as to persons remanded by magistrates' courts)—

      (a) in subsection (2), for "committed" there is substituted "sent",

      (b) in subsection (5), for "committed" there is substituted "sent",

      (c) in subsection (6), for "committed" there is substituted "sent", and

      (d) in subsection (7), for the words from "inquire" to "1980" there is substituted "send him to the Crown Court for trial under section 51 or 51A of the Crime and Disorder Act 1998", and in paragraph (b) of that subsection, the words "where the court proceeds under subsection (1) of that section" are omitted.

Police and Criminal Evidence Act 1984 (c. 60)

56 (1) The Police and Criminal Evidence Act 1984 is amended as follows.

  (2) In section 62 (intimate samples), in subsection (10)—

      (a) sub-paragraph (i) of paragraph (a) is omitted, and

      (b) in paragraph (aa), for sub-paragraphs (i) and (ii) there is substituted "paragraph 2 of Schedule 3 to the Crime and Disorder Act 1998 (applications for dismissal); and".

(3) In section 71 (microfilm copies), the paragraph beginning "Where the proceedings" is omitted.

(4) In section 76 (confessions), subsection (9) is omitted.

(5) In section 78 (exclusion of unfair evidence), subsection (3) is omitted.

Prosecution of Offences Act 1985 (c. 23)

57 (1) The Prosecution of Offences Act 1985 is amended as follows.

(2) In section 7A (powers of non-legal staff), for subsection (6) there is substituted—

"(6) This section applies to an offence if it is triable only on indictment or is an offence for which the accused has been sent for trial."

(3) In section 16 (defence costs)—

(a) in subsection (1), paragraph (b) is omitted, and

(b) in subsection (2)—

(i) in paragraph (a), for "committed" there is substituted "sent", and

(ii) paragraph (aa) is omitted, and

(c) subsection (12) is omitted.

(4) In section 21 (interpretation), in subsection (6)(b), for "committed" there is substituted "sent".

(5) In section 22 (power of Secretary of State to set time limits in relation to preliminary stages of criminal proceedings), in subsection (11)—

(a) in paragraph (a) of the definition of "appropriate court", for "committed for trial, sent for trial under section 51 of the Crime and Disorder Act 1998" there is substituted "sent for trial",

(b) for the definition of "custody of the Crown Court" there is substituted—

"custody of the Crown Court" includes custody to which a person is committed in pursuance of—

(a) section 43A of the Magistrates' Courts Act 1980 (magistrates' court dealing with a person brought before it following his arrest in pursuance of a warrant issued by the Crown Court); or

(b) section 52 of the Crime and Disorder Act 1998 (provisions supplementing section 51);".

(6) In section 23 (discontinuance of proceedings in magistrates' court), in subsection (2), for paragraphs (a) to (c) there is substituted—

"(a) any stage of the proceedings after the court has begun to hear evidence for the prosecution at a summary trial of the offence; or

(b) any stage of the proceedings after the accused has been sent for trial for the offence."

(7) In section 23A (discontinuance of proceedings after accused has been sent for trial)—

(a) in paragraph (b) of subsection (1), the words from "under" to "1998" are omitted, and

(b) in subsection (2), for "51(7)" there is substituted "51D(1)".

Criminal Justice Act 1987 (c. 38)

58 (1) The Criminal Justice Act 1987 is amended as follows.

(2) Sections 4 to 6 (which relate to the transfer of cases to the Crown Court) shall cease to have effect.

(3) In section 11 (restrictions on reporting)—

(a) in subsection (2), paragraph (a) is omitted,

(b) subsection (3) is omitted,

(c) in subsection (7), "(3)," is omitted,

(d) in subsection (8), "(3)," is omitted,

(e) subsections (9) and (10) are omitted,

(f) in subsection (11), paragraphs (a) and (d) are omitted.

Coroners Act 1988 (c. 13)

59 (1) The Coroners Act 1988 is amended as follows.

(2) In section 16 (adjournment of inquest in event of criminal proceedings)—

(a) in subsection (1)(b), for "charged before examining justices with" there is substituted "sent for trial for", and

(b) for subsection (8) there is substituted—

"(8) In this section, the "relevant criminal proceedings" means the proceedings—

(a) before a magistrates' court to determine whether the person charged is to be sent to the Crown Court for trial; or

        (b) before any court to which that person is sent for trial."
    (3) In section 17 (provisions supplementary to section 16)—
        (a) in subsection (2), for "committed" there is substituted "sent", and
        (b) in subsection (3)(b), for "committed" there is substituted "sent".

Criminal Justice Act 1988 (c. 33)

60   (1) The Criminal Justice Act 1988 is amended as follows.
    (2) In section 23 (first-hand hearsay), subsection (5) is omitted.
    (3) In section 24 (business etc documents), subsection (5) is omitted.
    (4) In section 26 (statements in certain documents), the paragraph beginning "This section shall not apply" is omitted.
    (5) In section 27 (proof of statements contained in documents), the paragraph beginning "This section shall not apply" is omitted.
    (6) In section 30 (expert reports), subsection (4A) is omitted.
    (7) In section 40 (power to join in indictment count for common assault etc), in subsection (1)—
        (a) the words "were disclosed to a magistrates' court inquiring into the offence as examining justices or" are omitted,
        (b) after "51" there is inserted "or 51A".
    (8) Section 41 (power of Crown Court to deal with summary offence where person committed for either way offence) shall cease to have effect.

Road Traffic Offenders Act 1988 (c. 53)

61   (1) The Road Traffic Offenders Act 1988 is amended as follows.
    (2) In section 11 (evidence by certificate as to driver, user or owner), subsection (3A) is omitted.
    (3) In section 13 (admissibility of records as evidence), subsection (7) is omitted.
    (4) In section 16 (documentary evidence as to specimens), subsection (6A) is omitted.
    (5) In section 20 (speeding offences etc), subsection (8A) is omitted.

Criminal Justice Act 1991 (c. 53)

62   (1) The Criminal Justice Act 1991 is amended as follows.
    (2) Section 53 (notices of transfer in certain cases involving children) shall cease to have effect.
    (3) Schedule 6 (notices of transfer: procedures in lieu of committal) shall cease to have effect.

Sexual Offences (Amendment) Act 1992 (c. 34)

63   In section 6 of the Sexual Offences (Amendment) Act 1992 (interpretation), in subsection (3)(c), for "commits him" there is substituted "sends him to the Crown Court".

Criminal Justice and Public Order Act 1994 (c. 33)

64   (1) The Criminal Justice and Public Order Act 1994 is amended as follows.
    (2) In section 34 (effect of accused's failure to mention facts when questioned or charged), in subsection (2)—
        (a) paragraph (a) is omitted, and
        (b) in paragraph (b), for sub-paragraphs (i) and (ii), there is substituted "paragraph 2 of Schedule 3 to the Crime and Disorder Act 1998".
    (3) In section 36 (effect of accused's failure or refusal to account for objects, substances or marks), in subsection (2)—
        (a) paragraph (a) is omitted, and
        (b) in paragraph (b), for sub-paragraphs (i) and (ii), there is substituted "paragraph 2 of Schedule 3 to the Crime and Disorder Act 1998".
    (4) In section 37 (effect of accused's failure or refusal to account for presence at a particular place), in subsection (2)—
        (a) paragraph (a) is omitted, and

(b) in paragraph (b), for sub-paragraphs (i) and (ii), there is substituted "paragraph 2 of Schedule 3 to the Crime and Disorder Act 1998".

Reserve Forces Act 1996 (c. 14)

65   In Schedule 2 to the Reserve Forces Act 1996 (deserters and absentees without leave), in paragraph 3, after sub-paragraph (2) there is inserted—
"(2A) The reference in sub-paragraph (2) to provisions of the Magistrates' Courts Act 1980 is to be taken to refer to those provisions as if no amendment to them had been made by the Criminal Justice Act 2003."

Criminal Procedure and Investigations Act 1996 (c. 25)

66   (1) The Criminal Procedure and Investigations Act 1996 is amended as follows.
      (2) In section 1 (application of this Part), in subsection (2)—
          (a) paragraphs (a) to (c) are omitted, and
          (b) in paragraph (cc), the words from "under" to the end are omitted.
      (3) In section 5 (compulsory disclosure by accused)—
          (a) in subsection (1), for "(2) to" there is substituted "(3A) and",
          (b) subsections (2) and (3) are omitted, and
          (c) in subsection (3A), in paragraph (b), for "subsection (7) of section 51" there is substituted "subsection (1) of section 51D".
      (4) In section 13 (time limits: transitional), in subsection (1), paragraphs (a) to (c) of the modified section 3(8) are omitted.
      (5) In section 21 (common law rules as to disclosure), in subsection (3), for paragraphs (b) and (c) there is substituted—
          "(b) the accused is sent for trial (where this Part applies by virtue of section 1(2)(cc)),".
      (6) In section 28 (introduction to Part 3), in subsection (1)—
          (a) for paragraph (a) there is substituted—
              "(a) on or after the appointed day the accused is sent for trial for the offence concerned,", and
          (b) paragraph (b) is omitted.
      (7) In section 39 (meaning of pre-trial hearing), in subsection (1), for paragraph (a) there is substituted—
          "(a) after the accused has been sent for trial for the offence, and".
      (8) Section 68 (use of written statements and depositions at trial) and Schedule 2 (statements and depositions) shall cease to have effect.

Sexual Offences (Protected Material) Act 1997 (c. 39)

67   In section 9 of the Sexual Offences (Protected Material) Act 1997 (modification and amendment of certain enactments), subsection (1) is omitted.

Crime and Disorder Act 1998 (c. 37)

68   The Crime and Disorder Act 1998 is amended as follows.
69   In section 52 (provisions supplementing section 51)—
          (a) in subsection (1), after "51" there is inserted "or 51A",
          (b) in subsection (3), after "51" there is inserted "or 51A",
          (c) in subsection (5), after "51" there is inserted "or 51A",
          (d) in subsection (6), after "51" there is inserted "or 51A", and
          (e) in the heading, after "**51**" there is inserted "**and 51A**".
70   In section 121 (short title, commencement and extent), in subsection (8), before "paragraphs 7(1)" there is inserted "paragraph 3 of Schedule 3 to this Act, section 52(6) above so far as relating to that paragraph,".
71   In paragraph 3 of Schedule 3 (reporting restrictions)—
          (a) in each of paragraphs (a) and (b) of sub-paragraph (1), for "Great Britain" there is substituted "the United Kingdom",
          (b) in sub-paragraph (8), after paragraph (b) there is inserted—
              "(bb) where the application made by the accused under paragraph 2(1) above relates to a charge for an offence in respect of which notice has been given to the court under section 51B of this Act, any relevant business information;",
          (c) after sub-paragraph (9) there is inserted—
              "(9A) The following is relevant business information for the purposes of sub-paragraph (8) above—
                  (a) any address used by the accused for carrying on a business on his own account;

(b) the name of any business which he was carrying on on his own account at any relevant time;

(c) the name of any firm in which he was a partner at any relevant time or by which he was engaged at any such time;

(d) the address of any such firm;

(e) the name of any company of which he was a director at any relevant time or by which he was otherwise engaged at any such time;

(f) the address of the registered or principal office of any such company;

(g) any working address of the accused in his capacity as a person engaged by any such company;

and here "engaged" means engaged under a contract of service or a contract for services.", and

(d) after sub-paragraph (11) there is inserted—

"(11A) Proceedings for an offence under this paragraph shall not, in Northern Ireland, be instituted otherwise than by or with the consent of the Attorney General for Northern Ireland."

72   In paragraph 4 of Schedule 3 (power of justice to take depositions etc), in sub-paragraph (12), for the definition of "the relevant date" there is substituted—

""the relevant date" means the expiry of the period referred to in paragraph 1(1) above."

Youth Justice and Criminal Evidence Act 1999 (c. 23)

73   (1) The Youth Justice and Criminal Evidence Act 1999 is amended as follows.

(2) In section 27 (video recorded evidence in chief), subsection (10) is omitted.

(3) In section 42 (interpretation and application of section 41), in subsection (3)—

(a) paragraphs (a) and (b) are omitted, and

(b) in paragraph (c), after "51" there is inserted "or 51A".

Powers of Criminal Courts (Sentencing) Act 2000 (c. 6)

74   (1) The Powers of Criminal Courts (Sentencing) Act 2000 is amended as follows.

(2) In section 8 (power and duty to remit young offenders to youth courts for sentence), in subsection (2), for paragraph (a) there is substituted—

"(a) if the offender was sent to the Crown Court for trial under section 51 or 51A of the Crime and Disorder Act 1998, to a youth court acting for the place where he was sent to the Crown Court for trial;".

(3) In section 89 (restriction on imposing imprisonment), in subsection (2)—

(a) in paragraph (b), the words "trial or" are omitted, and

(b) in paragraph (c), after "51" there is inserted "or 51A".

(4) In section 140 (enforcement of fines etc), in subsection (1)(b)—

(a) the words "was committed to the Crown Court to be tried or dealt with or by which he" are omitted, and

(b) after "51" there is inserted "or 51A".

(5) In section 148 (restitution orders), in subsection (6), for paragraph (b) there is substituted—

"(b) such documents as were served on the offender in pursuance of regulations made under paragraph 1 of Schedule 3 to the Crime and Disorder Act 1998."

(6) In Schedule 11, paragraph 9 is omitted.

Proceeds of Crime Act 2002 (c. 29)

75   (1) The Proceeds of Crime Act 2002 is amended as follows.

(2) In section 6 (making of confiscation order), in subsection (2)(b), for "section 3, 4 or 6" there is substituted "section 3, 3A, 3B, 3C, 4, 4A or 6".

(3) In section 27 (defendant absconds after being convicted or committed), in subsection (2)(b), for "section 3, 4 or 6" there is substituted "section 3, 3A, 3B, 3C, 4, 4A or 6".

(4) In section 70 (committal by magistrates' court), in subsection (5), after "way)" there is inserted "or under section 3B(2) of that Act (committal of child or young person)".

SCHEDULE 4   **Section 62**

QUALIFYING OFFENCES FOR PURPOSES OF SECTION 62

PART 1

LIST OF OFFENCES

Offences Against the Person

Murder

1   Murder.

Attempted murder

2   An offence under section 1 of the Criminal Attempts Act 1981 (c. 47) of attempting to commit murder.

Soliciting murder

3   An offence under section 4 of the Offences against the Person Act 1861 (c. 100).

Manslaughter

4   Manslaughter.

Wounding or causing grievous bodily harm with intent

5   An offence under section 18 of the Offences against the Person Act 1861 (c. 100).

Kidnapping

6   Kidnapping.

Sexual Offences

Rape

7   An offence under section 1 of the Sexual Offences Act 1956 (c. 69) or section 1 of the Sexual Offences Act 2003 (c. 42).

Attempted rape

8   An offence under section 1 of the Criminal Attempts Act 1981 (c. 47) of attempting to commit an offence under section 1 of the Sexual Offences Act 1956 or section 1 of the Sexual Offences Act 2003.

Intercourse with a girl under thirteen

9   An offence under section 5 of the Sexual Offences Act 1956.

Incest by a man with a girl under thirteen

10   An offence under section 10 of the Sexual Offences Act 1956 alleged to have been committed with a girl under thirteen.

Assault by penetration

11   An offence under section 2 of the Sexual Offences Act 2003.

Causing a person to engage in sexual activity without consent

12   An offence under section 4 of the Sexual Offences Act 2003 where it is alleged that the activity caused involved penetration within subsection (4)(a) to (d) of that section.

Rape of a child under thirteen

13   An offence under section 5 of the Sexual Offences Act 2003.

Attempted rape of a child under thirteen

14   An offence under section 1 of the Criminal Attempts Act 1981 of attempting to commit an offence under section 5 of the Sexual Offences Act 2003.

Assault of a child under thirteen by penetration

15   An offence under section 6 of the Sexual Offences Act 2003.

Causing a child under thirteen to engage in sexual activity

16   An offence under section 8 of the Sexual Offences Act 2003 (c. 42) where it is alleged that an activity involving penetration within subsection (2)(a) to (d) of that section was caused.

Sexual activity with a person with a mental disorder impeding choice

17   An offence under section 30 of the Sexual Offences Act 2003 where it is alleged that the touching involved penetration within subsection (3)(a) to (d) of that section.

Causing or inciting a person with a mental disorder impeding choice to engage in sexual activity

18   An offence under section 31 of the Sexual Offences Act 2003 where it is alleged that an activity involving penetration within subsection (3)(a) to (d) of that section was caused.

Drugs Offences

Unlawful importation of Class A drug

19   An offence under section 50(2) of the Customs and Excise Management Act 1979 (c. 2) alleged to have been committed in respect of a Class A drug (as defined by section 2 of the Misuse of Drugs Act 1971 (c. 38)).

Unlawful exportation of Class A drug

20   An offence under section 68(2) of the Customs and Excise Management Act 1979 alleged to have been committed in respect of a Class A drug (as defined by section 2 of the Misuse of Drugs Act 1971).

Fraudulent evasion in respect of Class A drug

21   An offence under section 170(1) or (2) of the Customs and Excise Management Act 1979 alleged to have been committed in respect of a Class A drug (as defined by section 2 of the Misuse of Drugs Act 1971).

Producing or being concerned in production of Class A drug

22   An offence under section 4(2) of the Misuse of Drugs Act 1971 alleged to have been committed in relation to a Class A drug (as defined by section 2 of that Act).

Supplying or offering to supply Class A drug

23   An offence under section 4(3) of the Misuse of Drugs Act 1971 alleged to have been committed in relation to a Class A drug (as defined by section 2 of that Act).

Theft Offences

Robbery

24   An offence under section 8(1) of the Theft Act 1968 (c. 60) where it is alleged that, at some time during the commission of the offence, the defendant had in his possession a firearm or imitation firearm (as defined by section 57 of the Firearms Act 1968 (c. 27)).

Criminal Damage Offences

Arson endangering life

25   An offence under section 1(2) of the Criminal Damage Act 1971 (c. 48) alleged to have been committed by destroying or damaging property by fire.

Causing explosion likely to endanger life or property

26   An offence under section 2 of the Explosive Substances Act 1883 (c. 3).

Intent or conspiracy to cause explosion likely to endanger life or property

27   An offence under section 3(1)(a) of the Explosive Substances Act 1883.

War Crimes and Terrorism

Genocide, crimes against humanity and war crimes

28   An offence under section 51 or 52 of the International Criminal Court Act 2001 (c. 17).

Grave breaches of the Geneva Conventions

29   An offence under section 1 of the Geneva Conventions Act 1957 (c. 52).

Directing terrorist organisation

30   An offence under section 56 of the Terrorism Act 2000 (c. 11).

Hostage-taking

31   An offence under section 1 of the Taking of Hostages Act 1982 (c. 28).

Hijacking and Other Offences Relating to Aviation, Maritime and Rail Security

Hijacking of aircraft

32   An offence under section 1 of the Aviation Security Act 1982 (c. 36).

Destroying, damaging or endangering the safety of an aircraft

33   An offence under section 2 of the Aviation Security Act 1982.

Hijacking of ships

34   An offence under section 9 of the Aviation and Maritime Security Act 1990 (c. 31).

Seizing or exercising control of fixed platforms

35   An offence under section 10 of the Aviation and Maritime Security Act 1990.

Destroying ships or fixed platforms or endangering their safety

36   An offence under section 11 of the Aviation and Maritime Security Act 1990.

Hijacking of Channel Tunnel trains

37   An offence under article 4 of the Channel Tunnel (Security) Order 1994 (S.I.1994/570).

Seizing or exercising control of the Channel Tunnel system

38   An offence under article 5 of the Channel Tunnel (Security) Order 1994 (S.I.1994/570).

Conspiracy

Conspiracy

39   An offence under section 1 of the Criminal Law Act 1977 (c. 45) of conspiracy to commit an offence listed in this Part of this Schedule.

PART 2

SUPPLEMENTARY

40   A reference in Part 1 of this Schedule to an offence includes a reference to an offence of aiding, abetting, counselling or procuring the commission of the offence.

41   A reference in Part 1 of this Schedule to an enactment includes a reference to the enactment as enacted and as amended from time to time.

SCHEDULE 5   **Section 75**

QUALIFYING OFFENCES FOR PURPOSES OF PART 10

PART 1

LIST OF OFFENCES FOR ENGLAND AND WALES

Offences Against the Person

Murder

1   Murder.

Attempted murder

2   An offence under section 1 of the Criminal Attempts Act 1981 (c. 47) of attempting to commit murder.

Soliciting murder

3   An offence under section 4 of the Offences against the Person Act 1861 (c. 100).

Manslaughter

4   Manslaughter.

Kidnapping

5   Kidnapping.

Sexual Offences

Rape

6   An offence under section 1 of the Sexual Offences Act 1956 (c. 69) or section 1 of the Sexual Offences Act 2003 (c. 42).

Attempted rape

7   An offence under section 1 of the Criminal Attempts Act 1981 of attempting to commit an offence under section 1 of the Sexual Offences Act 1956 or section 1 of the Sexual Offences Act 2003.

Intercourse with a girl under thirteen

8   An offence under section 5 of the Sexual Offences Act 1956.

Incest by a man with a girl under thirteen

9   An offence under section 10 of the Sexual Offences Act 1956 alleged to have been committed with a girl under thirteen.

Assault by penetration

10   An offence under section 2 of the Sexual Offences Act 2003 (c. 42).

Causing a person to engage in sexual activity without consent

11   An offence under section 4 of the Sexual Offences Act 2003 where it is alleged that the activity caused involved penetration within subsection (4)(a) to (d) of that section.

Rape of a child under thirteen

12   An offence under section 5 of the Sexual Offences Act 2003.

Attempted rape of a child under thirteen

13   An offence under section 1 of the Criminal Attempts Act 1981 (c. 47) of attempting to commit an offence under section 5 of the Sexual Offences Act 2003.

Assault of a child under thirteen by penetration

14   An offence under section 6 of the Sexual Offences Act 2003.

Causing a child under thirteen to engage in sexual activity

15   An offence under section 8 of the Sexual Offences Act 2003 where it is alleged that an activity involving penetration within subsection (2)(a) to (d) of that section was caused.

Sexual activity with a person with a mental disorder impeding choice

16   An offence under section 30 of the Sexual Offences Act 2003 where it is alleged that the touching involved penetration within subsection (3)(a) to (d) of that section.

Causing a person with a mental disorder impeding choice to engage in sexual activity

17   An offence under section 31 of the Sexual Offences Act 2003 where it is alleged that an activity involving penetration within subsection (3)(a) to (d) of that section was caused.

Drugs Offences

Unlawful importation of Class A drug

18   An offence under section 50(2) of the Customs and Excise Management Act 1979 (c. 2) alleged to have been committed in respect of a Class A drug (as defined by section 2 of the Misuse of Drugs Act 1971 (c. 38)).

Unlawful exportation of Class A drug

19   An offence under section 68(2) of the Customs and Excise Management Act 1979 alleged to have been committed in respect of a Class A drug (as defined by section 2 of the Misuse of Drugs Act 1971).

Fraudulent evasion in respect of Class A drug

20   An offence under section 170(1) or (2) of the Customs and Excise Management Act 1979 (c. 2) alleged to have been committed in respect of a Class A drug (as defined by section 2 of the Misuse of Drugs Act 1971 (c. 38)).

Producing or being concerned in production of Class A drug

21   An offence under section 4(2) of the Misuse of Drugs Act 1971 alleged to have been committed in relation to a Class A drug (as defined by section 2 of that Act).

Criminal Damage Offences

Arson endangering life

22   An offence under section 1(2) of the Criminal Damage Act 1971 (c. 48) alleged to have been committed by destroying or damaging property by fire.

Causing explosion likely to endanger life or property

23   An offence under section 2 of the Explosive Substances Act 1883 (c. 3).

Intent or conspiracy to cause explosion likely to endanger life or property

24   An offence under section 3(1)(a) of the Explosive Substances Act 1883.

War Crimes and Terrorism

Genocide, crimes against humanity and war crimes

25   An offence under section 51 or 52 of the International Criminal Court Act 2001 (c. 17).

Grave breaches of the Geneva Conventions

26   An offence under section 1 of the Geneva Conventions Act 1957 (c. 52).

Directing terrorist organisation

27   An offence under section 56 of the Terrorism Act 2000 (c. 11).

Hostage-taking

28   An offence under section 1 of the Taking of Hostages Act 1982 (c. 28).

Conspiracy

Conspiracy

29   An offence under section 1 of the Criminal Law Act 1977 (c. 45) of conspiracy to commit an offence listed in this Part of this Schedule.

PART 2

LIST OF OFFENCES FOR NORTHERN IRELAND

Offences Against the Person

Murder

30   Murder.

Attempted murder

31   An offence under Article 3 of the Criminal Attempts and Conspiracy (Northern Ireland) Order 1983 of attempting to commit murder.

Soliciting murder

32   An offence under section 4 of the Offences against the Person Act 1861 (c. 100).

Manslaughter

33   Manslaughter.

Kidnapping

34   Kidnapping.

Sexual Offences

Rape

35   Rape.

Attempted rape

36   An offence under section 2 of the Attempted Rape, etc., Act (Northern Ireland) 1960.

Intercourse with a girl under fourteen

37   An offence under section 4 of the Criminal Law Amendment Act 1885 (c. 69) of unlawfully and carnally knowing a girl under fourteen.

Incest by a man with a girl under fourteen

38   An offence under section 1(1) of the Punishment of Incest Act 1908 (c.45) alleged to have been committed with a girl under fourteen.

Drugs Offences

Unlawful importation of Class A drug

39   An offence under section 50(2) of the Customs and Excise Management Act 1979 (c. 2) alleged to have been committed in respect of a Class A drug (as defined by section 2 of the Misuse of Drugs Act 1971 (c. 38)).

Unlawful exportation of Class A drug

40   An offence under section 68(2) of the Customs and Excise Management Act 1979 alleged to have been committed in respect of a Class A drug (as defined by section 2 of the Misuse of Drugs Act 1971).

Fraudulent evasion in respect of Class A drug

41   An offence under section 170(1) or (2) of the Customs and Excise Management Act 1979 alleged to have been committed in respect of a Class A drug (as defined by section 2 of the Misuse of Drugs Act 1971).

Producing or being concerned in production of Class A drug

42   An offence under section 4(2) of the Misuse of Drugs Act 1971 alleged to have been committed in respect of a Class A drug (as defined by section 2 of that Act).

Criminal Damage Offences

Arson endangering life

43   An offence under Article 3(2) of the Criminal Damage (Northern Ireland) Order 1977 alleged to have been committed by destroying or damaging property by fire.

Causing explosion likely to endanger life or property

44   An offence under section 2 of the Explosive Substances Act 1883 (c. 3).

Intent or conspiracy to cause explosion likely to endanger life or property

45   An offence under section 3(1)(a) of the Explosive Substances Act 1883.

War Crimes and Terrorism

Genocide, crimes against humanity and war crimes

46   An offence under section 51 or 52 of the International Criminal Court Act 2001 (c. 17).

Grave breaches of the Geneva Conventions

47   An offence under section 1 of the Geneva Conventions Act 1957 (c. 52).

Directing terrorist organisation

48   An offence under section 56 of the Terrorism Act 2000 (c. 11).

Hostage-taking

49   An offence under section 1 of the Taking of Hostages Act 1982 (c. 28).

Conspiracy

Conspiracy

50   An offence under Article 9 of the Criminal Attempts and Conspiracy (Northern Ireland) Order 1983 of conspiracy to commit an offence listed in this Part of this Schedule.

PART 3

SUPPLEMENTARY

51   A reference in this Schedule to an offence includes a reference to an offence of aiding, abetting, counselling or procuring the commission of the offence.

52   A reference in this Schedule to an enactment includes a reference to the enactment as enacted and as amended from time to time.

SCHEDULE 6   Section 113

EVIDENCE OF BAD CHARACTER: ARMED FORCES

1   Sections 98 to 106, 109, 110 and 112, in so far as they are not applied in relation to proceedings before service courts by provision contained in or made under any other Act, have effect in relation to such proceedings (whether in the United Kingdom or elsewhere) as they have effect in relation to criminal proceedings.

2   Section 103, as it applies in relation to proceedings before service courts, has effect with the substitution in subsection (4)(a) of "charge sheet" for "written charge or indictment".

3   (1) Section 107 has effect in relation to proceedings before courts-martial (whether in the United Kingdom or elsewhere) with the following modifications.

        (2) In subsection (1)—

           (a) for "judge and jury" substitute "court-martial";

           (b) for "the court is satisfied" substitute "the judge advocate is satisfied";

           (c) for the words after paragraph (b) substitute "the judge advocate must either direct the court to acquit the defendant of the offence or, if he considers that there ought to be a retrial, dissolve the court."

        (3) In subsection (2)—

           (a) for "jury" substitute "court";

           (b) for "the court is satisfied" substitute "the judge advocate is satisfied".

        (4) In subsection (3)—

           (a) for paragraph (a) substitute—

             "(a) a court is required to determine under section 115B(2) of the Army Act 1955, section 115B(2) of the Air Force Act 1955 or section 62B(2) of the Naval Discipline Act 1957 whether a person charged with an offence did the act or made the omission charged,";

           (b) for "the court is satisfied" substitute "the judge advocate is satisfied";

           (c) for the words after paragraph (c) substitute "the judge advocate must either direct the court to acquit the defendant of the offence or, if he considers that there ought to be a rehearing, dissolve the court."

        (5) For subsection (4) substitute—

           "(4) This section does not prejudice any other power a judge advocate may have to direct a court to acquit a person of an offence or to dissolve a court."

4   Section 110, as it applies in relation to proceedings before service courts, has effect with the substitution of the following for subsection (1)—

        "(1) Where the court makes a relevant ruling—

           (a) it must state in open court (but, in the case of a ruling by a judge advocate in proceedings before a court-martial, in the absence of the other members of the court) its reasons for the ruling;

           (b) if it is a Standing Civilian Court, it must cause the ruling and the reasons for it to be entered in the note of the court's proceedings."

5   Section 111 has effect as if, in subsection (7), the definition of "rules of court" included rules regulating the practice and procedure of service courts.

6   (1) In this Schedule, and in section 107 as applied by this Schedule, "court-martial" means a court-martial constituted under the Army Act 1955 (3 & 4 Eliz. 2 c. 18), the Air Force Act 1955 (3 & 4 Eliz. 2 c. 19) or the Naval Discipline Act 1957 (c. 53).

        (2) In this Schedule "service court" means—

           (a) a court-martial;

           (b) a summary appeal court constituted under section 83ZA of the Army Act 1955, section 83ZA of the Air Force Act 1955 or section 52FF of the Naval Discipline Act 1957;

           (c) the Courts-Martial Appeal Court;

           (d) a Standing Civilian Court.

SCHEDULE 7   **Section 135**

HEARSAY EVIDENCE: ARMED FORCES

Application to proceedings before service courts

1   Sections 114 to 121, 123, 124, 126, 127 to 129 and 133 and 134, in so far as they are not applied in relation to proceedings before service courts by provision contained in or made under any other Act, have effect in relation to such proceedings (whether in the United Kingdom or elsewhere) as they have effect in relation to criminal proceedings.

2   (1) In their application to such proceedings those sections have effect with the following modifications.

        (2) In section 116(2)(c) for "United Kingdom" substitute "country where the court is sitting".

        (3) In section 117 insert after subsection (7)—

           "(8) In subsection (4) "criminal proceedings" includes summary proceedings under section 76B of the Army Act 1955, section 76B of the Air Force Act 1955 or section 52D of the Naval Discipline Act 1957; and the definition of "criminal proceedings" in section 134(1) has effect accordingly."

        (4) In section 123(4) for paragraph (a) substitute—

"(a) in the case of proceedings before a court-martial, proceedings held for the determination of the issue must take place before the judge advocate in the absence of the other members of the court;".

(5) In section 127, for subsection (7) substitute—

"(7) The appropriate rules are those regulating the practice and procedure of service courts."

(6) In section 132(10), at the end of the definition of "rules of court" insert—

"(d) rules regulating the practice and procedure of service courts."

(7) In section 134 insert after subsection (1)—

"(1A) In this Part "criminal investigation" includes any investigation which may lead—

(a) to proceedings before a court-martial or Standing Civilian Court, or

(b) to summary proceedings under section 76B of the Army Act 1955, section 76B of the Air Force Act 1955 or section 52D of the Naval Discipline Act 1957."

3   (1) Section 122 has effect in relation to proceedings before courts-martial (whether in the United Kingdom or elsewhere) with the following modifications.

(2) In subsection (1) for "judge and jury" substitute "court-martial".

(3) In subsection (2)—

(a) for "jury when they retire to consider their" substitute "court when it retires to consider its".

(b) for "the court" in paragraph (a) substitute "the judge advocate";

(c) for "the jury" in paragraph (b) substitute "the court".

4   (1) Section 125 has effect in relation to proceedings before courts-martial (whether in the United Kingdom or elsewhere) with the following modifications.

(2) In subsection (1)—

(a) for "judge and jury" substitute "court-martial";

(b) for "the court is satisfied" substitute "the judge advocate is satisfied";

(c) for the words after paragraph (b) substitute "the judge advocate must either direct the court to acquit the defendant of the offence or, if he considers that there ought to be a retrial, dissolve the court."

(3) In subsection (2)—

(a) for "jury" substitute "court";

(b) for "the court is satisfied" substitute "the judge advocate is satisfied".

(4) In subsection (3)—

(a) for paragraph (a) substitute—

"(a) a court is required to determine under section 115B(2) of the Army Act 1955, section 115B(2) of the Air Force Act 1955 or section 62B(2) of the Naval Discipline Act 1957 whether a person charged with an offence did the act or made the omission charged,";

(b) for "the court is satisfied" substitute "the judge advocate is satisfied";

(c) for the words after paragraph (b) substitute "the judge advocate must either direct the court to acquit the defendant of the offence or, if he considers that there ought to be a rehearing, dissolve the court."

(5) For subsection (4) substitute—

"(4) This section does not prejudice any other power a judge advocate may have to direct a court to acquit a person of an offence or to dissolve a court."

Amendments

5   For paragraph 1 of Schedule 1 to the Courts-Martial (Appeals) Act 1968 (c. 20) (use at retrial under Naval Discipline Act 1957 of record of evidence given at original trial) substitute—

"1 Evidence given at the retrial of any person under section 19 of this Act shall be given orally if it was given orally at the original trial, unless—

(a) all the parties to the retrial agree otherwise;

(b) section 116 of the Criminal Justice Act 2003 applies (admissibility of hearsay evidence where a witness is unavailable); or

(c) the witness is unavailable to give evidence, otherwise than as mentioned in subsection (2) of that section, and section 114(1)(d) of that Act applies (admission of hearsay evidence under residual discretion)."

6   For paragraph 3 of that Schedule (use at retrial under Army Act 1955 of record of evidence given at original trial) substitute—

"3 Evidence given at the retrial of any person under section 19 of this Act shall be given orally if it was given orally at the original trial, unless—

(a) all the parties to the retrial agree otherwise;

(b) section 116 of the Criminal Justice Act 2003 applies (admissibility of hearsay evidence where a witness is unavailable); or

(c) the witness is unavailable to give evidence, otherwise than as mentioned in subsection (2) of that section, and section 114(1)(d) of that Act applies (admission of hearsay evidence under residual discretion)."

7   For paragraph 5 of that Schedule (use at retrial under Air Force Act 1955 of record of evidence given at original trial) substitute—

"5 Evidence given at the retrial of any person under section 19 of this Act shall be given orally if it was given orally at the original trial, unless—

(a) all the parties to the retrial agree otherwise;

(b) section 116 of the Criminal Justice Act 2003 applies (admissibility of hearsay evidence where a witness is unavailable); or

(c) the witness is unavailable to give evidence, otherwise than as mentioned in subsection (2) of that section, and section 114(1)(d) of that Act applies (admission of hearsay evidence under residual discretion)."

Interpretation

8   In this Schedule, and in any provision of this Part as applied by this Schedule—

"court-martial" means a court-martial constituted under the Army Act 1955 (3 & 4 Eliz. 2 c. 18), the Air Force Act 1955 (3 & 4 Eliz. 2 c. 19) or the Naval Discipline Act 1957 (c. 53);

"service court" means—

(a) a court-martial;

(b) a summary appeal court constituted under section 83ZA of the Army Act 1955, section 83ZA of the Air Force Act 1955 or section 52FF of the Naval Discipline Act 1957;

(c) the Courts-Martial Appeal Court;

(d) a Standing Civilian Court.

SCHEDULE 8   **Section 179**

BREACH, REVOCATION OR AMENDMENT OF COMMUNITY ORDER

PART 1

PRELIMINARY

Interpretation

1   In this Schedule—

"the offender", in relation to a community order, means the person in respect of whom the order is made;

"the petty sessions area concerned", in relation to a community order, means the petty sessions area for the time being specified in the order;

"the responsible officer" has the meaning given by section 197.

2   In this Schedule—

(a) references to a drug rehabilitation requirement of a community order being subject to review are references to that requirement being subject to review in accordance with section 210(1)(b);

(b) references to the court responsible for a community order imposing a drug rehabilitation requirement which is subject to review are to be construed in accordance with section 210(2).

3   For the purposes of this Schedule—

(a) a requirement falling within any paragraph of section 177(1) is of the same kind as any other requirement falling within that paragraph, and

(b) an electronic monitoring requirement is a requirement of the same kind as any requirement falling within section 177(1) to which it relates.

Orders made on appeal

4   Where a community order has been made on appeal, it is to be taken for the purposes of this Schedule to have been made by the Crown Court.

PART 2

BREACH OF REQUIREMENT OF ORDER

Duty to give warning

5 (1) If the responsible officer is of the opinion that the offender has failed without reasonable excuse to comply with any of the requirements of a community order, the officer must give him a warning under this paragraph unless—

    (a) the offender has within the previous twelve months been given a warning under this paragraph in relation to a failure to comply with any of the requirements of the order, or

    (b) the officer causes an information to be laid before a justice of the peace in respect of the failure.

  (2) A warning under this paragraph must—

    (a) describe the circumstances of the failure,

    (b) state that the failure is unacceptable, and

    (c) inform the offender that, if within the next twelve months he again fails to comply with any requirement of the order, he will be liable to be brought before a court.

  (3) The responsible officer must, as soon as practicable after the warning has been given, record that fact.

  (4) In relation to any community order which was made by the Crown Court and does not include a direction that any failure to comply with the requirements of the order is to be dealt with by a magistrates' court, the reference in sub-paragraph (1)(b) to a justice of the peace is to be read as a reference to the Crown Court.

Breach of order after warning

6 (1) If—

    (a) the responsible officer has given a warning under paragraph 5 to the offender in respect of a community order, and

    (b) at any time within the twelve months beginning with the date on which the warning was given, the responsible officer is of the opinion that the offender has since that date failed without reasonable excuse to comply with any of the requirements of the order,

    the officer must cause an information to be laid before a justice of the peace in respect of the failure in question.

  (2) In relation to any community order which was made by the Crown Court and does not include a direction that any failure to comply with the requirements of the order is to be dealt with by a magistrates' court, the reference in sub-paragraph (1) to a justice of the peace is to be read as a reference to the Crown Court.

Issue of summons or warrant by justice of the peace

7 (1) This paragraph applies to—

    (a) a community order made by a magistrates' court, or

    (b) any community order which was made by the Crown Court and includes a direction that any failure to comply with the requirements of the order is to be dealt with by a magistrates' court.

  (2) If at any time while a community order to which this paragraph applies is in force it appears on information to a justice of the peace acting for the petty sessions area concerned that the offender has failed to comply with any of the requirements of the order, the justice may—

    (a) issue a summons requiring the offender to appear at the place and time specified in it, or

    (b) if the information is in writing and on oath, issue a warrant for his arrest.

  (3) Any summons or warrant issued under this paragraph must direct the offender to appear or be brought—

    (a) in the case of a community order imposing a drug rehabilitation requirement which is subject to review, before the magistrates' court responsible for the order, or

    (b) in any other case, before a magistrates' court acting for the petty sessions area concerned.

  (4) Where a summons issued under sub-paragraph (2)(a) requires the offender to appear before a magistrates' court and the offender does not appear in answer to the summons, the magistrates' court may issue a warrant for the arrest of the offender.

Issue of summons or warrant by Crown Court

8   (1) This paragraph applies to a community order made by the Crown Court which does not include a direction that any failure to comply with the requirements of the order is to be dealt with by a magistrates' court.

     (2) If at any time while a community order to which this paragraph applies is in force it appears on information to the Crown Court that the offender has failed to comply with any of the requirements of the order, the Crown Court may—

         (a) issue a summons requiring the offender to appear at the place and time specified in it, or

         (b) if the information is in writing and on oath, issue a warrant for his arrest.

     (3) Any summons or warrant issued under this paragraph must direct the offender to appear or be brought before the Crown Court.

     (4) Where a summons issued under sub-paragraph (2)(a) requires the offender to appear before the Crown Court and the offender does not appear in answer to the summons, the Crown Court may issue a warrant for the arrest of the offender.

Powers of magistrates' court

9   (1) If it is proved to the satisfaction of a magistrates' court before which an offender appears or is brought under paragraph 7 that he has failed without reasonable excuse to comply with any of the requirements of the community order, the court must deal with him in respect of the failure in any one of the following ways—

         (a) by amending the terms of the community order so as to impose more onerous requirements which the court could include if it were then making the order;

         (b) where the community order was made by a magistrates' court, by dealing with him, for the offence in respect of which the order was made, in any way in which the court could deal with him if he had just been convicted by it of the offence;

         (c) where—

            (i) the community order was made by a magistrates' court,

            (ii) the offence in respect of which the order was made was not an offence punishable by imprisonment,

            (iii) the offender is aged 18 or over, and

            (iv) the offender has wilfully and persistently failed to comply with the requirements of the order,

            by dealing with him, in respect of that offence, by imposing a sentence of imprisonment for a term not exceeding 51 weeks.

     (2) In dealing with an offender under sub-paragraph (1), a magistrates' court must take into account the extent to which the offender has complied with the requirements of the community order.

     (3) In dealing with an offender under sub-paragraph (1)(a), the court may extend the duration of particular requirements (subject to any limit imposed by Chapter 4 of Part 12 of this Act) but may not extend the period specified under section 177(5).

     (4) In dealing with an offender under sub-paragraph (1)(b), the court may, in the case of an offender who has wilfully and persistently failed to comply with the requirements of the community order, impose a custodial sentence (where the order was made in respect of an offence punishable with such a sentence) notwithstanding anything in section 152(2).

     (5) Where a magistrates' court deals with an offender under sub-paragraph (1)(b) or (c), it must revoke the community order if it is still in force.

     (6) Where a community order was made by the Crown Court and a magistrates' court would (apart from this sub-paragraph) be required to deal with the offender under sub-paragraph (1)(a), (b) or (c), it may instead commit him to custody or release him on bail until he can be brought or appear before the Crown Court.

     (7) A magistrates' court which deals with an offender's case under sub-paragraph (6) must send to the Crown Court—

         (a) a certificate signed by a justice of the peace certifying that the offender has failed to comply with the requirements of the community order in the respect specified in the certificate, and

         (b) such other particulars of the case as may be desirable;

         and a certificate purporting to be so signed is admissible as evidence of the failure before the Crown Court.

     (8) A person sentenced under sub-paragraph (1)(b) or (c) for an offence may appeal to the Crown Court against the sentence.

Powers of Crown Court

10 (1) Where under paragraph 8 or by virtue of paragraph 9(6) an offender appears or is brought before the Crown Court and it is proved to the satisfaction of that court that he has failed without reasonable excuse to comply with any of the requirements of the community order, the Crown Court must deal with him in respect of the failure in any one of the following ways—

(a) by amending the terms of the community order so as to impose more onerous requirements which the Crown Court could impose if it were then making the order;

(b) by dealing with him, for the offence in respect of which the order was made, in any way in which he could have been dealt with for that offence by the court which made the order if the order had not been made;

(c) where—

(i) the offence in respect of which the order was made was not an offence punishable by imprisonment,

(ii) the offender is aged 18 or over,

(iii) the offender has wilfully and persistently failed to comply with the requirements of the order,

by dealing with him, in respect of that offence, by imposing a sentence of imprisonment for a term not exceeding 51 weeks.

(2) In dealing with an offender under sub-paragraph (1), the Crown Court must take into account the extent to which the offender has complied with the requirements of the community order.

(3) In dealing with an offender under sub-paragraph (1)(a), the court may extend the duration of particular requirements (subject to any limit imposed by Chapter 4 of Part 12 of this Act) but may not extend the period specified under section 177(5).

(4) In dealing with an offender under sub-paragraph (1)(b), the Crown Court may, in the case of an offender who has wilfully and persistently failed to comply with the requirements of the community order, impose a custodial sentence (where the order was made in respect of an offence punishable with such a sentence) notwithstanding anything in section 152(2).

(5) Where the Crown Court deals with an offender under sub-paragraph (1)(b) or (c), it must revoke the community order if it is still in force.

(6) In proceedings before the Crown Court under this paragraph any question whether the offender has failed to comply with the requirements of the community order is to be determined by the court and not by the verdict of a jury.

Restriction of powers in paragraphs 9 and 10 where treatment required

11 (1) An offender who is required by any of the following requirements of a community order—

(a) a mental health treatment requirement,

(b) a drug rehabilitation requirement, or

(c) an alcohol treatment requirement,

to submit to treatment for his mental condition, or his dependency on or propensity to misuse drugs or alcohol, is not to be treated for the purposes of paragraph 9 or 10 as having failed to comply with that requirement on the ground only that he had refused to undergo any surgical, electrical or other treatment if, in the opinion of the court, his refusal was reasonable having regard to all the circumstances.

(2) A court may not under paragraph 9(1)(a) or 10(1)(a) amend a mental health treatment requirement, a drug rehabilitation requirement or an alcohol treatment requirement unless the offender expresses his willingness to comply with the requirement as amended.

Supplementary

12 Where a community order was made by a magistrates' court in the case of an offender under 18 years of age in respect of an offence triable only on indictment in the case of an adult, any powers exercisable under paragraph 9(1)(b) in respect of the offender after he attains the age of 18 are powers to do either or both of the following—

(a) to impose a fine not exceeding £5,000 for the offence in respect of which the order was made;

(b) to deal with the offender for that offence in any way in which a magistrates' court could deal with him if it had just convicted him of an offence punishable with imprisonment for a term not exceeding 51 weeks.

PART 3

REVOCATION OF ORDER

Revocation of order with or without re-sentencing: powers of magistrates' court

13 (1) This paragraph applies where a community order, other than an order made by the Crown Court and falling within paragraph 14(1)(a), is in force and on the application of the offender or the responsible officer it appears to the appropriate magistrates' court that, having regard to circumstances which have arisen since the order was made, it would be in the interests of justice—
 (a) for the order to be revoked, or
 (b) for the offender to be dealt with in some other way for the offence in respect of which the order was made.
 (2) The appropriate magistrates' court may—
 (a) revoke the order, or
 (b) both—
  (i) revoke the order, and
  (ii) deal with the offender, for the offence in respect of which the order was made, in any way in which it could deal with him if he had just been convicted by the court of the offence.
 (3) The circumstances in which a community order may be revoked under sub-paragraph (2) include the offender's making good progress or his responding satisfactorily to supervision or treatment (as the case requires).
 (4) In dealing with an offender under sub-paragraph (2)(b), a magistrates' court must take into account the extent to which the offender has complied with the requirements of the community order.
 (5) A person sentenced under sub-paragraph (2)(b) for an offence may appeal to the Crown Court against the sentence.
 (6) Where a magistrates' court proposes to exercise its powers under this paragraph otherwise than on the application of the offender, it must summon him to appear before the court and, if he does not appear in answer to the summons, may issue a warrant for his arrest.
 (7) In this paragraph "the appropriate magistrates' court" means—
 (a) in the case of an order imposing a drug rehabilitation requirement which is subject to review, the magistrates' court responsible for the order, and
 (b) in the case of any other community order, a magistrates' court acting for the petty sessions area concerned.

Revocation of order with or without re-sentencing: powers of Crown Court

14 (1) This paragraph applies where—
 (a) there is in force a community order made by the Crown Court which does not include a direction that any failure to comply with the requirements of the order is to be dealt with by a magistrates' court, and
 (b) the offender or the responsible officer applies to the Crown Court for the order to be revoked or for the offender to be dealt with in some other way for the offence in respect of which the order was made.
 (2) If it appears to the Crown Court to be in the interests of justice to do so, having regard to circumstances which have arisen since the order was made, the Crown Court may—
 (a) revoke the order, or
 (b) both—
  (i) revoke the order, and
  (ii) deal with the offender, for the offence in respect of which the order was made, in any way in which he could have been dealt with for that offence by the court which made the order if the order had not been made.
 (3) The circumstances in which a community order may be revoked under sub-paragraph (2) include the offender's making good progress or his responding satisfactorily to supervision or treatment (as the case requires).
 (4) In dealing with an offender under sub-paragraph (2)(b), the Crown Court must take into account the extent to which the offender has complied with the requirements of the order.
 (5) Where the Crown Court proposes to exercise its powers under this paragraph otherwise than on the application of the offender, it must summon him to appear before the court and, if he does not appear in answer to the summons, may issue a warrant for his arrest.

Supplementary

15   Paragraph 12 applies for the purposes of paragraphs 13 and 14 as it applies for the purposes of paragraph 9 above, but as if for the words "paragraph 9(1)(b)" there were substituted "paragraph 13(2)(b)(ii) or 14(2)(b)(ii)".

PART 4

AMENDMENT OF ORDER

Amendment by reason of change of residence

16   (1) This paragraph applies where, at any time while a community order is in force in respect of an offender, the appropriate court is satisfied that the offender proposes to change, or has changed, his residence from the petty sessions area concerned to another petty sessions area.

(2) Subject to sub-paragraphs (3) and (4), the appropriate court may, and on the application of the responsible officer must, amend the community order by substituting the other petty sessions area for the area specified in the order.

(3) The court may not under this paragraph amend a community order which contains requirements which, in the opinion of the court, cannot be complied with unless the offender continues to reside in the petty sessions area concerned unless, in accordance with paragraph 17, it either—

(a) cancels those requirements, or

(b) substitutes for those requirements other requirements which can be complied with if the offender ceases to reside in that area.

(4) The court may not amend under this paragraph a community order imposing a programme requirement unless it appears to the court that the accredited programme specified in the requirement is available in the other petty sessions area.

(5) In this paragraph "the appropriate court" means—

(a) in relation to any community order imposing a drug rehabilitation requirement which is subject to review, the court responsible for the order,

(b) in relation to any community order which was made by the Crown Court and does not include any direction that any failure to comply with the requirements of the order is to be dealt with by a magistrates' court, the Crown Court, and

(c) in relation to any other community order, a magistrates' court acting for the petty sessions area concerned.

Amendment of requirements of community order

17   (1) The appropriate court may, on the application of the offender or the responsible officer, by order amend a community order—

(a) by cancelling any of the requirements of the order, or

(b) by replacing any of those requirements with a requirement of the same kind, which the court could include if it were then making the order.

(2) The court may not under this paragraph amend a mental health treatment requirement, a drug rehabilitation requirement or an alcohol treatment requirement unless the offender expresses his willingness to comply with the requirement as amended.

(3) If the offender fails to express his willingness to comply with a mental health treatment requirement, drug rehabilitation requirement or alcohol treatment requirement as proposed to be amended by the court under this paragraph, the court may—

(a) revoke the community order, and

(b) deal with him, for the offence in respect of which the order was made, in any way in which he could have been dealt with for that offence by the court which made the order if the order had not been made.

(4) In dealing with the offender under sub-paragraph (3)(b), the court—

(a) must take into account the extent to which the offender has complied with the requirements of the order, and

(b) may impose a custodial sentence (where the order was made in respect of an offence punishable with such a sentence) notwithstanding anything in section 152(2).

(5) Paragraph 12 applies for the purposes of this paragraph as it applies for the purposes of paragraph 9, but as if for the words "paragraph 9(1)(b)" there were substituted "paragraph 17(3)(b)".

(6) In this paragraph "the appropriate court" has the same meaning as in paragraph 16.

Amendment of treatment requirements of community order on report of practitioner

18 (1) Where the medical practitioner or other person by whom or under whose direction an offender is, in pursuance of any requirement to which this sub-paragraph applies, being treated for his mental condition or his dependency on or propensity to misuse drugs or alcohol—
    (a) is of the opinion mentioned in sub-paragraph (3), or
    (b) is for any reason unwilling to continue to treat or direct the treatment of the offender,
    he must make a report in writing to that effect to the responsible officer and that officer must apply under paragraph 17 to the appropriate court for the variation or cancellation of the requirement.
(2) The requirements to which sub-paragraph (1) applies are—
    (a) a mental health treatment requirement,
    (b) a drug rehabilitation requirement, and
    (c) an alcohol treatment requirement.
(3) The opinion referred to in sub-paragraph (1) is—
    (a) that the treatment of the offender should be continued beyond the period specified in that behalf in the order,
    (b) that the offender needs different treatment,
    (c) that the offender is not susceptible to treatment, or
    (d) that the offender does not require further treatment.
(4) In this paragraph "the appropriate court" has the same meaning as in paragraph 16.

Amendment in relation to review of drug rehabilitation requirement

19 Where the responsible officer is of the opinion that a community order imposing a drug rehabilitation requirement which is subject to review should be so amended as to provide for each subsequent periodic review (required by section 211) to be made without a hearing instead of at a review hearing, or vice versa, he must apply under paragraph 17 to the court responsible for the order for the variation of the order.

Extension of unpaid work requirement

20 (1) Where—
    (a) a community order imposing an unpaid work requirement is in force in respect of any offender, and
    (b) on the application of the offender or the responsible officer, it appears to the appropriate court that it would be in the interests of justice to do so having regard to circumstances which have arisen since the order was made,
    the court may, in relation to the order, extend the period of twelve months specified in section 200(2).
(2) In this paragraph "the appropriate court" has the same meaning as in paragraph 16.

PART 5

POWERS OF COURT IN RELATION TO ORDER FOLLOWING SUBSEQUENT CONVICTION

Powers of magistrates' court following subsequent conviction

21 (1) This paragraph applies where—
    (a) an offender in respect of whom a community order made by a magistrates' court is in force is convicted of an offence by a magistrates' court, and
    (b) it appears to the court that it would be in the interests of justice to exercise its powers under this paragraph, having regard to circumstances which have arisen since the community order was made.
(2) The magistrates' court may—
    (a) revoke the order, or
    (b) both-
        (i) revoke the order, and

       (ii) deal with the offender, for the offence in respect of which the order was made, in any way in which he could have been dealt with for that offence by the court which made the order if the order had not been made.

  (3) In dealing with an offender under sub-paragraph (2)(b), a magistrates' court must take into account the extent to which the offender has complied with the requirements of the community order.

  (4) A person sentenced under sub-paragraph (2)(b) for an offence may appeal to the Crown Court against the sentence.

22 (1) Where an offender in respect of whom a community order made by the Crown Court is in force is convicted of an offence by a magistrates' court, the magistrates' court may commit the offender in custody or release him on bail until he can be brought before the Crown Court.

  (2) Where the magistrates' court deals with an offender's case under sub-paragraph (1), it must send to the Crown Court such particulars of the case as may be desirable.

Powers of Crown Court following subsequent conviction

23 (1) This paragraph applies where—

    (a) an offender in respect of whom a community order is in force—

      (i) is convicted of an offence by the Crown Court, or

      (ii) is brought or appears before the Crown Court by virtue of paragraph 22 or having been committed by the magistrates' court to the Crown Court for sentence, and

    (b) it appears to the Crown Court that it would be in the interests of justice to exercise its powers under this paragraph, having regard to circumstances which have arisen since the community order was made.

  (2) The Crown Court may—

    (a) revoke the order, or

    (b) both—

      (i) revoke the order, and

      (ii) deal with the offender, for the offence in respect of which the order was made, in any way in which he could have been dealt with for that offence by the court which made the order if the order had not been made.

  (3) In dealing with an offender under sub-paragraph (2)(b), the Crown Court must take into account the extent to which the offender has complied with the requirements of the community order.

PART 6

SUPPLEMENTARY

24 (1) No order may be made under paragraph 16, and no application may be made under paragraph 13, 17 or 20, while an appeal against the community order is pending.

  (2) Sub-paragraph (1) does not apply to an application under paragraph 17 which—

    (a) relates to a mental health treatment requirement, a drug rehabilitation requirement or an alcohol treatment requirement, and

    (b) is made by the responsible officer with the consent of the offender.

25 (1) Subject to sub-paragraph (2), where a court proposes to exercise its powers under Part 4 or 5 of this Schedule, otherwise than on the application of the offender, the court—

    (a) must summon him to appear before the court, and

    (b) if he does not appear in answer to the summons, may issue a warrant for his arrest.

  (2) This paragraph does not apply to an order cancelling a requirement of a community order or reducing the period of any requirement, or substituting a new petty sessions area or a new place for the one specified in the order.

26 Paragraphs 9(1)(a), 10(1)(a) and 17(1)(b) have effect subject to the provisions mentioned in subsection (2) of section 177, and to subsections (3) and (6) of that section.

27 (1) On the making under this Schedule of an order revoking or amending a community order, the proper officer of the court must—

    (a) provide copies of the revoking or amending order to the offender and the responsible officer,

    (b) in the case of an amending order which substitutes a new petty sessions area, provide a copy of the amending order to—

      (i) the local probation board acting for that area, and

      (ii) the magistrates' court acting for that area, and

(c) in the case of an amending order which imposes or amends a requirement specified in the first column of Schedule 14, provide a copy of so much of the amending order as relates to that requirement to the person specified in relation to that requirement in the second column of that Schedule.

(2) Where under sub-paragraph (1)(b) the proper officer of the court provides a copy of an amending order to a magistrates' court acting for a different area, the officer must also provide to that court such documents and information relating to the case as it considers likely to be of assistance to a court acting for that area in the exercise of its functions in relation to the order.

(3) In this paragraph "proper officer" means—
  (a) in relation to a magistrates' court, the justices' chief executive for the court; and
  (b) in relation to the Crown Court, the appropriate officer.

SCHEDULE 9   Section 180

TRANSFER OF COMMUNITY ORDERS TO SCOTLAND OR NORTHERN IRELAND

PART 1

SCOTLAND

1 (1) Where the court considering the making of a community order is satisfied that the offender resides in Scotland, or will reside there when the order comes into force, the court may not make a community order in respect of the offender unless it appears to the court—
  (a) in the case of an order imposing a requirement mentioned in sub-paragraph (2), that arrangements exist for persons to comply with such a requirement in the locality in Scotland in which the offender resides, or will be residing when the order comes into force, and that provision can be made for him to comply with the requirement under those arrangements, and
  (b) in any case, that suitable arrangements for his supervision can be made by the council constituted under section 2 of the Local Government etc. (Scotland) Act 1994 (c. 39) in whose area he resides, or will be residing when the order comes into force.

(2) The requirements referred to in sub-paragraph (1)(a) are—
  (a) an unpaid work requirement,
  (b) an activity requirement,
  (c) a programme requirement,
  (d) a mental health treatment requirement,
  (e) a drug rehabilitation requirement,
  (f) an alcohol treatment requirement, and
  (g) an electronic monitoring requirement.

(3) Where—
  (a) the appropriate court for the purposes of paragraph 16 of Schedule 8 (amendment by reason of change of residence) is satisfied that an offender in respect of whom a community order is in force proposes to reside or is residing in Scotland, and
  (b) it appears to the court that the conditions in sub-paragraph (1)(a) and (b) are satisfied,
  the power of the court to amend the order under Part 4 of Schedule 8 includes power to amend it by requiring it to be complied with in Scotland and the offender to be supervised in accordance with the arrangements referred to in sub-paragraph (1)(b).

(4) For the purposes of sub-paragraph (3), any reference in sub-paragraph (1)(a) and (b) to the time when the order comes into force is to be treated as a reference to the time when the amendment comes into force.

(5) The court may not by virtue of sub-paragraph (1) or (3) require an attendance centre requirement to be complied with in Scotland.

(6) A community order made or amended in accordance with this paragraph must—
  (a) specify the locality in Scotland in which the offender resides or will be residing when the order or amendment comes into force;
  (b) specify as the corresponding order for the purposes of this Schedule an order that may be made by a court in Scotland;
  (c) specify as the appropriate court for the purposes of subsection (4) of section 228 of the Criminal Procedure (Scotland) Act 1995 (c. 46) a court of summary

jurisdiction (which, in the case of an offender convicted on indictment, must be the sheriff court) having jurisdiction in the locality specified under paragraph (a); and section 216 (petty sessions area to be specified) does not apply in relation to an order so made or amended.

2 (1) Where a court is considering the making or amendment of a community order by virtue of paragraph 1, Chapter 4 of Part 12 of this Act has effect subject to the following modifications.

(2) Any reference to the responsible officer has effect as a reference to the officer of a council constituted under section 2 of the Local Government etc. (Scotland) Act 1994 (c. 39) responsible for the offender's supervision or, as the case may be, discharging in relation to him the functions in respect of community service orders assigned by sections 239 to 245 of the Criminal Procedure (Scotland) Act 1995.

(3) The following provisions are omitted—
  (a) subsection (7) of section 201 (activity requirement),
  (b) subsection (7) of section 202 (programme requirement),
  (c) subsection (4) of section 206 (residence requirement), and
  (d) subsection (4) of section 218 (availability of arrangements in local area).

(4) In section 207 (mental health treatment requirement), for subsection (2)(a) there is substituted—
  "(a) treatment as a resident patient in a hospital within the meaning of the Mental Health (Care and Treatment) (Scotland) Act 2003, not being a State hospital within the meaning of that Act;".

(5) In section 215 (electronic monitoring requirement), in subsection (3), the words from "and" onwards are omitted.

PART 2

NORTHERN IRELAND

3 (1) Where the court considering the making of a community order is satisfied that the offender resides in Northern Ireland, or will reside there when the order comes into force, the court may not make a community order in respect of the offender unless it appears to the court—
  (a) in the case of an order imposing a requirement mentioned in sub-paragraph (2), that arrangements exist for persons to comply with such a requirement in the petty sessions district in Northern Ireland in which the offender resides, or will be residing when the order comes into force, and that provision can be made for him to comply with the requirement under those arrangements, and
  (b) in any case, that suitable arrangements for his supervision can be made by the Probation Board for Northern Ireland.

(2) The requirements referred to in sub-paragraph (1) are—
  (a) an unpaid work requirement,
  (b) an activity requirement,
  (c) a programme requirement,
  (d) a mental health treatment requirement,
  (e) a drug rehabilitation requirement,
  (f) an alcohol treatment requirement,
  (g) an attendance centre requirement, and
  (h) an electronic monitoring requirement.

(3) Where—
  (a) the appropriate court for the purposes of paragraph 16 of Schedule 8 (amendment by reason of change of residence) is satisfied that the offender to whom a community order relates proposes to reside or is residing in Northern Ireland, and
  (b) it appears to the court that the conditions in sub-paragraphs (1)(a) and (b) are satisfied,
  the power of the court to amend the order under Part 4 of Schedule 8 includes power to amend it by requiring it to be complied with in Northern Ireland and the offender to be supervised in accordance with the arrangements referred to in sub-paragraph (1)(b).

(4) For the purposes of sub-paragraph (3), any reference in sub-paragraph (1)(a) and (b) to the time when the order comes into force is to be treated as a reference to the time when the amendment comes into force.

(5) A community order made or amended in accordance with this paragraph must specify the petty sessions district in Northern Ireland in which the offender resides or will be residing when the order or amendment comes into force; and section 216 (petty

sessions area to be specified) does not apply in relation to an order so made or amended.

(6) A community order made or amended in accordance with this paragraph must also specify as the corresponding order for the purposes of this Schedule an order that may be made by a court in Northern Ireland.

4   (1) Where a court is considering the making or amendment of a community order by virtue of paragraph 3, Chapter 4 of Part 12 of this Act has effect subject to the following modifications.

(2) Any reference to the responsible officer has effect as a reference to the probation officer responsible for the offender's supervision or, as the case may be, discharging in relation to the offender the functions conferred by Part 2 of the Criminal Justice (Northern Ireland) Order 1996 (S.I. 1996/3160 (N.I. 24)).

(3) The following provisions are omitted—

(a) subsection (7) of section 201 (activity requirement),

(b) subsection (7) of section 202 (programme requirement),

(c) subsection (4) of section 206 (residence requirement), and

(d) subsection (4) of section 218 (availability of arrangements in local area).

(4) In section 207 (mental health treatment requirement), for subsection (2)(a) there is substituted—

"(a) treatment (whether as an in-patient or an out-patient) at such hospital as may be specified in the order, being a hospital within the meaning of the Health and Personal Social Services (Northern Ireland) Order 1972, approved by the Department of Health, Social Services and Public Safety for the purposes of paragraph 4(3) of Schedule 1 to the Criminal Justice (Northern Ireland) Order 1996 (S.I. 1996/3160 (N.I. 24));".

(5) In section 214 (attendance centre requirement), any reference to an attendance centre has effect as a reference to a day centre, as defined by paragraph 3(6) of Schedule 1 to the Criminal Justice (Northern Ireland) Order 1996 (S.I. 1996/3160 (N.I. 24)).

(6) In section 215 (electronic monitoring requirement), in subsection (3), the words from "and" onwards are omitted.

PART 3

GENERAL PROVISIONS

5   In this Part of this Schedule—

"corresponding order" means the order specified under paragraph 1(6)(b) or 3(6);

"home court" means—

(a) if the offender resides in Scotland, or will be residing there at the relevant time, the sheriff court having jurisdiction in the locality in which he resides or proposes to reside, and

(b) if he resides in Northern Ireland, or will be residing there at the relevant time, the court of summary jurisdiction acting for the petty sessions district in which he resides or proposes to reside;

"the local authority officer concerned", in relation to an offender, means the officer of a council constituted under section 2 of the Local Government etc. (Scotland) Act 1994 (c. 39) responsible for his supervision or, as the case may be, discharging in relation to him the functions in respect of community service orders assigned by sections 239 to 245 of the Criminal Procedure (Scotland) Act 1995 (c. 46);

"the probation officer concerned", in relation to an offender, means the probation officer responsible for his supervision or, as the case may be, discharging in relation to him the functions conferred by Part 2 of the Criminal Justice (Northern Ireland) Order 1996;

"the relevant time" means the time when the order or the amendment to it comes into force.

6   Where a community order is made or amended in accordance with paragraph 1 or 3, the court which makes or amends the order must provide the home court with a copy of the order as made or amended, together with such other documents and information relating to the case as it considers likely to be of assistance to that court; and paragraphs (b) to (d) of subsection (1) of section 219 (provision of copies of relevant orders) do not apply.

7   In section 220 (duty of offender to keep in touch with responsible officer) the reference to the responsible officer is to be read in accordance with paragraph 2(2) or 4(2).

8   Where a community order is made or amended in accordance with paragraph 1 or 3, then, subject to the following provisions of this Part of this Schedule—

(a) the order is to be treated as if it were a corresponding order made in the part of the United Kingdom in which the offender resides, or will be residing at the relevant time, and

(b) the legislation relating to such orders which has effect in that part of the United Kingdom applies accordingly.

9 Before making or amending a community order in those circumstances the court must explain to the offender in ordinary language—

(a) the requirements of the legislation relating to corresponding orders which has effect in the part of the United Kingdom in which he resides or will be residing at the relevant time,

(b) the powers of the home court under that legislation, as modified by this Part of this Schedule, and

(c) its own powers under this Part of this Schedule.

10 The home court may exercise in relation to the community order any power which it could exercise in relation to the corresponding order made by a court in the part of the United Kingdom in which the home court exercises jurisdiction, by virtue of the legislation relating to such orders which has effect in that part, except the following—

(a) any power to discharge or revoke the order (other than a power to revoke the order where the offender has been convicted of a further offence and the court has imposed a custodial sentence),

(b) any power to deal with the offender for the offence in respect of which the order was made,

(c) in the case of a community order imposing an unpaid work requirement, any power to vary the order by substituting for the number of hours of work specified in it any greater number than the court which made the order could have specified, and

(d) in the case of a community order imposing a curfew requirement, any power to vary the order by substituting for the period specified in it any longer period than the court which made the order could have specified.

11 If at any time while legislation relating to corresponding orders which has effect in Scotland or Northern Ireland applies by virtue of paragraph 7 to a community order made in England and Wales—

(a) it appears to the home court—

(i) if that court is in Scotland, on information from the local authority officer concerned, or

(ii) if that court is in Northern Ireland, upon a complaint being made to a justice of the peace acting for the petty sessions district for the time being specified in the order,

that the offender has failed to comply with any of the requirements of the order, or

(b) it appears to the home court—

(i) if that court is in Scotland, on the application of the offender or of the local authority officer concerned, or

(ii) if it is in Northern Ireland, on the application of the offender or of the probation officer concerned,

that it would be in the interests of justice for a power conferred by paragraph 13 or 14 of Schedule 8 to be exercised,

the home court may require the offender to appear before the court which made the order or the court which last amended the order in England and Wales.

12 Where an offender is required by virtue of paragraph 11 to appear before a court in England and Wales that court—

(a) may issue a warrant for his arrest, and

(b) may exercise any power which it could exercise in respect of the community order if the offender resided in England and Wales,

and any enactment relating to the exercise of such powers has effect accordingly, and with any reference to the responsible officer being read as a reference to the local authority officer or probation officer concerned.

13 Paragraph 12(b) does not enable the court to amend the community order unless—

(a) where the offender resides in Scotland, it appears to the court that the conditions in paragraph 1(1)(a) and (b) are satisfied in relation to any requirement to be imposed, or

     (b) where the offender resides in Northern Ireland, it appears to the court that the conditions in paragraph 3(1)(a) and (b) are satisfied in relation to any requirement to be imposed.

14   The preceding paragraphs of this Schedule have effect in relation to the amendment of a community order by virtue of paragraph 12(b) as they have effect in relation to the amendment of such an order by virtue of paragraph 1(3) or 3(3).

15   Where an offender is required by virtue of paragraph (a) of paragraph 11 to appear before a court in England and Wales—

     (a) the home court must send to that court a certificate certifying that the offender has failed to comply with such of the requirements of the order as may be specified in the certificate, together with such other particulars of the case as may be desirable, and

     (b) a certificate purporting to be signed by the clerk of the home court is admissible as evidence of the failure before the court which made the order.

SCHEDULE 10   **Section 187**

REVOCATION OR AMENDMENT OF CUSTODY PLUS ORDERS AND AMENDMENT OF
INTERMITTENT CUSTODY ORDERS

Interpretation

1   (1) In this Schedule—

      "the appropriate court" means—

        (a) where the custody plus order or intermittent custody order was made by the Crown Court, the Crown Court, and

        (b) in any other case, a magistrates' court acting for the petty sessions area concerned;

      "the offender", in relation to a custody plus order or intermittent custody order, means the person in respect of whom the order is made;

      "the petty sessions area concerned", in relation to a custody plus order or intermittent custody order, means the petty sessions area for the time being specified in the order;

      "the responsible officer" has the meaning given by section 197.

     (2) In this Schedule any reference to a requirement being imposed by, or included in, a custody plus order or intermittent custody order is to be read as a reference to compliance with the requirement being required by the order to be a condition of a licence.

Orders made on appeal

2   Where a custody plus order or intermittent custody order has been made on appeal, it is to be taken for the purposes of this Schedule to have been made by the Crown Court.

Revocation of custody plus order or removal from intermittent custody order of requirements as to licence conditions

3   (1) Where at any time while a custody plus order or intermittent custody order is in force, it appears to the appropriate court on the application of the offender or the responsible officer that, having regard to circumstances which have arisen since the order was made, it would be in the interests of justice to do so, the court may—

      (a) in the case of a custody plus order, revoke the order, and

      (b) in the case of an intermittent custody order, amend the order so that it contains only provision specifying periods for the purposes of section 183(1)(b)(i).

     (2) The revocation under this paragraph of a custody plus order does not affect the sentence of imprisonment to which the order relates, except in relation to the conditions of the licence.

Amendment by reason of change of residence

4   (1) This paragraph applies where, at any time during the term of imprisonment to which a custody plus order or intermittent custody order relates, the appropriate court is satisfied that the offender proposes to change, or has changed, his residence during the licence period from the petty sessions area concerned to another petty sessions area.

     (2) Subject to sub-paragraphs (3) and (4), the appropriate court may, and on the application of the Secretary of State or the responsible officer must, amend the custody

plus order or intermittent custody order by substituting the other petty sessions area for the area specified in the order.

(3) The court may not amend under this paragraph a custody plus order or intermittent custody order which contains requirements which, in the opinion of the court, cannot be complied with unless the offender resides in the petty sessions area concerned unless, in accordance with paragraph 5, it either—

    (a) cancels those requirements, or

    (b) substitutes for those requirements other requirements which can be complied with if the offender does not reside in that area.

(4) The court may not amend under this paragraph any custody plus order or intermittent custody order imposing a programme requirement unless it appears to the court that the accredited programme specified in the requirement is available in the other petty sessions area.

Amendment of requirements of custody plus order or intermittent custody order

5 (1) At any time during the term of imprisonment to which a custody plus order or intermittent custody order relates, the appropriate court may, on the application of the offender, the Secretary of State or the responsible officer, by order amend any requirement of the custody plus order or intermittent custody order—

    (a) by cancelling the requirement, or

    (b) by replacing it with a requirement of the same kind imposing different obligations, which the court could include if it were then making the order.

(2) For the purposes of sub-paragraph (1)—

    (a) a requirement falling within any paragraph of section 182(1) is of the same kind as any other requirement falling within that paragraph, and

    (b) an electronic monitoring requirement is a requirement of the same kind as any requirement falling within section 182(1) to which it relates.

(3) Sub-paragraph (1)(b) has effect subject to the provisions mentioned in subsection (2) of section 182, and to subsections (3) and (5) of that section.

Alteration of pattern of temporary release

6 (1) At any time during the term of imprisonment to which an intermittent custody order relates, the appropriate court may, on the application of the offender, the Secretary of State or the responsible officer, amend the order—

    (a) so as to specify different periods for the purposes of section 183(1)(b)(i), or

    (b) so as to provide that he is to remain in prison until the number of days served by him in prison is equal to the number of custodial days.

(2) The appropriate court may not by virtue of sub-paragraph (1) amend an intermittent custody order unless it has received from the Secretary of State notification that suitable prison accommodation is available for the offender during the periods which, under the order as amended, will be custodial periods.

(3) In this paragraph "custodial period" has the same meaning as in section 184(3).

Supplementary

7 No application may be made under paragraph 3(1), 5(1) or 6(1) while an appeal against the sentence of which the custody plus or intermittent custody order forms part is pending.

8 (1) Subject to sub-paragraph (2), where a court proposes to exercise its powers under paragraph 5 or 6, otherwise than on the application of the offender, the court—

    (a) must summon him to appear before the court, and

    (b) if he does not appear in answer to the summons, may issue a warrant for his arrest.

(2) This paragraph does not apply to an order cancelling any requirement of a custody plus or intermittent custody order.

9 (1) On the making under this Schedule of an order revoking or amending a custody plus order or amending an intermittent custody order, the proper officer of the court must—

    (a) provide copies of the revoking or amending order to the offender and the responsible officer,

    (b) in the case of an amending order which substitutes a new petty sessions area, provide a copy of the amending order to—

  (i) the local probation board acting for that area, and

  (ii) the magistrates' court acting for that area,

(c) in the case of an order which cancels or amends a requirement specified in the first column of Schedule 14, provide a copy of so much of the amending order as relates to that requirement to the person specified in relation to that requirement in the second column of that Schedule.

(2) Where under sub-paragraph (1)(b) the proper officer of the court provides a copy of an amending order to a magistrates' court acting for a different area, the officer must also provide to that court such documents and information relating to the case as it considers likely to be of assistance to a court acting for that area in the exercise of its functions in relation to the order.

SCHEDULE 11   **Section 188**

TRANSFER OF CUSTODY PLUS ORDERS AND INTERMITTENT CUSTODY ORDERS TO SCOTLAND OR NORTHERN IRELAND

PART 1

INTRODUCTORY

1   In this Schedule—

  (a) "the 1997 Act" means the Crime (Sentences) Act 1997 (c. 43), and

  (b) any reference to a requirement being imposed by, or included in a custody plus order or intermittent custody order is a reference to compliance with the requirement being required by the order to be a condition of a licence.

PART 2

SCOTLAND

2   (1) Where the court making a custody plus order is satisfied that the offender resides in Scotland, or will reside there during the licence period, the court may, subject to sub-paragraph (2), impose requirements that are to be complied with in Scotland and require the offender's compliance with the order to be supervised in accordance with arrangements made by the local authority in Scotland in whose area he resides or will reside.

  (2) The court may not make an order by virtue of this paragraph unless it appears to the court—

  (a) in the case of an order imposing a requirement mentioned in sub-paragraph (3), that arrangements exist for persons to comply with such a requirement in the locality in Scotland in which the offender resides, or will be residing during the licence period, and that provision can be made for him to comply with the requirement under those arrangements, and

  (b) in any case, that suitable arrangements for supervising his compliance with the order can be made by the local authority in whose area he resides, or will be residing during the licence period.

  (3) The requirements referred to in sub-paragraph (2)(a) are—

  (a) an unpaid work requirement,

  (b) an activity requirement,

  (c) a programme requirement, and

  (d) an electronic monitoring requirement.

  (4) If an order has been made in accordance with this paragraph in relation to an offender but—

  (a) the Secretary of State decides not to make an order under paragraph 1 or 4 of Schedule 1 to the 1997 Act in relation to him, and

  (b) the offender has not applied under paragraph 22 of this Schedule for the amendment of the custody plus order or intermittent custody order,

  the Secretary of State must apply to the court under paragraph 22 of this Schedule for the amendment of the order.

3   Where—

  (a) the appropriate court for the purposes of paragraph 4 of Schedule 10 (amendment by reason of change of residence) is satisfied that the offender in respect of whom a custody plus order or intermittent custody order is in force is residing in Scotland, or proposes to reside there during the licence period, (b)　the Secretary of State has made, or has indicated his willingness to make, an order under paragraph 1 or 4 of Schedule 1 to the 1997 Act in relation to the offender, and

　(c)　it appears to the court that the conditions in paragraph 2(2)(a) and (b) are satisfied,

the power of the court to amend the order under Schedule 10 includes power to amend it by requiring the requirements included in the order to be complied with in Scotland and the offender's compliance with them to be supervised in accordance with the arrangements referred to in paragraph 2(2)(b).

4　　A court may not by virtue of paragraph 2 or 3 require an attendance centre requirement to be complied with in Scotland.

5　　A custody plus order made in accordance with paragraph 2 or a custody plus order or intermittent order amended in accordance with paragraph 3 must—

　(a)　specify the local authority area in which the offender resides or will reside during the licence period, and

　(b)　require the local authority for that area to appoint or assign an officer who will be responsible for discharging in relation to him the functions conferred on responsible officers by Part 12 of this Act;

and section 216 (petty sessions area to be specified) does not apply in relation to an order so made or amended.

6　(1)　Where a court makes a custody plus order in accordance with paragraph 2 or amends a custody plus order or intermittent custody order in accordance with paragraph 3, the court must provide the relevant documents to—

　(a)　the local authority for the area specified in the order, and

　(b)　the sheriff court having jurisdiction in the locality in which the offender resides or proposes to reside;

and paragraphs (b) to (d) of subsection (1) of section 219 (which relate to the provision of copies) do not apply in relation to an order so made or amended.

　(2)　In this paragraph, "the relevant documents" means—

　(a)　a copy of the order as made or amended, and

　(b)　such other documents and information relating to the case as the court making or amending the order considers likely to be of assistance.

7　(1)　In relation to the making of a custody plus order by virtue of paragraph 2, in relation to the amendment of a custody plus order or intermittent custody order by virtue of paragraph 3, and (except for the purposes of paragraph 22) in relation to an order so made or amended, Chapter 4 of Part 12 of this Act has effect subject to the following modifications.

　(2)　Any reference to the responsible officer has effect as a reference to the officer appointed or assigned under paragraph 5(b).

　(3)　The following provisions are omitted—

　(a)　subsection (7) of section 201 (activity requirement);

　(b)　subsection (7) of section 202 (programme requirement);

　(c)　subsection (4) of section 218 (availability of arrangements in local area).

　(4)　In section 215 (electronic monitoring requirement), in subsection (3), the words from "and" onwards are omitted.

8　　In this Part of this Schedule "local authority" means a council constituted under section 2 of the Local Government etc. (Scotland) Act 1994 (c. 39); and any reference to the area of such an authority is a reference to the local government area within the meaning of that Act.

PART 3

NORTHERN IRELAND

9　(1)　Where the court making a custody plus order is satisfied that the offender resides in Northern Ireland, or will reside there during the licence period, the court may, subject to sub-paragraph (2), impose requirements that are to be complied with in Northern Ireland and require the offender's compliance with the order to be supervised in accordance with arrangements made by the Probation Board for Northern Ireland.

　(2)　The court may not make an order by virtue of this paragraph unless it appears to the court—

　(a)　in the case of an order imposing a requirement mentioned in sub-paragraph (3), that arrangements exist for persons to comply with such a requirement in the petty sessions district in Northern Ireland in which the offender resides, or will be residing during the licence period, and that provision can be made for him to comply with the requirement under those arrangements, and

(b) in any case, that suitable arrangements for supervising his compliance with the order can be made by the Probation Board for Northern Ireland.

(3) The requirements referred to in sub-paragraph (1)(a) are—

(a) an unpaid work requirement,

(b) an activity requirement,

(c) a programme requirement,

(d) an attendance centre requirement, and

(e) an electronic monitoring requirement.

(4) If an order has been made in accordance with this paragraph in relation to an offender but—

(a) the Secretary of State decides not to make an order under paragraph 1 or 4 of Schedule 1 to the 1997 Act in relation to him, and

(b) the offender has not applied under paragraph 22 of this Schedule for the amendment of the custody plus order or intermittent custody order,

the Secretary of State must apply to the court under paragraph 22 for the amendment of the order.

10   Where—

(a) the appropriate court for the purposes of paragraph 4 of Schedule 10 (amendment by reason of change of residence) is satisfied that the offender in respect of whom a custody plus order or intermittent custody order is in force is residing in Northern Ireland, or proposes to reside there during the licence period,

(b) the Secretary of State has made, or has indicated his willingness to make, an order under paragraph 1 or 4 of Schedule 1 to the 1997 Act in relation to the offender, and

(c) it appears to the court that the conditions in paragraph 9(2)(a) and (b) are satisfied,

the power of the court to amend the order under Schedule 10 includes power to amend it by requiring the requirements included in the order to be complied with in Northern Ireland and the offender's compliance with them to be supervised in accordance with the arrangements referred to in paragraph 9(2)(b).

11   A custody plus order made in accordance with paragraph 9 or a custody plus order or intermittent custody order amended in accordance with paragraph 10 must—

(a) specify the petty sessions district in Northern Ireland in which the offender resides or will reside during the licence period, and

(b) require the Probation Board for Northern Ireland to appoint or assign a probation officer who will be responsible for discharging in relation to him the functions conferred on responsible officers by Part 11 of this Act;

and section 216 (petty sessions area to be specified) does not apply in relation to an order so made or amended.

12 (1) Where a court makes a custody plus order in accordance with paragraph 9 or amends a custody plus order or intermittent custody order in accordance with paragraph 10, the court must provide the relevant documents to—

(a) the Probation Board for Northern Ireland, and

(b) the court of summary jurisdiction acting for the petty sessions district in which the offender resides or proposes to reside;

and paragraphs (b) to (d) of subsection (1) of section 219 (which relate to the provision of copies) do not apply in relation to an order so made or amended.

(2) In this paragraph, "the relevant documents" means—

(a) a copy of the order as made or amended, and

(b) such other documents and information relating to the case as the court making or amending the order considers likely to be of assistance.

13 (1) In relation to the making of a custody plus order by virtue of paragraph 9, in relation to the amendment of a custody plus order or intermittent custody order by virtue of paragraph 10, and (except for the purposes of paragraph 22) in relation to an order so made or amended, Chapter 4 of Part 12 of this Act has effect subject to the following modifications.

(2) Any reference to the responsible officer has effect as a reference to the probation officer appointed or assigned under paragraph 11(b).

(3) The following provisions are omitted—
  (a) subsection (7) of section 201 (activity requirement);
  (b) subsection (7) of section 202 (programme requirement);
  (c) subsection (4) of section 218 (availability of arrangements in local area).
(4) In section 214 (attendance centre requirement), any reference to an attendance centre has effect as a reference to a day centre, as defined by paragraph 3(6) of Schedule 1 to the Criminal Justice (Northern Ireland) Order 1996 (S.I. 1996/3160 (N.I. 24).
(5) In section 215 (electronic monitoring requirement), in subsection (3), the words from "and" onwards are omitted.

PART 4

GENERAL PROVISIONS

14 This Part of this Schedule applies at any time while a custody plus order made in accordance with paragraph 2 or 9 or amended in accordance with paragraph 3 or 10, or an intermittent custody order amended in accordance with paragraph 3 or 10, is in force in respect of an offender.

15 In this Part of this Schedule—
"home court" means—
  (a) if the offender resides in Scotland, or will be residing there during the licence period, the sheriff court having jurisdiction in the locality in which the offender resides or proposes to reside, and
  (b) if he resides in Northern Ireland, or will be residing there during the licence period, the court of summary jurisdiction acting for the petty sessions district in which he resides or proposes to reside;
"local authority" and "local authority area" are to be read in accordance with paragraph 8;
"original court" means the court in England and Wales which made or last amended the custody plus order or intermittent custody order;
"the relevant officer" means—
  (a) where the order specifies a local authority area in Scotland, the local authority officer appointed or assigned under paragraph 5(b), and
  (b) where the order specifies a local authority district in Northern Ireland, the probation officer appointed or assigned under paragraph 11(b).

16 (1) Where this Part of this Schedule applies, Schedule 10 has effect subject to the following modifications.
(2) Any reference to the responsible officer has effect as a reference to the relevant officer.
(3) Any reference to the appropriate court has effect as a reference to the original court.
(4) Where the order specifies a local authority area in Scotland—
  (a) any reference to the petty sessions area concerned has effect as a reference to that local authority area, and
  (b) any other reference to a petty sessions area has effect as a reference to a local authority area.
(5) Where the order specifies a petty sessions district in Northern Ireland—
  (a) any reference to the petty sessions area concerned has effect as a reference to that petty sessions district, and
  (b) any other reference to a petty sessions area has effect as a reference to a petty sessions district.
(6) Paragraph 9 is omitted.

17 (1) The home court may exercise any power under paragraph 4 or 5 of Schedule 10 (amendment of custody plus order or intermittent custody order) as if it were the original court.
(2) Subject to sub-paragraph (3), where the home court proposes to exercise the power conferred by paragraph 5 of Schedule 10, otherwise than on the application of the offender, the court—
  (a) if it is in Scotland-
    (i) must issue a citation requiring the offender to appear before it, and
    (ii) if he does not appear in answer to the citation, may issue a warrant for the offender's arrest;
  (b) if it is in Northern Ireland—
    (i) must issue a summons requiring the offender to appear before it, and
    (ii) if he does not appear in answer to the summons, may issue a warrant for the offender's arrest;
and paragraph 8 of Schedule 10 does not apply to the home court.

(3) Sub-paragraph (2) does not apply to any order cancelling any requirement of a custody plus order or intermittent custody order.

(4) Where the home court is considering amending a custody plus or intermittent custody order, any reference in Chapter 4 of Part 12 of this Act to a local probation board has effect as a reference to a local authority in Scotland or, as the case may be, the Probation Board for Northern Ireland.

18   Where by virtue of paragraph 17 any application is made to the home court under paragraph 4 or 5 of Schedule 10, the home court may (instead of dealing with the application) require the offender to appear before the original court.

19   No court may amend or further amend a custody plus order or an intermittent custody order unless it appears to the court that the conditions in paragraph 2(2)(a) and (b) or, as the case may be, the conditions in paragraph 9(2)(a) and (b) are satisfied in relation to any requirement to be imposed; but this paragraph does not apply to any amendment made by virtue of paragraph 22(1).

20   The preceding paragraphs of this Schedule have effect in relation to any amendment of a custody plus or intermittent custody order by any court as they have effect in relation to the amendment of such an order by virtue of paragraph 3 or 10.

21   On the making of an order amending a custody plus order or intermittent custody order—

    (a) the court must provide copies of the amending order to the offender and the relevant officer, and

    (b) in the case of an amending order which substitutes a new local authority area or petty sessions district, paragraphs 5 and 6, or as the case may be paragraphs 11 and 12, have effect in relation to the order as they have effect in relation to an order made or amended in accordance with paragraph 2 or 3, or as the case may be, 9 or 10.

22   (1) Where—

    (a) a custody plus order has been made in accordance with paragraph 2 or 9 or a custody plus or intermittent custody order has been amended in accordance with paragraph 3 or 10, but (in any of those cases) the Secretary of State has not made an order under paragraph 1 or 4 of Schedule 1 to the 1997 Act in relation to the offender, or

    (b) the Secretary of State has made, or indicated his willingness to make, an order under paragraph 7(1) of Schedule 1 to the 1997 Act transferring the offender or his supervision back to England and Wales,

    the court may, on the application of the offender or the Secretary of State, amend the custody plus order or intermittent custody order by requiring it to be complied with in England and Wales.

(2) In sub-paragraph (1) "the court", in a case falling within paragraph (a) of that sub-paragraph, means the original court.

(3) In a case where paragraph 2(4) or 9(4) requires the Secretary of State to apply under this paragraph, the court must make an amending order under this paragraph.

(4) Where under this paragraph the court amends a custody plus order or intermittent custody order which contains requirements which, in the opinion of the court, cannot be complied with in the petty sessions area in which the offender is residing or proposes to reside, the court must, in accordance with paragraph 5 of Schedule 10, either—

    (a) cancel those requirements, or

    (b) substitute for those requirements other requirements which can be complied with if the offender resides in that area.

(5) Where the court amends under this paragraph any custody plus order or intermittent custody order imposing a programme requirement, the court must ensure that the requirement as amended specifies a programme which is available in the petty sessions area in England and Wales in which the offender is residing or proposes to reside.

(6) The custody plus order or intermittent custody order as amended under this paragraph must specify the petty sessions area in which the offender resides or proposes to reside in the licence period.

(7) On the making under this paragraph of an order amending a custody plus order or intermittent custody order, the court must—

    (a) provide copies of the amending order to the offender, the relevant officer and the local probation board acting for the new petty sessions area, and

(b) provide the magistrates' court acting for that area with a copy of the amending order and such other documents and information relating to the case as the home court considers likely to be of assistance to the court acting for that area in the exercise of its functions in relation to the order.

(8) Where an order has been amended under this paragraph, the preceding paragraphs of this Schedule shall cease to apply to the order as amended.

PART 5

SUPPLEMENTARY

23   Subsections (1) and (3) of section 245C of the Criminal Procedure (Scotland) Act 1995 (c. 46) (provision of remote monitoring) have effect as if they included a reference to the electronic monitoring of the requirements of a custody plus order made in accordance with paragraph 2 or a custody plus order or intermittent custody order made in accordance with paragraph 3.

24 (1) Section 4 of the Summary Jurisdiction (Process) Act 1881 (c. 24) (which provides, among other things, for service in England and Wales of Scottish citations or warrants) applies to any citation or warrant issued under paragraph 17(2)(a) as it applies to a citation or warrant granted under section 134 of the Criminal Procedure (Scotland) Act 1995.

(2) A summons issued by a court in Northern Ireland under paragraph 17(2)(b) may, in such circumstances as may be prescribed by rules of court, be served in England and Wales or Scotland.

SCHEDULE 12   **Section 193**

BREACH OR AMENDMENT OF SUSPENDED SENTENCE ORDER, AND EFFECT OF FURTHER CONVICTION

PART 1

PRELIMINARY

Interpretation

1   In this Schedule—
    "the offender", in relation to a suspended sentence order, means the person in respect of whom the order is made;
    "the petty sessions area concerned", in relation to a suspended sentence order, means the petty sessions area for the time being specified in the order;
    "the responsible officer" has the meaning given by section 197.

2   In this Schedule—
    (a) any reference to a suspended sentence order being subject to review is a reference to such an order being subject to review in accordance with section 191(1)(b) or to a drug rehabilitation requirement of such an order being subject to review in accordance with section 210(1)(b);
    (b) any reference to the court responsible for a suspended sentence order which is subject to review is to be construed in accordance with section 191(3) or, as the case may be, 210(2).

Orders made on appeal

3   Where a suspended sentence order is made on appeal it is to be taken for the purposes of this Schedule to have been made by the Crown Court.

PART 2

BREACH OF COMMUNITY REQUIREMENT OR CONVICTION OF FURTHER OFFENCE

Duty to give warning in relation to community requirement

4 (1) If the responsible officer is of the opinion that the offender has failed without reasonable excuse to comply with any of the community requirements of a suspended sentence order, the officer must give him a warning under this paragraph unless—

(a) the offender has within the previous twelve months been given a warning under this paragraph in relation to a failure to comply with any of the community requirements of the order, or

(b) the officer causes an information to be laid before a justice of the peace in respect of the failure.

(2) A warning under this paragraph must—

(a) describe the circumstances of the failure,

(b) state that the failure is unacceptable, and

(c) inform the offender that if within the next twelve months he again fails to comply with any requirement of the order, he will be liable to be brought before a court.

(3) The responsible officer must, as soon as practicable after the warning has been given, record that fact.

(4) In relation to any suspended sentence order which is made by the Crown Court and does not include a direction that any failure to comply with the community requirements of the order is to be dealt with by a magistrates' court, the reference in sub-paragraph (1)(b) to a justice of the peace is to be read as a reference to the Crown Court.

Breach of order after warning

5 (1) If—

(a) the responsible officer has given a warning under paragraph 4 to the offender in respect of a suspended sentence order, and

(b) at any time within the twelve months beginning with the date on which the warning was given, the responsible officer is of the opinion that the offender has since that date failed without reasonable excuse to comply with any of the community requirements of the order,

the officer must cause an information to be laid before a justice of the peace in respect of the failure in question.

(2) In relation to any suspended sentence order which is made by the Crown Court and does not include a direction that any failure to comply with the community requirements of the order is to be dealt with by a magistrates' court, the reference in sub-paragraph (1) to a justice of the peace is to be read as a reference to the Crown Court.

Issue of summons or warrant by justice of the peace

6 (1) This paragraph applies to—

(a) a suspended sentence order made by a magistrates' court, or

(b) any suspended sentence order which was made by the Crown Court and includes a direction that any failure to comply with the community requirements of the order is to be dealt with by a magistrates' court.

(2) If at any time while a suspended sentence order to which this paragraph applies is in force it appears on information to a justice of the peace acting for the petty sessions area concerned that the offender has failed to comply with any of the community requirements of the order, the justice may—

(a) issue a summons requiring the offender to appear at the place and time specified in it, or

(b) if the information is in writing and on oath, issue a warrant for his arrest.

(3) Any summons or warrant issued under this paragraph must direct the offender to appear or be brought—

(a) in the case of a suspended sentence order which is subject to review, before the court responsible for the order,

(b) in any other case, before a magistrates' court acting for the petty sessions area concerned.

(4) Where a summons issued under sub-paragraph (2)(a) requires the offender to appear before a magistrates' court and the offender does not appear in answer to the summons, the magistrates' court may issue a warrant for the arrest of the offender.

Issue of summons or warrant by Crown Court

7 (1) This paragraph applies to a suspended sentence order made by the Crown Court which does not include a direction that any failure to comply with the community requirements of the order is to be dealt with by a magistrates' court.

(2) If at any time while a suspended sentence order to which this paragraph applies is in force it appears on information to the Crown Court that the offender has failed to comply with any of the community requirements of the order, the Crown Court may—

    (a) issue a summons requiring the offender to appear at the place and time specified in it, or

    (b) if the information is in writing and on oath, issue a warrant for his arrest.

(3) Any summons or warrant issued under this paragraph must direct the offender to appear or be brought before the Crown Court.

(4) Where a summons issued under sub-paragraph (1)(a) requires the offender to appear before the Crown Court and the offender does not appear in answer to the summons, the Crown Court may issue a warrant for the arrest of the offender.

Powers of court on breach of community requirement or conviction of further offence

8   (1) This paragraph applies where—

    (a) it is proved to the satisfaction of a court before which an offender appears or is brought under paragraph 6 or 7 or by virtue of section 192(6) that he has failed without reasonable excuse to comply with any of the community requirements of the suspended sentence order, or

    (b) an offender is convicted of an offence committed during the operational period of a suspended sentence (other than one which has already taken effect) and either—

        (i) he is so convicted by or before a court having power under paragraph 11 to deal with him in respect of the suspended sentence, or

        (ii) he subsequently appears or is brought before such a court.

(2) The court must consider his case and deal with him in one of the following ways—

    (a) the court may order that the suspended sentence is to take effect with its original term and custodial period unaltered,

    (b) the court may order that the sentence is to take effect with either or both of the following modifications—

        (i) the substitution for the original term of a lesser term complying with section 181(2), and

        (ii) the substitution for the original custodial period of a lesser custodial period complying with section 181(5) and (6),

    (c) the court may amend the order by doing any one or more of the following—

        (i) imposing more onerous community requirements which the court could include if it were then making the order,

        (ii) subject to subsections (3) and (4) of section 189, extending the supervision period, or

        (iii) subject to subsection (3) of that section, extending the operational period.

(3) The court must make an order under sub-paragraph (2)(a) or (b) unless it is of the opinion that it would be unjust to do so in view of all the circumstances, including the matters mentioned in sub-paragraph (4); and where it is of that opinion the court must state its reasons.

(4) The matters referred to in sub-paragraph (3) are—

    (a) the extent to which the offender has complied with the community requirements of the suspended sentence order, and

    (b) in a case falling within sub-paragraph (1)(b), the facts of the subsequent offence.

(5) Where a court deals with an offender under sub-paragraph (2) in respect of a suspended sentence, the appropriate officer of the court must notify the appropriate officer of the court which passed the sentence of the method adopted.

(6) Where a suspended sentence order was made by the Crown Court and a magistrates' court would (apart from this sub-paragraph) be required to deal with the offender under sub-paragraph (2)(a), (b) or (c) it may instead commit him to custody or release him on bail until he can be brought or appear before the Crown Court.

(7) A magistrates' court which deals with an offender's case under sub-paragraph (6) must send to the Crown Court—

    (a) a certificate signed by a justice of the peace certifying that the offender has failed to comply with the community requirements of the suspended sentence order in the respect specified in the certificate, and

    (b) such other particulars of the case as may be desirable;

    and a certificate purporting to be so signed is admissible as evidence of the failure before the Crown Court.

(8) In proceedings before the Crown Court under this paragraph any question whether the offender has failed to comply with the community requirements of the suspended

sentence order and any question whether the offender has been convicted of an offence committed during the operational period of the suspended sentence is to be determined by the court and not by the verdict of a jury.

Further provisions as to order that suspended sentence is to take effect

9   (1) When making an order under paragraph 8(2)(a) or (b) that a sentence is to take effect (with or without any variation of the original term and custodial period), the court—

       (a) must also make a custody plus order, and

       (b) may order that the sentence is to take effect immediately or that the term of that sentence is to commence on the expiry of another term of imprisonment passed on the offender by that or another court.

   (2) The power to make an order under sub-paragraph (1)(b) has effect subject to section 265 (restriction on consecutive sentences for released prisoners).

   (3) For the purpose of any enactment conferring rights of appeal in criminal cases, any order made by the court under paragraph 8(2)(a) or (b) is to be treated as a sentence passed on the offender by that court for the offence for which the suspended sentence was passed.

Restriction of powers in paragraph 8 where treatment required

10   (1) An offender who is required by any of the following community requirements of a suspended sentence order—

       (a) a mental health treatment requirement,

       (b) a drug rehabilitation requirement, or

       (c) an alcohol treatment requirement,

       to submit to treatment for his mental condition, or his dependency on or propensity to misuse drugs or alcohol, is not to be treated for the purposes of paragraph 8(1)(a) as having failed to comply with that requirement on the ground only that he had refused to undergo any surgical, electrical or other treatment if, in the opinion of the court, his refusal was reasonable having regard to all the circumstances.

   (2) A court may not under paragraph 8(2)(c)(i) amend a mental health treatment requirement, a drug rehabilitation requirement or an alcohol treatment requirement unless the offender expresses his willingness to comply with the requirement as amended.

Court by which suspended sentence may be dealt with under paragraph 8(1)(b)

11   (1) An offender may be dealt with under paragraph 8(1)(b) in respect of a suspended sentence by the Crown Court or, where the sentence was passed by a magistrates' court, by any magistrates' court before which he appears or is brought.

   (2) Where an offender is convicted by a magistrates' court of any offence and the court is satisfied that the offence was committed during the operational period of a suspended sentence passed by the Crown Court—

       (a) the court may, if it thinks fit, commit him in custody or on bail to the Crown Court, and

       (b) if it does not, must give written notice of the conviction to the appropriate officer of the Crown Court.

Procedure where court convicting of further offence does not deal with suspended sentence

12   (1) If it appears to the Crown Court, where that court has jurisdiction in accordance with sub-paragraph (2), or to a justice of the peace having jurisdiction in accordance with that sub-paragraph—

       (a) that an offender has been convicted in the United Kingdom of an offence committed during the operational period of a suspended sentence, and

       (b) that he has not been dealt with in respect of the suspended sentence,

       that court or justice may, subject to the following provisions of this paragraph, issue a summons requiring the offender to appear at the place and time specified in it, or a warrant for his arrest.

   (2) Jurisdiction for the purposes of sub-paragraph (1) may be exercised—

       (a) if the suspended sentence was passed by the Crown Court, by that court;

       (b) if it was passed by a magistrates' court, by a justice acting for the petty sessions area for which that court acted.

   (3) Where—

(a) an offender is convicted in Scotland or Northern Ireland of an offence, and

(b) the court is informed that the offence was committed during the operational period of a suspended sentence passed in England or Wales,

the court must give written notice of the conviction to the appropriate officer of the court by which the suspended sentence was passed.

(4) Unless he is acting in consequence of a notice under sub-paragraph (3), a justice of the peace may not issue a summons under this paragraph except on information and may not issue a warrant under this paragraph except on information in writing and on oath.

(5) A summons or warrant issued under this paragraph must direct the offender to appear or be brought before the court by which the suspended sentence was passed.

PART 3

AMENDMENT OF SUSPENDED SENTENCE ORDER

Cancellation of community requirements of suspended sentence order

13 (1) Where at any time while a suspended sentence order is in force, it appears to the appropriate court on the application of the offender or the responsible officer that, having regard to the circumstances which have arisen since the order was made, it would be in the interests of justice to do so, the court may cancel the community requirements of the suspended sentence order.

(2) The circumstances in which the appropriate court may exercise its power under sub-paragraph (1) include the offender's making good progress or his responding satisfactorily to supervision.

(3) In this paragraph "the appropriate court" means—

(a) in the case of a suspended sentence order which is subject to review, the court responsible for the order,

(b) in the case of a suspended sentence order which was made by the Crown Court and does not include any direction that any failure to comply with the community requirements of the order is to be dealt with by a magistrates' court, the Crown Court, and

(c) in any other case, a magistrates' court acting for the petty sessions area concerned.

Amendment by reason of change of residence

14 (1) This paragraph applies where, at any time while a suspended sentence order is in force, the appropriate court is satisfied that the offender proposes to change, or has changed, his residence from the petty sessions area concerned to another petty sessions area.

(2) Subject to sub-paragraphs (3) and (4), the appropriate court may, and on the application of the responsible officer must, amend the suspended sentence order by substituting the other petty sessions area for the area specified in the order.

(3) The court may not amend under this paragraph a suspended sentence order which contains requirements which, in the opinion of the court, cannot be complied with unless the offender resides in the petty sessions area concerned unless, in accordance with paragraph 15 it either—

(a) cancels those requirements, or

(b) substitutes for those requirements other requirements which can be complied with if the offender does not reside in that area.

(4) The court may not amend under this paragraph any suspended sentence order imposing a programme requirement unless it appears to the court that the accredited programme specified in the requirement is available in the other petty sessions area.

(5) In this paragraph "the appropriate court" has the same meaning as in paragraph 13.

Amendment of community requirements of suspended sentence order

15 (1) At any time during the supervision period, the appropriate court may, on the application of the offender or the responsible officer, by order amend any community requirement of a suspended sentence order—

(a) by cancelling the requirement, or

(b) by replacing it with a requirement of the same kind, which the court could include if it were then making the order.

(2) For the purposes of sub-paragraph (1)—

(a) a requirement falling within any paragraph of section 190(1) is of the same kind as any other requirement falling within that paragraph, and

(b) an electronic monitoring requirement is a requirement of the same kind as any requirement falling within section 190(1) to which it relates.

(3) The court may not under this paragraph amend a mental health treatment requirement, a drug rehabilitation requirement or an alcohol treatment requirement unless the offender expresses his willingness to comply with the requirement as amended.

(4) If the offender fails to express his willingness to comply with a mental health treatment requirement, drug rehabilitation requirement or alcohol treatment requirement as proposed to be amended by the court under this paragraph, the court may—

    (a) revoke the suspended sentence order and the suspended sentence to which it relates, and

    (b) deal with him, for the offence in respect of which the suspended sentence was imposed, in any way in which it could deal with him if he had just been convicted by or before the court of the offence.

(5) In dealing with the offender under sub-paragraph (4)(b), the court must take into account the extent to which the offender has complied with the requirements of the order.

(6) In this paragraph "the appropriate court" has the same meaning as in paragraph 13.

Amendment of treatment requirements on report of practitioner

16 (1) Where the medical practitioner or other person by whom or under whose direction an offender is, in pursuance of any requirement to which this sub-paragraph applies, being treated for his mental condition or his dependency on or propensity to misuse drugs or alcohol—

    (a) is of the opinion mentioned in sub-paragraph (3), or

    (b) is for any reason unwilling to continue to treat or direct the treatment of the offender,

    he must make a report in writing to that effect to the responsible officer and that officer must apply under paragraph 15 to the appropriate court for the variation or cancellation of the requirement.

(2) The requirements to which sub-paragraph (1) applies are—

    (a) a mental health treatment requirement,

    (b) a drug rehabilitation requirement, and

    (c) an alcohol treatment requirement.

(3) The opinion referred to in sub-paragraph (1) is—

    (a) that the treatment of the offender should be continued beyond the period specified in that behalf in the order,

    (b) that the offender needs different treatment,

    (c) that the offender is not susceptible to treatment, or

    (d) that the offender does not require further treatment.

(4) In this paragraph "the appropriate court" has the same meaning as in paragraph 13.

Amendment in relation to review of drug rehabilitation requirement

17   Where the responsible officer is of the opinion that a suspended sentence order imposing a drug rehabilitation requirement which is subject to review should be so amended as to provide for each periodic review (required by section 211) to be made without a hearing instead of at a review hearing, or vice versa, he must apply under paragraph 15 to the court responsible for the order for the variation of the order.

Extension of unpaid work requirement

18 (1) Where—

    (a) a suspended sentence order imposing an unpaid work requirement is in force in respect of the offender, and

    (b) on the application of the offender or the responsible officer, it appears to the appropriate court that it would be in the interests of justice to do so having regard to circumstances which have arisen since the order was made,

    the court may, in relation to the order, extend the period of twelve months specified in section 200(2).

(2) In this paragraph "the appropriate court" has the same meaning as in paragraph 13.

Supplementary

19 (1) No application may be made under paragraph 13, 15 or 18, and no order may be made under paragraph 14, while an appeal against the suspended sentence is pending.

(2) Sub-paragraph (1) does not apply to an application under paragraph 15 which—

    (a) relates to a mental health treatment requirement, a drug rehabilitation requirement or an alcohol treatment requirement, and

(b) is made by the responsible officer with the consent of the offender.

20 (1) Subject to sub-paragraph (2), where a court proposes to exercise its powers under paragraph 15, otherwise than on the application of the offender, the court—

(a) must summon him to appear before the court, and

(b) if he does not appear in answer to the summons, may issue a warrant for his arrest.

(2) This paragraph does not apply to an order cancelling any community requirement of a suspended sentence order.

21   Paragraphs 8(2)(c) and 15(1)(b) have effect subject to the provisions mentioned in subsection (2) of section 190, and to subsections (3) and (5) of that section.

22 (1) On the making under this Schedule of an order amending a suspended sentence order, the proper officer of the court must—

(a) provide copies of the amending order to the offender and the responsible officer,

(b) in the case of an amending order which substitutes a new petty sessions area, provide a copy of the amending order to—

(i) the local probation board acting for that area, and

(ii) the magistrates' court acting for that area, and

(c) in the case of an amending order which imposes or amends a requirement specified in the first column of Schedule 14, provide a copy of so much of the amending order as relates to that requirement to the person specified in relation to that requirement in the second column of that Schedule.

(2) Where under sub-paragraph (1)(b) the proper officer of the court provides a copy of an amending order to a magistrates' court acting for a different area, the officer must also provide to that court such documents and information relating to the case as it considers likely to be of assistance to a court acting for that area in the exercise of its functions in relation to the order.

(3) In this paragraph "proper officer" means—

(a) in relation to a magistrates' court, the justices' chief executive for the court; and

(b) in relation to the Crown Court, the appropriate officer.

SCHEDULE 13   Section 194

TRANSFER OF SUSPENDED SENTENCE ORDERS TO SCOTLAND OR NORTHERN IRELAND

PART 1

SCOTLAND

1   (1) Where the court considering the making of a suspended sentence order is satisfied that the offender resides in Scotland, or will reside there when the order comes into force, the court may not make a suspended sentence order in respect of the offender unless it appears to the court—

(a) in the case of an order imposing a requirement mentioned in sub-paragraph (2), that arrangements exist for persons to comply with such a requirement in the locality in Scotland in which the offender resides, or will be residing when the order comes into force, and that provision can be made for him to comply with the requirement under those arrangements, and

(b) in any case, that suitable arrangements for his supervision can be made by the local authority in whose area he resides, or will be residing when the order comes into force.

(2) The requirements referred to in sub-paragraph (1)(a) are—

(a) an unpaid work requirement,

(b) an activity requirement,

(c) a programme requirement,

(d) a mental health treatment requirement,

(e) a drug rehabilitation requirement,

(f) an alcohol treatment requirement, and

(g) an electronic monitoring requirement.

(3) Where—

(a) the appropriate court for the purposes of paragraph 14 of Schedule 12 (amendment by reason of change of residence) is satisfied that an offender in respect of whom a suspended sentence order is in force proposes to reside or is residing in Scotland, and

(b) it appears to the court that the conditions in sub-paragraph (1)(a) and (b) are satisfied, the power of the court to amend the order under Part 3 of Schedule 12 includes power to amend it by requiring it to be complied with in Scotland and the offender to be supervised in accordance with the arrangements referred to in sub-paragraph (1)(b).

(4) For the purposes of sub-paragraph (3), any reference in sub-paragraph (1)(a) and (b) to the time when the order comes into force is to be treated as a reference to the time when the amendment comes into force.

(5) The court may not by virtue of sub-paragraph (1) or (3) require an attendance centre requirement to be complied with in Scotland.

(6) The court may not provide for an order made in accordance with this paragraph to be subject to review under section 191 or 210; and where an order which is subject to review under either of those sections is amended in accordance with this paragraph, the order shall cease to be so subject.

2   A suspended sentence order made or amended in accordance with paragraph 1 must—
   (a) specify the local authority area in which the offender resides or will be residing when the order or amendment comes into force, and
   (b) require the local authority for that area to appoint or assign an officer who will be responsible for discharging in relation to him the functions conferred on responsible officers by Part 12 of this Act;
   and section 216 (petty sessions area to be specified) does not apply in relation to an order so made or amended.

3 (1) Where a court makes or amends a suspended sentence order in accordance with paragraph 1, the court must provide the relevant documents to—
   (a) the local authority for the area specified in the order, and
   (b) the sheriff court having jurisdiction in the locality in which the offender resides or proposes to reside;
   and paragraphs (b) to (d) of subsection (1) of section 219 (provision of copies of relevant orders) do not apply in relation to an order so made or amended.

   (2) In this paragraph, "the relevant documents" means—
   (a) a copy of the order as made or amended, and
   (b) such other documents and information relating to the case as the court making or amending the order considers likely to be of assistance.

4 (1) In relation to the making or amendment of a suspended sentence order in accordance with paragraph 1, and (except for the purposes of paragraph 20) in relation to an order so made or amended, Chapter 4 of Part 12 of this Act has effect subject to the following modifications.

   (2) Any reference to the responsible officer has effect as a reference to the officer appointed or assigned under paragraph 2(b).

   (3) The following provisions are omitted—
   (a) subsection (7) of section 201 (activity requirement),
   (b) subsection (7) of section 202 (programme requirement),
   (c) subsection (4) of section 206 (residence requirement),
   (d) subsection (4) of section 218 (availability of arrangements in local area).

   (4) In section 207 (mental health treatment requirement), for subsection (2)(a) there is substituted—
   "(a) treatment as a resident patient in a hospital within the meaning of the Mental Health (Care and Treatment) (Scotland) Act 2003, not being a state hospital within the meaning of that Act;".

   (5) In section 215 (electronic monitoring requirement), in subsection (3), the words from "and" onwards are omitted.

5   In this Part of this Schedule "local authority" means a council constituted under section 2 of the Local Government etc. (Scotland) Act 1994 (c. 39); and any reference to the area of such an authority is a reference to the local government area within the meaning of that Act.

PART 2

NORTHERN IRELAND

6 (1) Where the court considering the making of a suspended sentence order is satisfied that the offender resides in Northern Ireland, or will reside there when the order comes into force, the court may not make a suspended sentence order in respect of the offender unless it appears to the court—
   (a) in the case of an order imposing a requirement mentioned in sub-paragraph (2), that arrangements exist for persons to comply with such a requirement in the petty

sessions district in Northern Ireland in which the offender resides, or will be residing when the order comes into force, and that provision can be made for him to comply with the requirement under those arrangements, and

(b) in any case, that suitable arrangements for his supervision can be made by the Probation Board for Northern Ireland.

(2) The requirements referred to in sub-paragraph (1)(a) are—

    (a) an unpaid work requirement,

    (b) an activity requirement,

    (c) a programme requirement,

    (d) a mental health treatment requirement,

    (e) a drug rehabilitation requirement,

    (f) an alcohol treatment requirement,

    (g) an attendance centre requirement, and

    (h) an electronic monitoring requirement.

(3) Where—

    (a) the appropriate court for the purposes of paragraph 14 of Schedule 12 (amendment by reason of change of residence) is satisfied that an offender in respect of whom a suspended sentence order is in force proposes to reside or is residing in Northern Ireland, and

    (b) it appears to the court that the conditions in sub-paragraphs (1)(a) and (b) are satisfied,

the power of the court to amend the order under Part 3 of Schedule 12 includes power to amend it by requiring it to be complied with in Northern Ireland and the offender to be supervised in accordance with the arrangements referred to in sub-paragraph (1)(b).

(4) For the purposes of sub-paragraph (3), any reference in sub-paragraph (1)(a) and (b) to the time when the order comes into force is to be treated as a reference to the time when the amendment comes into force.

(5) The court may not provide for an order made in accordance with this paragraph to be subject to review under section 191 or 210; and where an order which is subject to review under either of those sections is amended in accordance with this paragraph, the order shall cease to be so subject.

7   A suspended sentence order made or amended in accordance with paragraph 6 must—

    (a) specify the petty sessions district in Northern Ireland in which the offender resides or will be residing when the order or amendment comes into force, and

    (b) require the Probation Board for Northern Ireland to appoint or assign a probation officer who will be responsible for discharging in relation to him the functions conferred on responsible officers by Part 12 of this Act;

and section 216 (petty sessions area to be specified) does not apply in relation to an order so made or amended.

8   (1) Where a court makes or amends a suspended sentence order in accordance with paragraph 6, the court must provide the relevant documents to—

    (a) the Probation Board for Northern Ireland, and

    (b) the court of summary jurisdiction acting for the petty sessions district in which the offender resides or proposes to reside;

and paragraphs (b) to (d) of subsection (1) of section 219 (provision of copies of relevant orders) do not apply in relation to an order so made or amended.

(2) In this paragraph, "the relevant documents" means—

    (a) a copy of the order as made or amended, and

    (b) such other documents and information relating to the case as the court making or amending the order considers likely to be of assistance.

9   (1) In relation to the making or amendment of a suspended sentence order in accordance with paragraph 6, and (except for the purposes of paragraph 20) in relation to an order so made or amended, Chapter 4 of Part 12 of this Act has effect subject to the following modifications.

(2) Any reference to the responsible officer has effect as a reference to the probation officer appointed or assigned under paragraph 7(b).

(3) The following provisions are omitted—

    (a) subsection (7) of section 201 (activity requirement),

    (b) subsection (7) of section 202 (programme requirement),

    (c) subsection (4) of section 206 (residence requirement),

    (d) subsection (4) of section 218 (availability of arrangements in local area).

(4) In section 207 (mental health treatment requirement), for subsection (2)(a) there is substituted—

    "(a) treatment (whether as an in-patient or an out-patient) at such hospital as may be specified in the order, being a hospital within the meaning of the Health and Personal Social Services (Northern Ireland) Order 1972, approved by the Department of Health, Social Services and Public Safety for the purposes of paragraph 4(3) of Schedule 1 to the Criminal Justice (Northern Ireland) Order 1996 (S.I. 1996/ 3160 (N.I. 24));".

(5) In section 214 (attendance centre requirement), any reference to an attendance centre has effect as a reference to a day centre, as defined by paragraph 3(6) of Schedule 1 to the Criminal Justice (Northern Ireland) Order 1996 (S.I. 1996/3160 (N.I. 24).

(6) In section 215 (electronic monitoring requirement), in subsection (3), the words from "and" onwards are omitted.

PART 3

GENERAL PROVISIONS: BREACH OR AMENDMENT

10   This Part of this Schedule applies at any time while a suspended sentence order made or amended in accordance with paragraph 1 or 6 is in force in respect of an offender.

11   In this Part of this Schedule—

    "home court" means—

      (a) if the offender resides in Scotland, or will be residing there at the relevant time, the sheriff court having jurisdiction in the locality in which the offender resides or proposes to reside, and

      (b) if he resides in Northern Ireland, or will be residing there at the relevant time, the court of summary jurisdiction acting for the petty sessions district in which he resides or proposes to reside;

    "local authority" and "local authority area" are to be read in accordance with paragraph 5;

    "original court" means the court in England and Wales which made or last amended the order;

    "the relevant officer" means—

      (a) where the order specifies a local authority area in Scotland, the local authority officer appointed or assigned under paragraph 2(b), and

      (b) where the court specifies a petty sessions district in Northern Ireland, the probation officer appointed or assigned under paragraph 7(b);

    "the relevant time" means the time when the order or the amendment to it comes into force.

12 (1) Where this Part of this Schedule applies, Schedule 12 has effect subject to the following modifications.

(2) Any reference to the responsible officer has effect as a reference to the relevant officer.

(3) Any reference to a magistrates' court acting for the petty sessions area concerned has effect as a reference to a magistrates' court acting for the same petty sessions area as the original court; and any reference to a justice of the peace acting for the petty sessions area concerned has effect as a reference to a justice of the peace acting for the same petty sessions area as that court.

(4) Any reference to the appropriate court has effect as a reference to the original court.

(5) In paragraphs 4 and 5, any reference to causing an information to be laid before a justice of the peace has effect—

    (a) if the home court is in Scotland, as a reference to providing information to the home court with a view to it issuing a citation, and

    (b) if the home court is in Northern Ireland, as a reference to making a complaint to a justice of the peace in Northern Ireland.

(6) In paragraph 14—

(a) if the home court is in Scotland—

    (i) any reference to the petty sessions area concerned has effect as a reference to the local authority area specified in the order, and

    (ii) any other reference to a petty sessions area has effect as a reference to a local authority area, and

(b) if the home court is in Northern Ireland—

    (i) any reference to the petty sessions area concerned has effect as a reference to the petty sessions district specified in the order, and

    (ii) any other reference to a petty sessions area has effect as a reference to a petty sessions district.

(7) Paragraph 22 is omitted.

(8) No court in England and Wales may—

(a) exercise any power in relation to any failure by the offender to comply with any community requirement of the order unless the offender has been required in accordance with paragraph 14(1)(b) or (2)(a) of this Schedule to appear before that court;

(b) exercise any power under Part 3 of Schedule 12 unless the offender has been required in accordance with paragraph 15(2) or 16 of this Schedule to appear before that court.

13 (1) Sub-paragraph (2) applies where it appears to the home court—

(a) if that court is in Scotland, on information from the relevant officer, or

(b) if that court is in Northern Ireland, upon a complaint being made by the relevant officer,

that the offender has failed without reasonable excuse to comply with any of the community requirements of the suspended sentence order.

(2) The home court may—

(a) if it is in Scotland—

    (i) issue a citation requiring the offender to appear before it at the time specified in the citation, or

    (ii) issue a warrant for the offender's arrest;

(b) if it is in Northern Ireland—

    (i) issue a summons requiring the offender to appear before it at the time specified in the summons, or

    (ii) issue a warrant for the offender's arrest.

14 (1) The court before which an offender appears or is brought by virtue of paragraph 13 must—

(a) determine whether the offender has failed without reasonable excuse to comply with any of the community requirements of the suspended sentence order, or

(b) require the offender to appear before the original court.

(2) If the home court determines that the offender has failed without reasonable excuse to comply with any of the community requirements of the order—

(a) the home court must require the offender to appear before the original court, and

(b) when the offender appears before the original court, paragraph 8 of Schedule 12 applies as if it had already been proved to the satisfaction of the original court that the offender failed without reasonable excuse to comply with such of the community requirements of the order as may have been determined.

(3) An offender who is required by any of the following community requirements of a suspended sentence order—

(a) a mental health treatment requirement,

(b) a drug rehabilitation requirement, or

(c) an alcohol treatment requirement,

to submit to treatment for his mental condition, or his dependency on or propensity to misuse drugs or alcohol, is not to be treated for the purposes of sub-paragraph (2) as having failed to comply with that requirement on the ground only that he had refused to undergo any surgical, electrical or other treatment if, in the opinion of the court, his refusal was reasonable having regard to all the circumstances.

(4) The evidence of one witness shall, for the purposes of sub-paragraph (2), be sufficient.

(5) Where the home court is in Scotland and the order contains an electronic monitoring requirement, section 245H of the Criminal Procedure (Scotland) Act 1995 (c. 46)

(documentary evidence) applies to proceedings under this paragraph as it applies to proceedings under section 245F of that Act (breach of restriction of liberty order).

(6) Where an offender is required by virtue of sub-paragraph (2) to appear before the original court—

(a) the home court must send to the original court a certificate certifying that the offender has failed without reasonable excuse to comply with the requirements of the order in the respect specified, and

(b) such a certificate signed by the clerk of the home court is admissible before the original court as conclusive evidence of the matters specified in it.

15 (1) The home court may exercise any power under Part 3 of Schedule 12 (amendment of suspended sentence order) as if it were the original court, except that the home court may not exercise the power conferred by paragraph 15(4) of that Schedule.

(2) Where paragraph 15(4) of Schedule 12 applies the home court must require the offender to appear before the original court.

(3) Subject to sub-paragraph (4), where the home court proposes to exercise the power conferred by paragraph 15(1) of Schedule 12, otherwise than on the application of the offender, the court—

(a) if it is in Scotland—

(i) must issue a citation requiring the offender to appear before it, and

(ii) if he does not appear in answer to the citation, may issue a warrant for the offender's arrest;

(b) if it is in Northern Ireland—

(i) must issue a summons requiring the offender to appear before it, and

(ii) if he does not appear in answer to the summons, may issue a warrant for the offender's arrest;

and paragraph 20 of Schedule 12 does not apply to the home court.

(4) Sub-paragraph (3) does not apply to an order cancelling any community requirement of a suspended sentence order.

(5) Where the home court is considering amending a suspended sentence order, any reference in Chapter 4 of Part 12 of this Act to a local probation board has effect as a reference to a local authority in Scotland or, as the case may be, the Probation Board for Northern Ireland.

16 Where by virtue of paragraph 15 any application is made to the home court under Part 3 of Schedule 12, the home court may (instead of dealing with the application) require the offender to appear before the original court.

17 No court may amend or further amend a suspended sentence order unless it appears to the court that the conditions in paragraph 1(1)(a) and (b) or, as the case may be, paragraph 6(1)(a) and (b) are satisfied in relation to any requirement to be imposed; but this paragraph does not apply to any amendment by virtue of paragraph 20(2).

18 The preceding paragraphs of this Schedule have effect in relation to any amendment of a suspended order by any court as they have effect in relation to the amendment of such an order by virtue of paragraph 1(3) or 6(3).

19 On the making of an order amending a suspended sentence order—

(a) the court must provide copies of the amending order to the offender and the relevant officer, and

(b) in the case of an amending order which substitutes a new local authority area or petty sessions district, paragraphs 2 and 3 or, as the case may be, 7 and 8 have effect in relation to the order as they have effect in relation to an order made or amended in accordance with paragraph 1 or 6.

20 (1) This paragraph applies where the home court is satisfied that the offender is residing or proposes to reside in England and Wales.

(2) Subject to sub-paragraphs (3) and (4), the home court may, and on the application of the relevant officer must, amend the suspended sentence order by requiring it to be complied with in England and Wales.

(3) The court may not amend under this paragraph a suspended sentence order which contains requirements which, in the opinion of the court, cannot be complied with in the petty sessions area in which the offender is residing or proposes to reside unless, in accordance with paragraph 15 of Schedule 12 it either—

(a) cancels those requirements, or

(b) substitutes for those requirements other requirements which can be complied with if the offender resides in that area.

(4) The court may not amend under this paragraph any suspended sentence order imposing a programme requirement unless it appears to the court that the accredited programme specified in the requirement is available in the petty sessions area in England and Wales in which the offender is residing or proposes to reside.

(5) The suspended sentence order as amended must specify the petty sessions area in which the offender resides or proposes to reside.

(6) On the making under this paragraph of an order amending a suspended sentence order, the home court must—

(a) provide copies of the amending order to the offender, the relevant officer and the local probation board acting for the new petty sessions area, and

(b) provide the magistrates' court acting for that area with a copy of the amending order and such other documents and information relating to the case as the home court considers likely to be of assistance to a court acting for that area in the exercise of its functions in relation to the order.

(7) Where an order has been amended under this paragraph, the preceding paragraphs of this Schedule shall cease to apply to the order as amended.

PART 4

SUPPLEMENTARY

21   Subsections (1) and (3) of section 245C of the Criminal Procedure (Scotland) Act 1995 (c. 46) (provision of remote monitoring) have effect as if they included a reference to the electronic monitoring of the community requirements of a suspended sentence order made or amended in accordance with paragraph 1 of this Schedule.

22 (1) Section 4 of the Summary Jurisdiction (Process) Act 1881 (c. 24) (which provides, among other things, for service in England and Wales of Scottish citations or warrants) applies to any citation or warrant issued under paragraph 13(2)(a) or 15(3)(a) as it applies to a citation or warrant granted under section 134 of the Criminal Procedure (Scotland) Act 1995.

(2) A summons issued by a court in Northern Ireland under paragraph 13(2)(b) or 15(3)(b) may, in such circumstances as may be prescribed by rules of court, be served in England and Wales or Scotland.

SCHEDULE 14   **Section 219**

PERSONS TO WHOM COPIES OF REQUIREMENTS TO BE PROVIDED IN PARTICULAR CASES

Requirement	Person to whom copy of requirement is to be given
An activity requirement.	The person specified under section 201(1)(a).
An exclusion requirement imposed for the purpose (or partly for the purpose) of protecting a person from being approached by the offender.	The person intended to be protected.
A residence requirement relating to residence in an institution.	The person in charge of the institution.
A mental health treatment requirement.	The person specified under section 207(2)(c) or the person in charge of the institution or place specified under section 207(2)(a) or (b).
A drug rehabilitation requirement.	The person in charge of the institution or place specified under section 209(4)(a) or (b).
An alcohol treatment requirement.	The person specified under section 212(5)(c) or the person in charge of the institution or place specified under section 212(5)(a) or (b).
An attendance centre requirement.	The officer in charge of the attendance centre specified in the requirement.
An electronic monitoring requirement.	Any person who by virtue of section 215(3) will be responsible for the electronic monitoring. Any person by virtue of whose consent the requirement is included in the order.

Requirement	Person to whom copy of requirement is to be given

SCHEDULE 15   Section 224

SPECIFIED OFFENCES FOR PURPOSES OF CHAPTER 5 OF PART 12

PART 1

SPECIFIED VIOLENT OFFENCES

1   Manslaughter.

2   Kidnapping.

3   False imprisonment.

4   An offence under section 4 of the Offences against the Person Act 1861 (c. 100) (soliciting murder).

5   An offence under section 16 of that Act (threats to kill).

6   An offence under section 18 of that Act (wounding with intent to cause grievous bodily harm).

7   An offence under section 20 of that Act (malicious wounding).

8   An offence under section 21 of that Act (attempting to choke, suffocate or strangle in order to commit or assist in committing an indictable offence).

9   An offence under section 22 of that Act (using chloroform etc. to commit or assist in the committing of any indictable offence).

10   An offence under section 23 of that Act (maliciously administering poison etc. so as to endanger life or inflict grievous bodily harm).

11   An offence under section 27 of that Act (abandoning children).

12   An offence under section 28 of that Act (causing bodily injury by explosives).

13   An offence under section 29 of that Act (using explosives etc. with intent to do grievous bodily harm).

14   An offence under section 30 of that Act (placing explosives with intent to do bodily injury).

15   An offence under section 31 of that Act (setting spring guns etc. with intent to do grievous bodily harm).

16   An offence under section 32 of that Act (endangering the safety of railway passengers).

17   An offence under section 35 of that Act (injuring persons by furious driving).

18   An offence under section 37 of that Act (assaulting officer preserving wreck).

19   An offence under section 38 of that Act (assault with intent to resist arrest).

20   An offence under section 47 of that Act (assault occasioning actual bodily harm).

21   An offence under section 2 of the Explosive Substances Act 1883 (c. 3) (causing explosion likely to endanger life or property).

22   An offence under section 3 of that Act (attempt to cause explosion, or making or keeping explosive with intent to endanger life or property).

23   An offence under section 1 of the Infant Life (Preservation) Act 1929 (c. 34) (child destruction).

24   An offence under section 1 of the Children and Young Persons Act 1933 (c. 12) (cruelty to children).

25   An offence under section 1 of the Infanticide Act 1938 (c. 36) (infanticide).

26   An offence under section 16 of the Firearms Act 1968 (c. 27) (possession of firearm with intent to endanger life).

27   An offence under section 16A of that Act (possession of firearm with intent to cause fear of violence).

28   An offence under section 17(1) of that Act (use of firearm to resist arrest).

29   An offence under section 17(2) of that Act (possession of firearm at time of committing or being arrested for offence specified in Schedule 1 to that Act).

30   An offence under section 18 of that Act (carrying a firearm with criminal intent).

31   An offence under section 8 of the Theft Act 1968 (c. 60) (robbery or assault with intent to rob).

32   An offence under section 9 of that Act of burglary with intent to—
(a) inflict grievous bodily harm on a person, or
(b) do unlawful damage to a building or anything in it.

33   An offence under section 10 of that Act (aggravated burglary).

34   An offence under section 12A of that Act (aggravated vehicle-taking) involving an accident which caused the death of any person.

35   An offence of arson under section 1 of the Criminal Damage Act 1971 (c. 48).
36   An offence under section 1(2) of that Act (destroying or damaging property) other than an offence of arson.
37   An offence under section 1 of the Taking of Hostages Act 1982 (c. 28) (hostage-taking).
38   An offence under section 1 of the Aviation Security Act 1982 (c. 36) (hijacking).
39   An offence under section 2 of that Act (destroying, damaging or endangering safety of aircraft).
40   An offence under section 3 of that Act (other acts endangering or likely to endanger safety of aircraft).
41   An offence under section 4 of that Act (offences in relation to certain dangerous articles).
42   An offence under section 127 of the Mental Health Act 1983 (c. 20) (ill-treatment of patients).
43   An offence under section 1 of the Prohibition of Female Circumcision Act 1985 (c. 38) (prohibition of female circumcision).
44   An offence under section 1 of the Public Order Act 1986 (c. 64) (riot).
45   An offence under section 2 of that Act (violent disorder).
46   An offence under section 3 of that Act (affray).
47   An offence under section 134 of the Criminal Justice Act 1988 (c. 33) (torture).
48   An offence under section 1 of the Road Traffic Act 1988 (c. 52) (causing death by dangerous driving).
49   An offence under section 3A of that Act (causing death by careless driving when under influence of drink or drugs).
50   An offence under section 1 of the Aviation and Maritime Security Act 1990 (c. 31) (endangering safety at aerodromes).
51   An offence under section 9 of that Act (hijacking of ships).
52   An offence under section 10 of that Act (seizing or exercising control of fixed platforms).
53   An offence under section 11 of that Act (destroying fixed platforms or endangering their safety).
54   An offence under section 12 of that Act (other acts endangering or likely to endanger safe navigation).
55   An offence under section 13 of that Act (offences involving threats).
56   An offence under Part II of the Channel Tunnel (Security) Order 1994 (S.I. 1994/570) (offences relating to Channel Tunnel trains and the tunnel system).
57   An offence under section 4 of the Protection from Harassment Act 1997 (c. 40) (putting people in fear of violence).
58   An offence under section 29 of the Crime and Disorder Act 1998 (c. 37) (racially or religiously aggravated assaults).
59   An offence falling within section 31(1)(a) or (b) of that Act (racially or religiously aggravated offences under section 4 or 4A of the Public Order Act 1986 (c. 64)).
60   An offence under section 51 or 52 of the International Criminal Court Act 2001 (c. 17) (genocide, crimes against humanity, war crimes and related offences), other than one involving murder.
61   An offence under section 1 of the Female Genital Mutilation Act 2003 (c. 31) (female genital mutilation).
62   An offence under section 2 of that Act (assisting a girl to mutilate her own genitalia).
63   An offence under section 3 of that Act (assisting a non-UK person to mutilate overseas a girl's genitalia).
64   An offence of—
      (a) aiding, abetting, counselling, procuring or inciting the commission of an offence specified in this Part of this Schedule,
      (b) conspiring to commit an offence so specified, or
      (c) attempting to commit an offence so specified.
65   An attempt to commit murder or a conspiracy to commit murder.

PART 2

SPECIFIED SEXUAL OFFENCES

66   An offence under section 1 of the Sexual Offences Act 1956 (c. 69) (rape).
67   An offence under section 2 of that Act (procurement of woman by threats).
68   An offence under section 3 of that Act (procurement of woman by false pretences).
69   An offence under section 4 of that Act (administering drugs to obtain or facilitate intercourse).

70   An offence under section 5 of that Act (intercourse with girl under thirteen).

71   An offence under section 6 of that Act (intercourse with girl under 16).

72   An offence under section 7 of that Act (intercourse with a defective).

73   An offence under section 9 of that Act (procurement of a defective).

74   An offence under section 10 of that Act (incest by a man).

75   An offence under section 11 of that Act (incest by a woman).

76   An offence under section 14 of that Act (indecent assault on a woman).

77   An offence under section 15 of that Act (indecent assault on a man).

78   An offence under section 16 of that Act (assault with intent to commit buggery).

79   An offence under section 17 of that Act (abduction of woman by force or for the sake of her property).

80   An offence under section 19 of that Act (abduction of unmarried girl under eighteen from parent or guardian).

81   An offence under section 20 of that Act (abduction of unmarried girl under sixteen from parent or guardian).

82   An offence under section 21 of that Act (abduction of defective from parent or guardian).

83   An offence under section 22 of that Act (causing prostitution of women).

84   An offence under section 23 of that Act (procuration of girl under twenty-one).

85   An offence under section 24 of that Act (detention of woman in brothel).

86   An offence under section 25 of that Act (permitting girl under thirteen to use premises for intercourse).

87   An offence under section 26 of that Act (permitting girl under sixteen to use premises for intercourse).

88   An offence under section 27 of that Act (permitting defective to use premises for intercourse).

89   An offence under section 28 of that Act (causing or encouraging the prostitution of, intercourse with or indecent assault on girl under sixteen).

90   An offence under section 29 of that Act (causing or encouraging prostitution of defective).

91   An offence under section 32 of that Act (soliciting by men).

92   An offence under section 33 of that Act (keeping a brothel).

93   An offence under section 128 of the Mental Health Act 1959 (c. 72) (sexual intercourse with patients).

94   An offence under section 1 of the Indecency with Children Act 1960 (c. 33) (indecent conduct towards young child).

95   An offence under section 4 of the Sexual Offences Act 1967 (c. 60) (procuring others to commit homosexual acts).

96   An offence under section 5 of that Act (living on earnings of male prostitution).

97   An offence under section 9 of the Theft Act 1968 (c. 60) of burglary with intent to commit rape.

98   An offence under section 54 of the Criminal Law Act 1977 (c. 45) (inciting girl under sixteen to have incestuous sexual intercourse).

99   An offence under section 1 of the Protection of Children Act 1978 (c. 37) (indecent photographs of children).

100   An offence under section 170 of the Customs and Excise Management Act 1979 (c. 2) (penalty for fraudulent evasion of duty etc.) in relation to goods prohibited to be imported under section 42 of the Customs Consolidation Act 1876 (c. 36) (indecent or obscene articles).

101   An offence under section 160 of the Criminal Justice Act 1988 (c. 33) (possession of indecent photograph of a child).

102   An offence under section 1 of the Sexual Offences Act 2003 (c. 42) (rape).

103   An offence under section 2 of that Act (assault by penetration).

104   An offence under section 3 of that Act (sexual assault).

105   An offence under section 4 of that Act (causing a person to engage in sexual activity without consent).

106   An offence under section 5 of that Act (rape of a child under 13).

107   An offence under section 6 of that Act (assault of a child under 13 by penetration).

108   An offence under section 7 of that Act (sexual assault of a child under 13).

109   An offence under section 8 of that Act (causing or inciting a child under 13 to engage in sexual activity).

110   An offence under section 9 of that Act (sexual activity with a child).

111   An offence under section 10 of that Act (causing or inciting a child to engage in sexual activity).

112   An offence under section 11 of that Act (engaging in sexual activity in the presence of a child).

113   An offence under section 12 of that Act (causing a child to watch a sexual act).

114   An offence under section 13 of that Act (child sex offences committed by children or young persons).

115   An offence under section 14 of that Act (arranging or facilitating commission of a child sex offence).

116   An offence under section 15 of that Act (meeting a child following sexual grooming etc.).

117   An offence under section 16 of that Act (abuse of position of trust: sexual activity with a child).

118   An offence under section 17 of that Act (abuse of position of trust: causing or inciting a child to engage in sexual activity).

119   An offence under section 18 of that Act (abuse of position of trust: sexual activity in the presence of a child).

120   An offence under section 19 of that Act (abuse of position of trust: causing a child to watch a sexual act).

121   An offence under section 25 of that Act (sexual activity with a child family member).

122   An offence under section 26 of that Act (inciting a child family member to engage in sexual activity).

123   An offence under section 30 of that Act (sexual activity with a person with a mental disorder impeding choice).

124   An offence under section 31 of that Act (causing or inciting a person with a mental disorder impeding choice to engage in sexual activity).

125   An offence under section 32 of that Act (engaging in sexual activity in the presence of a person with a mental disorder impeding choice).

126   An offence under section 33 of that Act (causing a person with a mental disorder impeding choice to watch a sexual act).

127   An offence under section 34 of that Act (inducement, threat or deception to procure sexual activity with a person with a mental disorder).

128   An offence under section 35 of that Act (causing a person with a mental disorder to engage in or agree to engage in sexual activity by inducement, threat or deception).

129   An offence under section 36 of that Act (engaging in sexual activity in the presence, procured by inducement, threat or deception, of a person with a mental disorder).

130   An offence under section 37 of that Act (causing a person with a mental disorder to watch a sexual act by inducement, threat or deception).

131   An offence under section 38 of that Act (care workers: sexual activity with a person with a mental disorder).

132   An offence under section 39 of that Act (care workers: causing or inciting sexual activity).

133   An offence under section 40 of that Act (care workers: sexual activity in the presence of a person with a mental disorder).

134   An offence under section 41 of that Act (care workers: causing a person with a mental disorder to watch a sexual act).

135   An offence under section 47 of that Act (paying for sexual services of a child).

136   An offence under section 48 of that Act (causing or inciting child prostitution or pornography).

137   An offence under section 49 of that Act (controlling a child prostitute or a child involved in pornography).

138   An offence under section 50 of that Act (arranging or facilitating child prostitution or pornography).

139   An offence under section 52 of that Act (causing or inciting prostitution for gain).

140   An offence under section 53 of that Act (controlling prostitution for gain).

141   An offence under section 57 of that Act (trafficking into the UK for sexual exploitation).

142   An offence under section 58 of that Act (trafficking within the UK for sexual exploitation).
143   An offence under section 59 of that Act (trafficking out of the UK for sexual exploitation).
144   An offence under section 61 of that Act (administering a substance with intent).
145   An offence under section 62 of that Act (committing an offence with intent to commit a sexual offence).
146   An offence under section 63 of that Act (trespass with intent to commit a sexual offence).
147   An offence under section 64 of that Act (sex with an adult relative: penetration).
148   An offence under section 65 of that Act (sex with an adult relative: consenting to penetration).
149   An offence under section 66 of that Act (exposure).
150   An offence under section 67 of that Act (voyeurism).
151   An offence under section 69 of that Act (intercourse with an animal).
152   An offence under section 70 of that Act (sexual penetration of a corpse).
153   An offence of—
        (a) aiding, abetting, counselling, procuring or inciting the commission of an offence specified in this Part of this Schedule,
        (b) conspiring to commit an offence so specified, or
        (c) attempting to commit an offence so specified.

SCHEDULE 16   **Section 229**

SCOTTISH OFFENCES SPECIFIED FOR THE PURPOSES OF SECTION 229(4)

1   Rape.
2   Clandestine injury to women.
3   Abduction of woman or girl with intent to rape or ravish.
4   Assault with intent to rape or ravish.
5   Indecent assault.
6   Lewd, indecent or libidinous behaviour or practices.
7   Shameless indecency.
8   Sodomy.
9   An offence under section 170 of the Customs and Excise Management Act 1979 (c. 2) in relation to goods prohibited to be imported under section 42 of the Customs Consolidation Act 1876 (c. 36), but only where the prohibited goods include indecent photographs of persons.
10   An offence under section 52 of the Civic Government (Scotland) Act 1982 (c. 45) (taking and distribution of indecent images of children).
11   An offence under section 52A of that Act (possession of indecent images of children).
12   An offence under section 1 of the Criminal Law (Consolidation) (Scotland) Act 1995 (c. 39) (incest).
13   An offence under section 2 of that Act (intercourse with a stepchild).
14   An offence under section 3 of that Act (intercourse with child under 16 by person in position of trust).
15   An offence under section 5 of that Act (unlawful intercourse with girl under 16).
16   An offence under section 6 of that Act (indecent behaviour towards girl between 12 and 16).
17   An offence under section 8 of that Act (detention of woman in brothel or other premises).
18   An offence under section 10 of that Act (person having parental responsibilities causing or encouraging sexual activity in relation to a girl under 16).
19   An offence under subsection (5) of section 13 of that Act (homosexual offences).
20   An offence under section 3 of the Sexual Offences (Amendment) Act 2000 (c. 44) (abuse of position of trust).
21   An offence of—
        (a) attempting, conspiring or inciting another to commit any offence specified in the preceding paragraphs, or

(b) aiding, abetting, counselling or procuring the commission of any offence specified in paragraphs 9 to 20.

22 Any offence (other than an offence specified in any of the preceding paragraphs) inferring personal violence.

SCHEDULE 17 **Section 229**

NORTHERN IRELAND OFFENCES SPECIFIED FOR THE PURPOSES OF SECTION 229(4)

PART 1

VIOLENT OFFENCES

1 Manslaughter.
2 Kidnapping.
3 Riot.
4 Affray.
5 False imprisonment.
6 An offence under section 4 of the Offences against the Person Act 1861 (c. 100) (soliciting murder).
7 An offence under section 16 of that Act (threats to kill).
8 An offence under section 18 of that Act (wounding with intent to cause grievous bodily harm).
9 An offence under section 20 of that Act (malicious wounding).
10 An offence under section 21 of that Act (attempting to choke, suffocate or strangle in order to commit or assist in committing an indictable offence).
11 An offence under section 22 of that Act (using chloroform etc. to commit or assist in the committing of any indictable offence).
12 An offence under section 23 of that Act (maliciously administering poison etc. so as to endanger life or inflict grievous bodily harm).
13 An offence under section 27 of that Act (abandoning children).
14 An offence under section 28 of that Act (causing bodily injury by explosives).
15 An offence under section 29 of that Act (using explosives etc. with intent to do grievous bodily harm).
16 An offence under section 30 of that Act (placing explosives with intent to do bodily injury).
17 An offence under section 31 of that Act (setting spring guns etc. with intent to do grievous bodily harm).
18 An offence under section 32 of that Act (endangering the safety of railway passengers).
19 An offence under section 35 of that Act (injuring persons by furious driving).
20 An offence under section 37 of that Act (assaulting officer preserving wreck).
21 An offence under section 47 of that Act of assault occasioning actual bodily harm.
22 An offence under section 2 of the Explosive Substances Act 1883 (c. 3) (causing explosion likely to endanger life or property).
23 An offence under section 3 of that Act (attempt to cause explosion, or making or keeping explosive with intent to endanger life or property).
24 An offence under section 25 of the Criminal Justice (Northern Ireland) Act 1945 (c. 15) (child destruction).
25 An offence under section 1 of the Infanticide Act (Northern Ireland) 1939 (c. 5) (infanticide).
26 An offence under section 7(1)(b) of the Criminal Justice (Miscellaneous Provisions) Act (Northern Ireland) 1968 (c. 28) (assault with intent to resist arrest).
27 An offence under section 20 of the Children and Young Persons Act (Northern Ireland) 1968 (c. 34) (cruelty to children).
28 An offence under section 8 of the Theft Act (Northern Ireland) 1969 (c. 16) (robbery or assault with intent to rob).
29 An offence under section 9 of that Act of burglary with intent to—

(a) inflict grievous bodily harm on a person, or

(b) do unlawful damage to a building or anything in it.

30 An offence under section 10 of that Act (aggravated burglary).

31 An offence of arson under Article 3 of the Criminal Damage Northern Ireland) Order 1977 (S.I. 1977/426 (N.I. 4)).

32 An offence under Article 3(2) of that Order (destroying or damaging property) other than an offence of arson.

33 An offence under Article 17 of the Firearms (Northern Ireland) Order 1981 (S.I. 1981/155 (N.I. 2)) (possession of firearm with intent to endanger life).

34 An offence under Article 17A of that Order (possession of firearm with intent to cause fear of violence).

35 An offence under Article 18(1) of that Order (use of firearm to resist arrest).

36 An offence under Article 18(2) of that Order (possession of firearm at time of committing or being arrested for an offence specified in Schedule 1 to that Order).

37 An offence under Article 19 of that Order (carrying a firearm with criminal intent).

38 An offence under section 1 of the Taking of Hostages Act 1982 (c. 28) (hostage-taking).

39 An offence under section 1 of the Aviation Security Act 1982 (c. 36) (hijacking).

40 An offence under section 2 of that Act (destroying, damaging or endangering safety of aircraft).

41 An offence under section 3 of that Act (other acts endangering or likely to endanger safety of aircraft).

42 An offence under section 4 of that Act (offences in relation to certain dangerous articles).

43 An offence under section 1 of the Prohibition of Female Circumcision Act 1985 (c. 38) (prohibition of female circumcision).

44 An offence under Article 121 of the Mental Health (Northern Ireland) Order 1986 (S.I. 1986/595 (N.I.4) (ill-treatment of patients).

45 An offence under section 134 of the Criminal Justice Act 1988 (c. 33) (torture).

46 An offence under section 1 of the Aviation and Maritime Security Act 1990 (c. 31) (endangering safety at aerodromes).

47 An offence under section 9 of that Act (hijacking of ships).

48 An offence under section 10 of that Act (seizing or exercising control of fixed platforms).

49 An offence under section 11 of that Act (destroying fixed platforms or endangering their safety).

50 An offence under section 12 of that Act (other acts endangering or likely to endanger safe navigation).

51 An offence under section 13 of that Act (offences involving threats).

52 An offence under Part II of the Channel Tunnel (Security) Order 1994 (S.I. 1994/570) (offences relating to Channel Tunnel trains and the tunnel system).

53 An offence under Article 9 of the Road Traffic (Northern Ireland) Order 1995 (S.I. 1995/2994 (N.I. 18)) (causing death or grievous bodily injury by dangerous driving).

54 An offence under Article 14 of that Order (causing death or grievous bodily injury by careless driving when under the influence of drink or drugs).

55 An offence under Article 6 of the Protection from Harassment (Northern Ireland) Order 1997 (S.I. 1997/1180 (N.I. 9)) (putting people in fear of violence).

56 An offence under section 66 of the Police (Northern Ireland) Act 1998 (c. 32) (assaulting or obstructing a constable etc.).

57 An offence under section 51 or 52 of the International Criminal Court Act 2001 (c. 17) (genocide, crimes against humanity, war crimes and related offences), other than one involving murder.

58 An offence under section 1 of the Female Genital Mutilation Act 2003 (c. 31) (female genital mutilation).

59 An offence under section 2 of that Act (assisting a girl to mutilate her own genitalia).

60 An offence under section 3 of that Act (assisting a non-UK person to mutilate overseas a girl's genitalia).

61 An offence of—

(a) aiding, abetting, counselling, procuring or inciting the commission of an offence specified in this Part of this Schedule,

(b) conspiring to commit an offence so specified, or

(c) attempting to commit an offence so specified.

62   An attempt to commit murder or a conspiracy to commit murder.

PART 2

SEXUAL OFFENCES

63   Rape.

64   Indecent assault upon a female.

65   An offence under section 52 of the Offences against the Person Act 1861 (c. 100) (indecent assault upon a female).

66   An offence under section 53 of that Act (abduction of woman etc.).

67   An offence under section 54 of that Act (abduction of woman by force).

68   An offence under section 55 of that Act (abduction of unmarried girl under 16 from parent or guardian).

69   An offence under section 2 of the Criminal Law Amendment Act 1885 (c. 69) (procuration).

70   An offence under section 3 of that Act (procurement of woman or girl by threats etc. or administering drugs).

71   An offence under section 4 of that Act (intercourse or attempted intercourse with girl under 14).

72   An offence under section 5 of that Act (intercourse or attempted intercourse with girl under 17).

73   An offence under section 6 of that Act (permitting girl under 17 to use premises for intercourse).

74   An offence under section 7 of that Act (abduction of girl under 18 from parent or guardian).

75   An offence under section 8 of that Act (unlawful detention of woman or girl in brothel etc.).

76   An offence under section 1 of the Vagrancy Act 1898 (c. 39) (living on earnings of prostitution or soliciting or importuning in a public place).

77   An offence under section 1 of the Punishment of Incest Act 1908 (c. 45) (incest by a man).

78   An offence under section 2 of that Act (incest by a woman).

79   An offence under section 21 of the Children and Young Persons Act (Northern Ireland) 1968 (c. 34) (causing or encouraging seduction or prostitution of girl under 17).

80   An offence under section 22 of that Act (indecent conduct towards child).

81   An offence under section 9 of the Theft Act (Northern Ireland) 1969 (c. 16) of burglary with intent to commit rape.

82   An offence under Article 3 of the Protection of Children (Northern Ireland) Order 1978 (S.I. 1978/1047 (N.I. 17)) (indecent photographs of children).

83   An offence under section 170 of the Customs and Excise Management Act 1979 (c. 2) (penalty for fraudulent evasion of duty etc.) in relation to goods prohibited to be imported under section 42 of the Customs Consolidation Act 1876 (c. 36) (indecent or obscene articles).

84   An offence under Article 9 of the Criminal Justice (Northern Ireland) Order 1980 (S.I. 1980/704 (N.I. 6)) (inciting girl under 16 to have incestuous sexual intercourse).

85   An offence under Article 7 of the Homosexual Offences (Northern Ireland) Order 1982 (S.I. 1982/1536 (N.I. 19)) (procuring others to commit homosexual acts).

86   An offence under Article 8 of that Order (living on earnings of male prostitution).

87   An offence under Article 122 of the Mental Health (Northern Ireland) Order 1986 (S.I. 1986/595 (N.I. 4)) (protection of women suffering from severe mental handicap).

88   An offence under Article 123 of that Order (protection of patients).

89   An offence under Article 15 of the Criminal Justice (Evidence, etc.) (Northern Ireland) Order 1988 (S.I. 1988/1847 (N.I. 17) (possession of indecent photograph of a child).

90   An offence under section 15 of the Sexual Offences Act 2003 (c. 42) (meeting a child following sexual grooming etc.).

91   An offence under section 16 of that Act (abuse of position of trust: sexual activity with a child).

92   An offence under section 17 of that Act (abuse of position of trust: causing or inciting a child to engage in sexual activity).

93   An offence under section 18 of that Act (abuse of position of trust: sexual activity in the presence of a child).

94   An offence under section 19 of that Act (abuse of position of trust: causing a child to watch a sexual act).

95   An offence under section 47 of that Act (paying for sexual services of a child).

96   An offence under section 48 of that Act (causing or inciting child prostitution or pornography).

97   An offence under section 49 of that Act (controlling a child prostitute or a child involved in pornography).

98   An offence under section 50 of that Act (arranging or facilitating child prostitution or pornography).

99   An offence under section 52 of that Act (causing or inciting prostitution for gain).

100   An offence under section 53 of that Act (controlling prostitution for gain).

101   An offence under section 57 of that Act (trafficking into the UK for sexual exploitation).

102   An offence under section 58 of that Act (trafficking within the UK for sexual exploitation).

103   An offence under section 59 of that Act (trafficking out of the UK for sexual exploitation).

104   An offence under section 66 of that Act (exposure).

105   An offence under section 67 of that Act (voyeurism).

106   An offence under section 69 of that Act (intercourse with an animal).

107   An offence under section 70 of that Act (sexual penetration of a corpse).

108   An offence under Article 20 of the Criminal Justice (Northern Ireland) Order 2003 (S.I. 2003/1247 (N.I. 13)) (assault with intent to commit buggery).

109   An offence under Article 21 of that Order (indecent assault on a male).

110   An offence of—

   (a) aiding, abetting, counselling, procuring or inciting the commission of an offence specified in this Part of this Schedule,

   (b) conspiring to commit an offence so specified, or

   (c) attempting to commit an offence so specified.

SCHEDULE 18   Section 230

RELEASE OF PRISONERS SERVING SENTENCES OF IMPRISONMENT OR DETENTION FOR PUBLIC PROTECTION

Release on licence

1   (1) Section 31 of the Crime (Sentences) Act 1997 (c. 43) (duration and conditions of licences for life prisoners), is amended as follows.

   (2) In subsection (1) (licence to remain in force until death), after "life prisoner" there is inserted ", other than a prisoner to whom section 31A below applies,".

   (3) After that subsection there is inserted—

      "(1A) Where a prisoner to whom section 31A below applies is released on licence, the licence shall remain in force until his death unless—

         (a) it is previously revoked under section 32(1) or (2) below; or

         (b) it ceases to have effect in accordance with an order made by the Secretary of State under section 31A below."

2   After that section there is inserted—

   "31A mprisonment or detention for public protection: termination of licences

      (1) This section applies to a prisoner who—

         (a) is serving one or more preventive sentences, and

         (b) is not serving any other life sentence.

      (2) Where—

         (a) the prisoner has been released on licence under this Chapter; and

         (b) the qualifying period has expired,

            the Secretary of State shall, if directed to do so by the Parole Board, order that the licence is to cease to have effect.

      (3) Where—

         (a) the prisoner has been released on licence under this Chapter;

(b) the qualifying period has expired; and

(c) if he has made a previous application under this subsection, a period of at least twelve months has expired since the disposal of that application, the prisoner may make an application to the Parole Board under this subsection.

(4) Where an application is made under subsection (3) above, the Parole Board—

(a) shall, if it is satisfied that it is no longer necessary for the protection of the public that the licence should remain in force, direct the Secretary of State to make an order that the licence is to cease to have effect;

(b) shall otherwise dismiss the application.

(5) In this section—

"preventive sentence" means a sentence of imprisonment for public protection under section 225 of the Criminal Justice Act 2003 or a sentence of detention for public protection under section 226 of that Act;

"the qualifying period", in relation to a prisoner who has been released on licence, means the period of ten years beginning with the date of his release."

3   In section 34(2) of that Act (meaning of "life sentence"), after paragraph (c) there is inserted—

"(d) a sentence of imprisonment for public protection under section 225 of the Criminal Justice Act 2003, and

(e) a sentence of detention for public protection under section 226 of that Act."

Determination of tariffs

4   In section 82A of the Sentencing Act (determination of tariffs), after subsection (4) there is inserted—

"(4A) No order under subsection (4) above may be made where the life sentence is—

(a) a sentence of imprisonment for public protection under section 225 of the Criminal Justice Act 2003, or

(b) a sentence of detention for public protection under section 226 of that Act."

SCHEDULE 19   **Section 239(7)**

THE PAROLE BOARD: SUPPLEMENTARY PROVISIONS

Status and Capacity

1   (1) The Board is not to be regarded as the servant or agent of the Crown or as enjoying any status, immunity or privilege of the Crown; and the Board's property is not to be regarded as property of, or held on behalf of, the Crown.

(2) It is within the capacity of the Board as a statutory corporation to do such things and enter into such transactions as are incidental to or conducive to the discharge of—

(a) its functions under Chapter 6 of Part 12 in respect of fixed-term prisoners, and

(b) its functions under Chapter 2 of Part 2 of the Crime (Sentences) Act 1997 (c. 43) in relation to life prisoners within the meaning of that Chapter.

Membership

2   (1) The Board is to consist of a chairman and not less than four other members appointed by the Secretary of State.

(2) The Board must include among its members—

(a) a person who holds or has held judicial office;

(b) a registered medical practitioner who is a psychiatrist;

(c) a person appearing to the Secretary of State to have knowledge and experience of the supervision or after-care of discharged prisoners; and

(d) a person appearing to the Secretary of State to have made a study of the causes of delinquency or the treatment of offenders.

(3) A member of the Board—

(a) holds and vacates office in accordance with the terms of his appointment;

(b) may resign his office by notice in writing addressed to the Secretary of State; and a person who ceases to hold office as a member of the Board is eligible for re-appointment.

Payments to members

3   (1) The Board may pay to each member such remuneration and allowances as the Secretary of State may determine.

    (2) The Board may pay or make provision for paying to or in respect of any member such sums by way of pension, allowances or gratuities as the Secretary of State may determine.

    (3) If a person ceases to be a member otherwise than on the expiry of his term of office and it appears to the Secretary of State that there are special circumstances that make it right that he should receive compensation, the Secretary of State may direct the Board to make to that person a payment of such amount as the Secretary of State may determine.

    (4) A determination or direction of the Secretary of State under this paragraph requires the approval of the Treasury.

Proceedings

4   (1) Subject to the provisions of section 239(5), the arrangements relating to meetings of the Board are to be such as the Board may determine.

    (2) The arrangements may provide for the discharge, under the general direction of the Board, of any of the Board's functions by a committee or by one or more of the members or employees of the Board.

    (3) The validity of the proceedings of the Board are not to be affected by any vacancy among the members or by any defect in the appointment of a member.

Staff

5   (1) The Board may appoint such number of employees as it may determine.

    (2) The remuneration and other conditions of service of the persons appointed under this paragraph are to be determined by the Board.

    (3) Any determination under sub-paragraph (1) or (2) requires the approval of the Secretary of State given with the consent of the Treasury.

    (4) The Employers' Liability (Compulsory Insurance) Act 1969 (c. 57) shall not require insurance to be effected by the Board.

6   (1) Employment with the Board shall continue to be included among the kinds of employment to which a scheme under section 1 of the Superannuation Act 1972 (c. 11) can apply, and accordingly in Schedule 1 to that Act (in which those kinds of employment are listed) at the end of the list of Other Bodies there shall continue to be inserted—

        "Parole Board.".

    (2) The Board shall pay to the Treasury, at such times as the Treasury may direct, such sums as the Treasury may determine in respect of the increase attributable to this paragraph in the sums payable under the Superannuation Act 1972 out of money provided by Parliament.

Financial provisions

7   (1) The Secretary of State shall pay to the Board—

      (a) any expenses incurred or to be incurred by the Board by virtue of paragraph 3 or 5; and

      (b) with the consent of the Treasury, such sums as he thinks fit for enabling the Board to meet other expenses.

    (2) Any sums required by the Secretary of State for making payments under sub-paragraph (1) are to be paid out of money provided by Parliament.

Authentication of Board's seal

8   The application of the seal of the Board is to be authenticated by the signature of the Chairman or some other person authorised for the purpose.

Presumption of authenticity of documents issued by Board

9   Any document purporting to be an instrument issued by the Board and to be duly executed under the seal of the Board or to be signed on behalf of the Board shall be

received in evidence and shall be deemed to be such an instrument unless the contrary is shown.

Accounts and audit

10 (1) It is the duty of the Board—
    (a) to keep proper accounts and proper records in relation to the accounts;
    (b) to prepare in respect of each financial year a statement of accounts in such form as the Secretary of State may direct with the approval of the Treasury; and
    (c) to send copies of each such statement to the Secretary of State and the Comptroller and Auditor General not later than 31st August next following the end of the financial year to which the statement relates.
  (2) The Comptroller and Auditor General shall examine, certify and report on each statement of accounts sent to him by the Board and shall lay a copy of every such statement and of his report before each House of Parliament.
  (3) In this paragraph and paragraph 11 "financial year" means a period of 12 months ending with 31st March.

Reports

11   The Board must as soon as practicable after the end of each financial year make to the Secretary of State a report on the performance of its functions during the year; and the Secretary of State must lay a copy of the report before each House of Parliament.

SCHEDULE 20   **Section 262**

PRISONERS LIABLE TO REMOVAL FROM UNITED KINGDOM: MODIFICATIONS OF
CRIMINAL JUSTICE ACT 1991

1   In this Schedule "the 1991 Act" means the Criminal Justice Act 1991 (c. 53).
2   In section 42 of the 1991 Act (additional days for disciplinary offences), in subsection (2) before the word "and" at the end of paragraph (a) there is inserted—
        "(aa) any period which he must serve before he can be removed under section 46A below;".
3   (1) In section 46 of the 1991 Act (persons liable to removal from the United Kingdom) in subsection (3) after paragraph (d) there is inserted "or
        (e) he is liable to removal under section 10 of the Immigration and Asylum Act 1999".
    (2) Sub-paragraph (1) does not apply to any prisoner whose sentence relates to an offence committed before the commencement of this Schedule.
4   After section 46 of the 1991 Act there is inserted—

"46A Early removal of persons liable to removal from United Kingdom
    (1) Subject to subsection (2) below, where a short-term or long-term prisoner is liable to removal from the United Kingdom, the Secretary of State may under this section remove him from prison at any time after he has served the requisite period.
    (2) Subsection (1) above does not apply where—
        (a) the sentence is an extended sentence within the meaning of section 85 of the Powers of Criminal Courts (Sentencing) Act 2000,
        (b) the sentence is for an offence under section 1 of the Prisoners (Return to Custody) Act 1995,
        (c) the prisoner is subject to a hospital order, hospital direction or transfer direction under section 37, 45A or 47 of the Mental Health Act 1983,
        (d) the prisoner is subject to the notification requirements of Part 2 of the Sexual Offences Act 2003, or
        (e) the interval between—
            (i) the date on which the prisoner will have served the requisite period for the term of the sentence, and
            (ii) the date on which he will have served one-half of the sentence, is less than 14 days.
    (3) A prisoner removed from prison under this section—
        (a) is so removed only for the purpose of enabling the Secretary of State to remove him from the United Kingdom under powers conferred by—
            (i) Schedule 2 or 3 to the Immigration Act 1971, or

44–377

     (ii) section 10 of the Immigration and Asylum Act 1999, and
- (b) so long as remaining in the United Kingdom, remains liable to be detained in pursuance of his sentence until he falls to be released under section 33 or 35 above.

(4) So long as a prisoner removed from prison under this section remains in the United Kingdom but has not been returned to prison, any duty or power of the Secretary of State under section 33, 35 or 36 is exercisable in relation to him as if he were in prison.

(5) In this section "the requisite period" means—
- (a) for a term of three months or more but less than four months, a period of 30 days;
- (b) for a term of four months or more but less than 18 months, a period equal to one-quarter of the term;
- (c) for a term of 18 months or more, a period that is 135 days less than one-half of the term.

(6) The Secretary of State may by order made by statutory instrument—
- (a) amend the definition of "the requisite period" in subsection (5) above,
- (b) make such transitional provision as appears to him necessary or expedient in connection with the amendment.

(7) No order shall be made under subsection (6) above unless a draft of the order has been laid before and approved by a resolution of each House of Parliament.

(8) In relation to any time before the commencement of sections 80 and 81 of the Sexual Offences Act 2003, the reference in subsection (2)(d) above to Part 2 of that Act is to be read as a reference to Part 1 of the Sex Offenders Act 1997.

46B Early removal of persons liable to removal from United Kingdom

(1) This section applies in relation to a person who, after being removed from prison under section 46A above, has been removed from the United Kingdom before he has served one-half of his sentence.

(2) If a person to whom this section applies enters the United Kingdom at any time before his sentence expiry date, he is liable to be detained in pursuance of his sentence from the time of his entry into the United Kingdom until whichever is the earlier of the following—
- (a) the end of a period ("the further custodial period") beginning with that time and equal in length to the outstanding custodial period, and
- (b) his sentence expiry date.

(3) A person who is liable to be detained by virtue of subsection (2) above is, if at large, to be taken for the purposes of section 49 of the Prison Act 1952 (persons unlawfully at large) to be unlawfully at large.

(4) Subsection (2) above does not prevent the further removal from the United Kingdom of a person falling within that subsection.

(5) Where, in the case of a person returned to prison by virtue of subsection (2) above, the further custodial period ends before the sentence expiry date, subsections (1) and (2) of section 33 above apply in relation to him as if any reference to one-half or two-thirds of the prisoner's sentence were a reference to the further custodial period.

(6) If a person returned to prison by virtue of subsection (2) above falls by virtue of subsection (5) above to be released on licence under section 33(1) or (2) above after the date on which (but for his removal from the United Kingdom) he would have served three-quarters of his sentence, section 37(1) above has effect in relation to him as if for the reference to three-quarters of his sentence there were substituted a reference to the whole of his sentence.

(7) If a person who is released on licence under section 33(1) or (2) above at the end of the further custodial period is recalled to prison under section

39(1) or (2) above, section 33A(3) above shall not apply, but it shall be the duty of the Secretary of State—

    (a) if the person is recalled before the date on which (but for his removal from the United Kingdom) he would have served three-quarters of his sentence, to release him on licence on that date, and

    (b) if he is recalled after that date, to release him on the sentence expiry date.

(8) A licence granted by virtue of subsection (7)(a) above shall remain in force until the sentence expiry date.

(9) In this section—

    "further custodial period" has the meaning given by subsection (2)(a) above;

    "outstanding custodial period", in relation to a person to whom this section applies, means the period beginning with the date on which he was removed from the United Kingdom and ending with the date on which (but for his removal) he would have served one-half of his sentence;

    "sentence expiry date", in relation to a person to whom this section applies, means the date on which (but for his removal from the United Kingdom) he would have served the whole of this sentence."

SCHEDULE 21   **Section 269(5)**

DETERMINATION OF MINIMUM TERM IN RELATION TO MANDATORY LIFE SENTENCE

Interpretation

1   In this Schedule—

    "child" means a person under 18 years;

    "mandatory life sentence" means a life sentence passed in circumstances where the sentence is fixed by law;

    "minimum term", in relation to a mandatory life sentence, means the part of the sentence to be specified in an order under section 269(2);

    "whole life order" means an order under subsection (4) of section 269.

2   Section 28 of the Crime and Disorder Act 1998 (c. 37) (meaning of "racially or religiously aggravated") applies for the purposes of this Schedule as it applies for the purposes of sections 29 to 32 of that Act.

3   For the purposes of this Schedule an offence is aggravated by sexual orientation if it is committed in circumstances falling within subsection (2)(a)(i) or (b)(i) of section 146.

Starting points

4   (1) If—

    (a) the court considers that the seriousness of the offence (or the combination of the offence and one or more offences associated with it) is exceptionally high, and

    (b) the offender was aged 21 or over when he committed the offence,

        the appropriate starting point is a whole life order.

(2) Cases that would normally fall within sub-paragraph (1)(a) include—

    (a) the murder of two or more persons, where each murder involves any of the following-

      (i) a substantial degree of premeditation or planning,

      (ii) the abduction of the victim, or

      (iii) sexual or sadistic conduct,

    (b) the murder of a child if involving the abduction of the child or sexual or sadistic motivation,

    (c) a murder done for the purpose of advancing a political, religious or ideological cause, or

    (d) a murder by an offender previously convicted of murder.

5   (1) If—

    (a) the case does not fall within paragraph 4(1) but the court considers that the seriousness of the offence (or the combination of the offence and one or more offences associated with it) is particularly high, and

    (b) the offender was aged 18 or over when he committed the offence,

        the appropriate starting point, in determining the minimum term, is 30 years.

(2) Cases that (if not falling within paragraph 4(1)) would normally fall within sub-paragraph (1)(a) include—

    (a) the murder of a police officer or prison officer in the course of his duty,

    (b) a murder involving the use of a firearm or explosive,

    (c) a murder done for gain (such as a murder done in the course or furtherance of robbery or burglary, done for payment or done in the expectation of gain as a result of the death),

    (d) a murder intended to obstruct or interfere with the course of justice,

    (e) a murder involving sexual or sadistic conduct,

    (f) the murder of two or more persons,

    (g) a murder that is racially or religiously aggravated or aggravated by sexual orientation, or

    (h) a murder falling within paragraph 4(2) committed by an offender who was aged under 21 when he committed the offence.

6   If the offender was aged 18 or over when he committed the offence and the case does not fall within paragraph 4(1) or 5(1), the appropriate starting point, in determining the minimum term, is 15 years.

7   If the offender was aged under 18 when he committed the offence, the appropriate starting point, in determining the minimum term, is 12 years.

Aggravating and mitigating factors

8   Having chosen a starting point, the court should take into account any aggravating or mitigating factors, to the extent that it has not allowed for them in its choice of starting point.

9   Detailed consideration of aggravating or mitigating factors may result in a minimum term of any length (whatever the starting point), or in the making of a whole life order.

10   Aggravating factors (additional to those mentioned in paragraph 4(2) and 5(2)) that may be relevant to the offence of murder include—

    (a) a significant degree of planning or premeditation,

    (b) the fact that the victim was particularly vulnerable because of age or disability,

    (c) mental or physical suffering inflicted on the victim before death,

    (d) the abuse of a position of trust,

    (e) the use of duress or threats against another person to facilitate the commission of the offence,

    (f) the fact that the victim was providing a public service or performing a public duty, and

    (g) concealment, destruction or dismemberment of the body.

11   Mitigating factors that may be relevant to the offence of murder include—

    (a) an intention to cause serious bodily harm rather than to kill,

    (b) lack of premeditation,

    (c) the fact that the offender suffered from any mental disorder or mental disability which (although not falling within section 2(1) of the Homicide Act 1957 (c. 11)), lowered his degree of culpability,

    (d) the fact that the offender was provoked (for example, by prolonged stress) in a way not amounting to a defence of provocation,

    (e) the fact that the offender acted to any extent in self-defence,

    (f) a belief by the offender that the murder was an act of mercy, and

    (g) the age of the offender.

12   Nothing in this Schedule restricts the application of—

    (a) section 143(2) (previous convictions),

    (b) section 143(3) (bail), or

    (c) section 144 (guilty plea).

SCHEDULE 22   **Section 276**

MANDATORY LIFE SENTENCES: TRANSITIONAL CASES

Interpretation

1   In this Schedule—

    "the commencement date" means the day on which section 269 comes into force;

    "the early release provisions" means the provisions of section 28(5) to (8) of the Crime (Sentences) Act 1997 (c. 43);

"existing prisoner" means a person serving one or more mandatory life sentences passed before the commencement date (whether or not he is also serving any other sentence);

"life sentence" means a sentence of imprisonment for life or custody for life passed in England and Wales or by a court-martial outside England and Wales;

"mandatory life sentence" means a life sentence passed in circumstances where the sentence was fixed by law.

Existing prisoners notified by Secretary of State

2   Paragraph 3 applies in relation to any existing prisoner who, in respect of any mandatory life sentence, has before the commencement date been notified in writing by the Secretary of State (otherwise than in a notice that is expressed to be provisional) either—

    (a) of a minimum period which in the view of the Secretary of State should be served before the prisoner's release on licence, or

    (b) that the Secretary of State does not intend that the prisoner should ever be released on licence.

3   (1) On the application of the existing prisoner, the High Court must, in relation to the mandatory life sentence, either—

    (a) order that the early release provisions are to apply to him as soon as he has served the part of the sentence which is specified in the order, which in a case falling within paragraph 2(a) must not be greater than the notified minimum term, or

    (b) in a case falling within paragraph 2(b), order that the early release provisions are not to apply to the offender.

    (2) In a case falling within paragraph 2(a), no application may be made under this paragraph after the end of the notified minimum term.

    (3) Where no application under this paragraph is made in a case falling within paragraph 2(a), the early release provisions apply to the prisoner in respect of the sentence as soon as he has served the notified minimum term (or, if he has served that term before the commencement date but has not been released, from the commencement date).

    (4) In this paragraph "the notified minimum term" means the minimum period notified as mentioned in paragraph 2(a), or where the prisoner has been so notified on more than one occasion, the period most recently so notified.

4   (1) In dealing with an application under paragraph 3, the High Court must have regard to—

    (a) the seriousness of the offence, or of the combination of the offence and one or more offences associated with it,

    (b) where the court is satisfied that, if the prisoner had been sentenced to a term of imprisonment, the length of his sentence would have been treated by section 67 of the Criminal Justice Act 1967 (c. 80) as being reduced by a particular period, the effect which that section would have had if he had been sentenced to a term of imprisonment, and

    (c) the length of the notified minimum term or, where a notification falling within paragraph 2(b) has been given to the prisoner, to the fact that such a notification has been given.

    (2) In considering under sub-paragraph (1) the seriousness of the offence, or of the combination of the offence and one or more offences associated with it, the High Court must have regard to—

    (a) the general principles set out in Schedule 21, and

    (b) any recommendation made to the Secretary of State by the trial judge or the Lord Chief Justice as to the minimum term to be served by the offender before release on licence.

    (3) In this paragraph "the notified minimum term" has the same meaning as in paragraph 3.

Existing prisoners not notified by Secretary of State

5   Paragraph 6 applies in relation to any existing prisoner who, in respect of any mandatory life sentence, has not before the commencement date been notified as mentioned in paragraph 2(a) or (b) by the Secretary of State.

6   The Secretary of State must refer the prisoner's case to the High Court for the making by the High Court of an order under subsection (2) or (4) of section 269 in relation to the mandatory life sentence.

7   In considering under subsection (3) or (4) of section 269 the seriousness of an offence (or the combination of an offence and one or more offences associated with it) in a case referred to the High Court under paragraph 6, the High Court must have regard not only to the matters mentioned in subsection (5) of that section but also to any recommendation made to the Secretary of State by the trial judge or the Lord Chief Justice as to the minimum term to be served by the offender before release on licence.

8   In dealing with a reference under paragraph 6, the High Court—

     (a) may not make an order under subsection (2) of section 269 specifying a part of the sentence which in the opinion of the court is greater than that which, under the practice followed by the Secretary of State before December 2002, the Secretary of State would have been likely to notify as mentioned in paragraph 2(a), and

     (b) may not make an order under subsection (4) of section 269 unless the court is of the opinion that, under the practice followed by the Secretary of State before December 2002, the Secretary of State would have been likely to give the prisoner a notification falling within paragraph 2(b).

Sentences passed on or after commencement date in respect of offences committed before that date

9   Paragraph 10 applies where—

     (a) on or after the commencement date a court passes a life sentence in circumstances where the sentence is fixed by law, and

     (b) the offence to which the sentence relates was committed before the commencement date.

10   The court—

     (a) may not make an order under subsection (2) of section 269 specifying a part of the sentence which in the opinion of the court is greater than that which, under the practice followed by the Secretary of State before December 2002, the Secretary of State would have been likely to notify as mentioned in paragraph 2(a), and

     (b) may not make an order under subsection (4) of section 269 unless the court is of the opinion that, under the practice followed by the Secretary of State before December 2002, the Secretary of State would have been likely to give the prisoner a notification falling within paragraph 2(b).

Proceedings in High Court

11   (1) An application under paragraph 3 or a reference under paragraph 6 is to be determined by a single judge of the High Court without an oral hearing.

     (2) In relation to such an application or reference, any reference to "the court" in section 269(2) to (5) and Schedule 21 is to be read as a reference to the High Court.

Giving of reasons

12   (1) Where the High Court makes an order under paragraph 3(1)(a) or (b), it must state in open court, in ordinary language, its reasons for deciding on the order made.

     (2) Where the order is an order under paragraph 3(1)(a) specifying a part of the sentence shorter than the notified minimum term the High Court must, in particular, state its reasons for departing from the notified minimum term.

13   Where the High Court makes an order under subsection (2) or (4) of section 269 on a reference under paragraph 6, subsection (2) of section 270 does not apply.

Right of appeal

14   (1) A person who has made an application under paragraph 3 or in respect of whom a reference has been made under paragraph 6 may with the leave of the Court of Appeal appeal to the Court of Appeal against the decision of the High Court on the application or reference.

     (2) Section 1(1) of the Administration of Justice Act 1960 (c. 65) (appeal to House of Lords from decision of High Court in a criminal cause or matter) and section 18(1)(a) of the Supreme Court Act 1981 (c. 54) (exclusion of appeal from High Court to Court of Appeal in a criminal cause or matter) do not apply in relation to a decision to which sub-paragraph (1) applies.

     (3) The jurisdiction conferred on the Court of Appeal by this paragraph is to be exercised by the criminal division of that court.

     (4) Section 33(3) of the Criminal Appeal Act 1968 (c. 19) (limitation on appeal from criminal division of Court of Appeal) does not prevent an appeal to the House of Lords under this paragraph.

(5) In relation to appeals to the Court of Appeal or the House of Lords under this paragraph, the Secretary of State may make an order containing provision corresponding to any provision in the Criminal Appeal Act 1968 (subject to any specified modifications).

Review of minimum term on reference by Attorney General

15   Section 36 of the Criminal Justice Act 1988 (c. 33) applies in relation to an order made by the High Court under paragraph 3(1)(a) as it applies in relation to an order made by the Crown Court under section 269(2).

Modification of early release provisions

16 (1) In relation to an existing prisoner, section 28 of the Crime (Sentences) Act 1997 (c. 43) has effect subject to the following modifications.
   (2) Any reference to a life prisoner in respect of whom a minimum term order has been made includes a reference to—
      (a) an existing prisoner in respect of whom an order under paragraph 3(1)(a) has been made, and
      (b) an existing prisoner serving a sentence in respect of which paragraph 3(3) applies.
   (3) Any reference to the relevant part of the sentence is to be read—
      (a) in relation to a sentence in respect of which an order under paragraph 3(1)(a) has been made, as a reference to the part specified in the order, and
      (b) in relation to a sentence in respect of which paragraph 3(3) applies, as a reference to the notified minimum term as defined by paragraph 3(4).
   (4) In subsection (1B) (life prisoner serving two or more sentences), paragraph (a) is to be read as if it referred to each of the sentences being one—
      (a) in respect of which a minimum term order or an order under paragraph 3(1)(a) has been made, or
      (b) in respect of which paragraph 3(3) applies.

17   In section 34(1) of the Crime (Sentences) Act 1997 (c. 43) (interpretation of Chapter 2 of that Act), in the definition of "life prisoner", the reference to a transferred prisoner as defined by section 273 of this Act includes a reference to an existing prisoner who immediately before the commencement date is a transferred life prisoner for the purposes of section 33 of that Act.

Transferred life prisoners

18   In relation to an existing prisoner who immediately before the commencement date is a transferred life prisoner for the purposes of section 33 of the Crime (Sentences) Act 1997, this Schedule is to be read as if—
      (a) any certificate under subsection (2) of that section were a notification falling within paragraph 2(a) of this Schedule, and
      (b) references to any recommendation of the trial judge or the Lord Chief Justice were omitted.

SCHEDULE 23   **Section 278**

DEFERMENT OF SENTENCE

1   For sections 1 and 2 of the Sentencing Act (deferment of sentence) there is substituted—

"Deferment of sentence

1 Deferment of sentence
      (1) The Crown Court or a magistrates' court may defer passing sentence on an offender for the purpose of enabling the court, or any other court to which it falls to deal with him, to have regard in dealing with him to—
         (a) his conduct after conviction (including, where appropriate, the making by him of reparation for his offence); or
         (b) any change in his circumstances;
         but this is subject to subsections (3) and (4) below.
      (2) Without prejudice to the generality of subsection (1) above, the matters to which the court to which it falls to deal with the offender may have regard by virtue of paragraph (a) of that subsection include the extent to which the

offender has complied with any requirements imposed under subsection (3)(b) below.

(3) The power conferred by subsection (1) above shall be exercisable only if—
  (a) the offender consents;
  (b) the offender undertakes to comply with any requirements as to his conduct during the period of the deferment that the court considers it appropriate to impose; and
  (c) the court is satisfied, having regard to the nature of the offence and the character and circumstances of the offender, that it would be in the interests of justice to exercise the power.

(4) Any deferment under this section shall be until such date as may be specified by the court, not being more than six months after the date on which the deferment is announced by the court; and, subject to section 1D(3) below, where the passing of sentence has been deferred under this section it shall not be further so deferred.

(5) Where a court has under this section deferred passing sentence on an offender, it shall forthwith give a copy of the order deferring the passing of sentence and setting out any requirements imposed under subsection (3)(b) above—
  (a) to the offender,
  (b) where an officer of a local probation board has been appointed to act as a supervisor in relation to him, to that board, and
  (c) where a person has been appointed under section 1A(2)(b) below to act as a supervisor in relation to him, to that person.

(6) Notwithstanding any enactment, a court which under this section defers passing sentence on an offender shall not on the same occasion remand him.

(7) Where—
  (a) a court which under this section has deferred passing sentence on an offender proposes to deal with him on the date originally specified by the court, or
  (b) the offender does not appear on the day so specified,
the court may issue a summons requiring him to appear before the court at a time and place specified in the summons, or may issue a warrant to arrest him and bring him before the court at a time and place specified in the warrant.

(8) Nothing in this section or sections 1A to 1D below shall affect—
  (a) the power of the Crown Court to bind over an offender to come up for judgment when called upon; or
  (b) the power of any court to defer passing sentence for any purpose for which it may lawfully do so apart from this section.

1A Further provision about undertakings

(1) Without prejudice to the generality of paragraph (b) of section 1(3) above, the requirements that may be imposed by virtue of that paragraph include requirements as to the residence of the offender during the whole or any part of the period of deferment.

(2) Where an offender has undertaken to comply with any requirements imposed under section 1(3)(b) above the court may appoint—
  (a) an officer of a local probation board, or
  (b) any other person whom the court thinks appropriate,
to act as a supervisor in relation to him.

(3) A person shall not be appointed under subsection (2)(b) above without his consent.

(4) It shall be the duty of a supervisor appointed under subsection (2) above—
  (a) to monitor the offender's compliance with the requirements; and
  (b) to provide the court to which it falls to deal with the offender in respect of the offence in question with such information as the court may require relating to the offender's compliance with the requirements.

1B Breach of undertakings

(1) A court which under section 1 above has deferred passing sentence on an offender may deal with him before the end of the period of deferment if—

  (a) he appears or is brought before the court under subsection (3) below; and

  (b) the court is satisfied that he has failed to comply with one or more requirements imposed under section 1(3)(b) above in connection with the deferment.

(2) Subsection (3) below applies where—

  (a) a court has under section 1 above deferred passing sentence on an offender;

  (b) the offender undertook to comply with one or more requirements imposed under section 1(3)(b) above in connection with the deferment; and

  (c) a person appointed under section 1A(2) above to act as a supervisor in relation to the offender has reported to the court that the offender has failed to comply with one or more of those requirements.

(3) Where this subsection applies, the court may issue—

  (a) a summons requiring the offender to appear before the court at a time and place specified in the summons; or

  (b) a warrant to arrest him and bring him before the court at a time and place specified in the warrant.

1C Conviction of offence during period of deferment

(1) A court which under section 1 above has deferred passing sentence on an offender may deal with him before the end of the period of deferment if during that period he is convicted in Great Britain of any offence.

(2) Subsection (3) below applies where a court has under section 1 above deferred passing sentence on an offender in respect of one or more offences and during the period of deferment the offender is convicted in England and Wales of any offence ("the later offence").

(3) Where this subsection applies, then (without prejudice to subsection (1) above and whether or not the offender is sentenced for the later offence during the period of deferment), the court which passes sentence on him for the later offence may also, if this has not already been done, deal with him for the offence or offences for which passing of sentence has been deferred, except that—

  (a) the power conferred by this subsection shall not be exercised by a magistrates' court if the court which deferred passing sentence was the Crown Court; and

  (b) the Crown Court, in exercising that power in a case in which the court which deferred passing sentence was a magistrates' court, shall not pass any sentence which could not have been passed by a magistrates' court in exercising that power.

(4) Where a court which under section 1 above has deferred passing sentence on an offender proposes to deal with him by virtue of subsection (1) above before the end of the period of deferment, the court may issue—

  (a) a summons requiring him to appear before the court at a time and place specified in the summons; or

  (b) a warrant to arrest him and bring him before the court at a time and place specified in the warrant.

1D Deferment of sentence: supplementary

(1) In deferring the passing of sentence under section 1 above a magistrates' court shall be regarded as exercising the power of adjourning the trial conferred by section 10(1) of the Magistrates' Courts Act 1980, and accordingly sections 11(1) and 13(1) to (3A) and (5) of that Act (non-appearance of the accused) apply (without prejudice to section 1(7) above) if the offender does not appear on the date specified under section 1(4) above.

(2) Where the passing of sentence on an offender has been deferred by a court ("the original court") under section 1 above, the power of that court under

that section to deal with the offender at the end of the period of deferment and any power of that court under section 1B(1) or 1C(1) above, or of any court under section 1C(3) above, to deal with the offender—

(a) is power to deal with him, in respect of the offence for which passing of sentence has been deferred, in any way in which the original court could have dealt with him if it had not deferred passing sentence; and

(b) without prejudice to the generality of paragraph (a) above, in the case of a magistrates' court, includes the power conferred by section 3 below to commit him to the Crown Court for sentence.

(3) Where—

(a) the passing of sentence on an offender in respect of one or more offences has been deferred under section 1 above, and

(b) a magistrates' court deals with him in respect of the offence or any of the offences by committing him to the Crown Court under section 3 below,

the power of the Crown Court to deal with him includes the same power to defer passing sentence on him as if he had just been convicted of the offence or offences on indictment before the court.

(4) Subsection (5) below applies where—

(a) the passing of sentence on an offender in respect of one or more offences has been deferred under section 1 above;

(b) it falls to a magistrates' court to determine a relevant matter; and

(c) a justice of the peace is satisfied—

(i) that a person appointed under section 1A(2)(b) above to act as a supervisor in relation to the offender is likely to be able to give evidence that may assist the court in determining that matter; and

(ii) that that person will not voluntarily attend as a witness.

(5) The justice may issue a summons directed to that person requiring him to attend before the court at the time and place appointed in the summons to give evidence.

(6) For the purposes of subsection (4) above a court determines a relevant matter if it—

(a) deals with the offender in respect of the offence, or any of the offences, for which the passing of sentence has been deferred; or

(b) determines, for the purposes of section 1B(1)(b) above, whether the offender has failed to comply with any requirements imposed under section 1(3)(b) above."

2   In section 159 of the Sentencing Act (execution of process between England and Wales and Scotland), for "section 2(4)," there is substituted "section 1(7), 1B(3), 1C(4),".

SCHEDULE 24   **Section 279**

DRUG TREATMENT AND TESTING REQUIREMENT IN ACTION PLAN ORDER OR
SUPERVISION ORDER

1   (1) Section 70 of the Sentencing Act (requirements which may be included in action plan orders and directions) is amended as follows.

(2) After subsection (4) there is inserted—

"(4A) Subsection (4B) below applies where a court proposing to make an action plan order is satisfied—

(a) that the offender is dependent on, or has a propensity to misuse, drugs, and

(b) that his dependency or propensity is such as requires and may be susceptible to treatment.

(4B) Where this subsection applies, requirements included in an action plan order may require the offender for a period specified in the order ("the treatment period") to submit to treatment by or under the direction of a specified person having the necessary qualifications and experience ("the treatment provider") with a view to the reduction or elimination of the offender's dependency on or propensity to misuse drugs.

(4C) The required treatment shall be—
  (a) treatment as a resident in such institution or place as may be specified in the order, or
  (b) treatment as a non-resident at such institution or place, and at such intervals, as may be so specified;
  but the nature of the treatment shall not be specified in the order except as mentioned in paragraph (a) or (b) above.

(4D) A requirement shall not be included in an action plan order by virtue of subsection (4B) above—
  (a) in any case, unless—
    (i) the court is satisfied that arrangements have been or can be made for the treatment intended to be specified in the order (including arrangements for the reception of the offender where he is to be required to submit to treatment as a resident), and
    (ii) the requirement has been recommended to the court as suitable for the offender by an officer of a local probation board or by a member of a youth offending team; and
  (b) in the case of an order made or to be made in respect of a person aged 14 or over, unless he consents to its inclusion.

(4E) Subject to subsection (4F), an action plan order which includes a requirement by virtue of subsection (4B) above may, if the offender is aged 14 or over, also include a requirement ("a testing requirement") that, for the purpose of ascertaining whether he has any drug in his body during the treatment period, the offender shall during that period, at such times or in such circumstances as may (subject to the provisions of the order) be determined by the responsible officer or the treatment provider, provide samples of such description as may be so determined.

(4F) A testing requirement shall not be included in an action plan order by virtue of subsection (4E) above unless—
  (a) the offender is aged 14 or over and consents to its inclusion, and
  (b) the court has been notified by the Secretary of State that arrangements for implementing such requirements are in force in the area proposed to be specified in the order

(4G) A testing requirement shall specify for each month the minimum number of occasions on which samples are to be provided.

(4H) An action plan order including a testing requirement shall provide for the results of tests carried out on any samples provided by the offender in pursuance of the requirement to a person other than the responsible officer to be communicated to the responsible officer."

2   (1) Schedule 6 to the Sentencing Act (requirements which may be included in supervision orders) is amended as follows.

(2) In paragraph 1, after "6" there is inserted ",6A".

(3) After paragraph 6 there is inserted—
    "*Requirements as to drug treatment and testing*

6A (1) This paragraph applies where a court proposing to make a supervision order is satisfied—
    (a) that the offender is dependent on, or has a propensity to misuse, drugs, and
    (b) that his dependency or propensity is such as requires and may be susceptible to treatment.

    (2) Where this paragraph applies, the court may include in the supervision order a requirement that the offender shall, for a period specified in the order ("the treatment period"), submit to treatment by or under the direction of a specified person having the necessary qualifications and experience ("the treatment provider") with a view to the reduction or elimination of the offender's dependency on or propensity to misuse drugs.

    (3) The required treatment shall be—

       (a) treatment as a resident in such institution or place as may be specified in the order, or

       (b) treatment as a non-resident at such institution or place, and at such intervals, as may be so specified;

but the nature of the treatment shall not be specified in the order except as mentioned in paragraph (a) or (b) above.

    (4) A requirement shall not be included in a supervision order by virtue of sub-paragraph (2) above—

       (a) in any case, unless—

          (i) the court is satisfied that arrangements have been or can be made for the treatment intended to be specified in the order (including arrangements for the reception of the offender where he is to be required to submit to treatment as a resident), and

         (ii) the requirement has been recommended to the court as suitable for the offender by an officer of a local probation board or by a member of a youth offending team; and

       (b) in the case of an order made or to be made in respect of a person aged 14 or over, unless he consents to its inclusion.

    (5) Subject to sub-paragraph (6), a supervision order which includes a treatment requirement may also include a requirement ("a testing requirement") that, for the purpose of ascertaining whether he has any drug in his body during the treatment period, the offender shall during that period, at such times or in such circumstances as may (subject to the provisions of the order) be determined by the supervisor or the treatment provider, provide samples of such description as may be so determined.

    (6) A testing requirement shall not be included in a supervision order by virtue of sub-paragraph (5) above unless—

       (a) the offender is aged 14 or over and consents to its inclusion, and

       (b) the court has been notified by the Secretary of State that arrangements for implementing such requirements are in force in the area proposed to be specified in the order.

    (7) A testing requirement shall specify for each month the minimum number of occasions on which samples are to be provided.

    (8) A supervision order including a testing requirement shall provide for the results of tests carried out on any samples provided by the offender in pursuance of the requirement to a person other than the supervisor to be communicated to the supervisor."

3   In Schedule 7 to the Sentencing Act (breach, revocation and amendment of supervision orders), in paragraph 2(1), before "or 7" there is inserted ",6A".

SCHEDULE 25   **Section 280(1)**

SUMMARY OFFENCES NO LONGER PUNISHABLE WITH IMPRISONMENT

Vagrancy Act 1824 (c. 83)

1   The offence under section 3 of the Vagrancy Act 1824 (idle and disorderly persons) of causing or procuring or encouraging any child or children to wander abroad, or place himself or herself in any public place, street, highway, court, or passage, to beg or gather alms.

2   The following offences under section 4 of that Act (rogues and vagabonds)—

       (a) the offence of going about as a gatherer or collector of alms, or endeavouring to procure charitable contributions of any nature or kind, under any false or fraudulent pretence,

       (b) the offence of being found in or upon any dwelling house, warehouse, coach-house, stable, or outhouse, or in any inclosed yard, garden, or area, for any unlawful purpose, and

       (c) the offence of being apprehended as an idle and disorderly person, and violently resisting any constable, or other peace officer so apprehending him or her, and being subsequently convicted of the offence for which he or she shall have been so apprehended.

Railway Regulation Act 1842 (c. 55)

3   An offence under section 17 of the Railway Regulation Act 1842 (punishment of railway employees guilty of misconduct).

London Hackney Carriages Act 1843 (c. 86)

4　　　An offence under section 28 of the London Hackney Carriages Act 1843 (punishment for furious driving etc.).

Town Police Clauses Act 1847 (c. 89)

5　　　An offence under section 26 of the Town Police Clauses Act 1847 (unlawful release of impounded stray cattle).

6　　　An offence under section 28 of that Act (offences relating to obstructions and nuisances).

7　　　An offence under section 29 of that Act (drunken persons, etc. guilty of violent or indecent behaviour).

8　　　An offence under section 36 of that Act (keeping places for bear-baiting, cock-fighting etc.).

Ecclesiastical Courts Jurisdiction Act 1860 (c. 32)

9　　　An offence under section 2 of the Ecclesiastical Courts Jurisdiction Act 1860 (making a disturbance in churches, chapels, churchyards, etc.).

Town Gardens Protection Act 1863 (c. 13)

10　　　An offence under section 5 of the Town Gardens Protection Act 1863 (injuring gardens).

Public Stores Act 1875 (c. 25)

11　　　An offence under section 8 of the Public Stores Act 1875 (sweeping, etc., near dockyards, artillery ranges, etc.).

North Sea Fisheries Act 1893 (c. 17)

12　　　An offence under section 2 of the North Sea Fisheries Act 1893 (penalty for supplying, exchanging, or otherwise selling spirits).

13　　　An offence under section 3 of that Act (penalty for purchasing spirits by exchange or otherwise).

Seamen's and Soldiers' False Characters Act 1906 (c. 5)

14　　　An offence under section 1 of the Seamen's and Soldiers' False Characters Act 1906 (forgery of service or discharge certificate and personation).

Aliens Restriction (Amendment) Act 1919 (c. 92)

15　　　An offence under section 3(2) of the Aliens Restriction (Amendment) Act 1919 (promoting industrial unrest).

Children and Young Persons Act 1933 (c. 12)

16　　　An offence under section 4 of the Children and Young Persons Act 1933 (causing or allowing persons under sixteen to be used for begging).

Protection of Animals Act 1934 (c. 21)

17　　　An offence under section 2 of the Protection of Animals Act 1934 (offences relating to the prohibition of certain public contests, performances, and exhibitions with animals).

Public Health Act 1936 (c. 49)

18　　　An offence under section 287 of the Public Health Act 1936 (power to enter premises).

Essential Commodities Reserves Act 1938 (c. 51)

19　　　An offence under section 4(2) of the Essential Commodities Reserves Act 1938 (enforcement).

London Building Acts (Amendment) Act 1939 (c. xcvii)

20　　　An offence under section 142 of the London Building Acts (Amendment) Act 1939 (power of Council and others to enter buildings etc).

Cancer Act 1939 (c. 13)

21   An offence under section 4 of the Cancer Act 1939 (prohibition of certain advertisements).

Civil Defence Act 1939 (c. 31)

22   An offence under section 77 of the Civil Defence Act 1939 (penalty for false statements).

Hill Farming Act 1946 (c. 73)

23   An offence under section 19(2) or (3) of the Hill Farming Act 1946 (offences in relation to the control of rams).

Polish Resettlement Act 1947 (c. 19)

24   An offence under paragraph 7 of the Schedule to the Polish Resettlement Act 1947 (false representation or making a false statement).

Agriculture Act 1947 (c. 48)

25   An offence under section 14(7) of the Agriculture Act 1947, as remaining in force for the purposes of section 95 of that Act, (directions to secure good estate management and good husbandry).

26   An offence under section 95 of that Act (failure to comply with a direction to secure production).

Civil Defence Act 1948 (c. 5)

27   An offence under section 4 of the Civil Defence Act 1948 (powers as to land).

Agricultural Wages Act 1948 (c. 47)

28   An offence under section 12 of the Agricultural Wages Act 1948 (hindering investigation of complaints etc.).

Wireless Telegraphy Act 1949 (c. 54)

29   An offence under section 11(7) of the Wireless Telegraphy Act 1949 (enforcement of regulations as to use of apparatus), other than one within section 14(1A)(c) of that Act.

Prevention of Damage by Pests Act 1949 (c. 55)

30   An offence under section 22(5) of the Prevention of Damage by Pests Act 1949 (wrongful disclosure of information).

Coast Protection Act 1949 (c. 74)

31   An offence under section 25(9) of the Coast Protection Act 1949 (powers of entry and inspection).

Pet Animals Act 1951 (c. 35)

32   An offence under the Pet Animals Act 1951 (offences relating to licensing of pet shops and the sale of pets), other than one under section 4 of that Act.

Cockfighting Act 1952 (c. 59)

33   An offence under section 1 of the Cockfighting Act 1952 (possession of appliances for use in fighting of domestic fowl).

Agricultural Land (Removal of Surface Soil) Act 1953 (c. 10)

34   An offence under the Agricultural Land (Removal of Surface Soil) Act 1953 (removal of surface soil without planning permission).

Accommodation Agencies Act 1953 (c. 23)

35   An offence under section 1 of the Accommodation Agencies Act 1953 (illegal commissions and advertisements).

Army Act 1955 (3 & 4 Eliz. 2 c. 18)

36   An offence under section 19 of the Army Act 1955 (false answers in attestation paper).

37   An offence under section 161 of that Act (refusal to receive persons billeted, etc.).

38   An offence under section 171 of that Act (offences relating to the enforcement of provisions as to requisitioning).

39   An offence under section 191 of that Act (pretending to be a deserter).

40   An offence under section 193 of that Act (obstructing members of regular forces in execution of duty).

41   An offence under section 196 of that Act (illegal dealings in documents relating to pay, pensions, mobilisation etc.).

42   An offence under section 197 of that Act (unauthorised use of and dealing in decorations etc.).

Air Force Act 1955 (3 & 4 Eliz. 2 c. 19)

43   An offence under section 19 of the Air Force Act 1955 (false answers in attestation paper).

44   An offence under section 161 of that Act (refusal to receive persons billeted, etc.).

45   An offence under section 171 of that Act (offences relating to the enforcement of provisions as to requisitioning).

46   An offence under section 191 of that Act (pretending to be a deserter).

47   An offence under section 193 of that Act (obstructing members of regular air force in execution of duty).

48   An offence under section 196 of that Act (illegal dealings in documents relating to pay, pensions, mobilisation etc.).

49   An offence under section 197 of that Act (unauthorised use of and dealing in decorations etc.).

Naval Discipline Act 1957 (c. 53)

50   An offence under section 96 of the Naval Discipline Act 1957 (false pretence of desertion or absence without leave).

51   An offence under section 99 of that Act (illegal dealings in official documents).

Agricultural Marketing Act 1958 (c. 47)

52   An offence under section 45 of the Agricultural Marketing Act 1958 (failure to comply with demand for information or knowingly making any false statement in reply thereto).

Rivers (Prevention of Pollution) Act 1961 (c. 50)

53   An offence under section 12(1) of the Rivers (Prevention of Pollution) Act 1961 (restriction of disclosure of information).

Betting, Gaming and Lotteries Act 1963 (c. 2)

54   An offence under section 8 of the Betting, Gaming and Lotteries Act 1963 (betting in streets and public places).

Children and Young Persons Act 1963 (c. 37)

55   An offence under section 40 of the Children and Young Persons Act 1963 (offences relating to persons under 16 taking part in public performances etc.).

Animal Boarding Establishments Act 1963 (c. 43)

56   An offence under the Animal Boarding Establishments Act 1963 (offences in connection with the licensing and inspection of boarding establishments for animals), other than an offence under section 2 of that Act.

Agriculture and Horticulture Act 1964 (c. 28)

57   An offence under Part 3 of the Agriculture and Horticulture Act 1964 (offences relating to the grading and transport of fresh horticultural produce), other than an offence under section 15(1) of that Act.

Emergency Laws (Re-enactments and Repeals) Act 1964 (c. 60)

58   An offence under paragraph 1(3) or 2(4) of Schedule 1 to the Emergency Laws (Re-enactments and Repeals) Act 1964 (offences relating to the production of documents).

Riding Establishments Act 1964 (c. 70)

59   An offence under the Riding Establishments Act 1964 (offences relating to the keeping of riding establishments), other than an offence under section 2(4) of that Act.

Industrial and Provident Societies Act 1965 (c. 12)

60   An offence under section 16 of the Industrial and Provident Societies Act 1965 (cancellation of registration of society).
61   An offence under section 48 of that Act (production of documents and provision of information for certain purposes).

Cereals Marketing Act 1965 (c. 14)

62   An offence under section 17(1) of the Cereals Marketing Act 1965 (failure to comply with a requirement of a scheme).

Gas Act 1965 (c. 36)

63   An offence under paragraph 9 of Schedule 6 to the Gas Act 1965 (wrongful disclosure of information).

Armed Forces Act 1966 (c. 45)

64   An offence under section 8 of the Armed Forces Act 1966 (false statements on entry into Royal Navy).

Agriculture Act 1967 (c. 22)

65   An offence under section 6(9) of the Agriculture Act 1967 (compulsory use of systems of classification of carcases).
66   An offence under section 14(2) of that Act (levy schemes: requirements in relation to registration, returns and records).
67   An offence under section 69 of that Act (false statements to obtain grants etc).

Sea Fisheries (Shellfish) Act 1967 (c. 83)

68   An offence under section 14(2) of the Sea Fisheries (Shellfish) Act 1967 (offences relating to the deposit and importation of shellfish).

Theatres Act 1968 (c. 54)

69   An offence under section 13(1) or (2) of the Theatres Act 1968 (offences relating to licensing of premises for public performances of plays).

Theft Act 1968 (c. 60)

70   An offence under paragraph 2(1) of Schedule 1 to the Theft Act 1968 (taking or destroying fish).

Agriculture Act 1970 (c. 40)

71   An offence under section 106(8) of the Agriculture Act 1970 (eradication of brucellosis: obstructing or impeding an officer in the exercise of powers to obtain information).

Breeding of Dogs Act 1973 (c. 60)

72   An offence under the Breeding of Dogs Act 1973 (offences connected with the licensing of breeding establishments for dogs), other than under section 2 of that Act.

Slaughterhouses Act 1974 (c. 3)

73   An offence under section 4(5) of the Slaughterhouses Act 1974 (knacker's yard licences and applications for such licences).

National Health Service Act 1977 (c. 49)

74   An offence under paragraph 8(3) or 9(4) of Schedule 11 to the National Health Service Act 1977 (offences relating to the production of documents etc.).

Magistrates' Courts Act 1980 (c. 43)

75   An offence under section 84(3) of the Magistrates' Courts Act 1980 (making of false statement as to means).

Animal Health Act 1981 (c. 22)

76   An offence under paragraph 6 of Schedule 1 to the Animal Health Act 1981 (offences relating to the manufacture of veterinary therapeutic substances).

Fisheries Act 1981 (c. 29)

77   An offence under section 5(4) of the Fisheries Act 1981 (alteration of records or furnishing false information).

Civil Aviation Act 1982 (c. 16)

78   An offence under section 82 of the Civil Aviation Act 1982 (using an aircraft for advertising, etc.).

Mental Health Act 1983 (c. 20)

79   An offence under section 103 of the Mental Health Act 1983 (wrongful disclosure of a report made by a Visitor).
80   An offence under section 129 of that Act (obstruction).

Building Act 1984 (c. 55)

81   An offence under section 96(3) of the Building Act 1984 (wrongful disclosure of information).

Surrogacy Arrangements Act 1985 (c. 49)

82   An offence under section 2 of the Surrogacy Arrangements Act 1985 (negotiating surrogacy arrangements on a commercial basis, etc.).

Animals (Scientific Procedures) Act 1986 (c. 14)

83   An offence under section 22(3), 23 or 25(3) of the Animals (Scientific Procedures) Act 1986 (false statements and offences in relation to powers of entry).

Motor Cycle Noise Act 1987 (c. 34)

84   An offence under paragraph 1 of Schedule 1 to the Motor Cycle Noise Act 1987 (supply of exhaust systems etc. not complying with prescribed requirements).

Human Organ Transplants Act 1989 (c. 31)

85   An offence under section 2 of the Human Organ Transplants Act 1989 (restrictions on organ transplants).

Town and Country Planning Act 1990 (c. 8)

86   An offence under paragraph 14(4) of Schedule 15 to the Town and Country Planning Act 1990 (wrongful disclosure of information).

Environmental Protection Act 1990 (c. 43)

87   An offence under section 118(1)(g), (h) or (i) of the Environmental Protection Act 1990 (offences relating to inspection of genetically modified organisms).

Criminal Justice Act 1991 (c. 53)

88   An offence under section 20A of the Criminal Justice Act 1991 (false statements as to financial circumstances).

Deer Act 1991 (c. 54)

89   An offence under section 10(3) of the Deer Act 1991 (offences relating to sale and purchase etc. of venison).

Water Industry Act 1991 (c. 56)

90   An offence under section 206(2) of the Water Industry Act 1991 (wrongful disclosure of information).
91   An offence that falls within paragraph 5(5) of Schedule 6 to that Act (wrongful disclosure of information).

Social Security Administration Act 1992 (c. 5)

92   An offence under section 105 of the Social Security Administration Act 1992 (failure of person to maintain himself or another).
93   An offence under section 182 of that Act (illegal possession of documents).

Local Government Finance Act 1992 (c. 14)

94   An offence under section 27(5) of the Local Government Finance Act 1992 (false statements in relation to properties).

Trade Union and Labour Relations (Consolidation) Act 1992 (c. 52)

95   An offence under section 240 of the Trade Union and Labour Relations (Consolidation) Act 1992 (breach of contract involving injury to persons or property).

Merchant Shipping Act 1995 (c. 21)

96   An offence under section 57 of the Merchant Shipping Act 1995 (offences relating to merchant navy uniforms).

Reserve Forces Act 1996 (c. 14)

97   An offence under section 75(5) of the Reserve Forces Act 1996 (making false statements).
98   An offence under section 82(1) of that Act (offences in connection with regulations under sections 78 and 79 of that Act).
99   An offence under section 87(1) of that Act (offences in connection with claims for payment).
100   An offence under section 99 of that Act (false pretence of illegal absence).
101   An offence under paragraph 5(1) of Schedule 1 to that Act (false answers in attestation papers).

Housing Act 1996 (c. 52)

102   An offence under paragraph 23 or 24 of Schedule 1 to the Housing Act 1996 (contravening order not to part with money etc. held on behalf of a social landlord).

Broadcasting Act 1996 (c. 55)

103   An offence under section 144 of the Broadcasting Act 1996 (providing false information in connection with licences).

Breeding and Sale of Dogs (Welfare) Act 1999 (c. 11)

104   An offence under section 8 or 9(6) of the Breeding and Sale of Dogs (Welfare) Act 1999 (offences relating to the sale of dogs and connected matters).

Transport Act 2000 (c. 38)

105   An offence under section 82(2) of the Transport Act 2000 (wrongful disclosure of information).

SCHEDULE 26   **Section 280(2)**

INCREASE IN MAXIMUM TERM FOR CERTAIN SUMMARY OFFENCES

Railway Regulation Act 1840 (c. 97)

1   In section 16 of the Railway Regulation Act 1840 (obstructing officers or trespassing upon railway), for "one month", there is substituted "51 weeks".

Licensing Act 1872 (c. 94)

2   In section 12 of the Licensing Act 1872 (penalty for being found drunk), for "one month" there is substituted "51 weeks".

Regulation of Railways Act 1889 (c. 57)

3   In section 5 of the Regulation of Railways Act 1889 (avoiding payment of fares, etc.), in subsection (3), for "three months" there is substituted "51 weeks".

Witnesses (Public Inquiries) Protection Act 1892 (c. 64)

4   In section 2 of the Witnesses (Public Inquiries) Protection Act 1892 (persons obstructing or intimidating witnesses), for "three months" there is substituted "51 weeks".

Licensing Act 1902 (c. 28)

5   In section 2 of the Licensing Act 1902 (penalty for being drunk while in charge of a child), in subsection (1), for "one month" there is substituted "51 weeks".

Emergency Powers Act 1920 (c. 55)

6   In section 2 of the Emergency Powers Act 1920 (emergency regulations), in subsection (3), for "three months" there is substituted "51 weeks".

Judicial Proceedings (Regulation of Reports) Act 1926 (c. 61)

7   In section 1 of the Judicial Proceedings (Regulation of Reports) Act 1926 (restriction on publication of reports of judicial proceedings), in subsection (2), for "four months" there is substituted "51 weeks".

Public Order Act 1936 (1 Edw. 8 & 1 Geo. 6 c. 6)

8   In section 7 of the Public Order Act 1936 (enforcement), in subsection (2), for "three months" there is substituted "51 weeks".

Cinematograph Films (Animals) Act 1937 (c. 59)

9   In section 1 of the Cinematograph Films (Animals) Act 1937 (prohibition of films involving cruelty to animals), in subsection (3), for "three months" there is substituted "51 weeks".

House to House Collections Act 1939 (c. 44)

10   In section 8 of the House to House Collections Act 1939, in subsection (2), for "three months" there is substituted "51 weeks".

Fire Services Act 1947 (c. 41)

11   In section 31 of the Fire Services Act 1947 (false alarms of fire), in subsection (1), for "three months" there is substituted "51 weeks".

National Assistance Act 1948 (c. 29)

12   (1) The National Assistance Act 1948 is amended as follows.
(2) In section 51 (failure to maintain), in subsection (3)(a) and (b), for "three months" there is substituted "51 weeks".
(3) In section 52 (false statements), in subsection (1), for "three months" there is substituted "51 weeks".

Docking and Nicking of Horses Act 1949 (c. 70)

13   (1) The Docking and Nicking of Horses Act 1949 is amended as follows.
     (2) In section 1 (prohibition of docking and nicking except in certain cases), in subsection (3), for "three months" there is substituted "51 weeks".
     (3) In section 2 (restriction on landing docked horses)—
        (a) in subsection (3), and
        (b) in subsection (4),
           for "3 months" there is substituted "51 weeks".

Protection of Animals (Amendment) Act 1954 (c. 40)

14   In section 2 of the Protection of Animals (Amendment) Act 1954 (breach of disqualification order), for "three months" there is substituted "51 weeks".

Children and Young Persons (Harmful Publications) Act 1955 (c. 28)

15   In section 2 of the Children and Young Persons (Harmful Publications) Act 1955 (penalty for publishing certain works etc.), in subsection (1), for "four months" there is substituted "51 weeks".

Agriculture Act 1957 (c. 57)

16   In section 7 of the Agriculture Act 1957 (penalties)—
        (a) in subsection (1), for "three months" there is substituted "51 weeks", and
        (b) in subsection (2), for "one month" there is substituted "51 weeks".

Animals (Cruel Poisons) Act 1962 (c. 26)

17   In section 1 of the Animals (Cruel Poisons) Act 1962 (offences and penalties under regulations), in paragraph (b), for "three months" there is substituted "51 weeks".

Plant Varieties and Seeds Act 1964 (c. 14)

18   In section 27 of the Plant Varieties and Seeds Act 1964 (tampering with samples), in subsection (1), for "three months" there is substituted "51 weeks".

Agriculture Act 1967 (c. 22)

19   (1) The Agriculture Act 1967 is amended as follows.
     (2) In section 6 (penalties), in subsection (4), for "three months" there is substituted "51 weeks".
     (3) In section 21 (inquiry by Meat and Livestock Commission), in subsection (11), for "three months" there is substituted "51 weeks".

Firearms Act 1968 (c. 27)

20   (1) Part 1 of Schedule 6 to the Firearms Act 1968 (prosecution and punishment of offences) is amended as follows.
     (2) In the entry relating to section 3(6) of that Act (business and other transactions with firearms and ammunition), in the fourth column, for "3 months" there is substituted "51 weeks".
     (3) In the entry relating to section 6(3) of that Act (power to prohibit movement of arms and ammunition), in the fourth column, for "3 months" there is substituted "51 weeks".
     (4) In the entry relating to section 20(2) of that Act (trespassing with firearm), in the fourth column, for "3 months" there is substituted "51 weeks".
     (5) In the entry relating to section 22(1A) of that Act (acquisition and possession of firearms by minors), in the fourth column, for "3 months" there is substituted "51 weeks".
     (6) In the entry relating to section 25 of that Act (supplying firearm to person drunk or insane), in the fourth column, for "3 months" there is substituted "51 weeks".
     (7) In the entry relating to section 32C(6) of that Act (variation endorsement etc. of European documents), in the fourth column, for "3 months" there is substituted "51 weeks".
     (8) In the entry relating to section 42A of that Act (information as to transactions under visitors' permits), in the fourth column, for "3 months" there is substituted "51 weeks".
     (9) In the entry relating to section 47(2) of that Act (powers of constables to stop and search), in the fourth column, for "3 months" there is substituted "51 weeks".

(10) In the entry relating to section 49(3) of that Act (police powers in relation to arms traffic), in the fourth column, for "3 months" there is substituted "51 weeks".

Agriculture (Miscellaneous Provisions) Act 1968 (c. 34)

21   In section 7 of the Agriculture (Miscellaneous Provisions) Act 1968 (punishment of offences under Part 1), in subsection (1), for "three months" there is substituted "51 weeks".

Agriculture Act 1970 (c. 40)

22   (1) The Agriculture Act 1970 is amended as follows.
     (2) In section 68 (duty to give statutory statement), in subsection (4), for "three months" there is substituted "51 weeks".
     (3) In section 69 (marking of material prepared for sale), in subsection (4), for "three months" there is substituted "51 weeks".
     (4) In section 70 (use of names or expressions with prescribed meanings), in subsection (2), for "three months" there is substituted "51 weeks".
     (5) In section 71 (particulars to be given of attributes if claimed to be present), in subsection (2), for "three months" there is substituted "51 weeks".
     (6) In section 73 (deleterious ingredients in feeding stuff), in subsection (4), for "three months" there is substituted "51 weeks".
     (7) In section 73A (unwholesome feeding stuff), in subsection (4), for "three months" there is substituted "51 weeks".
     (8) In section 74A (regulations controlling the contents of feeding stuff), in subsection (3), for "three months" there is substituted "51 weeks".
     (9) In section 79 (supplementary provision relating to samples and analysis), in subsection (10), for "three months" there is substituted "51 weeks".
     (10) In section 83 (exercise of powers by inspectors), in subsection (3), for "three months" there is substituted "51 weeks".
     (11) In section 106 (eradication of brucellosis), in subsection (7), for "three months" there is substituted "51 weeks".

Slaughterhouses Act 1974 (c. 3)

23   (1) The Slaughterhouses Act 1974 is amended as follows.
     (2) In section 20 (wrongful disclosure of information), in subsection (4), for "three months" there is substituted "51 weeks".
     (3) In section 21 (obstruction), in subsection (1), for "one month" there is substituted "51 weeks".
     (4) In section 23 (prosecution and punishment of offences), in subsection (2)(a), for "three months" there is substituted "51 weeks".

Criminal Law Act 1977 (c. 45)

24   In section 8 of the Criminal Law Act 1977 (trespassing with a weapon of offence), in subsection (3), for "three months" there is substituted "51 weeks".

Refuse Disposal (Amenity) Act 1978 (c. 3)

25   In section 2 of the Refuse Disposal (Amenity) Act 1978 (penalty for unauthorised dumping), in subsection (1), for "three months" there is substituted "51 weeks".

Customs and Excise Management Act 1979 (c. 2)

26   (1) The Customs and Excise Management Act 1979 is amended as follows.
     (2) In section 21 (control of movement of aircraft), in subsection (6), for "3 months" there is substituted "51 weeks".
     (3) In section 33 (power to inspect aircraft etc.), in subsection (4), for "3 months" there is substituted "51 weeks".
     (4) In section 34 (power to prevent flight of aircraft)—
          (a) in subsection (2), and

        (b) in subsection (3),

              for "3 months" there is substituted "51 weeks".

Licensed Premises (Exclusion of Certain Persons) Act 1980 (c. 32)

27   In section 2 of the Licensed Premises (Exclusion of Certain Persons) Act 1980 (penalty for non-compliance with an exclusion order), in subsection (1), for "one month" there is substituted "51 weeks".

Criminal Attempts Act 1981 (c. 47)

28   In section 9 of the Criminal Attempts Act 1981 (interference with vehicles), in subsection (3), for "three months" there is substituted "51 weeks".

British Nationality Act 1981 (c. 61)

29   In section 46 of the British Nationality Act 1981 (offences and proceedings), in subsection (1) for "three months" there is substituted "51 weeks".

Civil Aviation Act 1982 (c. 16)

30   (1) The Civil Aviation Act 1982 is amended as follows.

      (2) In section 44 (offences relating to the power to obtain rights over land), in subsection (10), for "three months" there is substituted "51 weeks".

      (3) In section 75 (investigation of accidents), in subsection (5), for "three months" there is substituted "51 weeks".

Anatomy Act 1984 (c. 14)

31   In section 11 of the Anatomy Act 1984 (offences), in subsection (6), for "3 months" there is substituted "51 weeks".

Public Health (Control of Disease) Act 1984 (c. 22)

32   (1) The Public Health (Control of Disease) Act 1984 is amended as follows.

      (2) In section 29 (letting of house after recent case of notifiable disease), in subsection (1), for "one month" there is substituted "51 weeks".

      (3) In section 30 (duty on ceasing to occupy house after recent case of notifiable disease), in subsection (1), for "one month" there is substituted "51 weeks".

      (4) In section 62 (powers of entry), in subsection (3), for "3 months" there is substituted "51 weeks".

County Courts Act 1984 (c. 28)

33   (1) The County Courts Act 1984 is amended as follows.

      (2) In section 14 (penalty for assaulting officers), in subsection (1)(a), for "3 months" there is substituted "51 weeks".

      (3) In section 92 (penalty for rescuing goods seized), in subsection (1)(a), for "one month" there is substituted "51 weeks."

Animal Health and Welfare Act 1984 (c. 40)

34   In section 10 of the Animal Health and Welfare Act 1984 (artificial breeding of livestock), in subsection (6), for "three months" there is substituted "51 weeks".

Police and Criminal Evidence Act 1984 (c. 60)

35   In section 63C of the Police and Criminal Evidence Act 1984 (testing for presence of drugs), in subsection (1), for "three months" there is substituted "51 weeks".

Sporting Events (Control of Alcohol etc.) Act 1985 (c. 57)

36   In section 8 of the Sporting Events (Control of Alcohol etc.) Act 1985 (penalties for offences), in paragraph (b), for "three months" there is substituted "51 weeks".

Public Order Act 1986 (c. 64)

37   (1) The Public Order Act 1986 is amended as follows.

      (2) In section 12 (imposing conditions on public processions)—

(a) in subsection (8), and
(b) in subsection (10),
    for "3 months" there is substituted "51 weeks".
(3) In section 13 (prohibiting public processions)—
    (a) in subsection (11), and
    (b) in subsection (13),
        for"3 months" there is substituted "51 weeks".
(4) In section 14 (imposing conditions on public assemblies)—
    (a) in subsection (8), and
    (b) in subsection (10),
        for "3 months" there is substituted "51 weeks".
(5) In section 14B (offences in connection with trespassory assemblies and arrest therefor)—
    (a) in subsection (5), and
    (b) in subsection (7),
        for "3 months" there is substituted "51 weeks".

Road Traffic Offenders Act 1988 (c. 53)

38 (1) Part 1 of Schedule 2 to the Road Traffic Offenders Act 1988 (prosecution and punishment of offenders) is amended as follows.
    (2) In the entry relating to section 4(2) of the Road Traffic Act 1988 (driving, or being in charge, when under the influence of drink or drugs), in column 4, for "3 months" there is substituted "51 weeks".
    (3) In the entry relating to section 5(1)(b) of that Act (driving or being in charge of a motor vehicle with alcohol concentration above prescribed limit), in column 4, for "3 months" there is substituted "51 weeks".
    (4) In the entry relating to section 7 of that Act (provision of specimens for analysis), in column 4, for "3 months" there is substituted "51 weeks".
    (5) In the entry relating to section 7A of that Act (failing to allow specimen to be subjected to analysis), in column 4, for "3 months" there is substituted "51 weeks".

Official Secrets Act 1989 (c. 6)

39 In section 10 of the Official Secrets Act 1989 (penalties), in subsection (2), for "three months" there is substituted "51 weeks".

Human Organ Transplants Act 1989 (c. 31)

40 In section 1 of the Human Organ Transplants Act 1989 (prohibition of commercial dealings in human organs), in subsection (5), for "three months" there is substituted "51 weeks".

Football Spectators Act 1989 (c. 37)

41 In section 2 of the Football Spectators Act 1989 (unauthorised attendance at designated football matches), in subsection (3), for "one month" there is substituted "51 weeks".

Food Safety Act 1990 (c. 16)

42 In section 35 of the Food Safety Act 1990 (punishment of offences), in subsection (1), for "three months" there is substituted "51 weeks".

Deer Act 1991 (c. 54)

43 In section 9 of the Deer Act 1991 (penalties for offences relating to deer), in subsection (1), for "three months" there is substituted "51 weeks".

Social Security Administration Act 1992 (c. 5)

44 In section 112 of the Social Security Administration Act 1992 (false representations for obtaining benefit etc.), in subsection (2), for "3 months" there is substituted "51 weeks".

Criminal Justice and Public Order Act 1994 (c. 33)

45 (1) The Criminal Justice and Public Order Act 1994 is amended as follows.
    (2) In section 60 (failing to stop), in subsection (8), for "one month" there is substituted "51 weeks".

(3) In section 60AA (powers to require removal of disguises), in subsection (7), for "one month" there is substituted "51 weeks".

(4) In section 61 (power to remove trespasser on land), in subsection (4), for "three months" there is substituted "51 weeks".

(5) In section 62B (failure to comply with direction under section 62A: offences), in subsection (3), for "3 months" there is substituted "51 weeks".

(6) In section 63 (powers to remove persons attending or preparing for a rave), in subsections (6) and (7B), for "three months" there is substituted "51 weeks".

(7) In section 68 (offence of aggravated trespass), in subsection (3), for "three months" there is substituted "51 weeks".

(8) In section 69 (powers to remove persons committing or participating in aggravated trespass), in subsection (3), for "three months" there is substituted "51 weeks".

London Local Authorities Act 1995 (c. x)

46   In section 24 of the London Local Authorities Act 1995 (enforcement), in subsection (1), for "three months" there is substituted "51 weeks".

Police Act 1996 (c. 16)

47   In section 89 of the Police Act 1996 (assaults on constables etc.), in subsection (2), for "one month" there is substituted "51 weeks".

Treasure Act 1996 (c. 24)

48   In section 8 of the Treasure Act 1996 (duty of finder of treasure to notify coroner), in subsection (3)(a), for "three months" there is substituted "51 weeks".

Education Act 1996 (c. 56)

49   (1) The Education Act 1996 is amended as follows.
      (2) In section 444 (failure to secure regular attendance at school), in subsection (8A)(b), for "three months" there is substituted "51 weeks".
      (3) In section 559 (prohibition or restriction on employment of children), in subsection (4)(b), for "one month" there is substituted "51 weeks".

Government of Wales Act 1998 (c. 38)

50   In section 75 of the Government of Wales Act 1998 (witnesses and documents: supplementary), in subsection (3)(b), for "three months" there is substituted "51 weeks".

Access to Justice Act 1999 (c. 22)

51   In section 21 of the Access to Justice Act 1999 (misrepresentation etc), in subsection (2)(b), for "three months" there is substituted "51 weeks".

Greater London Authority Act 1999 (c. 29)

52   In section 64 of the Greater London Authority Act 1999 (failure to attend proceedings etc), in subsection (2)(b), for "three months" there is substituted "51 weeks".

Immigration and Asylum Act 1999 (c. 33)

53   (1) The Immigration and Asylum Act 1999 is amended as follows.
      (2) In section 105 (false representation), in subsection (2), for "three months" there is substituted "51 weeks".
      (3) In section 108 (failure of sponsor to maintain), in subsection (2), for "3 months" there is substituted "51 weeks".

Financial Services and Markets Act 2000 (c. 8)

54   (1) The Financial Services and Markets Act 2000 is amended as follows.
      (2) In section 177 (offences), in subsection (6), for "three months" there is substituted "51 weeks".

(3) In section 352 (offences), in subsection (5), for "three months" there is substituted "51 weeks".

Terrorism Act 2000 (c. 11)

55 (1) The Terrorism Act 2000 is amended as follows.
(2) In section 36 (police powers), in subsection (4)(a), for "three months" there is substituted "51 weeks".
(3) In section 51 (offences in relation to parking), in subsection (6)(a), for "three months" there is substituted "51 weeks".
(4) In Schedule 5 (terrorist investigations: information)—
    (a) in paragraph 3(8)(a), and
    (b) in paragraph 15(5)(a),
        for "three months" there is substituted "51 weeks".
(5) In Schedule 7 (ports and border controls), in paragraph 18(2)(a), for "three months" there is substituted "51 weeks".

Criminal Justice and Police Act 2001 (c. 16)

56 (1) The Criminal Justice and Police Act 2001 is amended as follows.
(2) In section 25 (enforcement of closure orders)—
    (a) in subsection (3)(a), for "one month" there is substituted "51 weeks", and
    (b) in subsections (4) and (5), for "three months" there is substituted "51 weeks".
(3) In section 42 (prevention of intimidation), in subsection (7), for "three months" there is substituted "51 weeks".

Police Reform Act 2002 (c. 30)

57 In section 46 of the Police Reform Act 2002 (offences against designated and accredited persons etc.), in subsection (2), for "one month" there is substituted "51 weeks".

Nationality, Immigration and Asylum Act 2002 (c. 41)

58 In section 137 of the Nationality, Immigration and Asylum Act 2002 (offences relating to the disclosure of information), in subsection (2)(a), for "three months" there is substituted "51 weeks".

Anti-social Behaviour Act 2003 (c. 38)

59 In section 40 of the Anti-social Behaviour Act 2003 (closure of noisy premises), in subsection (5)(a), for "three months" there is substituted "51 weeks".

SCHEDULE 27   **Section 283**

ENABLING POWERS: ALTERATION OF MAXIMUM PENALTIES ETC.

Plant Health Act 1967 (c. 8)

1 (1) Section 3 of the Plant Health Act 1967 (control of spread of pests in Great Britain) is amended as follows.
(2) In subsection (4A), for "three months" there is substituted "the prescribed term".
(3) After that subsection there is inserted—
    "(4B) In subsection (4A) above, "the prescribed term" means—
        (a) in relation to England and Wales, 51 weeks;
        (b) in relation to Scotland, three months."

Agriculture Act 1967 (c. 22)

2 (1) Section 9 of the Agriculture Act 1967 (powers to meet future developments in livestock and livestock products industries) is amended as follows.

(2) In subsection (10), for "three months" there is substituted "the prescribed term".

(3) After that subsection there is inserted—

"(10A) In subsection (10), "the prescribed term" means—

    (a) in relation to England and Wales, 51 weeks;

    (b) in relation to Scotland, three months."

European Communities Act 1972 (c. 68)

3   (1) Paragraph 1 of Schedule 2 to the European Communities Act 1972 (provisions as to powers conferred by section 2(2)) is amended as follows.

(2) In sub-paragraph (1)(d), for "three months" there is substituted "the prescribed term".

(3) After sub-paragraph (2) there is inserted—

"(3) In sub-paragraph (1)(d), "the prescribed term" means—

    (a) in relation to England and Wales, where the offence is a summary offence, 51 weeks;

    (b) in relation to England and Wales, where the offence is triable either way, twelve months;

    (c) in relation to Scotland and Northern Ireland, three months."

Slaughterhouses Act 1974 (c. 3)

4   In section 38(5) of the Slaughterhouses Act 1974 (maximum penalties to be prescribed by regulations), the words "or imprisonment for a term of three months or both" are omitted.

Anatomy Act 1984 (c. 14)

5   (1) Section 11 of the Anatomy Act 1984 (offences) is amended as follows.

(2) In subsection (7), for "3 months" there is substituted "the prescribed term".

(3) After that subsection there is inserted—

"(7A) In subsection (7), "the prescribed term" means—

    (a) in relation to England and Wales, 51 weeks;

    (b) in relation to Scotland, 3 months."

Environmental Protection Act 1990 (c. 43)

6   (1) Section 141 of the Environmental Protection Act 1990 (power to prohibit or restrict the importation or exportation of waste) is amended as follows.

(2) In paragraph (g) of subsection (5), for "six months" there is substituted "the prescribed term".

(3) After that subsection there is inserted—

"(5A) In subsection (5)(g), "the prescribed term" means—

    (a) in relation to England and Wales, where the offence is a summary offence, 51 weeks;

    (b) in relation to England and Wales, where the offence is triable either way, twelve months;

    (c) in relation to Scotland and Northern Ireland, six months."

Scotland Act 1998 (c. 46)

7   (1) Section 113 of the Scotland Act 1998 (subordinate legislation: scope of powers) is amended as follows.

(2) In paragraph (a) of subsection (10), for "three months" there is substituted "the prescribed term".

(3) After that subsection there is inserted—

"(10A) In subsection (10)(a), "the prescribed term" means—

    (a) in relation to England and Wales, where the offence is a summary offence, 51 weeks;

    (b) in relation to England and Wales, where the offence is triable either way, twelve months;

    (c) in relation to Scotland and Northern Ireland, three months."

Regulatory Reform Act 2001 (c. 6)

8   (1) Section 3 of the Regulatory Reform Act 2001 (limitations on order-making power) is amended as follows.

(2) In paragraph (b) of subsection (3), for "six months" there is substituted "the prescribed term".

(3) After that subsection there is inserted—

"(3A) In subsection (3)(b), "the prescribed term" means—

(a) in relation to England and Wales, where the offence is a summary offence, 51 weeks;

(b) in relation to England and Wales, where the offence is triable either way, twelve months;

(c) in relation to Scotland and Northern Ireland, six months."

SCHEDULE 28

Section 284

INCREASE IN PENALTIES FOR DRUG-RELATED OFFENCES

Misuse of Drugs Act 1971 (c. 38)

1   (1) Schedule 4 to the Misuse of Drugs Act 1971 (prosecution and punishment of offences) is amended as follows.

(2) In column 6 of that Schedule (punishments for offences under that Act committed in relation to Class C drugs), in each of the following entries, for "5 years" there is substituted "14 years".

(3) Those entries are the entries relating to the punishment, on conviction on indictment, of offences under the following provisions of that Act—

(a) section 4(2) (production, or being concerned in the production, of a controlled drug),

(b) section 4(3) (supplying or offering to supply a controlled drug or being concerned in the doing of either activity by another),

(c) section 5(3) (having possession of a controlled drug with intent to supply it to another),

(d) section 8 (being the occupier, or concerned in the management, of premises and permitting or suffering certain activities to take place there),

(e) section 12(6) (contravention of direction prohibiting practitioner etc from possessing, supplying etc controlled drugs), and

(f) section 13(3) (contravention of direction prohibiting practitioner etc from prescribing, supplying etc controlled drugs).

Customs and Excise Management Act 1979 (c. 2)

2   In Schedule 1 to the Customs and Excise Management Act 1979 (controlled drugs: variation of punishments for certain offences under that Act), in paragraph 2(c) (punishment on conviction on indictment of offences under that Act committed in relation to Class C drugs), for "5 years" there is substituted "14 years".

Criminal Justice (International Co-operation) Act 1990 (c. 5)

3   In section 19 of the Criminal Justice (International Co-operation) Act 1990 (ships used for illicit traffic), in subsection (4)(c)(ii) (punishment on conviction on indictment of offences under that section committed in relation to Class C drugs), for "five years" there is substituted "fourteen years".

SCHEDULE 29

Section 292

SENTENCING FOR FIREARMS OFFENCES IN NORTHERN IRELAND

1   The Firearms (Northern Ireland) Order 1981 (S.I. 1981/155 (N.I. 2)) is amended as follows.

2   In Article 2(2) (interpretation) after the definition of "firearms dealer" there is inserted—

""handgun" means any firearm which either has a barrel less than 30 centimetres in length or is less than 60 centimetres in length overall, other than an air weapon, a muzzle-loading gun or a firearm designed as signalling apparatus;".

3   In Article 3(1) (requirement of firearm certificate) for sub-paragraph (a) there is substituted—

"(aa) has in his possession, or purchases or acquires, a handgun without holding a firearm certificate in force at the time, or otherwise than as authorised by such a certificate;

(ab) has in his possession, or purchases or acquires, any firearm, other than a handgun, without holding a firearm certificate in force at the time, or otherwise than as authorised by such a certificate; or".

4   After Article 52 of that Order there is inserted—

"52A Minimum sentence for certain offences

(1) This Article applies where—

  (a) an individual is convicted of—

    (i) an offence under Article 3(1)(aa),

    (ii) an offence under Article 6(1)(a), (ab), (ac), (ad), (ae) or (c), or

    (iii) an offence under Article 6(1A)(a), and

  (b) the offence was committed after the commencement of this Article and at a time when he was aged 16 or over.

(2) The court shall—

  (a) in the case of an offence under Article 3(1)(aa) committed by a person who was aged 21 or over when he committed the offence, impose a sentence of imprisonment for a term of five years (with or without a fine), and

  (b) in any other case, impose an appropriate custodial sentence for a term of at least the required minimum term (with or without a fine)

unless (in any of those cases) the court is of the opinion that there are exceptional circumstances relating to the offence or to the offender which justify its not doing so.

(3) Where an offence is found to have been committed over a period of two or more days, or at some time during a period of two or more days, it shall be taken for the purposes of this Article to have been committed on the last of those days.

(4) In this Article—

"appropriate custodial sentence" means—

  (a) in the case of an offender who is aged 21 or over when convicted, a sentence of imprisonment, and

  (b) in the case of an offender who is aged under 21 at that time, a sentence of detention under section 5(1) of the Treatment of Offenders Act (Northern Ireland) 1968;

"the required minimum term" means—

  (a) in the case of an offender who was aged 21 or over when he committed the offence, five years, and

  (b) in the case of an offender who was aged under 21 at that time, three years."

5   After Article 52A there is inserted—

"52B Power by order to exclude application of minimum sentence to those under 18

(1) The Secretary of State may by order—

  (a) amend Article 52A(1)(b) by substituting for the word "16" the word "18", and

  (b) make such other provision as he considers necessary or expedient in consequence of, or in connection with, the provision made by virtue of sub-paragraph (a).

(2) The provision that may be made by virtue of paragraph (1)(b) includes, in particular, provision amending or repealing any statutory provision within the meaning of section 1(f) of the Interpretation Act (Northern Ireland) 1954 (whenever passed or made).

(3) An order under paragraph (1) shall be subject to annulment in pursuance of a resolution of either House of Parliament in like manner as a statutory instrument and section 5 of the Statutory Instruments Act 1946 shall apply accordingly."

6   (1) Schedule 2 (table of punishments) is amended as follows.

(2) For the entry relating to offences under Article 3(1) (purchase, acquisition or possession of firearm or ammunition without firearm certificate) there is substituted—

"Article 3(1)(aa)	Purchase, acquisition or possession of handgun without firearm certificate	Indictment	10 years or a fine, or both
Article 3(1)(ab)	Purchase, acquisition or possession without firearm certificate of firearm other than handgun	(a) Summary	1 year or a fine of the statutory maximum, or both
		(b) Indictment	5 years or a fine, or both
Article 3(1)(b)	Purchase, acquisition or possession of ammunition without firearm certificate	(a) Summary	1 year or a fine of the statutory maximum, or both
		(b) Indictment	5 years or a fine, or both"

(3) For the entries relating to offences under Article 6(1) (manufacture, dealing in or possession of prohibited weapons) and Article 6(1A) (possession of or dealing in other prohibited weapons) there is substituted—

"Article 6(1)(a), (ab), (ac), (ad), (ae) and (c)	Manufacture, dealing in or possession of prohibited weapons.	Indictment	10 years or a fine, or both
Article 6(1)(b)	Manfacture, dealing in or possession of prohibited weapon designed for discharge of noxious liquid etc.	(a) Summary	1 year or a fine of the statutory maximum, or both
		(b) Indictment	10 years or a fine, or both
Article 6 (1A)(a)	Possession of or dealing in firearm disguised as other object	Indictment	10 years or a fine, or both
Article 6(1A)(b), (c), (d), (e), (f) or (g)	Possession of or dealing in other prohibited weapons	(a) Summary	6 months or a fine of the statutory maximum, or both
		(b) Indictment	10 years or a fine, or both"

SCHEDULE 30   **Section 299**

DISQUALIFICATION FROM WORKING WITH CHILDREN

1   The Criminal Justice and Court Services Act 2000 (c. 43) is amended as follows.

2   After section 29 there is inserted—

"29A Disqualification at discretion of court: adults and juveniles

      (1) This section applies where—

          (a) an individual is convicted of an offence against a child (whether or not committed when he was aged 18 or over),

          (b) the individual is sentenced by a senior court, and

          (c) no qualifying sentence is imposed in respect of the conviction.

      (2) If the court is satisfied, having regard to all the circumstances, that it is likely that the individual will commit a further offence against a child, it may order the individual to be disqualified from working with children.

      (3) If the court makes an order under this section, it must state its reasons for doing so and cause those reasons to be included in the record of the proceedings.

29B Subsequent application for order under section 28 or 29

      (1) Where—

          (a) section 28 applies but the court has neither made an order under that section nor complied with subsection (6) of that section, or

          (b) section 29 applies but the court has not made an order under that section, and it appears to the prosecutor that the court has not considered the making of an order under that section,

      the prosecutor may at any time apply to that court for an order under section 28 or 29.

      (2) Subject to subsection (3), on an application under subsection (1)—

          (a) in a case falling within subsection (1)(a), the court—

              (i) must make an order under section 28 unless it is satisfied as mentioned in subsection (5) of that section, and

              (ii) if it does not make an order under that section, must comply with subsection (6) of that section,

          (b) in a case falling within subsection (1)(b), the court—

              (i) must make an order under section 29 if it is satisfied as mentioned in subsection (4) of that section, and

              (ii) if it does so, must comply with subsection (5) of that section.

      (3) Subsection (2) does not enable or require an order under section 28 or 29 to be made where the court is satisfied that it had considered the making of an order under that section at the time when it imposed the qualifying sentence or made the relevant order."

3   (1) Section 30 (supplemental provisions) is amended as follows.

      (2) In the heading for "and 29" there is substituted "to 29B".

      (3) In subsection (1)—

          (a) for "and 29" there is substituted "to 29B", and

          (b) in the definition of "qualifying sentence", after paragraph (d) there is inserted—

        "(dd) a sentence of detention under section 198 or 200 of the Criminal Justice Act 2003,".

      (4) In subsection (5)—

          (a) in paragraph (a), for "or 29" there is substituted ", 29 or 29A",

          (b) after paragraph (b) there is inserted—

        "(c) in relation to an individual to whom section 29A applies and on whom a sentence has been passed, references to his sentence are to that sentence."

4   In section 31 (appeals), in subsection (1), after paragraph (b) there is inserted—

    "(c) where an order is made under section 29A, as if the order were a sentence passed on him for the offence of which he has been convicted."

5   (1) Section 33 (conditions for application under section 32) is amended as follows.

      (2) In subsection (6), after paragraph (d) there is inserted—

      "(e) in relation to an individual not falling within any of paragraphs (a) to (d), the day on which the disqualification order is made.".

      (3) For subsection (8) there is substituted—

      "(8) In subsection (7) "detention" means detention (or detention and training)—

          (a) under any sentence or order falling within paragraphs (b) to (f) of the definition of "qualifying sentence" in section 30(1), or

(b) under any sentence or order which would fall within those paragraphs if it were for a term or period of 12 months or more.".

SCHEDULE 31   **Section 300**

DEFAULT ORDERS: MODIFICATION OF PROVISIONS RELATING TO COMMUNITY ORDERS

General

1   Any reference to the offender is, in relation to a default order, to be read as a reference to the person in default.

Unpaid work requirement

2   (1) In its application to a default order, section 199 (unpaid work requirement) is modified as follows.
     (2) In subsection (2), for paragraphs (a) and (b) there is substituted—
     "(a) not less than 20 hours, and
      (b) in the case of an amount in default which is specified in the first column of the following Table, not more than the number of hours set out opposite that amount in the second column.

TABLE

Amount	Number of Hours
An amount not exceeding £200	40 hours
An amount exceeding £20 but not exceeding £500	60 hours
An amount exceeding £500	100 hours"

     (3) Subsection (5) is omitted.

Curfew requirement

3   (1) In its application to a default order, section 204 (curfew requirement) is modified as follows.
     (2) After subsection (2) there is inserted—
     "(2A) In the case of an amount in default which is specified in the first column of the following Table, the number of days on which the person in default is subject to the curfew requirement must not exceed the number of days set out opposite that amount in the second column.

TABLE

Amount	Number of days
An amount not exceeding £200	20 days
An amount exceeding £200 but not exceeding £500	30 days
An amount exceeding £500 but not exceeding £1,000	60 days
An amount exceeding £1,000 but not exceeding £2,500	90 days
An amount exceeding £2,500	180 days"

Enforcement, revocation and amendment of default order

4   (1) In its application to a default order, Schedule 8 (breach, revocation or amendment of community orders) is modified as follows.
    (2) Any reference to the offence in respect of which the community order was made is to be taken to be a reference to the default in respect of which the default order was made.
    (3) Any power of the court to revoke the community order and deal with the offender for the offence is to be taken to be a power to revoke the default order and deal with him in any way in which the court which made the default order could deal with him for his default in paying the sum in question.
    (4) In paragraph 4 the reference to the Crown Court is to be taken as a reference to a magistrates' court.
    (5) The following provisions are omitted—
        (a) paragraph 9(1)(c), (5) and (8),
        (b) paragraph 12,
        (c) paragraph 13(5),
        (d) paragraph 15,
        (e) paragraph 17(5),
        (f) paragraph 21(4), and
        (g) paragraph 23(2)(b).

Power to alter amount of money or number of hours or days

5   The Secretary of State may by order amend paragraph 2 or 3 by substituting for any reference to an amount of money or a number of hours or days there specified a reference to such other amount or number as may be specified in the order.

Transfer of default orders to Scotland or Northern Ireland

6   In its application to a default order, Schedule 9 (transfer of community orders to Scotland or Northern Ireland) is modified as follows.
7   After paragraph 8 there is inserted—
    "8A Nothing in paragraph 8 affects the application of section 300(7) to a default order made or amended in accordance with paragraph 1 or 3."
8   In paragraph 10, after paragraph (b) there is inserted—
    "(bb) any power to impose a fine on the offender."

SCHEDULE 32   **Section 304**

AMENDMENTS RELATING TO SENTENCING

PART 1

GENERAL

Piracy Act 1837 (c. 88)

1   Section 3 of the Piracy Act 1837 (punishment for offence under certain repealed Acts relating to piracy) shall cease to have effect.

Children and Young Persons Act 1933 (c. 12)

2   (1) Section 49 of the Children and Young Persons Act 1933 (restrictions on reports of proceedings in which young persons are concerned) is amended as follows.
    (2) In subsection (4A)(d), for "section 62(3) of the Powers of Criminal Courts (Sentencing) Act 2000" there is substituted "section 222(1)(d) or (e) of the Criminal Justice Act 2003".
    (3) In subsection (11)—
        (a) in the definition of "sexual offence", for "has the same meaning as in the Powers of Criminal Courts (Sentencing) Act 2000" there is substituted "means an offence listed in Part 2 of Schedule 15 to the Criminal Justice Act 2003", and

(b) in the definition of "violent offence", for "has the same meaning as in the Powers of Criminal Courts (Sentencing) Act 2000" there is substituted "means an offence listed in Part 1 of Schedule 15 to the Criminal Justice Act 2003".

Prison Act 1952 (c. 52)

3   In section 53 of the Prison Act 1952 (interpretation), for "section 62 of the Powers of Criminal Courts (Sentencing) Act 2000" there is substituted "section 221 of the Criminal Justice Act 2003".

Criminal Justice Act 1967 (c. 80)

4   The Criminal Justice Act 1967 is amended as follows.
5   In section 32 (amendments of Costs in Criminal Cases Act 1952), in subsection (3)(a), for "make an order under paragraph 5 of Schedule 2 to the Powers of Criminal Courts (Sentencing) Act 2000 (probation orders requiring treatment for mental condition) or" there is substituted "include in a community order (within the meaning of Part 12 of the Criminal Justice Act 2003) a mental health requirement under section 207 of that Act or make an order under".
6   In section 104 (general provisions as to interpretation)_
        (a) in subsection (1), the definition of "suspended sentence" is omitted, and
        (b) subsection (2) is omitted.

Criminal Appeal Act 1968 (c. 19)

7   The Criminal Appeal Act 1968 is amended as follows.
8   (1) Section 10 (appeal against sentence in cases dealt with by Crown Court otherwise than on conviction on indictment) is amended as follows.
    (2) In subsection (2)—
        (a) in paragraph (b), for "or a community order within the meaning of the Powers of Criminal Courts (Sentencing) Act 2000" there is substituted "a youth community order within the meaning of the Powers of Criminal Courts (Sentencing) Act 2000 or a community order within the meaning of Part 12 of the Criminal Justice Act 2003", and
        (b) paragraph (c) and the word "or" immediately preceding it are omitted.
9   In section 11 (supplementary provisions as to appeal against sentence), subsection (4) is omitted.
10   In Schedule 2 (procedural and other provisions applicable on order for retrial), in paragraph 2(4), for the words from the beginning to "apply" there is substituted "Section 240 of the Criminal Justice Act 2003 (crediting of periods of remand in custody: terms of imprisonment and detention) shall apply".

Firearms Act 1968 (c. 27)

11   The Firearms Act 1968 is amended as follows.
12 (1) Section 21 (possession of firearms by persons previously convicted of crime) is amended as follows.
    (2) In subsection (2A), after paragraph (c) there is inserted—
        "(d) in the case of a person who has been subject to a sentence of imprisonment to which an intermittent custody order under section 183(1)(b) of the Criminal Justice Act 2003 relates, the date of his final release."
    (3) After subsection (2A) there is inserted—
      "(2B) A person who is serving a sentence of imprisonment to which an intermittent custody order under section 183 of the Criminal Justice Act 2003 relates shall not during any licence period specified for the purposes of subsection (1)(b)(i) of that section have a firearm or ammunition in his possession.".
    (4) In subsection (3)(b), for "probation order" there is substituted "community order".
    (5) After subsection (3) there is inserted—
    "(3ZA) In subsection (3)(b) above, "community order" means—
        (a) a community order within the meaning of Part 12 of the Criminal Justice Act 2003 made in England and Wales, or
        (b) a probation order made in Scotland."
    (6) In subsection (6), after "(2)" there is inserted ", (2B)".
13 (1) Section 52 (forfeiture and disposal of firearms; cancellation of certificate by convicting court) is amended as follows.
    (2) In subsection (1)(c), for "probation order" there is substituted "community order".

(3) After subsection (1) there is inserted —

"(1A) In subsection (1)(c) "community order" means—

    (a) a community order within the meaning of Part 12 of the Criminal Justice Act 2003 made in England and Wales, or

    (b) a probation order made in Scotland."

Social Work (Scotland) Act 1968 (c. 49)

14   In section 94 of the Social Work (Scotland) Act 1968 (interpretation), in the definition of "probation order" in subsection (1), for "community rehabilitation order" there is substituted "community order within the meaning of Part 12 of the Criminal Justice Act 2003".

Children and Young Persons Act 1969 (c. 54)

15   In section 23 of the Children and Young Persons Act 1969 (remands and committals to local authority accommodation), for the definition of "sexual offence" and "violent offence" in subsection (12) there is substituted—

    ""sexual offence" means an offence specified in Part 2 of Schedule 15 to the Criminal Justice Act 2003;

    "violent offence" means murder or an offence specified in Part 1 of Schedule 15 to the Criminal Justice Act 2003;".

Immigration Act 1971 (c. 77)

16   In section 7 of the Immigration Act 1971 (exemption from deportation for certain existing residents), in subsection (4), for "section 67 of the Criminal Justice Act 1967" there is substituted "section 240 of the Criminal Justice Act 2003".

Thames Barrier and Flood Prevention Act 1972 (c. xiv)

17   In section 56 of the Thames Barrier and Flood Prevention Act 1972 (orders for carrying out certain defence works), in subsection (3)(a)(ii), for "six months" there is substituted "12 months".

Rehabilitation of Offenders Act 1974 (c. 53)

18   (1) Section 5 of the Rehabilitation of Offenders Act 1974 (rehabilitation periods for particular offences) is amended as follows.

    (2) In subsection (1)—

      (a) at the end of paragraph (e), there is inserted "and", and

      (b) after that paragraph, there is inserted the following paragraph—

        "(f) a sentence of imprisonment for public protection under section 225 of the Criminal Justice Act 2003, a sentence of detention for public protection under section 226 of that Act or an extended sentence under section 227 or 228 of that Act"

    (3) In subsection (4A), after the words "probation order" there is inserted "or a community order under section 177 of the Criminal Justice Act 2003".

Armed Forces Act 1976 (c. 52)

19   (1) Section 8 of the Armed Forces Act 1976 (powers of Standing Civilian Courts in relation to civilians) is amended as follows.

    (2) In subsection (1)(a), for "six months" there is substituted "twelve months".

    (3) In subsection (2), for "12 months" there is substituted "65 weeks".

Bail Act 1976 (c. 63)

20   The Bail Act 1976 is amended as follows.

21   (1) Section 2 (other definitions) is amended as follows.

    (2) In subsection (1)(d)—

      (a) the words "placing the offender on probation or" are omitted, and

      (b) for "him" there is substituted "the offender".

    (3) In subsection (2), in the definition of "probation hostel", for the words from "by" onwards there is substituted "by a community order under section 177 of the Criminal Justice Act 2003".

22   In section 4 (general right to bail of accused persons and others), in subsection (3), for the words from "to be dealt with" onwards there is substituted "or the Crown Court to be dealt with under—

    (a) Part 2 of Schedule 3 to the Powers of Criminal Courts (Sentencing) Act 2000 (breach of certain youth community orders), or

    (b) Part 2 of Schedule 8 to the Criminal Justice Act 2003 (breach of requirement of community order)."

23   In Part 3 of Schedule 1 (interpretation), in the definition of "default" in paragraph 4, for the words from "Part II" onwards there is substituted "Part 2 of Schedule 8 to the Criminal Justice Act 2003 (breach of requirement of order)".

Criminal Law Act 1977 (c. 45)

24   In section 3 of the Criminal Law Act 1977 (penalties for conspiracy), in subsection (1), for "section 127 of the Powers of Criminal Courts (Sentencing) Act 2000" there is substituted "section 163 of the Criminal Justice Act 2003".

Magistrates' Courts Act 1980 (c. 43)

25   The Magistrates' Courts Act 1980 is amended as follows.

26   In section 11 (non appearance of accused), in subsection (3), for "section 119 of the Powers of Criminal Courts (Sentencing) Act 2000" there is substituted "paragraph 8(2)(a) or (b) of Schedule 12 to the Criminal Justice Act 2003".

27   In section 33 (maximum penalties on summary conviction in pursuance of section 22), in subsection (1)(a), for "3 months" there is substituted "51 weeks".

28   In section 85 (power to remit fine), in subsection (2A), for "section 35(2)(a) or (b) of the Crime (Sentences) Act 1997" there is substituted "section 300(2) of the Criminal Justice Act 2003".

29   In section 131 (remand of accused already in custody), after subsection (2) there is inserted—

    "(2A) Where the accused person is serving a sentence of imprisonment to which an intermittent custody order under section 183 of the Criminal Justice Act 2003 relates, the reference in subsection (2) to the expected date of his release is to be read as a reference to the expected date of his next release on licence.".

30   In section 133 (consecutive terms of imprisonment), in subsection (1), for "Subject to section 84 of the Powers of Criminal Courts (Sentencing) Act 2000," there is substituted "Subject to section 265 of the Criminal Justice Act 2003,".

Law Reform (Miscellaneous Provisions) (Scotland) Act 1980 (c. 55)

31   In Schedule 1 to the Law Reform (Miscellaneous Provisions) (Scotland) Act 1980 (ineligibility for and disqualification and excusal from jury service), in Part 2, in paragraph (bb), for sub-paragraph (v) there is substituted—

    "(v) a community order within the meaning of section 177 of the Criminal Justice Act 2003;

    (va) a youth community order as defined by section 33 of the Powers of Criminal Courts (Sentencing) Act 2000;".

Public Passenger Vehicles Act 1981 (c. 14)

32 (1) In Schedule 3 to the Public Passenger Vehicles Act 1981 (supplementary provisions as to qualifications for PSV operators licence), paragraph 1 is amended as follows.

    (2) In sub-paragraph (4)(a), for "a community service order for more than sixty hours" there is substituted "a community order requiring the offender to perform unpaid work for more than sixty hours".

    (3) In sub-paragraph (6), for the words from ""a community" onwards there is substituted ""a community order" means an order under section 177 of the Criminal Justice Act 2003, a community punishment order made before the commencement of that section or a community service order under the Community Service by Offenders (Scotland) Act 1978".

Criminal Attempts Act 1981 (c. 47)

33   In section 4 of the Criminal Attempts Act 1981 (trials and penalties), in subsection (5)(b), for sub-paragraph (ii) there is substituted—

"(ii) in section 154(1) and (2) (general limit on magistrates' court's powers to impose imprisonment) of the Criminal Justice Act 2003.".

Criminal Justice Act 1982 (c. 48)

34   The Criminal Justice Act 1982 is amended as follows.

35   In section 32 (early release of prisoners), in subsection (1)(a), after "life" there is inserted ", imprisonment for public protection under section 225 of the Criminal Justice Act 2003 or an extended sentence under section 227 of that Act".

36   (1) Part 3 of Schedule 13 (reciprocal arrangements (Northern Ireland): persons residing in England and Wales or Scotland) is amended as follows.

(2) In paragraph 7—

(a) in sub-paragraph (2)(b), for "such orders" there is substituted "an unpaid work requirement of a community order (within the meaning of Part 12 of the Criminal Justice Act 2003)", and

(b) in sub-paragraph (3)(b), for the words from "community service orders" onwards there is substituted "community orders within the meaning of Part 12 of the Criminal Justice Act 2003 conferred on responsible officers by that Part of that Act.".

(3) For paragraph 9(3) there is substituted—

"(3) Subject to the following provisions of this paragraph—

(a) a community service order made or amended in the circumstances specified in paragraph 7 above shall be treated as if it were a community order made in England and Wales under section 177 of the Criminal Justice Act 2003 and the provisions of Part 12 of that Act (so far as relating to such orders) shall apply accordingly; and

(b) a community service order made or amended in the circumstances specified in paragraph 8 above shall be treated as if it were a community service order made in Scotland and the legislation relating to community service orders in Scotland shall apply accordingly."

(4) In paragraph 9(4)(a), after "community service orders" there is inserted "or, as the case may be, community orders (within the meaning of Part 12 of the Criminal Justice Act 2003)".

(5) In paragraph 9(5), after "a community service order" there is inserted "or, as the case may be, a community order (within the meaning of Part 12 of the Criminal Justice Act 2003)".

(6) In paragraph 9(6)—

(a) after "community service orders", where first occurring, there is inserted "or, as the case may be, community orders (within the meaning of Part 12 of the Criminal Justice Act 2003)", and

(b) in paragraph (b)(i), for "the Powers of Criminal Courts (Sentencing) Act 2000" there is substituted "Part 12 of the Criminal Justice Act 2003".

Mental Health Act 1983 (c. 20)

37   The Mental Health Act 1983 is amended as follows.

38   In section 37 (powers of courts to order hospital admission or guardianship)—

(a) in subsection (1), the words "or falls to be imposed under section 109(2) of the Powers of Criminal Courts (Sentencing) Act 2000" are omitted,

(b) for subsections (1A) and (1B) there is substituted -

"(1A) In the case of an offence the sentence for which would otherwise fall to be imposed—

(a) under section 51A(2) of the Firearms Act 1968,

(b) under section 110(2) or 111(2) of the Powers of Criminal Courts (Sentencing) Act 2000, or

(c) under any of sections 225 to 228 of the Criminal Justice Act 2003,

nothing in those provisions shall prevent a court from making an order under subsection (1) above for the admission of the offender to a hospital.

(1B) References in subsection (1A) above to a sentence falling to be imposed under any of the provisions mentioned in that subsection are to be read in accordance with section 305(4) of the Criminal Justice Act 2003."

(c) in subsection (8), for "probation order" there is substituted "community order (within the meaning of Part 12 of the Criminal Justice Act 2003)".

39   In section 45A (powers of higher courts to direct hospital admission), in subsection (1)(b), the words from "except" to "1997" are omitted.

Repatriation of Prisoners Act 1984 (c. 47)

40   The Repatriation of Prisoners Act 1984 is amended as follows.

41   In section 2 (transfer out of the United Kingdom), in subsection (4)(b), for sub-paragraph (i) there is substituted—

"(i) released on licence under section 28(5) of the Crime (Sentences) Act 1997 or under section 244 or 246 of the Criminal Justice Act 2003; or".

42   In section 3 (transfer into the United Kingdom), subsection (9) is omitted.

43   (1) The Schedule (operation of certain enactments in relation to the prisoner) is amended as follows in relation to prisoners repatriated to England and Wales.

(2) In paragraph 2, for sub-paragraphs (1A) and (2) there is substituted—

"(2) If the warrant specifies a period to be taken into account for the purposes of this paragraph, the amount of time the prisoner has served shall, so far only as the question whether he has served a particular part of a life sentence is concerned, be deemed to be increased by that period.

(3) Where the prisoner's sentence is for a term of less than twelve months, Chapter 6 of Part 12 of the Criminal Justice Act 2003 shall apply as if the sentence were for a term of twelve months or more.

(4) In this paragraph—

"the enactments relating to release on licence" means section 28(5) and (7) of the Crime (Sentences) Act 1997 and Chapter 6 of Part 12 of the Criminal Justice Act 2003;

"sentence", means the provision included in the warrant which is equivalent to sentence.".

(3) Paragraph 3 is omitted.

Police and Criminal Evidence Act 1984 (c. 60)

44   In section 38 of the Police and Criminal Evidence Act 1984 (duties of custody officer after charge), for the definitions of "sexual offence" and "violent offence" in subsection (6A) there is substituted—

""sexual offence" means an offence specified in Part 2 of Schedule 15 to the Criminal Justice Act 2003;

"violent offence" means murder or an offence specified in Part 1 of that Schedule;".

Criminal Justice Act 1988 (c. 33)

45   The Criminal Justice Act 1988 is amended as follows.

46   In section 36 (reviews of sentencing), in subsection (2), for the words from "erred in law" onwards there is substituted—

"(a) erred in law as to his powers of sentencing; or

(b) failed to impose a sentence required by—

(i) section 51A(2) of the Firearms Act 1968;

(ii) section 110(2) or 111(2) of the Powers of Criminal Courts (Sentencing) Act 2000; or

(iii) any of sections 225 to 228 of the Criminal Justice Act 2003."

47   In section 50 (suspended and partly suspended sentences on certain civilians in courts-martial and Standing Civilian Courts), in subsection (3)(b)(i), for "Powers of Criminal Courts (Sentencing) Act 2000" there is substituted "Criminal Justice Act 2003".

Firearms (Amendment) Act 1988 (c. 45)

48   The Firearms (Amendment) Act 1988 is amended as follows.

49   In section 1 (prohibited weapons and ammunition), in subsection (4A) after paragraph (b) there is inserted—

"(bb) may amend subsection (1A)(a) of section 91 of the Powers of Criminal Courts (Sentencing) Act 2000 (offenders under 18 convicted of certain serious offences: power to detain for specified period) so as to include a reference to any provision added by the order to section 5(1) of the principal Act,

(bc) may amend section 50(5A)(a), 68(4A)(a) or 170(4A)(a) of the Customs and Excise Management Act 1979 (offences relating to improper importation or exportation) so as to include a reference to anything added by the order to section 5(1) of the principal Act,".

50   In section 27(4) (which relates to Northern Ireland), after "Except for" there is inserted "section 1, so far as enabling provision to be made amending the Customs and Excise Management Act 1979, and".

Road Traffic Act 1988 (c. 52)

51   In section 164 of the Road Traffic Act 1988 (power of constables to require production of driving licence and in certain cases statement of date of birth), in subsection (5), for "section 40 of the Crime (Sentences) Act 1997" there is substituted "section 301 of the Criminal Justice Act 2003".

Road Traffic Offenders Act 1988 (c. 53)

52   The Road Traffic Offenders Act 1988 is amended as follows.

53   In section 27 (production of licence), in subsection (3), for "section 40 of the Crime (Sentences) Act 1997" there is substituted "section 301 of the Criminal Justice Act 2003".

54   In section 46 (combination of disqualification and endorsement with probation orders and orders for discharge), in subsection (1), paragraph (a) and the word "or" following it shall cease to have effect.

Football Spectators Act 1989 (c. 37)

55   The Football Spectators Act 1989 is amended as follows.

56   In section 7 (disqualification for membership of scheme), subsection (9) is omitted.

57   In section 14E (banning orders: general), after subsection (6) there is inserted—

"(7) A person serving a sentence of imprisonment to which an intermittent custody order under section 183 of the Criminal Justice Act 2003 relates is to be treated for the purposes of this section as having been detained in legal custody until his final release; and accordingly any reference in this section to release is, in relation to a person serving such a sentence, a reference to his final release."

58   In section 18 (information), after subsection (4) there is inserted—

"(5) In relation to a person serving a sentence of imprisonment to which an intermittent custody order under section 183 of the Criminal Justice Act 2003 relates, any reference in this section to his detention or to his release shall be construed in accordance with section 14E(7)."

Children Act 1989 (c. 41)

59   The Children Act 1989 is amended as follows.

60 (1) Section 68 (persons disqualified from being foster parents) is amended as follows.

(2) In subsection (2)(d), the words "a probation order has been made in respect of him or he has been" are omitted.

(3) After subsection (2) there is inserted—

"(2A) A conviction in respect of which a probation order was made before 1st October 1992 (which would not otherwise be treated as a conviction) is to be treated as a conviction for the purposes of subsection (2)(d)."

61 (1) In Schedule 9A (child minding and day care for young children), paragraph 4 is amended as follows.

(2) In sub-paragraph (2)(g), the words "placed on probation or" are omitted.

(3) At the end there is inserted—

"(7) A conviction in respect of which a probation order was made before 1st October 1992 (which would not otherwise be treated as a conviction) is to be treated as a conviction for the purposes of this paragraph.".

Criminal Justice Act 1991 (c. 53)

62   The Criminal Justice Act 1991 is amended as follows.

63   Section 65 (supervision of young offenders after release) is omitted.

64 (1) Schedule 3 (reciprocal enforcement of certain orders) is amended as follows.

(2) In paragraph 10(3)(d), for the words from "paragraph 3 of Schedule 2" onwards there is substituted "section 201 of the Criminal Justice Act 2003".

(3) In paragraph 11(2) —

(a) in paragraph (a)—

(i) for "probation order" there is substituted "community order", and

(ii) after "England and Wales" there is inserted "under section 177 of the Criminal Justice Act 2003", and

(b) for paragraph (b) there is substituted—

"(b) the provisions of Part 12 of that Act (so far as relating to such orders) shall apply accordingly.".

(4) In paragraph 11(3), for paragraphs (a) and (b) there is substituted—

"(a) the requirements of Part 12 of the Criminal Justice Act 2003 relating to community orders (within the meaning of that Part);

(b) the powers of the home court under Schedule 8 to that Act, as modified by this paragraph; and".

(5) In paragraph 11(4), for the words from "probation order made by a court" onwards there is substituted "community order made by a court in England and Wales under section 177 of the Criminal Justice Act 2003, except a power conferred by paragraph 9(1)(b) or (c) or 13(2) of Schedule 8 to that Act".

(6) In paragraph 11(5), for "the Powers of Criminal Courts (Sentencing) Act 2000" there is substituted "Part 12 of the Criminal Justice Act 2003".

Aggravated Vehicle-Taking Act 1992 (c. 11)

65   In section 1 of the Aggravated Vehicle-Taking Act 1992 (new offence of aggravated vehicle taking), in subsection (2)(a), for "section 127 of the Powers of Criminal Courts (Sentencing) Act 2000" there is substituted "section 163 of the Criminal Justice Act 2003".

Prisoners and Criminal Proceedings (Scotland) Act 1993 (c. 9)

66   In section 10 of the Prisoners and Criminal Proceedings (Scotland) Act 1993 (life prisoners transferred to Scotland)—

(a) in subsection (1)—

(i) in paragraph (a), sub-paragraph (i), and the succeeding "or", are omitted, and

(ii) after paragraph (a)(ii) there is inserted "or

(iii) subsections (5) to (8) of section 28 (early release of life prisoners to whom that section applies) of the Crime (Sentences) Act 1997 (c. 43) (in this section, the "1997 Act") apply by virtue of an order made under section 28(2)(b) of that Act (while that provision was in force) or an order made under section 269(2) of, or paragraph 3(1)(a) of Schedule 22 to, the Criminal Justice Act 2003;", and

(iii) for "28(2)(b) or 82A(2) or paragraph" there is substituted "82A(2), 28(2)(b) or 269(2) or paragraph 3(1)(a) or";

(b) after subsection (1) there is inserted—

"(1AA) This Part of this Act, except section 2(9), applies also to a transferred life prisoner—

(a) who is transferred from England and Wales on or after the date on which section 269 of the Criminal Justice Act 2003 comes into force,

(b) in relation to whom paragraph 3 of Schedule 22 to that Act applies by virtue of paragraph 2(a) of that Schedule, but

(c) in respect of whom, under the paragraph so applying, no order has been made,

as if the prisoner were a life prisoner within the meaning of section 2 of this Act and the punishment part of his sentence within the meaning of that section were the notified minimum term defined by paragraph 3(4) of that Schedule."; and

(c) in subsection (5)(b)—

(i) for "the Crime (Sentences) Act 1997" there is substituted "the 1997 Act", and

(ii) after the words "Powers of Criminal Courts (Sentencing) Act 2000 (c. 6)" there is inserted "section 269(2) of, or paragraph 3(1)(a) of Schedule 22 to, the Criminal Justice Act 2003,".

Criminal Justice and Public Order Act 1994 (c. 33)

67   In section 25 of the Criminal Justice and Public Order Act 1994 (no bail for defendants charged with or convicted of homicide or rape after previous conviction of such offences), in paragraph (c) of the definition of "conviction" in subsection (5)—

(a) the words "placing the offender on probation or" are omitted, and

(b) for "him" there is substituted "the offender".

Goods Vehicles (Licensing of Operators) Act 1995 (c. 23)

68   (1) In Schedule 3 to the Goods Vehicles (Licensing of Operators) Act 1995 (qualifications for standard licence), paragraph 3 is amended as follows.

(2) In sub-paragraph (2)(a), for "exceeding three months" there is substituted "of 12 months or more or, before the commencement of section 181 of the Criminal Justice Act 2003, a term exceeding 3 months".

(3) In sub-paragraph (2)(c), for "community service order" there is substituted "community order".

(4) For sub-paragraph (3)(b), there is substituted—

"(b) "community order" means a community order under section 177 of the Criminal Justice Act 2003, a community punishment order made under section 46 of the Powers of Criminal Courts (Sentencing) Act 2000 or a community service order under the Community Service by Offenders (Scotland) Act 1978.".

Criminal Procedure (Scotland) Act 1995 (c. 46)

69   The Criminal Procedure (Scotland) Act 1995 is amended as follows.

70 (1) Section 234 (probation orders: persons residing in England and Wales) is amended as follows.

(2) In subsection (1), the words after paragraph (b) are omitted.

(3) For subsection (2) there is substituted—

"(2) Subsection (1) above applies to any probation order made under section 228 unless the order includes requirements which are more onerous than those which a court in England and Wales could impose on an offender under section 177 of the Criminal Justice Act 2003."

(4) In subsection (3), the words from "or to vary" to "one hundred" are omitted.

(5) In subsection (4)—

(a) in paragraph (a)—

(i) for "paragraph 5(3) of Schedule 2 to the 2000 Act" there is substituted "section 207(2) of the Criminal Justice Act 2003",

(ii) for "or, as the case may be, community rehabilitation orders" there is substituted "or, as the case may be, community orders under Part 12 of that Act", and

(iii) for "paragraph 5 of the said Schedule 2" there is substituted "section 207 of the Criminal Justice Act 2003", and

(b) in paragraph (b), for "sub-paragraphs (5) to (7) of the said paragraph 5" there is substituted "sections 207(4) and 208(1) and (2) of the Criminal Justice Act 2003".

(6) After subsection (4) there is inserted—

"(4A) A probation order made or amended under this section must specify as the corresponding requirements for the purposes of this section requirements which could be included in a community order made under section 177 of the Criminal Justice Act 2003."

(7) In subsection (5), for "Schedule 3" onwards there is substituted "Schedule 8 to the Criminal Justice Act 2003 shall apply as if it were a community order made by a magistrates' court under section 177 of that Act and imposing the requirements specified under subsection (4A) above".

(8) For subsection (6) there is substituted—

"(6) In its application to a probation order made or amended under this section, Schedule 8 to the Criminal Justice Act 2003 has effect subject to the following modifications—

(a) any reference to the responsible officer has effect as a reference to the person appointed or assigned under subsection (1)(a) above,

(b) in paragraph 9—

(i) paragraphs (b) and (c) of sub-paragraph (1) are omitted,

(ii) in sub-paragraph (6), the first reference to the Crown Court has effect as a reference to a court in Scotland, and

(iii) any other reference in sub-paragraphs (6) or (7) to the Crown Court has effect as a reference to the court in Scotland, and

(c) Parts 3 and 5 are omitted."

(9) In subsection (10)—

(a) for the words from "paragraph 6" to "community rehabilitation orders" there is substituted "paragraph 8 of Schedule 9 (which relates to community orders", and

(b) for "an order made under section 41" there is substituted "a community order made under Part 12".

71   In section 242 (community service orders: persons residing in England and Wales)—
(a) in subsection (1)—
(i) in paragraph (a)(ii), for "a community punishment order" there is substituted "an unpaid work requirement imposed by a community order (within the meaning of Part 12 of the Criminal Justice Act 2003)", and
(ii) in paragraph (a)(iii), for "community punishment orders made under section 46 of the Powers of Criminal Courts (Sentencing) Act 2000" there is substituted "unpaid work requirements imposed by community orders made under section 177 of the Criminal Justice Act 2003",
(b) in subsection (2)(b), for "community punishment orders made under section 46 of the Powers of Criminal Courts (Sentencing) Act 2000" there is substituted "unpaid work requirements imposed by community orders made under section 177 of the Criminal Justice Act 2003", and
(c) in subsection (3)(b), for "in respect of community punishment orders conferred on responsible officers by the Powers of Criminal Courts (Sentencing) Act 2000" there is substituted "conferred on responsible officers by Part 12 of the Criminal Justice Act 2003 in respect of unpaid work requirements imposed by community orders (within the meaning of that Part)".

72   In section 244 (community service orders: provisions relating to persons living in England and Wales or Northern Ireland)—
(a) in subsection (3)(a)—
(i) for "community punishment order" there is substituted "community order (within the meaning of Part 12 of the Criminal Justice Act 2003)", and
(ii) for "community punishment orders" there is substituted "such community orders",
(b) in subsection (4)(a), for "community punishment orders" there is substituted "community orders (within the meaning of Part 12 of the Criminal Justice Act 2003)",
(c) in subsection (5), for "community punishment order" there is substituted "a community order (within the meaning of Part 12 of the Criminal Justice Act 2003)", and
(d) in subsection (6)—
(i) for "community punishment orders", where first occurring, there is substituted "community orders (within the meaning of Part 12 of the Criminal Justice Act 2003)", and
(ii) in paragraph (b)(ii), for "the Powers of Criminal Courts (Sentencing) Act 2000" there is substituted "Part 12 of the Criminal Justice Act 2003".

Education Act 1996 (c. 56)

73   In section 562 of the Education Act 1996 (Act not to apply to persons detained under order of a court), for "probation order" there is substituted "community order under section 177 the Criminal Justice Act 2003".

Criminal Justice (Northern Ireland) Order 1996 (S.I. 1996/3160 (N.I.24))

74   The Criminal Justice (Northern Ireland) Order 1996 is amended as follows.
75   In Article 2 (interpretation) after paragraph (8) there is inserted—
"(9) For the purposes of this Order, a sentence falls to be imposed under paragraph (2) of Article 52A of the Firearms (Northern Ireland) Order 1981 if it is required by that paragraph and the court is not of the opinion there mentioned."
76   In Article 4 (absolute and conditional discharge), in paragraph (1), for "(not being an offence for which the sentence is fixed by law)" there is substituted "(not being an offence for which the sentence is fixed by law or falls to be imposed under Article 52A(2) of the Firearms (Northern Ireland) Order 1981)".
77   In Article 10 (probation orders), in paragraph (1) for "(not being an offence for which the sentence is fixed by law)" there is substituted "(not being an offence for which the sentence is fixed by law or falls to be imposed under Article 52A(2) of the Firearms (Northern Ireland) Order 1981)".

78 (1) Article 13 (community service orders) is amended as follows.

     (2) In paragraph (1) for "(not being an offence for which the sentence is fixed by law)" there is substituted "(not being an offence for which the sentence is fixed by law or falls to be imposed under Article 52A(2) of the Firearms (Northern Ireland) Order 1981)".

     (3) In paragraph (4)(b) as it has effect pursuant to paragraph 7(1) of Schedule 13 to the Criminal Justice Act 1982 (reciprocal arrangements), for "such orders" there is substituted "an unpaid work requirement of a community order (within the meaning of Part 12 of the Criminal Justice Act 2003)".

79   In Article 15 (orders combining probation and community service), in paragraph (1) for "(not being an offence for which the sentence is fixed by law)" there is substituted "(not being an offence for which the sentence is fixed by law or falls to be imposed under Article 52A(2) of the Firearms (Northern Ireland) Order 1981)".

80   In Article 19 (restrictions on imposing custodial sentences), at the end of paragraph (1) there is inserted "or falling to be imposed under Article 52A(2) of the Firearms (Northern Ireland) Order 1981".

81 (1) In Article 20 (length of custodial sentences), at the end of paragraph (1) there is inserted "or falling to be imposed under Article 52A(2) of the Firearms (Northern Ireland) Order 1981".

     (2) In Article 24 (custody probation orders), in paragraph (1) for "other than one fixed by law" there is substituted ", other than an offence for which the sentence is fixed by law or falls to be imposed under Article 52A(2) of the Firearms (Northern Ireland) Order 1981,".

Crime (Sentences) Act 1997 (c. 43)

82   The Crime (Sentences) Act 1997 is amended as follows.

83 (1) Section 31 (duration and conditions of licences) is amended as follows.

     (2) In subsection (3), for the words from "except" onwards there is substituted "except in accordance with recommendations of the Parole Board".

     (3) Subsection (4) is omitted.

     (4) In subsection (6), for "section 46(3) of the 1991 Act" there is substituted "section 259 of the Criminal Justice Act 2003".

84   In section 32 (recall of life prisoners while on licence) for subsection (5) there is substituted—

       "(5) Where on a reference under subsection (4) above the Parole Board directs the immediate release on licence under this section of the life prisoner, the Secretary of State shall give effect to the direction."

85 (1) Schedule 1 (transfers of prisoners within the British Islands) is amended as follows.

     (2) In paragraph 6, after sub-paragraph (3) there is inserted—

       "(4) In this Part of this Schedule—

         "the 2003 Act" means the Criminal Justice Act 2003;

         "custody plus order" has the meaning given by section 181(4) of that Act;

         "intermittent custody order" has the meaning given by section 183(2) of that Act."

     (3) In paragraph 8 (restricted transfers from England and Wales to Scotland)—

       (a) for sub-paragraph (2)(a) there is substituted—

         "(a) sections 241, 244, 247 to 252 and 254 to 264 of the 2003 Act (fixed-term prisoners) or, as the case may require, sections 102 to 104 of the Powers of Criminal Courts (Sentencing) Act 2000 (detention and training orders) or sections 28 to 34 of this Act (life sentences) shall apply to him in place of the corresponding provisions of the law of Scotland;

        (aa) sections 62 and 64 of the Criminal Justice and Court Services Act 2000 (which relate to licence conditions) shall apply to him in place of the corresponding provisions of the law of Scotland;

        (ab) where a custody plus order or intermittent custody order has effect in relation to him, the provisions of Chapters 3 and 4 of Part 12 of the 2003 Act relating to such orders shall also apply to him (subject to Schedule 11 to that Act); and",

       (b) for sub-paragraph (4)(a) there is substituted—

"(a) sections 241, 249 to 252 and 254 to 264 of the 2003 Act (fixed-term prisoners) or, as the case may require, sections 103 and 104 of the Powers of Criminal Courts (Sentencing) Act 2000 (detention and training orders) or sections 31 to 34 of this Act (life sentences) shall apply to him in place of the corresponding provisions of the law of Scotland;

(aa) sections 62 and 64 of the Criminal Justice and Court Services Act 2000 (which relate to licence conditions) shall apply to him in place of the corresponding provisions of the law of Scotland;

(ab) where a custody plus order or intermittent custody order has effect in relation to him, the provisions of Chapters 3 and 4 of Part 12 of the 2003 Act relating to such orders shall also apply to him (subject to Schedule 11 to that Act); and", and

(c) for sub-paragraphs (5) to (7) there is substituted—

"(5) Section 31(2A) of this Act (conditions as to supervision after release), as applied by sub-paragraph (2) or (4) above, shall have effect as if for paragraphs (a) to (c) there were substituted the words "a relevant officer of such local authority as may be specified in the licence".

"(6) Any provision of sections 102 to 104 of the Powers of Criminal Courts (Sentencing) Act 2000 which is applied by sub-paragraph (2) or (4) above shall have effect (as so applied) as if—

(a) any reference to secure accommodation were a reference to secure accommodation within the meaning of Part 2 of the Children (Scotland) Act 1995 or a young offenders institution provided under section 19(1)(b) of the Prisons (Scotland) Act 1989,

(b) except in section 103(2), any reference to the Secretary of State were a reference to the Scottish Ministers,

(c) any reference to an officer of a local probation board were a reference to a relevant officer as defined by section 27(1) of the Prisoners and Criminal Proceedings (Scotland) Act 1993,

(d) any reference to a youth court were a reference to a sheriff court,

(e) in section 103, any reference to a petty sessions area were a reference to a local government area within the meaning of the Local Government etc. (Scotland) Act 1994,

(f) in section 103(3), for paragraphs (b) and (c) there were substituted a reference to an officer of a local authority constituted under that Act for the local government area in which the offender resides for the time being,

(g) section 103(5) were omitted,

(h) in section 104, for subsection (1) there were substituted—

"(1) Where a detention and training order is in force in respect of an offender and it appears on information to a sheriff court having jurisdiction in the locality in which the offender resides that the offender has failed to comply with requirements under section 103(6)(b), the court may—

(a) issue a citation requiring the offender to appear before it at the time specified in the citation, or

(b) issue a warrant for the offender's arrest.",

(i) section 104(2) were omitted, and

(j) in section 104(6), the reference to the Crown Court were a reference to the High Court of Justiciary.""

(4) In paragraph 9 (restricted transfers from England and Wales to Northern Ireland)—

(a) for sub-paragraph (2)(a) there is substituted—

"(a) sections 241, 244, 247 to 252 and 254 to 264 of the 2003 Act (fixed-term prisoners) or, as the case may require, sections 102 to 104 of the Powers of Criminal Courts (Sentencing) Act 2000 (detention and training orders) or sections 28 to 34 of this Act (life sentences) shall apply to him in place of the corresponding provisions of the law of Northern Ireland;

(aa) sections 62 and 64 of the Criminal Justice and Court Services Act 2000 (which relate to licence conditions) shall apply to him in place of the corresponding provisions of the law of Northern Ireland;

           (ab) where a custody plus order or intermittent custody order has effect in relation to him, the provisions of Chapters 3 and 4 of Part 12 of the 2003 Act relating to such orders shall apply to him (subject to Schedule 11 to that Act); and",

      (b) for sub-paragraph (4)(a) there is substituted—

           "(a) sections 241, 249 to 252 and 254 to 264 of the 2003 Act (fixed-term prisoners) or, as the case may require, sections 103 and 104 of the Powers of Criminal Courts (Sentencing) Act 2000 (detention and training orders) or sections 31 to 34 of this Act (life sentences) shall apply to him in place of the corresponding provisions of the law of Northern Ireland;

           (aa) sections 62 and 64 of the Criminal Justice and Court Services Act 2000 (which relate to licence conditions) shall apply to him in place of the corresponding provisions of the law of Northern Ireland;

           (ab) where a custody plus order or intermittent custody order has effect in relation to him, the provisions of Chapters 3 and 4 of Part 12 of the 2003 Act relating to such orders shall apply to him (subject to Schedule 11 to that Act); and",

      (c) for sub-paragraphs (5) to (7) there is substituted—

           "(5) Section 31(2A) of this Act (conditions as to supervision after release), as applied by sub-paragraph (2) or (4) above, shall have effect as if for paragraphs (a) to (c) there were substituted the words "a probation appointed for or assigned to the petty sessions district within which the prisoner for the time being resides"."

  (5) In paragraph 15 (unrestricted transfers: general provisions), sub-paragraph (5) is omitted.

86   In Schedule 2 (repatriation of prisoners to the British Islands) paragraphs 2 and 3 are omitted.

Crime and Disorder Act 1998 (c. 37)

87   The Crime and Disorder Act 1998 is amended as follows.

88   In section 18 (interpretation etc. of Chapter 1)—

      (a) after the definition of "responsible officer" in subsection (1) there is inserted—

      ""serious harm" shall be construed in accordance with section 224 of the Criminal Justice Act 2003;"; and

      (b) subsection (2) is omitted.

89   (1) Section 38 (local provision of youth justice services) is amended as follows.

  (2) In subsection (4)(g), for "probation order, a community service order or a combination order" there is substituted "community order under section 177 of the Criminal Justice Act 2003".

  (3) In subsection (4)(i), after "1997 Act")" there is inserted "or by virtue of conditions imposed under section 250 of the Criminal Justice Act 2003".

Powers of Criminal Courts (Sentencing) Act 2000 (c. 6)

90   The Powers of Criminal Courts (Sentencing) Act 2000 is amended as follows.

91   (1) Section 6 (committal for sentence in certain cases where offender committed in respect of another offence) is amended as follows.

  (2) In subsection (3)(b), for "section 120(1) below" there is substituted "paragraph 11(1) of Schedule 12 to the Criminal Justice Act 2003".

  (3) For subsection (4)(e), there is substituted—

      "(e) paragraph 11(2) of Schedule 12 to the Criminal Justice Act 2003 (committal to Crown Court where offender convicted during operational period of suspended sentence).".

92   In section 7 (power of Crown Court on committal for sentence under section 6), in subsection (2), for "section 119 below" there is substituted "paragraphs 8 and 9 of Schedule 12 to the Criminal Justice Act 2003".

93   In section 12 (absolute and conditional discharge)—

      (a) in subsection (1) for "109(2), 110(2) or 111(2) below" there is substituted "section 110(2) or 111(2) below, section 51A(2) of the Firearms Act 1968 or section 225, 226, 227 or 228 of the Criminal Justice Act 2003)", and

      (b) subsection (4) (duty to explain effect of order for conditional discharge) is omitted.

94   In the heading to Part 4, and the heading to Chapter 1 of that Part, for "COMMUNITY ORDERS" there is substituted "YOUTH COMMUNITY ORDERS".

95   For section 33 there is substituted—

      "33 Meaning of "youth community order" and "community sentence"

    (1) In this Act "youth community order" means any of the following orders—

        (a) a curfew order;

        (b) an exclusion order;

        (c) an attendance centre order;

        (d) a supervision order;

        (e) an action plan order.

    (2) In this Act "community sentence" means a sentence which consists of or includes—

        (a) a community order under section 177 of the Criminal Justice Act 2003, or

        (b) one or more youth community orders."

96 (1) Section 36B (electronic monitoring of requirements in community orders) is amended as follows.

    (2) In the heading for "**community orders**" there is substituted "**youth community orders**", and

    (3) In subsection (1)—

     (a) for "to (4)" there is substituted "and (3)", and

     (b) for "community order" there is substituted "youth community order".

    (4) In subsection (2) and (6)(a), for "community order" there is substituted "youth community order".

97 (1) Section 37 (curfew orders) is amended as follows.

    (2) In subsection (1)—

     (a) after the word "person" there is inserted "aged under 16", and

     (b) for "sections 34 to 36 above" there is substituted "sections 148, 150 and 156 of the Criminal Justice Act 2003".

    (3) In subsection (5), for "community order" there is substituted "youth community order".

    (4) Subsection (10) is omitted.

98   In section 39 (breach, revocation and amendment of curfew orders), for "community orders" there is substituted "youth community orders".

99   In section 40 (curfew orders: supplementary), in subsection (3), for "paragraphs 2A(4) and (5) and 19(3)" there is substituted "paragraph 16(2)".

100 (1) Section 40A (exclusion orders) is amended as follows.

    (2) In subsection (1)—

     (a) after "person" there is inserted "aged under 16",

     (b) for "sections 34 to 36 above" there is substituted "sections 148, 150 and 156 of the Criminal Justice Act 2003", and

     (c) for "two years" there is substituted "three months".

    (3) In subsection (5), for "community order" there is substituted "youth community order".

    (4) Subsection (10) is omitted.

101   In section 40B (breach, revocation and amendment of exclusion orders), for "community orders" there is substituted "youth community orders".

102 (1) Section 60 (attendance centre orders) is amended as follows.

    (2) In subsection (1)—

     (a) in paragraph (a), for "sections 34 to 36 above" there is substituted "sections 148, 150 and 156 of the Criminal Justice Act 2003" and for "21" there is substituted "16", and

     (b) in paragraph (b), for "21" there is substituted "16", and

     (c) paragraph (c) and the word "or" immediately preceding it are omitted.

    (3) In subsection (4), for paragraphs (a) and (b) there is substituted "shall not exceed 24".

    (4) In subsection (7), for "community order" there is substituted "youth community order".

103   In section 63 (supervision orders), in subsection (1), for "sections 34 to 36 above" there is substituted "sections 148, 150 and 156 of the Criminal Justice Act 2003".

104 (1) Section 69 (action plan orders) is amended as follows.

    (2) In subsection (1), for "sections 34 to 36 above" there is substituted "sections 148, 150 and 156 of the Criminal Justice Act 2003", and

    (3) In subsection (5)(b), for "a community rehabilitation order, a community punishment order, a community punishment and rehabilitation order," there is substituted "a community order under section 177 of the Criminal Justice Act 2003".

(4) Subsection (11) is omitted.

105   In section 70 (requirements which may be included in action plan orders and directions), in subsection (5)(a), after the word "other" there is inserted "youth community order or any".

106 (1) Section 73 (reparation orders) is amended as follows.

(2) In subsection (4)(b), for "a community punishment order, a community punishment and rehabilitation order," there is substituted "a community order under section 177 of the Criminal Justice Act 2003".

(3) Subsection (7) is omitted.

107   In section 74 (requirements and provisions of reparation order, and obligations of person subject to it), in subsection (3)(a), after "community order" there is inserted "or any youth community order".

108   In section 76 (meaning of custodial sentence), in subsection (1) after paragraph (b) there is inserted—

"(bb) a sentence of detention for public protection under section 226 of the Criminal Justice Act 2003;

(bc) a sentence of detention under section 228 of that Act;".

109 (1) Section 82A (determination of tariffs) is amended as follows.

(2) In subsection (1), for the words from "where" onwards there is substituted "where the sentence is not fixed by law".

(3) In subsection (3)—

(a) in paragraph (b), for "section 87" there is substituted "section 240 of the Criminal Justice Act 2003", and

(b) in paragraph (c), for "sections 33(2) and 35(1) of the Criminal Justice Act 1991" there is substituted "section 244(1) of the Criminal Justice Act 2003".

(4) In subsection (4)—

(a) after "If" there is inserted "the offender was aged 21 or over when he committed the offence and", and

(b) the words "subject to subsection (5) below" are omitted.

(5) Subsections (5) and (6) are omitted.

110 (1) Section 91 (offenders under 18 convicted of certain serious offences) is amended as follows.

(2) In subsection (3), for "none of the other methods in which the case may legally be dealt with" there is substituted "neither a community sentence nor a detention and training order".

(3) In subsection (4), for "section 79 and 80 above" there is substituted "section 152 and 153 of the Criminal Justice Act 2003".

111 (1) Section 100 (detention and training orders) is amended as follows.

(2) In subsection (1)—

(a) for the words from the beginning to "subsection (2)" there is substituted "Subject to sections 90 and 91 above, sections 226 and 228 of the Criminal Justice Act 2003, and subsection (2)", and

(b) for paragraph (b) there is substituted—

"(b) the court is of the opinion that subsection (2) of section 152 of the Criminal Justice Act 2003 applies or the case falls within subsection (3) of that section,".

(3) Subsection (4) is omitted.

112   In section 106 (interaction of detention and training orders with sentences of detention in a young offender institution), subsections (2) and (3) are omitted.

113   After section 106 there is inserted—

"106A Interaction with sentences of detention

(1) In this section—

"the 2003 Act" means the Criminal Justice Act 2003;

"sentence of detention" means—

(a) a sentence of detention under section 91 above, or

(b) a sentence of detention under section 228 of the 2003 Act (extended sentence for certain violent or sexual offences: persons under 18).

(2) Where a court passes a sentence of detention in the case of an offender who is subject to a detention and training order, the sentence shall take effect as follows—

       (a) if the offender has at any time been released by virtue of subsection (2), (3), (4) or (5) of section 102 above, at the beginning of the day on which the sentence is passed, and

       (b) if not, either as mentioned in paragraph (a) above or, if the court so orders, at the time when the offender would otherwise be released by virtue of subsection (2), (3), (4) or (5) of section 102.

  (3) Where a court makes a detention and training order in the case of an offender who is subject to a sentence of detention, the order shall take effect as follows—

       (a) if the offender has at any time been released under Chapter 6 of Part 12 of the 2003 Act (release on licence of fixed-term prisoners), at the beginning of the day on which the order is made, and

       (b) if not, either as mentioned in paragraph (a) above or, if the court so orders, at the time when the offender would otherwise be released under that Chapter.

  (4) Where an order under section 102(5) above is made in the case of a person in respect of whom a sentence of detention is to take effect as mentioned in subsection (2)(b) above, the order is to be expressed as an order that the period of detention attributable to the detention and training order is to end at the time determined under section 102(5)(a) or (b) above.

  (5) In determining for the purposes of subsection (3)(b) the time when an offender would otherwise be released under Chapter 6 of Part 12 of the 2003 Act, section 246 of that Act (power of Secretary of State to release prisoners on licence before he is required to do so) is to be disregarded.

  (6) Where by virtue of subsection (3)(b) above a detention and training order made in the case of a person who is subject to a sentence of detention under section 228 of the 2003 Act is to take effect at the time when he would otherwise be released under Chapter 6 of Part 12 of that Act, any direction by the Parole Board under subsection (2)(b) of section 247 of that Act in respect of him is to be expressed as a direction that the Board would, but for the detention and training order, have directed his release under that section.

  (7) Subject to subsection (9) below, where at any time an offender is subject concurrently—

       (a) to a detention and training order, and

       (b) to a sentence of detention,

       he shall be treated for the purposes of the provisions specified in subsection (8) below as if he were subject only to the sentence of detention.

  (8) Those provisions are—

       (a) sections 102 to 105 above,

       (b) section 92 above and section 235 of the 2003 Act (place of detention, etc.), and

       (c) Chapter 6 of Part 12 of the 2003 Act.

  (9) Nothing in subsection (7) above shall require the offender to be released in respect of either the order or the sentence unless and until he is required to be released in respect of each of them."

114   In section 110 (required custodial sentence for third class A drug trafficking offence), subsection (3) is omitted.

115   In section 111 (minimum of three years for third domestic burglary) subsection (3) is omitted.

116   Sections 116 and 117 (return to prison etc. where offence committed during original sentence) shall cease to have effect.

117   In section 130 (compensation orders against convicted persons), in subsection (2), for "109(2), 110(2) or 111(2) above," there is substituted "110(2) or 111(2) above, section 51A(2) of the Firearms Act 1968 or section 225, 226, 227 or 228 of the Criminal Justice Act 2003,".

118   In section 136 (power to order statement as to financial circumstances of parent or guardian) in subsection (2), for "section 126 above" there is substituted "section 162 of the Criminal Justice Act 2003".

119 (1) Section 138 (fixing of fine or compensation to be paid by parent or guardian) is amended as follows.

(2) In subsection (1)(a), for "section 128 above" there is substituted "section 164 of the Criminal Justice Act 2003".

(3) In subsection (2), for "sections 128(1) (duty to inquire into financial circumstances) and" there is substituted "section 164(1) of the Criminal Justice Act 2003 and section".

(4) In subsection (4)—

    (a) for "section 129 above" there is substituted "section 165 of the Criminal Justice Act 2003",

    (b) for "section 129(1)" there is substituted "section 165(1)", and

    (c) for "section 129(2)" there is substituted "section 165(2)".

120   In section 146 (driving disqualification for any offence), in subsection (2), for "109(2), 110(2) or 111(2) above" there is substituted "110(2) or 111(2) above, section 51A(2) of the Firearms Act 1968 or section 225, 226, 227 or 228 of the Criminal Justice Act 2003".

121   In section 154 (commencement of Crown Court sentence), in subsection (2), for "section 84 above" there is substituted "section 265 of the Criminal Justice Act 2003".

122   In section 159 (execution of process between England and Wales and Scotland), for "10(7) or 24(1)" there is substituted "10(6) or 18(1)".

123 (1) Section 163 (interpretation) is amended as follows.

(2) In the definition of "attendance centre" for "section 62(2) above" there is substituted "section 221(2) of the Criminal Justice Act 2003".

(3) In the definition of "attendance centre order" for the words from "by virtue of" to "Schedule 3" there is substituted "by virtue of paragraph 4(2)(b) or 5(2)(b) of Schedule 3".

(4) In the definition of "community order", for "section 33(1) above" there is substituted "section 177(1) of the Criminal Justice Act 2003".

(5) For the definition of "curfew order" there is substituted—

    ""curfew order" means an order under section 37(1) above (and, except where the contrary intention is shown by paragraph 7 of Schedule 3 or paragraph 3 of Schedule 7 or 8, includes orders made under section 37(1) by virtue of paragraph 4(2)(a) or 5(2)(a) of Schedule 3 or paragraph 2(2)(a) of Schedule 7 or 8).".

(6) In the definition of "operational period", for "section 118(3) above" there is substituted "section 189(1)(b)(ii) of the Criminal Justice Act 2003".

(7) In the definition of "suspended sentence", for "section 118(3) above" there is substituted "section 189(7) of the Criminal Justice Act 2003".

(8) At the end there is inserted—

    ""youth community order" has the meaning given by section 33(1) above.".

124   In section 164 (further interpretative provision) for subsection (3) there is substituted—

    "(3) References in this Act to a sentence falling to be imposed—

      (a) under section 110(2) or 111(2) above,

      (b) under section 51A(2) of the Firearms Act 1968, or

      (c) under any of sections 225 to 228 of the Criminal Justice Act 2003,

    are to be read in accordance with section 305(4) of the Criminal Justice Act 2003."

125   For Schedule 3 (breach revocation and amendment of certain community orders) there is substituted—

"SCHEDULE 3

BREACH, REVOCATION AND AMENDMENT OF CURFEW ORDERS AND
EXCLUSION ORDERS

PART 1

PRELIMINARY

Definitions

1 In this Schedule—

    "the petty sessions area concerned" means—

      (a) in relation to a curfew order, the petty sessions area in which the place for the time being specified in the order is situated; and

      (b) in relation to an exclusion order, the petty sessions area for the time being specified in the order;

    "relevant order" means a curfew order or an exclusion order.

Orders made on appeal

2 Where a relevant order has been made on appeal, for the purposes of this Schedule it shall be deemed—

    (a) if it was made on an appeal brought from a magistrates' court, to have been made by a magistrates' court;

(b) if it was made on an appeal brought from the Crown Court or from the criminal division of the Court of Appeal, to have been made by the Crown Court.

PART 2

BREACH OF REQUIREMENT OF ORDER

Issue of summons or warrant

3 (1) If at any time while a relevant order is in force in respect of an offender it appears on information to a justice of the peace acting for the petty sessions area concerned that the offender has failed to comply with any of the requirements of the order, the justice may—

    (a) issue a summons requiring the offender to appear at the place and time specified in it; or

    (b) if the information is in writing and on oath, issue a warrant for his arrest.

(2) Any summons or warrant issued under this paragraph shall direct the offender to appear or be brought—

    (a) in the case of any relevant order which was made by the Crown Court and included a direction that any failure to comply with any of the requirements of the order be dealt with by the Crown Court, before the Crown Court; and

    (b) in the case of a relevant order which is not an order to which paragraph (a) above applies, before a magistrates' court acting for the petty sessions area concerned.

(3) Where a summons issued under sub-paragraph (1)(a) above requires an offender to appear before the Crown Court and the offender does not appear in answer to the summons, the Crown Court may issue a further summons requiring the offender to appear at the place and time specified in it.

(4) Where a summons issued under sub-paragraph (1)(a) above or a further summons issued under sub-paragraph (3) above requires an offender to appear before the Crown Court and the offender does not appear in answer to the summons, the Crown Court may issue a warrant for the arrest of the offender.

Powers of magistrates' court

4 (1) This paragraph applies if it is proved to the satisfaction of a magistrates' court before which an offender appears or is brought under paragraph 3 above that he has failed without reasonable excuse to comply with any of the requirements of the relevant order.

(2) The magistrates' court may deal with the offender in respect of the failure in one of the following ways (and must deal with him in one of those ways if the relevant order is in force)—

    (a) by making a curfew order in respect of him (subject to paragraph 7 below);

    (b) by making an attendance centre order in respect of him (subject to paragraph 8 below); or

    (c) where the relevant order was made by a magistrates' court, by dealing with him, for the offence in respect of which the order was made, in any way in which he could have been dealt with for that offence by the court which made the order if the order had not been made.

(3) In dealing with an offender under sub-paragraph (2)(c) above, a magistrates' court—

    (a) shall take into account the extent to which the offender has complied with the requirements of the relevant order; and

    (b) in the case of an offender who has wilfully and persistently failed to comply with those requirements, may impose a custodial sentence (where the relevant order was made in respect of an offence punishable with such a sentence) notwithstanding anything in section 152(2) of the Criminal Justice Act 2003.

(4) Where a magistrates' court deals with an offender under sub-paragraph (2)(c) above, it shall revoke the relevant order if it is still in force.

(5) Where a relevant order was made by the Crown Court and a magistrates' court has power to deal with the offender under sub-paragraph (2)(a) or (b) above, it may instead commit him to custody or release him on bail until he can be brought or appear before the Crown Court.

(6) A magistrates' court which deals with an offender's case under sub-paragraph (5) above shall send to the Crown Court—

    (a) a certificate signed by a justice of the peace certifying that the offender has failed to comply with the requirements of the relevant order in the respect specified in the certificate; and

    (b) such other particulars of the case as may be desirable;

and a certificate purporting to be so signed shall be admissible as evidence of the failure before the Crown Court.

(7) A person sentenced under sub-paragraph (2)(c) above for an offence may appeal to the Crown Court against the sentence.

Powers of Crown Court

5 (1) This paragraph applies where under paragraph 3 or by virtue of paragraph 4(5) above an offender is brought or appears before the Crown Court and it is proved to the satisfaction of that court that he has failed without reasonable excuse to comply with any of the requirements of the relevant order.

(2) The Crown Court may deal with the offender in respect of the failure in one of the following ways (and must deal with him in one of those ways if the relevant order is in force)—

    (a) by making a curfew order in respect of him (subject to paragraph 7 below);

    (b) by making an attendance centre order in respect of him (subject to paragraph 8 below); or

    (c) by dealing with him, for the offence in respect of which the order was made, in any way in which he could have been dealt with for that offence by the court which made the order if the order had not been made.

(3) In dealing with an offender under sub-paragraph (2)(c) above, the Crown Court—

    (a) shall take into account the extent to which the offender has complied with the requirements of the relevant order; and

    (b) in the case of an offender who has wilfully and persistently failed to comply with those requirements, may impose a custodial sentence (where the relevant order was made in respect of an offence punishable with such a sentence) notwithstanding anything in section 152(2) of the Criminal Justice Act 2003.

(4) Where the Crown Court deals with an offender under sub-paragraph (2)(c) above, it shall revoke the relevant order if it is still in force.

(5) In proceedings before the Crown Court under this paragraph any question whether the offender has failed to comply with the requirements of the relevant order shall be determined by the court and not by the verdict of a jury.

Exclusions from paragraphs 4 and 5

6 Without prejudice to paragraphs 10 and 11 below, an offender who is convicted of a further offence while a relevant order is in force in respect of him shall not on that account be liable to be dealt with under paragraph 4 or 5 in respect of a failure to comply with any requirement of the order.

Curfew orders imposed for breach of relevant order

7 (1) Section 37 of this Act (curfew orders) shall apply for the purposes of paragraphs 4(2)(a) and 5(2)(a) above as if for the words from the beginning to "make" there were substituted "Where a court has power to deal with an offender under Part 2 of Schedule 3 to this Act for failure to comply with any of the requirements of a relevant order, the court may make in respect of the offender".

(2) The following provisions of this Act, namely—

    (a) section 37(3) to (12), and

    (b) so far as applicable, sections 36B and 40 and this Schedule so far as relating to curfew orders;

have effect in relation to a curfew order made by virtue of paragraphs 4(2)(a) and 5(2)(a) as they have effect in relation to any other curfew order, subject to sub-paragraph (3) below.

(3) This Schedule shall have effect in relation to such a curfew order as if—

    (a) the power conferred on the court by each of paragraphs 4(2)(c), 5(2)(c) and 10(3)(b) to deal with the offender for the offence in respect of which the order was made were a power to deal with the offender, for his failure to comply with the relevant order, in any way in which the appropriate court could deal with him for that failure if it had just been proved to the satisfaction of the court;

(b) the reference in paragraph 10(1)(b) to the offence in respect of which the order was made were a reference to the failure to comply in respect of which the curfew order was made; and

(c) the power conferred on the Crown Court by paragraph 11(2)(b) to deal with the offender for the offence in respect of which the order was made were a power to deal with the offender, for his failure to comply with the relevant order, in any way in which the appropriate court (if the relevant order was made by the magistrates' court) or the Crown Court (if that order was made by the Crown Court) could deal with him for that failure if it had just been proved to its satisfaction.

(4) For the purposes of the provisions mentioned in paragraphs (a) and (c) of sub-paragraph (3) above, as applied by that sub-paragraph, if the relevant order is no longer in force the appropriate court's powers shall be determined on the assumption that it is still in force.

(5) Sections 148 and 156 of the Criminal Justice Act 2003 (restrictions and procedural requirements for community sentences) do not apply in relation to a curfew order made by virtue of paragraph 4(2)(a) or 5(2)(a) above.

Attendance centre orders imposed for breach of relevant order

8 (1) Section 60(1) of this Act (attendance centre orders) shall apply for the purposes of paragraphs 4(2)(b) and 5(2)(b) above as if for the words from the beginning to "the court may," there were substituted "Where a court has power to deal with an offender under Part 2 of Schedule 3 to this Act for failure to comply with any of the requirements of a relevant order, the court may,".

(2) The following provisions of this Act, namely—
  (a) subsections (3) to (11) of section 60, and
  (b) so far as applicable, section 36B and Schedule 5,
have effect in relation to an attendance centre order made by virtue of paragraph 4(2)(b) or 5(2)(b) above as they have effect in relation to any other attendance centre order, but as if there were omitted from each of paragraphs 2(1)(b), 3(1) and 4(3) of Schedule 5 the words ", for the offence in respect of which the order was made," and "for that offence".

(3) Sections 148 and 156 of the Criminal Justice Act 2003 (restrictions and procedural requirements for community sentences) do not apply in relation to an attendance centre order made by virtue of paragraph 4(2)(b) or 5(2)(b) above.

Supplementary

9 Any exercise by a court of its powers under paragraph 4(2)(a) or (b) or 5(2)(a) or (b) above shall be without prejudice to the continuance of the relevant order.

PART 3

REVOCATION OF ORDER

Revocation of order with or without re-sentencing: powers of magistrates' court

10 (1) This paragraph applies where a relevant order made by a magistrates' court is in force in respect of any offender and on the application of the offender or the responsible officer it appears to the appropriate magistrates' court that, having regard to circumstances which have arisen since the order was made, it would be in the interests of justice—
  (a) for the order to be revoked; or
  (b) for the offender to be dealt with in some other way for the offence in respect of which the order was made.

(2) In this paragraph "the appropriate magistrates' court" means a magistrates' court acting for the petty sessions area concerned.

(3) The appropriate magistrates' court may—
  (a) revoke the order; or
  (b) both—
    (i) revoke the order; and
    (ii) deal with the offender for the offence in respect of which the order was made, in any way in which he could have been dealt with for that

offence by the court which made the order if the order had not been made.

(4) In dealing with an offender under sub-paragraph (3)(b) above, a magistrates' court shall take into account the extent to which the offender has complied with the requirements of the relevant order.

(5) A person sentenced under sub-paragraph (3)(b) above for an offence may appeal to the Crown Court against the sentence.

(6) Where a magistrates' court proposes to exercise its powers under this paragraph otherwise than on the application of the offender, it shall summon him to appear before the court and, if he does not appear in answer to the summons, may issue a warrant for his arrest.

(7) No application may be made by the offender under sub-paragraph (1) above while an appeal against the relevant order is pending.

Revocation of order with or without re-sentencing: powers of Crown Court on conviction etc

11 (1) This paragraph applies where—

    (a) a relevant order made by the Crown Court is in force in respect of an offender and the offender or the responsible officer applies to the Crown Court for the order to be revoked or for the offender to be dealt with in some other way for the offence in respect of which the order was made; or

    (b) an offender in respect of whom a relevant order is in force is convicted of an offence before the Crown Court or, having been committed by a magistrates' court to the Crown Court for sentence, is brought or appears before the Crown Court.

(2) If it appears to the Crown Court to be in the interests of justice to do so, having regard to circumstances which have arisen since the order was made, the Crown Court may—

    (a) revoke the order; or

    (b) both—

        (i) revoke the order; and

        (ii) deal with the offender for the offence in respect of which the order was made, in any way in which he could have been dealt with for that offence by the court which made the order if the order had not been made.

(3) In dealing with an offender under sub-paragraph (2)(b) above, the Crown Court shall take into account the extent to which the offender has complied with the requirements of the relevant order.

Revocation following custodial sentence by magistrates' court unconnected with order

12 (1) This paragraph applies where—

    (a) an offender in respect of whom a relevant order is in force is convicted of an offence by a magistrates' court unconnected with the order;

    (b) the court imposes a custodial sentence on the offender; and

    (c) it appears to the court, on the application of the offender or the responsible officer, that it would be in the interests of justice to exercise its powers under this paragraph having regard to circumstances which have arisen since the order was made.

(2) In sub-paragraph (1) above "a magistrates' court unconnected with the order" means a magistrates' court not acting for the petty sessions area concerned.

(3) The court may—

    (a) if the order was made by a magistrates' court, revoke it;

    (b) if the order was made by the Crown Court, commit the offender in custody or release him on bail until he can be brought or appear before the Crown Court.

(4) Where the court deals with an offender's case under sub-paragraph (3)(b) above, it shall send to the Crown Court such particulars of the case as may be desirable.

13 Where by virtue of paragraph 12(3)(b) above an offender is brought or appears before the Crown Court and it appears to the Crown Court to be in the interests of justice to do so, having regard to circumstances which have arisen since the relevant order was made, the Crown Court may revoke the order.

Supplementary

14 (1) On the making under this Part of this Schedule of an order revoking a relevant order, the proper officer of the court shall forthwith give copies of the revoking order to the responsible officer.

(2) In sub-paragraph (1) above "proper officer" means—

(a) in relation to a magistrates' court, the justices' chief executive for the court; and

(b) in relation to the Crown Court, the appropriate officer.

(3) A responsible officer to whom in accordance with sub-paragraph (1) above copies of a revoking order are given shall give a copy to the offender and to the person in charge of any institution in which the offender was required by the order to reside.

PART 4

AMENDMENT OF ORDER

Amendment by reason of change of residence

15 (1) This paragraph applies where, at any time while a relevant order is in force in respect of an offender, a magistrates' court acting for the petty sessions area concerned is satisfied that the offender proposes to change, or has changed, his residence from that petty sessions area to another petty sessions area.

(2) Subject to sub-paragraph (3) below, the court may, and on the application of the responsible officer shall, amend the relevant order by substituting the other petty sessions area for the area specified in the order or, in the case of a curfew order, a place in that other area for the place so specified.

(3) The court shall not amend under this paragraph a curfew order which contains requirements which, in the opinion of the court, cannot be complied with unless the offender continues to reside in the petty sessions area concerned unless, in accordance with paragraph 16 below, it either—

(a) cancels those requirements; or

(b) substitutes for those requirements other requirements which can be complied with if the offender ceases to reside in that area.

Amendment of requirements of order

16 (1) Without prejudice to the provisions of paragraph 15 above but subject to the following provisions of this paragraph, a magistrates' court acting for the petty sessions area concerned may, on the application of an eligible person, by order amend a relevant order—

(a) by cancelling any of the requirements of the order; or

(b) by inserting in the order (either in addition to or in substitution for any of its requirements) any requirement which the court could include if it were then making the order.

(2) A magistrates' court shall not under sub-paragraph (1) above amend a curfew order by extending the curfew periods beyond the end of six months from the date of the original order.

(3) A magistrates' court shall not under sub-paragraph (1) above amend an exclusion order by extending the period for which the offender is prohibited from entering the place in question beyond the end of three months from the date of the original order.

(4) For the purposes of this paragraph the eligible persons are—

(a) the offender;

(b) the responsible officer; and

(c) in relation to an exclusion order, any affected person.

But an application under sub-paragraph (1) by a person such as is mentioned in paragraph (c) above must be for the cancellation of a requirement which was included in the order by virtue of his consent or for the purpose (or partly for the purpose) of protecting him from being approached by the offender, or for the insertion of a requirement which will, if inserted, be such a requirement.

Supplementary

17 No order may be made under paragraph 15 above, and no application may be made under paragraph 16 above, while an appeal against the relevant order is pending.

18 (1) Subject to sub-paragraph (2) below, where a court proposes to exercise its powers under this Part of this Schedule, otherwise than on the application of the offender, the court—

(a) shall summon him to appear before the court; and

(b) if he does not appear in answer to the summons, may issue a warrant for his arrest.

(2) This paragraph shall not apply to an order cancelling a requirement of a relevant order or reducing the period of any requirement, or to an order under paragraph 15 above substituting a new petty sessions area or a new place for the one specified in a relevant order.

19 (1) On the making under this Part of this Schedule of an order amending a relevant order, the justices' chief executive for the court shall forthwith—

(a) if the order amends the relevant order otherwise than by substituting, by virtue of paragraph 15 above, a new petty session area or a new place for the one specified in the relevant order, give copies of the amending order to the responsible officer;

(b) if the order amends the relevant order in the manner excepted by paragraph (a) above, send to the chief executive to the justices for the new petty sessions area or, as the case may be, for the petty sessions area in which the new place is situated—

(i) copies of the amending order; and

(ii) such documents and information relating to the case as he considers likely to be of assistance to a court acting for that area in the exercise of its functions in relation to the order;

and in a case falling within paragraph (b) above the chief executive of the justices for that area shall give copies of the amending order to the responsible officer.

(2) A responsible officer to whom in accordance with sub-paragraph (1) above copies of an order are given shall give a copy to the offender and to the person in charge of any institution in which the offender is or was required by the order to reside."

126 In Schedule 5 (breach, revocation and amendment of attendance centre orders)—

(a) in paragraph 1(1)(b), for "section 62(3) of this Act" there is substituted "section 222(1)(d) or (e) of the Criminal Justice Act 2003",

(b) in paragraph 2(5)(b), for "section 79(2) of this Act" there is substituted "section 152(2) of the Criminal Justice Act 2003", and

(c) in paragraph 3(3)(b), for "section 79(2) of this Act" there is substituted "section 152(2) of the Criminal Justice Act 2003".

127 In Schedule 6 (requirements which may be included in supervision orders)—

(a) in paragraph 2(7)(a), after the word "other" there is inserted "youth community order or any", and

(b) in paragraph 3(6)(a), for "community order" there is substituted "youth community order".

128 In Schedule 7 (breach, revocation and amendment of supervision orders)—

(a) in paragraph 3—

(i) in sub-paragraph (2), for "sub-paragraphs (4) and (5)" there is substituted "sub-paragraph (5)",

(ii) in sub-paragraph (3), for "Sections 35 and 36 of this Act" there is substituted "Sections 148 and 156 of the Criminal Justice Act 2003",

(iii) sub-paragraph (4) is omitted, and

(iv) in sub-paragraph (5)(a), for the words from the beginning to "and" there is substituted "the power conferred on the court by each of paragraphs 4(2)(c) and", and

(b) in paragraph 4(3), for "Sections 35 and 36 of this Act" there is substituted "Sections 148 and 156 of the Criminal Justice Act 2003".

129   In Schedule 8 (breach, revocation and amendment of action plan orders and reparation orders)—
    (a) in paragraph 3—
        (i) in sub-paragraph (2), for "sub-paragraphs (4) and (5)" there is substituted "sub-paragraph (5)",
        (ii) in sub-paragraph (3), for "Sections 35 and 36 of this Act" there is substituted "Sections 148 and 156 of the Criminal Justice Act 2003",
        (iii) sub-paragraph (4) is omitted, and
        (iv) in sub-paragraph (5)(a), for the words from the beginning to "and" there is substituted "The power conferred on the court by each of paragraphs 4(2)(c) and", and
    (b) in paragraph 4(3), for "Sections 35 and 36 of this Act" there is substituted "Sections 148 and 156 of the Criminal Justice Act 2003".

Child Support, Pensions and Social Security Act 2000 (c. 19)

130   The Child Support, Pensions and Social Security Act 2000 is amended as follows.
131 (1) Section 62 (loss of benefit for breach of community order) is amended as follows.
    (2) In subsection (8), for the definition of "relevant community order" there is substituted—
    ""relevant community order" means—
      (a) a community order made under section 177 of the Criminal Justice Act 2003; or
      (b) any order falling in England or Wales to be treated as such an order."
    (3) In subsection (11)(c)(ii), for "to (e)" there is substituted "and (b)".
132   In section 64 (information provision), in subsection (6)(a), after "community orders" there is inserted "(as defined by section 177 of the Criminal Justice Act 2003)".

Criminal Justice and Court Services Act 2000 (c. 43)

133   The Criminal Justice and Court Services Act 2000 is amended as follows.
134   In section 1 (purposes of Chapter 1 of Part 1 of the Act), in subsection (2)—
    (a) in paragraph (a), after "community orders" there is inserted "(as defined by section 177 of the Criminal Justice Act 2003)", and
    (b) after paragraph (c) there is inserted—
      "(d) giving effect to suspended sentence orders (as defined by section 189 of the Criminal Justice Act 2003)."
135   In section 42 (interpretation of Part 2), in subsection (2)(a), for "section 119 of the Powers of Criminal Court (Sentencing) Act 2000" there is substituted "paragraph 8(2)(a) or (b) of Schedule 11 of the Criminal Justice Act 2003".
136 (1) Section 62 (release on licence etc: conditions as to monitoring) is amended as follows.
    (2) For subsection (3) there is substituted—
    "(3) In relation to a prisoner released under section 246 of the Criminal Justice Act 2003 (power to release prisoners on licence before required to do so), the monitoring referred to in subsection (2)(a) does not include the monitoring of his compliance with conditions imposed under section 253 of that Act (curfew condition)."
    (3) In subsection (5) after paragraph (e) there is inserted ", and
      (f) a sentence of detention under section 226 or 228 of the Criminal Justice Act 2003".
137   In section 69 (duties of local probation boards in connection with victims of certain offences), in subsection (8), for paragraph (a) there is substituted—
    "(a) murder or an offence specified in Schedule 15 to the Criminal Justice Act 2003,".
138   In section 70 (general interpretation), in subsection (5), for the words "any community order" there is substituted "a curfew order, an exclusion order, a community rehabilitation order, a community punishment order, a community punishment and rehabilitation order, a drug treatment and testing order, a drug abstinence order, an attendance centre order, a supervision order or an action plan order".

International Criminal Court Act 2001 (c. 17)

139 (1) Schedule 7 to the International Criminal Court Act 2001 (domestic provisions not applicable to ICC prisoners), is amended as follows.
    (2) In paragraph 2(1), for paragraph (d) there is substituted—
    "(d) section 240 of the Criminal Justice Act 2003 (crediting of periods of remand in custody)."
    (3) In paragraph 3(1), for "Part 2 of the Criminal Justice Act 1991" there is substituted "sections 244 to 264 of the Criminal Justice Act 2003".

Armed Forces Act 2001 (c. 19)

140   In section 30 of the Armed Forces Act 2001 (conditional release from custody), in subsection (6)(a) for "six months" there is substituted "the term specified in subsection (1)(a) of section 8 of the Armed Forces Act 1976 (powers of courts in relation to civilians)".

Proceeds of Crime Act 2002 (c. 29)

141   In section 38 of the Proceeds of Crime Act 2002 (provisions about imprisonment or detention), in subsection (4)(a), for "section 118(1) of the Sentencing Act" there is substituted "section 189(1) of the Criminal Justice Act 2003".

Sexual Offences Act 2003 (c. 42)

142   The Sexual Offences Act 2003 is amended as follows.
143   In section 131 (application of Part 2 to young offenders), after paragraph (j) there is inserted—
       "(k) a sentence of detention for public protection under section 226 of the Criminal Justice Act 2003,
         (l) an extended sentence under section 228 of that Act,".
144   In section 133 (general interpretation), at the end of paragraph (a) of the definition of "community order" there is inserted "(as that Act had effect before the passing of the Criminal Justice Act 2003)".

PART 2

OFFENCES: ABOLITION OF IMPRISONMENT AND CONVERSION TO SUMMARY OFFENCE

Vagrancy Act 1824 (c. 83)

145   In section 3 of the Vagrancy Act 1824 (idle and disorderly persons), for the words from "subject to" to the end there is substituted "it shall be lawful for any justice of the peace to impose on such person (being thereof convicted before him by his own view, or by the confession of such person, or by the evidence on oath of one or more credible witnesses) a fine not exceeding level 3 on the standard scale".
146 (1) Section 4 of that Act (rogues and vagabonds) is amended as follows.
     (2) In that section, for the words from "shall be" to the end there is substituted "commits an offence under this section".
     (3) At the end of that section (which becomes subsection (1)) there is inserted—
       "(2) It shall be lawful for any justice of the peace to impose on any person who commits an offence under this section (being thereof convicted before him by the confession of such person, or by the evidence on oath of one or more credible witnesses)—
         (a) in the case of a person convicted of the offence of wandering abroad and lodging in any barn or outhouse, or in any deserted or unoccupied building, or in the open air, or under a tent, or in any cart or waggon, and not giving a good account of himself, a fine not exceeding level 1 on the standard scale, and
         (b) in the case of a person convicted of any other offence under this section, a fine not exceeding level 3 on the standard scale."

London Hackney Carriages Act 1843 (c. 86)

147   In section 28 of the London Hackney Carriages Act 1843, after "for every such offence", there is inserted "of which he is convicted before the justice".

Town Police Clauses Act 1847 (c. 89)

148   In section 26 of the Town Police Clauses Act 1847, for the words from "committed by them" to the end, there is substituted "liable to a fine not exceeding level 3 on the standard scale".
149   In section 28 of that Act, after "for each offence", there is inserted "of which he is convicted before the justice".
150   In section 29 of that Act, after "for every such offence", there is inserted "of which he is convicted before the justice".
151   In section 36 of that Act, after "liable", there is inserted "on conviction before the justices".

Seamen's and Soldiers' False Characters Act 1906 (c. 5)

152   In section 1 of the Seamen's and Soldiers' False Characters Act 1906, for "imprison-ment for a term not exceeding three months" there is substituted "a fine not exceeding level 2 on the standard scale".

Aliens Restriction (Amendment) Act 1919 (c. 92)

153   In section 3(2) of the Aliens Restriction (Amendment) Act 1919, for "imprisonment for a term not exceeding three months" there is substituted "a fine not exceeding level 3 on the standard scale".

Polish Resettlement Act 1947 (c. 19)

154   In the Schedule to the Polish Resettlement Act 1947, in paragraph 7, for "imprisonment for a term not exceeding three months" there is substituted "a fine not exceeding level 1 on the standard scale".

Army Act 1955 (3 & 4 Eliz. 2 c. 18)

155   In section 61 of the Army Act 1955, for the words from "the like" to "section nineteen of this Act" there is substituted "dismissal from Her Majesty's service with or without disgrace, to detention for a term not exceeding three months,".

Air Force Act 1955 (3 & 4 Eliz. 2 c. 19)

156   In section 61 of the Air Force Act 1955, for the words from "the like" to "section nineteen of this Act" there is substituted "dismissal from Her Majesty's service with or without disgrace, to detention for a term not exceeding three months,".

Naval Discipline Act 1957 (c. 53)

157   In section 34A of the Naval Discipline Act 1957, for the words "imprisonment for a term not exceeding three months" there is substituted "dismissal from Her Majesty's service with or without disgrace, detention for a term not exceeding three months,".

Slaughterhouses Act 1974 (c. 3)

158   In section 4 of the Slaughterhouses Act 1974, after subsection (5) there is inserted—
"(5A) A person guilty of an offence under subsection (5) above shall be liable to a fine not exceeding level 3 on the standard scale."

Water Industry Act 1991 (c. 56)

159   In Schedule 6 to the Water Industry Act 1991, in paragraph 5(4), for paragraphs (a) and (b) there is substituted ", on summary conviction, to a fine not exceeding level 5 on the standard scale".

Water Resources Act 1991 (c.57)

160   In section 205(6) of the Water Resources Act 1991, for paragraphs (a) and (b) there is substituted "on summary conviction to a fine not exceeding level 5 on the standard scale".

Transport Act 2000 (c. 38)

161   In section 82(4) of the Transport Act 2000, after "subsection (1)" there is inserted "or (2)".

Reserve Forces Act 1996 (c. 14)

162   In paragraph 5(3) of Schedule 1 to the Reserve Forces Act 1996, for the words "imprisonment for a term not exceeding three months" there is substituted "dismissal from Her Majesty's service with or without disgrace, to detention for a term not exceeding 3 months,".

SCHEDULE 33   **Section 321**

JURY SERVICE

1   The Juries Act 1974 (c. 23) is amended as follows.
2   For section 1 (qualification for jury service) there is substituted—

"1 Qualification for jury service

(1) Subject to the provisions of this Act, every person shall be qualified to serve as a juror in the Crown Court, the High Court and county courts and be liable accordingly to attend for jury service when summoned under this Act if—

    (a) he is for the time being registered as a parliamentary or local government elector and is not less than eighteen nor more than seventy years of age;

    (b) he has been ordinarily resident in the United Kingdom, the Channel Islands or the Isle of Man for any period of at least five years since attaining the age of thirteen;

    (c) he is not a mentally disordered person; and

    (d) he is not disqualified for jury service.

(2) In subsection (1) above "mentally disordered person" means any person listed in Part 1 of Schedule 1 to this Act.

(3) The persons who are disqualified for jury service are those listed in Part 2 of that Schedule."

3   Section 9(1) (certain persons entitled to be excused from jury service) shall cease to have effect.

4   In section 9(2) (discretionary excusal) after "may" there is inserted ", subject to section 9A(1A) of this Act,".

5   After section 9(2) (discretionary excusal) there is inserted—

"(2A) Without prejudice to subsection (2) above, the appropriate officer shall excuse a full-time serving member of Her Majesty's naval, military or air forces from attending in pursuance of a summons if—

    (a) that member's commanding officer certifies to the appropriate officer that it would be prejudicial to the efficiency of the service if that member were to be required to be absent from duty, and

    (b) subsection (2A) or (2B) of section 9A of this Act applies.

(2B) Subsection (2A) above does not affect the application of subsection (2) above to a full-time serving member of Her Majesty's naval, military or air forces in a case where he is not entitled to be excused under subsection (2A)."

6   In section 9(3) (discretionary excusal) after "above" there is inserted "or any failure by the appropriate officer to excuse him as required by subsection (2A) above".

7   In section 9A(1) (discretionary deferral) after "may" there is inserted ", subject to subsection (2) below,".

8   After section 9A(1) (discretionary deferral) there is inserted—

"(1A) Without prejudice to subsection (1) above and subject to subsection (2) below, the appropriate officer—

    (a) shall defer the attendance of a full-time serving member of Her Majesty's naval, military or air forces in pursuance of a summons if subsection (1B) below applies, and

    (b) for this purpose, shall vary the dates upon which that member is summoned to attend and the summons shall have effect accordingly.

(1B) This subsection applies if that member's commanding officer certifies to the appropriate officer that it would be prejudicial to the efficiency of the service if that member were to be required to be absent from duty.

(1C) Nothing in subsection (1A) or (1B) above shall affect the application of subsection (1) above to a full-time serving member of Her Majesty's naval, military or air forces in a case where subsection (1B) does not apply."

9   For section 9A(2) (discretionary deferral) there is substituted—

"(2) The attendance of a person in pursuance of a summons shall not be deferred under subsection (1) or (1A) above if subsection (2A) or (2B) below applies."

10   After section 9A(2) (discretionary deferral) there is inserted—

"(2A) This subsection applies where a deferral of the attendance of the person in pursuance of the summons has previously been made or refused under subsection (1) above or has previously been made under subsection (1A) above.

(2B) This subsection applies where—

    (a) the person is a full-time serving member of Her Majesty's naval, military or air forces, and

(b) in addition to certifying to the appropriate officer that it would be prejudicial to the efficiency of the service if that member were to be required to be absent from duty, that member's commanding officer certifies that this position is likely to remain for any period specified for the purpose of this subsection in guidance issued under section 9AA of this Act."

11   In section 9A(3) (discretionary deferral) after "above" there is inserted "or any failure by the appropriate officer to defer his attendance as required by subsection (1A) above".

12   After section 9A (discretionary deferral) there is inserted—

"9AA Requirement to issue guidance

(1) The Lord Chancellor shall issue guidance as to the manner in which the functions of the appropriate officer under sections 9 and 9A of this Act are to be exercised.

(2) The Lord Chancellor shall—

(a) lay before each House of Parliament the guidance, and any revised guidance, issued under this section, and

(b) arrange for the guidance, or revised guidance, to be published in a manner which he considers appropriate."

13   In section 19 (payment for jury service), after subsection (1) there is inserted—

"(1A) The reference in subsection (1) above to payments by way of allowance for subsistence includes a reference to vouchers and other benefits which may be used to pay for subsistence, whether or not their use is subject to any limitations."

14   In section 20 (offences), for subsection (5)(d) there is substituted—

"(d) knowing that he is disqualified under Part 2 of Schedule 1 to this Act, serves on a jury;"

15   For Schedule 1 (ineligibility and disqualification for and excusal from jury service) there is substituted—

"SCHEDULE 1

MENTALLY DISORDERED PERSONS AND PERSONS DISQUALIFIED FOR JURY SERVICE

PART 1

MENTALLY DISORDERED PERSONS

A person who suffers or has suffered from mental illness, psychopathic disorder, mental handicap or severe mental handicap and on account of that condition either—

(a) is resident in a hospital or similar institution; or

(b) regularly attends for treatment by a medical practitioner.

2 A person for the time being under guardianship under section 7 of the Mental Health Act 1983.

3 A person who, under Part 7 of that Act, has been determined by a judge to be incapable, by reason of mental disorder, of managing and administering his property and affairs.

4 (1) In this Part of this Schedule—

(a) "mental handicap" means a state of arrested or incomplete development of mind (not amounting to severe mental handicap) which includes significant impairment of intelligence and social functioning;

(b) "severe mental handicap" means a state of arrested or incomplete development of mind which includes severe impairment of intelligence and social functioning;

(c) other expressions are to be construed in accordance with the Mental Health Act 1983.

(2) For the purposes of this Part a person is to be treated as being under guardianship under section 7 of the Mental Health Act 1983 at any time while he is subject to guardianship pursuant to an order under section 116A(2)(b) of the Army Act 1955, section 116A(2)(b) of the Air Force Act 1955 or section 63A(2)(b) of the Naval Discipline Act 1957.

PART 2

PERSONS DISQUALIFIED

5 A person who is on bail in criminal proceedings (within the meaning of the Bail Act 1976).

6 A person who has at any time been sentenced in the United Kingdom, the Channel Islands or the Isle of Man—

(a) to imprisonment for life, detention for life or custody for life,

(b) to detention during her Majesty's pleasure or during the pleasure of the Secretary of State,

(c) to imprisonment for public protection or detention for public protection,

(d) to an extended sentence under section 227 or 228 of the Criminal Justice Act 2003 or section 210A of the Criminal Procedure (Scotland) Act 1995, or

(e) to a term of imprisonment of five years or more or a term of detention of five years or more.

7 A person who at any time in the last ten years has—

(a) in the United Kingdom, the Channel Islands or the Isle of Man—

(i) served any part of a sentence of imprisonment or a sentence of detention, or

(ii) had passed on him a suspended sentence of imprisonment or had made in respect of him a suspended order for detention,

(b) in England and Wales, had made in respect of him a community order under section 177 of the Criminal Justice Act 2003, a community rehabilitation order, a community punishment order, a community punishment and rehabilitation order, a drug treatment and testing order or a drug abstinence order, or

(c) had made in respect of him any corresponding order under the law of Scotland, Northern Ireland, the Isle of Man or any of the Channel Islands.

8 For the purposes of this Part of this Schedule—

(a) a sentence passed by a court-martial is to be treated as having been passed in the United Kingdom, and

(b) a person is sentenced to a term of detention if, but only if—

(i) a court passes on him, or makes in respect of him on conviction, any sentence or order which requires him to be detained in custody for any period, and

(ii) the sentence or order is available only in respect of offenders below a certain age,

and any reference to serving a sentence of detention is to be construed accordingly."

SCHEDULE 34 **Section 324**

PARENTING ORDERS AND REFERRAL ORDERS

Crime and Disorder Act 1998 (c. 37)

1 In section 8 of the Crime and Disorder Act 1998 (parenting orders), in subsection (2) the words from "and to section 19(5)" to "2000" shall cease to have effect.

2 (1) Section 9 of that Act (parenting orders: supplemental) is amended as follows.

(2) For subsection (1A) there is substituted—

"(1A) The requirements of subsection (1) do not apply where the court makes a referral order in respect of the offence."

(3) After subsection (2) there is inserted—

"(2A) In a case where a court proposes to make both a referral order in respect of a child or young person convicted of an offence and a parenting order, before making the parenting order the court shall obtain and consider a report by an appropriate officer—

(a) indicating the requirements proposed by that officer to be included in the parenting order;

(b) indicating the reasons why he considers those requirements would be desirable in the interests of preventing the commission of any further offence by the child or young person; and

(c) if the child or young person is aged under 16, containing the information required by subsection (2) above.

(2B) In subsection (2A) above "an appropriate officer" means—

(a) an officer of a local probation board;

(b) a social worker of a local authority social services department; or

(c) a member of a youth offending team."

(4) After subsection (7) there is inserted—

"(7A) In this section "referral order" means an order under section 16(2) or (3) of the Powers of Criminal Courts (Sentencing) Act 2000 (referral of offender to youth offender panel)."

Powers of Criminal Courts (Sentencing) Act 2000 (c. 6)

3   In section 19(5) of the Powers of Criminal Courts (Sentencing) Act 2000 (orders that cannot be made with referral orders)—
(a) at the end of paragraph (a) there is inserted "or", and
(b) paragraph (c) (parenting orders) and the word "or" immediately preceding it shall cease to have effect.

4   In section 22 of that Act (referral orders: attendance at panel meetings), after subsection (2) there is inserted—
"(2A) If—
(a) a parent or guardian of the offender fails to comply with an order under section 20 above (requirement to attend the meetings of the panel), and
(b) the offender is aged under 18 at the time of the failure,
the panel may refer that parent or guardian to a youth court acting for the petty sessions area in which it appears to the panel that the offender resides or will reside."

5   (1) Section 28 of that Act (which introduces Schedule 1) is amended as follows.
(2) In the sidenote, for "Offender referred back to court or" there is substituted "Offender or parent referred back to court: offender".
(3) After paragraph (a) there is inserted—
"(aa) in Part 1A makes provision for what is to happen when a youth offender panel refers a parent or guardian to the court under section 22(2A) above, and".

6   In Schedule 1 to that Act (youth offender panels: further court proceedings), after Part 1 there is inserted—

"PART 1A

REFERRAL OF PARENT OR GUARDIAN FOR BREACH OF SECTION 20 ORDER

Introductory
9A (1) This Part of this Schedule applies where, under section 22(2A) of this Act, a youth offender panel refers an offender's parent or guardian to a youth court.
(2) In this Part of this Schedule—
(a) "the offender" means the offender whose parent or guardian is referred under section 22(2A);
(b) "the parent" means the parent or guardian so referred; and
(c) "the youth court" means a youth court as mentioned in section 22(2A).

Mode of referral to court
9B The panel shall make the referral by sending a report to the youth court explaining why the parent is being referred to it.

Bringing the parent before the court
9C (1) Where the youth court receives such a report it shall cause the parent to appear before it.
(2) For the purpose of securing the attendance of the parent before the court, a justice acting for the petty sessions area for which the court acts may—
(a) issue a summons requiring the parent to appear at the place and time specified in it; or
(b) if the report is substantiated on oath, issue a warrant for the parent's arrest.
(3) Any summons or warrant issued under sub-paragraph (2) above shall direct the parent to appear or be brought before the youth court.

Power of court to make parenting order: application of supplemental provisions
9D (1) Where the parent appears or is brought before the youth court under paragraph 9C above, the court may make a parenting order in respect of the parent if—
(a) it is proved to the satisfaction of the court that the parent has failed without reasonable excuse to comply with the order under section 20 of this Act; and
(b) the court is satisfied that the parenting order would be desirable in the interests of preventing the commission of any further offence by the offender.
(2) A parenting order is an order which requires the parent—
(a) to comply, for a period not exceeding twelve months, with such requirements as are specified in the order, and

     (b) subject to sub-paragraph (4) below, to attend, for a concurrent period not exceeding three months, such counselling or guidance programme as may be specified in directions given by the responsible officer.

(3) The requirements that may be specified under sub-paragraph (2)(a) above are those which the court considers desirable in the interests of preventing the commission of any further offence by the offender.

(4) A parenting order under this paragraph may, but need not, include a requirement mentioned in subsection (2)(b) above in any case where a parenting order under this paragraph or any other enactment has been made in respect of the parent on a previous occasion.

(5) A counselling or guidance programme which a parent is required to attend by virtue of subsection (2)(b) above may be or include a residential course but only if the court is satisfied—

     (a) that the attendance of the parent at a residential course is likely to be more effective than his attendance at a non-residential course in preventing the commission of any further offence by the offender, and

     (b) that any interference with family life which is likely to result from the attendance of the parent at a residential course is proportionate in all the circumstances.

(6) Before making a parenting order under this paragraph where the offender is aged under 16, the court shall obtain and consider information about his family circumstances and the likely effect of the order on those circumstances.

(7) Sections 8(3) and (8), 9(3) to (7) and 18(3) and (4) of the Crime and Disorder Act 1998 apply in relation to a parenting order made under this paragraph as they apply in relation to any other parenting order.

Appeal

9E (1) An appeal shall lie to the Crown Court against the making of a parenting order under paragraph 9D above.

(2) Subsections (2) and (3) of section 10 of the Crime and Disorder Act 1998 (appeals against parenting orders) apply in relation to an appeal under this paragraph as they apply in relation to an appeal under subsection (1)(b) of that section.

Effect on section 20 order

9F (1) The making of a parenting order under paragraph 9D above is without prejudice to the continuance of the order under section 20 of this Act.

(2) Section 63(1) to (4) of the Magistrates' Courts Act 1980 (power of magistrates' court to deal with person for breach of order, etc) apply (as well as section 22(2A) of this Act and this Part of this Schedule) in relation to an order under section 20 of this Act."

SCHEDULE 35   **Section 328**

CRIMINAL RECORD CERTIFICATES: AMENDMENTS OF PART 5 OF POLICE ACT 1997

1   The Police Act 1997 (c. 50) is amended as follows.

2   In section 112 (criminal conviction certificates), in subsection (1)(a), after "prescribed" there is inserted "manner and".

3   (1) Section 113 (criminal record certificates) is amended as follows.

(2) In subsection (1)—

     (a) at the beginning there is inserted "Subject to subsection (4A)",

     (b) in paragraph (a), after "prescribed" there is inserted "manner and", and

     (c) in paragraph (b), after "pays" there is inserted "in the prescribed manner".

(3) After subsection (4) there is inserted—

"(4A) The Secretary of State may treat an application under this section as an application under section 115 if—

     (a) in his opinion the certificate is required for a purpose prescribed under subsection (2) of that section,

     (b) the registered person provides him with the statement required by subsection (2) of that section, and

     (c) the applicant consents and pays to the Secretary of State the amount (if any) by which the fee payable in relation to an application under section 115 exceeds the fee paid in relation to the application under this section.".

4   (1) Section 115 (enhanced criminal record certificates) is amended as follows.
    (2) In subsection (1)—
        (a) at the beginning there is inserted "Subject to subsection (9A),",
        (b) in paragraph (a), after "prescribed" there is inserted "manner and", and
        (c) in paragraph (b), after "pays" there is inserted "in the prescribed manner".
    (3) In subsection (2), for paragraphs (a) to (c) there is substituted "for such purposes as may be prescribed under this subsection".
    (4) Subsections (3) to (5) and subsections (6C) to (6E) are omitted.
    (5) After subsection (9) there is inserted—
    "(9A) The Secretary of State may treat an application under this section as an application under section 113 if in his opinion the certificate is not required for a purpose prescribed under subsection (2).
    (9B) Where by virtue of subsection (9A) the Secretary of State treats an application under this section as an application under section 113, he must refund to the applicant the amount (if any) by which the fee paid in relation to the application under this section exceeds the fee payable in relation to an application under section 113."

5   In section 116 (enhanced criminal record certificates: judicial appointments and Crown employment), in subsection (2)(b), for the words from "to which" onwards there is substituted "of such description as may be prescribed".

6   (1) Section 120 (registered persons) is amended as follows.
    (2) For subsection (2) there is substituted—
    "(2) Subject to regulations under section 120ZA and 120AA and to section 120A the Secretary of State shall include in the register any person who—
        (a) applies to him in writing to be registered,
        (b) satisfies the conditions in subsections (4) to (6), and
        (c) has not in the period of two years ending with the date of the application been removed from the register under section 120A or 120AA."

    (3) Subsection (3) is omitted.

7   After section 120 there is inserted—

"120ZA   Regulations about registration
        (1) The Secretary of State may by regulations make further provision about registration.
        (2) Regulations under this section may in particular make provision for—
            (a) the payment of fees,
            (b) the information to be included in the register,
            (c) the registration of any person to be subject to conditions,
            (d) the nomination by—
                (i) a body corporate or unincorporate, or
                (ii) a person appointed to an office by virtue of any enactment,
                of the individuals authorised to act for it or, as the case may be, him in relation to the countersigning of applications under this Part, and
            (e) the refusal by the Secretary of State, on such grounds as may be specified in or determined under the regulations, to accept or to continue to accept the nomination of a person as so authorised.
        (3) The provision which may be made by virtue of subsection (2)(c) includes provision—
            (a) for the registration or continued registration of any person to be subject to prescribed conditions or, if the regulations so provide, such conditions as the Secretary of State thinks fit, and
            (b) for the Secretary of State to vary or revoke those conditions.
        (4) The conditions imposed by virtue of subsection (2)(c) may in particular include conditions—
            (a) requiring a registered person, before he countersigns an application at an individual's request, to verify the identity of that individual in the prescribed manner,
            (b) requiring an application under section 113 or 115 to be transmitted by electronic means to the Secretary of State by the registered person who countersigns it, and
            (c) requiring a registered person to comply with any code of practice for the time being in force under section 122."

8   At the end of the sidenote to section 120A (refusal and cancellation of registration) there is inserted "on grounds related to disclosure".

9   After section 120A there is inserted—

"120AA Refusal, cancellation or suspension of registration on other grounds

(1) Regulations may make provision enabling the Secretary of State in prescribed cases to refuse to register a person who, in the opinion of the Secretary of State, is likely to countersign fewer applications under this Part in any period of twelve months than a prescribed minimum number.

(2) Subsection (3) applies where a registered person—

(a) is, in the opinion of the Secretary of State, no longer likely to wish to countersign applications under this Part,

(b) has, in any period of twelve months during which he was registered, countersigned fewer applications under this Part than the minimum number specified in respect of him by regulations under subsection (1), or

(c) has failed to comply with any condition of his registration.

(3) Subject to section 120AB, the Secretary of State may—

(a) suspend that person's registration for such period not exceeding 6 months as the Secretary of State thinks fit, or

(b) remove that person from the register.

120AB Procedure for cancellation or suspension under section 120AA

(1) Before cancelling or suspending a person's registration by virtue of section 120AA, the Secretary of State must send him written notice of his intention to do so.

(2) Every such notice must—

(a) give the Secretary of State's reasons for proposing to cancel or suspend the registration, and

(b) inform the person concerned of his right under subsection (3) to make representations.

(3) A person who receives such a notice may, within 21 days of service, make representations in writing to the Secretary of State as to why the registration should not be cancelled or suspended.

(4) After considering such representations, the Secretary of state must give the registered person written notice—

(a) that at the end of a further period of six weeks beginning with the date of service, the person's registration will be cancelled or suspended, or

(b) that he does not propose to take any further action.

(5) If no representations are received within the period mentioned in subsection (3) the Secretary of State may cancel or suspend the person's registration at the end of the period mentioned in that subsection.

(6) Subsection (1) does not prevent the Secretary of State from imposing on the registered person a lesser sanction than that specified in the notice under that subsection.

(7) Any notice under this section that is required to be given in writing may be given by being transmitted electronically.

(8) This section does not apply where—

(a) the Secretary of State is satisfied, in the case of a registered person other than a body, that the person has died or is incapable, by reason of physical or mental impairment, of countersigning applications under this Part, or

(b) the registered person has requested to be removed from the register.

(9) The Secretary of State may by regulations amend subsection (4)(a) by substituting for the period there specified, such other period as may be specified in the regulations."

10   After section 122 there is inserted—

"122A Delegation of functions of Secretary of State

(1) The Secretary of State may, to such extent and subject to such conditions as he thinks fit, delegate any relevant function of his under this Part to such person as he may determine.

(2) A function is relevant for the purposes of subsection (1) if it does not consist of a power—

(a) to make regulations, or

(b) to publish or revise a code of practice or to lay any such code before Parliament.

(3) A delegation under subsection (1) may be varied or revoked at any time."

11   After section 124 (offences: disclosure) there is inserted—

"124A Further offences: disclosure of information obtained in connection with delegated function

(1) Any person who is engaged in the discharge of functions conferred by this Part on the Secretary of State commits an offence if he discloses information which has been obtained by him in connection with those functions and which relates to a particular person unless he discloses the information, in the course of his duties,—

(a) to another person engaged in the discharge of those functions,

(b) to the chief officer of a police force in connection with a request under this Part to provide information to the Secretary of State, or

(c) to an applicant or registered person who is entitled under this Part to the information disclosed to him.

(2) Where information is disclosed to a person and the disclosure—

(a) is an offence under subsection (1), or

(b) would be an offence under subsection (1) but for subsection (3)(a), (d) or (e),

the person to whom the information is disclosed commits an offence if he discloses it to any other person.

(3) Subsection (1) does not apply to a disclosure of information which is made—

(a) with the written consent of the person to whom the information relates,

(b) to a government department,

(c) to a person appointed to an office by virtue of any enactment,

(d) in accordance with an obligation to provide information under or by virtue of any enactment, or

(e) for some other purpose specified in regulations made by the Secretary of State.

(4) A person who is guilty of an offence under this section shall be liable on summary conviction to imprisonment for a term not exceeding 51 weeks or to a fine not exceeding level 3 on the standard scale, or to both.

(5) In relation to an offence committed before the commencement of section 281(5) of the Criminal Justice Act 2003, the reference in subsection (4) to 51 weeks is to be read as a reference to 6 months."

12   In section 125 (regulations)—

(a) subsection (3) is omitted, and

(b) in subsection (4), the words "to which subsection (3) does not apply" are omitted.

SCHEDULE 36   **Section 331**

FURTHER MINOR AND CONSEQUENTIAL AMENDMENTS

PART 1

BAIL

Bail Act 1976 (c. 63)

1   The Bail Act 1976 is amended as follows.

2   (1) Section 5(6A)(a) (supplementary provisions about decisions on bail) is amended as follows.

(2) After "examination)" there is inserted ", section 52(5) of the Crime and Disorder Act 1998 (adjournment of proceedings under section 51 etc)".

(3) After sub-paragraph (ii) there is inserted—
      "(iia) section 17C (intention as to plea: adjournment), or".

(4) After sub-paragraph (iii) there is inserted "or
      (iiia) section 24C (intention as to plea by child or young person: adjournment),".

3   In Part 3 of Schedule 1 (interpretation) for paragraph 2 there is substituted—
      "2 References in this Schedule to previous grants of bail include—
      (a) bail granted before the coming into force of this Act;

    (b) as respects the reference in paragraph 2A of Part 1 of this Schedule (as substituted by section 14(1) of the Criminal Justice Act 2003), bail granted before the coming into force of that paragraph;

    (c) as respects the references in paragraph 6 of Part 1 of this Schedule (as substituted by section 15(1) of the Criminal Justice Act 2003), bail granted before the coming into force of that paragraph;

    (d) as respects the references in paragraph 9AA of Part 1 of this Schedule, bail granted before the coming into force of that paragraph;

    (e) as respects the references in paragraph 9AB of Part 1 of this Schedule, bail granted before the coming into force of that paragraph;

    (f) as respects the reference in paragraph 5 of Part 2 of this Schedule (as substituted by section 13(4) of the Criminal Justice Act 2003), bail granted before the coming into force of that paragraph."

Supreme Court Act 1981 (c. 54)

4   (1) Section 81 of the Supreme Court Act 1981 (bail) is amended as follows.

    (2) In subsection (1)(g) after "examination)" there is inserted ", section 52(5) of the Crime and Disorder Act 1998 (adjournment of proceedings under section 51 etc)".

    (3) In subsection (1)(g) the word "or" at the end of sub-paragraph (ii) is omitted and after that sub-paragraph there is inserted—

        "(iia) section 17C (intention as to plea: adjournment);".

    (4) In subsection (1)(g) after sub-paragraph (iii) there is inserted "or

        (iiia) section 24C (intention as to plea by child or young person: adjournment);".

Police and Criminal Evidence Act 1984 (c. 60)

5   In section 38(2A) of the Police and Criminal Evidence Act 1984 (bail granted by custody officer after charge)—

    (a) for "2" there is substituted "2(1)", and

    (b) after "1976" there is inserted "(disregarding paragraph 2(2) of that Part)".

PART 2

CHARGING ETC

Criminal Law Act 1977 (c. 45)

6   In section 39 of the Criminal Law Act 1977 (service of summons and citation throughout United Kingdom) for subsection (1) there is substituted—

    "(1) The following documents, namely—

    (a) a summons requiring a person charged with an offence to appear before a court in England or Wales,

    (b) a written charge (within the meaning of section 29 of the Criminal Justice Act 2003) charging a person with an offence,

    (c) a requisition (within the meaning of that section) requiring a person charged with an offence to appear before a court in England or Wales, and

    (d) any other document which, by virtue of any enactment, may or must be served on a person with, or at the same time as, a document mentioned in paragraph (a), (b) or (c) above,

    may, in such manner as may be prescribed by rules of court, be served on him in Scotland or Northern Ireland."

Magistrates' Courts Act 1980 (c. 43)

7   The Magistrates' Courts Act 1980 is amended as follows.

8   (1) Section 1 (issue of summons to accused or warrant for his arrest) is amended as follows.

    (2) In subsection (3) after "section" there is inserted "upon an information being laid".

    (3) In subsection (4) after "summons" there is inserted ", or a written charge and requisition,".

    (4) In subsection (6) after "has" there is inserted ", or a written charge and requisition have,".

    (5) After subsection (6) there is inserted—

    "(6A) Where the offence charged is an indictable offence and a written charge and requisition have previously been issued, a warrant may be issued under this section by a justice of the peace upon a copy of the written charge (rather than an information) being laid before the justice by a public prosecutor."

(6) After subsection (7) there is inserted—

"(7A) For the purposes of subsection (6A) above, a copy of a written charge may be laid before, and a warrant under this section may be issued by, a single justice of the peace."

9   In section 150(1) (interpretation of other terms) after the definition of "prescribed" there is inserted—

""public prosecutor", "requisition" and "written charge" have the same meaning as in section 29 of the Criminal Justice Act 2003;".

Prosecution of Offences Act 1985 (c. 23)

10   (1) Section 15 of the Prosecution of Offences Act 1985 (interpretation) is amended as follows.

(2) In subsection (1) after the definition of "public authority" there is inserted—

""public prosecutor", "requisition" and "written charge" have the same meaning as in section 29 of the Criminal Justice Act 2003;".

(3) In subsection (2), after paragraph (b) there is inserted—

"(ba) where a public prosecutor issues a written charge and requisition for the offence, when the written charge and requisition are issued;".

Criminal Justice and Public Order Act 1994 (c. 33)

11   (1) Section 51 of the Criminal Justice and Public Order Act 1994 (intimidation, etc, of witnesses, jurors and others) is amended as follows.

(2) In subsection (9), for the word "and" at the end of the definition of "potential" there is substituted—

""public prosecutor", "requisition" and "written charge" have the same meaning as in section 29 of the Criminal Justice Act 2003;"

(3) In subsection (10)(a), after sub-paragraph (i) there is inserted—

"(ia) when a public prosecutor issues a written charge and requisition in respect of the offence;".

Drug Trafficking Act 1994 (c. 37)

12   (1) Section 60 of the Drug Trafficking Act 1994 (prosecution by order of Commissioners of Customs and Excise) is amended as follows.

(2) In subsection (6) for the word "and" at the end of the definition of "officer" there is substituted—

""public prosecutor", "requisition" and "written charge" have the same meaning as in section 29 of the Criminal Justice Act 2003;".

(3) In subsection (6A), after paragraph (a) there is inserted—

"(aa) when a public prosecutor issues a written charge and requisition in respect of the offence;".

Merchant Shipping Act 1995 (c. 21)

13   (1) Section 145 of the Merchant Shipping Act 1995 (interpretation of section 144) is amended as follows.

(2) In subsection (2)(a), after sub-paragraph (i) there is inserted—

"(ia) when a public prosecutor issues a written charge and requisition in respect of the offence;".

(3) After subsection (2) there is inserted—

"(2A) In subsection (2) above "public prosecutor", "requisition" and "written charge" have the same meaning as in section 29 of the Criminal Justice Act 2003."

Terrorism Act 2000 (c. 11)

14   (1) Paragraph 11 of Schedule 4 to the Terrorism Act 2000 (proceedings for an offence: timing) is amended as follows.

(2) In sub-paragraph (1), after paragraph (a) there is inserted—

"(aa) when a public prosecutor issues a written charge and requisition in respect of the offence;".

(3) After sub-paragraph (2) there is inserted—

"(2A) In sub-paragraph (1) "public prosecutor", "requisition" and "written charge" have the same meaning as in section 29 of the Criminal Justice Act 2003."

Proceeds of Crime Act 2002 (c. 29)

15 (1) Section 85 of the Proceeds of Crime Act 2002 (proceedings) is amended as follows.

(2) In subsection (1), after paragraph (a) there is inserted—

"(aa) when a public prosecutor issues a written charge and requisition in respect of the offence;".

(3) After subsection (8) there is inserted—

"(9) In this section "public prosecutor", "requisition" and "written charge" have the same meaning as in section 29 of the Criminal Justice Act 2003."

Crime (International Co-operation) Act 2003 (c. 32)

16   After section 4 of the Crime (International Co-operation) Act 2003 there is inserted—

"4A General requirements for service of written charge or requisition

(1) This section applies to the following documents issued for the purposes of criminal proceedings in England and Wales by a prosecutor—

(a) a written charge (within the meaning of section 29 of the Criminal Justice Act 2003),

(b) a requisition (within the meaning of that section).

(2) The written charge or requisition may be issued in spite of the fact that the person on whom it is to be served is outside the United Kingdom.

(3) Where the written charge or requisition is to be served outside the United Kingdom and the prosecutor believes that the person on whom it is to be served does not understand English, the written charge or requisition must be accompanied by a translation of it in an appropriate language.

(4) A written charge or requisition served outside the United Kingdom must be accompanied by a notice giving any information required to be given by rules of court.

(5) If a requisition is served outside the United Kingdom, no obligation under the law of England and Wales to comply with the requisition is imposed by virtue of the service.

(6) Accordingly, failure to comply with the requisition is not a ground for issuing a warrant to secure the attendance of the person in question.

(7) But the requisition may subsequently be served on the person in question in the United Kingdom (with the usual consequences for non-compliance).

4B Service of written charge or requisition otherwise than by post

(1) A written charge or requisition to which section 4A applies may, instead of being served by post, be served on a person outside the United Kingdom in accordance with arrangements made by the Secretary of State.

(2) But where the person is in a participating country, the written charge or requisition may be served in accordance with those arrangements only if one of the following conditions is met.

(3) The conditions are—

(a) that the correct address of the person is unknown,

(b) that it has not been possible to serve the written charge or requisition by post,

(c) that there are good reasons for thinking that service by post will not be effective or is inappropriate."

PART 3

DISCLOSURE

Prosecution of Offences Act 1985 (c. 23)

17   In section 22B of the Prosecution of Offences Act 1985 (re-institution of proceedings stayed under section 22(4) or 22A(5)), in subsection (5)(a) for "section 3, 4, 7 or 9" there is substituted "section 3, 4 or 7A".

Criminal Justice Act 1987 (c. 38)

18   In section 9 of the Criminal Justice Act 1987 (preparatory hearings in serious fraud cases etc.), paragraphs (i) and (iii) of subsection (5) are omitted.

Criminal Justice (Serious Fraud) (Northern Ireland) Order 1988 (S.I. 1988/1846 (N.I. 16))

19   In Article 8 of the Criminal Justice (Serious Fraud) (Northern Ireland) Order 1988 (preparatory hearings in serious fraud cases etc.), sub-paragraphs (i) and (iii) of paragraph (5) are omitted.

Criminal Procedure and Investigations Act 1996 (c. 25)

20   The Criminal Procedure and Investigations Act 1996 is amended as follows.
21   In section 3 (primary disclosure by prosecutor), for the heading there is substituted "**Initial duty of prosecutor to disclose**".
22   In section 4 (primary disclosure: further provisions), in the heading for "**Primary disclosure**" there is substituted "**Initial duty to disclose**".
23   In section 5 (compulsory disclosure by accused), subsections (6) to (9) are omitted.
24   In section 6 (voluntary disclosure by accused), subsection (3) is omitted.
25   Section 7 (secondary disclosure by prosecutor) shall cease to have effect.
26   Section 9 (continuing duty of prosecutor to disclose) shall cease to have effect.
27   In section 10 (prosecutor's failure to observe time limits), in subsection (1), for paragraph (b) there is substituted—
    "(b) purports to act under section 7A(5) after the end of the period which, by virtue of section 12, is the relevant period for section 7A."
28   In section 12 (time limits)—
    (a) in subsection (1), for "and 7" there is substituted ", 6B, 6C and 7A(5)";
    (b) in subsection (5), for "7" there is substituted "7A(5)".
29   In section 13 (time limits: transitional), for subsection (2) there is substituted—
    "(2) As regards a case in relation to which no regulations under section 12 have come into force for the purposes of section 7A, section 7A(5) shall have effect as if—
        (a) in paragraph (a) for the words from "during the period" to the end, and
        (b) in paragraph (b) for "during that period",
        there were substituted "as soon as is reasonably practicable after the accused gives the statement in question"."
30   In section 14 (public interest: review for summary trials), in subsection (2)(a), for "7(5), 8(5) or 9(8)" there is substituted "7A(8) or 8(5)".
31   In section 15 (public interest: review in other cases), in subsection (2)(a), for "7(5), 8(5) or 9(8)" there is substituted "7A(8) or 8(5)".
32   In section 16 (applications: opportunity to be heard), in paragraph (a) and in the words after paragraph (c), for "7(5), 8(5), 9(8)" there is substituted "7A(8), 8(5)".
33   In section 17 (confidentiality of disclosed information), in subsection (1)(a), for "7, 9" there is substituted "7A".
34   In section 19 (rules of court) in subsection (2)(b) and (d), for "7(5), 8(2) or (5), 9(8)" there is substituted "5(5B), 6B(6), 6E(5), 7A(8), 8(2) or (5)".
35   In section 20 (other statutory rules as to disclosure)—
    (a) subsection (2) is omitted, and
    (b) in subsection (5)(a), for "sections 3 to 9" there is substituted "sections 3 to 8".
36   In section 31 (preparatory hearings in complex cases etc.), paragraphs (a) and (c) of subsection (6) are omitted.
37   (1) Section 77 (orders and regulations) is amended as follows.
    (2) In subsection (5)—
        (a) after "No" there is inserted "regulations or", and
        (b) after "section" there is inserted "6A or".
    (3) In subsection (6)(b) after "regulations" there is inserted "(other than regulations under section 6A)".
38   In Schedule 4 (modifications for Northern Ireland), in paragraph 7, for "3(6), 7(5), 8(5) or 9(8)" there is substituted "3(6), 7A(8) or 8(5)".

Sexual Offences (Protected Material) Act 1997 (c. 39)

39   In section 9(4) of the Sexual Offences (Protected Material) Act 1997 (which, when in force, will add a subsection (6) to section 1 of the Criminal Procedure and Investigations Act 1996), for "section 3, 7 or 9" there is substituted "section 3 or 7A".

PART 4

TRIALS ON INDICTMENT WITHOUT A JURY

Indictments Act 1915 (c. 90)

40 (1) Section 5 of the Indictments Act 1915 (orders for amendment of indictment, separate trial and postponement of trial) is amended as follows.
(2) In subsection (5)(a) for "are to" there is substituted "(if there is one)".
(3) In subsection (5)(b) after "discharged" there is inserted "under paragraph (a)".

Criminal Law Act 1967 (c. 58)

41 In section 6(4) of the Criminal Law Act 1967 (trial of offences) after "jury" there is inserted "or otherwise act".

Criminal Justice Act 1967 (c. 80)

42 In section 17 of the Criminal Justice Act 1967 (entry of verdict of not guilty by order of a judge)—
(a) for "the defendant being given in charge to a jury" there is substituted "any further steps being taken in the proceedings", and
(b) after "verdict of a jury" there is inserted "or a court".

Criminal Law Act (Northern Ireland) 1967 (c. 18)

43 In section 6(3) of the Criminal Law Act (Northern Ireland) 1967 (trial of offences) after "jury" there is inserted "or otherwise act".

Criminal Appeal Act 1968 (c. 19)

44 In section 7(2)(c) of the Criminal Appeal Act 1968 (power to order retrial)—
(a) for "the jury were discharged from giving a verdict" there is substituted "no verdict was given", and
(b) for "convicting him" there is substituted "his being convicted".

Judicature (Northern Ireland) Act 1978 (c. 23)

45 (1) Section 48 of the Judicature (Northern Ireland) Act 1978 (committal for trial on indictment) is amended as follows.
(2) In subsection (6A) for "the jury are sworn" there is substituted "the time when the jury are sworn".
(3) After subsection (6A) there is inserted—
"(6B) The reference in subsection (6A) to the time when the jury are sworn includes the time when the jury would be sworn but for—
(a) the making of an order under Part 7 of the Criminal Justice Act 2003, or
(b) the application of section 75 of the Terrorism Act 2000."

Criminal Appeal (Northern Ireland) Act 1980 (c. 47)

46 In section 6(3)(c) of the Criminal Appeal (Northern Ireland) Act 1980 (power to order retrial) for "the jury were discharged from giving a verdict" there is substituted "no verdict was given".

Supreme Court Act 1981 (c.54)

47 (1) Section 76 of the Supreme Court Act 1981 (committal for trial: alteration of place of trial) is amended as follows.
(2) In subsection (2A) for "the jury are sworn" there is substituted "the time when the jury are sworn"
(3) After subsection (2A) there is inserted—
"(2B) The reference in subsection (2A) to the time when the jury are sworn includes the time when the jury would be sworn but for the making of an order under Part 7 of the Criminal Justice Act 2003."

Police and Criminal Evidence Act 1984 (c. 60)

48 (1) Section 77 of the Police and Criminal Evidence Act 1984 (confessions of mentally handicapped persons) is amended as follows.

(2) In subsection (1) after "indictment" there is inserted "with a jury".

(3) In subsection (2) after "indictment" there is inserted "with a jury".

(4) After subsection (2) there is inserted—

"(2A) In any case where at the trial on indictment without a jury of a person for an offence it appears to the court that a warning under subsection (1) above would be required if the trial were with a jury, the court shall treat the case as one in which there is a special need for caution before convicting the accused on his confession."

Prosecution of Offences Act 1985 (c.23)

49   The Prosecution of Offences Act 1985 is amended as follows.

50   In section 7A(6)(a) (powers of non-legal staff) for "by a jury" there is substituted "on indictment".

51 (1) Section 22 (power of Secretary of State to set time limits in relation to preliminary stages of criminal proceedings) is amended as follows.

(2) In subsection (11A)—

   (a) for "when a jury is sworn" there is substituted "at the time when a jury is sworn",

   (b) for "a jury is sworn" there is substituted "the time when a jury is sworn".

(3) After that subsection there is inserted—

"(11AA) The references in subsection (11A) above to the time when a jury is sworn include the time when that jury would be sworn but for the making of an order under Part 7 of the Criminal Justice Act 2003."

Criminal Justice Act 1987 (c.38)

52   The Criminal Justice Act 1987 is amended as follows.

53 (1) Section 7 (power to order preparatory hearing) is amended as follows.

(2) In subsection (1) for "the jury are sworn" there is substituted "the time when the jury are sworn".

(3) After subsection (2) there is inserted—

"(2A) The reference in subsection (1) above to the time when the jury are sworn includes the time when the jury would be sworn but for the making of an order under Part 7 of the Criminal Justice Act 2003."

54 (1) Section 9 (the preparatory hearing) is amended as follows.

(2) In subsection (4)(b) for "the jury" there is substituted "a jury".

(3) In subsection (13) for "no jury shall be sworn" there is substituted "the preparatory hearing shall not be concluded".

55 (1) Section 10 (later stages of trial) is amended as follows.

(2) In subsection (2) after "jury" there is inserted "or, in the case of a trial without a jury, the judge".

(3) In subsection (3) for "deciding whether to give leave" there is substituted "doing anything under subsection (2) above or in deciding whether to do anything under it".

(4) In subsection (4) for "Except as provided by this section" there is substituted "Except as provided by this section, in the case of a trial with a jury".

Criminal Justice (Serious Fraud) (Northern Ireland) Order 1988 (S.I. 1988/1846 (N.I. 16))

56   The Criminal Justice (Serious Fraud) (Northern Ireland) Order 1988 is amended as follows.

57 (1) Article 6 (power to order preparatory hearing) is amended as follows.

(2) In paragraph (1) for "the jury are sworn" there is substituted "the time when the jury are sworn".

(3) After paragraph (2) there is inserted—

"(2A) The reference in paragraph (1) to the time when the jury are sworn includes the time when the jury would be sworn but for—

   (a) the making of an order under Part 7 of the Criminal Justice Act 2003, or

   (b) the application of section 75 of the Terrorism Act 2000."

58 (1) Article 8 (the preparatory hearing) is amended as follows.

(2) In paragraph (4)(b) for "the jury" there is substituted "a jury".

(3) In paragraph (12) for "no jury shall be sworn" there is substituted "the preparatory hearing shall not be concluded".

59 (1) Article 9 (later stages of trial) (as originally enacted) is amended as follows.

(2) In paragraph (1) after "jury" there is inserted "or, in the case of a trial without a jury, the judge".

(3) In paragraph (2) for "deciding whether to give leave" there is substituted "doing anything under paragraph (1) or in deciding whether to do anything under it".

(4) In paragraph (3) for "Except as provided by this Article" there is substituted "Except as provided by this Article, in the case of a trial with a jury".

60 (1) Article 9 (later stages of trial) (as substituted by paragraph 6 of Schedule 3 to the Criminal Procedure and Investigations Act 1996 (c. 25)) is amended as follows.

(2) In paragraph (2) after "jury" there is inserted "or, in the case of a trial without a jury, the judge".

(3) In paragraph (3) for "deciding whether to give leave" there is substituted "doing anything under paragraph (2) or in deciding whether to do anything under it".

(4) In paragraph (4) for "Except as provided by this Article" there is substituted "Except as provided by this Article, in the case of a trial with a jury".

Police and Criminal Evidence (Northern Ireland) Order 1989 (S.I. 1989/1341 (N.I. 12))

61 (1) Article 75 of the Police and Criminal Evidence (Northern Ireland) Order 1989 (confessions of mentally handicapped persons) is amended as follows.

(2) In paragraph (1) after "indictment" there is inserted "with a jury".

(3) In paragraph (2) after "indictment" there is inserted "with a jury".

(4) After paragraph (2) there is inserted—

"(2A) In any case where at the trial on indictment without a jury of a person for an offence it appears to the court that a warning under paragraph (1) would be required if the trial were with a jury, the court shall treat the case as one in which there is a special need for caution before convicting the accused on his confession."

Criminal Justice and Public Order Act 1994 (c. 33)

62   The Criminal Justice and Public Order Act 1994 is amended as follows.

63   In section 35(2) (effect of accused's silence at trial) after "indictment" there is inserted "with a jury".

64   In section 51(10)(b) (intimidation of witnesses, jurors and others) after "finding" there is inserted "otherwise than in circumstances where the proceedings are continued without a jury".

Criminal Procedure and Investigations Act 1996 (c.25)

65   The Criminal Procedure and Investigations Act 1996 is amended as follows.

66 (1) Section 29 (power to order preparatory hearing) is amended as follows.

(2) In subsection (1)(a) for "the jury are sworn" there is substituted "the time when the jury are sworn".

(3) After subsection (4) there is inserted—

"(5) The reference in subsection (1)(a) to the time when the jury are sworn includes the time when the jury would be sworn but for the making of an order under Part 7 of the Criminal Justice Act 2003."

67   In section 31(4)(b) (the preparatory hearing) for "the jury" there is substituted "a jury".

68 (1) Section 34 (later stages of trial) is amended as follows.

(2) In subsection (2) after "jury" there is inserted "or, in the case of a trial without a jury, the judge".

(3) In subsection (3) for "deciding whether to give leave" there is substituted "doing anything under subsection (2) or in deciding whether to do anything under it".

(4) In subsection (4) for "Except as provided by this section" there is substituted "Except as provided by this section, in the case of a trial with a jury".

69   In section 35(2) (appeals to Court of Appeal) for "no jury shall be sworn" there is substituted "the preparatory hearing shall not be concluded".

70   In section 36(2) (appeals to House of Lords) for "no jury shall be sworn" there is substituted "the preparatory hearing shall not be concluded".

71 (1) Section 39 (meaning of pre-trial hearing) is amended as follows.

(2) In subsection (3)—

(a) for "when a jury is sworn" there is substituted "at the time when a jury is sworn",

(b) for "a jury is sworn" there is substituted "the time when a jury is sworn".

(3) After that subsection there is inserted—

"(4) The references in subsection (3) to the time when a jury is sworn include the time when that jury would be sworn but for the making of an order under Part 7 of the Criminal Justice Act 2003."

72 (1) Schedule 4 (modifications for Northern Ireland) is amended as follows.

(2) In paragraph 15 after the substituted version of section 39(2) there is inserted—

"(2A) But, for the purposes of this Part, a hearing of the kind mentioned in section 45(2)(b) of the Criminal Justice Act 2003 is not a pre-trial hearing."

(3) In paragraph 15 in paragraph (b) of the substituted version of section 39(3)—

(a) for "when a jury is sworn" there is substituted "at the time when a jury is sworn", and

(b) for "a jury is sworn" there is substituted "the time when a jury is sworn".

(4) After paragraph 15 there is inserted—

"15A In section 39(4) for "(3)" substitute "(3)(b)"."

Crime and Disorder Act 1998 *(c. 37)*

73   In paragraph 2(2) of Schedule 3 to the Crime and Disorder Act 1998 (applications for dismissal) for "a jury properly to convict him" there is substituted "him to be properly convicted".

Youth Justice and Criminal Evidence Act 1999 *(c. 23)*

74   The Youth Justice and Criminal Evidence Act 1999 is amended as follows.

75   In section 32 (warning to jury) after "indictment" there is inserted "with a jury".

76   In section 39(1) (warning to jury) after "indictment" there is inserted "with a jury".

Anti-terrorism, Crime and Security Act 2001 *(c. 24)*

77   In paragraph 19(6)(c) of Schedule 1 to the Anti-terrorism, Crime and Security Act 2001 (general interpretation) after "finding" there is inserted "otherwise than in circumstances where the proceedings are continued without a jury".

Proceeds of Crime Act 2002 *(c. 29)*

78   In section 316(9)(c) of the Proceeds of Crime Act 2002 (general interpretation) after "finding" there is inserted "otherwise than in circumstances where the proceedings are continued without a jury".

PART 5

EVIDENCE

Criminal Procedure Act 1865 *(c. 18)*

79   In section 6 of the Criminal Procedure Act 1865 (witness's conviction for offence may be proved if not admitted)—

(a) for "A witness may be" there is substituted "If, upon a witness being lawfully";

(b) the words "and upon being so questioned, if" are omitted.

Criminal Evidence Act 1898 *(c. 36)*

80   In section 1 of the Criminal Evidence Act 1898 (defendant as witness)—

(a) at the beginning of subsection (2) there is inserted "Subject to section 101 of the Criminal Justice Act 2003 (admissibility of evidence of defendant's bad character),";

(b) subsection (3) is omitted.

Army Act 1955 *(c. 18)*

81   In section 99(1) of the Army Act 1955 (rules of evidence) after "courts-martial etc)" there is inserted "to Schedules 6 and 7 to the Criminal Justice Act 2003".

Air Force Act 1955 (c. 19)

82   In section 99(1) of the Air Force Act 1955 (rules of evidence) after "courts-martial etc)" there is inserted "to Schedules 6 and 7 to the Criminal Justice Act 2003".

Naval Discipline Act 1957 (c. 53)

83   In section 64A(1) of the Naval Discipline Act 1957 (rules of evidence) after "courts-martial etc)" there is inserted "to Schedules 6 and 7 to the Criminal Justice Act 2003".

Armed Forces Act 1976 (c. 52)

84   In paragraph 11(1) of Schedule 3 to the Armed Forces Act 1976 (rules of evidence) after "paragraph 12 below" there is inserted "to Schedules 6 and 7 to the Criminal Justice Act 2003".

Police and Criminal Evidence Act 1984 (c. 60)

85   (1) Section 74 of the Police and Criminal Evidence Act 1984 (conviction as evidence of commission of offence) is amended as follows.
     (2) In subsection (1) (commission of offence by non-defendant) for the words from ", where to do so" to "committed that offence" there is substituted "that that person committed that offence, where evidence of his having done so is admissible".
     (3) In subsection (3) (commission of offence by defendant) the words from "in so far" to "he is charged," are omitted.

PART 6

MISCELLANEOUS

Criminal Appeal Act 1968 (c. 19)

86   The Criminal Appeal Act 1968 is amended as follows.
87   In section 31(1) (powers of Court of Appeal exercisable by single judge) after paragraph (a) there is inserted—
        "(aa) the power to give leave under section 14(4B) of the Criminal Appeal Act 1995;".
88   In section 31A (powers of Court of Appeal exercisable by registrar) after subsection (4) there is inserted—
        "(5) In this section "respondent" includes a person who will be a respondent if leave to appeal is granted."
89   In section 45 (construction of references to Court of Appeal)—
            (a) in subsection (1), for "section 44A" there is substituted "sections 44A and 51",
            (b) in subsection (2) after "sections" there is inserted "23A,".
90   (1) Section 51 (interpretation) is amended as follows.
     (2) In subsection (1) the definition of "the defendant" is omitted.
     (3) After that subsection there is inserted—
        "(1A) In Part 2 of this Act "the defendant"—
            (a) in relation to an appeal under section 33(1) of this Act against a decision of the Court of Appeal on an appeal under Part 1 of this Act, means the person who was the appellant before the Court of Appeal,
            (b) in relation to an appeal under section 33(1) of this Act against any other decision, means a defendant in the proceedings before the Crown Court who was a party to the proceedings before the Court of Appeal, and
            (c) in relation to an appeal under section 33(1B) of this Act, shall be construed in accordance with section 33(4) of this Act;
        and, subject to section 33(1A) of this Act, "prosecutor" shall be construed accordingly."

Criminal Appeal (Northern Ireland) Act 1980 (c. 47)

91   The Criminal Appeal (Northern Ireland) Act 1980 is amended as follows.
92   (1) Section 19 (legal aid) is amended as follows.
     (2) In subsection (1) after "an appeal" there is inserted "under this Part of this Act".
     (3) In subsection (1A) for "for the purpose" there is substituted "in respect".
     (4) In subsection (1A)(a)—

    (a) the words "application for leave to" are omitted, and

    (b) after "hearings)" there is inserted "or section 47 of the Criminal Justice Act 2003".

  (5) For subsection (1A)(b) there is substituted—

    "(b) any other appeal to the Court of Appeal under any Northern Ireland legislation (whenever passed or made) from proceedings before the Crown Court; or

    (c) an application for leave to appeal in relation to an appeal mentioned in paragraph (a) or (b) above."

  (6) After subsection (1A) there is inserted—

    "(1B) The Crown Court or the Court of Appeal may order that an acquitted person shall be given legal aid in respect of an application made in relation to him under section 76 of the Criminal Justice Act 2003."

  (7) In subsection (3) for "an appellant" there is substituted "a person".

93 (1) Section 28 (costs) is amended as follows.

  (2) In subsection (2)(a) for "this Part" there is substituted "section 19(1)".

  (3) After subsection (2) there is inserted—

"(2AA) The expenses of any solicitor or counsel assigned to a person pursuant to a grant of legal aid under section 19(1A) or (1B) of this Act shall, up to an amount allowed by the Master (Taxing Office), be defrayed by the Lord Chancellor."

  (4) In subsection (2A) after "(2)(a)" there is inserted "or (2AA)".

  (5) In subsection (2G)—

    (a) after "(2)(a)" there is inserted "or (2AA)", and

    (b) for "subsection (2)" there is substituted "subsections (2) and (2AA)".

94   For section 31(3) (definition of defendant and prosecutor) there is substituted—

  "(3) In this Part of this Act "the defendant"—

    (a) in relation to an appeal under subsection (1) above against a decision of the Court on an appeal under Part 1 of this Act, means the person who was the appellant before the Court;

    (b) in relation to an appeal under subsection (1) above against any other decision, means a defendant in the proceedings before the Crown Court who was a party to the proceedings before the Court;

    (c) in relation to an appeal under subsection (1B) above, shall be construed in accordance with subsection (4) below;

    and, subject to subsection (1A) above, "prosecutor" shall be construed accordingly."

95   In section 45 (powers of Court of Appeal exercisable by single judge) after subsection (3B) there is inserted—

  "(3C) Subject to section 44(4) above, the power of the Court of Appeal to give leave under section 14(4B) of the Criminal Appeal Act 1995 may be exercised by a single judge of the Court."

Criminal Justice Act 1988 (c. 33)

96   In section 36 of the Criminal Justice Act 1988 (reviews of sentencing)—

    (a) in subsection (3), for "10" there is substituted "11",

    (b) in subsection (9)(b), for "10 and 35(1)" there is substituted "11 and 35(1)".

Criminal Appeal Act 1995 (c. 35)

97   In section 15(2)(a) of the Criminal Appeal Act 1995 (investigations by Criminal Cases Review Commission for Court of Appeal) for "case", in both places where it occurs, there is substituted "appeal or application for leave to appeal".

Powers of Criminal Courts (Sentencing) Act 2000 (c. 6)

98   In section 159 of the Powers of Criminal Courts (Sentencing) Act 2000 (execution of process between England and Wales and Scotland), for "paragraph 3(2) of Schedule 1" there is substituted "paragraph 3(2) or 9C(2) of Schedule 1".

SCHEDULE 37   **Section 332**

REPEALS

PART 1

REPEALS RELATING TO AMENDMENTS OF POLICE AND CRIMINAL EVIDENCE ACT 1984

Short title and chapter	Extent of repeal
Police and Criminal Evidence Act 1984 (c. 60)	In section 1(8), the word "and" at the end of paragraph (c). In section 54(1), the words "and record or cause to be recorded". In section 63(3)(a), the words "is in police detention or". In section 67— (a) the word "such" in subsections (9), (10)(a), (b) and (c) and in both places where it occurs in subsection (11), and (b) the words "of practice to which this section applies" in subsection (9A). In section 113— (a) in subsection (4), the words "issued under that subsection", (b) in subsection (8), the words "of practice issued under this section", and (c) in subsection (10), the word "such" in both places where it occurs.
Criminal Justice and Public Order Act 1994 (c. 33)	Section 29(3).
Armed Forces Act 2001 (c. 19)	In section 2(9), the word "and" at the end of paragraph (c).
Police Reform Act 2002 (c. 30)	In Schedule 7, paragraph 9(1) and (6).

PART 2

BAIL

Short title and chapter	Extent of repeal
Criminal Justice Act 1967 (c. 80)	In section 22, in subsection (1) the words "subject to section 25 of the Criminal Justice and Public Order Act 1994" and in subsection (3) the words from "except that" to the end.
Courts Act 1971 (c. 23)	In Schedule 8, in paragraph 48(b), the word "22(3)".
Bail Act 1976 (c. 63)	In section 3(6), the words "to secure that". In section 3A(5), the words "for the purpose of preventing that person from". In section 5, in subsection (3), the words from "with a view" to "another court", and in subsection (6), in paragraph (a) the words "to the High Court or" and paragraph (b). In section 5A(2), in the substituted version of section 5(3), the words from "with a view" to "vary the conditions".
Supreme Court Act 1981 (c. 54)	In section 81(1)(g), the word "or" at the end of sub-paragraph (ii).
Criminal Justice Act 1991 (c. 53)	In Schedule 11, in paragraph 22(2), the words "and the words" onwards.

Short title and chapter	Extent of repeal
Criminal Justice and Public Order Act 1994 (c. 33)	Section 26. In Schedule 10, paragraphs 15 and 34.
Powers of Criminal Courts (Sentencing) Act 2000 (c. 6)	In Schedule 9, paragraph 87(b).

PART 3

DISCLOSURE

Short title and chapter	Extent of repeal
Criminal Justice Act 1987 (c. 38)	In section 9(5)(i) and (iii).
Criminal Justice (Serious Fraud) (Northern Ireland) Order 1988 (S.I. 1988/1846 (N.I. 16))	Article 8(5)(i) and (iii).
Criminal Procedure and Investigations Act 1996 (c. 25)	Section 5(6) to (9). Section 6(3). Section 7. Section 9. Section 20(2). Section 31(6)(a) and (c).

PART 4

ALLOCATION AND SENDING OF OFFENCES

Short title and chapter	Extent of repeal
Bankers' Books Evidence Act 1879 (c. 11)	In section 4, the paragraph beginning "Where the proceedings". In section 5, the paragraph beginning "Where the proceedings".
Explosive Substances Act 1883 (c. 3)	Section 6(3).
Criminal Justice Act 1925 (c. 86)	Section 49(2).
Administration of Justice (Miscellaneous Provisions) Act 1933 (c. 36)	In section 2(2), paragraphs (aa) to (ac), paragraphs (iA) and (iB), and the words from "and in paragraph (iA)" to the end.
Criminal Justice Act 1948 (c. 58)	Section 41(5A). In section 80, the definition of "Court of summary jurisdiction".
Backing of Warrants (Republic of Ireland) Act 1965 (c. 45)	In the Schedule, in paragraph 4, the words "and section 2 of the Poor Prisoners Defence Act 1930 (legal aid before examining justices)".
Criminal Procedure (Attendance of Witnesses) Act 1965 (c. 69)	Section 2(5).
Criminal Justice Act 1967 (c. 80)	In section 9(1), the words ", other than committal proceedings". In section 36(1), the definition of "committal proceedings".
Criminal Appeal Act 1968 (c. 19)	In section 9(2), the words from "section 41" to "either way offence".
Firearms Act 1968 (c. 27)	In Schedule 6, in Part 2, paragraph 3.
Theft Act 1968 (c. 60)	Section 27(4A).
Criminal Justice Act 1972 (c. 71)	In section 46, subsections (1A) to (1C).
Bail Act 1976 (c. 63)	In section 3, subsections (8A) and (8B), and the subsection (10) inserted by paragraph 12(b) of Schedule 9 to the Criminal Justice and Public Order Act 1994 (c. 33). Section 5(6A)(a)(i).
Criminal Law Act 1977 (c. 45)	In Schedule 12, the entry relating to the Firearms Act 1968 (c. 27).
Interpretation Act 1978 (c. 30)	In Schedule 1, in the definition of "Committed for trial", paragraph (a).

Short title and chapter	Extent of repeal
Customs and Excise Management Act 1979 (c. 2)	Section 147(2).
Magistrates' Courts Act 1980 (c. 43)	Sections 4 to 8, and the cross-heading preceding section 4.
	In section 8B(6)(a), the words "commits or".
	Section 24(1A) and (2).
	In section 25, subsections (3) to (8).
	In section 33(1), paragraph (b) and the word "and" immediately preceding it.
	Section 42.
	Section 97A.
	Section 103.
	Section 106.
	In section 128, in subsection (1)(b), the words "inquiring into or", and in each of subsections (1A)(a), (3A), (3C)(a) and (3E)(a), the word "5,".
	In section 130(1), the word "5,".
	Section 145(1)(f).
	In section 150(1), the definition of "committal proceedings".
	In section 155(2)(a), the words "8 (except subsection (9))".
	In Schedule 3, paragraph 2(a).
	In Schedule 5, paragraph 2.
	In Schedule 7, paragraph 73.
Criminal Justice (Amendment) Act 1981 (c. 27)	The whole Act.
Criminal Attempts Act 1981 (c. 47)	In section 2(2)(g), the words "or committed for trial".
Contempt of Court Act 1981 (c. 49)	Section 4(4).
Supreme Court Act 1981 (c. 54)	Section 76(5).
	Section 77(4).
	In section 81—
	(a) in subsection (1)(a), the words "who has been committed in custody for appearance before the Crown Court or in relation to whose case a notice of transfer has been given under a relevant transfer provision or",
	(b) subsection (1)(g)(i),
	(c) subsection (7).
Criminal Justice Act 1982 (c. 48)	Section 61.
	In Schedule 9, paragraph 1(a).
Mental Health Act 1983 (c. 20)	In section 52(7)(b), the words "where the court proceeds under subsection (1) of that section,".
Police and Criminal Evidence Act 1984 (c. 60)	Section 62(10)(a)(i).
	In section 71, the paragraph beginning "Where the proceedings".
	Section 76(9).
	Section 78(3).
Prosecution of Offences Act 1985 (c. 23)	In section 16, subsections (1)(b), (2)(aa) and (12).
	In section 23A(1)(b), the words from "under" to "1998".
	In Schedule 1, paragraphs 2 and 3.
Criminal Justice Act 1987 (c. 38)	Sections 4 to 6.
	In section 11—
	(a) subsection (2)(a),
	(b) subsection (3),
	(c) in subsection (7), the word "(3),",
	(d) in subsection (8), the word "(3),",
	(e) subsections (9) and (10),
	(f) in subsection (11), paragraphs (a) and (d).
	In Schedule 2, paragraphs 1, 9 and 14.

Short title and chapter	Extent of repeal
Criminal Justice Act 1988 (c. 33)	Section 23(5). Section 24(5). In section 26, the paragraph beginning "This section shall not apply". In section 27, the paragraph beginning "This section shall not apply". Section 30(4A). Section 33. In section 40(1), the words "were disclosed to a magistrates' court inquiring into the offence as examining justices or". Section 41. Section 144. In Schedule 15, paragraphs 10, 66 and 104.
Road Traffic Offenders Act 1988 (c. 53)	Section 11(3A). Section 13(7). Section 16(6A). Section 20(8A).
Courts and Legal Services Act 1990 (c. 41)	In Schedule 18, paragraph 25(5).
Broadcasting Act 1990 (c. 42)	In Schedule 20, paragraph 29(1).
Criminal Justice Act 1991 (c. 53)	Section 53. Section 55(1). Schedule 6. In Schedule 11, paragraph 25.
Criminal Justice and Public Order Act 1994 (c. 33)	Section 34(2)(a). Section 36(2)(a). Section 37(2)(a). In Schedule 9, paragraphs 12, 17(c), 18(d), 25, 27, 29 and 49. In Schedule 10, paragraphs 40 and 71.
Criminal Procedure and Investigations Act 1996 (c. 25)	In section 1(2), paragraphs (a) to (c) and, in paragraph (cc), the words from "under" to the end. In section 5, subsections (2) and (3). In section 13(1), paragraphs (a) to (c) of the modified section 3(8). Section 28(1)(b). Section 44(3). Section 45. Section 49(4). Section 68. In Schedule 1, paragraphs 2 to 5, 8, 10, 12, 13, 15 to 19, 22(3), 24 to 26, 28 to 32, and 34 to 38. Schedule 2.
Sexual Offences (Protected Material) Act 1997 (c. 39)	Section 9(1).
Crime and Disorder Act 1998 (c. 37)	Section 47(6). In section 50(1), the words "unless the accused falls to be dealt with under section 51 below". In Schedule 3, in paragraph 2, sub-paragraphs (4) and (5), paragraph 12, and in paragraph 13(2), the words from "unless" to the end. In Schedule 8, paragraphs 8, 37, 40, 65 and 93.
Access to Justice Act 1999 (c. 22)	Section 67(3). In Schedule 4, paragraphs 16, 39 and 47. In Schedule 13, paragraphs 96, 111 and 137.

Short title and chapter	Extent of repeal
Youth Justice and Criminal Evidence Act 1999 (c. 23)	Section 27(10). In section 42(3), paragraphs (a) and (b).
Powers of Criminal Courts (Sentencing) Act 2000 (c. 6)	In section 89(2)(b), the words "trial or". In section 140(1)(b), the words "was committed to the Crown Court to be tried or dealt with or by which he". In Schedule 9, paragraphs 62, 63, 64(2), 65, 91 and 201. In Schedule 11, paragraph 9.

PART 5

EVIDENCE OF BAD CHARACTER

Short title and chapter	Extent of repeal
Criminal Procedure Act 1865 (c. 18)	In section 6, the words "and upon being so questioned, if".
Criminal Evidence Act 1898 (c. 36)	Section 1(3).
Children and Young Persons Act 1963 (c. 37)	Section 16(2) and (3).
Criminal Evidence Act 1979 (c. 16)	In section 1, the words from "each of the following" to "1898, and".
Police and Criminal Evidence Act 1984 (c. 60)	In section 74(3), the words from "in so far" to "he is charged,".
Criminal Justice and Public Order Act 1994 (c. 33)	Section 31.
Crime (Sentences) Act 1997 (c. 43)	In Schedule 4, paragraph 4.
Youth Justice and Criminal Evidence Act 1999 (c. 23)	In Schedule 4, paragraph 1(5).
Powers of Criminal Courts (Sentencing) Act 2000 (c. 6)	In Schedule 9, paragraph 23.

PART 6

HEARSAY EVIDENCE

Short title and chapter	Extent of repeal
Registered Designs Act 1949 (c. 88)	In section 17, in subsection (8) the words "Subject to subsection (11) below," and in subsection (10) the words ", subject to subsection (11) below,".
Patents Act 1977 (c. 37)	In section 32, in subsection (9) the words "Subject to subsection (12) below," and in subsection (11) the words ", subject to subsection (12) below,".
Criminal Justice Act 1988 (c. 33)	Part 2. Schedule 2. In Schedule 13, paragraphs 2 to 5. In Schedule 15, paragraph 32. In Schedule 4, paragraph 6(2).
Finance Act 1994 (c. 9)	Section 22(2)(b). In Schedule 7, paragraph 1(6)(b).
Value Added Tax Act 1994 (c. 23)	In Schedule 11, paragraph 6(6)(b).
Criminal Justice and Public Order Act 1994 (c. 33)	In Schedule 9, paragraph 31.
Civil Evidence Act 1995 (c. 38)	In Schedule 1, paragraph 12.
Finance Act 1996 (c. 8)	In Schedule 5, paragraph 2(6)(a).
Criminal Procedure and Investigations Act 1996 (c. 25)1	In Schedule 1, paragraphs 28 to 31.
Crime and Disorder Act 1998 (c. 37)	In Schedule 3, paragraph 5(4).
Youth Justice and Criminal Evidence Act 1999 (c. 23)	In Schedule 4, paragraph 16.
Finance Act 2000 (c. 17)	In Schedule 6, paragraph 126(2)(a).
Finance Act 2001 (c. 9)	In Schedule 7, paragraph 3(2)(a).
Crime (International Co-operation) Act 2003 (c. 32)	In section 9(4), the words "section 25 of the Criminal Justice Act 1988 or".

PART 7

SENTENCING: GENERAL

Short title and chapter	Extent of repeal
Piracy Act 1837 (c. 88)	Section 3.
Children and Young Persons Act 1933 (c. 12)	In section 16(3), the words "mandatory and".
Criminal Justice Act 1967 (c. 80)	In section 104, in subsection (1) the definition of "suspended sentence" and subsection (2).
Criminal Appeal Act 1968 (c. 19)	In section 10 subsection (2)(c) and the word "or" immediately preceding it. Section 11(4).
Social Work (Scotland) Act 1968 (c. 49)	In section 94(1), the definition of "community rehabilitation order".
Bail Act 1976 (c. 63)	In section 2(1)(d), the words "placing the offender on probation or".
Magistrates' Courts Act 1980 (c. 43)	In section 82(4A), paragraph (e) and the word "or" immediately preceding it. Section 133(2). In Schedule 6A, the entry relating to section 123(3) of the Powers of Criminal Courts (Sentencing) Act 2000.
Forgery and Counterfeiting Act 1981 (c. 45)	Section 23(1)(b), (2)(b) and (3)(b).
Mental Health Act 1983 (c. 20)	In section 37(1B), the words "109(2),". In section 45A(1)(b), the words from "except" to "1997".
Road Traffic Offenders Act 1988 (c. 53)	In section 46(1), paragraph (a) and the word "or" following it.
Football Spectators Act 1989 (c. 37)	In section 7, subsection (9) and in subsection (10)(b) the words from "(or" to the end.
Children Act 1989 (c. 41)	In section 68(2)(d), the words "a probation order has been made in respect of him or he has been". In Schedule 9A, in paragraph 4(2)(g), the words "placed on probation or".
Criminal Justice Act 1991 (c. 53)	Sections 32 to 51. Section 65. Schedule 5. In Schedule 12— (a) in paragraph 8(8), paragraph (d), and (b) in paragraph 9(3), paragraph (c).
Prisoners and Criminal Proceedings (Scotland) Act 1993 (c. 9)	In section 10(1)(a), sub-paragraph (i) and the succeeding "or".
Criminal Justice Act 1993 (c. 36)	Section 67(1).
Criminal Justice and Public Order Act 1994 (c. 33)	In section 25(3)(c), the words "placing the offender on probation or".
Criminal Procedure (Scotland) Act 1995 (c. 46)	In section 234— (a) in subsection (1), the words after paragraph (b), (b) in subsection (3), the words from "or to vary" to "one hundred", and (c) subsection (11).
Crime (Sentences) Act 1997 (c. 43)	Sections 35 and 40. In Schedule 1, paragraph 15(5). In Schedule 2, paragraphs 2 and 3. In Schedule 4, paragraphs 6(2), 7, 10(1), 12(1), 13 and 15(10).

Short title and chapter	Extent of repeal
Crime and Disorder Act 1998 (c. 37)	In section 18, subsection (2). In section 38(4)(i), the words "section 37(4A) or 65 of the 1991 Act or". Sections 59 and 60. Sections 80 and 81. Sections 99 and 100. Sections 101(1). Sections 103 to 105. In section 121(12), the words from the beginning to "paragraphs 56 to 60 of Schedule 8 to this Act;". In Schedule 7, paragraph 50. In Schedule 8, paragraphs 11, 13(2), 56, 58, 59, 79 to 84, 86 to 91, 94, 97, 132 and 135(3) and (4).
Criminal Justice (Children) (Northern Ireland) Order 1998 (S.I. 1998/1504 (N.I. 9))	In Schedule 5, paragraph 28(b).
Access to Justice Act 1999 (c. 22)	Section 58(5).
Powers of Criminal Courts (Sentencing) Act 2000 (c. 6)	Section 6(4)(d). Section 12(4). Sections 34 to 36A. In section 36B, subsections (4) and (8) and, in subsection (9), the words from "a community punishment order" to "a drug abstinence order". In section 37, in subsection (9) the words "who on conviction is under 16" and subsection (10). In section 40A, subsection (4), in subsection (9) the words "who on conviction is under 16" and subsection (10). Sections 41 to 59. In section 60, in subsection (1), paragraph (c) and the word "or" immediately preceding it. Section 62. Section 69(11). Section 73(7). Sections 78 to 82. Section 84. Section 85. Sections 87 and 88. Section 91(2). Section 100(4). Section 106(2) and (3). Section 109. Section 110(3). Section 111(3). In section 112(1)(a), the words "109,". In section 113, in subsection (1)(a), the words "a serious offence or" and in subsection (3), the words ""serious offence"," and "109,". In section 114(1)(b), the words "a serious offence,". In section 115, the word "109,". Sections 116 and 117. Sections 118 to 125. Sections 126 to 129. Sections 151 to 153. Sections 156 to 158. In section 159, the words ", 121(1) or 123(1)" and "paragraph 6(6) of Schedule 4 to this Act,".

Short title and chapter	*Extent of repeal*
	In section 160—
	(a) in subsection (2), in paragraph (a) the words from "42(2E)" to "Schedule 2" and in paragraph (b) the words from "122(7)" to the end,
	(b) in subsection (3), in paragraph (a) the words "45, 50, 58, 58A(4), 85(7)", paragraph (b) and the word "or" immediately preceding it,
	(c) subsection (4), and
	(d) in subsection (5), in paragraph (a) the words from "or paragraph 7" to the end, and in paragraph (b) the words from "42(2E)" to the end.
	Section 161(2) to (4).
	Section 162.
	In section 163, in the definition of "affected person", paragraphs (b) and (c), the definitions of "the appropriate officer of the court", "community punishment and rehabilitation order", "community rehabilitation order", "community rehabilitation period", "community punishment order", the definitions of "drug abstinence order", "drug treatment and testing order", "falling to be imposed under section 109(2), 110(2) or 11(2)", "pre-sentence report", "protecting the public from serious harm'", in the definition of "responsible officer", paragraphs (b) to (ee) and the words from "except that" to "that section;", the definitions of "review hearing", "sexual offence", "specified Class A drug", "suspended sentence supervision order", "the testing requirement", "the treatment provider", "the treatment requirement", "the treatment and testing period", "trigger offence" and "violent offence".
	In section 168—
	(a) in subsection (1), the words "to subsection (2) below and", and
	(b) subsections (2) and (3).
	Schedule 2.
	Schedule 4.
	In Schedule 7, paragraph 3(4).
	In Schedule 8, paragraph 3(4).
	In Schedule 9, paragraphs 7, 24(a), 26(2), 28, 29, 52, 54(3), 55, 61, 76, 81, 82, 89(2), 90(2), 94, 102, 137 to 145, 147(2) and (3)(a) to (d) and (e)(i), 151, 174, 176(2) to (5) and (7), 177(2) and (3), 184, 185, 186(3) and (4), 187(2), (3) and (5), 196 and 202.
Terrorism Act 2000 (c. 11)	In Schedule 15, paragraph 20.
Child Support, Pensions and Social Security Act 2000 (c. 19)	Section 62(10).
Criminal Justice and Court Services Act 2000 (c. 43)	Section 47 to 51.
	Sections 53 to 55.
	Section 63.
	Section 64(5)(e).
	In section 78(1), the definition of "community order".
	In Schedule 7, paragraphs 1 to 3, 104 to 107, 111(b), 123(a) and (c) to (f), 124(a) and (b), 133, 139, 140, 161, 162, 165 to 172, 177, 179, 189, 196(c)(ii) and (iii), 197(c) and (g)(ii), 198 to 200 and 206(a).

Short title and chapter	Extent of repeal
Anti-terrorism, Crime and Security Act 2001 (c. 24)	Section 39(7).
Proceeds of Crime Act 2002 (c. 29)	In Schedule 11, paragraph 32.

PART 8

LIFE SENTENCES

Short title and chapter	Extent of repeal
Murder (Abolition of Death Penalty) Act 1965 (c. 71)	Section 1(2).
Repatriation of Prisoners Act 1984 (c. 47)	In section 2(4)(b)(i), the words "or 29(1)".
	Section 3(9).
	Paragraph 3 of the Schedule.
Crime (Sentences) Act 1997 (c. 43)	Section 29.
	Section 31(4).
	Section 33.
	In section 34(3), the words from the beginning to "advocate; and".
Crime and Punishment (Scotland) Act 1977 (c. 48)	In Schedule 1, paragraph 10(3).
Crime and Disorder Act 1998 (c. 37)	In Schedule 8, paragraphs 57 and 60.
Powers of Criminal Courts (Sentencing) Act 2000 (c. 6)	In section 82A, in subsection (4) the words "subject to subsection (5) below", and subsections (5) and (6).

PART 9

ALTERATION OF PENALTIES FOR SUMMARY OFFENCES

Short title and chapter	Extent of repeal
Vagrancy Act 1824 (c. 83)	Section 5.
	Section 10.
Railway Regulation Act 1842 (c. 55)	In section 17, the words from "be imprisoned" (where first occurring) to "discretion of such justice, shall".
London Hackney Carriages Act 1843 (c. 86)	In section 28, the words from "; or it shall be lawful" to the end.
Town Police Clauses Act 1847 (c. 89)	In section 28, the words from ", or, in the discretion" to "fourteen days".
	In section 29, the words from ", or, in the discretion" to the end.
	In section 36, the words from ", or, in the discretion" to "one month".
Ecclesiastical Courts Jurisdiction Act 1860 (c. 32)	In section 2, the words from ", or may, if the justices" to the end.
Town Gardens Protection Act 1863 (c. 13)	In section 5, the words ", or to imprisonment for any period not exceeding fourteen days".
Public Stores Act 1875 (c. 25)	In section 8, the words from ", or, in the discretion" to the end.
North Sea Fisheries Act 1893 (c. 17)	In section 2—
	(a) in paragraph (a), the words from ", or, in the discretion" to the end, and
	(b) in paragraph (b), the words from ", or in the discretion" to the end.
	In section 3(a), the words from ", or, in the discretion" to the end.

Short title and chapter	Extent of repeal
Children and Young Persons Act 1933 (c. 12)	In section 4(1), the words from ", or alternatively" to the end.
Protection of Animals Act 1934 (c. 21)	In section 2, the words from ", or, alternatively" to the end.
Public Health Act 1936 (c. 49)	In section 287(5), the words from "or to imprisonment" to the end.
Essential Commodities Reserves Act 1938 (c. 51)	In section 4(2), the words from "or to imprisonment" to the end.
London Building Acts (Amendment) Act 1939 (c. xcvii)	In section 142(5), the words from "or to imprisonment" to the end.
Cancer Act 1939 (c. 13)	In section 4(2), the words from "or to imprisonment" to the end.
Civil Defence Act 1939 (c. 31)	In section 77, the words from "or to imprisonment" to the end.
Hill Farming Act 1946 (c. 73)	In section 19— (a) in subsection (2), the words from ", or to imprisonment" to the end, and (b) in subsection (3), the words from "or to imprisonment" to the end.
Agriculture Act 1947 (c. 48)	In section 14(7) (as remaining in force for the purposes of section 95), the words— (a) "to imprisonment for a term not exceeding three months or", and (b) "or to both such imprisonment and such fine". In section 95(3), the words— (a) "to imprisonment for a term not exceeding three months or", and (b) "or to both such imprisonment and such fine".
Civil Defence Act 1948 (c. 5)	In section 4(4), the words from "or to imprisonment" to the end.
Agricultural Wages Act 1948 (c. 47)	In section 12(7), the words from "or to imprisonment" to the end.
Wireless Telegraphy Act 1949 (c. 54)	In section 14(1B), the words— (a) "to imprisonment for a term not exceeding three months or", and (b) ", or both".
Prevention of Damage by Pests Act 1949 (c. 55)	In section 22(5), the words from "or to imprisonment" to the end.
Coast Protection Act 1949 (c. 74)	In section 25(9), the words from "or to imprisonment" to the end.
Pet Animals Act 1951 (c. 35)	In section 5— (a) in subsection (1), the words "other than the last foregoing section" and the words from "or to imprisonment" to the end, and (b) subsection (2).
Cockfighting Act 1952 (c. 59)	In section 1(1), the words— (a) "to imprisonment for a term not exceeding three months, or", and (b) ", or to both such imprisonment and such fine".
Agricultural Land (Removal of Surface Soil) Act 1953 (c. 10)	In section 2(1)— (a) paragraph (a) of the proviso, (b) the word "; or" immediately preceding paragraph (b) of the proviso, and (c) the words "or to both".
Accommodation Agencies Act 1953 (c. 23)	In section 1(5), the words from "or to imprisonment" to the end.

Short title and chapter	Extent of repeal
Army Act 1955 (3 & 4 Eliz. 2 c. 18)	In section 19(1), the words "to imprisonment for a term not exceeding three months or".
	In section 161, the words from ", or to imprisonment" to the end.
	In section 171(1), the words from ", or to imprisonment" to the end.
	In section 191, the words from "or to imprisonment" to the end.
	In section 193, the words from "or to imprisonment" to the end.
	In section 196(3), the words from "or to imprisonment" to the end.
	In section 197(3), the words from "or to imprisonment" to the end.
Air Force Act 1955 (3 & 4 Eliz. 2 c. 19)	In section 19(1), the words "to imprisonment for a term not exceeding three months or".
	In section 161, the words from ", or to imprisonment" to the end.
	In section 171(1), the words from ", or to imprisonment" to the end.
	In section 191, the words from "or to imprisonment" to the end.
	In sections 193, the words from "or to imprisonment" to the end.
	In section 196(3), the words from "or to imprisonment" to the end.
	In section 197(3), the words from "or to imprisonment" to the end.
Naval Discipline Act 1957 (c. 53)	In section 96, the words from "or to imprisonment" to the end.
	In section 99(3), the words from "or to imprisonment" to the end.
Agricultural Marketing Act 1958 (c. 47)	In section 45(6), the words— (a) "to imprisonment for a term not exceeding one month, or", and (b) ", or to both such imprisonment and such fine".
Rivers (Prevention of Pollution) Act 1961 (c. 50)	In section 12(2), the words from "or to imprisonment" to the end.
Betting, Gaming and Lotteries Act 1963 (c. 2)	In section 8(1), the words— (a) "or to imprisonment for a term not exceeding three months, or to both", and (b) "in any case".
Children and Young Persons Act 1963 (c. 37)	In section 40— (a) in subsection (1), the words from "or imprisonment" to the end, and (b) in subsection (2), the words from "or imprisonment" to the end.
Animal Boarding Establishments Act 1963 (c. 43)	In section 3— (a) in subsection (1), the words "other than the last foregoing section" and the words from "or to imprisonment" to the end, and (b) subsection (2).

Short title and chapter	Extent of repeal
Agriculture and Horticulture Act 1964 (c. 28)	In section 20(2), the words from "or to imprisonment" to the end.
Emergency Laws (Re-enactments and Repeals) Act 1964 (c. 60)	In Schedule 1— (a) in paragraph 1(3), the words "to imprisonment for a term not exceeding three months or" and ", or to both", and (b) in paragraph 2(4), the words "to imprisonment for a term not exceeding three months or" and ", or to both".
Riding Establishments Act 1964 (c. 70)	In section 4(1), the words from "or to imprisonment" to the end.
Industrial and Provident Societies Act 1965 (c. 12)	In section 16(5), the words from "or to imprisonment" to the end. In section 48(2), the words from "or to imprisonment" to the end.
Cereals Marketing Act 1965 (c. 14)	In section 17(1), the words from "or to imprisonment" to the end.
Gas Act 1965 (c. 36)	In Schedule 6, in paragraph 9, the words from "or to imprisonment" to the end.
Armed Forces Act 1966 (c. 45)	In section 8, the words "to imprisonment for a term not exceeding three months or".
Agriculture Act 1967 (c. 22)	In section 6(9), the words from "or to imprisonment" to the end. In section 14(2), the words from "or to imprisonment" to the end. In section 69, the words from "or imprisonment" to the end.
Criminal Justice Act 1967 (c. 80)	Section 20.
Sea Fisheries (Shellfish) Act 1967 (c. 83)	In section 14(2), the words from "or to imprisonment" to the end.
Theatres Act 1968 (c. 54)	In section 13(3), the words from "or to imprisonment" to the end.
Theft Act 1968 (c. 60)	In Schedule 1, in paragraph 2(1), the words— (a) "to imprisonment for a term not exceeding three months or", and (b) "or to both".
Agriculture Act 1970 (c. 40)	In section 106(8), the words from "or imprisonment" to the end.
Breeding of Dogs Act 1973 (c. 60)	In section 3(1)— (a) paragraph (a), (b) the word "; or" immediately preceding paragraph (b), and (c) the words "or to both".
Slaughterhouses Act 1974 (c. 3)	In section 38(5), the words "or imprisonment for a term of three months or both".
National Health Service Act 1977 (c. 49)	In Schedule 11— (a) in paragraph 8(3), the words "to imprisonment for a term not exceeding three months or" and ", or to both", and (b) in paragraph 9(4), the words "to imprisonment for a term not exceeding three months or" and ", or to both".
Magistrates' Courts Act 1980 (c. 43)	In section 84(3), the words— (a) "imprisonment for a term not exceeding 4 months or", and (b) "to both".

Short title and chapter	Extent of repeal
Animal Health Act 1981 (c. 22)	In paragraph 6 of Schedule 1, the words— (a) "or to imprisonment for a term not exceeding 2 months,", and (b) "in either case".
Fisheries Act 1981 (c. 29)	In section 5(4), the words from "or to imprisonment" to the end.
Civil Aviation Act 1982 (c. 16)	In section 82(2), the words from "or to imprisonment" to the end.
Criminal Justice Act 1982 (c. 48)	Section 70.
Mental Health Act 1983 (c. 20)	Section 43(5). In section 103(9), the words— (a) "to imprisonment for a term not exceeding three months or", and (b) "or both". In section 129(3), the words— (a) "to imprisonment for a term not exceeding three months or", and (b) "or to both".
Building Act 1984 (c. 55)	In section 96(3), the words "or to imprisonment for a tcrm not exceeding three months".
Surrogacy Arrangements Act 1985 (c. 49)	In section 4(1)— (a) paragraph (a), and (b) in paragraph (b), the words "in the case of an offence under section 3".
Animals (Scientific Procedures) Act 1986 (c. 14)	In section 22(3), the words— (a) "to imprisonment for a term not exceeding three months or", and (b) "or to both". In section 23(2), the words— (a) "to imprisonment for a term not exceeding three months or", and (b) "or to both". In section 25(3), the words— (a) "to imprisonment for a term not exceeding three months or", and (b) "or to both".
Motor Cycle Noise Act 1987 (c. 34)	In the Schedule, in paragraph 1(1), the words "to imprisonment for a term not exceeding three months or".
Human Organ Transplants Act 1989 (c. 31)	In section 2(5), the words— (a) "imprisonment for a term not exceeding three months or", and (b) "or both".
Town and Country Planning Act 1990 (c. 8)	In Schedule 15, in paragraph 14(4), the words from "or to imprisonment" to the end.
Environmental Protection Act 1990 (c. 43)	In section 118(7), the words from "or to imprisonment" to the end.
Criminal Justice Act 1991 (c. 53)	Section 26(5).
Deer Act 1991 (c. 54)	In section 10(3), the words from "or to imprisonment" to the end.
Water Industry Act 1991 (c. 56)	In section 206(9), the words— (a) "to imprisonment for a term not exceeding three months or", and (b) "or to both". In Schedule 6, in paragraph 5(5), the words— (a) "to imprisonment for a term not exceeding three months or", and (b) "or to both".

Short title and chapter	*Extent of repeal*
Social Security Administration Act 1992 (c. 5)	In section 105(1), the words— (a) "to imprisonment for a term not exceeding 3 months or", and (b) "or to both". In section 182(3), the words— (a) "to imprisonment for a term not exceeding 3 months or", and (b) "or to both".
Local Government Finance Act 1992 (c. 14)	In section 27(5), the words— (a) "imprisonment for a term not exceeding three months or", and (b) "or both".
Trade Union and Labour Relations (Consolidation) Act 1992 (c. 52)	In section 240(3), the words— (a) "to imprisonment for a term not exceeding three months or", and (b) "or both".
Merchant Shipping Act 1995 (c. 21)	In section 57(2)— (a) in paragraph (a), the words "except in a case falling within paragraph (b) below,", and (b) paragraph (b).
Reserve Forces Act 1996 (c. 14)	In section 75(5), the words— (a) "imprisonment for a term not exceeding 3 months or", and (b) "(or both)". In section 82(1), the words— (a) "imprisonment for a term not exceeding 3 months", and (b) "(or both)". In section 87(1), the words— (a) "imprisonment for a term not exceeding 3 months or", and (b) "(or both)". In section 99, the words— (a) "imprisonment for a term not exceeding 3 months", and (b) "(or both)". In Schedule 1, in paragraph 5(2), the words— (a) "imprisonment for a term not exceeding 3 months or", and (b) "(or both)".
Housing Act 1996 (c. 52)	In Schedule 1— (a) in paragraph 23(6), the words from "or imprisonment" to "or both", and (b) in paragraph 24(6), the words from "or imprisonment" to "or both".
Broadcasting Act 1996 (c. 55)	In section 144(4), the words— (a) "to imprisonment for a term not exceeding three months or", and (b) "or to both".
Breeding and Sale of Dogs (Welfare) Act 1999 (c. 11)	In section 9— (a) in subsection (1), paragraph (a), the word ", or" immediately preceding paragraph (b) and the words "or to both", and (b) in subsection (7), paragraph (a), the word ", or" immediately preceding paragraph (b) and the words "or to both".

Short title and chapter	Extent of repeal
Powers of Criminal Courts (Sentencing) Act 2000 (c. 6)	In section 6(4), paragraph (a).
Countryside and Rights of Way Act 2000 (c. 37)	In section 81, subsections (2) and (3).
Transport Act 2000 (c. 38)	In section 82, subsection (5).

PART 10

JURY SERVICE

Short title and chapter	Extent of repeal
Juries Act 1974 (c. 23).	In section 2(5)(a), the word "9(1),".
	In section 9, subsection (1) and in subsection (2) the words from "and" to the end.
Criminal Law Act 1977 (c. 45).	In Schedule 12, the entry relating to the Juries Act 1974.
Criminal Justice Act 1982 (c. 48).	In Schedule 14, paragraph 35.
Mental Health (Amendment) Act 1982 (c. 51).	In Schedule 3, paragraph 48.
Mental Health Act 1983 (c. 20).	In Schedule 4, paragraph 37.
Juries (Disqualification) Act 1984 (c. 34).	The whole Act.
Coroners Act 1988 (c. 13).	Section 9(2).
Criminal Justice Act 1988 (c. 33).	Section 119.
	In Schedule 8, paragraph 8.
Courts and Legal Services Act 1990 (c. 41).	In Schedule 17, paragraph 7.
	In Schedule 18, paragraph 5.
Criminal Justice Act 1991 (c. 53).	In Schedule 11, paragraph 18.
Probation Service Act 1993 (c. 47).	In Schedule 3, paragraph 5.
Police and Magistrates' Courts Act 1994 (c. 29).	In Schedule 8, paragraph 28.
Criminal Justice and Public Order Act 1994 (c. 33).	Section 40.
	Section 42.
	In Schedule 10, paragraph 29.
Criminal Appeal Act 1995 (c. 35).	In Schedule 2, paragraph 8.
Police Act 1996 (c. 16).	In Schedule 7, paragraph 23.
Police Act 1997 (c. 50).	In Schedule 9, paragraph 27.
Government of Wales Act 1998 (c. 38).	In Schedule 12, paragraph 18.
Scotland Act 1998 (c. 46).	Section 85(1).
Access to Justice Act 1999 (c. 22).	In Schedule 11, paragraph 22.
Criminal Justice and Court Services Act 2000 (c. 43).	In Schedule 7, paragraph 47.
European Parliamentary Elections Act 2002 (c. 24).	In Schedule 3, paragraph 2.

PART 11

REPEALS RELATING TO AMENDMENTS OF PART 5 OF POLICE ACT 1997

Short title and chapter	Extent of repeal
Police Act 1997 (c. 50)	In section 115, subsections (3) to (5) and subsections (6C) to (6E).
	Section 120(3).
	In section 125, subsection (3) and, in subsection (4), the words "to which subsection (3) does not apply".
Care Standards Act 2000 (c. 14)	Section 104(3)(a).
	In Schedule 4, paragraph 25(2)(a).
Private Security Industry Act 2001 (c. 12)	Section 21.
	Section 26(3)(a).
Health and Social Care Act 2001 (c. 15)	Section 19.
Criminal Justice and Police Act 2001 (c. 16)	Section 134(3) and (4).

Short title and chapter	Extent of repeal
National Health Service Reform and Health Care Professions Act 2002 (c. 17)	Section 42(7). In Schedule 2, paragraph 64.
Education Act 2002 (c. 32)	In Schedule 12, paragraph 15(2). In Schedule 13, paragraph 8(2).
Licensing Act 2003 (c. 17)	In Schedule 6, paragraph 116.

PART 12

MISCELLANEOUS

Short title and chapter	Extent of repeal
Criminal Appeal Act 1968 (c. 19) Section 10(4).	In section 11(2), the words from "(which expression" to "purposes of section 10)". In section 51(1), the definition of "the defendant".
Bail Act 1976 (c. 63)	In section 5(1)(c), the words "a court or officer of a court appoints".
Magistrates' Courts Act 1980 (c. 43)	In section 1(3), the words "and substantiated on oath". Section 12(1)(a)(i). In section 13(3)(a), the words "the information has been substantiated on oath and".
Criminal Appeal (Northern Ireland) Act 1980 (c. 47)	In section 19(1A)(a), the words "application for leave to".
Criminal Procedure and Investigations Act 1996 (c. 25)	In Schedule 4, paragraph 16.
Crime and Disorder Act 1998 (c. 37)	In section 8(2), the words from "and to section 19(5)" to "2000".
Youth Justice and Criminal Evidence Act 1999 (c. 23)	In Schedule 4, paragraphs 26 and 27.
Powers of Criminal Courts (Sentencing) Act 2000 (c. 6)	In section 19(5), paragraph (c) and the word "or" immediately preceding it. In Schedule 9, paragraphs 194 and 195.
Criminal Justice and Court Services Act 2000 (c. 43)	Sections 67 and 68.

SCHEDULE 38   **Section 333(6)**

TRANSITORY, TRANSITIONAL AND SAVING PROVISIONS

Sentencing of offenders aged 18 but under 21

1   If any provision of Part 12 ("the relevant provision") is to come into force before the day on which section 61 of the Criminal Justice and Court Services Act 2000 (abolition of sentences of detention in a young offender institution, custody for life, etc.) comes into force (or fully into force) the provision that may be made by order under section 333(1) includes provision modifying the relevant provision with respect to sentences passed, or other things done, at any time before section 61 of that Act comes into force (or fully into force).

Sentencing guidelines

2   The repeal by this Act of sections 80 and 81 of the Crime and Disorder Act 1998 does not affect the authority of any guidelines with respect to sentencing which have been included in any judgment of the Court of Appeal given before the commencement of that repeal ("existing guidelines"), but any existing guidelines may be superseded by sentencing guidelines published by the Sentencing Guidelines Council under section 170 of this Act as definitive guidelines.

3   (1) Subject to sub-paragraph (2), the repeal by this Act of section 81 of the Crime and Disorder Act 1998 does not affect the operation of subsection (4) of that section in relation to any notification received by the Panel under subsection (2) of that section, or proposal made by the Panel under subsection (3) of that section, before the commencement of the repeal.

(2) In its application by virtue of sub-paragraph (1) after the commencement of that repeal, section 81(4) of that Act is to have effect as if any reference to "the Court" were a reference to the Sentencing Guidelines Council.

(3) In this paragraph "the Panel" means the Sentencing Advisory Panel.

Drug treatment and testing orders

4   A drug treatment and testing order made under section 52 of the Powers of Criminal Courts (Sentencing) Act 2000 before the repeal of that section by this Act is in force (or fully in force) need not include the provision referred to in subsection (6) of section 54 of that Act (periodic review by court) if the treatment and testing period (as defined by section 52(1) of that Act) is less than 12 months.

Drug testing as part of supervision of young offenders after release

5   (1) Until the coming into force of the repeal by this Act of section 65 of the Criminal Justice Act 1991 (c. 53) (supervision of young offenders after release), that section has effect subject to the following modifications.

(2) In subsection (5B)—
  (a) in paragraph (a), for "18 years" there is substituted "14 years",
  (b) for paragraph (b) there is substituted—
    "(b) a responsible officer is of the opinion—
      (i) that the offender has a propensity to misuse specified Class A drugs, and
      (ii) that the misuse by the offender of any specified Class A drug caused or contributed to any offence of which he has been convicted, or is likely to cause or contribute to the commission by him of further offences; and".

(3) After subsection (5D) there is inserted—
  "(5E) A person under the age of 17 years may not be required by virtue of subsection (5A) to provide a sample otherwise than in the presence of an appropriate adult."

(4) For subsection (10) there is substituted—
  "(10) In this section—
    "appropriate adult", in relation to a person aged under 17, means—
    (a) his parent or guardian or, if he is in the care of a local authority or voluntary organisation, a person representing that authority or organisation,
    (b) a social worker of a local authority social services department, or
    (c) if no person falling within paragraph (a) or (b) is available, any responsible person aged 18 or over who is not a police officer or a person employed by the police;
    "responsible officer" means—
    (a) in relation to an offender aged under 18, an officer of a local probation board or a member of a youth offending team;
    (b) in relation to an offender aged 18 or over, an officer of a local probation board;
    "specified Class A drug" has the same meaning as in Part 3 of the Criminal Justice and Court Services Act 2000 (c. 43)."

Intermittent custody

6   If section 183 (intermittent custody) is to come into force for any purpose before the commencement of the repeal by this Act of section 78 of the Powers of Criminal Courts (Sentencing) Act 2000 (c. 6) (which imposes a general limit on the power of a magistrates' court to impose imprisonment), the provision that may be made by order under section 333(1) includes provision modifying any period or number of days specified in section 183 with respect to sentences passed by magistrates' courts before the commencement of that repeal.

Transfer to Scotland of community orders and suspended sentence orders

7   (1) Until the coming into force of the repeal by the Mental Health (Care and Treatment) (Scotland) Act 2003 of the Mental Health (Scotland) Act 1984 (c. 36), in the provisions mentioned in sub-paragraph (2) the reference to the Mental Health (Care and Treatment) (Scotland) Act 2003 has effect as a reference to the Mental Health (Scotland) Act 1984.

(2) Those provisions are—
  (a) paragraph 2(4) of Schedule 9 (transfer of community orders to scotland or Northern Ireland), and
  (b) paragraph 4 of Schedule 13 (transfer of suspended sentence orders to Scotland or Northern Ireland).

INDEX

References are to sections and Schedules